Wiley
CMA Learning System®
Exam Review 2013

About IMA® (Institute of Management Accountants)

IMA/The Association of Accountants and Financial Professionals in Business® is one of the largest and most respected associations focused exclusively on advancing the management accounting profession. Globally, IMA supports the profession through research, the CMA® (Certified Management Accountant) program, continuing education, networking, and advocacy of the highest ethical business practices. IMA has a global network of more than 50,000 members in 120 countries and 200 local chapter communities. IMA provides localized services through its offices in Montvale, NJ, USA; Zurich, Switzerland; Dubai, UAE; and Beijing, China. For more information about IMA, please visit www.imanet.org.

Wiley CMA Learning System® Exam Review 2013

Self-Study Guide

Part 1: Financial Planning, Performance and Control

The Association of
Accountants and
Financial Professionals
in Business®

Published by John Wiley & Sons, Inc., Hoboken, New Jersey.
Published simultaneously in Canada.

For general information on our other products and services or for technical support, please contact our Customer Care Department within the United States at (800) 762-2974, outside the United States at (317) 572-3993 or fax (317) 572-4002.

Wiley also publishes its books in a variety of electronic formats. Some content that appears in print may not be available in electronic books. For more information about Wiley products, visit our web site at www.wiley.com.

Library of Congress Cataloging-in-Publication Data

Wiley CMA exam review learning system.
     v. cm.
     Contents: pt. 1. Financial planning, performance and control—pt. 2. Financial decision making.
    Includes bibliographical references and index.
    ISBN 978-1-118-48058-8 (Part 1, 1 Year Subscription)
    ISBN 978-1-118-48060-1 (Part 2, 1 Year Subscription)
    ISBN 978-1-118-48057-1 (Set, 2 Year Subscription)
    ISBN 978-1-118-55110-3 (Part 1, 2 Year Subscription)
    ISBN 978-1-118-55191-2 (Part 2, 2 Year Subscription)
    ISBN 978-1-18-48068-7 (Part 1 + OIR 1 Year Subscription)
    ISBN 978-1-118-48070-0 (Part 2 + OIR 1 Year Subscription)
    ISBN 978-1-118-48066-3 (Set + OIR 2 Year Subscription)
      1. Accounting—Examinations—Study guides. 2. Accounting—Examinations, questions, etc.
 I. Title: Wiley Certified Management Accountant exam review learning system. II. Title: CMA exam review learning system.
    HF5661.W499   2013
    657.076—dc23

    2012022854

Printed in the United States of America

10 9 8 7 6 5 4 3 2 1

Contents

Acknowledgements of Subject Matter Experts

The CMA Learning System® (CMALS) content is written to help explain the concepts and calculations from the Certified Management Accountant (CMA) exam Learning Outcome Statements (LOS) published by the Institute of Certified Management Accountants (ICMA).

IMA would like to acknowledge the team of subject matter experts who worked together in conjunction with IMA staff to produce this version of the CMA Learning System®.

Saurav Dutta, CMA, is an associate professor and former chair of the Accounting Department at the State University of New York at Albany. Dutta is the author of some 20 research articles published in various academic journals. He received his Ph.D. in accounting from the University of Kansas and is also the recipient of the Robert Beyer Silver Medal for securing the second highest total score in a CMA examination.

Tony Griffin, CMA, is the accounting manager for Dayton Aerospace, Inc., a senior management consulting firm specializing in defense acquisition and logistics support to government and industry customers. Griffin has been actively involved in supporting the IMA and the CMA certification by serving as president of his local IMA chapter and by organizing and leading CMA review courses in the Dayton, Ohio, area. He also serves as the facilitator for the CMA Online Intensive Review course, where he supports online students around the world with their preparations for the CMA exams.

Karen L. Jett, CMA, is a consultant specializing in values-based organizational development and ethics training. Prior to starting her own business (Jett Excellence), she acquired over two decades of experience working in privately held companies and holds a degree in accounting from Temple University (Philadelphia, PA). Jett is author of *Grow Your People, Grow Your Business* (Mira Digital, 2008) and Questioning Ethics, an innovative ethics training system designed specifically for smaller businesses. She has taught the CMA Review Courses for many years, both as an adjunct professor at Villanova University (Villanova, PA) and directly to corporate clients.

Jan Kooiman holds a doctorate in business economics from the University of Amsterdam. He worked for an accounting and audit firm before stepping into the professional world as chief financial officer and board member of an international company. Kooiman is a qualified transactional Six Sigma Black Belt and Trainer and is adjunct professor of finance, business, and accounting at the Webster and Leiden University in the Netherlands, teaching MBA Finance and Management Accounting. He is also the program manager and instructor of the CMA program at the World Trade Center Amsterdam.

Lou Petro, CMA, CPA, CIA, CCP, CISA, CFE, CFM, PE, is a senior manager with a major fraud investigation firm and a former consultant and auditor. Petro specializes in fraud deterrence and investigation, corporate governance, bankruptcy, information systems auditing, production and inventory controls, internal controls, and cost and managerial accounting. He has also taught auditing, systems, accounting, and finance courses at colleges and universities in Michigan and Ontario.

Siaw-Peng Wan, CFA, is a professor of finance and the MBA program director at Elmhurst College (Elmhurst, IL). He received his Ph.D. in economics from the University of Illinois at Urbana-Champaign, and he recently became a CFA charter holder. His most recent articles on online investing and banking have appeared in *The Internet Encyclopedia* and *The Handbook of Information Security*. Wan has taught the CMA Review Courses at Northern Illinois University since 2004.

Candidate Study Information

CMA Certification from ICMA

The Certified Management Accountant (CMA) certification provides accountants and financial professionals with an objective measure of knowledge and competence in the field of management accounting. The CMA designation is recognized globally as an invaluable credential for professional accountancy advancement inside organizations and for broadening professional skills and perspectives.

The two-part CMA exam is designed to develop and measure critical thinking and decision-making skills and to meet these objectives:

- To establish management accounting and financial management as recognized professions by identifying the role of the professional, the underlying body of knowledge, and a course of study by which such knowledge is acquired.
- To encourage higher educational standards in the management accounting and financial management fields.
- To establish an objective measure of an individual's knowledge and competence in the fields of management accounting and financial management.
- To encourage continued professional development.

Individuals earning the CMA designation benefit by being able to:

- Communicate their broad business competency and strategic financial mastery.
- Obtain contemporary professional knowledge and develop skills and abilities that are valued by successful businesses.
- Convey their commitment to an exemplary standard of excellence that is grounded on a strong ethical foundation and lifelong learning.
- Enhance their career development, salary qualifications, and professional promotion opportunities.

The CMA certification is granted exclusively by the Institute of Certified Management Accountants (ICMA).

CMA Learning Outcome Statements (LOS)

The Certified Management Accountant exam is based on a series of Learning Outcome Statements (LOS) developed by the Institute of Certified Management Accountants (ICMA). The LOS describes the knowledge and skills that make up the CMA body of knowledge, broken down by part, section, and topic. The CMA Learning System® (CMALS) supports the LOS by addressing the subjects they cover. Candidates should use the LOS to ensure they can address the concepts in different ways or through a variety of question scenarios. Candidates should also be prepared to perform calculations referred to in the LOS in total or by providing missing components of a calculation. The LOS should not be used as proxies for exact exam questions; they should be used as a guide for studying and learning the content that will be covered on the exam.

A copy of the ICMA Learning Outcome Statements is included in Appendix A at the end of this book. Candidates are also encouraged to visit the IMA Web site to find other exam-related information at www.imanet.org.

CMA Exam Format

The content tested on the CMA exams is at an advanced level—which means that the passing standard is set for mastery, not minimum competence. Thus, there will be test questions for all major topics that require the candidate to synthesize information, evaluate a situation, and make recommendations. Other questions will test subject comprehension and analysis. However, compared to previous versions, this CMA exam will have an increased emphasis on the higher-level questions.

The content is based on a series of LOS that define the competencies and capabilities expected of a management accountant.

There are two exams, taken separately: Part 1: Financial Planning, Performance and Control; and Part 2: Financial Decision Making. Each exam is four hours in length and includes multiple-choice and essay questions. One hundred multiple-choice questions are presented first, followed by two essay questions. All of these questions—multiple-choice and essay—can address any of the LOS for the respective exam part. Therefore, your study plan should include learning the content of the part as well as practicing how to answer multiple-choice and essay questions against that content. The study plan tips and the final section of this CMA Learning System® book contain important information to help you learn how to approach the different types of questions.

Note on Candidate Assumed Knowledge

The CMA exam content is based on a set of assumed baseline knowledge that candidates are expected to have. Assumed knowledge includes economics, basic statistics, and financial accounting. Examples of how this assumed knowledge might be tested in the exam include:

- How to calculate marginal revenue and costs as well as understand the relevance of market structures when determining prices
- How to calculate variance when managing financial risk
- How to construct a cash flow statement as part of an analysis of transactions and assess the impact of the transactions on the financial statements

Please note this knowledge content is ***not covered*** in the CMA Learning System®. Therefore, prior courses in accounting and finance are highly recommended to ensure this knowledge competency when preparing for the exam.

Overall Expectations for the CMA Candidates

Completing the CMA exams requires a high level of commitment and dedication of up to 150 hours of study for each part of the CMA exam. Completing the two-part exam is a serious investment that will reap many rewards, helping you to build a solid foundation for your career, distinguish yourself from other accountants, and enhance your career in ways that will pay dividends for a lifetime.

Your success in completing these exams will rest heavily on your ability to create a solid study plan and to execute that plan. IMA offers many resources, tools, and programs to support you during this process—the exam content specifications, assessment tools to identify the content areas you need to study most, comprehensive study tools such as the Online Test Bank classroom programs, and online intensive review courses. We encourage you to register as a CMA candidate as soon as you begin the program to maximize your access to these resources and tools and to draw on these benefits with rigor and discipline that best supports your unique study needs. We also suggest candidates seek other sources if further knowledge is needed to augment knowledge and understanding of the ICMA LOS.

For more information about the CMA certification, the CMA exams, or the exam preparation resources offered through IMA, visit www.imanet.org.

Updates and Errata Notification

Please be advised that our materials are designed to provide thorough and accurate content with a high level of attention to quality. From time to time there may be clarifications, corrections, or updates that are captured in an Updates and Errata Notification.

To ensure you are kept abreast of changes, this notification will be available on Wiley's CMA update and errata page. You may review these documents by going to www.wiley.com/go/cmaerrata. For Part 1 of the Wiley CMA Learning System, click on the Wiley CMALS Part 1 link, for Part 2 of the Wiley CMA Learning System, click on the Wiley CMALS Part 2 link, and for the Online Intensive Review click on the OIR link.

How to Use the CMA Learning System®

This product is based on the CMA body of knowledge developed by the Institute of Certified Management Accountants (ICMA). This material is designed for learning purposes and is distributed with the understanding that the publisher and authors are not offering legal or professional services. Although the text is based on the body of knowledge tested by the CMA exam and the published Learning Outcome Statements (LOS) covering the two-part exams, CMA Learning System® (CMALS) program developers do not have access to the current bank of exam questions. It is critical that candidates understand all LOS published by the ICMA, learn all concepts and calculations related to those statements, and have a solid grasp of how to approach the multiple-choice and essay exams in the CMA program.

Some exam preparation tools provide an overview of key topics; others are intended to help you practice one specific aspect of the exams such as the questions. The CMALS is designed as a comprehensive exam preparation tool to help you study the content from the exam LOS, learn how to write the CMA exams, and practice answering exam-type questions.

Study the Book Content

The **table of contents** is set up using the CMA exam content specifications established by ICMA. Each section, topic, and subtopic is named according to the content specifications and the **Learning Outcome Statements (LOS)** written to correspond to these specifications. As you go through each section and major topic, refer to the related LOS found in Appendix A. Then review the CMALS book content to help learn the concepts and formulas covered in the LOS.

The **knowledge checks** are designed to be quick checks to verify that you understand and remember the content just covered by presenting questions and correct answers. The answers refer to the appropriate sections in the book for you to review the content and find the answer yourself.

The **practice questions** are a sampling of the type of exam questions you will encounter on the exam and are considered complex and may involve extensive written and/or calculation responses. Use these questions to begin applying what you have learned, recognizing there is a much larger sample of practice questions available in the Online Test Bank (described in the next section).

The CMALS also contains a **bibliography** in case you need to find more detailed content on an LOS. We encourage you to use published academic sources. While information can be found online, we discourage the use of open-source, unedited sites such as Wikipedia.

Suggested Study Process Using the CMALS

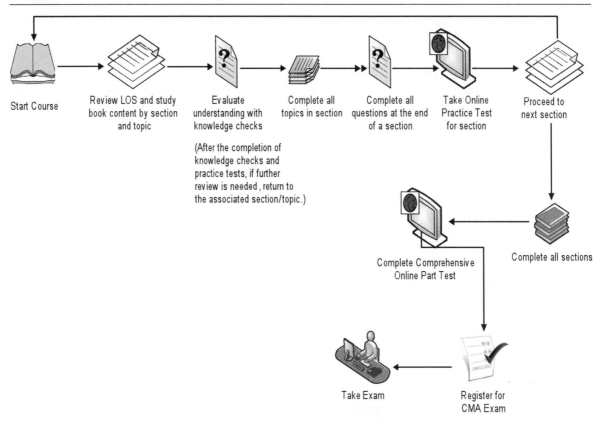

Start Course → Review LOS and study book content by section and topic → Evaluate understanding with knowledge checks → Complete all topics in section → Complete all questions at the end of a section → Take Online Practice Test for section → Proceed to next section

(After the completion of knowledge checks and practice tests, if further review is needed, return to the associated section/topic.)

Complete all sections → Complete Comprehensive Online Part Test → Register for CMA Exam → Take Exam

CMALS Book Features

The CMALS books use a number of features to draw your attention to certain types of content:

Key terms are **bolded** where they appear in the text with their definition, to allow you to quickly scan through and study them.

Key formulas are indicated with this icon. Be sure you understand these formulas and practice applying them.

Knowledge checks at the end of each topic are review questions that let you check your understanding of the content just read. (They are not representative of the type of questions that appear on the exam.)

 Study tips offer ideas and strategies for studying and preparing for the exam.

 Practice questions are examples of actual exam questions. Presented at the end of each section, these questions help you solidify your learning of that section and apply it to the type of questions that appear on the exam.

Online Test Bank

Included with your purchase of the CMA Learning System® Part 1 book is an Online Test Bank made available to you through the IMA's Learning Center. This course includes **five section-specific tests** that randomize questions from a selected section only. The course also includes **a comprehensive Part 1 test** that emulates the percentage weighting of each section on the actual Part 1 exam. All questions are drawn from a bank of more than 800 questions, so that each time you repeat the test, you will receive a different set of questions covering all the topics in the section. All the multiple-choice questions provide feedback in response to your answers. Also included is a **Resources** section that contains additional study documents.

It is suggested that you integrate Online Test Bank throughout your study program instead of leaving them until the end. The section-specific tests are designed for you to practice questions related to the section content—read and learn a section and then practice the online questions related to the section. This also will help you identify whether further study of the section content is required before moving to the next section.

The comprehensive Part 1 test is designed to help you simulate taking the actual CMA exam. Try the comprehensive Part 1 test after you have studied all the Part 1 content. You can take this exam multiple times. Each time you will receive a different combination of questions. It is recommended that you set up your own exam simulation—set aside four hours in a room without interruption, do not have any reference books open, and work through the comprehensive part exam as if you were taking the real exam. This will prepare you for the exam setting and give you a good idea of how ready you are.

The Resources section of the Online Test Bank Online Practice Tests contains example essay questions and answers. Use this document to practice the questions related to the essay portion of the exam. Be sure to review the sample grading guide in the CMALS book to understand how the essay questions are graded.

You are strongly encouraged to make full use of all online practice and review features as part of your study efforts. Please note that these features are subscription based and available only for a specific number of months from the time of purchase. (For more information on this feature and the terms of use, visit www.learncma.com.)

Learn to Write the CMA Exam

The four-hour CMA exam will test your understanding of each part's content using both multiple-choice and essay questions. This means you must learn to write two types of tests in one sitting. The CMALS® books contain tips, instruction, and examples to help you learn to write an essay exam. Be sure to study the Essay Exam Support Materials section so that in addition to practicing with the Online Test Bank, you also learn to respond to the part content in essay format.

Create a Study Plan

Each part of the two-part CMA exam uses a combination of a multiple-choice format and an essay format to test your understanding of the part concepts, terms, and calculations. Creating a study plan is an essential ingredient to planning a path to success. Managing your plan is critical to achieving success. The next tips and tactics are included to help you prepare and manage your study plan.

Study Tips

There are many ways to study, and the plan you create will depend on things such as your lifestyle (when and how you can schedule study time), your learning style, how familiar you are with the content, and how practiced you are at writing a formal exam. Only you can assess these factors and create a plan that will work for you. Some suggestions that other exam candidates have found helpful follow.

- Schedule regular study times and stay on schedule.
- Avoid cramming by breaking your study times into small segments. For example, you may want to work intensely for 45 minutes with no interruptions, followed by a 15-minute break during which time you do something different. You may want to leave the room, have a conversation, or exercise.
- When reading, highlight key ideas, especially unfamiliar ones. Reread later to ensure comprehension.
- Pay particular attention to the terms and equations highlighted in this book, and be sure to learn the acronyms in the CMA body of knowledge.
- Create personal mnemonics to help you memorize key information. For example, CCIC to remember the four ethical standards: Competence, Confidentiality, Integrity, and Credibility.
- Create study aids such as flash cards.
- Use index cards, and write a question on one side and the answer on the other. This helps reinforce the learning because you are writing the information as well as reading it. Examples: What is ____? List the five parts of ____.
- In particular, make flash cards of topics and issues that are unfamiliar to you, key terms and formulas, and anything you highlighted while reading.
- Keep some cards with you at all times to review at when you have times, such as in an elevator, while waiting for an appointment, and so on.

- Use a flash card partner. This person does not need to understand accounting. He or she only needs the patience to sit with you and read the questions off the flash card.
- As test time approaches, start to eliminate the questions you can easily answer from your stack so you can concentrate on the more challenging topics and terms.
- If particular topics are difficult, tap into other resources, such as the Internet, library, accountant colleagues, or professors, to augment your understanding.
- Use your study plan—treat it as a living document and update it as you learn more about what you need to do to prepare for the exam.
- Use the knowledge checks in the book to assess how well you understand the content you just completed.
- Use the Online Test Bank to test your ability to answer multiple-choice practice questions on each section's content as you finish it. After completing the first 40 questions presented, review areas in the book that you were weak on in the practice test. Then try the section test again.
- Be sure to learn how to write a multiple-choice question exam—there are many online resources with tips and guidance that relate to answering multiple-choice exams.
  - Make an attempt to answer all questions. There is no penalty for an incorrect answer—if you don't try, even when you are uncertain, you eliminate the potential of getting a correct answer.
  - Create your own "simulated" multiple-choice trial exam using the full part Online Practice Test.
- Learn to write an effective essay answer.
  - Use the Essay Exam Support Materials section of this book. This content shows a sample grading guide and includes a sample of a good, a better, and a best answer in addition to some helpful tips for writing an essay answer.
  - Learn how points are awarded for an essay answer so that you can ensure you get the most points possible for your answers, even when you are very challenged by a question.
  - Practice essay responses using the questions in this CMALS book and in the Resources section of the Online Test Bank.
- Be sure to access the Online Test Bank and Essay Questions in the Resources section until you are comfortable with the content.

Ensure you are both well rested and physically prepared for the exam day as each exam is four hours in length with no break for meals. Learning how to answer a multiple-choice and essay exam and being mentally and physically prepared can improve your grade significantly. Know the content and be prepared to deal with challenges with a focused, confident, and flexible attitude.

 Be sure to check the **Resources** section of your Online Practice Test course on a regular basis. This section is used to post new study resource documents for CMALS students, updates and errata notifications for the CMALS books, and any other important exam study update information.

Introduction

Welcome to Part 1: Financial Planning, Performance and Control of the Institute of Management Accountants' CMA Learning System®.

This Part 1 textbook is composed of five sections:

Section A: Planning, Budgeting, and Forecasting, looks at basic budgeting concepts and forecasting techniques that provide the information a company can use to execute its strategy and pursue its short- and long-term goals.

Section B: Performance Management, deals with the methods of comparing actual financial performance to the budget. It also describes tools that incorporate both financial and nonfinancial measures to aid an organization in matching its planning to its overall strategy.

Section C: Cost Management, describes various costing systems that can be used to monitor a company's costs and provide management with information it needs to manage the company's operations and performance.

Section D: Internal Controls, begins with a discussion of the assessment and management of risk. Understanding risk provides the basis for internal auditing activities and the means of ensuring the security and reliability of the information on which the company bases its decisions.

Section E: Professional Ethics, presents the *IMA Statement of Ethical Professional Practice* in the context of the ethical demands individuals within an organization need to face.

Many of these subjects, tested in the Part 1 CMA exam, provide a foundation for the concepts and methodologies that will be the subject of the Part 2 exam.

Planning, Budgeting, and Forecasting

How do some companies become great successes while others flounder? Successful companies have a strategy that is based on accurate information from both external and internal sources. They match their internal strengths to the best external opportunities available. But a good strategy is not enough. Companies need to convert an overall strategy into action. This is the purpose of a budget. A budget is a detailed plan for executing both long-term and short-term goals. A successful budget not only provides cost controls but also makes sure that day-to-day operations take the company where it wants to be in the future.

This section covers basic budgeting concepts and forecasting techniques that provide the assumptions on which budgets are based. It discusses various budget methodologies and their applications and explores the master budget in detail. It demonstrates, with case study examples, how a company can use components of a master budget to analyze its performance and operations.

Budgeting Concepts

PLANNING IS THE PROCESS OF mapping out the organization's future direction to attain desired goals. Strategy is the organization's plan to match its strengths with the opportunities in the marketplace to accomplish its desired goals over the short and long term. A budget provides the foundation for planning, because a successful budget is created by a process of aligning the company's resources with its strategy.

This topic introduces the concepts underlying budgeting, the processes used, the people involved, and their roles. It also examines the standards that may be employed in developing budget expectations and evaluating performance against these expectations. This topic provides an overview of the elements of a budget that are explored in greater detail in subsequent topics.

 READ the Learning Outcome Statements (LOS) for this topic as found in Appendix A and then study the concepts and calculations presented here to be sure you understand the content you could be tested on in the CMA exam.

Fundamentals: Terminology, Budget Cycle, and Reasons for Budgeting

These budget terms are used in this section.

Budget. A budget is an operational plan and a control tool for an entity that identifies the resources and commitments needed to satisfy the entity's goals over a period. Budgets are primarily quantitative, not qualitative. They set specific goals for income, cash flows, and financial position.

Budgeting. Budgeting is undertaking the steps involved in preparing a budget. Along with clear communication of organizational goals, the ideal budget also contains budgetary controls.

Budgetary control. Without a formal system of control, a budget is little more than a forecast. Budgetary control is a management process to help ensure that a budget is achieved by instituting a systematic budget approval process, by coordinating the efforts of all involved parties and operations, and by analyzing variances from the plan and providing appropriate feedback to responsible parties. The goals identified in the budget must be perceived by employees as realistic if those employees are to be motivated to achieve the goals.

Pro forma statement. A pro forma statement is a budgeted financial statement based on historical documents that is adjusted for events as if they had occurred. Budgeted balance sheets, budgeted statements of cash flows, and budgeted income statements are forecasts of goals for a future period that assist in the allocation of resources.

Budget Cycle

A budget cycle usually involves four steps:

1. A budget is created that addresses the entity as a whole as well as its subunits, and all managers of the subunits agree to fulfill their part of the budget.
2. The budget is used to test current performance against expectations.
3. Variations from the plan are examined, and corrective actions are taken when possible.
4. Feedback is collected, and the plan is revisited and revised if needed. Figure 1A-1 shows how these steps revolve back to the beginning to form a cycle.

Figure 1A-1 Budget Cycle

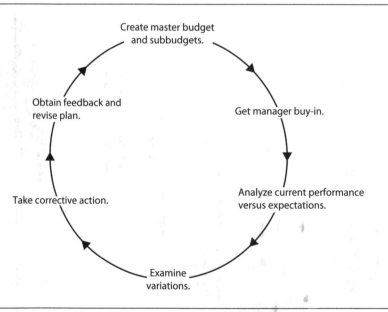

Reasons for Budgeting

There are four main reasons a company creates a budget: planning, communication and coordination, monitoring, and evaluation.

Planning

One of the major benefits of budgeting is that it forces the organization to examine the future. Expectations must be established for income, expenses, personnel needs, future growth (or contraction), and the like. Planning allows for the input of ideas from multiple sources within the organization and allows for input from different viewpoints. The planning process may generate new ideas for the organization's direction, or it may provide insight into better ways to achieve goals that have already been established. The budget process provides a framework to achieve the goals of the organization. Without the framework of a budget, individual managers would improvise decisions without the direction and coordination provided by a budget. Without a budget, the organization would be operating in a reactive manner rather than in a proactive manner.

Communication and Coordination

Budgeting also promotes communication and coordination of efforts within the organization. The different parts of the organization (production, marketing, materials management, etc.) must communicate their plans and needs to each other during the budget process so that all can evaluate the effect that the plans and needs of others have on their own. Each part of the organization must coordinate its activities to attain the budgeted goals and objectives. For example, if new products are to be developed, funds must be provided for development, materials will have to be purchased to produce the products, marketing and sales must have sufficient resources to promote and sell the products, and shipping and distribution may need additional space to store the products or additional resources to distribute them. Budgeting also allows the organization to communicate its goals to everyone in the organization, including those not involved in the budget process. Budgeting sets the stage for everyone in the organization to work toward the goals of the organization.

Monitoring

The budget sets standards, or performance indicators, by which managers can monitor the organization's progress in meeting its goals. By comparing the actual results for a period to the budgeted results for that period, managers can see whether the organization is on track to achieving its goals. Breaking down the organization's master budget to divisional and departmental levels allows each level of the organization to be evaluated. The organization as a whole may be meeting its goals while individual divisions and departments are failing. The difference between the actual results and the expected results is called a variance. A negative, or unfavorable, variance may indicate a need to take corrective action. Positive, or favorable, variances can reflect opportunities to make adjustments to take advantage of the conditions creating the variance—that is, if sales are up, then perhaps production should be increased.

Evaluation

Budgets also serve as guides or instruments for employee evaluations. Once the budget is set and managers have been advised of their responsibilities in relation to budget performance, they can be held responsible for their portion of the budget. By comparing actual results to the budget for a given period, a manager's performance can be evaluated. Having negative or unfavorable results does not necessarily mean that a manager is not performing well, but it does provide an indication that a specific part of the business should be focused on, in order to determine the root cause of the unfavorable variance. Likewise, positive, or favorable, results do not necessarily mean that a manager is performing in an exceptional way. Performance evaluations allow an organization to motivate employees by rewarding them for good performance in a number of ways, such as through performance-based bonuses and/or by including performance evaluations in the decision process for future compensation or promotion decisions.

Economic Considerations in the Budgeting Process

There are a significant number of interrelationships among economic conditions, industry situations, organizational plans, and the budgeting process. Budgeting is most effective when the budgeting process is linked to the overall strategy of the organization. Managers should build their strategy and organizational objectives to focus on all economic factors, including the financial impact of the decision-making process and understanding factors of competition.

When developing an organizational strategy, managers should ask these questions:

- What are our organizational objectives?
- How can we relate our organizational objectives to the budgeting process?
- Who are our competitors, and how can we differentiate ourselves from them?
- How are we affected by the competition and trends in the marketplace?
- What organizational risks exist that may impact the budgeting process?
- What organizational opportunities exist that may impact the budgeting process?

Operations and Performance Goals

A prerequisite for budget development is a strategic analysis that matches an entity's capabilities with available marketplace opportunities. Strategy addresses the objectives of the organization; locates potential markets; considers the impact of events, competitors, and the economy; addresses the structure of the organization; and evaluates the risks of alternative strategies. Strategic analysis is the basis for both long-term and short-term planning. These plans lead, respectively, to long-term and short-term budgets, as summarized in Figure 1A-2. These budgets lead in turn to the master budget and its components.

Figure 1A-2 Strategy, Planning, and Budgets

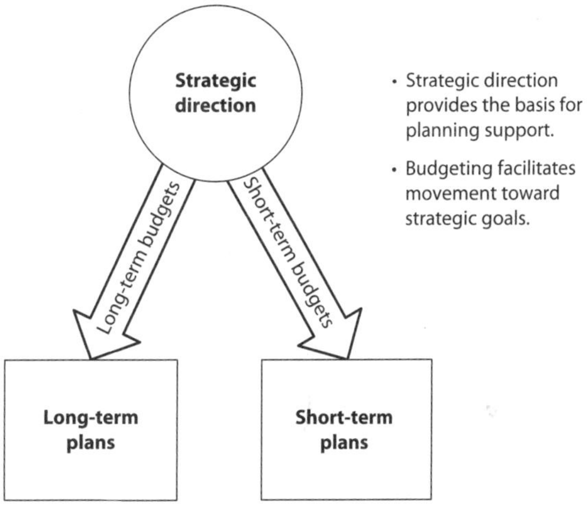

Budgets play a role in measuring performance against established goals. When using past performance solely to evaluate present results, the mistakes and problems that occurred in the past are automatically factored in to the benchmark that is being used.

For example: A company reports poor sales because of a new and inexperienced sales force. If this year's data are used as the next year's sales benchmark, the mark would be set lower than necessary and the sales team would not be motivated to work as hard. However, if the benchmark is set too high, employees may not strive to achieve amounts they view as unrealistic. This can be the case when an anomaly produces better-than-average results one year.

Employing a forecasted budget as a plan allows for the use of the expected results as the benchmark. Another benefit of using a budget instead of historical results is that past performance is not always indicative of future results. A budget may be able to predict and account for such shifts, but relying only on historical data leads to a sense that the past year must always be improved on, no matter the circumstances.

Costs are considered "controllable" or "discretionary" when the purchaser or manager has discretion in whether to incur the charge or alter the level of the charge within a short amount of time. Variable costs and other costs directly under the control of the manager are controllable costs. The manager can cut workers' hours, use cheaper materials, or otherwise restrict such controllable costs. A division manager can control maintenance and advertising costs to a certain degree.

Fixed costs, such as administrative salaries or rent, usually are not controllable and are therefore called "committed" costs.

Controllable costs are useful for performance evaluation and budgeting.

- Rating a manager's use of funds based on divisional net revenue less controllable costs will be perceived, by those being rated, as a more reasonable approach than being held accountable for uncontrollable costs—which can be very unmotivating.

- Focusing on controllable costs places the emphasis where the most benefit can be achieved from the effort of budgeting.

Characteristics of Successful Budgeting

Many factors characterize a successful budget, but no single factor can lead to a successful budget. Here is a list of the common factors in a successful budget:

- The budget must be aligned with the corporate strategy.
- The budget process should be kept separate but should flow from the strategic planning and forecasting processes.
- **Strategic plans** are higher level, longer term, and structured in companywide terms, such as product lines, rather than responsibility centers. However, early budgeting steps can be used to refine the strategic direction of the company because they use more current information.
- **Forecasts** often have lower accountability than a budget, usually are not approved by management, and often are not formally analyzed against variances. For instance, a manager may create a forecast for direct materials needed in next week's production to ensure adequate inventory levels. However, budgets must use the forward-looking information from more comprehensive forecasts. Therefore, the forecasts directly used in the budgeting process, such as the sales forecast, must be kept accountable.
- The budget should be used to alleviate potential bottlenecks and to allocate resources to those areas that will use the funds most efficiently and effectively.
- The budget must contain technically correct and reasonably accurate numbers and facts.
- Management (including top management) must fully endorse the budget—they must accept responsibility for reaching the budget goals.
- Employees must consider the budget as a planning, communication, and coordinating tool, and not as a pressure or blame device.
- The budget must be characterized as a motivating tool to help employees work toward organizational goals.
- The budget must be seen as an internal control device, where internal-use budgets base employee evaluations on controllable or discretionary costs.
- Sales and administrative budgets need to be detailed in order that key assumptions can be better understood.
- A higher authority than the team that developed the budget must review and approve the budget.

The final budget should not be easily changed, but it must be flexible enough to be useful. Budgets should compel planning, promote communication and coordination, and provide performance criteria. The budget process must balance input from those who will need to follow the budget against a thorough and fair review of the budget by upper management.

Characteristics of a Successful Budget Process

Whether the organization and its budget are very simple or highly complex, the characteristics of a successful budget process include: the budget period, the participants in the budget process, the basic steps in budgeting, and the use of cost standards.

Budget Period

Budgets are most commonly prepared for the company's fiscal year, but often three-, five-, and ten-year budgets are planned, as well as budgets of shorter durations. Management must consider what the most suitable length of time would be to suit the needs of the organization. The most frequently used budget timeframe is one year, although often the year is divided into months and quarters. A different year basis other than fiscal year is possible but is not recommended because fiscal-year financial statements can be easily compared to the budget. Budgets are often further broken into continuous (rolling) budgets. A continuous budget has a month, quarter, or year basis, and as each period ends, the upcoming period's budget is revised and another period is added to the end of the budget. Software is available for implementing this type of budget.

Budget Process

Methods of budget preparation differ between companies, but all fall somewhere on a continuum between entirely authoritative and entirely participative. In an **authoritative budget** (top-down budget), top management sets everything from strategic goals down to the individual items of the budget for each department and expects lower managers and employees to adhere to the budget and meet the goals. In a **participative budget** (bottom-up or self-imposed budget), managers at all levels and certain key employees cooperate to set budgets for their areas, and top management usually retains final approval. The ideal process combines the features of each and falls somewhere between these methods.

Figure 1A-3 lists benefits and limitations of purely authoritative and participative budgeting and shows how a combined approach provides the greatest number of checks and balances over a budgetary process. Note that the combination approach sometimes is considered to be a form of the participative approach.

The five steps in a combined approach include:

1. Budget participants are identified, including representatives of all levels of management as well as key employees with expertise in particular areas.
2. Top management communicates the strategic direction to budget participants.
3. Budget participants create the first draft of their budget.
4. Lower levels submit budgets to the next higher level for review in an iterative process stressing communication in both directions.
5. Rigorous but fair review and budget approval sets the final budget.

Figure 1A-3 Comparison of Authoritative, Combined, and Participative Budgeting

Authoritative Approach	Combination Approach	Participative Approach
Top management incorporates strategic goals into its budgets.	Strategic goals are communicated topdown and implemented bottomup.	Strategic goals do not receive priority in the budgetary process.
Better control over decisions.	Control retained and expertise gained at cost of a slightly longer process.	Expertise leads to informed budget decisions.
Dictates instead of communicates.	Two-way communication: Top management understands participants' difficulties and needs. Participants understand management's dilemmas.	Communicates lower-level perspective (of product/service or market) to management.
Employees: Resentful Unmotivated	Personal control leads to acceptance, which leads to greater personal commitment.	Employees: Involved Empowered
Stringent budgets may not be strictly followed at lower levels.	Ownership of budget and thorough review leads to tight budgets that get followed.	Easy or abdicated approval can lead to loose budgets and budget slack.
Not a recommended approach but could work in small or slow-changing environments.	Best for most companies; provides balance between strategic and tactical inputs.	Best for responsibility centers with highly variable situations where area manager has best data.

Budget Participants

Three groups make or break a budget: the board of directors, top management, and the budget committee. Middle and lower management also play a significant role, because they create detailed budgets based on upper management's plan. Depending on the size of the company and the type of budget being created, a budget coordinator and process experts may be involved in budget development.

Board of Directors

The board of directors does not create the budget, but it cannot abdicate its responsibility to review the budget and either approve or send it back for revision. The board usually appoints the members of the budget committee.

Top Management

Top management is ultimately responsible for the budgets, and the primary means top managers have of exercising this responsibility is to ensure that all levels of management understand and support the budget and the overall budget control process. If top management is not perceived to endorse a budget, line managers will be less likely to follow the budget precisely. Also, top managers should pay close attention to how they are affecting each line manager's budget, because insensitive policies could result in creative budgeting on the part of staff.

Top managers should give their subordinates incentives for making truthful and complete budgets, such as rewarding accuracy. A common problem that needs to be avoided is budget slack. **Budget slack** occurs when budgeted performance differs from actual performance because managers tend to build in some extra money for their budget to deal with the unexpected. Budget slack is built-in freedom to fail, and cumulative budget slack at each sublevel can result in a very inaccurate master budget.

However, rigid enforcement of budgets will, in some situations, cost an organization more in the long run than if some flexibility is allowed. For example, a manufacturer could lose thousands of dollars if the maintenance manager refuses to approve overtime for its mechanics to make an urgent repair because "it would use up too much of the maintenance budget."

Budget Committee

Large corporations usually need to form a budget committee composed of senior management and often led by the chief executive officer (CEO) or a vice president. The size of the committee will vary depending on the organization. The committee directs budget preparation, approves budgets, rules on disagreements, monitors the budget, reviews results, and approves revisions.

Middle and Lower Management

Once the budget committee sets the tone for the budget process, many others in the organization have some role to play. Middle and lower management do much of the specific budgeting work. These managers follow budget guidelines, which are general guidelines for responsibility centers preparing individual budgets set by either top management or the budget committee. A responsibility center, cost center, or strategic business unit (SBU) is a segment of a company in which the manager is vested with the authority to make cost, revenue, and/or investment decisions and therefore also set budgets. The budget guidelines are formed around the company's strategy and long-term plans. The guidelines govern preparation methods, layout, and new events that have occurred since the publication of the master budget, such as new downsizing needs, changes in the economy, and year-to-date operating results.

Budget Coordinator

The more people who are involved in a budget process, the greater the need for an individual or team who can identify and resolve discrepancies between the budgets of the various responsibility centers and between various portions of a master budget.

Process Experts

When participative budgeting is used, often certain key nonmanagerial employees are added to the team. Team participants tend to be those who have a detailed understanding of the costs for a particular area, especially those areas that are extremely complex or variable. Such participants will not only bring more focus to a budget but will also take ownership of the budget and increase its likelihood of being followed at the operational level.

Budgeting Steps

The steps that responsibility centers take in preparing their budgets include the initial budget proposal, budget negotiation, review and approval, and revision.

Budget Proposal

After the CEO decides on the company strategy, a memo or directive is sent to all line managers or responsibility centers so they can start aligning their budget process with the strategic plan (i.e., a top-down implementation). With this strategy in mind, each responsibility center prepares an initial budget, taking both internal and external factors into account. Internal factors include: changes in price, availability, and manufacturing processes; new products or services; changes in related or intertwined responsibility centers; and staff changes. External factors include changes in the economy and the labor market, the price and availability of goods and services, industry trends, and actions of competitors.

Budget Negotiation

When the initial budget proposal is submitted to a superior or to the budget committee, the budget is reviewed to see if it meets the organization's strategic goals, falls within an acceptable range, and is consistent with similar budgets. Reviewers also determine if the budget is feasible and if it fits within the goals of units the next level up. Negotiations take up the bulk of time in budget preparations because push-back from a superior will result in renegotiation of priorities for both the superior and the responsibility center.

Budget Review and Approval

Budgets are reviewed and approved up the chain of command to the level of the budget committee, where the combined budgets become the master budget, after review for consistency with the budget guidelines, short- and long-term goals, and strategic plans. Once the committee and the committee leader approve the plan, it is submitted to the board of directors for final approval.

Budget Revision

The rigidity of a budget varies from organization to organization. Some budgets must be followed absolutely; others can be revised only under specific circumstances; and others are subject to continuous revision. Rigidly following a budget in the face of changing circumstances has the potential for disaster. Management should not be required to rely on the budget as the sole operational guideline. Regular revisions may provide better operating guidelines; however, this may lead managers to anticipate regular changes and not prepare budgets as carefully as they should. Organizations that allow regular revisions should make sure that the threshold for revision is set high enough to keep employees working as efficiently as possible. When regular revisions occur, a copy of the original budget should be kept for comparison with actual results at the end of the period.

Cost Standards

Organizations set different types of standards that they strive to achieve. A **standard** is any carefully determined price, quantity, service level, or cost. Standards in manufacturing are usually set on a per-unit basis. A standard cost is how much an operation or service should cost, or the cost an entity expects to incur assuming that all goes as planned (e.g, expected time and capacity). Budget planners use standard costs to prepare budgets and then update standard costs as circumstances change. In practice, there is not a precise dividing line between a budgeted amount and a standard amount. With shorter time frames, there is little distinction between a budgeted amount and a standard amount.

Types of Standards

Standards can be either authoritative or participative.

Authoritative Standards

Authoritative standards are determined solely by management. They are more speedily set and can closely match overall company goals but may be a cause for resentment or may not be followed at all.

Participative Standards

Participative standards are set by holding a dialogue between management and all involved parties. They are more likely to be adopted than authoritative standards, but they take more time and require negotiation to ensure that operating goals are still met.

Specific types of standard costs include ideal standards and reasonably attainable standards.

Ideal Standards

An ideal standard is a forward-looking goal; it is currently attainable only if all circumstances result in the best possible outcome. Ideal standards work into a continuous improvement strategy and total quality management philosophies. They allow for no work delays, interruptions, waste, or machine breakdown. Ideal standards require a level of effort that can be attained only by the most skilled and efficient employees working at their best efficiency all of the time. Some firms use progress toward an ideal standard instead of deviations from the ideal to measure and reward success. However, ideal standards are very difficult to attain, and their frequent use can become frustrating. If difficult-to-attain ideal standards are constantly required, they can be a disincentive to productivity, because workers will not even attempt to meet such "impossible" goals and may become used to missing goals.

Reasonably Attainable Standards

A reasonably attainable standard is closer to a historical standard; it sets goals at a level that is attainable by properly trained individuals operating at a normal pace. The standard is expected to be reached most of the time. They allow for normal work delays, spoilage, waste, employee rest periods, and machine downtime. Practical standards can be attained by efficient efforts from an average worker. Variances from practical standards represent deviations caused by abnormal conditions and can be used in forecasting and inventory. In comparison, ideal standards cannot be used in forecasting and planning since they may result in unrealistic planning and forecasting figures that are not attainable even under the best of circumstances. Setting such a standard too low will encourage employees to work less diligently than needed. In addition, using reasonably attainable standards tends to discourage continuous improvement strategies.

Standard Costs for Direct Materials and Labor

Direct cost items, such as direct materials and direct labor, are measured by determining the number of units of each type of input required to get one unit of output. This amount is multiplied by the standard cost per input unit.

For example: If three input units are allowed for producing one output unit and an input unit costs $10, then the standard cost would be $30 per output unit. For direct labor, if 0.7 manufacturing labor hours of input are allowed for producing one output unit and labor hours cost $10, then the standard cost would be $7 per output unit.

Of course, real standard costs are developed by adding together multiple direct materials and labor costs. More specific guidelines for determining the prices for direct materials and labor are described next.

Standard Costs for Direct Materials

Standard costs are determined by quality, quantity, and price. Quality must be determined first, because it affects all the other variables. Quality level is determined by the product's targeted market niche. The standard is developed by engineers, production managers, and management accountants working together, on the basis of the production facilities, the quality of the product, the costs of manufacturing, and the equipment to be used. Direct material usage standards should allow for losses, spoilage, scrap, and waste normally expected in the production process. A price is set as a combination of all prior work done, including quality, quantity, and supply chain costs. Determining supply chain costs includes such considerations as whether to select the lowest-cost vendor each time (costs will vary) or to establish a relationship with one reliable vendor (costs will be more stable).

Standard Costs for Direct Labor

Product complexity, personnel skill levels, the type and condition of equipment, and the nature of the manufacturing process will all affect the direct labor costs. Management accountants, engineers, production managers, labor unions, human resources, and others affect the direct labor standards. Labor usage standards should consider normally expected equipment downtime and worker breaks that slow the production process. The cost of direct labor is based on gross base pay, not net base pay. Fringe benefits, overtime, and shift premiums are normally considered labor-related overhead costs.

Sources for Standards Setting

Several sources often are used simultaneously when setting standards: activity analysis, historical data, market expectations, strategic decisions, and benchmarking.

Activity Analysis

An activity analysis, as part of activity-based costing (ABC), identifies, codifies, and analyzes the activities needed to finish a job or operation. (ABC is discussed in more detail in Section C: Cost Management.) The most efficient combination of resources and other inputs is derived by interviewing personnel directly involved with various aspects of the operation. Engineers are involved in calculating the product ingredients and determining the specific steps required in the process. Management accountants help analyze the direct costs of the inputs and allocate an appropriate amount of the indirect costs (lighting, rent, repairs, etc.) to the operation. Such analyses also evaluate the skill levels required of those who perform the tasks. Activity analyses in activity-based costing are the most thorough costing method—and are the most expensive to implement.

Historical Data

Relying on historical data for determining costs is relatively inexpensive but is less reliable than activity analysis. When reliable, historical data can be used to find the average or median historical cost for an operation. To implement continuous improvement, the best performance recorded could be used as a standard or, at least, as an ideal standard. However, historical data can perpetuate past inefficiencies or fail to take into account the impact of new technologies.

Market Expectations and Strategic Decisions

Market expectations and strategic decisions can determine a maximum cost level that is allowed for a product, as is the case when using target costing. Target costing is a product design technique in which the product reaches a particular target cost at the end of the production process. However, when a company is a price taker in the market (in other words, it must take the going rate for materials or labor), target costing must take these actual costs into account when setting standards. Strategic objectives, such as a program of continuous improvement or zero defects, will be accomplished only if the standards are set high.

Benchmarking

Benchmarking is the continuous, systematic process of measuring products, services, and practices against the best levels of performance. Benchmarking is frequently thought of as capturing best-in-class information, but the practice has a much wider application. Quite often, "best levels" are comparisons to external benchmarks of industry leaders. However, they may also be based on internal benchmarking information or measures from other organizations (outside an industry) that have similar processes. Good benchmarks can lead a company toward continuous improvement. However, a poor benchmark can have significant negative results. For example, using an incompatible industry as a benchmark can produce either unreachable or unchallenging goals. Also, benchmarking typically does not produce breakthroughs that lead to sustainable competitive advantage.

Resource Allocation

All entities have a finite amount of resources and want to make the most of their capital. The allocation of scarce resources among competing opportunities is accomplished through implementation of a strategy.

Master Budget

A master budget is a plan based on a company's strategy for controlling its operations for a specific period of time. A key point is that master budgets are fixed at an expected level of business activity.

Strategy

A company analyzes external factors to identify opportunities and threats; it analyzes internal factors to identify competitive advantages and weaknesses. When a company sees how it can match its strengths to market opportunities, it has a strategy that can be applied to the budget.

When a budget exists without consideration of strategy, it usually begins with the prior year's budget and misses opportunities to change the direction of the company, causing stagnation. Many once-great companies have met their demise because they failed to change in response to market demands. Implementing the strategy requires formulation of long-term plans, and long-term plans are implemented using a budget process.

Long-Term Planning

While a strategy is the starting point for achieving organizational goals, a long-term plan is needed to ensure that the strategy is implemented. A long-term plan is usually a five- to ten-year plan of actions required to achieve the company's goals. Planning for the long term can involve discontinuing certain operations over time, arranging for equity or debt financing, and allocating resources gradually to new branches of business. Such major reorganizations can be accomplished only over a period of time and usually involve the use of capital budgeting (part of the master budget). Capital budgeting is the process of allocating resources to an entity's proposed long-term projects. Because buildings, equipment, and hiring and training staff are all extremely expensive, such allocations must be made in accordance with strategy.

Short-Term Objectives

Short-term objectives are the variations in the long-term plan that result from capital budgeting, the operating results of past periods, and expected future results caused by the current economic, social, industrial, and technological environment. These variations are fed into each year's master budget.

Components of a Master Budget

The **master budget** is the overall plan for operations for a company or business unit over a year, an operating period, or a shorter duration. The master budget sets quantitative goals for all operations, including detailed plans for raising the required capital. Figure 1A-4 shows how the factors behind a master budget relate to it.

Figure 1A-4 Strategic Goals, Long-Term Objectives, Budgets, and Operations

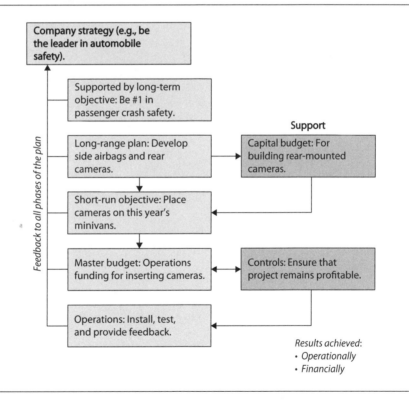

The master budget is a map showing where the company is heading. If it is properly designed, it will show the company heading in the same direction as the strategy and the long-term plan. The budget is more precise and of shorter duration than long-term plans, and it is more focused on responsibility centers than longer-term planning tools.

A master budget is broken down into an operating budget, a financial budget, and a capital budget.

- An **operating budget** identifies resources that are needed for operations and is concerned with the acquisition of these resources through purchase or manufacture. Production budgets, purchasing budgets, sales promotion budgets, and staffing budgets are all operating budgets.
- A **financial budget** matches sources of funds with uses of funds in order to achieve the goals of the firm, including budgets for cash inflows, outflows, financial position, operating income, and capital expenditures.
- A **capital budget** is used to plan how resources will be used to support significant investments in projects that have long-term implications. These projects could include the purchase of new equipment or investment in new facilities.

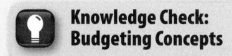

Knowledge Check: Budgeting Concepts

The next questions are intended to help you check your understanding and recall of the material presented in this topic. They do not represent the type of questions that appear on the CMA exam.

Directions: Answer each question in the space provided. Correct answers and section references appear after the knowledge check questions.

1. A management representative interviews the manager of the firm's tennis ball line and the tennis ball machine operators. The objective is to define a cost standard that each of these parties believes is the best result that could be achieved assuming that nothing went wrong. What sort of standard is being set?

   ☐ **a.** Authoritative ideal standard

   ☐ **b.** Participative ideal standard

   ☐ **c.** Authoritative currently attainable standard

   ☐ **d.** Participative currently attainable standard

2. Number the following steps in forming a master budget in the correct order:

   _____ Create master budget

   _____ Create long-term plans

   _____ Create short-term plans

   _____ Analyze the internal and external environment

   _____ Form strategic goals

3. Which of the following groups is most likely to introduce slack into a budget?

   ☐ **a.** Board of directors

   ☐ **b.** Top management

   ☐ **c.** Budget committee

   ☐ **d.** Middle and lower management

4. In setting standard costs for direct materials, what element must be determined first and why?

   _____

5. Identify at least three component budgets of a financial budget.

   _____, _____, and _____.

Knowledge Check Answers: Budgeting Concepts

1. A management representative interviews the manager of the firm's tennis ball line and the tennis ball machine operators. The objective is to define a cost standard that each of these parties believes is the best result that could be achieved assuming that nothing went wrong. What sort of standard is being set? *[See Types of Standards]*

    ☐ **a.**   Authoritative ideal standard

    ☑ **b.**   Participative ideal standard

    ☐ **c.**   Authoritative currently attainable standard

    ☐ **d.**   Participative currently attainable standard

2. Number the following steps in forming a master budget in the correct order: *[See Master Budget.]*

    5   Create master budget.

    3   Create long-term plans.

    4   Create short-term plans.

    1   Analyze the internal and external environment.

    2   Form strategic goals.

3. Which of the following groups is most likely to introduce slack into a budget? *[See Middle and Lower Management.]*

    ☐ **a.**   Board of directors

    ☐ **b.**   Top management

    ☐ **c.**   Budget committee

    ☑ **d.**   Middle and lower management

4. In setting standard costs for direct materials, what element must be determined first and why? *[See Standard Costs for Direct Materials and Labor.]*

    Quality must be determined first, because it affects all the other variables.

5. Identify at least three component budgets of a financial budget. *[See Components of a Master Budget.]*

    Component budgets of a financial budget include budgets for: cash inflows, outflows, financial position, operating income, and capital expenditures.

Forecasting Techniques

A VITAL FUNCTION OF MANAGING any business is planning for the future. Experienced judgment, intuition, and awareness of economic conditions may give business leaders a rough idea of what may happen in the future. However, this experience must be supported by various quantitative methods that can be used to forecast such outcomes as next quarter's sales volume or the viability of introducing a new product line. In addition, a degree of uncertainty needs to be incorporated into the decision-making process.

This topic looks at a number of forecasting techniques that companies can use to plan for future financial performance. The quantitative methods discussed here are regression analysis, time series analysis, smoothing, learning curve analysis, expected value, and sensitivity analysis.

 READ the Learning Outcome Statements (LOS) for this topic as found in Appendix A and then study the concepts and calculations presented here to be sure you understand the content you could be tested on in the CMA exam.

Quantitative Methods

When planning for the future, a company faces some degree of uncertainty and will rely on a variety of quantitative methods to help it make better decisions. This content focuses on quantitative methods in three areas:

Data analysis involves analyzing a given set of data to establish the relationship and/or pattern in the data. These analyses can be used to predict the outcome based on a given set of conditions (i.e., regression analysis), or they can be used to forecast the outcome based on an established pattern (i.e., time series analysis and smoothing).

Model building involves creating a mathematical model that establishes the relationship between different factors. Learning curve analysis is one type of model that is used to determine how the amount of time required to produce a product changes as the number of units produced changes.

Decision theory deals with uncertainty by looking at various potential outcomes that can happen in the future, along with the likelihood of these outcomes occurring. Expected value and sensitivity analysis are two methods that deal with uncertainty.

Regression Analysis

Linear regression analysis is a statistical method used to determine the impact one variable (or a group of variables) has on another variable. It provides the best, linear, unbiased estimate of the relationship between the dependent variable (Y) and one or more independent variables (X or X's). Linear regression often is used by management accountants to analyze cost behavior (i.e., determine the fixed and variable portions of a total cost) or to forecast future events such as sales levels.

The assumptions underlying linear regression are:

- Linearity. The relationship between the dependent variable and the independent variable(s) is linear.
- Stationary. The process underlying the relationship is stationary. This assumption is often called the constant process assumption.
- The differences between the actual values of the dependent variable and its predicted values (the error or residual terms) are normally distributed with a mean of zero and a constant standard deviation. In other words, the dependent variable is not correlated with itself; that is, it is not autocorrelated or serialcorrelated.
- The independent variables (X's) in multiple regression analysis are independent of each other. There is no multi-colinearity.

Regression analysis creates a linear equation based on the relationship between a dependent variable and one or more independent variables. The dependent variable (Y) is the value being forecast, such as sales or total costs. The independent variables (X's) are the factors that are assumed to influence or drive the variations seen in the dependent variable. It is assumed that the relationship between the dependent variable and the independent variable remains constant (hence the linear relationship).

There are two main types of regression analysis: **simple regression analysis**, which uses only one independent variable; and **multiple regression analysis**, which uses two or more independent variables.

Regression analysis equations systematically reduce estimation errors and are therefore also called least square regression. Regression analysis fits a line (the regression line) through data points—a line that minimizes the difference between the line (prediction) and the data point (actual). The statistical formula that the regression is based on produces the least amount of error between these two items.

Simple Linear Regression

Simple linear regression analysis can be used to analyze the relationship between sales and marketing costs.

For example: A retail firm called Build and Fix is trying to forecast sales and believes that store sales depend on marketing costs. To forecast sales for year 4, Build and Fix management collects data about its past sales and marketing expenditures. Figure 1A-5 summarizes the data.

Figure 1A-5 Data on Marketing Costs and Sales for Build and Fix

Quarter	Marketing Costs ($000)	Sales ($000)	Marketing Costs ($000)	Sales ($000)	Marketing Costs ($000)	Sales ($000)
	Year 1		Year 2		Year 3	
Q1	$50	$48,000	$100	$89,000	$40	$62,000
Q2	30	40,000	90	105,000	90	130,000
Q3	40	62,000	80	73,000	70	80,000
Q4	60	75,000	110	105,000	50	50,000

Figure 1A-6 shows the data from Figure 1A-5 on a scatter diagram. Note in the scatter diagram that the data exhibit an upward trend, indicating that there is a positive relationship between sales and marketing costs. This means that when marketing costs increase, sales also increase. Regression analysis attempts to estimate the linear relationship between sales and marketing costs. The result is a linear regression line, shown in Figure 1A-6.

Figure 1A-6 Marketing Costs as a Predictor of Sales

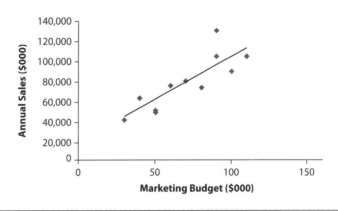

The dependent variable (Y), which is always plotted on the vertical axis, is sales. The independent variable (X) is plotted on the horizontal axis. In this example, it represents marketing costs. A mathematical expression of the original data points can be developed that can be used to forecast sales (Y) based on a given marketing budget. Since the regression line is a straight line that best fits the set of data points, it can be represented mathematically as the next equation:

$$Y = a + bX$$

where:

Y = annual sales; it is the dependent variable to be forecast.

a = amount of Y when X = 0. This value is also called the Y intercept, because when X = 0, Y = a, and on a graph, the line will intercept the Y axis at the value of a.

b = slope of the line, also known as the regression coefficient. It represents the "impact" X has on Y. For every 1 unit change in X, Y is expected to change by b units.

X = value for the independent variable (in this case, marketing costs) or the driver for the dependent variable to be forecast (in this case, annual sales).

Figure 1A-7 represents the results of the simple linear regression analysis performed on the given set of sales and marketing data in Figure 1A-5.

Figure 1A-7 Regression Values for Marketing Costs as Predictor of Sales

	Coefficients	T-Value	Standard Error
Intercept	$18,444,808.74	1.48	$12,460,200.96
Marketing costs	$861.31	4.98	$172.93

In the example shown in Figures 1A-6 and 1A-7, the regression equation is:

$$Y = \$18,444,809 + \$861(X)$$

where X represents the marketing budget. This formula can be used to go beyond the table and forecast sales with a marketing budget of $75,000.

$$Y = \$18,444,809 + \$861(75,000) = \$83,019,809 \text{ Forecast Sales}$$

Regression analysis also provides a number of objective benchmarks that allow users to evaluate the reliability of the regression equation. Three common measures are R-squared, T-value, and standard error of estimate (SE).

R-squared

R-squared (goodness of fit or coefficient of determination) is a value between 0 and 1 indicating the degree to which changes in a dependent variable can be predicted by changes in independent variables. R-squared shows how much of the variation in total cost is accounted for by the cost driver(s). It is the percentage of the variation in the dependent variable accounted for by the variability in the independent variable. A regression with an R-squared value closer to 1 has more explanatory power than a regression with an R-squared value closer to 0. Graphs of regressions with high R-squared values show data points lying near the regression line, while regressions with low R-squared values show more widely scattered data points.

The R-squared value for Build and Fix's sales and marketing costs is 0.7127. This means that approximately 71.27% of the variation in sales is accounted for by variation in marketing costs.

T-value

T-value measures whether an independent variable (X) has a valid, long-term relationship to a dependent variable. Generally, the T-value should be more than 2. A variable with a low T-value indicates little or no statistically significant relationship between the independent and dependent variables, and the variable should be removed from the regression because it can lead to inaccurate forecasts.

For Build and Fix, the T-value is greater than 2 for the marketing costs, which indicates that the impact marketing cost has on sales is statistically significant.

Standard Error of Estimate

The SE measures the dispersion around the regression line and allows the user to assess the accuracy of the predictions. That is, a user can build a confidence interval around the estimate. For normal (i.e., mound-shaped) distributions, approximately 68% of measurements will fall within plus or minus 1 standard error (depends on sample size). Approximately 95% will fall within plus or minus 2 standard errors.

Multiple Linear Regression

In the Build and Fix example, a simple linear regression analysis was used to estimate the impact that the amount of money spent on marketing would have on the company's sales. Using a simple regression analysis, it is assumed that marketing expenditures are the only factor that explain (or have an impact) on a company's sales level. Based on the results of the analysis, the R-squared is only 0.7127. That means only 71.27% of the variation in sales can be explained by changes in marketing expenditures, and the remaining 28.73% (100% – 71.27%) is explained by changes in other factors that are not included in the regression model.

In forecasting sales, an organization needs to take into consideration not only its marketing efforts but other factors, such as the economic conditions, its competitors' actions, its pricing strategy, and so on. All of these other factors can be incorporated into a multiple regression model, where they become the additional independent variables that can help to explain the other 28.73% in sales variation that cannot be explained by marketing expenditures.

In general, a multiple regression model looks very similar to a simple regression model, except that it has two or more independent variables (X_1, X_2, etc). The regression "line" from a multiple regression model can be represented mathematically as shown:

$$Y = a + b_1 X_1 + b_2 X_2 + b_3 X_3 + \ldots b_n X_n$$

For a multiple regression analysis, the interpretation of the Y-intercept (i.e., *a*), the regression coefficient of each of the independent variables (*b1*, *b2*, etc.), the R-square, and the T-value of each independent variable are similar to that of a simple regression analysis.

In addition to the R-squared, T-value, and standard error of the estimate, evaluating a multiple regression model requires the user to evaluate the correlation between the independent variables (X's) to assure the lack of multi-colinearity. A correlation matrix of the independent variables is used to accomplish this. As a general rule of thumb, as long as the correlation between any two independent variables is 0.7 or below, there is no problem. If the correlation between two of the independent variables is 0.7 or above, then one must be eliminated and the regression analysis must be run again.

Benefits and Shortcomings of Regression Analysis

Regression analysis gives management accountants an objective measure to use in evaluating the precision and reliability of estimations.

It is important to prepare a graph of the data prior to using regression analysis and determine whether any unusual data points, called outliers, are present. Regression analysis can be influenced strongly by outliers, which may result in an estimation line that is not representative of most of the data. If present, each outlier should be reviewed to determine whether it is due to a data recording error, a normal operating condition, or a unique and nonrecurring event. Regression analysis requires a collection of data points—preferably 30 or more—to be accurate.

Regression analysis assumes a linear relationship between one dependent variable and one or more independent variables. In the case of analyzing cost behavior, this linear assumption can be problematic if it is expected that costs decline due to learning curves (see the Learning Curve Analysis later in this topic) or when there are different relevant ranges of activity that cause costs to shift.

Regression analysis also assumes that past relationships between dependent and independent variables will hold into the future. When using regression analysis as a forecasting tool, it is important to evaluate or make adjustments for changes in the relationship between the variables over time. For example, clear knowledge that one part of a variable cost element is increasing makes the *b* coefficient less reliable for future periods.

When using the results of a regression analysis to make any prediction, it is important to remember that the dependent variables used for the prediction must fall within the range of the data set used to establish the regression line. For the Build and Fix sales and marketing costs, the marketing costs used to estimate the regression line fall in the range of $30,000 and $110,000. The company can reliably predict its sales for any marketing cost that falls within this range, but it cannot rely on the result if the marketing cost used in the prediction falls outside this range (e.g, $10,000 or $200,000).

One caveat regarding regression analysis is that the user must evaluate the reasonableness of the relationship between the dependent and independent variables.

Does it make sense that X causes Y to change? Any numbers can be input as X and Y variables and will result in an equation, but whether the equation makes sense must be based on the user's judgment.

Time Series Analysis

A **time series analysis** is a series of measurements of a variable taken at any time interval (hour, day, month, etc.), with the objective of finding patterns in the data that can aid in making forecasts or predictions of future values. Essentially, time series analysis involves using time as the independent variable in a regression analysis.

For example: FunMart, a retail store, tracks sales (the dependent variable) to determine whether they increase or decrease over time (the independent variable). Figure 1A-8 shows a table of time series data for FunMart, and Figure 1A-9 shows a scatter diagram of the data.

Figure 1A-8 Time Series Data—Retail Sales at FunMart

Quarter	Sales* ($000)	Quarter	Sales* ($000)	Quarter	Sales* ($000)	Quarter	Sales* ($000)
1	$120	5	$128	9	$135	13	$140
2	$136	6	$138	10	$144	14	$166
3	$134	7	$175	11	$139	15	$160
4	$145	8	$152	12	$152	16	$180

* In thousands of dollars

Figure 1A-9 Scatter Diagram of FunMart Time Series Data

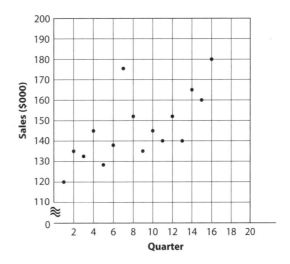

The ability to find patterns in data of these sorts helps the business owner make decisions, such as staffing requirements, how much merchandise should be ordered at a given time of year, or the state of the economy. Four components combine to provide the overall pattern in a time series analysis: trend, cycles, seasonality, and irregular variations.

Trend

Time series data may show a gradual shift to higher (up-sloping) or lower (down-sloping) values, called a trend. A long-term trend is usually the result of factors such as changes in population, technology, and consumer preferences. Figure 1A-10 shows the data for FunMart with a trend line drawn through it.

Figure 1A-10 Trend Line in FunMart Data

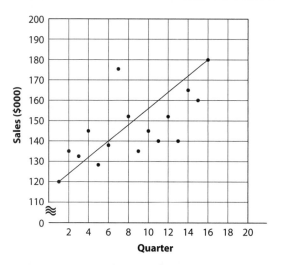

A trend line is used to predict, as closely as possible, future values of the dependent variable—in this case, sales. This can be accomplished by using the simple regression analysis discussed earlier, where sales will be the dependent variable and time (as measured in quarters) will be the independent variable. Analysts can use the trend to make decisions about planning and actions. If a trend line is upward, the company may gear up for increased sales and production. If the trend line is downward, the company may consider exit strategies.

Cycles

There may also be cyclical fluctuations in the time series analysis that are explained by a cycle in the overall economy. In this case, there may be an independent variable that is some form of economic indicator or index.

Some companies, such as those that sell inferior goods, do better in a poor economy. These are called countercyclical businesses or industries, because they go against the normal economic cycle. Others, called cyclical industries, do well in a good economy; these include producers of luxury goods. Noncyclical companies, such as the food industry, are more constant.

A recurring sequence of points above or below the trend line lasting more than one year can be attributed to the cyclical component of the time series.

Seasonality

The seasonal component is a measure of data with time as the independent variable within a single fiscal or calendar year. Unlike a straight trend line, there are peaks and troughs over time with regular patterns. Results from seasonal sales are due to changes in seasonal activities and preferences. The travel industry usually shows a seasonal rise in family travel in the summer months and a dip in business travel near holidays.

Irregular Variations

The irregular component represents the random variability in a time series; it is any deviation of data on the time series from values that can be observed as trend, cyclical, and seasonal components. The irregular component is often called noise.

Irregular variations are caused by short-term, unanticipated, and nonrecurring factors, such as natural or man-made disasters. Analysts cannot predict the impact of irregular factors on the time series.

Benefits and Limitations of Time Series Analysis

Time series analysis helps analysts to see patterns that are clearly upward or downward so managers can make decisions to expand or exit the business or product market. Businesses that show cyclical trends can match production and expenditures to leading economic indicators, and businesses that show seasonal patterns can stock up and increase production to meet high seasonal needs.

Time series analysis is limited in that it is assumed that past patterns will continue into the future. However, there are often other missing variables that also affect results, and analysts cannot predict irregular events such as natural disasters.

Smoothing

Time series data generally exhibit a great deal of random fluctuation, and patterns are difficult to detect. **Smoothing** is an analytical method that levels out the random fluctuations from the irregular component of the time series. Smoothing methods are effective for time series that do not exhibit significant patterns due to trend, cyclical, or seasonal effects. Smoothing generally provides a high level of accuracy for short-range forecasts, such as a forecast for the next time period. There are three smoothing methods: moving averages, weighted moving averages, and exponential smoothing.

Moving Averages

The moving averages method uses the average of the most recent data value set of a given time period. The mathematical formula for the moving average is:

$$\text{Moving Average} = \frac{\Sigma \text{ Most Recent Data Values for } n}{n}$$

The variable n in the equation represents the number of time periods.

For example: FunMart has sales of $166 million, $160 million, and $180 million in the three most recent quarters.

The moving average is:

$$\frac{\Sigma\,(166 + 160 + 180)}{3} = \frac{506}{3} = 168.67$$

This moving average is used to predict sales in the next quarter.

Weighted Moving Averages

When taking the average of the last n quarters of data in the moving averages method, each quarter is given equal weighting (in the example, one-third for each quarter). The weighted moving average assumes that the most recent data has more power of prediction than data that came before, so more weight is given to the most recent data than to earlier data.

For example: Consider the calculation of the weighted moving average for sales in three quarters at FunMart as a forecast of sales in the forthcoming quarter. Each of the first three quarters is given a different weighting, by a fraction of a whole, so that the total of all the weightings equals 1. Assume that quarter 16 is assigned a weight of 0.5, quarter 15 a weight of 0.3, and quarter 14 a weight of 0.2. Using a weighted moving average, quarter 17 sales would be forecasted as shown:

$$0.2(166) + 0.3(160) + 0.5(180) = 171.2$$

Exponential Smoothing

Exponential smoothing uses a weighted average of past time series, selecting only one weight—that of the most recent set of data. The weights for the other data values are automatically computed, getting smaller as the time period moves farther into the past. The basic exponential smoothing model is:

$$F_{t+1} = aY_t + (1 - a)F_t$$

where:

F_{t+1} = forecast of the time series for the period $t + 1$ (e.g, the fifth quarter for FunMart), where t is the current time period. This is the objective of the current forecast.

Y_t = actual value of the time series in period t (e.g, sales in the fourth quarter for FunMart).

F_t = forecast of the time series for period t (forecast for the fourth quarter). This was the objective of the previous forecast. Notice that the right side of the equation relates forecast sales to actual sales (for quarter 4 at FunMart).

a = smoothing constant ($0 \leq a \leq 1$). The smoothing constant is derived through trial and error on an initial set of data to determine what value of a, which must be between 0 and 1, results in the forecast closest to the actual sales for the period. Mean standard error can be used to find the best approximation of an effective smoothing constant.

If the time series data contain substantial random variability, a small value for a is preferable, because the forecasts should not be adjusted too quickly. If time series data contain relatively little random variability, larger values for the smoothing constant have the advantage of quickly adjusting forecasts, allowing the forecast to react more quickly to changing conditions.

Notice that the formula is essentially forecasting sales in the period $t + 1$ by adding the value of the smoothing constant times actual sales for period t to the complement of the smoothing constant times the forecast for period t.

For example:

If $a = 0.2$, $Y_2 = 180$, and $F_2 = 150$, then:

$$F_3 = a(Y_2) + (1 - a)F_2 = 0.2(180) + 0.8(150) = 36 + 120 = 156$$

Exponential smoothing has minimal data requirements and is therefore a good smoothing method to use when forecasts are required for a large number of dependent variables. Not all past data need be saved in order to compute the forecast for the next period. Once the smoothing constant has been selected, the exponential smoothing method requires only two pieces of information to compute the forecast: the forecast and actual values for the last (current) period.

Smoothing techniques, such as exponential smoothing, work well when the time series is stable, exhibiting no significant trends, cyclical effects, or seasonal effects. However, unless modified appropriately, smoothing methods will not work as well when there are significant trends or seasonal variations. In fact, the point of smoothing techniques is to reduce the impact of changes in the data to avoid placing too much weight on random variations. Smoothing, therefore, can make trends harder to spot. Other techniques or modification (e.g, seasonal adjustments) need to be adopted in such situations.

Learning Curve Analysis

Learning curve analysis is a systematic method for estimating costs based on increased learning by the business, group, or individual, which allows them to become more efficient at completing tasks. As a result, costs will decrease as learning increases. However, this happens only to a certain point, and then costs level off. The learning curve is sometimes also called the experience curve.

Calculation of the learning curve is based on the learning rate, which is the percentage by which average time decreases from the previous level as output doubles. The learning curve can be measured in two ways:

1. Incremental unit-time learning model (also called the Crawford method)
2. Cumulative average-time learning model (also called the Wright method)

The cumulative average-time learning model (Wright method) is the generally accepted model.

Typical decreases in time based on learning range from 10% to 20% each time production doubles. A learning curve for a 20% reduction is called an 80% learning curve; a 10% reduction arises from a 90% curve.

Because of their different approaches, the incremental unit-time and cumulative average-time methods produce different results for the same data. The incremental method is considered more appropriate for large-scale, complex operations, while the cumulative method is considered to be simpler.

Incremental Unit-Time Learning Model

The incremental unit-time learning model measures increased efficiency by adding the incremental time for each unit to the previous total time. Average time per unit is then calculated by dividing total time by the number of units.

For example: Assume that one new worker can assemble his or her first widget in 10 hours. If two new workers each build one widget, then it would take 10 hours to assemble each widget, for a total of 20 hours of production time and an average production time of 10 hours per widget. However, if one worker assembles both widgets, the first unit will take 10 hours, but because of the worker's learning experience, the second unit will take only 8 hours—assuming learning takes place at a rate of 80% (.8 $\times$ 10 hours = 8 hours). The total time to build the two widgets is 18 hours, so the average production time per widget is 9 hours.

Figure 1A-11 shows the effect of the learning curve on average production time, as calculated by the incremental unit-time learning model. Assuming an 80% curve, production time (Y) decreases by 20% for each doubling of widget production (X). Total hours in column three results from adding the current production time (Y) to the previous total (a).

Figure 1A-12 is a graph of the average time, or cost, per widget with a learning curve. It is a visual representation of the impact of the 80% learning rate assumed in the example.

Figure 1A-11 Incremental Unit-Time Learning Model

Widget (X)	Hours for This Widget * (Y)	Total Hours (c = a + Y)	Average Time per Widget (c ÷ X)
1	10 (value of a)	10	10 (10 ÷ 1)
2	8 (10 × 0.8) = Y	18 (10 + 8)	9 (18 ÷ 2)
4	6.4 (8 × 0.8) = Y	31.42**	7.855 (31 ÷ 4)
8	5.12 (6.4 × 0.8) = Y	53.47**	6.68 (53.47 ÷ 8)

* Previous value of Y × learning curve rate (assumed to be 80% in this example).

** The total hours for four and eight widgets (31.42 and 53.47) are calculated by using a formula that is not shown here. The formula is complex, and calculations are usually done by software or numbers are read from standard tables. It may appear from this table that the total hours to produce eight widgets would simply be derived by multiplying 8 × 5.12. However, 5.12 is the amount of time that it took to produce the eighth unit. The seventh unit took more time to produce than the eighth unit; the sixth unit took more time to produce than the fifth unit, and so on. Learning curve calculators can be found through an Internet search.

Notice that the learning curve levels off. Learning increases efficiency up to a certain point, at which productivity reaches equilibrium and then levels off.

Figure 1A-12 Incremental Unit-Time Learning Curve

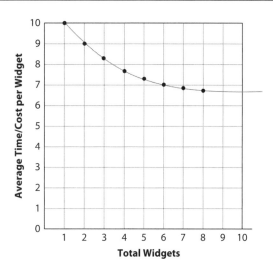

Cumulative Average-Time Learning Model

The cumulative average-time learning model also measures increased efficiency due to learning. It calculates cumulative total time by multiplying the incremental unit by the cumulative average time per unit.

For the widget learning curve example, the cumulative total time for assembling two widgets would be 16 hours (8 hours × 2 units). The individual unit time for the last unit then is 6 hours (16 hours total cumulative time minus the previous total of 10 hours).

Figure 1A-13 shows the previous learning curve example applied to the cumulative average-time learning model.

Figure 1A-13 Cumulative Average-Time Learning Model

X	Cumulative Average Time per Widget* (c)	Cumulative Total Time (c × X)	Individual Time for xth Widget
1	10 (value of c)	10 (10 × 1)	10
2	8 (10 × 0.8)	16 (8 × 2)	6 (16 – 10)
4	6.4 (8 × 0.8)	25.6 (6.4 × 4)	4.54[†]
8	5.12 (6.4 × 0.8)	40.96 (5.12 × 8)	3.55[†]

* Each c = rate (0.8 here) × the preceding value of the variable c.

[†] Calculated by a formula not shown here.

Note the difference in assumptions from before.

Here, for example, the first two units take an average time of 8 hours to produce (0.8 × 10 for the 80% curve). In the previous calculations, the second unit required 8 hours to produce, for an average of 9 hours when combined with the 10 hours required for the first unit.

Here the 0.8 multiplier is applied to the time required to produce all accumulated units, in other words, not only to the time required to produce the incremental unit.

Figure 1A-14 is a graph of the increase in efficiency from learning as measured by the cumulative average-time learning model.

Figure 1A-14 Cumulative Average-Time Learning Curve

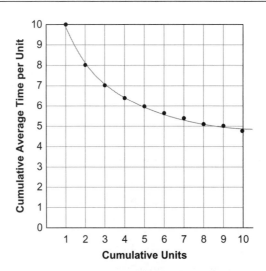

Benefits and Limitations of Learning Curve Analysis

Companies use learning curves to make a number of decisions, including setting prices. A company may set a price lower than the initial costs of production in order to gain market share, based on the assumption that as learning increases, production costs will decrease. Some companies use learning curve analysis when evaluating performance, because it expects an individual's productivity to increase with the individual's learning curve. Learning affects quality and improves productivity. Other factors contribute to the learning curve besides production output. These include job rotation, work teams, and total quality management.

Next are listed the limitations of learning curve analysis.

- The learning curve approach is not as effective when machinery performs repetitive tasks, such as robotics. It is most appropriate for labor-intensive contexts that involve repetitive tasks, long production runs, and repeated trials.
- The learning rate is assumed to be constant in the calculations, but actual declines in labor time are not constant. The analyst needs to update projections based on the observed progression of learning.
- Conclusions might be unreliable because observed changes in productivity actually may be due to factors other than learning, such as a change in the labor mix, the product mix, or some combination of the two.

Expected Value

When a company is trying to forecast its sales for the upcoming year, the results can vary depending on the economic conditions. If the economy is booming, the company's sales may be higher, but if the economy is in a recession, the company's sales will likely be lower. Thus, future sales are considered to be a random variable because their outcome is uncertain.

After creating sales forecasts based on various economic conditions and assigning a probability for the likelihood of each economic scenario, the company can lay out the sales forecasts and probabilities for the various scenarios in a table. An example of such a table for Hardware Haven is presented in Figure 1A-15.

Figure 1A-15 Hardware Haven Sales Forecasts Based on Economic Conditions

Economic Condition	Sales Forecast	Probability
Boom	$3,000,000	0.1
Average	$2,000,000	0.8
Recession	$600,000	0.1

Using the information shown in the figure, the company can determine the expected value of its sales by using the next formula:

$$\text{Expected Value (EV)} = \Sigma\, S \times (P_x)$$

where:

EV = expected value

Σ = sum of the variables that follow in the equation

S = amount associated with a specific outcome

P_x = probability associated with a specific outcome

To calculate the expected value , simply multiply the outcome of each possible outcome by the probability associated with that possible outcome, and then add all of them together. The expected value of the sales in Figure 1A-15 is calculated as shown next:

$$\text{Expected sales} = \$3,000,000(0.1) + \$2,000,000(0.8) + \$600,000(0.1)$$
$$= \$1,960,000$$

In this example, given the uncertainties associated with the economic conditions, the company expects its sales, on average, to be \$1,960,000 for the upcoming year. It is important to note that this is not the actual outcome the company will see in the upcoming year. The expected value simply represents the long-run average of the outcome (in this case, sales) based on the given uncertainties (represented by the probability assigned to the different outcomes).

Benefits and Limitations of Expected Value

The expected value technique helps an organization determine the average outcome of an event when faced with uncertainties. These averages often help the organization decide whether it should undertake certain actions.

For example: An organization may be presented with an investment option with a 60% chance of making a profit of \$300,000 and a 40% chance of incurring a loss of \$500,000. The calculation of the expected value of this investment reveals that the expected profit is:

$$\text{Expected Profit: } (\$300,000 \times 0.6) + (-\$500,000 \times 0.4) = -\$20,000$$

In other words, this investment is expected to lose, on average, \$20,000. Given this information, it would not be a good idea for the organization to pursue this investment.

However, the expected value calculation is only as good as the estimated potential outcomes for each scenario and the probability assigned to each scenario. If any of these assumptions is unreliable, then the expected value that is calculated cannot be trusted in making sound decisions.

Expected value analysis assumes that the decision maker is risk neutral. If the decision maker is either a risk taker or risk averse, then the expected value model would not be appropriate.

Sensitivity Analysis

Decision makers use sensitivity analysis to help decide what changes in a given situation (called the "state of nature") are most likely to produce a particular outcome (called a "payoff"). For example, to reduce the level of crime in a neighborhood, actions might include increasing the amount of street lighting, putting more police officers on the streets, or providing supervised activities for local teenagers. The question is: How sensitive is the crime rate to changes in these variables?

Sensitivity analysis can be used to study impacts on qualitative, or subjective, states of nature and payoffs as well as quantifiable outcomes like amount of crime. The neighborhood improvement analysis, for example, could focus on perceived quality-of-life improvements rather than number of crimes committed.

Sensitivity analysis is a form of what-if analysis, because it is conducted by changing a specific variable (i.e., an input) and determining how sensitive the outcome is to the changes in the input. It helps the decision maker determine which points of input are critical to the choice of the best decision alternative.

The outcome (i.e., solution to a particular problem) is sensitive to a particular input if a small change in the input results in a significant change in the outcome. In such a case, input at this point should be very accurate to aid in making decisions.

The outcome is not sensitive to a particular input if a small, or even large, change in the input does not result in a change in the outcome.

For example: Hardware Haven is changing the probability assigned to the various economic conditions.

Figure 1A-16 Hardware Haven's Alternative Probabilities for Economic Conditions

Economic Condition	Sales Forecast	Original Probability	Alternative Probability 1	Alternative Probability 2
Boom	$3,000,000	0.1	0.6	0.1
Average	2,000,000	0.8	0.3	0.2
Recession	600,000	0.1	0.1	0.7

In the scenario shown in Figure 1A-16, the changes in the probability assigned to the various economic conditions reflect Hardware Haven's outlook regarding the economic condition in the upcoming year. In the original scenario, the company expects the economic condition to most likely be "average" and thus, assigns an 80% probability to its occurrence. If the company is optimistic about the economic condition in the upcoming year, the probability distribution will be represented by alternative probability 1 (as indicated by a higher probability assigned to an economic boom). However, if Hardware Haven is pessimistic about the economic condition in the upcoming year, the probability distribution will be represented by alternative probability 2 (as indicated by a higher probability assigned to an economic recession).

Using the information presented in Figure 1A-16, Hardware Haven's expected sales using the original probability scenario as well as the alternative probabilities 1 and 2 are calculated as shown next.

Original Probability

Expected Sales = ($3,000,000 × 0.1) + ($2,000,000 × 0.8) + ($600,000 × 0.1)
$$= \$1,960,000$$

Alternative Probability 1

Expected Sales = ($3,000,000 × 0.6) + ($2,000,000 × 0.3) + ($600,000 × 0.1)
$$= \$2,460,000$$

Alternative Probability 2

Expected Sales = ($3,000,000 × 0.1) + ($2,000,000 × 0.2) + $600,000 × 0.7)
$$= \$1,120,000$$

When Hardware Haven becomes more optimistic, expected sales increase from the original level of $1,960,000 to $2,460,000 (a 25.51% increase); and when the company becomes more pessimistic, expected sales decrease from $1,960,000 to $1,120,000 (a 42.86% decrease). These results indicate that the company's expected sales are very sensitive to its outlook regarding the upcoming economic conditions.

Benefits and Limitations of Sensitivity Analysis

Sensitivity analysis shows managers how susceptible the outcomes of decisions are to changes in any parameter or estimate. Managers may be faced with a situation in which any slight variance in an estimate will result in a large change in the outcome, or, just as important, a large variance in an estimate may not result in a noticeable change in the outcome.

In addition, the change in one estimate or parameter could have an impact on another. If managers are not aware of this mutual relationship and make only one change, the results of their sensitivity analysis will not be reliable.

Sensitivity analysis can be used to estimate the impact on the outcome of decisions of occurrences that may or may not happen. This is sometimes called the what-if approach. *For example:* What if workers strike and hold up production? What will be the impact on the bottom line?

Knowledge Check: Forecasting Techniques

The next questions are intended to help you check your understanding and recall of the material presented in this topic. They do not represent the type of questions that appear on the CMA exam.

Directions: Answer each question in the space provided. Correct answers and section references appear after the knowledge check questions.

1. An analyst generates a regression equation of $Y = \$1,125,000 + \$2(X)$ as a predictor of a company's sales of cough syrup, where X = marketing costs. If the firm spends $50,000 on marketing, what will expected sales be?

    _____.

2. Using the cumulative average-time method and a 90% learning rate, what would be the total time required to produce 4 units of a product if the first unit was produced in 5 hours?

    ☐ **a.** 20 total hours

    ☐ **b.** 18 total hours

    ☐ **c.** 17.6 total hours

    ☐ **d.** 16.2 total hours

3. Which of the following is **not** an assumption of simple regression analysis?

    ☐ **a.** There is a linear relationship between variables.

    ☐ **b.** There is only one independent variable.

    ☐ **c.** There may be several dependent variables.

    ☐ **d.** Past relationships will continue in the future.

4. A time series analysis of a business's sales shows a decline in sales every summer, with a peak during the winter. These results could be:

    ☐ **a.** a downward trend.

    ☐ **b.** cyclical fluctuations.

    ☐ **c.** an upward trend.

    ☐ **d.** seasonal fluctuations.

5. Exponential smoothing

    ☐ **a.** places the greatest emphasis on the most recent data set.

    ☐ **b.** places the greatest emphasis on the earliest data set.

    ☐ **c.** places the same value on every data set.

    ☐ **d.** forecasts the dependent variable by increasing the R-squared value.

6. Sensitivity analysis can be used for all of the following except:

   ☐ **a.** figuring out potential outcomes if probabilities are different than anticipated.

   ☐ **b.** figuring out how to best allocate limited resources among alternatives.

   ☐ **c.** figuring out whether slight differences in anticipated events will affect a decision.

   ☐ **d.** figuring out whether changes in payoff dollars impact a decision.

7. Match each measure to its description by drawing a line between them:

Measures	Definitions
R-squared	Measures the dispersion around the regression line and allows the user to assess the accuracy of the predictions.
SE	Measures whether an independent variable (X) is significant (i.e., does not equal zero).
T-value	Shows how much of the variation in the dependent variable is accounted for by variation in the independent variable(s).

8. Identify what the following formula calculates, and then define the component factors:

$$F_{t+1} = aY_t + (1 - a) F_t$$

9. Hardware Haven is considering expanding its product line to offer a full range of plants and garden supplies. The marketing director says that he is giving the project an 80% chance of delivering a profit of $600,000. The operations manager believes that the market for garden supplies will not support the investment, the facility is not well suited to maintaining plants and that, overall, there is a 20% chance that they will lose $1.4 million. Strictly on the basis of these numbers, should the firm make the investment?

10. An organization has potential cash inflows of $10,000, $15,000, and $40,000. The probability of the entity receiving them is 50%, 35% and 15%, respectively. Using this information, compute the expected cash flow.

Knowledge Check Answers: Forecasting Techniques

1. An analyst generates a regression equation of Y = $1,125,000 + $2(X) as a predictor of a company's sales of cough syrup, where X = marketing costs. If the firm spends $50,000 on marketing, what will expected sales be? *[See Simple Linear Regression.]*

   $1,125,000 + $2($50,000) = $1,125,000 + $100,000 = $1,225,000

2. Using the cumulative average-time method and a 90% learning rate, what would be the total time required to produce 4 units of a product if the first unit was produced in 5 hours? *[See Cumulative Average-Time Learning Model.]*

   ☐ **a.** 20 total hours

   ☐ **b.** 18 total hours

   ☐ **c.** 17.6 total hours

   ☑ **d.** 16.2 total hours

   At a 90% learning rate, if the first unit takes 5 hours to produce, 2 units will take an average of 4.5 hours (0.9 × 5) and 4 will take an average of 4.05 hours each (0.9 × 4.5), for a total of 16.2 hours (4.05 × 4 units).

3. Which of the following is **not** an assumption of simple regression analysis? *[See Mutiple Linear Regression.]*

   ☐ **a.** There is a linear relationship between variables.

   ☐ **b.** There is only one independent variable.

   ☑ **c.** There may be several dependent variables.

   ☐ **d.** Past relationships will continue in the future.

   Simple regression analysis assumes one dependent and one independent variable; multiple regression assumes more than one independent variable but only one dependent variable.

4. A time series analysis of a business's sales shows a decline in sales every summer, with a peak during the winter. These results could be: *[See Seasonality.]*

   ☐ **a.** a downward trend.

   ☐ **b.** cyclical fluctuations.

   ☐ **c.** an upward trend.

   ☑ **d.** seasonal fluctuations.

5. Exponential smoothing *[See Exponential Smoothing.]*
   - ☑ **a.** places the greatest emphasis on the most recent data set.
   - ☐ **b.** places the greatest emphasis on the earliest data set.
   - ☐ **c.** places the same value on every data set.
   - ☐ **d.** forecasts the dependent variable by increasing the R-squared value.

6. Sensitivity analysis can be used for all of the following except: *[See Sensitivity Analysis.]*
   - ☐ **a.** figuring out potential outcomes if probabilities are different than anticipated.
   - ☑ **b.** figuring out how to best allocate limited resources among alternatives.
   - ☐ **c.** figuring out whether slight differences in anticipated events will affect a decision.
   - ☐ **d.** figuring out whether changes in payoff dollars impact a decision.

7. Correct matches are shown. *[See Simple Linear Regression.]*

Measures	Definitions
R-squared	Shows how much of the variation in the dependent variable is accounted for by variation in the independent variable(s).
SE	Measures the dispersion around the regression line and allows the user to assess the accuracy of the predictions.
T-value	Measures whether an independent variable (X) is significant (i.e., does not equal zero).

8. Identify what the following formula calculates, and then define the component factors: *[See Exponential Smoothing.]*

   $$F_{t+1} = aY_t + (1 - a) F_t$$

   Basic exponential smoothing model.

   F_{t+1} = forecast of the time series for the period $t + 1$

   Y_t = actual value of the time series in period t

   F_t = forecast of the time series for period t

9. Hardware Haven is considering expanding its product line to offer a full range of plants and garden supplies. The marketing director says that he is giving the project an 80% chance of delivering a profit of $600,000. The operations manager believes that the market for garden supplies will not support the investment, the facility is not well suited to maintaining plants and that overall there is a 20% chance that they will lose $1.4 million. Strictly on the basis of these numbers, should the firm make the investment? *[See Expected Value.]*

Yes, based on calculation of expected value:

Expected Value, Marketing Director Estimate = **0.8** × **$600,000** = **$480,000**

Expected Value, Operations Manager Estimate = **0.2** × **$1,400,000** = **$280,000**

Total Expected Value = **$480,000 – $280,000** = **$200,000**

10. An organization has potential cash inflows of $10,000, $15,000, and $40,000. The probability of the entity receiving them is 50%, 35% and 15%, respectively. Using this information, compute the expected cash flow.

$$\$10,000 \times 50\% = \$5,000$$

$$\$15,000 \times 35\% = \$5,250$$

$$\$40,000 \times 15\% = \$6,000$$

The expected cash flow is $16,250

Budgeting Methodologies

T O USE ITS BUDGET AS an effective planning and management tool, a company must choose a budget methodology that supports and reinforces its management approach. A firm looking to continuously improve and reinvent its operations may not be well served by an incremental budget system. For a stable operation with a few products, the investment in an activity-based budget effort may not be worth the effort. However, the availability of a range of budget methods enables an organization, and its constituent departments and divisions, to create budgets that are meaningful and appropriate to their requirements.

This topic covers the different types of budget systems, including master budgets, project budgets, activity-based budgets, incremental budgets, zero-based budgets, continuous (rolling) budgets, and flexible budgets.

 READ the Learning Outcome Statements (LOS) for this topic as found in Appendix A and then study the concepts and calculations presented here to be sure you understand the content you could be tested on in the CMA exam.

Options for Budget Creation

An organization's **master budget**, also known as an annual business plan or profit plan, is a comprehensive budget for a year or less. Every aspect of the company's revenue and cost flows are projected, starting with the sales budget, based on its forecasted sales for the upcoming periods, and ending with a set of pro forma financial statements, which include the income statement and balance sheet. The benefits of having a master budget are numerous and the drawbacks are few. Virtually every company needs some form of master budget.

Depending on the types of business, organizational structure, complexity of operations, and management philosophy, a company can choose different approaches in formulating its master budget. The company can even adopt different approaches for different pieces of its master budget. Six different budgeting systems that a company can use to create its budgets are:

1. **Project budgeting.** Used for creating a budget for specific projects rather than for an entire company
2. **Activity-based budgeting.** Focuses on classifying costs based on activities rather than based on departments or products
3. **Incremental budgeting.** Starts with the prior year's budget and produces increments into the future based on the prior year's results and coming year's expectations
4. **Zero-based budgeting.** Starts each new budgeting cycle from scratch as though the budgets are prepared for the first time
5. **Continuous (or rolling) budgeting.** Allows the budget to be continually updated by removing information for the period just ended (e.g, March of this year) and adding estimated data for the same period next year (e.g, March of next year)
6. **Flexible budgeting.** Serves as a control mechanism that evaluates the performance of managers by comparing actual revenue and expenses to the budgeted amount for the actual activities (and not the budgeted activities)

These budgeting systems are not mutually exclusive; a company can choose to adopt several of them simultaneously.

Project Budgeting

Project budgets are used when a project is completely separate from other elements of a company or is the only element of the company. A motion picture has a crew and costs that are related solely to that movie. A ship, a road, an aircraft, or other major capital asset is also often budgeted using a project budget. The time frame for a project budget is simply the duration of the project, but a multiyear project could be broken down by year. Successful past project budgets for similar projects should be used as benchmarks when developing project budgets. Project budgets are developed using the same techniques and components as shown for master budgeting, except that the focus will be solely on costs related to the project instead of the company as a whole. The overhead budget is simplified because the company will allocate certain portions of the company's fixed and variable overhead to the project, and all remaining overhead for the company is excluded from the project budget.

Project budget advantages include the ability to contain all of a project's costs so that its individual impact can be easily measured. Project budgets work well on both large and small scales, and project management software can facilitate developing and tracking these budgets. A potential limitation of project budgets occurs when projects use resources and staff that are committed to the entire organization rather than dedicated to the project. In such situations, the budget will contain links to these resource centers, and affected individuals may be reporting to two or more supervisors. Care must be taken in dividing costs and lines of authority.

Activity-Based Budgeting

An **activity-based budget** (ABB) focuses on activities instead of departments or products. Each activity is matched with the most appropriate cost driver, which is any volume-based (e.g, labor hours or square feet) or activity-based (e.g, number of parts to assemble for a machine) unit of measurement of the cost of a job or activity needed to sustain operations. Costs are divided into cost pools, such as unit, batch, product, and facility. Cost pools include homogeneous costs that all vary in the same proportion to the rise and fall of production. Fixed costs are in one pool, and different levels of variable costs are in their own pools. The accuracy of these groupings should be evaluated each time a master budget is prepared. The concept of activity-based costing (ABC) is discussed in greater detail in Section C: Cost Management.

Whereas traditional budgeting focuses on input resources and expresses budgeting units in terms of functional areas, ABB focuses on value-added activities and expresses budgeting units in terms of activity costs. Traditional budgeting places emphasis on increasing management performance; ABB places emphasis on teamwork, synchronized activity, and customer satisfaction.

ABB proponents believe that traditional costing obscures the relationships between costs and outputs by oversimplifying the measurements into such categories as labor hours, machine hours, or output units for an entire process or department. Instead of using only volume drivers as a measurement tool, ABB uses activity-based cost drivers, such as number of setups, to make a clear connection between resource consumption and output. ABB will also use volume-based drivers if they are the most appropriate measurement unit for a particular activity. If the relationships are made clear, managers can see how resource demands are affected by changes in products offered, product designs, manufacturing techniques, customer base, and market share. Each planned activity will have its cost implications highlighted. Because of this, companies using ABB will be able to continuously improve their budgeting. Conversely, traditional budgets focus on past (historical) budgets and often continue funding items that would be cut if their cost-effectiveness were better known.

ABB can be used as the foundation of a master budgeting process. The resulting subbudgets would be based on different ways of measuring the costs, so the resulting proportions of costs would be weighted differently. For instance, some portion of the indirect materials or labor that would be part of overhead could be tracked more carefully and included in direct materials and direct labor amounts.

For example: Figure 1A-17 displays an overhead budget created for Bluejay Manufacturing Company using an activity-based approach. It shows overhead cost by activities, such as production setup, fabrication, assembly, quality control inspections, and engineering changes.

A key advantage of ABB is greater precision in determining costs, especially when multiple departments or products need to be tracked. This advantage comes at a cost, and a potential drawback to ABB can occur if the cost of designing and maintaining the ABB system exceeds the cost savings from better planning. Therefore,

Figure 1A-17 Activity-Based Overhead Budget for Bluejay Manufacturing Company

Activity	Usage	Activity Rate	Activity Cost
Machine setup	80 setup	$4000/setup	$320,000
Fabrication	1,700 DLH*	$5/DLH	8,500
Assembly	6,000 DLH	$12/DLH	72,000
Inspection	100 inspections	$2,500/inspection	250,000
Engineering changes	15 changes	$10,000/changes	150,000
Total overhead cost			$800,500

* DLH = direct labor hours.

ABB is most appropriate in businesses that have complexity in their number of products, number of departments, or other factors, such as setups. This is because the more complex a situation becomes, the less useful is the broad brush of traditional costing.

Incremental Budgeting

An **incremental budget** is a general type of budget that starts with the prior year's budget and uses projected changes in sales and the operating environment to adjust individual items in the budget upward or downward. It is the opposite of a zero-based budget. The main drawback to using this type of budget (and the reason that some companies use zero-based budgets) is that the budgets tend to only increase in size over the years. A sense of entitlement may also arise with the use of an incremental budget.

Zero-Based Budgeting

In order to avoid situations in which ineffective elements of a business continue to exist simply because they were on the prior budget, some companies use zero-based budgets , which, as the name implies, start with zero dollars allocated. While the traditional budget focuses on changes to the past budget, the **zero-based budget** focuses on constant cost justification of each and every item in a budget. Managers must conduct in-depth reviews of each area under their control to provide such justification.

The strength of the zero-based budget is that it forces review of all elements of a business. Zero-based budgets can create efficient, lean organizations and therefore are popular with government and nonprofit organizations. A zero-based budget is a way of taking a new look at an old problem.

The first step in developing a zero-based budget is to have each department manager rank all department activities from most to least important and assign a cost to each activity. Upper management reviews these lists, called "decision packages," and cuts items that lack justification or are less critical. Upper management asks questions, such as "Should the activity be performed and if it is not, what will happen?" or "Are there substitute methods of providing this function such as outsourcing or customer self-service?" Managers may also use benchmark figures and cost-benefit analysis to help decide what to cut. Only those items approved appear in the budget. The cost of the accepted items may be arrived at through discussion and negotiation with the department managers. Once the budget figures are determined, the zero-based budget becomes the basis for a master budget.

Theoretically, zero-based budgets have the advantage of focusing on every line item instead of just the exceptions. They should motivate managers to identify and remove items that are more costly than the benefits provided. These budgets are especially useful when new management is hired. Zero-based budgets have a major drawback in that they encourage managers to exhaust all of their resources during a budget period for fear that they will be allocated less during the next budget cycle. If a manager has incorporated budget slack into the budget, a zero-based budget can encourage a significant amount of waste and unnecessary purchasing.

One issue with zero-based budgeting is the time-consuming and expensive annual review process. As a result, the review often may be less thorough than it is intended to be. In addition, by not using prior budgets, the firm may be ignoring lessons learned from prior years. If used every year, a zero-based budget actually may become little more than an incremental budget with a little extra processing. Managers simply remember their old justifications and figures and use them the following year.

The time and expense of a zero-based budget often is mitigated by performing zero-based budgets only on a periodic basis, such as once every five years, and applying a different budget method in the other years. Or the firm might rotate the use of zero-based budgeting for a different division each year.

Continuous (Rolling) Budgets

A **continuous budget**, or rolling budget, adds a new period onto the budget at the end of each period so there are always several periods planned for the future and the budgets remain uptodate with the operating environment. As with the other budget types, this budget becomes the master budget for an entity. However, while other budgets will expire at the end of the budgeted time period, the time frame for this budget always remains the same—for example, one year, no matter if it is viewed in January or July.

Therefore, if the period is a month, each month a new set of monthly financial statements is issued to each person responsible for preparing the budget. In a monthly budget meeting, managers report on the variances from the past month's budget and make projections for the next month. After review, a budget coordinator updates the master budget, performing the calculations not performed by line managers, such as depreciation or inventory valuation.

A continuous budget will be more relevant than a budget prepared once a year. It can reflect current events and changes in its estimates, and it has the advantage of breaking down a large process into manageable steps. Because managers always have a full period of budgeted data, they tend to view decisions in a longer-term perspective than with a one-year budget, which will cover a shorter and shorter period of time as the year progresses.

Potential disadvantages of continuous budgets include the need to have a budget coordinator and/or the opportunity cost of having managers use part of each month working on the next month's budget. Continuous budgets are appropriate for firms that cannot devote a large block of time to a once-a-year budget process. These types of budgets are also useful for companies that want their managers to have a longer-term view of the firm.

Flexible Budgeting

Flexible budgeting establishes a base cost budget for a particular level of output (a cost-volume relationship), plus an incremental cost-volume amount that shows the behavior of costs at various volumes. Only the variable costs are adjusted; fixed costs remain unchanged. The most common use of a flexible budget is to show the budget that would have been made if the organization had exactly matched its sales forecast. While flexible budgets from prior periods can be helpful in determining how to modify the next budget, a flexible budget that applies actual production output cannot be used as a type of master budget because the actual production output is not known until the period is complete. Therefore, flexible budgets are used more as an analysis tool for determining variances from plan than for creating the original budget.

The benefits of using a flexible budget include the ability to make better use of historical budget information to improve future planning. There are few disadvantages to using flexible budgeting, but there is the potential for the firm to focus principally on the flexible budget level of output and disregard the fact that the sales target was missed. However, most businesses use flexible budgets because they allow for extremely detailed variance analysis. The use of flexible budgeting in variance analysis is covered in Section C: Cost Management.

For example: Robin Manufacturing Company uses flexible budgeting to evaluate how closely its direct labor usage was to the budgeted amount (i.e., perform a variance analysis). For the month of July, the company has projected a production of 72,000 units each requiring 0.5 direct labor hours, with a budgeted hourly rate of $15. However, the actual production turns out to be only 68,000 units, and the actual hourly rate turns out to be $15.50. Figure 1A-18 presents the company's budgeted and actual cost of direct labor used:

Based on the information presented, it seems the company is $13,000 under its direct labor budget for the month of July. However, this is misleading because the company is not producing at its budgeted level of production. To truly evaluate its performance, the company needs to create a flexible budget where the standard cost

Figure 1A-18 Original Budget versus Actual Budget for Robin Manufacturing Company

	Original Budget	Actual Budget
Production (units)	72,000	68,000
DLH* per unit	× 0.5	× 0.5
DLH needed (or used)	36,000	34,000
Hourly rate	× $15	×$15.50
Total direct labor cost	$540,000	$527,000

* DLH = direct labor hours.

per unit (and not the actual cost per unit) is applied to the actual production and not the budgeted production. Figure 1A-19 shows the company's flexible budget.

Figure 1A-19 Flexible Budget versus Actual Budget

	Original Budget	Flexible Budget	Actual Budget
Production	72,000	68,000 ←	68,000
DLH* per unit	× 0.5	× 0.5	× 0.5
DLH needed (or used)	36,000	34,000	34,000
Hourly rate	× $15 →	× $15	$15.50
Total direct labor cost	$540,000	$510,000	$527,000

* DLH = direct labor hours.

From Figure 1A-19, it is clear that when evaluated at the actual production level of 68,000 units, Robin Manufacturing Company is actually $17,000 over its direct labor budget, not $13,000 under the budget.

Knowledge Check: Budgeting Methodologies

The next questions are intended to help you check your understanding and recall of the material presented in this topic. They do not represent the type of questions that appear on the CMA exam.

Directions: Answer each question in the space provided. Correct answers and section references appear after the knowledge check questions.

1. Which of the following budgeting methods might use a cost driver such as number of setups to measure the costs of a batch mixing production job?
   - ☐ **a.** Activity-based budgeting
   - ☐ **b.** Continuous (or rolling) budgeting
   - ☐ **c.** Flexible budgeting
   - ☐ **d.** Incremental budgeting
   - ☐ **e.** Project budgeting
   - ☐ **f.** Zero-based budgeting

2. Which of the following budgeting methods establishes a base cost budget for a particular level of output plus a marginal cost-volume amount that shows the behavior of costs at various volumes?
   - ☐ **a.** Activity-based budgeting
   - ☐ **b.** Continuous (or rolling) budgeting
   - ☐ **c.** Flexible budgeting
   - ☐ **d.** Incremental budgeting
   - ☐ **e.** Project budgeting
   - ☐ **f.** Zero-based budgeting

3. Department B must justify each of its programs annually to its parent agency, which then submits its budget request to the city council. Which budget system is most appropriate?
   - ☐ **a.** Activity-based budgeting
   - ☐ **b.** Continuous (or rolling) budgeting
   - ☐ **c.** Flexible budgeting
   - ☐ **d.** Incremental budgeting
   - ☐ **e.** Project budgeting
   - ☐ **f.** Zero-based budgeting

4. Company D completed its reorganization three years ago and has experienced steady sales in that time. It is now looking to add to its sales force, marketing, and production but maintain its current organization and direction. What budget method might be most appropriate?

   ☐ **a.** Activity-based budgeting

   ☐ **b.** Continuous (or rolling) budgeting

   ☐ **c.** Flexible budgeting

   ☐ **d.** Incremental budgeting

   ☐ **e.** Project budgeting

   ☐ **f.** Zero-based budgeting

5. Company C is a consulting firm that designs customized marketing plans and product launches for a variety of clients. Which budget system might work best for the firm, and what might be its disadvantages?

Knowledge Check Answers: Budgeting Methodologies

1. Which of the following budgeting methods might use a cost driver such as number of setups to measure the costs of a batch mixing production job? *[See Activity-Based Budgeting.]*

   ☒ **a.**   Activity-based budgeting

   ☐ **b.**   Continuous (or rolling) budgeting

   ☐ **c.**   Flexible budgeting

   ☐ **d.**   Incremental budgeting

   ☐ **e.**   Project budgeting

   ☐ **f.**   Zero-based budgeting

2. Which of the following budgeting methods establishes a base cost budget for a particular level of output plus a marginal cost-volume amount that shows the behavior of costs at various volumes? *[See Flexible Budgeting.]*

   ☐ **a.**   Activity-based budgeting

   ☐ **b.**   Continuous (or rolling) budgeting

   ☒ **c.**   Flexible budgeting

   ☐ **d.**   Incremental budgeting

   ☐ **e.**   Project budgeting

   ☐ **f.**   Zero-based budgeting

3. Department B must justify each of its programs annually to its parent agency, which then submits its budget request to the city council. Which budget system is most appropriate? *[See Zero-Based Budgeting.]*

   ☐ **a.**   Activity-based budgeting

   ☐ **b.**   Continuous (or rolling) budgeting

   ☐ **c.**   Flexible budgeting

   ☐ **d.**   Incremental budgeting

   ☐ **e.**   Project budgeting

   ☒ **f.**   Zero-based budgeting

4. Company D completed its reorganization three years ago and has experienced steady sales in that time. It is now looking to add to its sales force, marketing, and production but maintain its current organization and direction. What budget method might be most appropriate? *[See Incremental Budgeting.]*

   ☐ **a.**   Activity-based budgeting

   ☐ **b.**   Continuous (or rolling) budgeting

☐ **c.**   Flexible budgeting

☑ **d.**   Incremental budgeting

☐ **e.**   Project budgeting

☐ **f.**   Zero-based budgeting

5. Company C is a consulting firm that designs customized marketing plans and product launches for a variety of clients. Which budget system might work best for the firm, and what might be the disadvantages of that system? *[See Project Budgeting.]*

Project budgeting would allow tracking and evaluating the costs of each client project, but shared resources would have to be allocated among the projects.

Annual Profit Plan and Supporting Schedules

T HE MASTER BUDGET, OR ANNUAL profit plan, has many components and supporting schedules. Each of these pieces provides specific information that the organization can use to review its current operations and develop its plans for the short and long term. The forecasts and assumptions used in creating each component and the interplay of the components present not just an analytical challenge but an opportunity for effectively managing the organization toward its objectives.

This topic looks at the individual elements that come together to form the master budget. It describes the budgets for sales, production, direct materials, direct labor, overhead, cost of goods sold, and selling and administrative expenses that are used in developing the operating budget and the pro forma financial statement. It also discusses the cash budget, the capital expenditure budget, and the pro forma balance sheet and statement of cash flows and their place in the financial budget.

 READ the Learning Outcome Statements (LOS) for this topic as found in Appendix A and then study the concepts and calculations presented here to be sure you understand the content you could be tested on in the CMA exam.

Master Budget

The master budget provides a comprehensive summation of all of an entity's budgets and plans for the operating activities of its subunits. It is the place where everything must add up, where strategy and long-term plans meet up with short-term objectives and current realities.

The master budget is basically made up of financial projections of many different budgets for a company on an annual basis, although other short-duration time periods are also used. The master budget can be broken down into two major components: the operating budget and the financial budget.

The operating budget makes up the bulk of the master budget. It includes the sales budget, the production budget, the direct materials budget, the direct labor budget, the overhead budget, and the selling and administrative (S&A) expense budget. All of these budgets culminate in the formation of the pro forma (or budgeted) income statement. The financial budget includes the cash budget, the capital expenditure budget, and the pro forma (or budgeted) balance sheet and statement of cash flows.

Figure 1A-20 shows how the components of the master budget are related.

Figure 1A-20 Master Budget

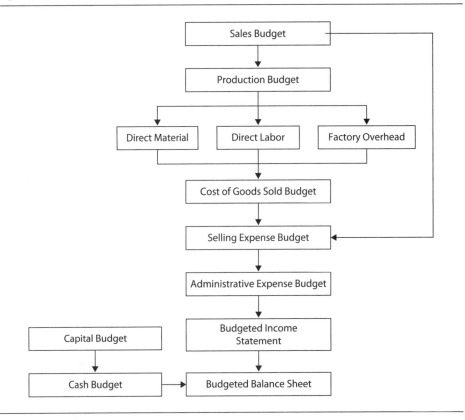

Operating Budget

In creating an operating budget, the various pieces are assembled, including, for instance, the sales budget, the production budget, the direct materials budget, the direct labor budget, the overhead budget, and the S&A expense budget. All of these budgets are then used to create the pro forma (or budgeted) income statement.

Sales Budget

Before creating a sales budget, an accurate sales forecast is needed. A **sales forecast** is a subjective estimate of the entity's future sales for the upcoming period.

Without an accurate sales forecast, all other budget elements will be inaccurate. Forecasters consider not only historical trends for sales but also economic and industry conditions and indicators, competitors' actions, rising costs, policies on pricing and extending credit, the amount of advertising and marketing expenditures, the number of unfilled back orders, and sales in the sales pipeline (unsigned prospects).

Sales forecasts should use statistical analysis techniques such as regression analysis and time series analysis (discussed in Section A, Topic 2: Forecasting Techniques) and rely on sales managers' knowledge about their market and customer needs. Once a company has determined its forecasted sales level, based on its long- and short-term objectives, it forms a sales budget to accomplish its goals. The two key components of the sales budget are the projected number of units of sales and the projected selling prices for the upcoming periods.

For example: Figure 1A-21 shows the sales budget of Robin Manufacturing Company for the third quarter.

Figure 1A-21 Sales Budget

Robin Manufacturing Company Sales Budget **for the Quarter Ended September 30, Year 1**				
	July	**August**	**September**	**Quarter**
Sales in units	70,000	72,000	77,000	219,000
Selling price per unit	$110.80	$110.80	$112.00	(varies)
Total sales	$7,756,000	$7,977,600	$8,624,000	$24,357,600

It is important to note that the sales budget basically drives the operating budget because it helps define the formation of the other budgets.

Production Budget

Once the desired level of sales is determined, the production budget is created to satisfy the expected demand. The **production budget** is a plan for acquiring resources and combining them to meet sales goals and maintain a certain level of inventory. The budgeted production is calculated as shown next.

Budgeted Production = Budgeted Sales + Desired Ending Inventory − Beginning Inventory

Budgeted sales are an integral part of the production budget. Sales are the basis of what logistics managers use to plan resource needs for the coming year, develop manufacturing schedules, and create shipping policies. When actual sales either fall short or significantly exceed projected revenue, the entire inventory system is affected. Inventory on hand needs to be adjusted to reflect the change in production needs. Often inventory purchasing is planned in advance to take advantage of bulk pricing deals that may be negotiated with suppliers. If costs suddenly increase, the financial burden of buying and carrying inventory becomes greater. Changes in the operating and purchasing costs for a company can cause inventory purchase levels to change. For example, an organization may wish to increase or decrease purchasing volumes at various times during the year to try to take advantage of price fluctuations.

During the planning stages of a production budget, the production managers will complete a production schedule outlining how they will meet expected demand. The estimates should include the cost of production equipment, inventory, and personnel. Other factors that can affect the production budget include investment in new equipment, hiring necessary personnel, capacity constraints, and scheduling issues. *For example:* Figure 1A-22 shows a production budget for several months.

Figure 1A-22 Production Budget

	July	August	September	Quarter
Robin Manufacturing Company **Production Budget** **for the Quarter Ended September 30, Year 1**				
Budgeted sales in units	70,000	72,000	77,000	219,000
Add: Desired ending inventory of finished goods	10,000	11,000	12,000	12,000
Total units needed	80,000	83,000	89,000	231,000
Less: Beginning inventory of finished goods	8,000	10,000	11,000	8,000
Budgeted production in units	72,000	73,000	78,000	223,000

Direct Materials Budget

The **direct materials budget** (or the direct materials usage budget) determines the required materials and the quality level of the materials used to meet production. While the production budget specifies only the number of units to be produced, the usage budget specifies the amount and cost of materials needed for the production and the amount and cost of materials that must be purchased to meet the production requirement. A direct materials purchase budget will need to be prepared to determine the amount and cost of materials that need to be purchased. This is determined as shown next.

Direct Materials Purchased = Direct Materials Used in Production + Desired Ending Inventory of Direct Materials − Beginning Inventory of Direct Materials

For example: Figure 1A-23 illustrates Robin Manufacturing's direct materials usage budget. Figure 1A-24 illustrates the company's direct materials purchase budget.

Figure 1A-23 Direct Materials Usage Budget

Robin Manufacturing Company Direct Materials Usage Budget for the Quarter Ended September 30, Year 1				
	July	**August**	**September**	**Quarter**
Production requirement				
Budgeted production	72,000	73,000	78,000	223,000
Pounds of resin per unit of product	× 5	× 5	× 5	× 5
Total pounds of resin required	360,000	365,000	390,000	1,115,000
Pounds of resin in beginning inventory	35,000	35,000	35,000	35,000
Cost per pound	$13.00	$13.00	$13.25	$13.00
Total cost of beginning inventory	$455,000	$455,000	$463,750	$455,000
Total cost of resin purchases	4,680,000	4,836,250	5,253,500	14,769,750
Cost of resin available for production	$5,135,000	$5,291,250	$5,717,250	$15,224,750
Desired ending inventory in pounds	35,000	35,000	40,000	40,000
Cost of desired ending inventory per pound	× $13.00	× $13.25	× $13.30	× $13.30
Total cost of desired ending inventory	$455,000	$463,750	$532,000	$532,000
Cost of resin used in production (Cost Available for Production – Cost of Desired Ending Inventory)	$4,680,000	$4,827,500	$5,185,250	$14,692,750

Figure 1A-24 Direct Materials Purchase Budget

Robin Manufacturing Company Direct Materials Purchase Budget for the Quarter Ended September 30, Year 1				
	July	**August**	**September**	**Quarter**
Total direct materials needed in production	360,000	365,000	390,000	1,115,000
Add: Desired ending inventory	35,000	35,000	40,000	40,000
Total direct materials required	395,000	400,000	430,000	1,155,000
Less: Direct materials beginning inventory	35,000	35,000	35,000	35,000
Direct materials purchases	360,000	365,000	395,000	1,120,000
Purchase price per pound	$13.00	$13.25	$13.30	
Total cost for direct materials purchases	$4,680,000	$4,836,250	$5,253,500	$14,769,750

Direct Labor Budget

The production requirement laid out in the production budget, which determines the direct materials needed, also determines the direct labor needed for production. The **direct labor budget**, which is prepared by the production manager and human resources, specifies the direct labor requirement needed to meet the production need. The direct labor requirement is determined by multiplying the expected production by the number of direct labor hours (DLH) required to produce a unit. This number is then multiplied by the direct labor cost per hour to calculate the budgeted direct labor cost.

Direct Labor Requirement = (Expected Production × Direct Labor Hours per Unit)

Budgeted Direct Labor Cost = Direct Labor Requirement × Direct Labor Cost per Hour

The direct labor budget can help firms plan production processes to smooth out production over a year and keep a consistent workforce size throughout the year. Labor budgets are usually broken down into categories, such as semiskilled, unskilled, and skilled.

For example: Figure 1A-25 illustrates a direct labor budget for Robin Manufacturing.

Figure 1A-25 Direct Labor Budget

Robin Manufacturing Company Direct Labor Budget for the Quarter Ended September 30, Year 1				
	July	**August**	**September**	**Quarter**
Budgeted production	72,000	73,000	78,000	223,000
DLH* required per unit	× 0.5	× 0.5	× 0.5	
DLH needed	36,000	36,500	39,000	111,500
Hourly rate	× $15	× $15	× $15	
Total wages for direct labor	$540,000	$547,500	$585,000	$1,672,500

* DLH = direct labor hours.

In addition to the cost of wages, an organization can estimate the cost of employee benefits. Employers match the Federal Insurance Contributions Act (FICA) contribution (7.65%) and may pay a share of health insurance, life insurance, or pension matching plans on behalf of their employees. Employee benefits can be included in direct labor costs or can be classified as overhead. The effect on cost of goods sold is the same regardless of whether it is classified as a direct labor cost or a soverhead.

Overhead Budget (Factory Overhead Budget)

All other production costs that are not in the direct materials and direct labor budgets are in the **overhead budget**, sometimes called a fixed costs budget because most of the costs in this category do not vary with the rise and fall of production. Rent and insurance, for instance, remain stable even if production goes up or down. However, there are some overhead costs that do vary with production—variable costs such as batch setup costs or the costs of electricity and other utilities. Fixed costs are easy to budget, but variable costs require forecasting the number of units to be produced, the production methods used, and other external factors. *For example:* Figure 1A-26 illustrates Robin Manufacturing's overhead budget.

Figure 1A-26 Factory Overhead Budget

Robin Manufacturing Company Factory Overhead Budget
for the Quarter Ended September 30, Year 1

	Rate per DLH*	July	August	September	Quarter
Total DLHs (See Figure 1A-25)		36,000	36,500	39,000	111,500
Variable factory overhead					
Supplies	$0. 20	$7,200	$7,300	$7,800	$22,300
Fringe benefits	4. 10	147,600	149,650	159,900	457,150
Utilities	1. 00	36,000	36,500	39,000	111,500
Maintenance	0. 50	18,000	18,250	19,500	55,750
Total variable factory overhead	$5. 80	$208,800	$211,700	$226,200	$646,700
Fixed factory overhead					
Depreciation		$20,000	$20,000	$20,000	$60,000
Plant insurance		800	800	800	2,400
Property taxes		1,200	1,200	1,200	3,600
Salary supervision		10,000	10,000	10,000	30,000
Indirect labor		72,000	72,000	72,000	216,000
Utilities		4,000	4,000	4,000	12,000
Maintenance		900	900	900	2,700
Total fixed factory overhead		$108,900	$108,900	$108,900	$326,700
Total factory overhead		$317,700	$320,600	$335,100	$973,400

* Direct labor hour (DLH) is assumed to be the cost driver for factory overhead in this example.

For Robin Manufacturing, employee benefits such as health and dental insurance, short-term and long-term disability insurance, and retirement benefits are considered to be part of the overhead budget, and they are rolled up as fringe benefits in Figure 1A-26. The company could also choose to allocate a portion of these employee benefits into the direct labor budget.

Cost of Goods Sold Budget

The **cost of goods sold budget** indicates the total cost of producing the product sold for a period. This budget is sometimes called the cost of goods manufactured and sold budget , because it often also includes items budgeted to be in inventory. This budget is created only after the production, direct materials, direct labor, and overhead budgets are formed, because it is basically a summary of these budgets.

For example: Figure 1A-27 illustrates a cost of goods sold budget for Robin Manufacturing.

In Figure 1A-27, the cost of goods manufactured is composed of the cost of direct materials used, costs of direct labor used, and the overhead cost. This means that the cost of goods manufactured can be recategorized into a variable cost component made up of the cost of direct materials used, the cost of direct labor materials used, and the variable overhead cost and a fixed cost component, or the fixed

Figure 1A-27 Cost of Goods Sold Budget

Robin Manufacturing Company Cost of Goods Sold Budget
for the Quarter Ended September 30, Year 1

	July	August	September	Quarter
Beginning finished goods inventory, 7/1/Year 1				$626,400
Direct materials used (see Figure 1A-23)	$4,680,000	$4,827,500	$5,185,250	14,692,750
Direct labor used (see Figure 1A-25)	540,000	547,500	585,000	1,672,500
Manufacturing overhead (see Figure 1A-26)	317,700	320,600	335,100	973,400
Cost of goods manufactured	$5,537,700	$5,695,600	$6,105,350	$17,338,650
Cost of goods available for sale				$17,965,050
Less: Ending finished goods inventory				939,600
Cost of goods sold				$17,025,450

overhead cost. Dividing the costs of goods manufactured into the two components can assist the company in determining the unit and total contribution margins of its product, as shown next.

$$\text{Unit Contribution Margin} = \text{Price Per Unit} - \text{Variable Cost Per Unit}$$

$$\text{Total Contribution Margin} = \text{Total Revenue} - \text{Total Variable Cost}$$

The contribution margin represents the portion of the revenue, less the total variable costs, that is used to recoup the fixed costs. Once the fixed costs have been recouped, the remaining contribution margin will go toward the company's operating income. When calculating the contribution, both per unit and in total, other nonmanufacturing-related variable costs, such as variable selling or administrative expenses, need to be taken into consideration. For more information on calculating contribution margins, see Section C: Cost Management.

Selling and Administrative Expense Budget

Nonmanufacturing expenses are often grouped into a single budget called a S&A expense budget or nonmanufacturing costs budget. The selling expense components of this budget include salaries and commissions for the sales department, travel and entertainment, advertising expenditures, shipping supplies, postage and stationery (related to sales), and so on. Sales expenses are included in this category because they are not allowed to be allocated to production processes but must be expensed in the period in which they are incurred. The administrative expense components of this budget, however, include management salaries, legal and professional services, utilities, insurance expense, non–sales-related stationery, supplies, postage, and the like.

Just as with overhead expenses, S&A expenses can be categorized into fixed costs and variable costs. In general, selling expenses are made up of both fixed and variable cost components, whereas the administrative expenses tend to include more fixed costs.

The costs in this budget usually satisfy long-term goals, such as customer service, so it is not easy to make cuts in these expense items. When using a contribution margin format for S&A expenses, all variable selling and administrative costs as well as variable manufacturing costs are deducted from net sales to find the contribution margin. This allows the budget to be used for internal performance measurement and to help show where costs can be controlled.

For example: Robin Manufacturing Company's S&A expense budget (nonmanufacturing costs) is shown in Figure 1A-28.

Figure 1A-28 Selling and Administrative Expense Budget

Robin Manufacturing Company Selling and Administrative Expense Budget for the Quarter Ended September 30, Year 1				
	July	August	September	Quarter
Research/design	$95,000	$95,000	$100,000	$290,000
Marketing	240,000	280,000	290,000	810,000
Shipping	135,000	140,000	150,000	425,000
Product support	90,000	90,000	95,000	275,000
Administration	185,000	190,000	192,000	567,000
Total	$745,000	$795,000	$827,000	$2,367,000

Pro Forma (or Budgeted) Income Statement

Various pieces of the operating budget developed earlier are used to put together the **pro forma (or budgeted) income statement** , which shows what the profits for the company will be at the end of the year if the company meets its budget and if its assumptions prove to be correct. When budgeted income falls short of the goal, management knows it must take corrective action. The budget is revised to account for these actions. A budgeted income statement is therefore a benchmark to use in evaluating progress.

For example: Figure 1A-29 shows the pro forma income statement for Robin Manufacturing Company compiled using information from the sales budget, the cost of goods sold budget, and the S&A expense budget. In addition, the company is expected to pay an interest expense of $140,361 and a tax installment of $1,702,165 for the quarter.

Financial Budgets

Once a company completes the various pieces of the operating budget and creates the pro forma (or budgeted) income statement, it next develops the necessary financial budgets to identify the assets and capital (both debt and equity) needed

Figure 1A-29 Pro Forma Income Statement

Robin Manufacturing Company
Pro Forma Income Statement
for the Quarter Ended September 30, Year 1

Sales (see Figure 1A-21)	$24,357,600
Less: Cost of goods sold (see Figure 1A-27)	17,026,650
Gross margin	$7,330,950
Less: S&A expenses (see Figure 1A-28)	2,367,000
Operating income	$4,963,950
Less: Interest expenses	140,361
Earnings before taxes	$4,823,589
Less: Taxes	1,702,165
Net income	$3,121,424

to support the operation. These financial budgets include the capital expenditure budget, the cash budget, the pro forma (or budgeted) balance sheet, and the pro forma (or budgeted) statement of cash flows. Figure 1A-29a shows the flow of the financial budgets.

Figure 1A-29a Financial Budget Flow

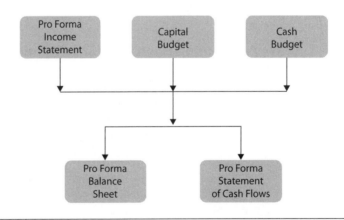

Capital Budget

The **capital budget** represents the amount of money the company plans to invest in selected capital projects, which include purchases of property, plant, or equipment, as well as purchases of new businesses or operating capabilities. This budget often categorizes the capital projects by categories (e.g, machines, buildings, etc.), the amount of funding, the timing of the funding need, and the reasons for investing in the capital projects (e.g, process improvement, replacement of obsolete equipment, etc.).

The capital budget is used for evaluating and selecting projects that require large amounts of funding, which will provide benefits far into the future. Because all businesses face a scarcity of resources, capital must be rationed. Therefore, capital budgets must first be aligned with the company strategy, and that strategy must be continually refined to take advantage of internal strengths and external opportunities.

Cash Budget

Maintaining adequate liquidity is a requirement for staying in business, and a cash budget is a plan to ensure liquidity. Financing can be arranged in an orderly fashion, and investment durations can be planned so that they can be liquidated at the time the funds are needed. Cash budgets are commonly formulated for monthly periods, but many companies find it useful to have even finer divisions, such as by week or even by day.

Because cash is needed in all areas of operations, the cash budget gets data from all parts of the master budget. A cash budget is divided into four sections: the cash receipt section, the cash disbursement section, the cash excess or deficiency section, and the financing section.

The cash budget combines the results of the operating, cash collections, and cash disbursements budgets to provide an overall picture of where an organization expects its cash to come from and be paid to for a given period. The capital expenditure budget is a line item that is included in the cash disbursements section of the cash budget. A pro forma income statement is completed to determine if an acceptable level of income is possible. This estimated income and changes to the cash budget are used to create a pro forma balance sheet. The pro forma cash flow statement classifies all of the cash receipts and disbursements based on activity—that is, operating activities, investing activities, and financial activities.

Cash Receipts

Cash receipts are all collections in the current period from sales made in the current and prior periods (from collections of accounts receivable) and from other sources, such as interest income from investments.

Cash Disbursements

The cash disbursements section includes all outgoing cash payments. These include payments for purchases of materials, wages, operating expenses, taxes, and interest expenses.

Cash Excess or Deficiency

The cash excess or deficiency section is calculated as the beginning cash balance plus receipts and less disbursements and minimum cash balance requirements. The result is either an excess or a deficiency of cash for the period. Excess cash can be invested (per the company's policy) and deficiencies must be financed.

Financing

Financing includes finding sources of cash when liquidity levels fall below a point set by management or the board of directors as well as using excess cash for temporary and short-term investments to make use of cash above a certain level. Most firms value capital preservation over returns on investment when choosing investments, so they choose relatively safe investments, such as money market securities.

The more complex aspects of the financing section involve calculating interest and loan repayments. If financing is needed in one month, the amount of financing must include enough for the minimum cash balance to be satisfied. Conversely, when calculating the amount of principle and interest that can be repaid, the minimum cash balance must be deducted first. Furthermore, it is important to note when the principal and interest are to be repaid (at the beginning or the end of a period), in order to determine what principal the interest charge will be based on. Calculation of interest must take into account partial periods (e.g, 1/12th of 10% per annum for a month's interest).

The cash receipts and cash disbursements sections of the budget are influenced by a number of factors. Companies generally create a pro forma schedule to estimate their cash receipts and another to estimate cash disbursements. The pro forma cash receipts schedule estimates percentages of collections for each period using the same method as the accounts receivable balance pattern, which is discussed next. The pro forma cash disbursements schedule can also use payment percentage patterns, but these are based on payment history instead of collection history. Often these disbursements are broken down by materials purchases, direct wages (based on current sales), general and administrative expenses, and income taxes. Other schedules separate fixed and variable expenses.

An accounts receivable (A/R) balance pattern estimates cash inflows, but the same methods can be applied to cash outflows.

An A/R balance pattern is a forecasting tool to estimate timing of cash inflows and A/R levels resulting from making sales on credit. Companies use great care in analyzing historical collection trends and use such patterns as assumptions in forecasting cash collections. An A/R balance pattern is derived from a company's collection history and results in a percentage estimate of uncollected credit sales at the end of a specific period, such as a month.

For example: Figure 1A-30 shows an A/R sales collection history for Robin Manufacturing Company.

Figure 1A-30 A/R Sales Collection History

Robin Manufacturing Company A/R Sales Collection History

Interval Since Month Sales	Percentage Collected
Month 0 (current month)	40%
Month 1 (next month)	30%
Month 2 (month after next)	20%
Month 3 (three months after)	10%

Using this information, an A/R balance pattern can be applied to monthly sales to predict collections from an upcoming period.

Assume that Robin Manufacturing has actual March sales of $9,200,000, April sales of $9,500,000, May sales of $9,032,000, June sales of $8,520,000, and July through September estimated sales taken from the sales budget in Figure 1A-21. This is shown in Figure 1A-31.

Figure 1A-31 A/R Balance Pattern

		Robin Manufacturing Company		
		A/R Balance Pattern for August with Forecast Inflows through September		
Month Sales	**Sales**	**Cash Inflows for Month**	**A/R Remaining from Month Sales at End of August**	**Remaining A/R as a % of Month Sales**
June	$8,520,000	$8,937,600	$852,000	10%
July	$7,756,000	$8,414,800	$2,326,800	30%
August	$7,977,600	$8,125,040	$4,786,560	60%
September	$8,624,000	$8,246,080		

Cash inflows from sales for the month are calculated using the next formula.

Cash Inflows for Month

= (Month zero % Collected × Sales Current Month)

+ (Month one % Collected × Sales Last Month)

+ (Month two % Collected × Sales Two Months Ago)

+ (Month three % Collected × Sales Three Months Ago)

For example: The final forecast amount for September was determined using the next calculation.

For September = (0.4 × $8,624,000) + (0.3 × $7,977,600)
+ (0.2 × $7,756,000) + (0.1 × $8,520,000)
= $3,449,600 + $2,393,280 + $1,551,200 + $852,000 = $8,246,080

Calculating accounts receivable from month sales at the end of the month and the remaining A/R percentage of month sales uses this formula:

A/R Remaining from Month Sales at End of Current Month

= (Month Sales − [(Month zero % Collected × Month Sales)

+ (Month one % Collected × Month Sales)

+ (Month two % Collected × Month Sales)

+ (Month three % Collected × Month Sales)]

A/R Remaining from June Sales at End of August

$$= \$8,520,000 - [(0.4 \times \$8,520,000)$$
$$+ (0.3 \times \$8,520,000) + (0.2 \times \$8,520,000) + 0^*]$$
$$= \$8,520,000 - (\$3,408,000 + \$2,556,000 + \$1,704,000)$$
$$= \$8,520,000 - \$7,668,000 = \$852,000$$

* Not yet collected

For example: For Robin Manufacturing, A/R remaining from month sales at the end of August and the remaining A/R as a percentage of month sales are calculated as shown next.

A/R Remaining in Current Month as a % of Month Sales

$$= \frac{\text{A/R Remaining from Month Sales at End of Current Month}}{\text{Month Sales}}$$

A/R Remaining in August as a % of June Sales

$$= \frac{\$852,000}{\$8,520,000} = 0.1 = 10\%$$

Note that it is possible that the firm would have additional planned cash collections from nonsales sources, such as investment income. In this case, those cash receipts would be added to the cash receipts from sales to find total cash receipts. Using these methods, a pro forma schedule of cash receipts and disbursements can be made.

For example: Figure 1A-32 shows Robin Manufacturing's pro forma schedule of cash receipts and disbursements. In addition to the information stated previously in the direct materials, direct labor, and overhead budgets for Robin Manufacturing, assume that, in June, actual direct material purchases were $3,280,000, actual variable factory overhead was $188,500, actual fixed factory overhead (less depreciation) was $88,900, and actual S&A expenses were $705,000. Half of Robin Manufacturing's purchases are paid in the same month as the purchase, and the other half are paid one month later. Direct labor is paid in the same month. Overhead is paid the next month. In the meantime, the company's interest expense on its long-term debt for the quarter of $120,000 will be paid in July, and its tax installment for the quarter of $1,702,165 will be paid in August. The company has also budgeted the capital expenditures: July, $880,000; August, $5,360,000: September, $51,000. The amounts calculated on this schedule are used in the cash budget.

Once the company has determined its cash receipts and cash disbursements, and with the beginning cash balance for the quarter, it can then put together its cash budget for the quarter. The cash budget will help the company determine if it has surplus cash or insufficient cash.

Figure 1A-32 Pro Forma Schedule of Cash Receipts and Cash Disbursements

Robin Manufacturing Company Pro Forma Schedule of Cash Receipts and Cash Disbursements
For the 3rd Quarter, Year 1

	July Expected	August Expected	September Expected
Sales (see Figure 1A-21)	$7,756,000	$7,977,600	$8,624,000
DM* purchases (see Figure 1A-23)	$4,680,000	$4,836,250	$5,253,500
Cash receipts			
Sales—40% same month	$3,102,400	$3,191,040	$3,449,600
30%—1-month lag	$2,556,000	$2,326,800	$2,393,280
20%—2-month lag	$1,806,400	$1,704,000	$1,551,200
10%—3-month lag	$950,000	$903,200	$852,000
Total cash receipts	$8,414,800	$8,125,040	$8,246,080
Cash disbursements			
DM purchases—50% same month	$2,340,000	$2,418,125	$2,626,750
50% following month	$1,640,000	$2,340,000	$2,418,125
Direct labor paid same month (Fig. 1A-25)	$540,000	$547,500	$585,000
Variable factory overhead paid following month (Fig. 1A-26)	$188,500	$208,800	$211,700
Fixed factory overhead paid following month† (Figure 1A-26)	$88,900	$88,900	$88,900
S&A expenses paid following month (Figure 1A-28)	$705,000	$745,000	$795,000
Interest expense on long-term debt	$120,000		
Tax installment		$1,702,165	
Capital expenditure	$880,000	$5,360,000	$51,000
Total cash disbursements	$6,502,400	$13,410,490	$6,776,475

*DM = direct materials.

†Since depreciation is a noncash expense, the $20,000 of depreciation was removed from each month's fixed factory overhead.

For example: It is assumed that Robin Manufacturing will not invest its surplus cash and will borrow with short-term loans to bring its cash balance to the minimum required level if it has insufficient cash. It is assumed that the company has an established policy to keep its minimum cash balance at $250,000. Figure 1A-33 illustrates the cash budget for Robin Manufacturing Company for the quarter ended September 30.

In Figures 1A-32 and 1A-33, the information from various pieces of the master budget is used to create the cash budget of Robin Manufacturing Company, which helps demonstrate the relationship between the cash budget and the rest of the master budget.

The cash receipt portion of the cash budget is influenced by the figures projected in the sales budget. The cash disbursement portion is influenced by the figures projected in the direct materials budget, the direct labor budget, the overhead budget, the S&A budget, and the capital expenditure budget.

Figure 1A-33 Cash Budget

Robin Manufacturing Company Cash Budget
for the Quarter Ended September 30, Year 1

	July	August	September	Quarter
Cash balance, beginning	$1,587,000	$3,499,400	$250,000	$1,587,000
Add cash receipts	8,414,800	8,125,040	8,246,080	24,785,920
Total cash available for needs	$10,001,800	$11,624,440	$8,496,080	$26,372,920
Deduct cash disbursements	6,502,400	13,410,490	6,776,475	26,689,365
Minimum cash needed	250,000	250,000	250,000	250,000
Total cash needed	$6,752,400	$13,660,490	$7,026,475	$26,939,365
Cash excess (deficiency)	3,249,400	(2,036,050)	1,469,605	($566,445)
Financing				
Borrowing (beginning balance)	–	–	2,036,050	0
Borrowing	–	2,036,050	–	2,036,050
Repayment (end of period)	–	–	(1,449,244)*	(1,449,244)
Interest expense	–	–	(20,361)†	(20,361)
Borrowing (ending balance)		$2,036,050	$586,806‡	$586,806
Total financing needs (adjusted for interest payments)	–	2,036,050	(1,469,605)	586,806
Cash balance, ending	$3,499,400	$250,000	$250,000	$250,000

* Only $1,449,244 could be paid back at this time.

† Interest on short-term borrowings.

‡ Note that interest for the following month will be $5,868.

General notes: Robin Manufacturing Company requires a cash balance of $250,000 at all times. In the month of August, the need to borrow over $2 million was financed with a short-term loan at 12% per annum interest. Note also that the example assumes that excess cash is not being invested (see July).

In the meantime, the cash budget is also influencing other pieces of the master budget. The financing portion of the cash budget will determine the borrowing needed (i.e., if the company has insufficient cash). This short-term borrowing will contribute to the current liabilities of the pro forma balance sheet, and the interest expense on the short-term borrowings will count toward the interest expense in the pro forma income statement. Similarly, any short-term investments made using surplus cash will contribute to the current assets of the pro forma balance sheet.

Pro Forma (or Budgeted) Balance Sheet

A pro forma balance sheet (also known as budget balance sheet or statement of financial position) illustrates how operations should affect the company's assets, liabilities, and stockholders' equity. The budgeted balance sheet is usually the last item prepared in a master budget and is based in part on the budgeted balance sheet at the end of the current period. The effects of operations for the budget period are added to the data in the prior balance sheet.

Pro Forma (or Budgeted) Statement of Cash Flows

A company's pro forma statement of cash flows represents its projected sources and uses of funds. Using information from the income statement and balance sheet, it groups the company's cash flows into one of three activities: operating, investing, and financing activities.

The operating activity portion tracks the cash flows generated by the operation itself. Cash flows that are included in this category include net income (after adding back depreciation, because it is a noncash expense) plus net changes to its non-cash working capital accounts (i.e., accounts payable and receivable, inventory, accrued and prepaid expenses, and deferred taxes).

The investing activity portion tracks the cash flows associated with the buying and selling of capital assets.

The financing activity portion tracks the cash flows from the sale and repayment of the company's debt, both short-term and long-term, the sale and repurchase of its equity, both preferred and common stocks, and the payment of cash dividends. Note that the interest payments on debt appear in the operating activity portion and not in the financing activity portion.

Relationship Among Cash Budget, Capital Expenditure Budget, and Pro Forma Financial Statements

The cash budget combines the results of the operating, cash collections, and cash disbursements budgets to provide an overall picture of where an organization expects its cash to come from and be paid to for a given period. The capital expenditure budget is a line item that is included in the cash disbursements section of the cash budget. A pro forma income statement is completed to determine if an acceptable level of income is possible. This estimated income and changes to the cash budget are used to create a pro forma balance sheet. The pro forma cash flow statement classifies all of the cash receipts and disbursements based on activity; i.e.operating activities, investing activities, and financial activities.

Comprehensive Problem: Budgeting Methodologies

Happy New Year! The date is January 2. You are the newly hired Assistant Controller for Pile Driver, Inc. , and you have been asked to produce the following schedules and budgets for the current quarter:

a) Sales budget

b) Production budget

c) Finished goods inventory budget (in units)

d) Direct materials usage budget

e) Direct materials purchase budget

f) Direct labor budget

g) Factory overhead budget (variable and fixed)

h) Cost of goods sold budget and projected value of ending finished goods inventory

i) Selling & administrative budget

j) Pro forma schedule of cash receipts and cash disbursements

k) Cash budget

l) Pro forma income statement

After hours of research, you have collected the following information. Use this information to produce the required schedules in a format that will clearly document your calculations and communicate the important management accounting information.

Budgeted Sales Information

January	5,000 units
February	5,500 units
March	6,050 units
Selling price per unit	$60

Opening Balances as of January 1

Cash balance, January 1	$110,000
Accounts receivable balance, January 1	$39,150
Accounts payable balance, January 1	$11,750
Finished goods inventory quantity, January 1	900 units
Finished goods inventory value, January 1	$37,019
Direct materials inventory quantity, January 1	5,000 pounds
Direct materials inventory value, January 1	$3,750

Desired Monthly Closing Balances

Cash-desired minimum closing balance each month	$100,000
Finished goods inventory: 20% of next month's sales	
Direct materials inventory: 20% of next month's production	
The company uses a simple average cost method to calculate the value of the projected ending monthly finished goods inventory	

March 31 — Special Assumptions

Desired finished goods inventory, March 31	1,230 units
Desired direct materials inventory, March 31	7,000 pounds

Production Cost Information

Direct materials needed per unit	6 pounds
Total direct labor hours needed per unit	2 hours
Direct materials cost per pound	$0.75
Direct labor cost per hour	$9.00

Overhead Costs

Variable	
Supplies	$0.10 per DLH
Fringe benefits	$5.00 per DLH
Utilities	$0.80 per DLH
Maintenance	$0.75 per DLH
Fixed (monthly)	
Depreciation	$15,000
Plant insurance	$800
Property taxes	$1,200
Salary supervision	$10,000
Indirect labor	$35,000
Utilities	$3,000
Maintenance	$1,100

Selling and Administrative Costs (monthly)

Research/design (January and February)	$5,000
Research/design (March)	$6,000
Marketing (monthly)	$1,000
Shipping	10% of sales
Product support (January and February)	$1,200
Product support (March)	$1,500
Administration (January)	$10,000
Administration (February)	$11,000
Administration (March)	$12,000

Additional Cash Flow Information

Collections: 70% of each month's sales are collected in the same month; 30% are collected the following month.

Payables: 50% of direct materials purchases are paid within the same month; 50% are paid the following month; assume all other cash expenses are paid in the month incurred.

Capital expenditures: no capital expenditures are planned for the quarter.

The company makes monthly payments of $5,000 on a term loan, with approximately $4,000 going against principal and $1,000 as interest.

The company also has access to a revolving line of credit with an interest rate of 10%.

As of January 1, the company had no borrowings against the line of credit.

Corporate income tax rate is 35% and the company pays quarterly installments.

Tax installment of $22,000 is due in January.

Use this information to create the required schedules. Good luck in your new position! Your success with this assignment will convince the management of Pile Driver, Inc. that they made a good decision when they hired you.

Solution to Comprehensive Problem: Budgeting Methodologies

a)

Sales Budget

	January	February	March	Quarter
Expected unit sales	5,000	5,500	6,050	16,550
Selling price per unit	$60	$60	$60	$60
Total Sales	$300,000	$330,000	$363,000	$993,000

b)

Production Budget

	January	February	March	Quarter
Budgeted unit sales	5,000	5,500	6,050	16,550
Add: desired ending finished goods inventory	1,100	1,210	1,230	
Total units needed	6,100	6,710	7,280	20,090
Less: beginning finished goods inventory	(900)	(1,100)	(1,210)	
Total budgeted production units	5,200	5,610	6,070	16,880

c)

Finished Goods Inventory Budget (units)

	January	February	March	Quarter
Beginning finished goods inventory	900	1,100	1,210	900
Units produced	5,200	5,610	6,070	16,880
Units available for sale	6,100	6,710	7,280	17,780
Budgeted unit sales	(5,000)	(5,500)	(6,050)	(16,550)
Ending finished goods inventory	1,100	1,210	1,230	1,230

d)

Direct Materials Usage Budget

	January	February	March	Quarter
Direct materials needed for production:				
Total budgeted production units	5,200	5,610	6,070	16,880
Direct materials needed per unit (pounds)	6	6	6	6
Direct materials needed for production (pounds)	31,200	33,660	36,420	101,280
Direct materials cost per pound	$0.75	$0.75	$0.75	$0.75
Total cost of direct materials used in production	$23,400	$25,245	$27,315	$75,960

e)

Direct Materials Purchase Budget

	January	February	March	Quarter
Direct materials needed for production	31,200	33,660	36,420	101,280
Add: Desired direct materials ending inventory	6,732	7,284	7,000	7,000
Less: beginning direct materials inventory	(5,000)	(6,732)	(7,284)	(5,000)
Direct materials to be purchased	32,932	34,212	36,136	103,280
Direct materials cost per pound	$0.75	$0.75	$0.75	$0.75
Total value of direct materials purchased	$24,699	$25,659	$27,102	$77,460

f)

Direct Labor Budget

	January	February	March	Quarter
Total budgeted production units	5,200	5,610	6,070	16,880
Direct labor hours needed per unit	2	2	2	2
Total hours needed for production	10,400	11,220	12,140	33,760
Labor rate per hour	$9.00	$9.00	$9.00	$9.00
Total direct labor cost	$93,600	$100,980	$109,260	$303,840

g)

Factory Overhead Budget

	Rate per direct labor hour	January	February	March	Quarter
Total direct labor hours		10,400	11,220	12,140	33,760
Variable Factory Overhead					
Supplies	$0.10	$1,040	$1,122	$1,214	$3,376
Fringe benefits	5.00	52,000	56,100	60,700	168,800
Utilities	0.80	8,320	8,976	9,712	27,008
Maintenance	0.75	7,800	8,415	9,105	25,320
Total variable factory overhead		$69,160	$74,613	$80,731	$224,504
Fixed Factory Overhead					
Depreciation		$15,000	$15,000	$15,000	$45,000
Plant insurance		$800	$800	$800	2,400
Property taxes		$1,200	$1,200	$1,200	3,600
Salary supervision		$10,000	$10,000	$10,000	30,000
Indirect labor		$35,000	$35,000	$35,000	105,000
Utilities		$3,000	$3,000	$3,000	9,000
Maintenance		$1,100	$1,100	$1,100	3,300
Total fixed factory overhead		$66,100	$66,100	$66,100	$198,300
Total overhead		$135,260	$140,713	$146,831	$422,804

h)

Cost of Goods Sold Budget

	January	February	March	Quarter
Direct materials used in production	$23,400	$25,245	$27,315	$75,960
Direct labor used in production	93,600	100,980	109,260	303,840
Manufacturing overhead (see schedule)	135,260	140,713	146,831	422,804
Cost of goods manufactured	252,260	266,938	283,406	$802,604
Beginning finished goods inventory	37,019	52,179	57,537	37,019
Cost of goods available for sale	$289,279	$319,117	$340,943	$839,623
Units available for sale	6,100	6,710	7,280	17,780
Average cost per unit available for sale	$47.42	$47.56	$46.83	n/a
Units sold	5,000	5,500	6,050	16,550
Cost of goods sold	$237,100	$261,580	$283,322	$782,002
Ending finished goods inventory	$52,179	$57,537	$57,621	$57,621

i)

Selling and Administrative Budget

	January	February	March	Quarter
Research/design	$5,000	$5,000	$6,000	$16,000
Marketing	1,000	1,000	1,000	$3,000
Shipping	30,000	33,000	36,300	$99,300
Product support	1,200	1,200	1,500	$3,900
Administration	10,000	11,000	12,000	$33,000
Total S&A	$47,200	$51,200	$56,800	$155,200

j)

Pro Forma Schedule of Cash Receipts and Cash Disbursements

	January	February	March	Quarter
Cash Receipts				
Collections from customers (70% same month)	$210,000	$231,000	$254,100	$695,100
Collections from customers (30% next month)	39,150	90,000	99,000	228,150
Total cash receipts	$249,150	$321,000	$353,100	$923,250
Cash Disbursements				
Direct materials purchases (50% same month)	$12,350	$12,830	$13,551	$38,731
Direct materials purchases (50% following month)	11,750	12,349	12,829	36,928
Direct labor (paid same month)	93,600	100,980	109,260	303,840
Variable factory overhead	69,160	74,613	80,731	224,504
Fixed factory overhead	66,100	66,100	66,100	198,300
Less depreciation (non-cash expense)	(15,000)	(15,000)	(15,000)	(45,000)
S&A expense	$47,200	$51,200	$56,800	$155,200

Pro Forma Schedule of Cash Receipts and Cash Disbursements

	January	February	March	Quarter
Term loan payment	5,000	5,000	5,000	15,000
Tax installment	22,000	-	-	22,000
Capital expenditures	-	-	-	-
Total cash disbursements	$312,160	$308,072	$329,271	$949,503

k)

Cash Budget

	January	February	March	Quarter
Cash Balance, beginning	$110,000	$100,000	$100,000	$110,000
Add: Cash receipts	249,150	321,000	353,100	923,250
Total cash available for use	$359,150	$421,000	$453,100	$1,033,250
Cash disbursements	(312,160)	(308,072)	(329,271)	(949,503)
Cash balance before financing	$46,990	$112,928	$123,829	$83,747
Minimum cash requied	(100,000)	(100,000)	(100,000)	(100,000)
Cash excess (deficiency)	$(53,010)	$12,928	$23,829	$(16,253)

Line of Credit (LOC)

	January	February	March	Quarter
LOC interest expense	$-	$(442)	$(338)	$(780)
Borrowing (at end of month)	53,010	-	-	53,010
LOC repayment (at end of month)	-	(12,486)	(23,491)	(35,977)
Total effects of LOC financing	$53,010	$(12,928)	$(23,829)	$16,253
Cash balance, ending	$100,000	$100,000	$100,000	$100,000

l)

Pro Forma Income Statement

	January	February	March	Quarter
Sales	$300,000	$330,000	$363,000	$993,000
Cost of goods sold	(237,100)	(261,580)	(283,322)	(782,002)
Gross profit	$62,900	$68,420	$79,678	$210,998
Less: S&A expenses	(47,200)	(51,200)	(56,800)	(155,200)
Operating income (EBIT)	$15,700	$17,220	$22,878	$55,798
Less: Interest expense	$(1,000)	$(1,442)	$(1,338)	$(3,780)
Earnings before taxes	$14,700	$15,778	$21,540	$52,018
Less: Tax expense	(5,145)	(5,522)	(7,539)	(18,206)
Net income (loss)	$9,555	$10,256	$14,001	$33,812

Knowledge Check:
Annual Profit Plan and Supporting Schedules

The following questions are intended to help you check your understanding and recall of the material presented in this topic. They do not represent the type of questions that appear on the CMA exam.

Directions: Answer in the space provided. Correct answers and section references appear after the knowledge check questions.

1. Which of the following budgets is the first operating budget prepared because it defines needed capacity for operations?
   - ☐ **a.** Production/inventory budget
   - ☐ **b.** Direct labor budget
   - ☐ **c.** Sales budget
   - ☐ **d.** Overhead budget

2. Which of the following internal pro forma financial statements is usually the last budget prepared at the end of a period?
   - ☐ **a.** Pro forma income statement
   - ☐ **b.** Pro forma balance sheet
   - ☐ **c.** Pro forma statement of stockholders' equity
   - ☐ **d.** Cash budget

3. Which of the following budgets is designed to ensure that the company maintains adequate liquidity?
   - ☐ **a.** Overhead budget
   - ☐ **b.** Sales budget
   - ☐ **c.** Production/inventory budget
   - ☐ **d.** Cash budget

4. What factors are used to calculate the production budget? Complete the equation:

   Budgeted production = _____ + _____ − _____

5. Calculate the budgeted direct labor cost for Company D for January.

   Direct labor hours per unit = 7 direct labor hours

   Expected production = 5,700 units

   Direct labor cost per hour = $19 per hour

6. In a pro forma statement of cash flows, which activity tracks each of the following cash flows?

	Operating Activity	Investing Activity	Financing Activity
Net changes to non-cash working capital accounts			
Repayment of company debt			
Interest payment on debt			
Sales of capital assets			

Knowledge Check Answers:
Annual Profit Plan and Supporting Schedules

1. Which of the following budgets is the first operating budget prepared because it defines needed capacity for operations? *[See Sales Budget]*
   - ☐ **a.** Production/inventory budget
   - ☐ **b.** Direct labor budget
   - ☑ **c.** Sales budget
   - ☐ **d.** Overhead budget

2. Which of the following internal pro forma financial statements is usually the last budget prepared at the end of a period? *[See Pro Forma (or Budgeted) Balance Sheet]*
   - ☐ **a.** Pro forma income statement
   - ☑ **b.** Pro forma balance sheet
   - ☐ **c.** Pro forma statement of stockholders' equity
   - ☐ **d.** Cash budget

3. Which of the following budgets is designed to ensure that the company maintains adequate liquidity? *[See Cash Budget]*
   - ☐ **a.** Overhead budget
   - ☐ **b.** Sales budget
   - ☐ **c.** Production/inventory budget
   - ☑ **d.** Cash budget

4. What factors are used to calculate the production budget? Complete the equation: *[See Production Budget]*

   Budgeted Production = Budgeted Sales + Desired Ending Inventory − Beginning Inventory

5. Calculate the budgeted direct labor cost for Company D for January. *[See Direct Labor Budget]*

   Direct Labor Hours Requirement = 7 Direct Labor Hours × 5,700 units = 39,900 Direct Labor Hours

   Direct Labor Costs = 39,900 Direct Labor Hours × $19 per Hour = $758,100

6. In a pro forma statement of cash flows, which activity tracks each of the following cash flows? *[See Pro Forma (or Budgeted) Statement of Cash Flows]*

	Operating Activity	Investing Activity	Financing Activity
Net changes to non-cash working capital accounts	X		
Repayment of company debt			X
Interest payment on debt	X		
Sales of capital assets		X	

Top-Level Planning and Analysis

THE MASTER BUDGET, OR ANNUAL profit plan, includes a set of pro forma financial statements. These financial statements are key elements in helping a company plan for the future. Based on these pro forma statements, a company can: determine if it is meeting its predetermined targets; estimate the amount of external funding needed to support its projected sales growth; and perform sensitivity analysis to identify the impacts of estimates, operating, and policy changes on selected financial ratios.

This topic traces the process of creating pro forma financial statements using the percentage of sales method, which builds a pro forma income statement and then a pro forma balance sheet, and it shows an example of creating a pro forma statement of cash flows. It describes the process of assessing anticipated performance using pro forma financial statements, including performing sensitivity analyses.

 READ the Learning Outcome Statements (LOS) for this topic as found in Appendix A and then study the concepts and calculations presented here to be sure you understand the content you could be tested on in the CMA exam.

Pro Forma Financial Statements and Budgets

The concept of a master budget was introduced in Topic 4: Annual Profit Plan and Supporting Schedule. The master budget is composed of the operating budgets and the financial budgets. The final product of the operating budget is the pro forma income statement, which basically shows a company's projected sales revenue, costs, and profit (i.e., net income). Once the company's dividend policy has been factored in to determine the amount of dividends to be paid, the amount of projected retained earnings will then be added to its current balance sheet to create the pro forma balance sheet. Information from the company's capital expenditure budget and cash budget will also be used to help formulate the pro forma balance sheet. Once the pro forma income statement and balance sheet are compiled, the information can then be used to create the pro forma statement of cash flows.

The relationship among the various pro forma financial statements and budgets are illustrated in Figure 1A-34.

Figure 1A-34 Relationship Among Pro Forma Financial Statements and Budgets

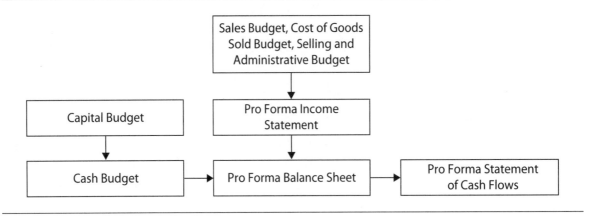

Pro forma statements represent a company's projected financial statements. They are useful in the company's planning process because these statements support three major functions. They help a company to:

1. Assess whether its anticipated performance is in line with its established targets.
2. Anticipate the amount of funding needed to achieve its forecasted sales growth.
3. Estimate the effects of changes in assumptions of key numbers by performing sensitivity analysis (i.e., what-if analysis). Sensitivity analysis helps to identify potential conditions that could lead to major problems for the company. This enables the company to plan for appropriate actions in case such an event should occur. In addition, sensitivity analysis also provides the company with the opportunity to analyze the impact of changing its operating plans.

Creating a Pro Forma Income Statement with the Percentage-of-Sales Method

In Topic 4: Annual Profit Plan and Supporting Schedules, various pieces of the operating budget were projected and used to ultimately form the pro forma income statement. The process to complete these schedules is very complex and time consuming. Here a short-cut approach, known as the percentage-of-sales method, is used to create a pro forma income statement and a pro forma balance sheet.

The percentage-of-sales method is a simple approach that ties many of the items in the pro forma income statement and balance sheet to future sales revenue. It assumes that the relationship between these income statement and balance sheet items and sales revenue remains constant, which means that they grow proportionally with sales growth. Any activity that is needed to directly support the operations that will generate the specific sales level is assumed to grow proportionately with sales. On the income statement, these items include the cost of goods sold (COGS) and selling and administrative (S&A) expense; on the balance sheet, it includes current assets, net fixed assets, accounts payables, and accruals.

None of the financing activities—namely, notes payable (short-term borrowing), long-term debt, and owners' equity—is assumed to grow proportionately with sales.

For example: Heavenly Furniture Company uses the percentage-of-sales method to forecast its pro forma financial statements. Based on historical financial statements, these relationships can be established between several items and sales:

- COGS is 80% of sales.
- S&A expense is 5% of sales.
- Cash and equivalent are 3% of sales.
- Account receivables are 18% of sales.
- Inventories are 25% of sales.
- Net fixed assets are 35% of sales.
- Accounts payables are 12% of sales.
- Accruals are 8% of sales.

Heavenly Furniture is projecting a sales revenue growth of 18% in the upcoming year. The company currently has 12,000 shares of common stocks outstanding, and it plans on maintaining its dividend policy of paying out 40% of its net income as dividends. It is currently paying 8% interest on its notes payable and 10% on its long-term debt. The company has a 35% tax rate.

The process it uses is:

1. Create the pro forma income statement.
2. Create the pro forma balance sheet.
3. Create the pro forma statement of cash flows.

Creating a Pro Forma Income Statement

To create the pro forma income statement, it is necessary to first estimate the sales revenue for the upcoming year. Given the current-year sales revenue of $100,000 and a projected growth rate of 18%, the upcoming-year sale revenue will be $118,000. The projected sales revenue is then used to determine the COGS and S&A. Since COGS is assumed to remain at 80% of sales, the forecasted COGS is projected to be $94,400. S&A is assumed to remain at 5% of sales, so the upcoming S&A is projected to be $5,900.

To simplify the calculations, it is assumed that Heavenly Furniture's interest expense is calculated based on its beginning-of-period debt balance. Since the company is carrying a $5,000 note payable and $20,000 of long-term debt at the beginning of the upcoming year, the total interest expense is $2,400—the interest expense on the note payable is $400 ($5,000 note payable multiplied by the 8% annual interest rate), and the interest expense on the long-term debt is $2,000 ($20,000 long-term debt multiplied by the 10% annual interest rate).

These numbers are then used to create the upcoming year's pro forma income statement, presented along with the current year's income statement in Figure 1A-35.

Figure 1A-35 Heavenly Furniture Company Pro Forma Income Statement

	Current Year	Upcoming Year
Sales	$100,000	$118,000
COGS	80,000	94,400
Gross Margin	20,000	23,600
S&A Expenses	5,000	5,900
EBIT (Operating Income)	15,000	17,700
Interest	1,800	2,400
EBT	13,200	15,300
Taxes (35%)	4,620	5,355
Net Income	$8,580	$9,945
EPS	$0.72	$0.83
Dividends (40%)	$3,432	$3,978
Addition to retained earnings	$5,148	$5,967

EBIT = earnings before interest and taxes; EBT = earnings before taxes; EPS = earnings per share.

With a projected 18% sales growth, Heavenly Furniture expects to generate a net income of $9,945 and EPS of $0.83 (= $9,945/12,000 shares). Given the current dividend policy of paying out 40% of earnings as dividends, the company will be paying out $3,978 (= $9,945 ×0.40) in dividends and retaining $5,967 (= $9,945 − $3,978) in earnings.

Creating a Pro Forma Balance Sheet and Determining Additional Funding Needed

After creating the pro forma income statement for the upcoming year, Heavenly Furniture Company's pro forma balance sheet can be created. Once again, based on a projected sales revenue of $118,000 and the assumed relationships:

Cash and cash equivalents are projected to be $3,540 (3% of sales).

Accounts receivables are projected to be $21,240 (18% of sales).

Inventories are projected to be $29,500 (25% of sales).

Net fixed assets are projected to be $41,300 (35% of sales).

Accounts payables are projected to be $14,160 (12% of sales).

Accruals are projected to be $9,440 (8% of sales).

In addition, based on the pro forma statement for the upcoming year, Heavenly Furniture Company is expected to retain $5,967 in earnings. The earnings will be added to the current year's retained earnings of $16,000 in the balance sheet to derive the upcoming year's retained earnings of $21,967.

Two iterations will be completed to derive Heavenly Furniture Company's pro forma balance sheet. In the first iteration, all financing activities (i.e., notes payables, long-term debt, and common stock) are assumed to remain at the current year's levels. This will help to determine if the company needs any additional external funding to support the projected sales growth. Once the level of external funding has been determined, it will be incorporated to create the final pro forma balance sheet in the second iteration.

Using the estimated balance sheet items calculated earlier, Heavenly Furniture's pro forma balance sheet (before any additional financing) is presented in Figure 1A-36.

Figure 1A-36 Heavenly Furniture Pro Forma Balance Sheet Before Additional Financing

	Current Year	Upcoming Year
Assets		
Cash and equivalents	$3,000	$3,540
Receivables	18,000	21,240
Inventories	25,000	29,500
Total Current Assets	46,000	54,280
Net Fixed Assets	35,000	41,300
Total Assets	$81,000	$95,580
Liabilities and Equity		
Accounts payable	$12,000	$14,160
Accruals	8,000	9,440
Notes payable	5,000	5,000
Total Current Liabilities	25,000	28,600
Long-term debt	20,000	20,000
Total Liabilities	45,000	48,600
Common stock	20,000	20,000
Retained earnings	16,000	21,967
Total Equity	36,000	41,967
Total liabilities and equity	$81,000	$90,567
Additional Funding Needed		$5,013

Since the company needed $95,580 in assets to support its estimated sales revenue of $118,000 but only has $90,567 in financing (i.e., total liabilities and equity), the company will need $5,013 ($95,580 − $90,567) in external funding.

Heavenly Furniture Company has several options for raising the $5,013 of external funding it needs. The company can raise the funds using notes payable, long-term debt, common stocks, or any combination of the three—such as $2,000 from notes payable and $3,013 from long-term debt. However, if the company is unwilling to seek that much external funding, it can lower its external funding need by increasing the amount of internal funding (i.e., retained earnings) available by altering its dividend policy. The company can lower its dividend payout ratio (e.g, from 40% to 30%) to reduce the amount of dividends paid out and to increase the amount of earnings retained. For every additional dollar of internal funding (in the form of retained earnings) raised, the company will need one less dollar of external funding.

In this scenario, it is assumed that Heavenly Furniture Company will acquire the $5,013 of external funding it needs using notes payable. This will be added to the company's current $5,000 of notes payable for a total of $10,013. Figure 1A-37 shows the company's pro forma balance sheet after taking on the additional funding.

Figure 1A-37 Heavenly Furniture Pro Forma Balance Sheet After Additional Financing

	Current Year	**Upcoming Year**
Assets		
Cash and equivalents	$3,000	$3,540
Receivables	18,000	21,240
Inventories	25,000	29,500
Total Current Assets	$46,000	$54,280
Net Fixed Assets	35,000	41,300
Total Assets	$81,000	$95,580
Liabilities and Equity		
Accounts payable	$12,000	$14,160
Accruals	8,000	9,440
Notes payable	5,000	10,013
Total Current Liabilities	$25,000	$33,613
Long-term debt	20,000	20,000
Total Liabilities	$45,000	$53,613
Common stock	20,000	20,000
Retained earnings	16,000	21,967
Total Equity	36,000	41,967
Total liabilities and equity	$81,000	$95,580

Creating a Pro Forma Statement of Cash Flows

Once Heavenly Furniture Company's pro forma income statement and balance sheet have been completed, that information can be used to create the company's pro forma statement of cash flows. There are two approaches to creating a statement of cash flows: the direct method and the indirect method. Heavenly Furniture Company's pro forma statement of cash flows will be created using the indirect method.

A key concept in dealing with cash flows is:

- Any increase in accounts receivables, inventories, net fixed assets, net income generated, and dividends paid represents a cash outflow, and vice versa.
- Any increase in accounts payables, accruals, and financing activities (i.e., notes payable, long-term debt, and common stock issued) represents a cash inflow, and vice versa.

For example: According to Figure 1A-37, Heavenly Furniture's accounts receivables increases by $3,240 (from $18,000 to $21,240). This represents a cash flow of −$3,240 (a cash outflow). Its accounts payable amount increases by $2,160 (from $12,000 to

$14,160). This represents a cash flow of +$2,160. The pro forma statement of cash flows groups cash flows as a result of various activities into three major categories:

1. Cash flows from operating activities
2. Cash flows from investing activities
3. Cash flows from financing activities

For example: Using information from the company's pro forma income statement and balance sheet (see Figures 1A-35 and 1A-36):

- Cash flow from operating activities = $5,805
- Cash flow from investing activities   = −$6,300
- Cash flows from financing activities = $1,035

Heavenly Furniture's pro forma statement of cash flows is shown in Figure 1A-38.

Figure 1A-38 Heavenly Furniture Pro Forma Statement of Cash Flows

Net income	$9,945
Receivables	(3,240)
Inventories	(4,500)
Payables	2,160
Accruals	1,440
Cash flow from operating activities	$5,805
Capital expenditure (net fixed assets)	$(6,300)
Cash flow from investing activities	$(6,300)
Notes payables	$5,013
Dividends	(3,978)
Cash flow from financing activities	$1,035
Net change in cash flow	$540
Beginning cash	3,000
Ending cash	$3,540

The company's combined cash flow for the upcoming year totals $540 (= $5,805 − $6,300 + $1,035). Together with a beginning cash balance of $3,000, the additional cash flow of $3,000 will result in an ending cash balance of $3,540. This matches Heavenly Furniture Company's cash position in the pro forma balance sheet (see Figure 1A-37).

Assessing Anticipated Performance Using Pro Forma Financial Statements

Once a company creates its pro forma financial statements, the statements need to be analyzed to determine if the company is meeting its predetermined financial targets. This can be accomplished by calculating a variety of financial ratios and comparing them to predetermined targets and industry averages. These calculations can help answer questions such as:

- Is the company's leverage (as measured by its debt ratio) within an acceptable range?
- Is its return on equity (ROE) acceptable in relation to the industry average?

A more detailed discussion on financial statement analysis using ratios and the formulas for additional ratios is covered in Part 2 of the CMA Learning System®.

For example: Figure 1A-39 presents a few selected financial ratios for Heavenly Furniture, calculated using the current and pro forma income statement and balance sheets (Figures 1A-35 and 1A-37).

Figure 1A-39 Heavenly Furniture Selected Financial Ratios

	Current Year	Upcoming Year
Current ratio	1.8400	1.6149
Quick ratio	0.8400	0.7372
Return on assets (ROA)	0.1059	0.1040
Return on equity (ROE)	0.2383	0.2370
Gross profit margin	0.2000	0.2000
Operating profit margin	0.1500	0.1500
Net profit margin	0.0858	0.0843
Debt ratio	0.5556	0.5609
Times interest earned (TIE)	8.3333	7.3750
EPS	$0.72	$0.83

The ratios shown are calculated using these formulas:

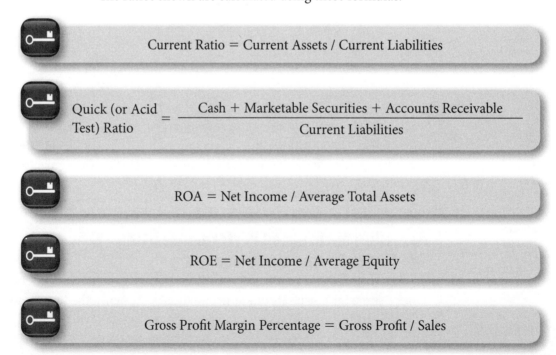

Current Ratio = Current Assets / Current Liabilities

$$\text{Quick (or Acid Test) Ratio} = \frac{\text{Cash} + \text{Marketable Securities} + \text{Accounts Receivable}}{\text{Current Liabilities}}$$

ROA = Net Income / Average Total Assets

ROE = Net Income / Average Equity

Gross Profit Margin Percentage = Gross Profit / Sales

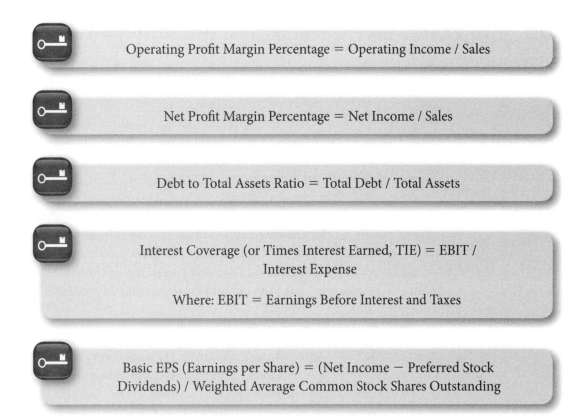

Operating Profit Margin Percentage = Operating Income / Sales

Net Profit Margin Percentage = Net Income / Sales

Debt to Total Assets Ratio = Total Debt / Total Assets

Interest Coverage (or Times Interest Earned, TIE) = EBIT / Interest Expense

Where: EBIT = Earnings Before Interest and Taxes

Basic EPS (Earnings per Share) = (Net Income − Preferred Stock Dividends) / Weighted Average Common Stock Shares Outstanding

In order to support a projected 18% sales growth, Heavenly Furniture Company is raising $5,013 of external funding via notes payable. Because the company is tapping short-term borrowing for its external funding needs, its liquidity position will deteriorate as the current ratio and quick ratio are expected to decrease in the upcoming year. Its profit position, in terms of return on assets (ROA), return on equity (ROE), and net profit margin, are also expected to decrease in the upcoming year.

Because the company is relying on notes payable to raise its needed external funding, it is important that it pay close attention to its debt ratio and interest coverage (in terms of times interest earned [TIE]) to ensure that it has not violated its debt covenants. The company's debt ratio is expected to increase from 55.56% to 56.09%, and its TIE is expected to decrease from 8.333 to 7.3750. Both of these changes are relatively minor, so the company should be able to meet its debt covenant.

Earnings per share (EPS) is expected to increase from $0.72 to $0.83 (a 15.28% increase) as a result of the sales growth that is funded by additional debt.

Performing Sensitivity Analysis

The pro forma statements in Figures 1A-35, 1A-36, 1A-37, 1A-38, and the selected ratios in Figure 1A-39 are based on Heavenly Furniture Company's assumptions of a projected 18% sales growth and certain assumed relationships between sales revenue and selected items in the income statement and balance sheet. Since the company is dealing with the future when projecting its pro forma statements, there is always a chance that these initial assumptions will change. What if the projected sales growth is 20% rather than 18%? What if the cost of production has increased and the COGS is actually 85% of sales rather than 80% of sales?

The company can analyze these alternatives by performing a series of what-if analyses. Doing this involves systematically changing one of the assumptions and analyzing the impact that these changes have on the pro forma statements and on the selected financial ratios. What-if analysis that changes one assumption (or variable) at a time is also known as sensitivity analysis. (See Section A, Topic 2: Forecasting Techniques, for more information on sensitivity analysis.)

For example: Heavenly Furniture Company is performing a sensitivity analysis to determine the effects of changing one or more of its initial assumptions. The original pro forma income statement and balance sheet (from Figures 1A-35 and 1A-37) and the selected ratios (from Figure 1A-39) serve as the base scenario.

Their first analysis focuses on changing two of the income statement–related assumptions: sales revenue growth rate and the relationship between COGS and sales.

Sensitivity Analysis Based on Growth Rate Changes

Heavenly Furniture Company initially projected a sales revenue growth rate of 18% for the upcoming year. However, this projected growth rate might be as high as 20% or as low as 16%, depending on the economic conditions in the upcoming year. The company can reproject its pro forma income statement and balance sheet first based on a 16% growth rate and then based on a 20% growth rate. All other assumptions are assumed to remain the same.

The 16% growth rate will lead to projected sales of $116,000. The 20% growth rate will lead to projected sales of $120,000. Using the methods discussed earlier in creating the initial pro forma financial statements, the pro forma income statement and balance sheet for the various growth rate assumptions are presented in Figure 1A-40.

Figure 1A-40 Sensitivity Analysis with Different Growth Rates

Heavenly Furniture Company Pro Forma Income Statement			
	Growth = 16%	**Base =18%**	**Growth = 20%**
Sales	$116,000	$118,000	$120,000
COGS	92,800	94,400	96,000
Gross Margin	23,200	23,600	24,000
S&A Expenses	5,800	5,900	6,000
EBIT (Operating Income)	17,400	17,700	18,000
Interest	2,400	2,400	2,400
EBT	15,000	15,300	15,600
Taxes	5,250	5,355	5,460
Net Income	$9,750	$9,945	$10,140
EPS	$0.81	$0.83	$0.85
Dividends	$3,900	$3,978	$4,056
Addition to retained earnings	$5,850	$5,967	$6,084

Heavenly Furniture Company Pro Forma Balance Sheet			
	Growth = 16%	**Base=18%**	**Growth = 20%**
Assets			
Cash and equivalents	$3,480	$3,540	$3,600
Receivables	20,880	21,240	21,600
Inventories	29,000	29,500	30,000
Total Current Assets	$53,360	$54,280	$55,200
Net Fixed Assets	40,600	41,300	42,000
Total Assets	$93,960	$95,580	$97,200
Liabilities and Equity			
Accounts payable	$13,920	$14,160	$14,400
Accruals	9,280	9,440	9,600
Notes payable	8,910	10,013	11,116
Total Current Liabilities	$32,110	$33,613	$35,116
Long-term debt	20,000	20,000	20,000
Total Liabilities	$52,110	$53,613	$55,116
Common stock	20,000	20,000	20,000
Retained earnings	21,850	21,967	22,084
Total Equity	$41,850	$41,967	$42,084
Total liabilities and equity	$93,960	$95,580	$97,200

The sensitivity analysis for Heavenly Furniture Company was done by varying its projected sales growth within the range of 16% to 20%. The pro forma income statement and balance sheet will provide the company an opportunity to determine how various items in the income statement and balance sheet change as the projected growth rate changes.

For example: In Figure 1A-40, the company's EPS drops to $0.81 when the growth rate is 16%, and the EPS rises to $0.85 when the growth rate is 20%. This means that a 2% change in growth rate leads to a $0.02 change in EPS.

The new pro forma income statement and balance sheet can also be used to create new sets of financial ratios, as shown in Figure 1A-41. Once again, the company will be able to analyze how each financial ratio changes when the growth rate changes.

In addition to the financial ratios, the additional amounts of external funding needed for the various growth rates are also presented in Figure 1A-41. Since the company relies solely on the use of notes payable to meet its external funding need, the amount of external funding needed can be determined by subtracting the amount of notes payable in the current year ($5,000) from the amount of notes payable in the upcoming year. For instance, the amount of notes payable is $8,910 when the growth rate is 16%, so the amount of external funding needed is $3,910 (= $8,910 − $5,000). It is important for Heavenly Furniture to pay close attention to how the amount of external funding needed changes when the growth rate assumption changes. The company might not be comfortable raising the amount

Figure 1A-41 Selected Financial Ratio Sensitivity Analysis with Different Growth Rates

	Growth = 16%	Base = 18%	Growth = 20%
Current ratio	1.6618	1.6149	1.5719
Quick ratio	0.7586	0.7372	0.7176
ROA	0.1038	0.1040	0.1043
ROE	0.2330	0.2370	0.2409
Gross profit margin	0.2000	0.2000	0.2000
Operating profit margin	0.1500	0.1500	0.1500
Net profit margin	0.0841	0.0843	0.0845
Debt ratio	0.5546	0.5609	0.5670
TIE	7.2500	7.3750	7.5000
Additional funding needed	$3,910	$5,013	$6,116

of external funding if the growth rate is higher than anticipated, or the company may need to arrange for a line of credit and be prepared to pursue other external funding options if needed.

Sensitivity Analysis Based on COGS Changes

In the previous scenario, a sensitivity analysis was performed by changing Heavenly Furniture Company's revenue (i.e., the sales growth rate). Now the analysis is repeated, but this time one of its expenses, namely COGS, will be changed.

In the base scenario, it was initially assumed that COGS is 80% of sales. However, the cost of its production (e.g, labor and materials) might increase in the upcoming year, and COGS could become 85% of sales. Due to a more streamlined production process or a drop in material costs, the COGS could decrease to 75% of sales in the upcoming year. Once again, assuming all the other assumptions remain the same (e.g, sales growth rate of 18%), the company's pro forma income statement and balance sheet can be prepared for each of the alternative COGS scenarios. The results are shown in Figure 1A-42.

Once again, the company can determine how various items in the income statement and balance sheet change when COGS changes. In Figure 1A-42, the company's EPS rises to $1.15 when COGS is 75% of sales, and the EPS drops to $0.51 when COGS is 85% of sales. This means that a 5% change in COGS (in relation to sales) leads to a $0.32 change in EPS.

Similarly, the new pro forma income statement and balance sheet, based on various COGS rates, are used to create new sets of financial ratios. The results (including the external funding needed) are presented in Figure 1A-43.

Heavenly Furniture Company can continue to perform additional sensitivity analysis by changing other income statement–related assumptions, such as the relationship between S&A and sales.

In addition, the company can analyze the impact of varying its operating plans by changing its balance sheet–related assumptions. For example, if the company

Figure 1A-42 Sensitivity Analysis with Different COGS Rates

Heavenly Furniture Company Pro Forma Income Statement

	COGS = 75%	Base = 80%	COGS = 85%
Sales	$118,000	$118,000	$118,000
COGS	88,500	94,400	100,300
Gross Margin	29,500	23,600	17,700
S&A Expenses	5,900	5,900	5,900
EBIT (Operating Income)	23,600	17,700	11,800
Interest	2,400	2,400	2,400
EBT	21,200	15,300	9,400
Taxes	7,420	5,355	3,290
Net Income	$13,780	$9,945	$6,110
EPS	$1.15	$0.83	$0.51
Dividends	$5,512	$3,978	$2,444
Addition to retained earnings	$8,268	$5,967	$3,666
Assets			
Cash and equivalents	$3,540	$3,540	$3,540
Receivables	21,240	21,240	21,240
Inventories	29,500	29,500	29,500
Total Current Assets	54,280	54,280	54,280
Net Fixed Assets	41,300	41,300	41,300
Total Assets	$95,580	$95,580	$95,580
Liabilities and Equity			
Accounts payable	$14,160	$14,160	$14,160
Accruals	9,440	9,440	9,440
Notes payable	7,712	10,013	12,314
Total Current Liabilities	31,312	33,613	35,914
Long-term debt	20,000	20,000	20,000
Total Liabilities	51,312	53,613	55,914
Common stocks	20,000	20,000	20,000
Retained earnings	24,268	21,967	19,666
Total Equity	44,268	41,967	39,666
Total liabilities and equity	$95,580	$95,580	$95,580

plans on installing a new inventory control system, how would that affect its pro forma financial statements, including additional funding needed and selected financial ratios? The company can accomplish this by varying the relationship between inventories and sales. Since the new inventory control system will allow the company to hold less inventory, the inventory assumption can be changed from 25% of sales to a lower number.

Figure 1A-43 Selected Financial Ratios Sensitivity Analysis with Different COGS Rates

	COGS = 75%	Base = 80%	COGS = 85%
Current ratio	1.7335	1.6149	1.5114
Quick ratio	0.7914	0.7372	0.6900
ROA	0.1442	0.1040	0.0639
ROE	0.3113	0.2370	0.1540
Gross profit margin	0.2500	0.2000	0.1500
Operating profit margin	0.2000	0.1500	0.1000
Net profit margin	0.1168	0.0843	0.0518
Debt ratio	0.5368	0.5609	0.5850
TIE	9.8333	7.3750	4.9167
Additional funding needed	$2,712	$5,013	$7,314

Overall, sensitivity analysis encourages a company to manage by exception. Performing sensitivity analysis by changing different variables allows a company to determine which sets of variables have the greatest impact on items of interest (e.g, EPS and additional funding needed) and which sets of variables have negligible impacts on the items of interest. This allows the company to focus its attention (and effort) on the most critical assumptions. In the Heavenly Furniture Company example, changes in COGS have a bigger impact on financial ratios (such as EPS) and additional funding needed than changes in the sales growth rate. As demonstrated, a 2% change in sales growth rate will lead to a $0.02 change in EPS, whereas a 5% change in COGS leads to a $0.32 change in EPS.

Knowledge Check:
Top-Level Planning and Analysis

The next questions are intended to help you check your understanding and recall of the material presented in this topic. They do not represent the type of questions that appear on the CMA exam.

Directions: Answer in the space provided. Correct answers and section references appear after the knowledge check questions.

1. What planning functions do pro forma statements support?

   a. _____

   b. _____

   c. _____

2. Robin Manufacturing Company has projected a sales growth rate of 15% for the upcoming year. The pro forma balance sheet created based on this growth rate shows that total assets are $4,300,000 and the total liabilities and owner's equity are $3,950,000. This indicates that the amount of external funding the company needs is:

   ☐ a. $4,300,000

   ☐ b. $3,950,000

   ☐ c. $350,000

   ☐ d. $8,250,000

3. If the amount of external funding is too high for the company, which of the following actions can it take?

   ☐ a.   Reduce its dividend payout.

   ☐ b.   Increase its dividend payout.

   ☐ c.   Increase its sales growth rate.

   ☐ d.   Reduce its accounts payables (in relation to sales).

4. Which of the following actions is not permitted in a sensitivity analysis?

   ☐ a.   Changing the projected growth rate

   ☐ b.   Changing the dividend payout ratio

   ☐ c.   Changing the cost of goods sold (COGS)

   ☐ d.   Changing the projected growth rate and COGS

5. Indicate whether each situation listed represents a cash inflow or cash outflow.

Situation	Cash Inflow	Cash Outflow
Increase in inventories		
Increase in long-term debt		
Increase in accounts payable		
Decrease accruals		
Decrease in net fixed assets		
Decrease in accounts payable		

Knowledge Check Answers: Top-Level Planning and Analysis

1. What planning functions do pro forma statements support? *[See Creating a Pro Forma Income Statement with the Percentage of Sales Method.]*

   a. **Assess whether anticipated performance is in line with its established targets**

   b. **Anticipate the amount of funding needed to achieve its forecasted sales growth**

   c. **Estimate effects of changes in assumptions of key numbers**

2. Robin Manufacturing Company has projected a sales growth rate of 15% for the upcoming year. The pro forma balance sheet created based on this growth rate shows that total assets are $4,300,000 and the total liabilities and owner's equity are $3,950,000. This indicates that the amount of external funding the company needs is: *[See Creating a Pro Forma Balance Sheet and Determining Additional Funding Needed.]*

   ☐ a. $4,300,000

   ☐ b. $3,950,000

   ☑ c. $350,000

   ☐ d. $8,250,000

3. If the amount of external funding is too high for the company, which of the following actions can it take? *[See Creating a Pro Forma Balance Sheet and Determining Additional Funding Needed.]*

   ☑ a. Reduce its dividend payout.

   ☐ b. Increase its dividend payout.

   ☐ c. Increase its sales growth rate.

   ☐ d. Reduce its accounts payables (in relation to sales).

4. Which of the following actions is not permitted in a sensitivity analysis? *[See Performing Sensitivity Analysis.]*

   ☐ a. Changing the projected growth rate

   ☐ b. Changing the dividend payout ratio

   ☐ c. Changing the cost of goods sold (COGS)

   ☑ d. Changing the projected growth rate and COGS5. Indicate whether each situation listed represents a cash inflow or cash outflow. *[See Creating a Pro Forma Statement of Cash Flows.]*

Situation	Cash Inflow	Cash Outflow
Increase in inventories		X
Increase in long-term debt	X	
Increase in accounts payable	X	
Decrease accruals		X
Decrease in net fixed assets	X	
Decrease in accounts payable		X

Directions: This sampling of questions is designed to emulate actual exam questions. Read each question and write your response on another sheet of paper. Use the answer and explanation (given later in the book) to assess your response. Validate or improve the answer you wrote. For a more robust selection of practice questions, access the **Online Test Bank** found on the IMA's Learning Center Web site. See the "Answers to Section Practice Questions" section at the end of this book.

Question 1A4-CQ02

Topic: Annual Profit Plan and Supporting Schedules

Troughton Company manufactures radio-controlled toy dogs. Summary budget financial data for Troughton for the current year are shown next.

Sales (5,000 units at $150 each)	$750,000
Variable manufacturing cost	400,000
Fixed manufacturing cost	100,000
Variable selling and administrative cost	80,000
Fixed selling and administrative cost	150,000

Troughton uses an absorption costing system with overhead applied based on the number of units produced, with a denominator level of activity of 5,000 units. Underapplied or overapplied manufacturing overhead is written off to cost of goods sold in the year incurred.

The $20,000 budgeted operating income from producing and selling 5,000 toy dogs planned for this year is of concern to Trudy George, Troughton's president. She believes she could increase operating income to $50,000 (her bonus threshold) if Troughton produces more units than it sells, thus building up the finished goods inventory.

How much of an increase in the number of units in the finished goods inventory would be needed to generate the $50,000 budgeted operating income?

- ☐ **a.** 556 units
- ☐ **b.** 600 units
- ☐ **c.** 1,500 units
- ☐ **d.** 7,500 units

Question 1A4-CQ04

Topic: Annual Profit Plan and Supporting Schedules

Hannon Retailing Company prices its products by adding 30% to its cost. Hannon anticipates sales of $715,000 in July, $728,000 in August, and $624,000 in

September. Hannon's policy is to have on hand enough inventory at the end of the month to cover 25% of the next month's sales. What will be the cost of the inventory that Hannon should budget for purchase in August?

- ☐ **a.** $509,600
- ☐ **b.** $540,000
- ☐ **c.** $560,000
- ☐ **d.** $680,000

Question 1A4-CQ06

Topic: Annual Profit Plan and Supporting Schedules

Tyler Company produces one product and budgeted 220,000 units for the month of August with these budgeted manufacturing costs:

	Total Costs	Cost per Unit
Variable costs	$1,408,000	$6.40
Batch setup cost	880,000	4.00
Fixed costs	1,210,000	5.50
Total	$3,498,000	$15.90

The variable cost per unit and the total fixed costs are unchanged within a production range of 200,000 to 300,000 units per month. The total for the batch setup cost in any month depends on the number of production batches that Tyler runs. A normal batch consists of 50,000 units unless production requires less volume. In the prior year, Tyler experienced a mixture of monthly batch sizes of 42,000 units, 45,000 units, and 50,000 units. Tyler consistently plans production each month in order to minimize the number of batches. For the month of September, Tyler plans to manufacture 260,000 units. What will be Tyler's total budgeted production costs for September?

- ☐ **a.** $3,754,000
- ☐ **b.** $3,930,000
- ☐ **c.** $3,974,000
- ☐ **d.** $4,134,000

Question 1A4-CQ08

Topic: Annual Profit Plan and Supporting Schedules

Savior Corporation assembles backup tape drive systems for home microcomputers. For the first quarter, the budget for sales is 67,500 units. Savior will finish the fourth quarter of last year with an inventory of 3,500 units, of which 200 are obsolete. The target ending inventory is 10 days of sales (based on 90 days in a quarter). What is the budgeted production for the first quarter?

- ☐ **a.** 75,000
- ☐ **b.** 71,700
- ☐ **c.** 71,500
- ☐ **d.** 64,350

Question 1A4-CQ09

Topic: Annual Profit Plan and Supporting Schedules

Streeter Company produces plastic microwave turntables. Sales for the next year are expected to be 65,000 units in the first quarter, 72,000 units in the second quarter, 84,000 units in the third quarter, and 66,000 units in the fourth quarter.

Streeter usually maintains a finished goods inventory at the end of each quarter equal to one half of the units expected to be sold in the next quarter. However, due to a work stoppage, the finished goods inventory at the end of the first quarter is 8,000 units less than it should be.

How many units should Streeter produce in the second quarter?

- ☐ **a.** 75,000 units
- ☐ **b.** 78,000 units
- ☐ **c.** 80,000 units
- ☐ **d.** 86,000 units

Question 1A4-CQ10

Topic: Annual Profit Plan and Supporting Schedules

Data regarding Rombus Company's budget are shown next.

Planned sales	4,000 units
Material cost	$2.50 per pound
Direct labor	3 hours per unit
Direct labor rate	$7 per hour
Finished goods beginning inventory	900 units
Finished goods ending inventory	600 units
Direct materials beginning inventory	4,300 units
Direct materials ending inventory	4,500 units
Materials used per unit	6 pounds

Rombus Company's production budget will show total units to be produced of:

- ☐ **a.** 3,700
- ☐ **b.** 4,000
- ☐ **c.** 4,300
- ☐ **d.** 4,600

Question 1A4-CQ11

Topic: Annual Profit Plan and Supporting Schedules

Krouse Company is in the process of developing its operating budget for the coming year. Given next are selected data regarding the company's two products, laminated putter heads and forged putter heads, sold through specialty golf shops.

	Putter Heads	
	Forged	**Laminated**
Raw materials		
Steel	2 pounds @ $5/pound	1 pound @ $5/pound
Copper	None	1 pound @ $15/pound
Direct labor	1/4 hour @ $20/hour	1 hour @ $22/hour
Expected sales	8,200 units	2,000 units
Selling price per unit	$30	$80
Ending inventory target	100 units	60 units
Beginning inventory	300 units	60 units
Beginning inventory (cost)	$5,250	$3,120

Manufacturing overhead is applied to units produced on the basis of direct labor hours. Variable manufacturing overhead is projected to be $25,000, and fixed manufacturing overhead is expected to be $15,000.

The estimated cost to produce one unit of the laminated putter head (PH) is:

- ☐ **a.** $42
- ☐ **b.** $46
- ☐ **c.** $52
- ☐ **d.** $62

Question 1A4-CQ12

Topic: Annual Profit Plan and Supporting Schedules

Tidwell Corporation sells a single product for $20 per unit. All sales are on account, with 60% collected in the month of sale and 40% collected in the following month. A partial schedule of cash collections for January through March of the coming year reveals these receipts for the period:

	Cash Receipts		
	January	**February**	**March**
December receivables	$32,000		
From January sales	$54,000	$36,000	
From February sales		$66,000	$44,000

Other information includes:

- Inventories are maintained at 30% of the following month's sales.
- Assume that March sales total $150,000.

The number of units to be purchased in February is

- ☐ **a.** 3,850 units
- ☐ **b.** 4,900 units
- ☐ **c.** 6,100 units
- ☐ **d.** 7,750 units

Question 1A4-CQ13

Topic: Annual Profit Plan and Supporting Schedules

Stevens Company manufactures electronic components used in automobile manufacturing. Each component uses two raw materials, Geo and Clio. Standard usage of the two materials required to produce one finished electronic component, as well as the current inventory, are shown next.

Material	Standard Usage per Unit	Price	Current Inventory
Geo	2.0 pounds	$15/pound	5,000 pounds
Clio	1.5 pounds	$10/pound	7,500 pounds

Stevens forecasts sales of 20,000 components for each of the next two production periods. Company policy dictates that 25% of the raw materials needed to produce the next period's projected sales be maintained in ending direct materials inventory.

Based on this information, what would the budgeted direct material purchases for the coming period be?

	Geo	Clio
☐ **a.**	$450,000	$450,000
☐ **b.**	$675,000	$300,000
☐ **c.**	$675,000	$400,000
☐ **d.**	$825,000	$450,000

Question 1A4-CQ14

Topic: Annual Profit Plan and Supporting Schedules

Petersons Planters Inc. budgeted these amounts for the coming year:

Beginning inventory, finished goods	$10,000
Cost of goods sold	400,000
Direct material used in production	100,000
Ending inventory, finished goods	25,000
Beginning and ending work-in-process inventory	Zero

Overhead is estimated to be two times the amount of direct labor dollars. The amount that should be budgeted for direct labor for the coming year is:

☐ **a.** $315,000

☐ **b.** $210,000

☐ **c.** $157,500

☐ **d.** $105,000

Question 1A4-CQ15

Topic: Annual Profit Plan and Supporting Schedules

Over the past several years, McFadden Industries has experienced the costs shown regarding the company's shipping expenses:

Fixed costs	$16,000
Average shipment	15 pounds
Cost per pound	$0.50

Shown next are McFadden's budget data for the coming year.

Number of units shipped	8,000
Number of sales orders	800
Number of shipments	800
Total sales	$1,200,000
Total pounds shipped	9,600

McFadden's expected shipping costs for the coming year are:

☐ **a.** $4,800

☐ **b.** $16,000

☐ **c.** $20,000

☐ **d.** $20,800

Question 1A4-CQ18

Topic: Annual Profit Plan and Supporting Schedules

In preparing the direct material purchases budget for next quarter, the plant controller has this information available:

Budgeted unit sales	2,000
Pounds of materials per unit	4
Cost of materials per pound	$3
Pounds of materials on hand	400
Finished units on hand	250
Target ending units inventory	325
Target ending inventory of pounds of materials	800

How many pounds of materials must be purchased?

- ☐ **a.** 2,475
- ☐ **b.** 7,900
- ☐ **c.** 8,700
- ☐ **d.** 9,300

Question 1A4-CQ22

Topic: Annual Profit Plan and Supporting Schedules

Given the next data for Scurry Company, what is the cost of goods sold?

Beginning inventory of finished goods	$100,000
Cost of goods manufactured	700,000
Ending inventory of finished goods	200,000
Beginning work-in-process inventory	300,000
Ending work-in-process inventory	50,000

- ☐ **a.** $500,000
- ☐ **b.** $600,000
- ☐ **c.** $800,000
- ☐ **d.** $950,000

Question 1A4-CQ23

Topic: Annual Profit Plan and Supporting Schedules

Tut Company's selling and administrative costs for the month of August, when it sold 20,000 units, were:

	Cost per Unit	Total Cost
Variable costs	$18.60	$372,000
Step costs	4.25	85,000
Fixed costs	8.80	176,000
Total selling and administrative costs	$31.65	$633,000

The variable costs represent sales commissions paid at the rate of 6.2% of sales.

The step costs depend on the number of salespersons employed by the company. In August there were 17 persons on the sales force. However, 2 members have taken early retirement effective August 31. It is anticipated that these positions will remain vacant for several months.

Total fixed costs are unchanged within a relevant range of 15,000 to 30,000 units per month.

Tut is planning a sales price cut of 10%, which it expects will increase sales volume to 24,000 units per month. If Tut implements the sales price reduction, the total budgeted selling and administrative costs for the month of September would be:

- ☐ **a.** $652,760
- ☐ **b.** $679,760
- ☐ **c.** $714,960
- ☐ **d.** $759,600

Question 1A4-CQ36

Topic: Annual Profit Plan and Supporting Schedules

Data regarding Johnsen Inc. 's forecasted dollar sales for the last seven months of the year and Johnsen's projected collection patterns are shown next.

Forecasted sales

June	$700,000
July	600,000
August	650,000
September	800,000
October	850,000
November	900,000
December	840,000

Types of sales

Cash sales	30%
Credit sales	70%

Collection pattern on credit sales (5% determined to be uncollectible)

During the month of sale	20%
During the first month following the sale	50%
During the second month following the sale	25%

Johnsen's budgeted cash receipts from sales and collections on account for September are:

- ☐ **a.** $635,000
- ☐ **b.** $684,500
- ☐ **c.** $807,000
- ☐ **d.** $827,000

Question 1A4-CQ37

Topic: Annual Profit Plan and Supporting Schedules

The Mountain Mule Glove Company is in its first year of business. Mountain Mule had a beginning cash balance of $85,000 for the quarter. The company has a

$50,000 short-term line of credit. The budgeted information for the first quarter is shown next.

	January	February	March
Sales	$60,000	$40,000	$50,000
Purchases	$35,000	$40,000	$75,000
Operating costs	$25,000	$25,000	$25,000

All sales are made on credit and are collected in the second month following the sale. Purchases are paid in the month following the purchase while operating costs are paid in the month that they are incurred. How much will Mountain Mule need to borrow at the end of the quarter if the company needs to maintain a minimum cash balance of $5,000 as required by a loan covenant agreement?

- ☐ **a.** $0
- ☐ **b.** $5,000
- ☐ **c.** $10,000
- ☐ **d.** $45,000

Question 1A2-CQ05

Topic: Forecasting Techniques

Aerosub, Inc. has developed a new product for spacecraft that includes the manufacture of a complex part. The manufacturing of this part requires a high degree of technical skill. Management believes there is a good opportunity for its technical force to learn and improve as it becomes accustomed to the production process. The production of the first unit requires 10,000 direct labor hours. If an 80% learning curve is used, the cumulative direct labor hours required for producing a total of eight units would be:

- ☐ **a.** 29,520 hours
- ☐ **b.** 40,960 hours
- ☐ **c.** 64,000 hours
- ☐ **d.** 80,000 hours

Question 1A2-CQ09

Topic: Forecasting Techniques

Sales of big-screen televisions have grown steadily during the past five years. A dealer predicted that the demand for February would be 148 televisions. Actual demand in February was 158 televisions. If the smoothing constant is $a=0.3$, the demand forecast for March, using the exponential smoothing model, will be:

- ☐ **a.** 148 televisions
- ☐ **b.** 151 televisions

☐ **c.** 153 televisions

☐ **d.** 158 televisions

Question 1A2-CQ14

Topic: Forecasting Techniques

Scarf Corporation's controller has decided to use a decision model to cope with uncertainty. With a particular proposal, currently under consideration, Scarf has two possible actions: invest or not invest in a joint venture with an international firm. The controller has determined this information:

Action 1: Invest in the Joint Venture

Events and Probabilities:

Probability of success = 60%

Cost of investment = $9.5 million

Cash flow if investment is successful = $15.0 million

Cash flow if investment is unsuccessful = $2.0 million

Additional costs to be paid = $0

Costs incurred up to this point = $650,000

Action 2: Do Not Invest in the Joint Venture

Events:

Costs incurred up to this point = $650,000

Additional costs to be paid = $100,000

Which one of the next alternatives correctly reflects the respective expected values of investing versus not investing?

☐ **a.** $300,000 and ($750,000)

☐ **b.** ($350,000) and ($100,000)

☐ **c.** $300,000 and ($100,000)

☐ **d.** ($350,000) and ($750,000)

To further assess your understanding of the concepts and calculations covered in Part 1, Section A: Planning, Budgeting, and Forecasting, practice with the **Online Test Bank** for this section.

REMINDER: See the "Answers to Section Practice Questions" section at the end of this book.

Performance Management

Once an organization has established a master budget, it is critical to compare actual financial performance against the master budget plan to measure variances and in turn, success in achieving goals. This financial measure comparison or feedback process allows an organization to confirm the overall vision of where it wants to be against actual results. Without this feedback, the budgeting process is not very useful.

This section reviews the process of how to:

- Break down variances from the master budget into subcategories so an organization can better assess the specific reasons for the variance.
- Utilize performance feedback from responsibility centers or strategic business units (SBUs) to help manage profitability.
- Understand the financial measures of profitability used in responsibility centers and in the organization as a whole.

After covering financial measures, this section also shows a balanced approach to performance measurement. The balanced scorecard measures both financial and nonfinancial aspects of an organization and is integrated with strategy so that reading the scorecard will tell anyone in the organization what the strategy is and how the organization plans to achieve it.

Cost and Variance Measures

FEEDBACK IS A NECESSARY ELEMENT OF CONTROL. Feedback in financial management is the comparison of planned (expected) results or the budget to actual outcomes, and is known as a variance. A **variance** is the difference between the actual and planned results.

This topic covers how flexible budgets and variances aid in financial management control and planning, thereby making the business as efficient as possible. It includes a look at the use of flexible budgets in analyzing performance, a discussion of the role of management by exception, and an analysis of variation from standard cost expectations using a case study.

 READ the Learning Outcome Statements (LOS) for this topic as found in Appendix B and then study the concepts and calculations presented here to be sure you understand the content you could be tested on in the CMA exam.

Comparison of Actual to Planned Results

A successful budget cycle generally follows a process of:

- Creating a master budget that sets out plans for the performance of the organization as a whole as well as for each subunit.
- Establishing standards or specific expectations against which actual results can be compared.
- Investigating variations from plans and taking corrective action, if necessary.
- Planning for continuous improvement, taking into consideration feedback and changed conditions.

When comparing actual to planned results, managers are concerned with the efficiency of the operation and its effectiveness in meeting organizational goals.

Efficiency is the budgeted amounts or standards set for a particular resource compared to the actual resources consumed. Typically, resources are categorized into direct material, direct labor, and manufacturing overhead. For example, if a cost is estimated to be $2 per unit, an efficient operation that sells 1,000 units should have a cost of $2,000 or less. An inefficient operation would incur costs in excess of that amount.

Effectiveness is measured by how well a firm attains its goals. If the master budget calls for net operating income to be $300 million, an effective operation would have earned that amount or more and an ineffective operation would have earned less than that amount. An operation can be effective but not efficient or efficient but not effective. An inefficient but effective operation is one that meets its primary goals even though it had cost overruns.

In order to attain both objectives of efficiency and effectiveness, it is important to know how an operation is performing and how it should be performing. Determining how an operation is doing involves standard costing, but such methods will not alleviate any issues unless combined with variance analysis to determine actual operational behavior. Determining how the operation should perform depends on selecting appropriate benchmarks with an appropriate level of stringency—for example, whether to use kaizen with continually increasing goals, target costing with specific types of standards, and so on, in the measure.

A primary means of assessing effectiveness is through the **operating income variance**, or the difference between budgeted operating income and actual operating income. Such a measure looks at the bottom line of operations. A secondary means of assessing effectiveness is to do a line-by-line comparison of actual to planned results.

Figure 1B-1 shows variances from a **static budget**, which is a budget that is set at the beginning of the year and not changed. Flexible budgets are covered later in the section.

Favorable/Unfavorable Variances

Some variances are favorable and others are unfavorable. A **favorable variance** exceeds the planned amount of earnings or was less than the planned costs. An **unfavorable variance** is the opposite. A general rule of thumb is that if a variance helps the bottom line, it is favorable; if it hurts the bottom line, it is unfavorable.

For example: Bounce Sporting Goods' budget analysis in Figure 1B-1 shows both favorable (F) and unfavorable (U) variances.

Note that in Figure 1B-1 there is a favorable direct materials variance, $1,491,840 – $1,800,000 = ($308,160), which is a negative but favorable amount. Positive and negative signs are very important to track for variance calculations but do not indicate favorableness or unfavorableness by themselves. Taken together with the fact that this is a cost, a negative number means that the cost is reduced, increasing net income, and therefore the variance is favorable.

In contrast, the $600,000 unfavorable revenue variance in Figure 1B-1 is unfavorable because it is lower than the planned revenue, adversely affecting net income. Some of the illustrations in this text drop the negative and positive signs to focus more on favorable and unfavorable variances, but if a favorable variance is added to an unfavorable variance, they have to be netted against each other.

Is the $308,160 favorable direct material variance a good thing for the company? Even though the operation was ineffective, was it at least efficient? Not necessarily.

Figure 1B-1 Analysis of Variance Between Actual and Static Budget for Bounce Sporting Goods Company

High-Level Analysis — Overview	
Actual operating income	$35,760
Budgeted operating income	270,000
Static-budget variance of operating income	$234,240 U

Midlevel Analysis	Actual Results	Static Budget	Variance (Actual − Static)
Units sold	24,000	30,000	6,000 U*
Revenues variable costs	$3,000,000	$3,600,000	$600,000 U
Direct materials	1,491,840	1,800,000	308,160 F†
Direct manufacturing labor	475,200	480,000	4,800 F
Variable manufacturing overhead	313,200	360,000	46,800 F
Total variable costs	2,280,240	2,640,000	359,760 F
Contribution margin	719,760	960,000	240,240 U
Fixed costs	684,000	690,000	6,000 F
Operating income	$35,760	$270,000	$234,240 U

*U = Unfavorable effect on operating income
†F = Favorable effect on operating income

Because the operation had an unfavorable number of units sold, the primary reason for the operation being ineffective was that sales were lower than budgeted. Because fewer goods were produced, the direct material costs were lower. The budgeted direct material costs were $1,800,000 for 30,000 units, or $60 per unit. The actual number of units produced was 24,000 units at an actual cost of $1,491,840, so the actual cost was $62.16 per unit.

Therefore, favorable and unfavorable are not necessarily indications of a good or bad result per se but show whether the firm is or is not meeting its plan. Budget variances on line items can be misleading and may not indicate either effectiveness or efficiency. Furthermore, variances should be tested against a materiality threshold. If they are individually immaterial, they should be ignored. However, several small variances could point to a much larger problem.

Consistent budget variances usually point to a systematic fault in the operation, which should be rectified to improve efficiency. However, budget variances can also occur because of flawed assumptions when preparing the budget, inefficiencies in execution of the budget, or unforeseen internal or external changes in the environment. Additional analyses that assess the efficiency of operations are needed to determine why targets were missed. One approach is to use a flexible budget.

Use of Flexible Budgets to Analyze Performance

Using a flexible budget provides more meaningful analysis than using a static budget when determining why a budget has variances.

The primary difference between a static budget and a flexible budget is that while both are planned and originally created in the same manner, at the end of the period, a **static budget** is left unchanged and all comparisons are made to the expected output, while a **flexible budget** alters the budget amounts to reflect actual output levels. Output levels and types of output vary across industries and businesses. A manufacturing company would base changes on units of output, but a hospital could use number of patient days, and a service company could use billed hours of service.

Referring again to the sales situation illustrated in Figure 1B-1, if sales were supposed to be 30,000 units but were actually 24,000 units, the flexible budget would be altered to show 24,000 units, and all other corresponding budgeted amounts would change accordingly. This means that variable costs would be adjusted to the actual output level and that fixed costs would most likely remain the same. The result would be a budget that is "flexed," or adjusted, to the actual level of output.

Creating a flexible budget from a static budget allows managers to make direct comparisons. Using a flexible budget, the favorable variance in direct material costs changes to an unfavorable variance, because instead of a budgeted amount of $1,800,000 for direct materials, the new budgeted amount of $1,440,000 ($60 per unit × 24,000 units) would be used, and the actual amount of $1,491,840 would be $51,840 unfavorable.

When compared to static budgets, flexible budgets yield better managerial control results. The reason for better control lies in the concept of variable and fixed expenses. In general, management has more control over variable costs because their cost behavior is directly tied to units of production. If a business lowers the number of units produced from the number suggested in the static budget, the variable costs incurred should go down in equal proportion with the drop in units of production.

Characteristics of Flexible Budgets

A detailed analysis of variances in a static budget can be misleading, because the static budget is prepared at the beginning of the budgeting period and is valid only for the planned level of activity. It is not adjusted to the actual level of activity. By contrast, analyzing a flexible budget's variances in detail can be informative. A flexible budget alters the output units and corresponding total variable costs related to a specific level of output but does not alter unit prices, unit costs, or other items not tied to output. Fixed expenses are also not usually changed because they are by nature fixed over the operating period.

For example: Bounce Sporting Goods' flexible budget has been altered for an unfavorable and a favorable variance in output units, along with changes in other items, and is shown in Figure 1B-2.

Figure 1B-2 shows how flexible budgets can be prepared either after the actual results are known or before, as a pro forma flexible budget. Unit changes alter total sales and total variable expenses. Therefore, the total contribution margin and operating income change correspondingly. However, the percentage of the contribution

Figure 1B-2 Flexible Budgets for Bounce Sporting Goods Company

	Flexible Budget at 80%		Flexible Budget at 100% Static or Master Budget		Flexible Budget at 110%	
Units sold	24,000		30,000		33,000	
Sales	$2,880,000		$3,600,000		$3,960,000	
Variable expenses	2,112,000		2,640,000		2,904,000	
Contribution margin	$768,000	26.67%	$960,000	26.67%	$1,056,000	26.67%
Fixed expenses	690,000		690,000		690,000	
Operating income	$78,000	2.7%	$270,000	7.5%	$366,000	9.2%

margin stays the same while the percentage of operating income changes. This is because when the flexible budget has an unfavorable output variance, the fixed costs assume a larger percentage of the costs. In a favorable output variance, the opposite is true.

Flexible budgets can be prepared without any reference to the master budget. A master budget must be prepared before the accounting period, but flexible budgets can be prepared any time and with varying levels of detail to highlight particular items that need attention. Managers can also use flexible budgets to analyze operating results and determine reasons for changes in operating conditions.

Steps in Preparing a Flexible Budget

Four steps are used when developing a flexible budget.

1. **Prepare a static master budget.** Determine a budgeted selling price, budgeted variable costs per unit, and budgeted fixed costs, as these amounts will continue to be used in the flexible budget. Additionally, output has to be estimated.
2. **Find the actual quantity of output.** The quantity of output is the cost driver for the variable costs.
3. **Calculate the flexible budget amounts for total sales.** The next formula is used to calculate total sales in a flexible budget:

Total Sales = # of Units Sold × Budgeted Selling Price per Unit

For example: Bounce Sporting Goods' flexible budget revenues are calculated as shown:

$$\text{Flexible Budget Revenues} = \$120/\text{unit} \times 24,000 \text{ units}$$
$$= \$2,880,00$$

4. **Calculate the flexible budget amounts for expenses.** The next formula is used to calculate total expenses in a flexible budget:

Total Expenses = Total Variable Expenses + Total Fixed Expenses

Total variable expenses equal the number of units sold multiplied by the budgeted variable costs per unit. *For example:* Bounce's flexible budget calculated for actual results is shown in Figure 1B-3.

Figure 1B-3 Flexible Budget Amounts for Expenses

Flexible budget variable costs	
Direct materials, $60 × 24,000	$1,440,000
Direct manufacturing labor, $16 × 24,000	384,000
Variable manufacturing overhead, $12 × 24,000	288,000
Total variable costs	2,112,000
Flexible budget fixed costs	690,000
Flexible budget total costs	$2,802,000

Flexible Budget Variance and Sales Volume Variance

A flexible budget can be used to analyze the efficiency of an operation.

The difference between the actual results and the static budget is called the **static budget variance**. This variance can be broken down into two different types of variances when a flexible budget is created:

1. The **flexible budget variance** is calculated by taking the actual results less the flexible budget amount (adjusted for actual output). This variance identifies the difference in operating income when the budget is flexed, or adjusted to the actual level of sales.
2. The **sales volume variance** is calculated by taking the flexible budget amount adjusted for actual output less the static budget amount. This variance provides information on how operating income is affected by the difference in the volume of budgeted sales compared to the volume of actual sales.

For example: Bounce's actual results are compared against the flexible and static budgets in Figure 1B-4. These comparisons provide the foundation for calculating the flexible budget variance and sales volume variance. A summary of these variances is included in Figure 1B-5.

The flexible budget variance is calculated as shown:

Flexible Budget Variance = Actual Results − Flexible Budget Amount
(adjusted for actual output)

Flexible Budget Variance = $35,760 − $78,000 = $42,240 U

Figure 1B-4 Calculating Flexible Budget Variance and Sales Volume Variance for Bounce Sporting Goods

	Actual Results	Flexible Budget	Flexible Budget Variances (Actual – Flexible)	Static Budget	Sales Volume Variances (Flexible – Static)
Units sold	24,000	24,000	0	30,000	6,000 U
Revenues	$3,000,000	$2,880,000	$120,00 F	$3,600,000	$720,000 U
Variable costs					
Direct materials	1,491,840	1,440,000	51,840 U	1,800,000	360,000 F
Direct manufacturing labor	475,200	384,000	91,200 U	480,000	96,000 F
Variable mfg. overhead	313,200	288,000	25,200 U	360,000	72,000 F
Total variable costs	2,280,240	2,112,000	168,240 U	2,640,000	528,000 F
Contribution margin	719,760	768,000	48,240 U	960,000	192,000 U
Fixed costs	684,000	690,000	6,000 F	690,000	0
Operating income	$35,760	$78,000	$42,240 U	$270,000	$192,000 U

$42,240 U
Total flexible budget variance

$192,000 U
Total sales volume variance

Total static budget variance
$234,240 U

The sales volume variance is calculated as shown:

Sales Volume Variance = Flexible Budget Amount (adjusted for actual output) − Static Budget Amount

Sales Volume Variance = $78,000 − $270,000 = $192,000 U

Figure 1B-5 Flexible Budget Variances and Sales Volume Variances for Bounce Sporting Goods

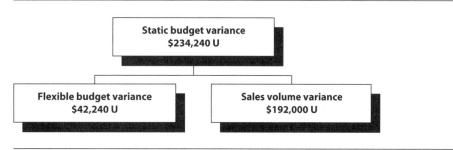

The sales volume variance shows the effect of the difference in actual output quantity from the budgeted amounts. The flexible budget variance, however, shows the effects of differences due to actual selling price, variable expenses, and fixed expenses. An unfavorable sales volume variance indicates that the firm does not have as much market share as was assumed or that the market is smaller than anticipated; favorable sales volume variance indicates higher-than-anticipated demand for the product. Insignificant sales volume variances mean that the budget predicted accurate sales. An unfavorable flexible budget variance indicates that the input costs were higher than budgeted. A favorable flexible budget variance indicates that the input costs were lower than budgeted. Analysis of both variances together will help assess whether an operation is effective and/or efficient.

Management by Exception

The breakdown of variances into flexible budget variances and sales budget variances can allow a firm to make business decisions based on these variances. **Management by exception** is a method of focusing management attention on only significant variances from the budget. Significant variances are the exceptions that require more attention than other areas. Some management software automatically creates exception reports. Management by exception flags unfavorable as well as favorable variances. Favorable variances should be tracked to determine if the performance is truly exceptional or perhaps the standard is set too low. Exceptional performance over time should be incorporated into standard practice.

Knowing which exceptions to investigate requires managerial experience, but the size and frequency of the variances are primary considerations. The relative size of the variance is more important than the absolute size, but managers often have set a general rule for both—for example, flag all variances over $30,000 or 5% of the budgeted cost.

Small but frequent variances are also worth investigating. Other considerations include following trends, such as a cost that continuously gets larger over time, and the level of control that can be directed to change the cost, such as not paying as much attention to a cost that is rising solely due to market demand.

Management by exception is a good management technique in that it focuses a manager's attention only on exceptions that are tracked, and each exception is tracked or not tracked based on a cost-benefit decision. However, because this method requires management discretion, poor management judgment can cause this benefit to become a drawback. For example, if management believes that a rising raw material cost cannot be controlled and therefore does not flag the cost, it might be overlooking an alternative, such as finding a different vendor or a replacement material. When properly implemented, exception tracking can reduce future costs when causes for unfavorable variances are removed or when causes for favorable variances can be extended.

Use of Standard Cost Systems

A **standard cost** is any carefully determined price, quantity, service level, or cost, usually expressed in a per-unit amount, which is determined before actual costs are available. Standard costs are used for planning purposes, because actual costs usually are not available until after a product is produced or a service is rendered. A standard cost is a predetermined amount based on experience and represents the amount that a unit of output is expected to cost. A standard costing system uses standard costs for all elements of a product or service, including standard expenses for manufacturing, administration, and sales. A standard costing system can be a valuable management tool, because it enables the firm to identify variances from what was planned. When a variance arises between actual and standard costs, management becomes aware that costs have differed from the standard (planned, expected) costs. Standard cost systems allow for the use of management by exception and provide the foundation for variance analysis, which allows management to gain an understanding of what is causing favorable or unfavorable performance.

Analysis of Variation from Standard Cost Expectations

A flexible budget provides a high-level overview of budget variances, and flexible budget and sales volume variances provide a more detailed view, a third level of detail is possible by analyzing the cause of these flexible budget variances.

Recall that all standards have two components:

1. A standard rate per unit of the cost driver. A cost driver is an activity, such as direct labor hours, machine hours, level of output, and so on, that affects the level of costs that are incurred.
2. A standard number of units of a cost driver for a given output level—the flexible budget level.

Focusing on changes in each of these two components allows flexible budget variances to be broken down into price (rate) variances and efficiency (usage) variances. The total of these two variances equals the flexible budget variance, as shown in Figure 1B-6 (where DM is direct materials and DL is direct labor).

Note that in Figure 1B-6, for direct materials, the price variance plus the efficiency variance will equal the flexible budget variance only when the amount of material purchased in the period exactly equals the amount used in production during the period, which means that the inventory balance does not change—and that is a rare event. This problem does not occur in direct labor or overhead because these items cannot be inventoried (i.e., the amount purchased always equals the amount used). Direct costs and fixed and variable overhead require different methods of calculating these variances.

A discussion of sales mix variances and their breakdown into mix variances and yield variances appears later in this topic.

Price and Efficiency Variances for Direct Labor and Direct Material Inputs

Price and efficiency variances result from variances from budgeted input prices or input quantities. A **standard input** is a predetermined quantity of direct inputs,

Figure 1B-6 Variance Breakdown for Direct Costs

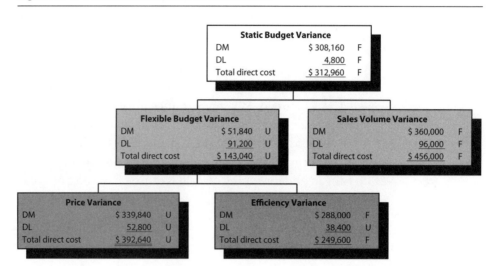

such as labor hours or gallons of a fluid needed to make one unit of output. A price variance for direct labor is often referred to as a rate variance , and an efficiency variance for direct material is often referred to as a quantity or usage variance.

Price (Rate) Variances for Direct Costs

A **price variance** is the actual input quantity of an item multiplied by the difference between the actual input price and the budgeted (or standard) input price.

> Price (Rate) Variance = Actual Input Quantity × (Actual Input Price − Budgeted Input Price)

Suppose the standards for a unit were:

Direct Materials (DM): 10.0 Pounds DM/Unit @ $6.00/Pound = $60/Unit Standard
 (24,000 Units × 10.0 Pounds/Unit = 240,000 Pounds Standard)

Direct Labor (DL): 2.0 Labor Hours/Unit @ $8.00/Hour = $16/Unit Standard
 (24,000 Units × 2.0 Labor Hours/Unit = 48,000 Labor Hours Standard)

Assume that for a period, the actual price paid for direct materials was $7.77/pound and the process purchased and consumed 192,000 pounds of material to produce 24,000 units. The price variance for direct materials would be calculated as shown:

> DM Price Variance = Actual Input Quantity × (Actual Input Price − Budgeted Input Price)

$$\text{DM Price Variance} = 192{,}000 \text{ Pounds} \times (\$7.77/\text{Pound} - \$6/\text{Pound})$$

$$= \$339{,}840 \text{ U}$$

If the quantity purchased is not equal to the quantity used, the quantity purchased should be used in the DM price variance calculation.

For the same period, if the actual price paid for labor hours was \$9.00/hour and the number of hours logged was 52,800 to produce 24,000 units, the price (rate) variance for labor would be calculated as shown:

> DL Rate Variance = Actual Input Quantity × (Actual Input Price
> − Budgeted Input Price)

$$\text{DL Rate Variance} = 52{,}800 \text{ Hours} \times (\$9/\text{Hour} - \$8/\text{Hour}) = \$52{,}800 \text{ U}$$

Favorable direct materials price variances can be caused by quantity discounts, better negotiations, unforeseen price or shipping cost changes, or lack of demand for an item (high availability lowering the price). Unfavorable direct materials price variances can be caused by the opposite situations. Either type of variance could also be caused by poor budgeting or by receiving materials of better or worse quality than expected. Direct labor rate variances are caused by changes in market demand for the appropriate labor, labor shortages, overtime rates, or requiring different skill levels to be used, which requires different rates to be paid from those set in the standards.

The effect of a variance, whether it is favorable or unfavorable, should be studied. For example, a favorable materials price variance caused by purchasing in bulk could cause a firm to have greater inventory holding costs. Moreover, if the standards reflect the company's strategy, such as differentiation for quality, variations should be studied for their effect on the company's strategy and corrected when they differ from that strategy.

Efficiency (Quantity or Usage) Variances for Direct Costs

An **efficiency variance** is the budgeted input price multiplied by the difference between the actual input quantity and the budgeted (or standard) input quantity. This formula is:

> Efficiency Variance = Budgeted Input Price × (Actual Input Quantity
> − Budgeted Input Quantity)

Continuing with the prior example, for direct materials, the actual input quantity was 192,000 pounds, or 8 pounds/unit (192,000/24,000). Because the budgeted input quantity was 240,000 pounds and the budgeted price was $6/pound, the efficiency (quantity) variance would be calculated as shown:

> DM Efficiency (Quantity) Variance = Budgeted Input Price × (Actual Input Quantity − Budgeted Input Quantity)

DM Efficiency (Quantity) Variance = $6/Pound × (192,000 Pounds − 240,000 Pounds)
= $288,000 F

The direct materials efficiency variance is normally referred to as the direct materials quantity variance or the direct materials usage variance.

For direct labor, the actual input quantity was 52,800 labor hours, or 2.2 hours per unit (52,800/24,000). Because the budgeted input quantity was 48,000 labor hours and the budgeted price was $8/labor hour, the efficiency variance would be calculated as shown:

> DL Efficiency Variance = Budgeted Input Price × (Actual Input Quantity − Budgeted Input Quantity)

DL Efficiency Variance = $8/Hour × (52,800 Hours − 48,000 Hours)
= $38,400 U

Because the price variance plus the efficiency variance equals the flexible budget variance, the flexible budget variance can be verified by totaling the price and efficiency variances as shown:

DM Flexible Budget Variance = $339,840 U (price) + $288,000 F (efficiency)
= $51,840 U

DL Flexible Budget Variance = $52,800 U (price) + $38,400 F (efficiency)
= $91,200 U

Both direct material and direct labor efficiency variances can be caused by poor budgeting or by variances in worker skill level, scheduling, supervision, or setup efficiency. Improperly maintained machines or improper training can also lead to direct material and direct labor efficiency variances.

Spending and Efficiency Variances for Variable and Fixed Overhead

As with direct costs, variable overhead cost variances can be further broken down into price and efficiency variances. Because of the fixed nature of fixed overhead costs, the fixed overhead cost variances are further broken down into the fixed overhead spending variance and the fixed overhead production volume variance.

Variances for Variable Overhead

Breaking down the variable overhead flexible budget variance requires knowing three calculated amounts:

1. **Actual variable overhead:** Actual overhead incurred during the period
2. **Predicted variable overhead:** Actual quantity of cost driver times the standard rate
3. **Applied variable overhead:** Standard allowed quantity of cost driver times the standard rate

The variable overhead flexible budget variance can be broken down into a variable overhead spending variance (1 minus 2 in the list shown above) and a variable overhead efficiency variance (2 minus 3 in the list shown above).

Variable Overhead Spending Variance

The **variable overhead spending variance** is calculated by taking the difference between actual overhead cost and the standard variable overhead rate multiplied by the actual quantity of the cost driver. This variance tells management how much should have been spent in total on variable overhead items during the period.

Variable Overhead Spending (or Price) Variance = Actual Overhead Cost − (Actual Quantity of Cost Driver × Standard Variable Overhead Rate)

Variable overhead standards are created using a cost driver and a number of units of the cost driver.

For example: If machine hours are used as the cost driver for variable overhead and 1.2 machine hours at \$10/machine hour are set as the standard for one unit (\$12/unit), then 24,000 units should require 28,800 machine hours, or \$288,000 (see Figure 1B-4).

Actual variable overhead costs allocated to these 24,000 units are \$313,200, which then makes the variable overhead flexible budget variance \$25,200 unfavorable (\$288,000 − \$313,200 = \$25,200 U).

Therefore, if the actual number of machine hours is 28,000, the variable overhead spending variance would be calculated as:

Variable Overhead Spending Variance = Actual Cost − (Actual Units of Cost Driver × Standard Cost Driver Rate)

$$\begin{aligned}
\text{Variable Overhead Spending Variance} &= \$313{,}200 - (28{,}000 \text{ Machine Hours} \\
&\qquad \times \$10/\text{Machine Hour}) \\
&= \$313{,}200 - \$280{,}000 \\
&= \$33{,}200 \text{ U}
\end{aligned}$$

Variable Overhead Efficiency Variance

The **variable overhead efficiency variance** is the product of the actual quantity of the cost driver multiplied by the standard variable overhead rate, less the product of the standard quantity of the cost driver multiplied by the standard variable overhead rate.

> Variable Overhead Efficiency Variance =
> (Actual Units of Cost Driver × Standard Cost Driver Rate) − (Standard
> Units of Cost Driver × Standard Cost Driver Rate)

The variable overhead efficiency variance is shown next, along with an example.

$$\begin{aligned}
&\text{Variable Overhead Efficiency Variance} \\
&= (28{,}000 \text{ Machine Hours} \times \$10/\text{Machine Hour}) \\
&\quad - (28{,}800 \text{ Machine Hours} \times \$10/\text{Machine Hour}) \\
&= \$280{,}000 - \$288{,}000 \\
&= \$8{,}000 \text{ F}
\end{aligned}$$

> Variable Overhead Flexible Budget Variance = Variable Overhead Spending
> Variance + Variable Overhead Efficeincy Variance

The variable overhead spending plus efficiency variances aggregate to the variable overhead flexible budget variance.

$$\begin{aligned}
\text{Variable Overhead Flexible Budget Variance} &= \$33{,}200 \text{ U} + \$8{,}000 \text{ F} \\
&= \$25{,}200 \text{ U}
\end{aligned}$$

A variable overhead variance is more likely caused by the imprecision inherent in choosing a single cost driver for overhead that is likely made up of very different costs. In contrast, variance measures for direct materials and direct labor have accurate cost drivers. For greater accuracy in calculating overhead, activity-based overhead variance measures could perform the variance measures using a variety of cost pools, each with its own cost driver, but the higher administrative cost may be prohibitive. Variable overhead may also have variances because many types of variable overhead costs are not based on output measures, such as units of output, but on input measures, such as number of setups or batches.

Variable Overhead Accounting

The variable overhead flexible budget variance of $25,200 unfavorable in the prior example represents the amount of underapplied overhead, because this is the amount by which actual costs exceed applied overhead. If favorable, the amount would represent the amount of overapplied overhead.

However, by breaking this variance down into spending and efficiency variances, the accounting for the differences can also become more specific. (See Figure 1B-7.)

Figure 1B-7 Journal Entries for Variable Overhead (Actual and Applied)

Variable Manufacturing Overhead Control	$313,200	
Accounts Payable Control and Other Accounts		$313,200
To record actual variable manufacturing overhead costs incurred.		
Work-in-Process Control	$288,000	
Variable Manufacturing Overhead Applied		$288,000
To record applied variable manufacturing overhead costs (1.2 machine hours/unit × $10/machine hour × 24,000 units).		

The costs in the work-in-process (WIP) control account would be transferred to the finished goods control account when production is finished. The costs of items sold are transferred from the finished goods control account to the cost of goods sold account when sales are made.

The entry shown in Figure 1B-8 would be made to record the variances. (Note that the two variance accounts now replace the single overhead applied account.)

Figure 1B-8 Journal Entry to Record Variable Overhead Variances

Variable Manufacturing Overhead Applied	$288,000	
Variable Manufacturing Overhead Spending Variance	$33,200	
Variable Manufacturing Overhead Control		$313,200
Variable Manufacturing Overhead Efficiency Variance		$8,000
To record variable overhead variances for the accounting period.		

Assuming that the amount of overhead that is underapplied (or overapplied) is immaterial, the accounting entries shown in Figure 1B-9 would be made to write off the difference to the cost of goods sold account at the end of the period.

Figure 1B-9 Disposition of Variable Overhead Variance Accounts

Cost of Goods Sold	$25,200	
Variable Manufacturing Overhead Efficiency Variance	$8,000	
Variable Manufacturing Overhead Spending Variance		$33,200
To record the disposition of variable overhead variance accounts.		

If the amount of overapplied or underapplied overhead is material and unavoidable, the amounts must be prorated among the ending WIP inventory, ending finished goods inventory, and the cost of goods sold based on the relative variable manufacturing overhead allocated to each account during the accounting period.

Variances for Fixed Overhead

The total **fixed overhead variance** represents the difference between actual fixed overhead and applied fixed overhead.

Total Fixed Overhead Variance = Actual Fixed Overhead
− Applied Fixed Overhead

The total fixed overhead variance is also called the underapplied or overapplied fixed overhead.

Just like the other cost variances, the fixed overhead variance can also be broken down further, so that management can gain a better understanding of performance for this cost category. To break down the total fixed overhead variance into two subcategories, three amounts must be known:

1. **Actual fixed overhead:** Actual overhead incurred in the period.
2. **Budgeted fixed overhead:** A fixed cost, usually assessed as a lump sum and not on a per-unit basis. The fixed overhead standard rate per unit is the total static budgeted quantity cost driver times the standard fixed overhead rate.
3. **Applied fixed overhead:** Standard allowed quantity times the standard fixed overhead rate.

Actual fixed overhead is the actual amount of overhead incurred in a period. **Budgeted fixed overhead** uses the standard quantity set in the static budget. Note that the flexible budget cost for fixed overhead is equal to the static budget cost, as the fixed overhead cost is, by definition, fixed and is independent of output. Therefore, the sales volume variance for fixed overhead is always zero.

The fixed overhead flexible budget variance can be broken down into a fixed overhead spending variance (1 minus 2 in the prior list) and a fixed overhead production volume variance (2 minus 3 in the list). The fixed overhead spending variance is actual fixed overhead minus budgeted fixed overhead. The fixed overhead production volume variance is the budgeted fixed overhead minus applied fixed overhead.

Continuing the prior example (see Figure 1B-4), the actual fixed overhead is $684,000. The budgeted fixed overhead is calculated by taking 30,000 units and multiplying them by the standard fixed overhead rate of $23/unit ($690,000/30,000 = $23/unit), which equals $690,000. The applied fixed overhead is the actual quantity of 24,000 units multiplied by the standard rate of $23/unit, which equals $552,000.

The fixed overhead spending variance and the fixed overhead production volume variance are calculated as shown:

Fixed Overhead Spending Variance = Actual Fixed Overhead
− Budgeted Fixed Overhead

Fixed Overhead Spending Variance = $684,000 − $690,000 = $6,000 F

Fixed Overhead Production Volume Variance = Budgeted Fixed Overhead
− Applied Fixed Overhead

Fixed Overhead Volume Variance = $690,000 − $552,000 = $138,000 U

Total Fixed Overhead Variance (Equal to the Amount of Overapplied or
Underapplied Overhead) = Fixed Overhead Spending Variance + Fixed
Overhead Production Volume Variance

Total Fixed Overhead Variance = $6,000 Favorable + $138,000 U

= $132,000 U

or

Total Fixed Overhead Variance = Actual Fixed Overhead
− Applied Fixed Overhead

Total Fixed Overhead Variance = $684,000 − $552,000 = $132,000 U

A fixed overhead spending variance shows that the budget procedure either missed or failed to predict changes in certain fixed costs. Unfavorable spending variances can also occur if inadequate control is exercised over departmental spending or because of accidents and unexpected repairs. The breakdown of fixed costs into these two categories can highlight when certain variable costs are misclassified as fixed costs, because changes in production volume will be accompanied by changes in some portion of the fixed costs that may be discretionary. Also, as with the variable overhead variances, the total fixed overhead variance of $132,000 unfavorable is the total amount of fixed overhead underapplied and would be accounted for using the combination of the fixed overhead spending variance and the fixed overhead production volume variance accounts. The entries would be similar to those shown previously for variable overhead, with the entry shown in Figure 1B-10 to record the variances.

Figure 1B-10 Journal Entry to Record Fixed Manufacturing Overhead Variances

Fixed Manufacturing Overhead Applied	$552,000	
Fixed Manufacturing Overhead Production Volume Variance	$138,000	
Fixed Manufacturing Overhead Control		$684,000
Fixed Manufacturing Overhead Spending Variance		$6,000
To record variances for the accounting period.		

The final entry to adjust the cost of goods sold (if immaterial) is shown in Figure 1B-11.

Figure 1B-11 Disposition of Fixed Overhead Variances

Cost of Goods Sold	$132,000	
Fixed Manufacturing Overhead Spending Variance	$6,000	
Fixed Manufacturing Overhead Production Volume Variance		$138,000
To record the disposition of fixed overhead variance account.		

Again, if material and unavoidable, such costs would be prorated among the inventory accounts and the cost of goods sold.

The fixed overhead production volume variance can occur when demand for a product changes from what was expected. Often some measurement of a production variable (e.g., labor hours or machine hours) is used as the allocation base for overhead. If the labor usage being measured (actual quantity of allocation base as measured in applied fixed overhead) differs from the budgeted amount used to compute the overhead rate (standard quantity of allocation base as measured in budgeted fixed overhead), this will result in fixed overhead variances being either overapplied or underapplied.

Other causes of the fixed overhead production volume variance include changes in strategy or unexpected breakdowns. If the company made as many units in the period as it budgeted, there should be no fixed overhead production volume variance. The production volume variance reflects the company's use of its capacity. When volume is low, the price per unit of fixed overhead is higher and capacity is underutilized. The production volume variance does not indicate efficiency but its effectiveness in attaining its cost goals.

Using Overhead Variance Data to Solve for Other Unknowns

Sometimes the variances for a situation are known but some other variables are not known. In such situations, the equation can be solved for the variable in question.

For example: Assume that Bounce Sporting Goods is benchmarking a competitor, SportCo. SportCo's actual variable overhead is $432,000, and its actual sales are 28,250 units. SportCo stated in a magazine article that it uses labor hours when allocating variable overhead, and it allows a budgeted input of 1.6 labor hours per unit. The article did not mention the variable overhead allocation rates or actual number of labor hours used for the period. SportCo's variable overhead variances are \$58,000 unfavorable efficiency variance and \$20,000 favorable spending variance. Standard flexible budget units of the cost driver can thus be derived: 28,250 actual units $\times$ 1.6 labor hours per unit = 45,200 labor hours.

Based on this information, what is the variable overhead allocation rate per unit? Per labor hour? What was the actual number of labor hours? To find the answers, input the known amounts into the formulas for variances and then solve for the unknown variable. Note that because the actual units of the labor hours cost driver is not known, the first calculation uses units as its cost driver and solves for the answer in units and then uses the answer to solve for the standard labor hours cost driver rate.

Variable Overhead (OH) Spending Variance = Actual Cost −
(Actual Units of Cost Driver $\times$ Standard Cost Driver Rate)

The variable overhead spending variance formula can be used to solve for the standard cost per unit as shown:

$$- \$20,000\ F\ =\ \$432,000\ -\ (28,250\ \text{Units} \times \$X/\text{Unit})$$

$$- \$20,000\ -\ \$432,000\ =\ -\ (28,250\ \text{Units} \times \$X/\text{Unit})$$

$$\$452,000\ =\ 28,250\ \text{Units} \times \$X/\text{Unit}$$

$$\frac{\$452,000}{28,250\ \text{Units}}\ =\ \$X/\text{Unit}\ =\ \$16/\text{Unit}$$

Budgeted Variable OH Cost Rate/Unit =
Budgeted Input/Unit $\times$ Budgeted Variable OH Cost Rate/Input Unit

The last formula can be used to solve for the budgeted variable overhead rate as shown:

$$\$16/\text{Unit}\ =\ 1.6\ \text{Labor Hours/Unit} \times \$X/\text{Labor Hour}$$

$$\frac{\$16/\text{Unit}}{1.6\ \text{Labor Hours/Unit}}\ =\ \$X/\text{Labor Hour}\ =\ \$10/\text{Labor Hour}$$

Once the budgeted variable overhead cost rate per labor hour is known, the next steps show one way to determine the actual number of labor hours used based on the known variable overhead efficiency variance.

Variable Overhead Efficiency Variance = (Actual Units of Cost Driver $\times$
Standard Cost Driver Rate) − (Standard Units of Cost Driver $\times$
Standard Cost Driver Rate)

The variable overhead efficiency variance is calculated as shown:

Variable Overhead Efficiency Variance

= (× Labor Hours × $10/Labor Hour) − (45,200 Labor Hours × $10/Labor Hour)

= $58,000 Unfavorable

= (× Labor Hours × $10/Labor Hour) − $452,000 = $58,000 U

= (× Labor Hours × $10/Labor Hour) = $58,000 U + $452,000

= (× Labor Hours × $10/Labor Hour) = $510,000

= × Labor Hours = $\dfrac{\$510,000}{\$10/\text{Labor Hour}}$ = 51,000 Labor Hours (Actual)

Sales Volume, Mix, and Quantity Variances

When there are multiple products, the sales volume variance can be broken down into a sales mix variance and a sales quantity variance.

> Sales Volume Variance = Sales Mix Variance × Sales Quantity Variance

The **sales volume variance** is the sum of the individual sales volume variances. Each individual sales volume variance is calculated as:

> Sales Volume Variance =
>
> (Units Sold − Units in Static Budget) × Budgeted Standard Contribution Margin per Unit

The contribution margin is calculated by taking total sales less all variable expenses. The portion of sales volume variance that is not attributable to sales quantity is caused by variations in the mix of various products a firm offers.

For example: If a tennis ball company also makes racquet balls, its sales mix variance would arise from variations in the actual sales mix of these two products compared to the budgeted sales mix. A sales mix is the ratio of any single product or service to the total of all products or services. Sales mix variance is a company-wide measure and is the sum of the sales mix variance of each type of merchandise sold by the company.

Sales Mix Variance

A sales mix variance for a particular type of product is calculated by multiplying the budgeted contribution margin per unit for that merchandise, the total number of all merchandise sold, and the difference between the actual sales mix ratio and the budgeted sales mix ratio. The sales mix variance formula is:

Sales Mix Variance = (Actual Sales Mix Ratio for a Product − Budgeted Sales Mix Ratio for a Product) × Actual Units Sold × Budgeted Contribution Margin per Unit of Product

Consider a situation in which the master budget calls for 10,000 cans of tennis balls to be sold at a unit contribution margin of $8 each and for 6,000 cans of racquet balls to be sold at a contribution margin of $4 each. The budgeted sales mix ratio for tennis balls is 10,000/16,000, or 0.625, and for racquet balls is 6,000/16,000, or 0.375. Suppose the actual sales for the period were 9,000 cans of tennis balls and 9,000 cans of racquet balls. The sales mix ratios change to 0.5 for tennis balls and 0.5 for racquet balls.

Product A Sales Volume Variance = Sales Mix Variance
+ Sales Quantity Variance

Tennis Ball Sales Volume Variance = (9,000 − 10,000) × 8

Tennis Ball Sales Volume Variance = −1,000 × 8

Tennis Ball Sales Volume Variance = $8,000 U

Product B Sales Volume Variance = Sales Mix Variance
× Sales Quantity Variance

Racquet Ball Sales Volume Variance = (9,000 − 6,000) × 4

Racquet Ball Sales Volume Variance = 3,000 × 4

Racquet Ball Sales Volume Variance = $12,000 F

Total Sales Volume Variance = (Product A Sales Volume Variance
+ Product B Sales Volume Variance)

Total Sales Volume Variance = ($8,000 U) + ($12,000 F)

Total Sales Volume Variance = $4,000 F

Product A Sales Mix Variance = (Actual Sales Mix Ratio for a Product − Budgeted Sales Mix Ratio for a Product) × Actual Units Sold × Budgeted Contribution Margin per Unit of Product

Tennis Ball Sales Mix Variance = (0.5 − 0.625) × 18,000 units × $8

Tennis Ball Sales Mix Variance = −0.125 × $144,000

Tennis Ball Sales Mix Variance = $18,000 U

Racquet Ball Sales Mix Variance = (0.5 − 0.375) × 18,000 units × $4

Racquet Ball Sales Mix Variance = 0.125 × $72,000

Racquet Ball Sales Mix Variance = $9,000 F

Total Sales Mix Variance = (Product A Sales Mix Variance + Product B Sales Mix Variance)

Total Sales Mix Variance = ($18,000 U) + ($9,000 F)

Total Sales Mix Variance = 9,000 U

Total Quantity Variance

The next formula can be used to calculate the total quantity variance for each of the products:

Sales Quantity Variance = Sales Volume Variance − Sales Mix Variance

Tennis Ball Sales Quantity Variance = $8,000 U − ($18,000 U)
= $10,000 F

Racquet Ball Sales Quantity Variance = $12,000 F − $9,000 F
= $3,000 F

The total quantity variances for each of the products can then be added together to arrive at a total quantity variance for both products.

Total Quantity Variance (Overall) = Quantity Variance (Product A) + Quantity Variance (Product B)

Total Quantity Variance (Overall) = $10,000 Favorable + $3,000 Favorable

Total Quantity Variance (Overall) = $13,000 Favorable

Mix and Yield Variances for Direct Materials and Direct Labor

The efficiency (usage) variance for direct costs can be further broken down into two components when a product has two or more ingredients or labor costs that can be substituted for one another. The efficiency variance can be broken down into a direct materials (or labor) mix variance and a direct materials (or labor) yield variance. Three amounts must be known to break an efficiency variance down into its subcomponents:

1. Budgeted Cost/Unit × Actual Total Quantity Used
   × Actual Mix Ratio for the Item

2. Budgeted Cost/Unit × Actual Total Quantity Used
   × Budgeted Mix Ratio for the Item

3. Budgeted Cost/Unit × Budgeted Total Quantity Used
   × Budgeted Mix Ratio for the Item

The **mix variance** is calculated by taking the amount from item 1 above and subtracting the amount in item 2 above (1 − 2 = mix variance). The **yield variance** is calculated by taking the amount from item 2 above and subtracting the amount of item 3 above (2 − 3 = yield variance). The **mix ratio** is the amount of one substitutable item divided by the total of all substitutable items.

$$\text{Mix Ratio} = \frac{\text{Amount of Substitutable Items}}{\text{Total of All Substitutable Items}}$$

For example: Assume that synthetic rubber and natural rubber can be substituted to produce tennis balls and that the standard amounts and prices in the product mix call for 1,000 pounds of synthetic rubber at $2 per pound ($2,000 standard cost) and 600 pounds of natural rubber at $3 per pound ($1,800) to produce 1,000 cans of tennis balls ($3,800 total standard cost). The standard mix ratio for synthetic rubber would be 1,000/1,600 = 0.625, or 62.5%. Similarly the standard mix ratio for natural rubber would be 0.375, or 37.5%. Assume also that the production manager can substitute up to 5% of either product for the other product. In reality, only 988 pounds of synthetic rubber ($1,976 actual cost) and only 532 pounds of natural rubber ($1,596 actual cost) actually are used, for a total of 1,520 pounds (total cost = $3,572, a variance of $228 favorable). This makes the actual mix ratio 65% (988/1,520) for synthetic rubber and 35% for natural rubber.

Using these data, the mix variance is calculated as:

1. Budgeted Cost/Unit $\times$ Actual Total Quantity Used $\times$ Actual Mix Ratio
for the item

Synthetic Rubber = $2/Pound $\times$ 1,520 Pounds $\times$ 0.65 = $1,976

Natural Rubber = $3/Pound $\times$ 1,520 Pounds $\times$ 0.35 = $\underline{$1,596}$
$\underline{$3,572}$

2. Budgeted Cost/Unit $\times$ Actual Total Quantity Used $\times$ Budgeted Mix
Ratio for the item

Synthetic Rubber = $2/Pound $\times$ 1,520 Pounds $\times$ 0.625 = $1,900

Natural Rubber = $3/Pound $\times$ 1,520 Pounds $\times$ 0.375 = $\underline{$1,710}$
$\underline{$3,610}$

The yield variance is calculated as:

Step 1 − Step 2 = $3,572 − $3,610 = $38 Favorable Mix Variance

2. Budgeted Cost/Unit $\times$ Actual Total Quantity Used $\times$ Budgeted
Mix Ratio for the item

Synthetic Rubber = $2/Pound $\times$ 1,520 Pounds $\times$ 0.625 = $1,900

Natural Rubber = $3/Pound $\times$ 1,520 Pounds $\times$ 0.375 = $\underline{$1,710}$
$\underline{$3,610}$

3. Budgeted Cost/Unit $\times$ Actual Total Quantity Used $\times$ Budgeted Mix
Ratio for the item

Synthetic Rubber = $2/Pound $\times$ 1,600 Pounds $\times$ 0.625 = $2,000

Natural Rubber = $3/Pound $\times$ 1,600 Pounds $\times$ 0.375 = $\underline{$1,800}$
$\underline{$3,800}$

Step 2 − Step 3 = $3,610 − $3,800 = $190 Favorable Yield Variance

Total Efficiency Variance = ($38) + ($190) = $228 Favorable

The mix variance results from using direct material and/or labor inputs in a ratio that differs from standard specifications. The mix variance is favorable in the preceding example because a larger percentage of cheaper materials were used to create the product than was budgeted. The yield variance results because the yield (output) obtained differs from the one expected on the basis of input. The larger favorable amount for the yield variance in the example results from the fact that 10% less in materials was used than was expected in order to produce the 1,000 cans of tennis balls. Knowing the breakdown between mix and yield variances can help managers determine how an efficiency variance should be dealt with.

Extension of Variance Analyses

Each of the prior variances can be broken down into subclasses using the same formulas given. For example, the price (rate) variance can be used to differentiate labor classes to determine more specifically where a favorable or unfavorable variance originated.

Other similar breakdowns or variations include:

- Using mix variance to calculate labor substitution variance (e.g., professional versus unskilled labor substitution)
- Labor variance from using substandard materials
- Price (rate) variance formula to measure the sales price variance or the cost price variance without changing the formula

In some situations, some variances are known but other variables must be found. The next example shows a highly detailed variance analysis.

For example: The following description traces the variance analysis for Bounce Sporting Goods.

Bounce Sporting Goods had a very poor month in June, according to a flexible budget variance of $76,370 unfavorable. Key data for June follow.

Budgeted production was for 12,000 units, but a rush order for 8,000 units was added at the last minute, and the sales team promised end-of-month delivery.

Standard Costs:

Direct material (DM) (from supplier A): 1.5 pounds @ $8/pound = $12/unit

Direct labor (DL) (standard Class III, unskilled): 1.2 direct labor hours (DLH) @ $14/DLH = $16.80/unit

Total standard direct costs = $28.80/unit

Actual Costs:

After Bounce purchased (and used) 18,200 pounds of DM from supplier A for $144,690, the supplier could not provide more for the rush order, so the purchasing department had to use supplier B, which supplied 18,000 pounds for $142,200 (of which only 15,800 pounds were used, at a cost of $126,400).

Actual DM costs charged to production:

Supplier A DM—18,200 pounds $\times$ $8/pound = $145,600

Supplier B DM—15,800 pounds $\times$ $8/pound = $126,400

To meet the new production quota, Bounce had to transfer some Class II semi-skilled employees from a different department, paid on average $16/DLH. These employees, though more skilled, are not familiar with the task and will not be as efficient as employees who are trained in this task.

Actual DL costs charged to production:

Class III DL (15,200 hours) = $216,600

Class II DL (10,300 hours) = $163,770

Total production costs: $145,600 + $126,400 + $216,600 + $163,770 = $652,370

Total standard costs at flexible budget level: 20,000 units × $28.80/unit = $576,000

Flexible budget variance = $652,370 − $576,000 = $76,370 U

Because the DM from supplier B turned out to be very poor, the manager made a breakdown of the time spent by each class of labor in producing units with each set of DM, as shown in Figure 1B-12.

Figure 1B-12 Units Produced and Labor Used by DM Type

	Supplier A DM		Supplier B DM	
DM used	18,200	pounds	15,800	pounds
Production output				
Class III	7,200	units	4,800	units
Class II	4,800	units	3,200	units
Total output	12,000	units	8,000	units
Actual DLH				
Class III DLH	8,600	hours	6,600	hours
Class II DLH	5,900	hours	4,400	hours
Total DLH	14,500	hours	11,000	hours

What is the DM efficiency (quantity or usage) variance for supplier A materials? For supplier B materials? Figure 1B-13 shows how these variances are calculated. Note that in the next calculations, the order of the variance calculations is reversed. Earlier the text presented this formula:

Efficiency Variance = (Actual Input Quantity − Budgeted Input Quantity) × Budgeted Input Price

but the next calculations consistently reverse the order of budgeted versus actual inputs:

Efficiency Variance = (Budgeted Input Quantity − Actual Input Quantity) × Budgeted Input Price

This formula will result in the same number, but it will be positive instead of negative (or vice versa). If this reversal is done for one of the variances, it must be done consistently for all of the variances in a set of data. Therefore, in Figure 1B-13, the $32,000 unfavorable material usage variance indicates that materials cost $32,000 more than was allocated in the flexible budget.

Bounce Sporting Goods also has enough data to break its direct labor variance down into four components: labor rate variance, labor substitution variance, labor variance from substandard materials (supplier B DM), and labor efficiency

Figure 1B-13 DM Efficiency (Quantity or Usage) Variance with Multiple Materials

	Supplier A DM	Supplier B DM	Total
Output—units produced	12,000	8,000	20,000
Material requirements per unit	× 1.5	× 1.5	
Total standard material requirements	18,000	12,000	30,000
Actual material consumed	– 18,200	– 15,800	– 34,000
Usage variance in units (unfavorable)	(200) U	(3,800) U	(4,000) U
Standard cost per unit	× $8	× $8	
Material usage variance	($1,600) U	($30,400) U	($32,000) U
Percent variance from standard	1.1% U	31.7% U	

variance on regular materials (supplier A DM). Figure 1B-14 shows the computation of these variances.

The Total Flexible Budget Variance of $76,370 Unfavorable is made up of:

- $32,000 Unfavorable Material Usage Variance (from Figure 1B-13)
- $2,770 Unfavorable Labor Rate Variance (from Figure 1B-14)
- $20,600 Unfavorable Labor Substitution Variance (from Figure 1B-14)
- $19,600 Unfavorable Substandard Material Labor Variance (from Figure 1B-14)
- $1,400 Unfavorable Labor Efficiency Variance on Regular Material (from Figure 1B-14)

Note that the final line of Figure 1B-14 is the sum of all variances for each column. What can be learned from this analysis? First, the rush order can be shown to have caused several of the problems. Supplier B's materials accounted for a material usage variance of $30,400 unfavorable (see Figure 1B-13), which is much greater than that for supplier A's materials, so the alternate supplies must have had much more scrap or waste. This could have been avoided if the rush order had not been submitted. Second, the labor substitution variance of $20,600 unfavorable is the result of needing to use labor that costs more than the regular workers. Third, the total direct labor variance from use of substandard materials is $19,600 unfavorable, which once again reinforces the conclusion that both types of workers had to waste time working with unsuitable materials.

A detailed analysis such as this can be used for performance evaluation. For example, in keeping with the tenets of responsibility accounting, perhaps the unfavorable variances related to the rush order could be charged to the sales department because it did not provide enough time to produce the rush order, or perhaps purchasing could be charged for the variances related to the substandard materials. Decisions such as these will force the other departments to work more carefully with the production department in the future.

Note that the measures used for the variances discussed here make direct use of the most likely cost drivers or revenue drivers that would be used in activity-based costing, such as measuring direct labor hours for a rate variance. Measuring performance against operational goals can take a variety of forms, and here,

Figure 1B-14 DL Variance with Multiple Materials and Multiple Types of Labor

	Class III DL	Class II DL	Total DL
Actual DL cost	$216,600	$163,770	$380,370
DL rate variance			
Actual direct labor hours	15,200	10,300	
Standard labor rate	$14.00	$16.00	
Actual labor rate (cost/hours)	− $14.25	− $15.90	
Rate variance per hour	($.25) U	$.10 F	
× Actual direct labor hours	× 15,200	× 10,300	
Labor rate variance	($3,800) U	$1,030 F	($2,770) U
Actual labor hours at standard rate	$212,800	$164,800	$377,600
DL substitution variance			
Class III standard labor rate		$14.00	
Class II standard labor rate		− $16.00	
Substitution rate variance per hour		($2.00) U	
× Actual direct labor hours		× 10,300	
Labor substitution variance		($20,600) U	($20,600) U
Actual labor hours at Class III standard rate	$212,800	$144,200	$357,000
DL variance from substandard materials (Supplier B)			
Units produced—alternative materials	4,800	3,200	
Labor standard per unit	× 1.2	× 1.2	
Standard hours allowed	5,760	3,840	
Actual hours	− 6,600	− 4,400	
Saved/(excess) hours	(840)	(560)	
× Class III standard rate	× $14.00	× $14.00	
Substandard materials labor variance	($11,760) U	($7,840) U	($19,600) U
Subtotal labor costs after substandard materials	$201,040	$136,360	$337,400
DL efficiency variance on regular materials (Supplier A)			
Units produced—regular materials	7,200	4,800	
Labor standard per unit	× 1.2	× 1.2	
Standard hours allowed	8,640	5,760	
Actual hours	− 8,600	− 5,900	
Saved/(excess) hours	40	(140)	
× Class III standard rate	× $14.00	× $14.00	
Labor efficiency variance on regular materials	$560 F	($1,960) U	($1,400) U
Flexible budget labor costs	$201,600	$134,400	$336,000
Total direct labor variances (Flexible − Actual)	($15,000) U	($29,370) U	($44,370) U

measuring performance was based mostly on manufacturing costs. However, other performance measures are based on revenue, nonmanufacturing costs, and profit, depending on the type of unit being measured. Analyzing and reporting on costs for various operations of an organization is covered in Topic 2: Responsibility Centers and Reporting Segments.

Using Variance Analysis in Nonmanufacturing Organizations

Although the previous discussion focuses on calculating variances in a manufacturing organization, the concepts can also be applied to service industries, with minor modifications. Typically, in a service industry setting, the material price and usage variances are less significant, because direct materials constitute a very small percentage of total costs for firms in service industry. Consequently, the labor and overhead variances are more important. For example, in a hospital, the hours and costs of various categories of labor (e.g., nurses, interns, general practitioners, surgeons, etc.) and overhead (e.g., medical equipment, support staff, etc.) are of greater importance. Therefore, variance analysis in a service company will focus mostly on direct labor and overhead variances.

Many firms in service industries have implemented activity-based costing systems by going through the process of identifying various cost drivers within the organization. This causes some components of fixed costs (such as setup, quality assurance, secretarial services, etc.) to become variable with respect to the appropriate cost drivers. Analysis of the flexible budget could easily be extended to service companies to provide a more accurate benchmark against which to compare actual costs.

Furthermore, while the production volume variance is applicable to manufacturing companies, it has limited applicability to service companies, which have little or no production activity. However, certain service industries have developed their own well-accepted measures of production, such as the use of revenue passenger mile (RPM) or available seat mile (ASM) in the airline industry. Production volume variances can be modified to use these measures instead of units of output.

Knowledge Check: Cost and Variance Measures

The next questions are intended to help you check your understanding and recall of the material presented in this topic. They do not represent the type of questions that appear on the CMA exam.

Directions: Answer each question in the space provided. Correct answers and section references appear after the knowledge check questions.

1. The purpose of a flexible budget is to:

   ☐ **a.** provide management with slack in their budget.

   ☐ **b.** eliminate fluctuations in production reports.

   ☐ **c.** compare actual and budgeted results at various levels of activity.

   ☐ **d.** make the annual budget process more efficient.

2. Which variance would be added to the flexible budget variance to arrive at the total static budget variance?

   ☐ **a.** Efficiency variance

   ☐ **b.** Price variance

   ☐ **c.** Sales mix variance

   ☐ **d.** Sales volume variance

3. What is meant by the term *management by exception*?

4. What is the formula for calculating total fixed overhead variance?

   ☐ **a.** Total Fixed Overhead Variance = Actual Fixed Overhead − Budgeted Fixed Overhead

   ☐ **b.** Total Fixed Overhead Variance = Actual Fixed Overhead − Applied Fixed Overhead

   ☐ **c.** Total Fixed Overhead Variance = Budgeted Fixed Overhead − Applied Fixed Overhead

   ☐ **d.** Total Fixed Overhead Variance = Budgeted Fixed Overhead − Actual Fixed Overhead

5. Combo Company uses a standard cost system. Information for raw materials for Product #4 for the month of June is shown next:

Standard price per pound of raw materials	$1.60
Actual purchase price per pound of raw materials	$1.55
Actual quantity of raw materials purchased	2,000 pounds
Actual quantity of raw materials used	1,900 pounds
Standard quantity allowed for actual production	1,800 pounds

What is the materials purchase price variance?

☐ **a.** $90 favorable

☐ **b.** $90 unfavorable

☐ **c.** $100 favorable

☐ **d.** $100 unfavorable

6. Craig Corporation has provided the following data concerning its direct labor costs for January:

Standard wage rate	$13.30 per direct labor hour (DLH)
Standard hours	5.5 DLHs per unit
Actual wage rate	$13.20 per DLH
Actual hours	45,880 DLHs
Actual output	8,400 units

The labor rate variance for January would be:

☐ **a.** $4,588 unfavorable

☐ **b.** $4,588 favorable

☐ **c.** $4,620 unfavorable

☐ **d.** $4,620 favorable

7. The following labor standards have been established for product T3:

Standard labor hours per unit of output	5.0 hours
Standard labor rate	$18.25 per hour

The following data are for product T3 for the month of July:

Actual hours worked	9,800 hours
Actual total labor cost	$176,400
Actual output	1,900 units

What is the labor efficiency variance for the month?

☐ **a.** $3,025 unfavorable

☐ **b.** $5,400 unfavorable

☐ **c.** $3,025 favorable

☐ **d.** $5,475 unfavorable

Knowledge Check Answers: Cost and Variance Measures

1. The purpose of a flexible budget is to: *[See Characteristics of Flexible Budgets.]*

   ☐ **a.** provide management with slack in their budget.

   ☐ **b.** eliminate fluctuations in production reports.

   ☑ **c.** compare actual and budgeted results at various levels of activity.

   ☐ **d.** make the annual budget process more efficient.

2. Which variance would be added to the flexible budget variance to arrive at the total static budget variance? *[See Flexible Budget Variance and Sales Volume Variance.]*

   ☐ **a.** Efficiency variance

   ☐ **b.** Price variance

   ☐ **c.** Sales mix variance

   ☑ **d.** Sales volume variance

3. What is meant by the term *management by exception*? *[See Management by Exception.]*

   When using a management by exception approach, managers focus their attention on results that are different from what was expected. This approach assumes that results that meet expectations do not require investigation.

4. What is the formula for calculating total fixed overhead variance? *[See Variances for Fixed Overhead.]*

   ☐ **a.** Total Fixed Overhead Variance = Actual Fixed Overhead − Budgeted Fixed Overhead

   ☑ **b.** Total Fixed Overhead Variance = Actual Fixed Overhead − Applied Fixed Overhead

   ☐ **c.** Total Fixed Overhead Variance = Budgeted Fixed Overhead − Applied Fixed Overhead

   ☐ **d.** Total Fixed Overhead Variance = Budgeted Fixed Overhead − Actual Fixed Overhead

5. Combo Company uses a standard cost system. Information for raw materials for Product #4 for the month of June is shown next. *[See Price (Rate) Variances for Direct Costs.]*

Standard price per pound of raw materials	$1.60
Actual purchase price per pound of raw materials	$1.55
Actual quantity of raw materials purchased	2,000 pounds
Actual quantity of raw materials used	1,900 pounds
Standard quantity allowed for actual production	1,800 pounds

What is the materials purchase price variance?

- ☐ **a.** $90 favorable
- ☐ **b.** $90 unfavorable
- ☑ **c.** $100 favorable
- ☐ **d.** $100 unfavorable

Solution:

Materials Price Variance = Actual Quantity Purchased
                              × (Actual Price − Standard Price)
Materials Price Variance = 2,000 ×($1.55 − $1.60)
Materials Price Variance = $100 Favorable

6. Craig Corporation has provided the following data concerning its direct labor costs for January: *[See Price and Efficiency Variances for Direct Labor and Direct Material.]*

Standard wage rate	$13.30 per direct labor hour (DLH)
Standard hours	5.5 DLHs per unit
Actual wage rate	$13.20 per DLH
Actual hours	45,880 DLHs
Actual output	8,400 Units

The labor rate variance for January would be:

- ☐ **a.** $4,588 unfavorable
- ☑ **b.** $4,588 favorable
- ☐ **c.** $4,620 unfavorable
- ☐ **d.** $4,620 favorable

Solution:

Labor Rate Variance = Actual Hours ×(Actual Rate − Standard Rate)
Labor Rate Variance = 45,880 × ($13.20 − $13.30)
Labor Rate Variance = $4,588 Favorable

7. The following labor standards have been established for product T3: *[See Efficiency (Quantity or Usage) Variances for Direct Costs.]*

Standard labor-hours per unit of output	5.0 hours
Standard labor rate	$18.25 per hour

The following data are for product T3 for the month of July:

Actual hours worked	9,800 hours
Actual total labor cost	$176,400
Actual output	1,900 units

What is the labor efficiency variance for the month?

☐ **a.** $3,025 unfavorable

☐ **b.** $5,400 unfavorable

☐ **c.** $3,025 favorable

☑ **d.** $5,475 unfavorable

Solution:

Standard Hours = Standard Hours per Unit × Actual Output

Standard Hours = 5 × 1,900 = 9,500

Labor Efficiency Variance = Standard Rate × (Actual Hours − Standard Hours)

= $18.25 × (9,800 − 9,500) = $5,475 Unfavorable

Responsibility Centers and Reporting Segments

A CENTRALIZED ORGANIZATION ALLOWS MANAGERS very little freedom to make decisions. In contrast, a decentralized organization spreads decision making to managers at different responsibility center levels. A responsibility center, also called a strategic business unit (SBU), is any portion of a business that grants the center's manager responsibility over costs, profits, revenues, or investments.

This topic covers different types of responsibility centers, including cost centers, profit centers, and investment centers. Reporting segments and contribution reporting are also discussed in this topic.

 READ the Learning Outcome Statements (LOS) for this topic as found in Appendix A and then study the concepts and calculations presented here to be sure you understand the content you could be tested on in the CMA exam.

Types of Responsibility Centers

Responsibility accounting is a method of defining segments or subunits in an organization as types of responsibility centers based on their level of autonomy and the responsibilities of their managers, and then basing performance evaluations on these factors. Responsibility centers are classified by their primary effect on the company as a whole. Revenue or profit centers sell their product or service to outside customers, generating revenues. Cost centers provide service to other parts of the organization and are not responsible for generating revenue through sales to outside customers. However, a cost center such as a service department may generate some revenues, but the department usually has a net cost. Investment centers not only generate revenues but also have authority on making investments.

Revenue Centers

Revenue centers are responsible for sales but not for the manufacturing costs of the sales. A revenue center obtains products from either a cost center or a profit center (discussed below). Revenue centers are evaluated on their ability to provide a contribution: sales less the direct revenue center costs. They are not responsible for the costs of the items obtained from cost or profit centers. A captive marketing division of a corporation would be an example of a revenue center.

Cost Centers

A manager for a **cost center** is responsible for controlling costs in a department that generates little or no revenue. Therefore, the manager is not responsible for revenue or investments but is rewarded whenever he or she can minimize costs while maintaining an expected level of quality. Finance, administration, human resources, accounting, customer service, and help desks are all examples of cost centers. If the cafeteria is not expected to make a profit, it is also a cost center. Even plants and manufacturing facilities sometimes are considered cost centers, assuming that the profit center would then be the sales department or a different production department.

Common costs are allocated among all cost centers involved in proportion to the amounts of a selected cost driver. Managers of cost centers usually are responsible for direct material and labor efficiency variances as well as the variable overhead variance. Removing unfavorable variances and analyzing favorable variances are often part of the manager's responsibility.

Profit Centers

Profit centers are responsible for both costs and revenues. Since profit is a function of both revenue and costs, a manager for a profit center is responsible for generating profits, managing revenue, and controlling costs. Managers of these departments usually do not have control over investments. Profit centers are often separate reporting segments. A grocery store that is part of a chain of stores could be a profit center and a separate reporting segment. Managers of profit centers would be evaluated based on actual profits versus expected profits.

Investment Centers

Managers for **investment centers** are responsible for investments, costs, and revenues in their department. Investment centers can be centered primarily on internal or external investments. Internal investment managers are responsible for reviewing and approving capital budgeting and other investments, such as in research and development. External investment managers are responsible for reviewing and approving temporary and long-term investments for capital maintenance, return on investment, and strategic investments. Managers in such centers would be evaluated not only by the center's profit but by relating the profit to its invested capital.

Strategic investments would be evaluated for their fit with company strategy, while other investments would be judged on their return on investment and preservation of capital.

For example: Consider an office supply store. If there is an employee cafeteria, it is probably a cost center, responsible only for controlling the costs of the cafeteria. Each product line, such as printers, is a revenue center, responsible to account for the revenues from the product line's sales. Each department is a profit center, such as paper supplies, which accounts for the revenues and the expenses (i.e., the profitability) of that department. Finally, each store is an investment center, responsible for the revenues and expenses and also for the capital project budgets and the assets and liabilities of the store.

Contribution and Segment Reporting

Managing the performance of the various responsibility centers depends on an analysis of their costs and revenue contributions to the organization. Two approaches that are used to aid in this type of analysis are contribution reporting and segment reporting.

Contribution Reporting

The contribution approach to reporting on an income statement is useful for internal decision making. It separates fixed from variable expenses, deducting variable expenses first to arrive at the contribution margin and then deducting fixed expenses to arrive at net operating income. The **contribution margin** is the amount that contributes toward fixed expenses and profits. The contribution margin shows managers how profits are affected by changes in volume, because fixed costs and operating capacity are kept constant.

The primary advantage of such an income statement format is that profit center managers can view the costs by their behavior (e.g., fixed or variable) instead of by departments, such as sales, administration, and production (cost of goods sold). Managers can use a contribution income statement when analyzing product lines and when deciding on prices for goods, whether to expand a segment or discontinue it, or whether to make or buy a good.

Evaluating a contribution margin report often involves the use of cost-volume-profit (CVP) ratios such as the contribution margin, the contribution margin ratio, and breakeven sales in dollars. Alternatively, a balanced scorecard is a more comprehensive tool used in evaluating performance.

Management performance can be evaluated more easily using a contribution income statement because the items outside managers' control are separated from the items within their control. However, many fixed costs are controllable, so managers often have their fixed costs further divided into controllable fixed costs and uncontrollable fixed costs. Controllable fixed costs are those that can be changed within a year; uncontrollable costs take over a year to influence. Uncontrollable fixed costs can also come from a nonnegotiable corporate allocation of headquarters expenses. The controllable margin is the contribution margin less the controllable fixed costs.

Figure 1B-15 shows two versions of the same income statement, in traditional and contribution formats. If a prior period's statement showed that the uncontrollable fixed production costs were rising and the variable production costs were falling, a traditional statement would not show this fact, but the contribution format could show that the manager has been successful at keeping costs relatively the same even in the face of rising fixed costs outside his or her control. Note also that the traditional income statement's cost of goods sold, selling, and administrative costs include both fixed and variable expenses, but there is no way to determine how the amounts are broken down.

Figure 1B-15 Income Statements in Traditional versus Contribution Format

Traditional Approach (Costs Organized by Function)			Contribution Approach (Costs Organized by Behavior)		
Sales		$31,200	Sales		$31,200
Less cost of goods sold		15,600	Less variable expenses:		
Gross margin		$15,600	Variable production	$5,200	
Less operating expenses:			Variable selling expenses	1,560	
Selling expenses	$8,060		Variable admin. expenses	1,040	$7,800
Administrative expenses	4,940	$13,000	Contribution margin		$23,400
Net operating income		$2,600	Less fixed expenses:		
			Fixed production	$10,400	
			Fixed selling	6,500	
			Fixed administrative	3,900	$ 20,800
			Net operating income		$2,600

Segment Reporting

Reporting segments are portions of a business divided for reporting purposes along product lines, geographical areas, or other meaningful segments to provide individual information about that area. *For example:* Consider a grocery chain. Each store is a segment. Also, if the accounting and decision-making systems evaluate product lines separately, each product line (such as produce, dairy, meats, etc.) is a segment as well.

Segmented financial statements are the same as nonsegmented statements except that each segment has its own costs traced back to it so that the report shows how profitable each segment is by itself. The **segment margin** is the segment's contribution margin less all traceable fixed costs for the segment. The segment margin is a useful indication of a segment's profitability. If it is not positive, the segment may need to be discontinued unless it adds value to other segments.

Traceable fixed costs that are included in a segment's margin are costs that would not exist were it not for the segment. Administrative salaries for segment managers are an example of a fixed cost that can be traced directly to a segment. Similarly, building maintenance costs or insurance premiums for a specific business segment can be traced to the segment.

Common Cost Allocation

Unlike traceable fixed costs, common fixed costs (such as the chief executive's salary) cannot be traced to a specific department because they are shared costs and must be apportioned between two or more departments using some allocation basis that may or may not provide an accurate allocation. Additionally, common costs are often uncontrollable to some extent by the department manager who is held responsible for the cost and thus make it more difficult to determine the profitability of an individual segment. A **common cost** is any cost that is shared by two or more segments or entities. When common costs are allocated to segments, the value of the segment margin on reporting profitability is diluted; therefore some businesses allocate common costs to segments only when all or most of the cost would disappear if the segment were to be discontinued. Two methods of allocating common costs are the stand-alone method and the incremental method.

Stand-alone cost allocation is a method that determines the relative proportion of cost driver for each party that shares a common cost and allocates the costs by those percentages.

For example: Company A has a new plant and an older plant, but both plants require some workers to be given on-site training. The traveling trainer's salary of $60,000 plus $10,000 travel and lodging expenses can be allocated based on the number of users who need to be trained at each location or some other cost driver, such as days spent at each location. If the old plant has 40 trainees and the new plant has 60 trainees, the old plant would receive $28,000 of the cost (40%) and the new plant would receive $42,000 of the cost. This method has the benefit of fairness and is easy to implement.

Incremental cost allocation is a method that allocates costs by ranking the parties by a primary user and incremental users, or those users who add an additional cost due to the fact that there is now more than one user of the cost.

For example: Company A, just described, hires a trainer because the new plant is being opened. The trainer is based in the new plant's city, so the new plant is the primary user of the trainer's time. If the trainer works at the new plant for three quarters of the time and at the old plant for one quarter of the time, the new plant is allocated $45,000 of the costs, while the old plant is allocated the remaining $15,000 plus all $10,000 of the travel expenses because these are an incremental cost of having the trainer relocate to serve the incremental user.

Conversely, if management wanted to reduce start-up costs for the new plant, it could choose to designate the old plant as the primary user and allocate only a small amount of the costs to the new plant. Because this method allows managers to manipulate how costs are allocated, it is not as balanced as the stand-alone method.

Also, when common costs are allocated in this manner, most of the segments want to be incremental users, so this method can cause interdepartmental contention.

Transfer Pricing Models

Allocating costs to a responsibility center or segment involves assigning pricing for the goods and services that pass between segments. **Transfer pricing** sets prices for internally exchanged goods and services. An **intermediate product** is a good or service that is transferred between two segments of a company. Company strategy is greatly affected by choice of transfer prices. If the company wants the business units to behave independently and keep managers motivated to achieve company goals, transfer prices should be set at arm's length, as if the party were any other external client. When no external suppliers or customers exist for a product or service, the arm's-length price (an impartial or fair market price) is more difficult to determine than simply checking market prices. The amounts set for transfer prices require cooperation among many departments, including finance, production, marketing, and tax planning.

Firms that have a high degree of vertical integration will need to set transfer prices carefully. For example, a corporation that owns farms, food warehouses, distributors, and grocery stores will need to set prices for each service that will be considered fair by all segments and also allow each portion of the business to be financially flexible.

Four models that can be used to set transfer prices are market price, negotiated price, variable cost, and full cost. Firms often combine various methods (dual pricing) to match their needs.

Market Price Model

The market price model is a true arm's-length model because it sets the price for a good or service at going market prices. This model can be used only when an item has a market; items such as work-in-process inventory may not have a market price. The market price model keeps business units autonomous, forces the selling unit to be competitive with external suppliers, and is preferred by tax authorities. Businesses that use this model should account for the reduced selling and marketing costs in the price.

Negotiated Price Model

The negotiated price model sets the transfer price through negotiation between the buyer and the seller. When different business units experience conflicts, negotiation or even arbitration may be needed to keep the company as a whole functioning efficiently. Negotiated prices can make both buying and selling units less autonomous.

Variable Cost Model

The variable cost model sets transfer prices at the unit's variable cost, or the actual cost to produce the good or service less all fixed costs. This method will lower the selling unit's profits and increase the buying unit's profits due to the low price. This model is advantageous for selling units that have excess capacity or for situations when a buying unit could purchase from external sources but the company wants to encourage internal purchases. Among the disadvantages of this method is the fact that it is not viewed favorably by tax authorities because it lowers the profits, and thereby taxes, for the location where the product was manufactured.

Full Cost (Absorption) Model

The full cost (absorption) model starts with the seller's variable cost for the item and then allocates fixed costs to the price. Some companies allocate standard fixed costs because this allows the buying unit to know the cost in advance and keeps the seller from becoming too inefficient due to a captive buyer that pays for the inefficiencies. Adding fixed costs is relatively straightforward and fair. However, it can alter a business unit's decision making.

Although fixed costs should not be included in the decision to purchase items internally or externally, often managers will purchase the "lower-cost" external item even though the internal fixed costs still will be incurred.

To illustrate: Hopkins Company has two operating divisions, North and South. One of the products of the North division is a raw material used in the South division. Income statements for the two divisions, excluding interdivisional operations, are shown in Figure 1B-16.

Figure 1B-16 North and South Division Income Statements

	North Division (30% Tax Rate)	North Division (40% Tax Rate)	Total Both Divisions
Sales			
10,000 units × $15 per unit	$ 150,000	–	$ 150,000
20,000 units × $18 per unit	–	$ 360,000	$ 360,000
Total sales	$ 150,000	$ 360,000	$ 510,000
Expenses			
Variable:			
10,000 units × $7 per unit	$ 70,000	–	$ 70,000
20,000 units × $10 per unit	–	$ 200,000	$ 200,000
Fixed*:	50,000	65,000	$ 115,000
Total expenses	$ 120,000	$ 265,000	$ 385,000
Operating income	$ 30,000	$ 95,000	$ 125,000

Under the market price model, assuming that the North division is currently operating at full capacity and can sell all of the products it can produce, North will sell one unit to South for $15 (the price at which all products of North are sold).

Under the negotiated price model, assuming there is some excess capacity in the North division, if North sells to South at the market price ($15), South may prefer to purchase from an outside vendor, and company profit may not be maximized.

Therefore, North and South may negotiate a price between $15 (the market price) and $7 (the variable cost), which will provide some contribution toward North's fixed costs and contribute to overall company profits.

Under the variable cost model, North will sell to South at a price of $7 per unit (the variable costs).

Under the full cost (absorption) model, at this level of production and sales, North will sell to South at a price of $12 per unit ($7 variable plus $5 fixed costs per unit).

Choosing Transfer Price Models

In general, the market price method is preferred in situations when the market price for a good or service is available. When a market price is not available, the negotiated price method is preferred. When neither is acceptable, companies may turn to one of the cost models. Cost-based methods are not recommended because they can lead to motivation problems between parties such as the seller not actively controlling costs because they are simply passed on to the buyer.

The logic of choosing a transfer price model and setting transfer prices starts with a make-or-buy decision. If there are outside suppliers for a product or service, the market price model should be used. The company should compare the selling unit's variable costs to the market price for the external substitute. If the external market price is lower than the internal variable cost, the buyer should purchase externally to motivate the internal supplier to find ways to lower costs.

When the internal variable cost is less than the external market price, the buying unit should purchase internally, as long as the selling unit has excess capacity. The variable cost model is best for low capacity, and the market price model is best for high capacity. If the selling unit is at full capacity, the buying unit should purchase externally, as long as the selling unit can generate more profit from a sale to an external source than will be lost if the buying unit pays the external market price for the item. When the opposite is true, the buying unit should purchase internally and pay market price for the item.

Reporting of Organizational Segments

Performance measurement reports for various organizational segments are created for internal use and are focused on providing the information management needs to address problems and design improvements.

Performance Measurement Reports

Performance measurement reports should be tailored to the audience and level of management to which they are directed. Too much information can cloud an issue as easily as not enough information can, so the amount and timing of information delivery is critical to the success of each manager. Timing of performance measurement reports such as variance reports is critical; the information must be relevant for it to be useful. However, if a manager is flooded with information and cannot discern which information is important,reporting may be too frequent.

Effective performance measures lead to a desired strategic result by causing the manager and other employees to strive for organizational goals, simultaneously maximizing company goals and individual goals. The objectives of a performance evaluation system include:

- Goal congruence (e.g., aligning the individual's goals with those of the organization)
- Clear communication of expectations
- Opportunities to motivate the individual to perform in a way that will maximize organizational goals
- Providing communication between the individual and the organization
- Articulation of the organization's benchmarks

Improper motivation can occur when feedback is ineffective or when benchmarks are improperly matched with cost and/or revenue drivers of an operation, causing organizations to be counterproductive. Each performance measure selected needs to have these elements:

- A time period for performance measurement (e.g., view one year's results or several years' results simultaneously)
- Common definitions for items (e.g., assets are defined as total assets available regardless of function or usage)
- Definitions of specific measurement units used (e.g., historical cost, current cost)
- A target level of performance for each performance measure and each segment
- A feedback timing schedule (e.g., feedback supplied daily, weekly, quarterly)

Specific financial performance measurements and the balanced scorecard method of evaluating financial and nonfinancial performance are covered in Section B, Topic 3: Performance Measures.

Multinational Company Performance Measurement

The nonfinancial differences among countries—in economy, laws, customs, and politics—should play a part in evaluating a foreign division's results.

Multinational companies must account for additional concerns, such as how tariffs, exchange rates, taxes, currency restrictions, expropriation risk, and the availability and relative cost of materials and skills could affect performance evaluations. The use of transfer pricing by multinationals to gain tax and income advantages can conflict with the use of transfer pricing to evaluate performance or to create performance incentives.

For example: Some pharmaceutical companies produce their goods in Puerto Rico and sell the majority of the product in the mainland United States. Because

Puerto Rico has a relatively lower tax status than the rest of the United States, the incentive is for the pharmaceutical company to charge the highest transfer price possible for drugs sold to their U. S. divisions (such as market price), thus retaining the profits in the territory that has a lower tax rate. Because the Puerto Rican subsidiary essentially has a captive market, it may not be as efficient as overall corporate management would like.

Conversely, if the producing country has relatively higher taxes than the primary country in which sales occur, the incentive will be to charge the lowest price possible (such as cost) for the goods so that the profits end up in the selling-country division. The resulting performance could be that the producing country fails to meet total demand. Also, if the price is actual cost, the producer will not have any incentive to control those costs because they are merely transferred to the other division. One solution to such a dilemma is to use standard costs instead of actual costs. (The standard could be made more stringent over time through continuous improvement efforts.) Another solution is to change the accountability structure of the segments, making them more centralized if decentralized transfer prices fail to create the desired incentives.

As with any performance evaluation, a multinational company should focus on separating controllable from noncontrollable costs, basing assessments only on costs that can be affected by the managers' choices. If a foreign currency becomes devalued, this will affect profits but is outside management's control. When foreign governments impose trade restrictions, such as tariffs, the performance measurement should take into account the reduced profits from such sources. When managers in foreign countries keep their books in a foreign country's currency, their supervisors should consider the effects of currency fluctuations, inflation, and differences in relative purchasing power in the foreign country. For example, a country with lower costs of labor and goods will also have to price goods for sale in that country much lower than in a country where labor and goods are more costly.

However, because performance evaluations should provide incentives for managers to improve overall operations, it is important to determine if any portion of a noncontrollable event actually could have been prevented or deflected. For example, if managers know they will not be held accountable for a devalued currency, they may not be as quick to move funds out of the country as if they were accountable for a portion of such losses. Managers evaluated in such a fashion might employ market analysts or economists specializing in currency exchange to help forecast such changes.

Another way of enhancing the value of performance measurement is by using benchmark values from other managers or companies in similar local environments. Each distinct area would have its own comparison group, which would provide an opportunity to evaluate performance across companies.

Finally, because profits can be so distorted by various international issues, performance evaluations could avoid focusing on profit and instead focus on more stable indicators, such as revenues, market share, or operating costs.

**Knowledge Check:
Responsibility Centers and Reporting Segments**

The next questions are intended to help you check your understanding and recall of the material presented in this topic. They do not represent the type of questions that appear on the CMA exam.

Directions: Answer each question in the space provided. Correct answers and section references appear after the knowledge check questions.

1. Which of the following responsibility centers usually makes a manager responsible for all financial business decisions?

   ☐ **a.** Revenue center

   ☐ **b.** Cost center

   ☐ **c.** Investment center

   ☐ **d.** Profit center

2. Which of the following transfer pricing models sets prices at actual cost less all fixed costs?

   ☐ **a.** Variable cost

   ☐ **b.** Full cost (absorption)

   ☐ **c.** Market price

   ☐ **d.** Negotiated price

3. Match each of term to its corresponding description by drawing a line between them.

Term	Description
Common cost	Allows reporting based on product line or geographic location
Contribution margin	Shows how profits are affected by changes in volume
Incremental cost allocation	May allow managers to manipulate how costs are allocated
Segment reporting	Any cost that is shared by two or more segments or entities

Knowledge Check Answers: Responsibility Centers and Reporting Segments

1. Which of the following responsibility centers usually makes a manager responsible for all financial business decisions? *[See Investment Centers.]*

   ☐ **a.** Revenue center

   ☐ **b.** Cost center

   ☑ **c.** Investment center

   ☐ **d.** Profit center

2. Which of the following transfer pricing models sets prices at actual cost less all fixed costs? *[See Variable Cost Model.]*

   ☑ **a.** Variable cost

   ☐ **b.** Full cost (absorption)

   ☐ **c.** Market price

   ☐ **d.** Negotiated price

3. Correct matches of term and description are shown here. *[See Contribution and Segment Reporting.]*

Term	Description
Common cost	Any cost that is shared by two or more segments or entities
Contribution margin	Shows how profits are affected by changes in volume
Incremental cost allocation	May allow managers to manipulate how costs are allocated
Segment reporting	Allows reporting based on product line or geographic location

Performance Measures

PROFITABILITY ANALYSES MEASURE THE RELATIVE success or failure of a company over a period. A variety of measures can be used to help an organization analyze the performance of specific products, business units, and customers. In addition to discussions of product, business unit, and customer profitability analysis, this topic covers performance analysis techniques, including return on investment, residual income, and balanced scorecard.

READ the Learning Outcome Statements (LOS) for this topic as found in Appendix A and then study the concepts and calculations presented here to be sure you understand the content you could be tested on in the CMA exam.

Product Profitability Analysis

Product profitability analysis shows which products are the most profitable, which need to have their prices and costs reevaluated, and which should get the greatest amount of marketing and support attention. Product line managers often use a product profitability analysis as the basis for compensation or bonuses.

Product lines that are unprofitable in the long run will be discontinued. When determining whether to discontinue a product line, the first step is to remove from the analysis all per-unit fixed costs that would not be eliminated if the product line were discontinued. The product profitability analysis sums up the benefits of removing all fixed costs that are traceable to the affected unit, plus all variable costs for the unit. Then the analysis sums up the opportunity cost of all sales that would be lost if the product line were discontinued. The difference between these amounts is the increase or decrease in profit that would occur from discontinuing the product line.

For example: If Bounce Sporting Goods had a profitable tennis ball line and an unprofitable racquet ball line, the racquet ball line could be analyzed to determine what effect removing it would have on company profits. In Figure 1B-17, the contribution margin for both product lines shows a positive amount of profit. However, after traceable costs are allocated to each department, the racquet ball department shows a loss. Note that all common costs are deducted only from the total amount for the entire company, so these costs do not play a part in management's decision to discontinue the operation.

Figure 1B-17 Profitability Analysis for Bounce Sporting Goods

	Tennis Balls	Racquet Balls	Total
Last year's sales	$780,000	$195,000	$975,000
Relevant costs			
Variable cost	585,000	175,500	760,500
Contribution margin	$195,000	$19,500	$214,500
Other relevant costs (traceable)			
Advertising	19,500	26,000	45,500
Contribution after all relevant costs	$175,500	$(6,500)	$169,000
Nonrelevant costs (not traceable)			
Fixed cost			100,000
Net income with racquet balls			$69,000

In addition to financial measures, a product line profitability analysis needs to analyze how the line affects overall company strategy. These questions illustrate types of nonfinancial considerations:

- How will dropping the product line affect company morale?
- If the product line is dropped, how will sales of related product lines be affected?
- Is the product line used as a component of another, moreprofitable product?
- Would investing more resources into marketing and sales increase product profitability?
- Could the product become more profitable in the long run?
- Would increasing the price of the product increase profitability or just lower sales even more?

Business Unit Profitability Analysis

A business unit, often referred to as a **strategic business unit** or SBU, is an entity or operating unit within a larger organization. An SBU has its own business strategy and objectives, which may differ from that of its parent organization.

Business unit profitability analysis is measured using contribution margin, direct profit, controllable profit, income before taxes, or net income.

For example: Figure 1B-18 shows how an income statement could be formed to include these measures for a business unit.

Figure 1B-18 Business Unit Income Statement

Sales revenue	$780,000
Variable expenses	585,000
Contribution margin	195,000
Fixed expenses controllable by the profit center	19,500
Direct/controllable profit	175,500
Corporate charges allocated to the SBU	52,500
Income before taxes	123,000
Taxes	49,200
Net income	$73,800

Contribution Margin

Contribution margin measures the difference between revenue and variable expenses. It is useful for management performance analysis because it eliminates the fixed expenses that are perceived to be beyond the manager's control. However, not all fixed expenses are uncontrollable, so focusing on contribution margin can lead a manager to ignore possible cost reductions. Furthermore, even fixed costs that cannot be altered still must be managed for efficient use—for example, maintaining and improving performance standards for salaried employees.

Direct/Controllable Profit

Direct profit is the business unit's contribution margin less its fixed costs. Direct profit does not include fixed costs common to the organization as a whole. Managers evaluated using this measure may be content with a lower level of success than if common costs were also deducted from the measurement. This is the metric that should be used for the SBU's performance. Because corporate charges are beyond SBU management control, they should not be considered when measuring SBU performance.

Income Before Taxes

Income before taxes deducts all costs for a business unit other than taxes. However, using this measure makes the business unit manager seem accountable for costs that are not under the manager's control, such as the costs of the human resources department that are allocated to the business unit. Therefore, care must be exercised in conducting evaluations in this way. One advantage of using this measure is that the manager will have a realistic view of the level of profitability needed to make the business unit a successful part of the company, and thereby would affect its pricing and productivity decisions. The amount can be compared easily to the profitability of competitors. Managers rewarded for maintaining profitability in the face of all overhead may make better long-term decisions, such as decisions related to product mix and marketing.

Net Income

Net income is income after taxes. Using net income has the same benefits and drawbacks as using income before taxes in profitability analysis. It also has other drawbacks: First, tax rates are often the same for each area, so there may be little benefit to examining this amount. Second, when tax rates differ, it is usually a result of corporate manipulation for tax purposes, a factor beyond the manager's control. Third, taxes and tax-related decisions are made at the corporate level, not at the SBU level. Net income measurement is useful in evaluating foreign business units because the different tax rates in each country affect overall profitability for a business unit.

Organizational policies can alter the net income of a business unit and a company. For example, choosing the first-in, first-out (FIFO) method of cost flow assumption in valuing inventories causes the oldest inventory prices to be included in cost of goods sold on the income statement and the newest prices to be included in the balance sheet's inventory. In times of rising prices, FIFO will provide a higher inventory valuation and a higher net income than the last-in, first-out (LIFO) method or the average method. Similarly, the choice of depreciation methods (e.g., straight-line, declining balance, and units-of-production) will yield different amounts of expense that will, in turn, yield different balances in net income. In addition, when two companies have chosen different inventory or depreciation methods, comparability is more difficult because the same operations will yield different balance sheet and income statement results.

Customer Profitability Analysis

Customer profitability analysis evaluates the costs and benefits of providing goods or services to a particular customer or customer segment. This analysis is undertaken to enhance the overall profitability of the organization. This cost management tool is relatively new, although it is increasingly popular. This analysis has two primary objectives: measuring customer profitability and identifying effective and ineffective customer-related activities and services.

Measuring profitability at the level of the customer involves determining the benefits received from the customer and the costs incurred to service the customer. The benefits include nonfinancial and financial measures. Nonfinancial measures include customer acquisition, customer retention, customer satisfaction, and overall market share. Financial measures usually can be collected on a customer level only if the company uses financial software that breaks out costs by customer. This feature is typically found in activity-based costing (ABC) software. The financial measures serve as a balance to a company that puts customers first in its strategy, because retaining customers even when the costs outweigh the revenues is a losing strategy. Sometimes organizations seek to increase market share and customer satisfaction without fully evaluating the costs of doing so. This leads organizations to spend significant resources to satisfy customers, often without knowing whether such efforts will be profitable. The customer profitability analysis will show when a customer demand should be satisfied, when it should be declined, and when it should include an additional fee for the service. At the extreme, the organization may decide to drop unprofitable customers or find ways to serve them while making a profit. Some academic studies have shown that for a typical business, only 20% of customers contribute to profits; the remaining 80% either break even or generate losses.

For strategic reasons, some customer demands will be satisfied even when they are not financially profitable, but an advanced financial management software system such as ABC would at least bring the cost issue to the attention of managers so that a long-term solution can be formed. The emphasis should be on transforming the unprofitable customer into a profitable customer. Lifetime profitability is one reason to retain customers that are initially unprofitable. If customers can be retained for the long term, the overall profits can be very positive.

For example, a real estate agent who spends time with a client trying to purchase a lower-cost home may not realize much profit on the sale, but the customer's lifetime repeat business could be significant. Similarly, an unprofitable customer would be retained if having that customer attracts or influences other, more profitable customers.

The other objective of performing customer profitability analysis is to identify effective and ineffective customer-related activities, to determine which ones to enhance or eliminate, and to determine how such decisions will affect profitability. Banks, for example, may use this method to determine the classes of customers that are profitable or unprofitable and then use that information in deciding on the location of their branches, effectively adding or dropping customers.

Return on Investment

Return on investment (ROI) measures profitability by dividing the net profit of the business unit by the investment in assets made to attain that income. ROI is also called the accounting rate of return or the accrual accounting rate of return.

The formula used by the ICMA for ROI is:

$$\text{Return on Investment} = \frac{\text{Net Profit of Business Unit}}{\text{Assets of Business Unit}}$$

The formula used to calculate ROI may have many variations in regard to how to derive profit for the numerator and assets for the denominator. However, the formula shown here is the one that is tested on the CMA exam.

Although the timeline for the net profit and the investment in assets is not always equal—for example, investment in a bond in Year 1, with interest returns for the next five years—when comparing two or more investment opportunities, it is important that the time horizons be the same for each project so that a fair comparison can be made. When using ROI for a cost-benefit analysis, it is also important to account for any ongoing costs of the investment over the period that the benefits are tracked—that is, net benefit per year.

ROI can be measured for the short term (a single month or year) or the long term (e.g., investing in a computer system that will generate six years of benefits and six years of costs). However, when dealing with long-term analyses, using a discounted cash flow model will be more appropriate because such models take into account the time value of money.

Both the net profit and the assets of the business unit can be defined in different ways to measure different types of profitability, which are outlined in this topic.

ROI is a broad measure of what you get from what you put in. As mentioned earlier, the numerator and denominator of the ROI formula can be adapted in many different ways. How a particular company decides to calculate ROI may depend on industry conventions or internal company conventions. Knowing what figures were used to generate a ratio is the only way to be able to rely on those ratios. If the ratios for a firm are given without any context, it may be more reliable to generate ratios again, directly from the firm's financial statements. Doing this ensures that each ratio is computed using the same methodology and source data. Similarly, the disclosures to financial statements provide important information regarding what method the company used to, for example, account for inventory. Because of the various methods each firm may use, the results will not be comparable unless data is converted to a common methodology. For example, companies using LIFO for inventory valuation will report a FIFO equivalent in their disclosures, and this amount can be used when comparing results to another company also using FIFO.

ROI can be expressed as a percentage, and the greater the percentage, the greater the return on investment. ROI is a popular measure of profitability because it combines revenues, investments, and costs all in one figure. However, no financial ratio has meaning by itself; ROI should be used with other financial measures and should be compared to industry averages or to other possible investments.

For internal use, companies use various definitions of income (or profits) and investments. For external use, U. S. companies currently use generally accepted accounting principles (GAAP) definitions of each. However, both internal and external ratios may be hard to compare if the ratios were prepared using different methods of allocating common costs—that is, comparing ROI between business units.

When ROI uses average total assets in its investment denominator, it becomes **return on assets (ROA)**, which shows how successful a company is at making a profit using a given level of assets. Firms that are more efficient with their assets are more likely to be profitable.

When ROI uses ownership interest for the investment denominator, it is called **return on equity (ROE)**. ROE is calculated only for common equity because preferred stockholders have a set return that is the preferred dividend rate.

There is a relationship between ROE and ROA. In general, a company's ROE should be higher than its ROA, because this implies that the funds borrowed (e.g., at 9%) were reinvested to earn a higher rate of return (e.g., 15% ROE) than was used in borrowing the funds. A firm uses financial leverage to achieve this difference, which is called trading on the equity. Financial leverage is calculated as shown:

$$\text{Financial Leverage} = \frac{\text{Assets}}{\text{Equity}} = \frac{\text{Total Assets}}{\text{Average Shareholders' Equity}}$$

Having relatively more assets with relatively less equity increases the financial leverage ratio. From a shareholder's perspective, a higher financial leverage is preferred. For companies making profit above the financing costs, this would yield higher return on invested capital (equity). However, higher financial leverage also exposes the company to greater bankruptcy risk in situations when the company earns less than the interest costs. When revenues are increasing, profits for shareholders are multiplied. However, when revenues are decreasing, profits shrink at the same accelerated rate because interest costs must be paid regardless of profits.

For example: A sporting goods manufacturer analyzes ROI for two business units using operating income for income and net assets for investment:

Tennis ball business unit: income of $100,000; net assets of $400,000

$$\text{ROI} = \frac{\$100,000}{\$400,000} = 25\%$$

Racquet ball business unit: income of $60,000; net assets of $300,000

$$\text{ROI} = \frac{\$60,000}{\$300,000} = 20\%$$

Residual Income

Residual income (RI) is a dollar amount of income less a chosen required rate of return for an investment. The formula used by the ICMA for RI is:

Residual Income (RI) = Net Operating Profits of Business Unit
— (Assets of Business Unit × Required Rate of Return)

The imputed cost of an investment (asset) is the required rate of return multiplied by the investment (asset), a measure of the opportunity cost of not being able to invest the funds elsewhere. Imputed costs attempt to add up the costs of an investment (asset) that are not always recognized under accrual accounting, such as the cost of raising capital, such as a 6% interest rate on long-term debt.

For example, assume that the same sporting goods manufacturer from the ROI example decided that the required rate of return for tennis balls was 10% but that the required rate of return for racquet balls was 12% due to greater risks involved in this business unit. The residual income of each business unit is calculated as shown:

$$\text{RI, tennis balls} = \$100,000 - (\$400,000 \times 0.1) = \$60,000$$

$$\text{RI, racquet balls} = \$60,000 - (\$300,000 \times 0.12) = \$24,000$$

RI implies that as long as the tennis ball unit earns more than \$40,000 RI ($0.1 \times \$400,000$) and the racquet ball unit earns more than \$36,000 RI ($0.12 \times \$300,000$), the sporting goods manufacturer should continue to invest in assets to grow these operations. Using RI instead of ROI makes managers aim for an actual dollar amount rather than a percentage.

Just as ROI can measure a specific business segment's returns, RI can be used for a business segment, in which case it uses segment income, segment investment, and a segment-specific required rate of return.

RI versus ROI

Financial ratios must be used in the context of the business and its industry. The nature of a company's business will affect how financial ratios such as ROI are perceived. For example, a particular industry may have lower average ROIs, and the market will view a slightly higher ROI favorably even though it is lower than ROIs for most industries. The maturity of the business also is considered; a firm in its first year of business is not expected to generate as high a return as an established business. Firms entering new markets must set their expectations appropriately. For example, a firm used to a particular ROI for its television division would have to use a different set of criteria for a new aerospace division. To get past these comparability issues, it is useful to compute the ratios for the company and for relevant benchmark firms (such as rivals) using the same methodology. Then the company can be compared to others at the same maturity level.

Focusing only on ROI is not a good general business policy. Instead, firms should take many factors into account, both financial and nonfinancial. Perhaps for business development reasons, a firm should take a low ROI project because it promises to add a new long-term client and therefore a long-term positive ROI.

When ROI is used as a primary performance evaluation tool, managers of business units with higher profits according to ROI may reject capital investments that do not promise as good or better an ROI than the rate being currently earned—even if the investment is strategically beneficial to the organization as a whole.

For example: If Bounce's tennis ball unit was considering purchasing a new machine for \$100,000 that would produce additional revenue of \$20,000, the ROI of 20% would lower the business unit's overall ROI of 25%:

$$\text{Tennis Ball Unit with Expansion} = \frac{\$100,000 + \$20,000}{\$400,000 + \$100,000} = 24\%$$

A manager compensated on ROI would be less likely to make this investment. Conversely, if the same situation used RI instead, the calculation is:

Tennis Ball Unit with Expansion $= \$120,\!000 - (0.1 \times \$500,\!000) = \$70,\!000$

Because RI increases with this investment, a manager compensated based on total RI would have the incentive to make this expansion. Assuming the expansion earns the revenue it promises to earn, the manager will be rewarded for increasing RI.

RI gives managers the incentive to select any project that generates returns above the required rate of return. However, RI is a flat dollar amount, so it is less useful for comparing business units of different sizes (using a percentage value). Also, large business units, even with poor efficiency, still will have a larger RI than a small business unit with good efficiency. Therefore, the measure tends to favor large business units over smaller ones. In contrast, ROI is a more robust measure in some ways because RI is very sensitive to the required rate of return and as the investments become larger, this sensitivity becomes more pronounced.

The objective of maximizing ROI may induce managers of highly profitable subunits to reject projects that, from the viewpoint of the organization as a whole, should be accepted. Such situations occur, as in the last example, when the subunit is operating at a higher ROI (22%) than the cost of capital for the organization (12%). In that case, a new project with an ROI of 18% would be beneficial to the organization but would be rejected by the subunit because it would reduce the overall ROI of the subunit. Conversely, a manager of an unprofitable subunit will accept projects that, from the viewpoint of the organization, should be rejected. Consider another subunit whose ROI is 8%, and the organization has a cost of capital of 12%. The manager of this subunit will accept a project with ROI of 10% even though it will yield a negative residual income for the organization. Generally, goal congruence between subunits and the organization is promoted by using RI rather than ROI as a measure of a manager's performance.

ROI and RI have similar problems. The maximization of either ROI or RI involves maximizing profits (maximizing sales while minimizing costs) and minimizing the investment base. Maximizing sales and minimizing costs promotes transfer price disputes among SBUs, because the transfer price is recorded as revenue to the seller and cost to the buyer. Cost minimization encourages SBUs to cut discretionary costs to maximize profits. The discretionary costs most likely to be cut in the short term are:

- Research and development
- Quality control
- Maintenance
- Human resource development
- Advertising and promotion

The cutting of such costs raises ROI or RI in the short run while creating long-term problems that could be quite detrimental to the SBU as well as to the overall organization.

Maximizing ROI or RI encourages SBU management to reduce the investment base by not replacing assets in need of replacement, not purchasing needed new assets or technology, or unwarranted disposal of assets. All of these actions tend to produce long-term problems.

Investment Base Issues

Using ROI and RI as performance measurement tools may present challenges when attempting to compare competing companies or various internal business units. This is due to the fact that organizations may use different approaches to measure their financial performance. Among the differences that may make these types of comparisons less useful are:

- Differing revenue and expense recognition policies
- Differing inventory measurement policies
- Possession of joint or shared assets between business units
- Differing choices on what to consider an asset and how to value those assets

Joint or shared assets are similar to other common costs that must be assigned to business units, as covered earlier in this section.

Balanced Scorecard

Traditionally, most companies focus the analysis of performance solely on financial measures. Although these measures are objective and quantitative, they are entirely historical in nature. Moreover, they are better at providing short-term forecasts than long-term ones. Although these lagging indicators are important in tracking what has been done, companies must now also focus on the leading indicators, or indicators of future success. The **balanced scorecard** (BSC) and similar holistic techniques provide this broader focus.

The BSC gives companies a simple tool that shows them specific financial and nonfinancial indicators. It is a strategic measurement and management system that translates a company's strategy into four balanced categories: Financial measures show the past performance of a firm; customer, internal business process, and learning and growth measures drive future financial performance.

BSC was created by Robert Kaplan and David Norton as a means of moving organizations away from concentrating solely on financial data. The objective is to focus simultaneously on financial information and on creating the abilities and intangible assets required for long-term growth. This is done by translating a company's strategy into specific measures within each category. Companies use the BSC as a management tool to:

- Clarify and communicate strategy
- Align individual and unit goals to strategy
- Link strategy to the budgeting process
- Get feedback for continuous strategy improvement

Critical Success Factors for a Balanced Scorecard

To effectively develop its strategies, a firm needs to analyze its internal **s̲trengths** and **w̲eaknesses** and then analyze its external **o̲pportunities** and **t̲hreats**. Combined, this effort is termed a **SWOT analysis** .

Strengths include the organization's core competencies, or skills the company performs especially well. Weaknesses are those characteristics that place the company at some disadvantage. Opportunities are chances to increase revenues or profits, and threats are elements in the company environment that may provide trouble for the company. Analysis of these factors helps a company determine its critical success factors (CSFs).

CSFs are specific, measurable goals that must be met in order to achieve a firm's strategy. The BSC identifies CSFs and arranges them into the SWOT categories.

Figure 1B-19 presents an example of one company's CSFs.

Figure 1B-19 CSF Measurement

Factor	Critical Success Factor	Measurement Examples
Financial	Sales	Sales forecast accuracy, return on sales, sales trends
	Liquidity	Asset, inventory, and receivables turnover; cash flow
	Profitability	ROI, residual income, economic value added
	Market value	Market value added, share price
Customer	Market share	Trade association analyses, market definitions
	Customer acquisition	Number of new customers, total sales to new customers
	Customer satisfaction	Customer returns, complaints, surveys
	Customer retention	Customer retention by category, percentage growth with existing customers
	Quality	Warranty expense
	Timeliness	Time from order to door, number of on-time deliveries
Internal business process	Productivity	Cycle time, effectiveness, efficiency, variances, scrap
	Quality	Defects, returns, scrap, rework, surveys, warranty
	Safety	Accidents, insurance claims, result of accidents
	Process time	Setup time, turnaround, lead time
	Brand management	Number of advertisements, surveys, new accounts
Learning and growth	Skill development	Training hours or trainees, skill improvement
	Motivation, empowerment	Suggestions per employee, suggestions implemented
	New products	New patents, number of design changes, research and development skills
	Competence	Employee turnover, experience, customer satisfaction
	Team performance	Surveys, number of gains shared with other teams, number of multi-team projects, percentage of shared incentives

After defining the CSFs, a measurement unit must be assigned to each one. According to Kaplan and Norton, "If you can't measure it, you can't manage it. "

In developing CSFs, it is very possible that some measures may conflict with or be counterproductive to others. To avoid this, the BSC uses a process of integrating the CSFs into the firm's strategy.

Effective Use of a Balanced Scorecard

Once the CSFs and their measurements are defined, they must be linked back to the strategy of the firm. No set of measurement tools will be successful if each manager is motivated to achieve his or her goals at the expense of the other goals. A successful BSC will create a shared understanding within the organization. The BSC creates an overall view of how the individual contributes to strategic success. The elements of the BSC not only should be created from the strategy; study of the factors should show what the strategy is. Linking the four categories together with strategy requires understanding three principles: cause-and-effect relationships; outcome measures and performance drivers; and links to financial measures.

Cause-and-Effect Relationships

All of the CSFs just described should fit within an overall cause-and-effect relationship chain that ends with a relevant financial measure and the achievement of part of the company's strategy. Cause-and-effect situations can be hypothesized using if-then statements: If the firm introduces a new product line, then the firm will attract a new customer base. If the firm attracts a new customer base, then all existing product lines will have new customers . . . and so on. These chains of cause-and-effect relationships should progress through each of the four areas where possible, and the net result of all of the chains should explicitly describe the company's strategy, how to measure each element, and, therefore, how to provide feedback to the process. In the end, all CSFs should be incorporated into one of these cause-and-effect chains.

Outcome Measures and Performance Drivers

For the cause-and-effect chains of CSFs to be useful, they must be linked to a definite outcome and a performance driver that says how the outcome can be met. Outcome measures are lagging indicators, or historic indicators of success such as measures of profitability, market share, employee skills, or customer retention. Outcome measures tend to be general measures of what must be achieved at the end of several cause-and-effect chains. Performance drivers are leading indicators, or drivers that are specific to the strategy of a particular business unit, such as cycle times, setup times, or new patents. Performance drivers without outcome measures will show how to perform in the short term but will not indicate whether the strategy is successful in the long term. Outcome measures without performance drivers will indicate where the department or team needs to be but will not show the path to achieve the goal and will not give relevant information at the time the information is needed.

Links to Financial Measures

No matter how focused an organization is on an initiative such as total quality management or employee empowerment, without linkage to the bottom line, such programs can become goals in themselves. Furthermore, the lack of a link to a tangible benefit from the program can cause disillusionment because there is no way of measuring its success. Therefore, all cause-and-effect chains need to be linked to financial outcome measures.

Nonfinancial Balanced Scorecard Measures

To drive future financial performance, the BSC requires assessment of customer, internal business process, and learning and growth measures.

Customer Measures

Because customers create all of a company's revenue, customer identification and classification into market segments are of vital importance to all companies. The customer perspective must include specific outcome measures and specific performance drivers. Because a company cannot target everyone without losing its focus on its core customers, a company must shape performance drivers (also known as value propositions) that are specific to market segments and their strategy.

The primary customer outcome measures include:

- Market share
- Acquisition
- Satisfaction
- Retention
- Profitability

These elements work together in a cause-and-effect relationship chain, as shown in Figure 1B-20.

Figure 1B-20 Customer Outcome Measures

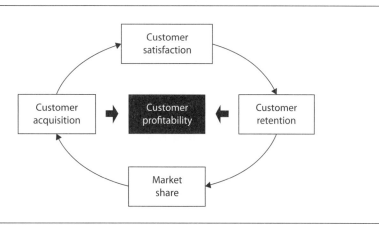

Market share is the proportion of customers that use a company's product or service out of the total of all users in that particular market segment. A subdivision of market share is account share. **Account share** is the proportion of a customer's business out of its total spending in the area the company represents. For example, a food distributor may measure the amount of purchases of its products over all of the targeted customers' food purchases as "share of the pantry. "

Data on the size of the total market segment for a business can be gained from trade associations, industry groups, government studies, and customer surveys. The share of this market controlled by the company can be measured using metrics such as total number of customers, unit volume sold, or dollars spent. Account share is measured using surveys or approximation techniques that estimate the spending of an average user compared to the spending with the company itself. Companies with few customers can track individual customers, whereas companies with many customers must track customer segments.

Customer Acquisition

Companies with a growth strategy will focus strongly on the customer acquisition measure, but all companies need to add new customers because customer retention is never 100%. Customer acquisition is a measure of the success of the funds spent on acquiring the new customers, such as advertising costs and other marketing efforts. Customer acquisition can be measured in absolute terms (number of new customers) or relative terms (net gain in customers). It can also be measured as total sales to customers and acquisition divided by customer market segment. Other measures focus on customer conversion rate: the number of new customers divided by the total number of prospect contacts.

Customer Satisfaction

Measures of customer satisfaction show how successfully a company has met the needs of its consumers. When a firm's customers are corporations, a measurement of customer satisfaction often can be acquired through a formal process of having the customer rank its vendors on a variety of factors. Retail customer satisfaction similarly can be measured using surveys or, conversely, customer complaints. Customer surveys range from relatively inexpensive to very expensive, depending on the medium used and the number of desired responses. Web-based surveys and Web tracking have made the data-gathering process relatively inexpensive.

Customer Retention

Customer retention is an ongoing process that can be measured directly by companies that maintain lists of their customers, such as magazines, auto dealerships, distributors, and banks. Similar to account share, customer retention can be further broken down into the percentage change of business with each customer. For retailers, some customer retention data can be gained from credit card receipts. A major source of retention data for some retailers are "loyalty" programs that provide enrolled customers with discounts and enable the firm to precisely track customer purchases.

Customer Performance Drivers

Although outcome measures may be broadly defined for most industries, performance drivers are specific to each company's strategy and market. The performance drivers for customer acquisition, retention, and satisfaction are based on meeting the needs of customers. Examples of some common performance drivers include:

- Response time
- Delivery performance
- Defects
- Lead time

Internal Business Process Measures

After the financial and customer measures are created to meet company strategy, the internal business process measures can be designed to link to these metrics and achieve customer and shareholder value. Instead of creating measures that merely attempt to improve existing business processes, the BSC suggests that companies start with current and future customer needs, progressing through the cause-and-effect chain via operations, marketing, and other areas all the way to sales and service, keeping only the elements that add value to customers.

Internal business process measures go beyond simple financial variance measures to include output measures such as quality, cycle time, yield, order fulfillment, production planning, throughput, and turnover. However, improving such measures may not be enough to differentiate a company from its competitors, when these firms are working toward the same goals. Entirely new internal processes may be needed to make the company a leader in all of these measures simultaneously. A SWOT analysis can help identify weaknesses that require new solutions rather than just incremental improvements. For example, a business could radically improve cycle time by eliminating its warehouse and directly shipping goods to retail locations on a just-in-time basis.

The BSC identifies three business process areas that contribute to most companies' business strategies for internal business processes: innovation, operations, and postsale service.

Innovation

The innovation process starts with the SWOT analysis to identify customer needs that the company can satisfy. Research and development can be extremely expensive and must be written off as a period expense. Therefore, becoming efficient and effective at producing new products can be just as or more important than concentrating on the efficiency of ongoing production operations. Because the first company to introduce a new product has a distinct edge in market share, time to market is a key metric for evaluating the success of a new product introduction. Other measures employed include percentage of sales from new or proprietary products, new products versus competitors' new products, and variation from project budgets.

Product development processes can include performance measurements, such as yield, cycle time, and cost. For example, research into new computer chips could test numerous materials, and the yield of materials to warrant further study can be judged against the total number tested. The material in each stage can have its time in that phase measured (cycle time), and the overall cost of processing and research can be measured. Thus, the progress toward the outcome measurement of time to market and overall cost can be measured.

Operations

The operations process is the area that has garnered the majority of performance measurements in the past, and it continues to be important in reducing costs or increasing capabilities. Using only financial measures for operations, such as variances and standard costs, can lead to line managers making decisions that run counter to the organization's strategy—for example, creating too much inventory to keep a financial ratio in line with expectations rather than adjusting it to fit customer demand. Although the financial measurements continue to be important, the BSC recommends supplementing them with measures of quality, technological capabilities, and reducing cycle time to build the company's long-term strategy for differentiation over its competitors.

Postsale Service

Postsale service is a method of adding value to a product or service while simultaneously gaining feedback on customer satisfaction. Many companies that sell complex goods or services include postsale service in their strategic plans. Metrics such as response time for equipment failures and promptness of maintenance calls can be employed to measure the success of postsale service.

Learning and Growth Measures

A company develops learning and growth measures after identifying its financial, customer, and internal process strategic needs. If the company created its strategy with ambition and innovation, the company will need to achieve new capabilities through learning and growth. Although it is the last step designed in a BSC strategy, it will be the first step performed. Learning and growth measures are performance drivers for the desired strategic outcomes. Measuring learning and growth using financial measures alone usually tends to show only the short-term results, and short-term training results usually show that the training is unprofitable. However, because the long-term consequences of ignoring this element of an organization can be devastating, new measures must be introduced to guide management's decisions in this area.

The learning and growth perspective can be broken down into three categories: employee skill sets; information system capabilities; and empowerment, motivation, and organizational alignment.

Employee Skill Sets

The automation of repetitive tasks has transformed employee management from an industrial model to a knowledge-based model. Specific outcome measurements of employee results include employee satisfaction, employee retention, and employee productivity. Satisfied employees produce satisfied customers. Employee satisfaction can be measured through employee annual reviews or surveys. Employee retention is measured by employee turnover and by numbers of years of service. Employees with greater investment in a company tend to be more satisfied. The employee productivity outcome measure is a product of performance drivers, such as employee training, autonomy in decision making versus results, and output versus numbers of employees needed to produce the output. Another common and simple productivity measure is revenue per employee, but it should not be the sole measure because overly stressing revenue can lead employees to accept revenue even while the profit level is negative, such as salespersons offering huge price discounts to make sales.

Employees needing new skill sets can be measured using the amount of training needed per employee, the proportion of the workforce needing training, or the training and experience required to advance from an unqualified to a qualified employee. Such measures will indicate the amount of work required to raise the organization's capabilities to the desired strategic level. The strategic job coverage ratio is another metric that tracks the number of employees qualified for a strategic job divided by total organizational needs. This ratio exposes gaps in organizational skill sets.

Information System Capabilities

Measurements of the time needed to access or process business information can assess the capabilities of the current information systems and indicate need for continued investment in such infrastructure. A strategic information coverage ratio can be used to measure current information system capabilities divided by anticipated system needs.

Empowerment, Motivation, and Organizational Alignment

Empowerment and motivation can be measured using metrics such as the number and impact of employee-initiated improvements and innovations. Empowerment and motivation can be enhanced when employees are encouraged in and recognized for suggesting improvements in the organization's products and processes. Organizational alignment, organizational learning, and teamwork measurements include the goals set versus goals achieved for a department and team-based measures that include team-based rewards. The linking of personal goals and rewards to organizational outcomes is key to achieving the overall company strategy. Performance drivers for organizational alignment include periodic surveys of employees to determine their level of motivation to achieve the critical success factors in the BSC.

A Balanced Scorecard Example

Acme Company's BSC, shown in Figure 1B-21, gives the company's overall strategic goal and the associated targets. It then covers the specific objectives from each of the four perspectives. Each objective has a specific measurable tool and a target for each of the next two years. The "Programs" column is the result of a survey Acme performed that matched planned programs to particular strategic objectives. The targets were set under the assumption that these programs would go forward.

Figure 1B-21 Acme Company's Balanced Scorecard (Planned Results)

Overall goal: Grow sales by 20% over the next two years. Targets					
			Current Year (Y0)	**Year 1 (Y1)**	**Year 2 (Y2)**
Revenues:			$400,000	$432,000	$484,000
Perspective	**Strategic Objectives**	**Measurements**	**Y1 Target**	**Y2 Target**	**Programs**
Financial	F1: Maximize return on equity	Return on equity	9%	13%	
	F2: Positive economic value added (EVA)	EVA	$20,000	$30,000	
	F3: 10% revenue growth	% change in revenues	8%	12%	
	F4: Asset utilization	Utilization rates	85%	88%	
Customer	C1: Price	Competitive comparison	−4%	−5%	
	C2: Customer retention	Retention %	75%	75%	Implement customer relationship management (CRM) program
	C3: Lowest-cost suppliers	Total cost relative to competition	−6%	−7%	Implement supplier relationship management (SRM) program
	C4: Product innovation	% of sales from new products	10%	15%	
Internal business process	P1: Improve production work flow	Cycle time	0.3 days	0.25 days	Upgrade enterprise resource planning (ERP) system
	P2: New product success	Number of orders	1,000	1,500	
	P3: Sales penetration	Actual versus plan (variance)	0%	0%	
	P4: Reduce inventory	Inventory as a % of sales	30%	28%	
Learning and growth	L1: Link strategy to reward system	Net income per dollar of variable pay (aggregate)	65%	68%	Implement CRM
	L2: Fill critical competency gaps	% of critical competencies satisfied on tracking matrix	75%	80%	Tuition reimbursement
	L3: Become customer-driven culture	Survey index	77%	79%	Implement CRM
	L4: Quality leadership	Average ranking (on 10-point scale) of executives	8.9	9.2	Tuition reimbursement

At the end of Year 1, the results were as shown in Figure 1B-22.

Figure 1B-22 Acme Company's Balanced Scorecard (Actual Results)

Overall goal: Grow sales by 20% over the next two years. (Actual)

		Y1 Target	Y1 Actual	Variance*	
Revenues:		$432,000	$424,000	$8,000	U
Perspective	**Strategic Objectives**				
Financial	F1: Maximize return on equity	9%	8%	1%	U
	F2: Positive EVA	$20,000	$18,000	$2,000	U
	F3: 10% revenue growth	8%	6%	2%	U
	F4: Asset utilization	85%	87%	2%	F
Customer	C1: Price	–4%	–4%	0	
	C2: Customer retention	75%	70%	5%	U
	C3: Lowest-cost suppliers	–6%	–7%	–1%	F
	C4: Product innovation	10%	8%	2%	U
Internal business process	P1: Improve production work flow	0.3 days	0.25 days	0.05 days	F
	P2: New product success	1,000 orders	800 orders	200 orders	U
	P3: Sales penetration	0%	–7%	–7%	U
	P4: Reduce inventory	30%	29%	1%	F
Learning and growth	L1: Link strategy to reward system	65%	63%	2%	U
	L2: Fill critical competency gaps	75%	75%	0	
	L3: Become customer-driven culture	77%	74%	3%	U
	L4: Quality leadership	8.9	8.9	0	

*U = Unfavorable variance; F = Favorable variance.

What can Acme learn from the results of Year 1? It may have had trouble implementing its CRM program (poorly planned, project canceled, delayed, etc.) because each of the measures that was linked to that program had an unfavorable variance. A reexamination of that program may find ways to refocus on the customers' needs.

Acme's production costs and production efficiencies all have favorable variances, meaning that the SRM and ERP initiatives seem to have been successful. Acme's workforce is progressing on pace, and its tuition reimbursement program is a likely aid to this success. However, although the workforce is strong in core competencies and in leadership, its members have not become customer-oriented enough, which is the primary reason for Acme's loss of customers and its inability to penetrate new markets and sell new products (which were likely designed with poor information on actual market needs). If Acme wants to turn things around and meet its goals, it must increase its investment in its CRM initiative, including training to change its employees' mind-sets toward a customer orientation.

Implementing the Balanced Scorecard

The next information on implementing the BSC was drawn from *The Strategy-Focused Organization* by Kaplan and Norton (Harvard Business Review Press,

2000). Implementing the BSC is basically executing strategy. Without execution, even the best vision remains a dream. In the past few decades, the average company has gone from about two-thirds of its value being based on tangible assets to about one-third, meaning that companies are moving from being able to describe and measure their success solely in financial terms to needing knowledge-based strategies that rely on more than just slow-reacting tools such as budgets. The BSC lends itself well to strategy execution, because the scorecard itself is a method of describing strategy in a way that can be acted on. A strategy-focused organization has these aspects:

- All of the measures used in the BSC (financial and nonfinancial) should be derived from the firm's vision and strategy.
- Processes become participative rather than directive.
- Change is not limited to cost cutting and downsizing but includes repositioning the firm (new or more specialized competitive markets, a customer focus, a performance mind-set, etc.).
- The organization must adopt new cultural values and priorities.

Aligning and Focusing Resources on Strategy

Rather than encouraging a general effort toward "improvement" or "efficiency," the executive team, business units, information technology, human resources, budgets, and capital investments must all be aligned and focused toward narrower and more intense (but not necessarily more capital-intensive) goals. To accomplish this, a firm must implement continuous improvement cycle consisting of five steps:

1. Translate the strategy in operational terms.
2. Align the organization to the firm's strategy.
3. Make strategy everybody's everyday job.
4. Make strategy a continual process.
5. Mobilize change through executive leadership.

1. **Translate the strategy into operational terms using strategy maps and the BSC**. A **strategy map** helps provide a high-level view of the organization's strategy and associated priorities so that it can design metrics that will enable it to evaluate its performance against strategies.

    For example: Figure 1B-23 shows a strategy map that Mobil North America Marketing and Refining (NAM&R) created to address a new focus on the customer and on those factors aimed at making customers want to use Mobil stations and products more.

2. **Align the organization to the firm's strategy using corporate scorecards as well as business unit and support unit synergies.** Synergies make the whole worth more than the sum of its parts. Break down functional area silos not by replacing departments or organizational charts but by replacing formal reporting structures with strategic priorities across business units (e.g., by having common themes across each unit's different scorecards). Examples of linked scorecards can be found in Kaplan and Norton's *The Strategy-Focused Organization*.

3. **Make strategy everyone's daily job using personal scorecards, strategic awareness, and balanced paychecks.** Replacing top-down direction with top-down communication means that every employee has a clear set of expectations that are already in line with strategy. The BSC becomes the educational tool showing how to measure success, but it may need to be backed up with more formal training (e.g., if employees must refine customer segments, they must first be taught about customer segmentation). Also, the lowest or personal-level scorecards can be left to the end users to create based on the higher-level priorities communicated. Often this leads to unsought-for synergies when an individual finds ways to help other areas of the company. Such a process helps create a strategic awareness at every level.

   Balanced paychecks link pay to the BSC measures, usually by business unit performance instead of individual performance. Balanced paychecks apply financial and nonfinancial BSC measures by weighting their importance. Some measures have an individual performance portion and a unit performance portion; and most also tie the compensation to some external factors, such as an industry benchmark to compensate for factors outside of employees' control. Using some form of balanced paycheck raises the interest level of all employees in using the BSC. Although employees may be studying the BSC to see what their compensation will be, they are also simultaneously working to improve corporate goals through their diligence. In the Mobil example in Figure 1B-23, when truck drivers delivered gasoline to stores, they started reporting poor station conditions because they knew their own compensation was partly based on customer perceptions at the stations.

4. **Make strategy a continual process by linking strategy to budgeting, using analytical automation, holding strategy meetings, and implementing strategic learning.** Strategy often is neglected in favor of tactical decisions, such as setting a budget, so the BSC uses a "double-loop" process. For example, two budgets are created, a strategic budget and an operational budget, thus protecting the long-term objectives from suboptimization in the short term. Regular strategy meetings organized around the BSC allow input from a broader group of managers while keeping the meeting focused. Instead of talking about variances or other specifics, managers will use their own BSC to measure their own performance and then use the meeting to talk about what has gone right and/or wrong and what should be continued or discontinued.

   Analytical tool automation found in today's enterprise resource and other sophisticated analytical systems can provide feedback to a broader audience than was traditionally possible, and a BSC can include such analysis. The firm must teach employees how to learn and adapt the strategy, such as by providing simple internal brochures explaining how to use a particular type of measure in its specific business context. Other firms may have employees use and then test the cause-and-effect linkages in a scorecard by analyzing actual results.

5. **Mobilize change through executive leadership using mobilization, governance processes, and a strategic management system.** Active executive

Figure 1B-23 Strategy Maps for Mobil NAM&R

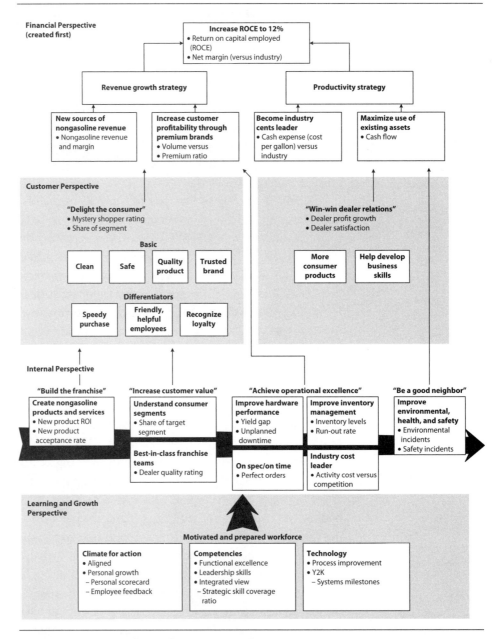

involvement is a must, and it involves a focus more on mobilization or getting momentum started than on the metrics in the BSC itself. Governance processes involve how to manage the process once it has begun, using team-based approaches that break up old power structures and focus on executing strategy. In the final phase of implementing the BSC, governance becomes a strategic management system that transforms the new methods and values into the new business culture. Governance processes reinforce positive changes, such as by determining when and how to link the executive level and other levels of the firm to the BSC, for example, using executive compensation. This last phase is dangerous, as the desire for stability can make future changes more difficult. However, this tendency toward setting standards is universal in organizations and so should be planned for, embraced for a time, and then evaluated and changed to fit evolving strategy.

Performance Measures and Reporting Mechanisms

Management control systems, such as the BSC, aid in communication and coordination of an organization's goals to all employees. If carefully designed and properly implemented, these systems also can motivate employee behavior. Implementing a thorough BSC or any other strategic mechanism requires the development of a corresponding performance measurement system that supports the achievement of strategic goals and prevents dysfunctional behaviors that are not in alignment with strategic goals. A well-designed management control system will measure and report both financial as well as nonfinancial metrics of performance.

For performance measures to be effective in achieving the organization's goals, they must be related to the strategic goals of the organization. When performance measures are not aligned with the goals of the organization, they may induce behavior that is detrimental to the organization. It is often said that "You get what you reward." Hence, when performance measures are not linked to organizational goals, employees receive a mixed message as to which objectives management deems important. Measuring and rewarding behavior not aligned to organizational goals would induce behavior that is detrimental to the goals of the organization.

Performance measures need to be reasonably objective and easy to measure. Very complex performance measurement systems traditionally have not been successful in practice. Employees should be able to comprehend what is being measured, how the measurement system works, and how to relate the effects of their actions to those measures. This knowledge will help employees align their actions with the organization's goals.

It is important that performance measures be applied in a uniform, consistent, and regular manner. Inconsistent or irregular application of these measures has a negative impact on employee morale and motivation.

While traditional performance measurement systems focus more on financial measures, such as profits and cost variances, lately the emphasis has shifted toward the use of nonfinancial measures, such as those obtained from a BSC. It has been demonstrated that focusing on nonfinancial measures improves operational control. Moreover, such measures are more directly linked to the performance of lower-level employees.

Finally, the cost of measurement has to be considered. Since measuring performance requires the collection and analysis of data, the cost of such processes has to be considered prior to implementing a performance measurement system. A very costly performance measurement system may report very accurate results, but the additional costs may not be justified. Hence, the performance measurement system is the result of a trade-off between accuracy and cost.

**Knowledge Check:
Performance Measures**

The next questions are intended to help you check your understanding and recall of the material presented in this topic. They do not represent the type of questions that appear on the CMA exam.

Directions: Answer each question in the space provided. Correct answers and section references appear after the knowledge check questions.

1. A business unit has $100,000 in net profit, assets of $500,000, and revenues of $200,000. Calculate its ROI.

   _____

2. Complete the following equation:

   Net Profit of Business Unit − (Assets of Business Unit × _____)
   = Residual Income

3. Which of the following perspectives of the balanced scorecard should every cause-and-effect chain be linked to?

   ☐ **a.** Financial

   ☐ **b.** Customer

   ☐ **c.** Internal business process

   ☐ **d.** Learning and growth

4. Which of the following is a customer performance driver?

   ☐ **a.** Market share

   ☐ **b.** Lead time

   ☐ **c.** Retention

   ☐ **d.** Profitability

5. Periodic surveys of employee motivation are an example of a

   ☐ **a.** learning and growth outcome measure.

   ☐ **b.** learning and growth performance driver.

   ☐ **c.** customer outcome measure.

   ☐ **d.** customer performance driver.

6. The process time critical success factor would be measured best by which of the following?

   ☐ **a.** Surveys

   ☐ **b.** ROI

   ☐ **c.** Customer returns

   ☐ **d.** Turnaround

7. Define the five steps firms must use to implement a continuous improvement cycle.

1. _____

2. _____

3. _____

4. _____

5. _____

Knowledge Check Answers: Performance Measures

1. A business unit has $100,000 in net profit, assets of $500,000, and revenues of $200,000. Calculate its ROI. *[See Return on Investment.]*

    $$\text{Return on Investment (ROI)} = \frac{\text{Net profit of business unit}}{\text{Assets of business unit}}$$

    ROI = $100,000/$500,000

    ROI = 20%

2. Complete the following equation: *[See Residual Income.]*

    Net Profit of Business Unit – (Assets of Business Unit × Required Rate of Return) = Residual Income

3. Which of the following perspectives of the balanced scorecard should every cause-and-effect chain be linked to? *[See Links to Financial Measures.]*

    ☑ **a.** Financial

    ☐ **b.** Customer

    ☐ **c.** Internal business process

    ☐ **d.** Learning and growth

4. Which of the following is a customer performance driver? *[See Customer Performance Drivers.]*

    ☐ **a.** Market share

    ☑ **b.** Lead time

    ☐ **c.** Retention

    ☐ **d.** Profitability

5. Periodic surveys of employee motivation are an example of a *[See Empowerment, Motivation, and Organizational Alignment.]*

    ☐ **a.** learning and growth outcome measure.

    ☑ **b.** learning and growth performance driver.

    ☐ **c.** customer outcome measure.

    ☐ **d.** customer performance driver.

6. The process time critical success factor would be measured best by which of the following? *[See Critical Success Factors for a Balanced Scorecard.]*

    ☐ **a.** Surveys

    ☐ **b.** ROI

    ☐ **c.** Customer returns

    ☑ **d.** Turnaround

7. Define the five steps firms must use to implement a continuous improvement cycle. *[See Aligning and Focusing Resources on Strategy.]*

1. Translate the strategy in operational terms.
2. Align the organization to the firm's strategy.
3. Make strategy everybody's everyday job.
4. Make strategy a continual process.
5. Mobilize change through executive leadership.

Directions: This sampling of questions is designed to emulate actual exam questions. Read each question and write your response on another sheet of paper. Use the answer and explanation (given later in the book) to assess your response. Validate or improve the answer you wrote. For a more robust selection of practice questions, access the **Online Test Bank** found on the IMA's Learning Center Web site. See the "Answers to Section Practice Questions" section at the end of the book.

Question 1B1-CQ01

Topic: Cost and Variance Measures

The following performance report was prepared for Dale Manufacturing for the month of April.

	Actual Results	**Static Budget**	**Variance**
Sales units	100,000	80,000	20,000F
Sales dollars	$190,000	$160,000	$30,000F
Variable costs	125,000	96,000	29,000U
Fixed costs	45,000	40,000	5,000U
Operating income	$20,000	$ 24,000	$ 4,000U

Using a flexible budget, Dale's total sales-volume variance is:

- ☐ **a.** $4,000 unfavorable.
- ☐ **b.** $6,000 favorable.
- ☐ **c.** $16,000 favorable.
- ☐ **d.** $20,000 unfavorable.

Question 1B1-CQ02

Topic: Cost and Variance Measures

MinnOil performs oil changes and other minor maintenance services (e.g., tire pressure checks) for cars. The company advertises that all services are completed within 15 minutes for each service.

On a recent Saturday, 160 cars were serviced resulting in the following labor variances: rate, $19 unfavorable; efficiency, $14 favorable. If MinnOil's standard labor rate is $7 per hour, determine the actual wage rate per hour and the actual hours worked.

	Wage Rate	Hours Worked
☐ **a.**	$6.55	42.00
☐ **b.**	$6.67	42.71
☐ **c.**	$7.45	42.00
☐ **d.**	$7.50	38.00

Question 1B1-CQ03

Topic: Cost and Variance Measures

Frisco Company recently purchased 108,000 units of raw material for $583,200. Three units of raw materials are budgeted for use in each finished good manufactured, with the raw material standard set at $16.50 for each completed product.

Frisco manufactured 32,700 finished units during the period just ended and used 99,200 units of raw material. If management is concerned about the timely reporting of variances in an effort to improve cost control and bottom-line performance, the materials purchase price variance should be reported as

☐ **a.** $6,050 unfavorable.

☐ **b.** $9,920 favorable.

☐ **c.** $10,800 unfavorable.

☐ **d.** $10,800 favorable.

Question 1B1-CQ04

Topic: Cost and Variance Measures

Christopher Akers is the chief executive officer of SBL Inc., a masonry contractor. The financial statements have just arrived showing a $3,000 loss on the new stadium job that was budgeted to show a $6,000 profit. Actual and budget information relating to the materials for the job are shown next.

	Actual	Budget
Bricks — number of bundles	3,000	2,850
Bricks — cost per bundle	$7.90	$8.00

Which one of the following is a **correct** statement regarding the stadium job for SBL?

☐ **a.** The price variance was favorable by $285.

☐ **b.** The price variance was favorable by $300.

☐ **c.** The efficiency variance was unfavorable by $1,185.

☐ **d.** The flexible budget variance was unfavorable by $900.

Question 1B1-CQ05

Topic: Cost and Variance Measures

A company isolates its raw material price variance in order to provide the earliest possible information to the manager responsible for the variance. The budgeted amount of material usage for the year was computed as shown:

150,000 Units of Finished Goods $\times$ 3 Pounds/Unit $\times$ \$2.00/Pound = \$900,000

Actual results for the year were the following:

Finished goods produced	160,000 units
Raw materials purchased	500,000 pounds
Raw materials used	490,000 pounds
Cost per pound	\$2.02

The raw material price variance for the year was

- ☐ **a.** \$9,600 unfavorable.
- ☐ **b.** \$9,800 unfavorable.
- ☐ **c.** \$10,000 unfavorable.
- ☐ **d.** \$20,000 unfavorable.

Question 1B1-CQ06

Topic: Cost and Variance Measures

Lee Manufacturing uses a standard cost system with overhead applied based on direct labor hours. The manufacturing budget for the production of 5,000 units for the month of May included the following information.

Direct labor cost (10,000 hours at \$15/hour)	\$150,000
Variable overhead	\$30,000
Fixed overhead	\$80,000

During May, 6,000 units were produced and the direct labor efficiency variance was \$1,500 unfavorable. Based on this information, the actual number of direct labor hours used in May was:

- ☐ **a.** 9,900 hours.
- ☐ **b.** 10,100 hours.
- ☐ **c.** 11,900 hours.
- ☐ **d.** 12,100 hours.

Question 1B1-CQ07

Topic: Cost and Variance Measures

At the beginning of the year, Douglas Company prepared this monthly budget for direct materials.

Units produced and sold	10,000	15,000
Direct material cost	$15,000	$22,500

At the end of the month, the company's records showed that 12,000 units were produced and sold and $20,000 was spent for direct materials. The variance for direct materials is:

- ☐ **a.** $2,000 favorable.
- ☐ **b.** $2,000 unfavorable.
- ☐ **c.** $5,000 favorable.
- ☐ **d.** $5,000 unfavorable.

Question 1B1-CQ08

Topic: Cost and Variance Measures

A company had a total labor variance of $15,000 favorable and a labor efficiency variance of $18,000 unfavorable. The labor price variance was:

- ☐ **a.** $3,000 favorable.
- ☐ **b.** $3,000 unfavorable.
- ☐ **c.** $33,000 favorable.
- ☐ **d.** $33,000 unfavorable.

Question 1B1-CQ09

Topic: Cost and Variance Measures

Lee Manufacturing uses a standard cost system with overhead applied based on direct labor hours. The manufacturing budget for the production of 5,000 units for the month of June included 10,000 hours of direct labor at $15 per hour, or $150,000. During June, 4,500 units were produced, using 9,600 direct labor hours, incurring $39,360 of variable overhead, and showing a variable overhead efficiency variance of $2,400 unfavorable. The standard variable overhead rate per direct labor hour was:

- ☐ **a.** $3.85.
- ☐ **b.** $4.00.
- ☐ **c.** $4.10.
- ☐ **d.** $6.00.

Question 1B1-CQ10

Topic: Cost and Variance Measures

Cordell Company uses a standard cost system. On January 1 of the current year, Cordell budgeted fixed manufacturing overhead cost of $600,000 and production at 200,000 units. During the year, the firm produced 190,000 units and incurred fixed manufacturing overhead of $595,000. The production volume variance for the year was:

- ☐ **a.** $5,000 unfavorable.
- ☐ **b.** $10,000 unfavorable.
- ☐ **c.** $25,000 unfavorable.
- ☐ **d.** $30,000 unfavorable.

Question 1B1-CQ11

Topic: Cost and Variance Measures

Harper Company's performance report indicated this information for the past month:

Actual total overhead	$1,600,000
Budgeted fixed overhead	$1,500,000
Applied fixed overhead at $3 per labor hour	$1,200,000
Applied variable overhead at $.50 per labor hour	$200,000
Actual labor hours	430,000

Harper's total overhead spending variance for the month was:

- ☐ **a.** $100,000 favorable.
- ☐ **b.** $115,000 favorable.
- ☐ **c.** $185,000 unfavorable.
- ☐ **d.** $200,000 unfavorable.

Question 1B1-CQ12

Topic: Cost and Variance Measures

The JoyT Company manufactures Maxi Dolls for sale in toy stores. In planning for this year, JoyT estimated variable factory overhead of $600,000 and fixed factory overhead of $400,000. JoyT uses a standard costing system, and factory overhead is allocated to units produced on the basis of standard direct labor hours. The denominator level of activity budgeted for this year was 10,000 direct labor hours, and JoyT used 10,300 actual direct labor hours.

Based on the output accomplished during this year, 9,900 standard direct labor hours should have been used. Actual variable factory overhead was $596,000, and actual fixed factory overhead was $410,000 for the year. Based on this information, the variable overhead spending variance for JoyT for this year was:

- ☐ **a.** $24,000 unfavorable.
- ☐ **b.** $2,000 unfavorable.
- ☐ **c.** $4,000 favorable.
- ☐ **d.** $22,000 favorable.

Question 1B1-CQ13

Topic: Cost and Variance Measures

Johnson Inc. has established per unit standards for material and labor for its production department based on 900 units normal production capacity as shown.

3 pounds of direct materials @ $4 per pound	$12
1 direct labor hour @ $15 per hour	15
Standard cost per unit	$27

During the year, 1,000 units were produced. The accounting department has charged the production department supervisor with the next unfavorable variances.

Material Quantity Variance		**Material Price Variance**	
Actual usage	3,300 pounds	Actual cost	$4,200
Standard usage	3,000 pounds	Standard cost	4,000
Unfavorable	300 pounds	Unfavorable	$200

Bob Sterling, the production supervisor, has received a memorandum from his boss stating that he did not meet the established standards for material prices and quantity and corrective action should be taken. Sterling is very unhappy about the situation and is preparing to reply to the memorandum explaining the reasons for his dissatisfaction.

All of the following are valid reasons for Sterling's dissatisfaction **except** that the:

- ☐ **a.** material price variance is the responsibility of the purchasing department.
- ☐ **b.** cause of the unfavorable material usage variance was the acquisition of substandard material.
- ☐ **c.** standards have not been adjusted to the engineering changes.
- ☐ **d.** variance calculations fail to properly reflect that actual production exceeded normal production capacity.

Question 1B2-CQ01

Topic: Responsibility Centers and Reporting Segments

Manhattan Corporation has several divisions that operate as decentralized profit centers. At the present time, the Fabrication Division has excess capacity of 5,000 units with respect to the UT-371 circuit board, a popular item in many digital applications. Information about the circuit board is presented next.

Market price	$48
Variable selling/distribution costs on external sales	$5
Variable manufacturing cost	$21
Fixed manufacturing cost	$10

Manhattan's Electronic Assembly Division wants to purchase 4,500 circuit boards either internally or else use a similar board in the marketplace that sells for $46. The Electronic Assembly Division's management feels that if the first alternative is pursued, a price concession is justified, given that both divisions are part of the same firm. To optimize the overall goals of Manhattan, the minimum price to be charged for the board from the Fabrication Division to the Electronic Assembly Division should be:

- ☐ **a.** $21.
- ☐ **b.** $26.
- ☐ **c.** $31.
- ☐ **d.** $46.

Question 1B3-CQ01

Topic: Performance Measures

Performance results for four geographic divisions of a manufacturing company are shown next.

Division	Target Return on Investment	Actual Return on Investment	Return on Sales
A	18%	18.1%	8%
B	16%	20.0%	8%
C	14%	15.8%	6%
D	12%	11.0%	9%

The division with the **best** performance is:

- ☐ **a.** Division A.
- ☐ **b.** Division B.
- ☐ **c.** Division C.
- ☐ **d.** Division D.

Question 1B3-CQ02

Topic: Performance Measures

KHD Industries is a multidivisional firm that evaluates its managers based on the return on investment (ROI) earned by its divisions. The evaluation and compensation plans use a targeted ROI of 15% (equal to the cost of capital), and managers receive a bonus of 5% of basic compensation for every one percentage point that the division's ROI exceeds 15%.

Dale Evans, manager of the Consumer Products Division, has made a forecast of the division's operations and finances for next year that indicates the ROI would be 24%. In addition, new short-term programs were identified by the Consumer Products Division and evaluated by the finance staff as shown.

Program	Projected ROI
A	13%
B	19%
C	22%
D	31%

Assuming no restrictions on expenditures, what is the optimal mix of new programs that would add value to KHD Industries?

☐ **a.** A, B, C, and D

☐ **b.** B, C, and D only

☐ **c.** C and D only

☐ **d.** D only

Question 1B1-AT03

Topic: Cost and Variance Measures

Franklin Products has an estimated practical capacity of 90,000 machine hours, and each unit requires two machine hours. The next data apply to a recent accounting period.

Actual variable overhead	$240,000
Actual fixed overhead	$442,000
Actual machine **hours** worked	88,000
Actual finished **units** produced	42,000
Budgeted variable overhead at 90,000 machine hours	$200,000
Budgeted fixed overhead	$450,000

Of the following factors, the production volume variance is **most** likely to have been caused by:

☐ **a.** acceptance of an unexpected sales order.

☐ **b.** a wage hike granted to a production supervisor.

☐ **c.** a newly imposed initiative to reduce finished goods inventory levels.

☐ **d.** temporary employment of workers with lower skill levels than originally anticipated.

Question 1B3-AT03

Topic: Performance Measures

Which one of the following **best** identifies a profit center?

- ☐ **a.**   A new car sales division for a large local auto agency
- ☐ **b.**   The information technology department of a large consumer products company
- ☐ **c.**   A large toy company
- ☐ **d.**   The production operations department of a small job-order machine shop company

Question 1B3-AT20

Topic: Performance Measures

Teaneck Inc. sells two products, Product E and Product F, and had these data for last month:

	Product E		Product F	
	Budget	Actual	Budget	Actual
Unit sales	5,500	6,000	4,500	6,000
Unit contribution margin (CM)	$4.50	$4.80	$10.00	$10.50

The company's sales mix variance is:

- ☐ **a.** $3,300 favorable.
- ☐ **b.** $3,420 favorable.
- ☐ **c.** $17,250 favorable.
- ☐ **d.** $18,150 favorable.

Question 1B3-AT05

Topic: Performance Measures

The balanced scorecard provides an action plan for achieving competitive success by focusing management attention on critical success factors. Which one of the following is **not** one of the critical success factors commonly focused on in the balanced scorecard?

- ☐ **a.**   Financial performance measures
- ☐ **b.**   Internal business processes
- ☐ **c.**   Competitor business strategies
- ☐ **d.**   Employee innovation and learning

 To further assess your understanding of the concepts and calculations covered in Part 1, Section B: Performance Management, practice with the **Online Test Bank** for this section. REMINDER: See the "Answers to Section Practice Questions" section at the end of this book.

Cost Management

Cost management requires the ability to measure, accumulate, assign, and classify all of the costs involved in running a modern business enterprise. A costing system is used to monitor a company's costs, thereby providing management with information on operations and performance. Various costing systems, such as job order costing, process costing, activity-based costing (ABC), throughput costing, and life-cycle costing, can be implemented to monitor costs.

Cost management involves the actions undertaken by managers to satisfy customers while also monitoring and controlling costs. In the modern manufacturing environment, every resource is monitored very closely to ensure the company is receiving the best return for its investment. The use of resources, such as direct materials, direct labor, and manufacturing overhead, are analyzed carefully with the appropriate measurement system. Operational efficiency and overall business performance can be sustained and improved through the knowledgeable application of the right systems.

Measurement Concepts

MEASUREMENT CONCEPTS MAKE USE OF cost behavior relationships to analyze the effect that changes in costs will have on the firm's profitability. Defining and classifying costs is essential to understanding how they can be used to measure performance.

This topic discusses types and classification of costs, including fixed, variable, and step costs; cost drivers; actual, normal, and standard costing; absorption and variable costing; and joint and by-product costing.

 READ the Learning Outcome Statements (LOS) for this topic as found in Appendix A and then study the concepts and calculations presented here to be sure you understand the content you could be tested on in the CMA exam.

Cost Behavior and Cost Objects

The first step in classifying a cost is to understand its behavior over a specific period of time. This period of time is called the *relevant range*, and the cost may be fixed or variable over the relevant range. A fixed cost will remain the same over the relevant range. A variable cost will vary in proportion to activity, volume, or some other cost driver. Total cost is the sum of all variable and fixed costs.

Relevant Range

Fixed and variable costs are defined with respect to specific cost drivers for a specific duration of time. Change any quantity by a large enough degree, and the fixed costs will no longer remain fixed. Change the quantity to zero, and typically all fixed costs will end, along with the product they are used to produce. Change the quantity above a certain level, and new plants or other capacity must be added. Therefore, fixed and variable costs are constrained by a **relevant range**. Fixed costs will remain constant over a discrete range of production activity.

For example: A manufacturing plant has fixed costs, such as rent and management salaries, and variable costs, such as production labor and material costs. The fixed costs will remain constant regardless of whether the plant has zero output or full production. The variable costs will not be incurred until production starts and then will increase as production increases.

Variable Costs

A **variable cost** includes changes in total for a cost object in proportion to each change in the quantity of a cost driver over a relevant range. Variable cost measured on a per-unit basis will remain constant over a relevant range (e.g., $5/unit within a relevant range of 1 to 5,000 units). Direct materials and direct labor are both variable costs because more materials and labor are needed if more units of a product are produced. Some indirect costs are also variable costs, such as sealants and adhesives used in the process that are difficult to track per unit but must be accounted for in the cost of each item.

For example: For a tennis ball manufacturer, as the quantity of tennis balls increases, the quantity of direct materials, such as rubber, and the quantity of direct labor will increase across the relevant range defined as the minimum and maximum output of the tennis ball machine (without having to change the size of the workforce).

Fixed Costs

Fixed costs are the portion of total costs that do not change when the quantity of a cost driver changes over a relevant range and duration. The duration is important because fixed costs may be constant one year and at a constant but higher level the next year. Fixed cost measured on a per-unit basis will decline (become less significant) as quantities increase: At 100 units, a $1,000 fixed cost is $10/unit, but at 1,000 units, it is only $1/unit.

Fixed costs can also be further classified as discretionary or committed:

- **Discretionary costs**, which are also known as managed or budgeted fixed costs, can be included or excluded from the budget at the discretion of the managers. Examples of discretionary costs include advertising, training, or internships, as well as indirect manufacturing labor and selling and administrative labor.
- **Committed costs** are costs that cannot be omitted due to strategic or operational priorities in the short run. An example is depreciation on equipment previously purchased. Committed fixed costs tend to be facilities related and result from prior capacity-related decisions.

Fixed costs include many indirect costs, such as depreciation, taxes, employees paid on salary, insurance, and lease costs. These costs usually are fixed because no matter the level of output within the relevant range, these costs will remain the same.

Figure 1C-1 shows both fixed and variable costs over a relevant range.

Figure 1C-1　Fixed and Variable Costs

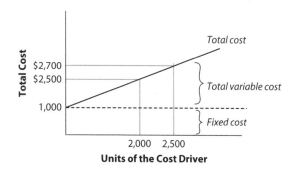

For a given output level, the next formula holds true:

Total Cost/Unit at a Given Output Level = Fixed Cost/Unit + Variable Cost/Unit

Total cost per unit will decline as output increases because the fixed costs are being allocated over greater quantities.

Step Costs

Step costs are fixed costs with very narrow relevant ranges. Step costs tend to be considered fixed costs over the short run but become variable costs over the long run.

For example: A company operates one plant. In the short run, the plant overhead is a fixed cost. If the plant's capacity is 100 units a day, an additional plant must be purchased to produce 200 units per day. A doubling in production capacity will also double the plant overhead cost (assuming that each plant has the same capacity and costs). In the long run, plant overhead becomes a variable cost.

The narrow relevant ranges on step costs can be step-fixed or step-variable. Step-fixed ranges increase in equal-size chunks over an equal number of cost drivers, such as plant overhead increasing by $100,000 for each plant added. Step-variable ranges go up to a higher constant cost in either increasingly larger or increasingly smaller amounts of a cost driver. Step-variable costs can increase or decrease at a predictable rate when they are caused by factors such as increasing learning curve rates for workers, diminishing marginal returns, or economies of scale.

For example, if one worker can produce 0.5 units per day, two workers can produce 1.0 unit, three workers can produce 1.5 units, and four workers can produce 3.0 units, the resulting step-variable costs would look like those in the right side of Figure 1C-2. The left side of this figure shows step-fixed costs using the plant overhead example.

Figure 1C-2 Step-Fixed and Step-Variable Costs

Total Cost and Mixed Cost

Total costs are all fixed and variable costs for a cost object. Total costs are also called **mixed costs** when they include both fixed and variable components.

Cost Type Relationships

Direct costs can be fixed or variable, and indirect costs can also be fixed or variable.

Capacity

Capacity measures the constraints or bottlenecks keeping a system from expanding in output or some other measure. Manufacturing capacity can be increased by adding plants, employees, or equipment. Financial capacity can be increased by gaining access to new debt or equity. Capacity relates to the relevant range, because the capacity limits often are reached at the upper limit of the relevant range. Furthermore, as capacity limits are approached, operations lose efficiency and increase in cost. This leads to the need to define a company's **practical capacity**, which is the highest output level a resource such as a plant can achieve without increasing its costs due to bottlenecks. When output exceeds the practical capacity, marginal costs begin to exceed marginal benefits. Practical capacity also takes into account normal operating conditions, such as the average number of errors or breakdowns, holidays and vacation time, and other realistic factors.

When such real-world factors are omitted, capacity is defined as **theoretical capacity**, or the upper limit on output assuming that nothing goes wrong, everything operates at full speed, and no holidays or other scheduling conflicts are included. Theoretical capacity is an ideal.

Capacity decisions made in the past generally will determine a company's present fixed costs. Fixed costs related to capacity choices include everything from the amount of space and resources devoted to each business unit, the size and cost of plants, to the amount of depreciation. These fixed costs are generally noncontrollable by division managers, who nevertheless feel the effect of these costs. If too much capacity is created, there are opportunity costs and high fixed costs at risk. If too little capacity is created, companies face other costs, such as overtime, lost sales, and higher wear and tear on facilities. Tracking the cost of excess capacity separately from the overall cost of an item can help show the cost of underutilized assets.

For example: If a plant's budgeted fixed overhead is $500,000 and overhead is applied by the units produced, the plant has a practical capacity level of 5,000 units per period, and overhead would by applied at $100/unit. If the plant budgeted only 4,000 units at $100/unit, $400,000 would be allocated to operations, and the remaining $100,000 would be treated as a separate period expense, tracked as the cost of having excess capacity. It is important to match the manager's incentives to the plant's practical capacity so that any decisions made to increase output can be weighed against the costs of increasing that output, holding inventory, and the like.

Although the prior definitions of capacity hinged on output, when capacity is defined by the expected demand for output or budgeted demand, it is called capacity utilization. **Normal capacity utilization** is a level of capacity utilization that will meet the average customer demand over a period, including the seasonal and cyclical variations or trends. Normal capacity utilization is a long-term tool that often is used over a period of several years. **Master budget capacity utilization** is normal capacity utilization for the current budget period, such as a year. It is important to use normal capacity utilization for long-term planning and master budget capacity utilization for shorter-term planning, or else the end costs can be inaccurate. Each of these capacity levels can be used to allocate costs, and each generally shows a different amount.

For example: In a plant with $500,000 in budgeted fixed overhead, if theoretical capacity is 8,000 units/period, practical capacity is 5,000 units/period, normal capacity utilization is 4,500 units/period, and master budget capacity is 4,000 units/period, the budgeted fixed cost per case would be $62.50, $100, $111, and $125 respectively. Similar results can be found with variable costs. Correct choice of capacity is therefore the key to cost analysis, management incentives, and performance evaluation decisions.

Cost Drivers

Firms manage their costs by determining how cost drivers affect a particular cost object. There are four types of cost drivers:

1. **Activity-based cost drivers** focus on operations that involve manufacturing or service activity, such as machine setup, machine use, or packaging.
2. **Volume-based cost drivers** focus on output, which involves aggregate measures, such as units produced or labor hours.
3. **Structural cost drivers** focus on company strategy, which involves long-term plans for scale, complexity, amount of experience in an area, or level of technical expertise.

4. **Executional cost drivers** focus on short-term operations, which involve reducing costs through concern with workforce commitment and involvement, production design, and supplier relationships.

Activity-Based Cost Drivers

Firms use an activity analysis to determine a detailed description of each type of activity. These descriptions form the basis for the activity-based cost drivers. The descriptions then are broken down into steps, and each step in the description becomes a different cost driver. The intent is to determine how changing the steps will change the overall cost of the operation. The cost of each step or activity can also be determined, and therefore the overall cost of a cost object can be determined. This detailed breakdown can help firms determine which activities add value for customers and which do not. Furthermore, when an activity costs more than is expected, activity-based cost drivers will highlight this discrepancy.

For example: Figure 1C-3 illustrates a few of the activities and cost drivers for a retailer.

Figure 1C-3 Retailer Activities and Cost Drivers

Activity	Cost Driver
Accepting cash	Number of cash transactions
Processing of credit card	Number of credit transactions
Payment of credit card fee	Dollar size of transactions
Close-out and supervisor review of clerk	Number of close-outs
Consolidation and deposit of receipts	Number of deposits
Bank account reconciliation	Number of accounts
Updating of customer account balances via computer	Number of accounts updated
Investigation of unusual transactions	Number of transactions investigated
Processing of returns and chargebacks	Number of chargebacks
Maintenance of computer equipment	Number of computer terminals
Training	Number of stores
Mailing of customer statements	Number of accounts

Volume-Based Cost Drivers

Volume-based cost drivers are aggregations of activities based on volume of use. Some cost drivers, such as direct materials and direct labor, are inherently volume-based. Direct labor is, by definition, the level of output for a volume of work at an hourly rate. Volume-based drivers such as direct labor often have a sloped curve in relation to output levels, as shown in Figure 1C-4.

Figure 1C-4 Total Cost and the Effect of Capacity Limits

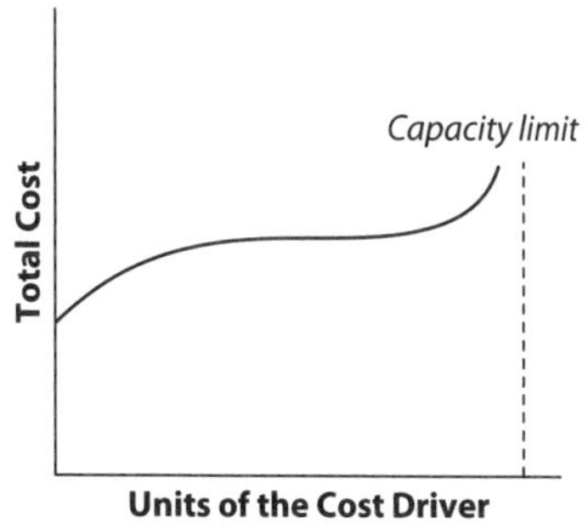

When a volume-based cost driver is very low, factors such as learning curves and efficient use of resources will cause costs to increase more slowly as production increases. This is called increasing marginal productivity, because the increasing output will use the inputs more efficiently. At a certain level, the total costs will level off, and a rise in volume will have a proportional rise in cost within the relevant range, until a certain point at which the capacity of the persons or equipment will reach the limit. As the volume increases toward the limit, the costs will rise dramatically because of increased need for repairs, more overtime, and other similar factors. This is called the law of diminishing marginal capacity.

Determining costs across the entire range of productivity would be hard to estimate without using complex calculations, which is why the relevant range is an important element of cost drivers.

Structural Cost Drivers

Structural cost drivers are long-term cost drivers based on the overall strategy of the company. There are four types of structural cost drivers: scale, experience level, technology, and complexity.

Scale

The scale of a project or the speed at which a company grows will affect all of the costs of the company overall. Deciding how many stores to open, how many employees to hire, or how much capital to devote to a project will affect costs directly.

Experience Level

The experience level of the company for a particular strategic desire will affect the overall cost of achieving that goal. The areas in which the company has the most expertise will be the cheapest areas to develop further, but if the market no longer needs such expertise, developing a new area of expertise could be more cost effective in the long run.

Technology

Changing the level of technology for a process can make that process more efficient and therefore less costly. The other benefit of investing in technology is that the products may be of higher quality; therefore, the firm may be able to increase market share with a cheaper and better product.

Complexity

The more complex a firm gets (more products, more levels of hierarchy), the more it costs to sustain that complexity. Reducing complexity will reduce both the costs of product development and the costs of distribution and service. Strategic decisions related to complexity usually are made to reduce overall complexity and cost. Conversely, a firm that has too few products or too small a staff may be missing out on market opportunities.

Executional Cost Drivers

Executional cost drivers are the short-term decisions that can be made to reduce operational costs. There are three types: workforce involvement, production process design, and supplier relationships.

Workforce Involvement

The greater the commitment of the workforce, the lower the labor costs will be in proportion to the amount of work that gets done. Many firms have been successful in improving quality and reducing labor costs by working to foster pride and commitment in the workplace through creative team building and an emphasis on consensus and employee input.

Production Process Design

Analyzing and redesigning production processes and incorporating software applications to streamline workflow have been key factors in reducing production costs for many firms.

Supplier Relationships

Close relationships with suppliers can reduce overall costs, especially inventory costs. With electronic data interchange (EDI) and similar applications, a firm can allow its supplier to view the company's inventory levels directly and automatically ship items as needed, resulting in a more efficient production flow.

Actual, Normal, and Standard Costing

Cost allocation is a method of applying costs to products, jobs, or services. Actual, normal, and standard costing are types of cost allocation. The terms *actual* and *normal* refer to the means of applying or allocating overhead costs to cost objects.

Actual costing uses the actual amounts for overhead costs. **Normal costing** uses the actual costs for labor and direct materials and uses a predetermined overhead rate for overhead. **Standard costing** uses a predetermined standard cost, also known as a "should" cost, for overhead, direct materials, and direct labor. All three of these methods are types of job order costing, in which costs are accumulated in inventory accounts (such as work-in-process [WIP] and finished goods inventory) and are recorded on the income statement as cost of goods sold (COGS) once the product is sold.

Actual Costing

An actual costing system records the actual costs incurred for *all* costs—including direct labor, direct material, and overhead. The actual costs are determined by waiting until the end of the accounting period and then calculating the actual costs based on the recorded amounts.

The primary benefit of actual costs is that they are more accurate than other costing systems. However, this reliability also means a delay in information, because the costs cannot be known until all of the invoices are received, which may not be until the end of the fiscal year or later. Because the number of units produced varies from period to period, and because the fixed costs do not vary with these production changes, actual costing makes costs per unit vary for products produced in different periods. To smooth out these fluctuations in the actual cost per unit, firms often turn to normal costing as an alternative method.

Normal Costing

Similar to actual costing, normal costing applies actual costs for direct materials and direct labor to a job, process, or other cost object and then uses a predetermined overhead rate to assign overhead to a cost object. This method allows current calculation of product costs and, by normalizing the fluctuations in overhead rates, enables comparisons between periods.

A predetermined factory overhead rate is applied to a job or other cost object, as determined in four steps:

1. Create an annual (or other period) budget for overhead costs.
2. Choose cost drivers (usually activity or volume) for charging overhead.
3. Estimate the total annual amount or volume of the selected cost driver for the total overhead costs or each cost pool.
4. Calculate the predetermined factory overhead rate by dividing the budgeted factory overhead costs by the estimated cost driver activity level:

$$\text{Predetermined Factory Overhead Rate} = \frac{\text{Budgeted Factory Overhead Costs}}{\text{Estimated Cost Driver Activity Level}}$$

Factory overhead using normal costing will be underapplied in some months and overapplied in others. The net amount overapplied is the amount of applied overhead that exceeds actual costs, and the net amount underapplied is the opposite. The net amount over- or underapplied is disposed of either by adjusting the COGS account or by prorating the net difference between the current period's applied overhead balances in the WIP inventory, finished goods inventory, and COGS accounts.

Adjusting Cost of Goods Sold

Suppose that $1,530,000 of actual overhead was incurred and $1,490,000 of overhead was allocated to products under normal costing. This means that overhead was underapplied by $40,000. Assuming that this underapplied amount is not material, the COGS should be increased by $40,000. The adjusting entry to the COGS account is shown in Figure 1C-5.

Figure 1C-5 Journal Entry to Record Disposition of Underapplied Overhead

	COGS Method	
Cost of Goods Sold	$40,000	
Factory Overhead Applied	$1,490,000	
Factory Overhead		$1,530,000

To record the disposition of underapplied overhead.

This entry closes the factory overhead applied and factory overhead accounts and debits (or increases) the cost of goods sold.

Under a different scenario, if $1,600,000 of overhead was allocated under normal costing and the actual overhead remained the same at $1,530,000 and if the $70,000 in overapplied overhead is not material, the adjusting entry to the COGS account would be as shown in Figure 1C-6. Note that the entry credits (decreases) cost of goods sold.

Figure 1C-6 Journal Entry to Record Disposition of Overapplied Overhead

	COGS Method	
Factory Overhead Applied	$1,600,000	
Factory Overhead		$1,530,000
Costs of Goods Sold		$70,000

To record the disposition of overapplied overhead.

Prorating Net Difference Between Inventories and Cost of Goods Sold

Factory overhead is accounted for in the WIP inventory, finished goods inventory, and COGS accounts, so when the net variance is material, it should be accounted for in each of these accounts in proportion to their relative size. If all production is complete, all goods are sold by the end of a period, and there is no balance in the WIP and finished goods inventory accounts, the simple COGS approach can be used. However, because production usually never ceases, the amount to be prorated to each account should be calculated. To determine the amount of overhead to apply to each account, the applied overhead in the ending inventories of each of these three accounts at the end of the period is divided by the sum of the applied overhead in the three accounts together.

For example: Assume that the applied overhead for each account is:

- Ending WIP inventory is $200,000.
- Ending finished goods inventory is $300,000.
- COGS is $1,000,000.

The ending WIP inventory proration is calculated as:

$$\frac{\$200,000}{\$1,500,000} = 0.133 = 13.3\%$$

If the finished goods are prorated at 20% and the COGS at 66.7% and if the variance were an underapplied overhead of $100,000, the WIP account would need to be increased by $13,300. Figure 1C-7 shows the adjusting entries.

Figure 1C-7 Journal Entry to Record Disposition of Underapplied Overhead

Inventory Account Allocation Method		
Factory Overhead Applied	$1,500,000	
Work-in Process Inventory	$13,300	
Finished Goods Inventory	$20,000	
Cost of Goods Sold	$66,700	
Factory Overhead		$1,600,000

To record the disposition of underapplied overhead.

Each inventory account is debited (or increased) by the amount shown. If $100,000 of overhead was overapplied (other factors staying the same), the adjusting entries would be as shown in Figure 1C-8.

Figure 1C-8 Journal Entry to Record Disposition of Overapplied Overhead

Inventory Account Allocation Method		
Factory Overhead Applied	$1,500,000	
Work-in-Process Inventory		$13,300
Finished Goods Inventory		$20,000
Cost of Goods Sold		$66,700
Factory Overhead		$1,400,000

To record the disposition of overapplied overhead.

Each inventory account is credited (or decreased) by the amount shown. If the difference is immaterial, COGS is adjusted; if the difference is material, the pro-rated method is used.

Standard Costing

Standard costing applies all product costs (direct materials, direct labor, and overhead) using a predetermined (standard) rate. A standard cost is an expected or target cost for an operation. Standard costing is designed to point out where variances occur so that the company can achieve a better operating result. Each standard cost is usually broken down into these two parts:

1. A standard number of units of a cost driver adjusted for actual unit production (e.g., labor hours divided by the units produced, such as 40,000 labor hours divided by 80,000 units produced = 0.5 labor hours per unit).
2. A standard rate per unit of the cost driver (e.g., $20 per labor hour)

Knowing the standard rate and the number of units produced allows calculation of the standard cost of direct labor or direct materials. Standard costs (e.g., standard number of hours times the standard rate per hour) then can be compared to actual total costs (e.g., total direct labor costs).

For example: In a given month with the same 80,000 units produced, actual labor hours may have been 42,000 at an actual rate of $18 per labor hour. These differences between standard costs and actual costs lead to budget variances.

Standards can be ideal or currently attainable, as set by company policy, activity analysis, historical data, market expectations, strategy, and benchmarking.

Two of the advantages of using standard costs are they are less likely to incorporate past inefficiencies and that they can be adapted as new data indicate expected changes during the budget period.

The disadvantages in standard costing include the problems associated with unreasonable standards, when the process used to set the standards are authoritarian or secretive, or when the standards are poorly communicated. Inflexible standards or those that place undue emphasis on profits are likely to fail.

Absorption (Full) and Variable (Direct) Costing

Absorption costing (or full costing) is an inventory costing system that includes both variable and fixed manufacturing costs. Under absorption costing, inventory absorbs all costs of manufacturing. **Variable costing** (or direct costing) is an inventory costing method that includes only the variable manufacturing costs in the inventory costs and excludes fixed manufacturing costs. Variable costing expenses fixed manufacturing costs in the period in which the costs are incurred. Each method expenses all nonmanufacturing costs (both fixed and variable) in the period in which they occur. Therefore, these two methods differ only in how they account for fixed manufacturing costs.

Figure 1C-9 Variable versus Absorption Costing

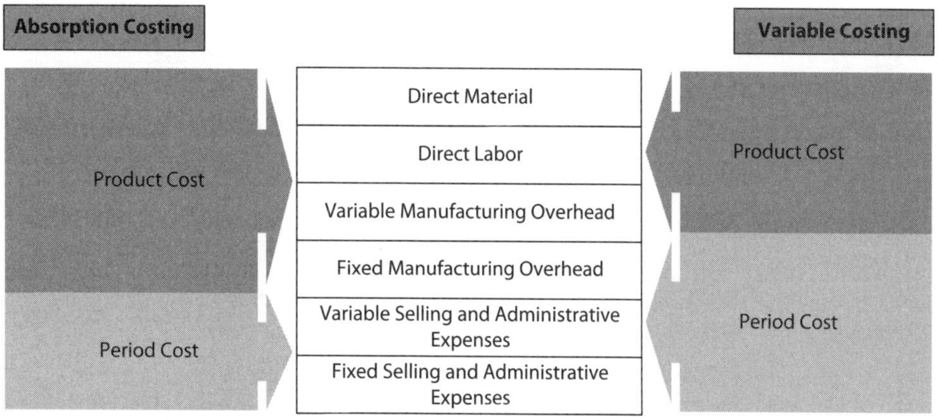

The difference between variable and absorption costing lies with the treatment of fixed manufacturing overhead. Absorption costing treats fixed manufacturing overhead as a product cost. Variable costing treats it as a period cost.

Income Statement Preparation Using Absorption and Variable Costing

Because variable costing and absorption costing have different objectives concerning the importance of the information presented on the income statement, each is usually presented in its own format. The variable costing method uses a contribution margin format, which highlights the distinction between fixed and variable costs. The absorption method uses the gross margin format, which highlights the differences between manufacturing and nonmanufacturing costs. The variable manufacturing costs are accounted for in the same manner in both income statements. The absorption method is the format required for external reporting.

The primary differences between the two statements are that under variable costing, the fixed manufacturing costs are deducted as an expense, whereas under absorption costing, each finished unit absorbs its share of the fixed manufacturing costs, which flows through to the finished goods inventory accounts. When production does not equal sales, net income will differ between absorption and variable costing. If more units are produced than sold, absorption costing will have higher net income because costs are all sitting in inventory, whereas variable costing will have lower net income because not as many costs end up in inventory compared to cost of goods sold.

Another difference is that when using absorption costing, fixed manufacturing costs in ending inventory are deferred to future periods whereas variable costing expenses the entire amount in the period in which the inventory is created.

Figure 1C-10 Variable Costing versus Absorption Costing Example

Variable Costing			Absorption Costing		
Revenues:			**Revenues:**		
$200 × 500 units		$100,000	$200 × 500 units		$100,000
Variable costs			**Costs of goods sold**		
Beginning inventory	$0		Beginning inventory	$0	
+ Variable manufacturing costs: $30 × 700	+21,000		+ Variable manufacturing costs: $30 × 700	+21,000	
= Cost of goods available for sale	21,000		+ Fixed manufacturing costs: $25 × 700	+17,500	
− Ending inventory: $30 × 200	− 6,000		= Cost of goods available for sale	38,500	
= Variable cost of goods Sold	15,000		− Ending inventory: ($30 variable + $25 fixed) × 200	−11,000	
+ Variable marketing costs: $20 × 500	+10,000		= Cost of goods sold		−27,500
= Total variable costs		−25,000			
= Contribution margin		75,000	= Gross margin		72,500
Fixed costs			**Operating costs**		
Fixed manufacturing costs: $25 × 700	17,500		Variable marketing costs: $20 × 500	10,000	
+ = Fixed marketing costs	+14,000		+ Fixed marketing costs	+14,000	
+/− Adjustment for fixed cost variances	0		+/− Adjustment for operating cost variances	0	
= Total fixed costs		−31,500	= Total operating costs		−24,000
= **Operating income**		**$43,500**	= **Operating income**		**$48,500**

For example: Figure 1C-10 shows each type of costing and each type of format. The data used for both sides of the table are the same.

- Units made: 700
- Units sold: 500
- Variable manufacturing costs per unit: $30
- Variable selling (marketing) costs per unit: $20
- Fixed manufacturing costs per unit: $25
- Fixed selling (marketing) costs: $14,000

In summary, when inventory increases, net income under absorption costing will be greater than under variable costing by the amount of the fixed cost of the change in inventory (200 units × $25 = $5,000 in Figure 1C-10). When inventory decreases, net income under absorption costing will be less than under variable costing by the amount of the change in inventory fixed cost. However, as methods such as just-in-time production and other inventory reduction methods increase in importance, the differences between variable and absorption costing will grow less material because inventory levels are less significant. In fact, if a company has zero inventory at the beginning and end of each accounting period, there is no difference between these two methods of costing.

Benefits and Limitations of Absorption and Variable Costing

Absorption costing is the standard method because both the U. S. Internal Revenue Service (IRS) and generally accepted accounting principles (GAAP) require its use. However, absorption costing allows managers to manipulate operating income simply by increasing production. If bonuses or other incentives are tied to operating income, managers may increase inventory even if no additional demand exists. Managers also may choose to produce items that absorb the highest fixed manufacturing costs instead of what is best for the company. To fix this and other improper management incentives, the company could switch to variable costing for internal reporting, allow managers less latitude in selecting what to produce, or provide a disincentive for accumulating inventory, such as a percentage carrying charge for all ending inventory.

Variable costing is used when the emphasis is on what items can be traced to and controlled by a responsibility center. Because fixed costs generally are outside the control of the center's manager, many companies focus only on the areas that can be controlled.

Variable costing is very effective in supporting internal decision making and is required for cost-volume-profit analysis.

Joint Product and By-Product Costing

Joint products are products that share a portion of the production process and have relatively the same sales value. **By-products** are products that share the same production process with a product or joint product but have relatively minor value in comparison to the main product. The oil industry uses a joint manufacturing process, where crude oil is refined into joint products, such as diesel, gasoline, motor oil, and plastic. A lumber mill may have finished boards and the scrap that could be used in plywood (a joint product), whereas the sawdust is used in other products (by-products). Both joint products and by-products share at least some of the same raw materials and initial processing costs. The split-off point is the point at which products diverge and become separately identifiable. The split-off point is not necessarily the point at which the products become finished goods.

Costing for joint products and by-products includes all manufacturing costs incurred before and after the split-off point. For financial reporting, joint costs incurred before the split-off point are allocated among the joint products. Additional processing costs (separable costs) are any costs that can be specifically identified with a product because the cost occurs after the split-off point where the costs are assigned to the separate products.

Two basic approaches can be taken for allocating joint costs to joint products: using data based on the market (such as revenues) or using data based on physical measures (such as weight or volume).

Market-Based Methods of Allocating Joint Costs to Joint Products

The market-based methods include:

- Sales value at split-off method
- Gross profit method
- NRV method

Sales Value at Split-off Method

The **sales value at split-off method** (also known as the sales value method) is widely used because of its simplicity. The sales value method can be used only when sales values are available at the split-off point. It allocates joint costs to joint products using their proportional sales value at the split-off point.

For example: A paper mill incurs $8,000 in joint costs when selling finished paper for $4 a pound and semifinished paper for $2 a pound. The process produces 1,000 pounds of finished paper and 3,000 pounds of semifinished paper. The steps for allocating this cost to each product are described next.

1. Calculate the total sales value for each joint product, which is the price per unit multiplied by the number of units. The sales value is not the record of actual sales but a calculation of value.

$$1,000 \text{ pounds} \times \$4 = \$4,000$$
$$3,000 \text{ pounds} \times \$2 = \$6,000$$

2. Calculate the proportion of the sales value for each joint product to the total sales value.

$$\frac{\$4,000}{\$10,000} = 0.4 = 40\% \qquad \frac{\$6,000}{\$10,000} = 0.6 = 60\%$$

3. Multiply the joint cost by the proportional amount of the sales value. This becomes the COGS and is the amount allocated to each product cost.

$$\$8,000 \times 0.4 = \$3,200 \qquad \$8,000 \times 0.6 = \$4,800$$

4. Calculate the cost per unit (pound) by dividing the COGS (proportional cost) from the previous step by the number of units (pounds). (Note that although the remaining methods do not show this step, the cost per unit can be calculated in the same manner.)

$$\frac{\$3,200}{1,000 \text{ pounds}} = \$3.20/\text{pound} \qquad \frac{\$4,800}{1,000 \text{ pounds}} = \$1.60/\text{pound}$$

5. Calculate the gross margin for each product by subtracting the sales value from the proportional cost:

$$\$4,000 - \$3,200 = \$800 \qquad \$6,000 - \$4,800 = \$1,200$$

Assuming that the sales prices are accurate estimates and if no extra processing is needed on the joint products, the sales value method has the advantage of providing the same gross margin percentage for both joint products. The gross margin percentage is calculated by dividing the gross margin by the sales value:

$$\frac{\$800}{\$4,000} = 0.2 = 20\% \qquad\qquad \frac{\$1,200}{\$6,000} = 0.2 = 20\%$$

The sales value method is widely used because it is both simple to calculate and allocates costs according to the value of the products. Other methods, such as the physical measure method, do not allocate costs according to value and therefore sometimes can allocate so much cost to a product that it has no gross profit margin whereas its counterpart joint product has a huge profit margin. The sales value method has the limitation of not being useful for products that need additional processing after the split-off point before a sales value is established. This method also may be less useful for products that have frequent market price fluctuations.

Gross Profit (Constant Gross Margin Percentage) Method

The **gross profit method,** also called the constant gross margin percentage method, allocates joint costs so as to provide the same gross margin percentage of profit for each joint product.

For example: Assume the same data from the paper mill example, except that in this case, the joint products share $5,000 in joint costs, finished paper has $2,000 in additional processing costs, and semifinished paper has $1,000 in additional processing costs after the split-off point. The steps for the gross profit method are:

1. Calculate the total gross margin percentage. To do this, first determine the final sales value by multiplying the price per unit by the number of units produced.

    $$1,000 \text{ Pounds} \times \$4 = \$4,000$$
    $$3,000 \text{ Pounds} \times \$2 = \$6,000$$

    The total of these amounts ($10,000) less all joint and separable costs is the gross margin:

    $$\$10,000 - \$5,000 - \$2,000 - \$1,000 = \$2,000 \text{ Gross Margin}$$

    The gross margin percentage is the gross margin divided by the total sales value:

    $$\frac{\$2,000}{\$10,000} = 0.2 = 20\%$$

2. To determine the total costs that each product will bear, multiply the gross margin percentage by each individual sales value amount, and then deduct this amount from the sales value to determine the cost:

    $$\$4,000 \times 0.2 = \$800 \qquad\qquad \$6,000 \times 0.2 = \$1,200$$
    $$\$4,000 - \$800 = \$3,200 \qquad\qquad \$6,000 - \$1,200 = \$4,800$$

3. Deduct the additional processing costs from the total costs to determine the joint cost that must be allocated to each product:

$3,200 − $2,000 = $1,200 Joint Cost Allocated to Finished Paper
$4,800 − $1,000 = $3,800 Joint Cost Allocated to Semifinished Paper
$5,000 Total Joint Costs

The final step in this method distinguishes the gross profit method from the other methods because it takes into account the costs incurred before and after the split-off point. Thus, this method is not only a joint cost allocation method but also a profit allocation method. Both the joint costs and the total gross margin are allocated to a joint product to maintain a constant gross margin.

One benefit of the gross profit method is that it can be used even when there are additional processing costs. The amount of the joint costs allocated to each product is not always a positive number; a joint product could get a negative allocation of joint costs in order to make the gross margin percentage equal to the overall average for the entity. This is an advantage for companies that wish to keep the same margin for each product, but it could lead to a distortion in the fairness of how costs are allocated.

Net Realizable Value Method

The **net realizable value** (NRV) method, also known as the estimated NRV method, is used when the market price for one or more of the joint products cannot be determined at the split-off point, usually because additional processing is needed. The product's final sales value less additional processing costs is its NRV.

NRV = Sales Value − Additional Processing Cost

For example: Assume the same paper mill example, except that an additional 1,000 pounds of scrap can now be sold directly to a paper recycling business, with no additional cost, for $1 per pound.

The steps for calculating the NRV are shown next.

1. Calculate the NRV for each joint product. To do this, start by calculating the sales value for each unit, which is the price per unit multiplied by the number of units.

Finished Paper 1,000 Pounds × $4 = $4,000
Semifinished Paper 3,000 Pounds × $2 = $6,000
By-Products 1,000 Pounds × $1 = $1,000

The NRV is calculated using this final sales value. (For products with no additional processing cost, the sales value is the NRV.)

	Final Sales Value	−	**Additional Processing Costs**	=	**NRV**
Finished Paper	$4,000	−	$2,000	=	$2,000
Semifinished Paper	$6,000	−	$1,000	=	$5,000
By-Products					$1,000
			Total NRV		$8,000

2. Calculate the proportion of the NRV for each joint and by-product to the total NRV:

<table>
<tr><td>Finished Paper</td><td>Semifinished Paper</td><td>By-Products</td></tr>
<tr><td>$\dfrac{\$2,000}{\$8,000} = 25\%$</td><td>$\dfrac{\$5,000}{\$8,000} = 62.5\%$</td><td>$\dfrac{\$1,000}{\$8,000} = 12.5\%$</td></tr>
</table>

3. Multiply the joint cost by the proportional amount of the NRV. This is the amount allocated to each product cost.

$$\$5,000 \times 0.25 = \$1,250$$
$$\$5,000 \times 0.625 = \$3,125$$
$$\$5,000 \times 0.25 = \$625$$

Like the sales value method, this method allocates values in proportion to the value of the product and produces predictable profit margins.

Physical Measure Methods of Allocating Joint Costs to Joint Products

The physical measure, or units-of-production, method uses a physical measurement to allocate joint costs to joint products. Physical measures include weight, number, and volume. Measures can be input measures, such as pounds of paper, or output measures, such as pounds, cans, packages, or crates. The physical measure method is called the average cost method when output is used to allocate joint costs.

For example: A paper mill sells finished paper for $4 a pound and semifinished paper for $2 a pound; the process produces 1,000 pounds of finished paper, 3,000 pounds of semifinished paper, and 1,000 pounds of scrap. It costs $8,000 for the entire process, with no additional processing costs.

The steps for allocating joint costs using the physical measure method with an input measure of pounds are shown next.

1. Calculate the average cost per unit of the total joint cost by dividing the total joint costs by the total number of pounds (ignoring scrap, waste, and by-products):

$$\text{Average Cost/Unit} = \frac{\$8,000}{4,000 \text{ Pounds}} = \$2/\text{Pound}$$

2. Multiply the average cost per unit by the total number of units to determine the amount of the joint cost to allocate to each product:

$2/Pound $\times$ 1,000 Pounds = $2,000 Cost Allocated to Finished Paper

$2/Pound $\times$ 3,000 Pounds = $6,000 Cost Allocated to Semifinished Paper

Thus the gross margin for finished paper is $2,000 ($4,000 gross profit − $2,000 cost), making the profit margin for finished paper 50% ($2,000/ $4,000). The gross margin for semifinished paper is $0 ($6,000 gross profit − $6,000 cost). Semifinished paper has no profit margin.

Although the physical measure method is easy to use and employs objective criteria for measurement, it has more drawbacks than benefits. As shown in the example, the physical measure method can produce gross profit margins that could frustrate managers and distort profits. This is because the value of the joint product is not accounted for at all, unless the relevant physical measure conveys the value of each of the items. For example, gold melted into ounces or bars measured by weight would still be correctly valued (unless the processing added artistic or utilitarian value). Another limitation would be for processes that cannot all be measured using the same units, such as pounds and gallons. Lastly the physical units method is not considered GAAP.

Accounting Treatment of Joint Products and By-Products

Joint product costs, once allocated using one of the methods just discussed, become part of inventory costs and are divided among the various finished goods. According to GAAP, all joint costs that can be considered manufacturing costs should be allocated to joint products for purposes of financial reporting and taxation.

By-products can be accounted for in two different ways: the asset recognition approach or the revenue method. If the firm can assign an inventoriable value to by-products at the split-off point, it uses an asset recognition approach. In this case, in the period in which the by-product is produced, it can record the NRV (NRV = Sales Value − Additional Processing Cost) of the by-products as inventory on the balance sheet and as a deduction from the total manufacturing cost on the income statement.

Alternatively, in the period in which the by-product is produced, the firm can record the NRV of the by-products as other income (or other sales revenue item) on the income statement. These methods follow the matching principle of accrual accounting because the firm matches the value of the by-product with its cost to manufacture. Therefore, recognition at the time of production is considered more appropriate if the amounts are material. When by-product is sold, the inventory cost is recorded as the cost of sales.

If the firm cannot assign an inventoriable value to by-products at the split-off point, it can recognize the by-product at the time of sale using a revenue method. The firm can record the net sales revenue from a by-product as other income (or other sales revenue item) on the income statement. Alternately, at the time of sale, it can record the net sales revenue as a reduction of the total manufacturing cost on the income statement.

The revenue methods are simpler to use and are based on the concepts of revenue realization but should be reserved for immaterial amounts.

Exercise: Absorption versus Full Costing

Consider the following information:

Units made	1,000
Units sold	750
Variable manufacturing costs per unit	$ 35
Variable selling costs per unit	$ 25
Fixed manufacturing costs per unit	$ 20
Fixed selling costs	$ 20,000
Beginning inventory (in units)	0
Ending inventory (in units)	250
Unit selling price	$150

In the space provided, prepare a variable costing and absorption costing income statement.

Exercise Solution

Variable Costing Operating Income Statement

Revenues		$ 112,500
Variable cost of goods sold:		
Beginning Inventory	$ –	
Variable manufacturing costs	35,000	
Cost of goods available for sale	35,000	
Less Ending Inventory	(8,750)	
Variable cost of goods sold	26,250	
Variable selling costs	18,750	
Total variable costs		45,000
Contribution margin		$ 67,500
Fixed costs		
Fixed manufacturing costs	$ 20,000	
Fixed selling costs	20,000	
Total fixed costs		$ 40,000
Operating income		$ 27,500

Absorption Costing Operating Income Statement

Revenues		$112,500
Variable cost of goods sold:		
Beginning inventory	0	
Variable manufacturing costs	$ 35,000	
Fixed manufacturing costs	20,000	
Cost of goods available for sale	$ 55,000	
Less: ending Inventory*	(13,750)	
Cost of goods sold		$ 41,250
Gross margin		$ 71,250
Operating costs:		
Variable selling costs	18,750	
Fixed selling costs	20,000	
Total operating costs		$ 38,750
Operating income		$ 32,500
Difference in absorption costing versus variable Costing		**$ 5,000**

*Includes both fixed and variable costs

**Knowledge Check:
Measurement Concepts**

The next questions are intended to help you check your understanding and recall of the material presented in this topic. They do not represent the type of questions that appear on the CMA exam.

Directions: Answer each question in the space provided. Correct answers and section references appear after the knowledge check questions.

1. Match the following types of cost drivers with an appropriate example of that cost driver.

   _____ Activity-based cost driver   a. Redesigning a production process to remove unnecessary steps

   _____ Volume-based cost driver   b. High-technology machine replacing an older unit

   _____ Structural cost driver   c. Labor hours spent driving a truck

   _____ Executional cost drivers   d. Number of invoices processed for billing

2. A plant meters electricity usage at the department level. The department contains several product operations, including the manufacturing of tennis balls. For a can of tennis balls, electricity is considered which of the following?

   ☐ **a.** A variable indirect cost

   ☐ **b.** A variable direct cost

   ☐ **c.** A fixed indirect cost

   ☐ **d.** A fixed direct cost

3. If a firm is more concerned with reliability of data than with the speed at which the data are available, which of the following costing methods would be the best fit?

   ☐ **a.** Variable (direct) costing

   ☐ **b.** Standard costing

   ☐ **c.** Normal costing

   ☐ **d.** Actual costing

4. Using variable costing, fixed manufacturing overhead costs are treated as _____ costs. Using absorption costing, fixed manufacturing overhead costs are treated as _____ costs.

5. Three market-based methods of allocating joint costs to joint products are:

    a. NRV method

    b. Sales value at split-off method

    c. _____

6. Complete the equation for NRV:

    NRV = Sales Value − _____

Knowledge Check Answers: Measurement Concepts

1. Match the following types of cost drivers with an appropriate example of that cost driver. *[See Cost Drivers.]*

   __d__   Activity-based cost driver

   __c__   Volume-based cost driver

   __b__   Structural cost driver

   __a__   Executional cost drivers

   a. Redesigning a production process to remove unnecessary steps

   b. High technology machine replacing an older unit

   c. Labor hours spent driving a truck

   d. Number of invoices processed for billing

2. A plant meters electricity usage at the department level. The department contains several product operations, including the manufacturing of tennis balls. For a can of tennis balls, electricity is considered which of the following? *[See Variable Costs.]*

   ☑ **a.** A variable indirect cost

   ☐ **b.** A variable direct cost

   ☐ **c.** A fixed indirect cost

   ☐ **d.** A fixed direct cost

3. If a firm is more concerned with reliability of data than with the speed at which the data are available, which of the following costing methods would be the best fit? *[See Actual Costing.]*

   ☐ **a.** Variable (direct) costing

   ☐ **b.** Standard costing

   ☐ **c.** Normal costing

   ☑ **d.** Actual costing

4. Using variable costing, fixed manufacturing overhead costs are treated as **period** costs. Using absorption costing, fixed manufacturing overhead costs are treated as **product** costs. *[See Absorption (Full) and Variable (Direct) Costing.]*

5. Three market-based methods of allocating joint costs to joint products are: *[See Market-Based Methods of Allocating Joint Costs to Joint Products.]*

   a. NRV method

   b. Sales value at split-off method

   c. Gross profit method

6. Complete the equation for net realizable value: *[See Net Realizable Value Method.]*

   NRV = Sales Value − Additional Processing Cost

Costing Systems

COSTING SYSTEMS ARE USED TO accumulate costs and assign them to a particular cost object, such as a product or service. Costing systems and the cost data they contain provide strategic value by helping businesses manage costs and price their products and services appropriately.

This topic covers job order costing, process costing, activity-based costing (ABC), life-cycle costing, and other methods of cost accumulation.

 READ the Learning Outcome Statements (LOS) for this topic as found in Appendix A and then study the concepts and calculations presented here to be sure you understand the content you could be tested on in the CMA exam.

Cost Flows in a Manufacturing Organization

It is important to understand how cost flows are processed in a manufacturing organization. Certain inputs are fed into the cost of the product to determine the product's total cost. A representation of this cost flow is presented in Figure 1C-10a.

Figure 1C-10a Cost Flows in a Manufacturing Organization

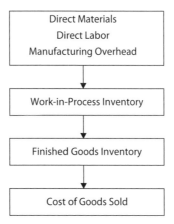

Job Order versus Process Costing

Companies typically adopt one of two basic types of costing systems when they need to assign costs to products or services:

1. **Job order costing (job costing)** assigns costs to a specific job (a distinct unit, batch, or lot of a product or service).
2. **Process costing** accumulates product or service costs by process or department and then assigns them to a large number of nearly identical products by dividing the total costs by the total number of units produced.

Job order costing is used when the product or service has costs that can be, and often need to be, tracked and assigned to a specific job or service. For example, job costing is used for capital asset construction (buildings, ships) in the manufacturing sector; advertising campaigns, research and development, and repair jobs in the service sector; and custom mail-order items and special promotions in the merchandising sector. Costs for these products, projects, or services can be easily tracked to the product, project, or service.

Process costing is used for multiple, nearly identical units that can be organized into a flow. A process costing system would be suitable for products and services such as newspapers, books, and soft drinks in the manufacturing sector; check processing and postal delivery in the service sector; and magazine subscription receipts in the merchandising sector. These products tend to be homogeneous in nature, meaning they are all alike or very similar, and therefore it is not necessary to track costs to a specific unit of product or service.

Both costing systems share the overall purpose of assigning direct materials, direct labor, and manufacturing overhead to products. Both use the same accounts, including direct materials inventory, work-in-process (WIP) inventory, finished goods inventory, and cost of goods sold (COGS). Job costing differs from process costing in how costs are accumulated. In a job costing system, costs are accumulated by job. In a process costing system, costs are accumulated by department. Job costing uses a job sheet or equivalent software to track specific items, whereas process costing uses a production cost report to track all department costs. Job costing computes unit cost by job at the end of the job. Under process costing, unit costs are computed at the end of the accounting period, after total department costs are available. Most companies use a combination of the two methods, especially when they have some specific and some mass-produced products or services.

Job Order Costing

The procedures outlined previously for actual, normal, and standard costing can be used in job order costing. The basic steps in using job costing to assign costs to a job are:

1. Identify the job, typically with a unique code or hierarchical reference, including a date.
2. Trace the direct costs for the job (direct materials, direct labor).

3. Identify indirect cost pools associated with the job (overhead).
4. Select the cost allocation base (cost drivers) to be used in allocating indirect cost pools to the job.
5. Calculate the rate per unit of each cost allocation base. The actual indirect cost rate is calculated as shown:

$$\text{Actual Indirect Cost Rate} = \frac{\text{Actual Total Cost in Indirect Cost Pool}}{\text{Actual Total Quantity of Cost Driver}}$$

6. Assign cost to the cost object by adding all direct costs and indirect costs.

For example: Smith Company is a shipbuilding firm that manufactures yachts. It uses actual costing.

1. The yacht in question is identified as job number 123.
2. The direct costs for the job are $40,000 in direct materials and $60,000 in direct labor.
3. The total annual indirect cost for all projects is $60,000 for the first pool and $120,000 for the second pool.
4. The first pool is measured in machine hours: 20,000. The second pool is measured in direct labor hours: 30,000 for all projects for the entire year.
5. The actual indirect cost rate is calculated as:

$$\text{Actual Indirect Cost Rate} = \frac{\$60,000}{20,000 \text{ Machine Hours}} = \$3/\text{Machine Hour}$$

$$= \frac{\$120,000}{30,000 \text{ Labor Hours}} = \$4/\text{Labor Hour}$$

6. All direct costs are added to indirect costs. Indirect costs are based on a combination of machine and labor hours:

Direct costs:	
Direct materials	$40,000
Direct labor	60,000
Total direct costs	100,000
Indirect costs:	
2,000 machine hours @ $3/MH	$6,000
3,000 direct labor hours @ $4/DLH	12,000
Total indirect costs	18,000
Total manufacturing costs	$118,000
Yacht selling price	$140,000
Less total manufacturing costs	118,000
Gross profit margin	$22,000

Gross margin % = $22,000 / $140,000 = 15.7%

Spoilage, Rework, and Scrap in Job Costing

Companies want to reduce the amount of spoilage, rework, and scrap they produce in order to maximize the value of their raw materials.

Spoilage

Spoilage is any material or good that is considered unacceptable and is discarded or sold for its disposal value. Spoilage can be normal or abnormal. Normal spoilage is any unit of production that is deemed unacceptable during the normal production process, assuming efficient operating conditions. Normal spoilage is considered part of the cost of operations and therefore is part of the cost of good units produced. Normal spoilage can be a direct cost to a particular job or an indirect cost to production in general (allocated to factory overhead). If charged directly to a job, spoilage can be reduced by any estimated salvage value.

Abnormal spoilage is any unacceptable product that should not normally exist under efficient and normal operating conditions. Any spoilage over the amount considered normal is allocated to a loss from abnormal spoilage account.

Use the next formula to calculate total spoilage:

 Total Spoilage = Beginning Inventory + Units Started − Units Completed and Transferred Out − Ending Inventory

A variation of this formula would be:

 Total Spoilage = Beginning Inventory + Units Started = (Units Complete and Transferred Out + Spoilage) + Ending Inventory

For example: At Peter's Plastics, the manufacturing cost per unit is $15. During the month, Peter's produces 10,000 good units. Despite efficient operations, limitations on the plastic molds produces 100 units of normal spoilage. In addition, 50 units spoiled because of unusual machine breakdowns.

The calculation of total good units completed (including normal spoilage) is:

Manufacturing costs of good units (units × manufacturing costs per unit)	$150,000
Normal spoilage costs (normal spoilage units × manufacturing costs per unit)	1,500
	$151,500

The calculation of total good units completed (including normal spoilage) is:

Manufacturing costs per good unit (total cost with spoilage/good units)	$15.15
Normal spoilage rate (spoiled units/good units)	1%

The cost of abnormal spoilage is calculated as:

Units lost from abnormal spoilage	50
Manufacturing cost per unit	$15
Cost of abnormal spoilage	$750

Rework

Rework is any finished product that must have additional work performed on it before it can be sold. It is divided into categories as rework needed on:

- Normal defective units for a specific job. Charged to a specific job's WIP inventory account (increasing the cost and reducing profits)
- Normal defective units common with all jobs. Charged to factory overhead
- Abnormal defective units. Charged to loss from abnormal rework account

Scrap

Scrap is a portion of a product or leftover material that has no economic value. It can be categorized by whether it relates to a specific job or is common to all jobs. Specific job scrap is charged to the job's WIP inventory account. Scrap that is common to all jobs is charged to factory overhead. Either method increases the cost from the affected account. Scrap costs are not accounted for separately, but if scrap is sold, the accountant will credit (reduce) either WIP inventory or overhead accounts by the price received for the scrap.

Job Order Costing Benefits and Limitations

Job order costing can provide very detailed results of a specific job or operation so it is ideal for specific jobs. For large processes, job order costing is less valuable because it is impractical to assign individual costs to mass-produced items on a daily basis. Job order costing can accommodate multiple costing methods, such as actual, normal, and standard costing, so it is flexible enough to be used by a wide variety of companies.

Job order costing can have a strategic value for a business because it gives a detailed breakdown of all of the different types of costs. The gross margin and gross profit margin can be used to compare the company's profitability across different jobs. For jobs that did poorly, the company can analyze whether the cost overruns were from direct labor costs, direct materials costs, or one of the indirect cost pools.

Process Costing

Process costing is recommended for companies that have mass production processes of identical or nearly identical products. Such companies track their quantities and costs on a departmental production cost report and calculate the unit cost at the end of a period by dividing the total cost of an operation or department by the total units produced.

Process costing is good for any highly automated or repetitive process. The strategic value of process costing for such companies is that they can be in continuous operations while still receiving timely, accurate, and relatively inexpensive cost information each period, due in part to the use of equivalent units. Process costing also uses production cost reports, which have built-in checks, such as balancing units to be accounted for against units accounted for.

Equivalent Units in Process Costing

Unlike job costing, in which partially completed units have a cost already attached to them, process costing cannot easily determine values for partially completed units because the accounting highlights costs for processes or departments, not jobs or items. Therefore, process costing must find the combined cost for all units, including all units partially complete at the beginning and end of the accounting period. *Partially complete* means that the item is still in WIP inventory so items that are considered complete by one department are not actually complete until they enter finished goods inventory. At the end of the period, either a production manager or an engineer gives an estimate of what percentage of units remains on the production line or in WIP inventory.

Because product cost is calculated by determining the cost per unit in each department, partially completed units must be factored into these calculations. At the end of an accounting period, a process costing system accounts for any WIP inventory as equivalent units. An **equivalent unit (EU)** is a measure of the amount of work done on partially completed units expressed in terms of how many complete units could have been created with the same amount of work. EUs are necessary because a continuous process is being divided into artificial time periods.

Engineers calculate EUs separately for direct labor, direct materials, and overhead because one category may be more complete than another for the same product. Each category is calculated in a similar fashion: Multiply the number of units that are partially complete by the estimated percentage that are complete overall.

For example: If direct labor on 1,000 cans of tennis balls is 30% complete, they would total 300 equivalent direct labor units. If the same tennis balls were complete but needed to be canned, the material costs could be 90% complete and therefore would total 900 equivalent direct materials units.

Beginning Inventory

Beginning inventory items that are a certain percentage complete were accounted for in the last accounting period at that percentage of completion, so the remaining percentage that needs to be completed is used instead. Therefore, if an item in beginning inventory is 30% complete, the remaining 70% incomplete is the basis for the EU calculation. (1,000 actual units would be 700 EUs.) However, not all methods account for beginning inventory in their calculations.

The formula for calculating the total EUs of production is:

Equivalent Production Units = [Beginning Inventory Units × (100% − % Complete Beginning Inventory] + Units Started and Completed During the Period + Equivalent Units in Ending WIP Inventory

Conversion Costs

Some firms measure only direct materials separately and combine direct labor and overhead, which are collectively called **conversion costs**. When the direct labor is not a significant portion of the costs due to a highly automated environment, such firms combine direct labor with overhead when performing calculations, such as determining EUs.

Conversion cost works well for companies using labor-based cost drivers, but those companies that use nonlabor-based drivers, such as number of setups or machine hours, find it better to calculate labor and overhead separately.

Process Costing Cost Flows

Unlike job costing, which moves costs through jobs directly, the cost flow in process costing is routed through processes and departments. In process costing, each department must have its own WIP inventory account. Because direct materials, direct labor, and overhead are incurred by each department involved, these charges can be made to each department, not just the first department. When departments complete their portion of work on a product, all of the costs are transferred to the next department's WIP inventory account by debiting a transferred-in costs account on the next department's books. When goods are completed, the cost of goods completed is transferred to finished goods inventory.

For example: The accounting entries for two different departments working on the same product are shown in Figure 1C-11.

Steps in Preparing a Production Cost Report

Individual departments prepare a production cost reports that contain all physical units and EUs, ending WIP inventories, costs incurred during the period, costs assigned to units completed, and costs assigned to units transferred out. Production cost reports are prepared using five steps:

1. Determine the flow of physical units. Both input and output units are accounted for when determining the units that are on hand at the beginning of the period, the units that are initiated or received, the units that are finished and transferred out, and the units that are in ending WIP inventory. Beginning WIP inventory and the units that enter the production department during the period are input

Figure 1C-11 T-Account Cost Flow Model Using Process Costing

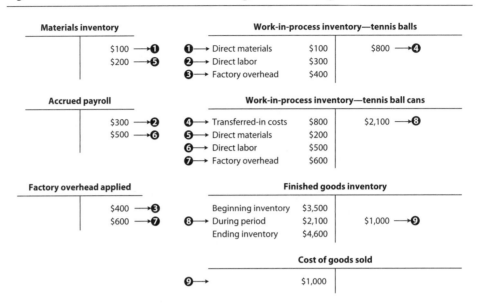

Note: Circled numbers indicate cost inputs and outputs of the process.

units. For a particular department, units that are completed and transferred out and units remaining in WIP inventory at the end of the period are output units.

2. Determine the equivalent units.

   (Steps 1 and 2 analyze production quantities and measure the total work effort for production).

3. Calculate total manufacturing costs. The costs of any items in the WIP beginning inventory and any current costs are included in the total manufacturing costs that must be accounted for. Material requisition forms, time tickets, and factory overhead allocation sheets collect these costs.

4. Calculate unit costs. To determine product costing and income for a period, the costs per unit are calculated for overall costs as well as for direct materials, direct labor, and factory overhead.

   (Steps 3 and 4 are sometimes called unit cost determination).

5. Assign total manufacturing costs to units (cost assignment). Units completed and transferred out and units remaining in WIP inventory receive the period's manufacturing costs.

Production Cost Report Preparation Methods

When using process costing, the production cost report can be prepared according to the first-in, first-out (FIFO) method or the weighted-average method.

First-In, First-Out Costing Method

The **FIFO** costing method is an inventory valuation method that calculates the unit cost using only costs incurred and work performed during the current period.

FIFO keeps the beginning WIP inventory separated from the inventory that begins and ends during the current period. FIFO also assumes that the beginning WIP inventory is the first inventory to be completed in the period and therefore must be complete by the end of the period. The method requires two categories of completed units to correctly cost all inventory: beginning WIP units, and units started and completed during the current period.

The costs of work done before the current period on beginning WIP inventory are kept separate from work done in the current period. However, these prior-period costs are still included when calculating the costs of units completed from beginning inventory.

EU costing is a five-step process:

1. Determine the flow of physical units ("units to be accounted for").
2. Determine the EUs ("units accounted for").
3. Calculate total manufacturing costs (using work done in the current period only).
4. Calculate unit costs (beginning WIP plus current-period costs; "costs to be accounted for").
5. Assign total manufacturing costs to units (cost assignment; "costs accounted for").

Note that units to be accounted for should equal the units accounted for; similarly, the costs to be accounted for should equal the costs accounted for.

By definition, the beginning WIP will always be partially complete; otherwise, it would have been moved to the next department. Therefore, the objective is to obtain the correct cost of items completed during the month and items left in WIP at the end of the month.

For example: The EU costing for firm described in Figure 1C-12 starts with an assumption that 100% of the material is added to the product at the beginning of the production process and is thus 100% complete for beginning inventory but that beginning WIP conversion costs are only 40% complete. The example also shows how to deal with a partially complete ending inventory (100% complete direct materials and 80% complete conversion costs).

Note that in the costs to be accounted for area, the beginning WIP costs are determined using the prior month's direct material (DM) and conversion costs.

1. **Determine the flow of physical units.**

   Input units:
   WIP beginning of month: 100 units
   Units started in production: 700 units
   Units to be accounted for: 800 units
   Output units:
   Units completed: 600 units
   Ending WIP inventory: 200 units
   Units accounted for: 800 units (should match the units to be accounted for)

2. **Determine the equivalent units.**

Because direct materials are 100% complete and conversion costs are 40% complete, the beginning inventory of 100 physical units calculates to zero EUs of direct materials [$100 \times (100\% - 100\%)$] and 60 EU of conversion costs [$100 \times (100\% - 40\%)$].

In addition, because direct materials are 100% complete and conversion costs are 80% complete, the ending inventory of 200 physical units calculates to 200 EUs of direct materials and 160 EUs of conversion costs.

Taking into account the 500 units completed, direct materials EUs equal 700 and conversion cost EUs equal 660.

3. **Calculate costs accounted for.**

To calculate the cost of the units transferred to next department (600 units):

Determine the costs accounted for in the WIP beginning for (100 units) which is $5,800 plus the DM cost of $0.00 plus the conversion cost of $1,916.40 equals the WIP beginning total cost of $7,716.40.

The cost of the units started and completed (500 units) is $37,400.00.

The cost of the total units completed and transferred is $7,716.40 plus $37,400.00 equals $45,116.40.

To calculate the cost of the WIP month-end (200 units): Take the DM cost of $8,572.00 plus the conversion cost of $5,110.40 which equals the total cost of the WIP month-end of $13,682.40.

The total of costs accounted for is the cost of the total units completed and transferred of $45,116.40 plus the total cost of the WIP month-end of $13,682.40, which equals $58,798.80.

4. **Calculate unit costs (beginning WIP plus current period costs; "costs to be accounted for").**

Take the $29,998.80 cost of EUs DM added in the current month divided by the 700 units EUs of production to find the cost per EU of $42.86.

Take the $23,000 cost of EU conversion added in the current month divided by the 720 EUs of production to find the cost per EU of $31.94.

5. **Assign total manufacturing costs to units (cost assignment; "costs accounted for").**

Add the EU DM of $42.86 to the EU conversion of $31.94 to determine the whole cost per unit of $74.80.

Weighted-Average Method

The **weighted-average inventory valuation method** calculates the unit cost using all costs including both those for the current period and those for prior periods that are part of the current period's beginning WIP inventory. The weighted-average method finds the average of cost for prior periods and the current period. Whereas the FIFO method is concerned with both input and output measures (i.e., the beginning and ending status of products for the period), the weighted-average method is concerned only with the status of the products at the end of the period.

Figure 1C-12 FIFO Method Production Cost Report

		Physical Quantity	EU DM	EU Conversion
Units to be accounted for	WIP beginning of month	100		
	Units started in production	700		
	Total units	800		
Units accounted for	Transfers to next department:			
	From beginning WIP, direct material (DM) 100 × (100% − 100%); conversion 100 × (100% − 40%):	100	0	60
	Started and completed (800 units − 200 ending WIP − 100 beginning WIP completed first)	500	500	500
	From WIP month-end, DM 200 × 100%, conversion 200 × 80%	200	200	160
	Accounted for:	800		
	Work done in current period only:		700	720

		Total Cost	Direct Materials Cost	Conversion Costs	Whole Unit
Calculate EU/Unit costs and costs to be accounted for	WIP, Beginning of month (cost of work done before current period: (100 DM × $40) + (60 conversion × $30)):	$5,800.00	Not included	Not included	
	Costs added in the current month:	52,998.80	$29,998.80	$23,000.00	
	EUs of production (see above):		700	720	
	Cost per EU:		$42.86	$31.94	$74.80
	Total costs to account for:	**$58,798.80**			
Costs accounted for	Transferred to next department (600 units):				
	WIP, beginning (100 units)	$5,800.00			
	DM	$0	0 × $42.86		
	Conversion	$1,916.40		60 × $31.94	
	WIP, beginning total	$7,716.40			
	Started and completed (500 units):	$37,400.00	500 × $42.86	500 × $31.94	
	Total units completed and transferred:	$45,116.40			
	WIP, month-end (200 units):				
	DM	$8,572.00	200 × $42.86		
	Conversion	$5,110.40		160 × $31.94	
	Total WIP, month-end	$13,682.40			
	Total cost	**$58,798.80**			

For example: For this firm, all costs on the current period's production cost sheet are included in cost calculations, whether the cost actually was incurred in the current period or not. The production cost report using the weighted-average method can be prepared using the same five steps that were used in the FIFO example:

1. Determine the flow of physical units. ("Units to be accounted for")
2. Determine the equivalent units. ("Units accounted for")
3. Calculate total manufacturing costs (using work done in the current period only).
4. Calculate unit costs (beginning WIP plus current period costs; "costs to be accounted for").
5. Assign total manufacturing costs to units (cost assignment; "costs accounted for").

1. **Determine the flow of physical units.**

   Input units:

   > Partially complete beginning WIP inventory: 5,000 units

   > Work begun or received during the period: 30,000 units

   These 35,000 units are called "units to account for. "

   Output units:

   > Units completed: 20,000 units

   > Ending WIP inventory: 15,000 units

   These 35,000 units are called "number of units accounted for" and should match the units to account for.

2. **Determine the equivalent units.** Beginning WIP inventory units are not included in EUs because they are already included in physical units under this method. Because direct materials are 100% complete and conversion costs are 47% complete, the ending inventory of 15,000 physical units calculates to 15,000 EUs of direct materials and 7,050 EUs of conversion costs (direct labor plus factory overhead). This, plus the 20,000 units completed, equals 35,000 direct materials EUs and 27,050 conversion cost EUs.

3. **Calculate total manufacturing costs.** The beginning WIP for direct materials, $10,000, is added to conversion costs, $10,043, for a total of $20,043. The current period's costs for direct materials, $60,000, are added to conversion costs, $40,000, for a total of $100,000. Total manufacturing costs are $120,043.

4. **Calculate equivalent unit costs as shown:**

Direct Materials	=	$10,000 Beginning WIP Inventory
		$60,000 Current-Period Costs
		$70,000 Total Costs

$$\frac{\$70,000}{35,000\ \text{Units}} = \$2/\text{Unit Direct Materials}$$

$$\frac{\$50,043}{27,050\ \text{Units}} = \$1.85/\text{Unit Conversion Costs}$$

$$\$2.00 + \$1.85 = \$3.85/\text{Unit Total Cost}$$

5. **Assign total manufacturing costs to units in the ending inventory and to units transferred out.** The unit costs just calculated are multiplied by the number of units in each category, as shown at the bottom of Figure 1C-13 (Step 5) in a sample production cost report.

Figure 1C-13 Production Cost Report—Weighted-Average Method

1. *Quantity Schedule and Equivalent Units (EUs)*

Quantity Schedule					
Units to be accounted for:					
Work in process, January 1	5,000				
Started into production	30,000				
Total units	35,000				

		EUs			
		Materials		Conversion	
		units	%	Units	%
Units accounted for as follows:					
Units completed and transferred out	20,000	20,000	100%	20,000	100%
Work in process, ending	15,000	15,000	100%	7,050	47%
Total units and EUs of production	35,000	35,000		27,050	

2. *Costs per EU*

	Total Cost	Materials	Conversion Costs		Whole Unit
Cost to be accounted for:					
Work in process, beginning	$20,043	$10,000	$10,043		
Cost added during the month	100,000	60,000	40,000		
Total cost (a)	$ 120,043	$70,000	$50,043		
EUs of production (b)		35,000	27,050		
Cost per EU (a/b)		$2.00 +	$1.85	=	$3.85

3. *Cost Reconciliation*

	Total Cost	EUs (above)	
		Materials	Conversion
Cost accounted for as follows:			
Transferred out (20,000 × $3.85)	$77,000	20,000	20,000
Work in process, ending			
Materials (15,000 × $2.00)	30,000	15,000	
Conversion (7,050 × $1.85)	13,043		7,050
Total work in process, ending	43,043		
Total Cost	**$ 120,043**		

Note that the total costs calculated using unit costs should match the total costs calculated in the third step of $120,043.

Production Costing in a Multi-department Company

Because most processes usually involve more than one department, a more complex example will help show how to deal with costs transferred in from a prior department. This example also illustrates how to calculate inventory values and the COGS in process costing using both the FIFO and the weighted-average methods.

Transferred-in costs are any costs accumulated by prior departments. These are charged to the current department upon assumption of the partially completed units. Thus, each department is treated as a separate entity, and the prior department is like a vendor that supplies a semifinished good for a price (cost).

Unlike job order costing, with process costing, each production department will have its own WIP account. The completed production of a prior department is transferred to the next department's WIP account.

For example: Robusto Soup Company has three departments that operate in a continuous process, starting with the mixing department, then the cooking department, and finally the canning department. When each department finishes its work (measured in cans-worth of finished product) and transfers the materials to the next department, it also transfers the costs of the batch to that department as transferred-in costs (or prior department costs).

Figure 1C-14 shows how Robusto's materials and conversion costs are added by department.

Figure 1C-14 Percentage of Costs by Department

	Mixing Department	Cooking Department	Canning Department
Direct materials	90%	0%	10%
Conversion costs	60%	20%	20%
Transferred-in costs	N/A	100%	100%

Robusto Soup moves inventory between its accounts as shown in Figure 1C-15.

Figure 1C-15 Movement of Robusto's Inventory in Units for July

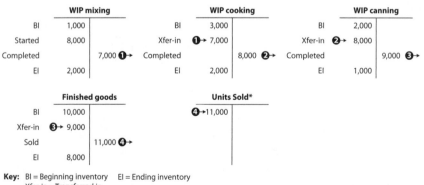

Key: BI = Beginning inventory   EI = Ending inventory
      Xfer-in = Transferred in

* This account corresponds to cost of goods sold when viewed in dollars instead of in units.

Note: Circled numbers indicate flow of cost inputs and outputs.

Note that this table shows movements in units and not in costs.

FIFO Method for the Canning Department at Robusto

If the company uses the FIFO method, its canning department has these costs:

Work-in-process (WIP) beginning (2,000 units):
- Cost of work done before current month: (1,800 DM × $1. 25/unit) + (1,600 conversion × $2. 50/unit) = $6,250

Costs added in current month:
- Transferred in from cooking department = $24,000
- DM = $990
- Conversion = $4,000

Figure 1C-16 shows a completed FIFO method production cost report using this data.

Figure 1C-16 Canning Department Equivalent Unit Calculation — FIFO Method

1. *Quantity Schedule and Equivalent Units (EUs)*

Quantity Schedule

Units to be accounted for:								
Work in process, beginning of month	2,000							
Started into production	8,000							
Total units	10,000							

		EUs						
		Transferred In		Materials		Conversion		
		units	%	units	%	units	%	
Units accounted for as follows:								
From beginning WIP	2,000	-	100%	200	10%	400	20%	
Units completed and transferred out	7,000	7,000	100%	7,000	100%	7,000	100%	
Work in process, ending	1,000	1,000	100%	900	90%	800	80%	
Total units and EUs of production	10,000	8,000		8,100		8,200		

2. *Costs per EU*

	Total Cost	Transferred In	Materials	Conversion Costs	Whole Unit
Cost to be accounted for:					
Work in process, beginning	$6,250	not included	not included	not included	
Cost added during the month	28,990	$24,000	$990	$4,000	
Total cost (a)	$35,240	$24,000	$990	$4,000	
EUs of production (b)		8,000	8,100	8,200	
Cost per EU (a/b)		$3.00 +	$0.12 +	$0.49 =	$3.61

3. Cost Reconciliation

		EUs			
	Total Cost	**Transferred In**	**Materials**	**Conversion**	**Whole Units**
Cost accounted for as follows:					
Work in process, beginning (2,000 units)	$6,250				
Transferred in (0 × $3.00):	–	–			
Direct Materials (200 × $0.12)	24		200		
Conversion (400 × $0.49)	196			400	
Total work in process, beginning:	$6,470				
Started and completed (7,000 × $3.61)	$25,270				7,000
Total of units completed and transferred out:	$31,740				
Work in process, ending					
Transferred in (1,000 × $3.00)	$3,000	1,000			
Direct Materials (900 × $0.12)	108		900		
Conversion (800 × $0.49)	392			800	
Total work in process, ending	$3,500				
Total Cost	$35,240				

Weighted-Average Method for the Canning Department at Robusto

If the weighted-average method were used instead, the number of units transferred (Figure 1C-17) would remain the same, but the transferred-in costs would differ because each department would include the work done in prior periods (whereas the FIFO method includes only the work done in the current period). Therefore, although all other aspects of the example remain the same, assume that the transferred-in costs to the canning department are now $25,005. Figure 1C-17 shows a completed weighted-average method production cost report.

Figure 1C-17 Canning Department Production Cost Report—Weighted-Average Method

1. *Quantity Schedule and Equivalent Units (EUs)*

Quantity Schedule							
Units to be accounted for:							
Work in process, beginning	2,000						
Transferred in	8,000						
Total units	10,000						

		EUs					
		Transferred In		Materials		Conversion	
		Units	%	units	%	units	%
Units accounted for as follows:							
Units completed and transferred out	9,000	9,000	100%	9,000	100%	9,000	100%
Work in process, ending	1,000	1,000	100%	900	90%	800	80%
Total units and EUs of production	10,000	10,000		9,900		9,800	

2. *Costs per EU*

	Total Cost	Transferred-In	Materials	Conversion Costs	Whole Unit
Cost to be accounted for:					
Work in process, beginning	$7,500	$6,250	$250	$1,000	
Cost added during the month	29,995	25,005	990	4,000	
Total cost (a)	$ 37,495	$ 31,255	$1,240	$5,000	
EUs of production (b)		10,000	9,900	9,800	
Cost per EU (a/b)		$3. 13 +	$0. 13 +	$0. 51 =	$3. 76

3. Cost Reconciliation

	Total Cost	EUs			Whole Units
		Transferred In	Materials	Conversion	
Cost accounted for as follows:					
Goods completed and transferred out (9,000 × $3.76):	$33,840				9,000
Work in process, ending					
Transferred in (1,000 × $3.13)	3,130	1,000			
Direct Materials (900 × $0.13)	117		900		
Conversion (800 × $0.51)	408			800	
Total work in process, ending	3,655				
Total Cost	$37,495				

Figure 1C-18 summarizes the data for Robusto Soup, showing the types of T-account transactions and journal entries that would coincide with the data from the weighted-average production cost report.

Separate production cost reports for the mixing department and the cooking department would also be needed. (Data for these two accounts are for illustrative purposes only.)

Note that each of the base accounts (raw materials, wages payable, and factory overhead) feeds not only into the first department but into the other departments, as indicated by the percentage of inputs shown in Figure 1C-18. The costs transferred out by that department do not directly equal the costs added during the current period; however, beginning inventory plus the costs added in the current month always equal the ending inventory plus the costs transferred out.

Note also that each inventory account's beginning and ending inventory levels are broken down by direct materials, conversion costs, and transferred-in costs.

Determining Inventory Levels in Process Costing

There may be considerable complexity in determining inventory levels in process costing.

For example: Bounce Sporting Goods buys rubber as a direct material for racquet balls. The molding department processes the racquet balls and then transfers the balls to the finishing department, where a coating and a label are applied. The

Figure 1C-18 T-Account and Journal Entries for Robusto (Weighted-Average Method)

Raw materials

BI	$15,000		
CM	$5,000	$9,000 → ❶	
		$990 → ❽	
EI	$10,010		

Wages payable

	$8,000	$4,800 → ❷
		$1,600 → ❺
		$1,600 → ❾

Factory overhead

$12,000	$7,200 → ❸
	$2,400 → ❻
	$2,400 → ❿

WIP mixing

BI	DM $1,250		
	Conv $2,500		
CM ❶→	DM $9,000		
❷ ❸→	Conv $12,000	$18,375 → ❹	
EI	DM $2,375		
	Conv $4,000		
	Total $6,375		

WIP cooking

BI	DM $0		
	Conv $1,875		
	Xfer-in $9,375		
CM ❹→	Xfer-in $18,375		
	DM $0	$25,005 → ❼	
❺ ❻→	Conv $4,000		
EI	Xfer-in $7,125		
	DM $0		
	Conv $1,500		
	Total $8,620		

WIP canning

BI	DM $250		
	Conv $1,000		
	Xfer-in $6,250		
CM ❼→	Xfer-in $25,005		
❽→	DM $990	$33,853 → ⓫	
❾ ❿→	Conv $4,000		
EI	Xfer-in $3,125		
	DM $114		
	Conv $408		
	Total $3,647		

Finished goods

BI	$37,500		
⓫→	Xfer-in $33,853	$41,371 → ⓬	
CM			
EI	$29,982		

Cost of goods sold

⓬→ $41,371	

Selected journal entries:

❶→ WIP mixing $9,000
      Raw materials $9,000

❷→ WIP mixing $4,800
      Salaries & wages payable $4,800

❸→ WIP mixing $7,200
      Factory overhead $7,200

❼→ WIP canning $25,005
      WIP cooking $25,005

⓫→ Finished goods $33,853
      WIP canning $33,853

⓬→ Cost of goods sold $41,371
      Finished goods $41,371
   Accounts receivable $55,000
      Sales $55,000

   To record 11,000 units sold at $5/unit

Key: Xfer-in = Transferred-in costs   BI = Beginning inventory   EI = Ending inventory
         CM = Current month   WIP = Work-in-process
                                          inventory

Note: Circled numbers indicate flow of cost inputs and outputs.

forming department began manufacturing 15,000 balls (called "Bouncers") during the month of June. There was no beginning inventory.

Costs for the molding department for the month of June are:

Direct materials:	$60,000
Conversion costs:	46,200
Total	$106,200

A total of 12,000 balls were completed and transferred to the finishing department; the remaining 3,000 balls were still in the molding process at the end of the month. All of the molding department's direct materials were placed in process but, on average, only 40% of the conversion cost was applied to the ending WIP inventory.

What is the cost of the units transferred to the finishing department? To find the answer, first determine whether the operation uses the weighted-average or FIFO method. In this example, either method will arrive at the same answer because there is no beginning inventory: Beginning WIP EUs are 0 for DMs and 0 for conversion costs.

The answer, $90,000, is calculated as shown:

Determine units started and completed:

DM: 12,000 Units × 100% Complete = 12,000 EU

Conv: 12,000 Units × 100% Complete = 12,000 EU

Determine WIP month-end:

DM: 3,000 Units × 100% Complete = 3,000 EU

Conv: 3,000 Units × 40% Complete = 1,200 EU

Determine total EU:

DM: 0 + 12,000 + 3,000 = 15,000 EU

Conv: 0 + 12,000 + 1,200 = 13,200 EU

Calculate EU/unit costs:

$$\text{DM: } \frac{\$60,000}{15,000 \text{ EU}} = \$4.00/\text{EU}$$

$$\text{Conv: } \frac{\$46,200}{13,200 \text{ EU}} = \$3.50/\text{EU}$$

Cost of units started and completed (transferred to finishing department):

(12,000 × $4) + (12,000 × $3.50) = $90,000

To verify, calculate ending WIP:

(3,000 EU DM × $4) + (1,200 EU conv × $3.50) = $16,200

Note that $90,000 + $16,200 = $106,200, the total cost.

Spoilage in Process Costing

Process costing can have normal and abnormal spoilage (as defined in the discussion of job costing). Spoilage in process costing is handled in one of two ways. The first method counts the number of spoiled units, separately computes the total cost per unit, and then allocates this cost to the good units. The second method omits the spoiled units in the totals so that the cost per unit does not include any spoiled units, making the spoilage cost part of the total manufacturing costs. The first method provides more precise product costs because the individually calculated spoilage cost is spread over only the good units produced. The second method is less precise because the costs are spread to all units including good completed units, units in ending WIP inventory, and abnormal spoiled units.

Benefits and Limitations of Process Costing

Process costing is useful for any highly repetitive flow process, such as mass production of homogeneous items. Conversely, it is not useful for custom orders or other individual jobs. Process costing allocates costs not only by cost per unit but also to specific departments, allowing individual managers to control their own costs.

Another commonly used costing system is ABC, which allows companies to gain a more accurate understanding of its overhead costs, leading to better information about the profitability of its products and services.

Activity-Based Costing

ABC is a method of assigning costs to customers, services, and products based on an activity's consumption of resources. An activity is any type of action, work, or movement performed within an entity. An activity center is a logical grouping of activities, actions, movements, or sequences of work. A resource is an element with economic value that is consumed or applied when performing an activity.

Other terms important to ABC include resource cost drivers and activity cost drivers.

A resource cost driver measures the amount of resources consumed by an activity. Resource costs used in an activity are assigned to a cost pool using a resource cost driver. In manufacturing, a resource cost driver could be the amount of rubber required to make a batch of tennis balls. In an engineering services firm, a resource cost driver could be the number of hours used by an engineer to design, build, and maintain a project schedule.

An activity cost driver is a measurement of the amount of an activity used by a cost object. Activity cost drivers assign costs in cost pools to cost objects. For example, an activity cost driver is the number of labor hours required for the activity of performing a setup for a particular product.

The basis for ABC is that activities use resources but produce products or services. The resource cost is calculated using a cost driver; the amount of an activity consumed in a period is multiplied by the cost of the activity. The calculated costs are assigned to the product or service.

ABC is especially appropriate for companies that have expanded to multiple products and/or products that use varying amounts of resources, which include not only raw materials and other direct costs but also indirect costs such as customer service, quality control, and supervision. When each product or product line consumes each of these costs at different rates, a broad brush or uniform cost allocation for all items will make some products appear more profitable and others less profitable than they are. As a result, products can be overcosted or undercosted: Overcosted items consume few actual resources but are charged as if they had consumed more; undercosted items consume more actual resources than they are charged for.

Strategically, ABC should be used when the cost of making decisions based on inaccurate costing data exceeds the added expense of collecting more information and implementing the system. An effective ABC system can be particularly important to a firm in its decision to drop or add a product line. It can also aid in decisions related to product pricing and where to allocate funds to improve processes.

ABC uses a two-stage approach to allocate costs:

Stage 1: Resource cost assignment of overhead costs to activity cost pools or activity centers using pertinent resource cost drivers

Stage 2: Activity cost assignment of activity costs to cost objects using pertinent activity cost drivers (to measure a cost object's drain on an activity)

Key Steps in ABC

The steps for designing an ABC system are: identifying activities and resource costs, assigning resource costs to activities, and assigning activity costs to cost objects.

Step 1. Identify Activities and Resource Costs

An activity analysis identifies the resource costs of performing particular activities by determining the work performed for each activity. The project team makes detailed lists of activities and organizes them into activity centers as well as into these levels:

Unit-level activities include activities that are performed for each unit produced, such as direct materials or direct labor hours. In other words, these are the same as volume-based or unit-based activities.

Batch-level activities include activities that are performed for each batch of units, such as machine setup, purchase orders, batch inspections, batch mixing, or production scheduling.

Product-sustaining activities include activities that are performed to support the production process, such as product design, expediting, and implementing engineering changes.

Facility-sustaining activities include activities that support production for an entire facility, such as environmental health and safety, security, plant management, depreciation, property taxes, and insurance.

Customer-level activities include activities that are performed to support customer needs, such as customer service, phone banks, or custom orders.

Step 2. Assign Resource Costs to Activities

Resource costs are assigned to activities using resource cost drivers. A cause-and-effect relationship must be established between the driver and the activity. Resource cost drivers and the related activity that companies often use include:

Number of employees: personnel activities

Time worked: personnel activities

Setup hours: setup or machine activities

Number or distance of movements: materials-handling activities

Meters: utilities (flow meters, electricity meters, etc.)

Machine hours: machine-running activities

Number of orders: production orders

Square feet: cleaning activities

Amount of value added: general and administrative

Step 3. Assign Activity Costs to Cost Objects

After determining activity costs, the activity costs per unit are measured using an appropriate cost driver. The activity cost driver should show a cause-and-effect relationship or, in other words, be directly related to the rise and fall of the cost.

The activity cost drivers determine the proportion of a cost to allocate to each product or service using the next formula:

$$\text{Rate} = \frac{\text{Cost Pool}}{\text{Driver}}$$

When to Use ABC

ABC helps managers understand their costs, thus highlighting the competitive advantages and weaknesses of their process or product. As more firms adopt ABC, it will become increasingly difficult for companies using a less accurate costing system to compete, because they will find themselves at a competitive disadvantage.

ABC is particularly important for:

- Firms that have high product diversity, complexity, or volume
- Firms that have a high likelihood of cost distortion, such as those with both mass-produced and custom orders, both mature and new products, and both custom delivery and standard delivery channels

ABC was first adopted by manufacturing companies. Now it is also used by service companies such as hospitals, banks, and insurance companies, not only to account for costs but also to make strategic decisions by analyzing processes, assessing management performance, and assessing profitability.

Differences Between ABC and Traditional Costing

The three primary differences between ABC and traditional costing are shown in Figure 1C-19.

Figure 1C-19 ABC versus Traditional Costing

	ABC	Traditional Costing
Cost drivers	Multiple cost drivers: activity and volume-based drivers (whichever fits the cost best)	Up to three cost drivers: only volume-based, chosen for best general fit
Overhead	Overhead assigned to activities and then from activities to products or services	Overhead assigned to departments and then from departments to products or services
Focus	Focus on solving costing and processing issues that cross departmental lines	Focus on assigning responsibility to departmental managers for individual cost and process improvements within their department

Benefits and Limitations of ABC

Benefits of using ABC include these:

- ABC reduces distortions found in traditional cost allocation methods that allocate overhead by department. ABC gives managers access to relevant costs so they can compete better in the marketplace.
- ABC measures activity-driving costs, allowing management to alter product designs and activity designs and know how overall cost and value are affected.
- ABC normally results in substantially greater unit costs for low-volume products than is reported by traditional product costing (meaning better decisions can be made to add or drop a product line).

The limitations of ABC include these:

- Not all overhead costs can be related to a particular cost driver and may need to be arbitrarily allocated, especially when the cost of tracing is greater than the benefit.
- ABC requires substantial development and maintenance time, even with available software. ABC changes the rules for managers, so resistance to change is common. Without top management support, managers could find workarounds.
- ABC, if viewed only as an accounting initiative, will likely fail.
- ABC generates vast amounts of information. Too much information can mislead managers into concentrating on the wrong data.
- ABC reports do not conform to generally accepted accounting principles (GAAP), so restating financial data adds an expense and causes confusion, leaving users unsure as to whether they should rely on the ABC or external data.

Life-Cycle Costing

When a longer-term perspective is needed than other costing methods provide (usually a year), life-cycle costing may be used. Life-cycle costing considers the entire life cycle of a product or service, from concept through sales and warranty service.

For example: The life cycle for a pharmaceutical product starts with research and development and moves through multiple stages of testing and approvals, product design, manufacturing, marketing and distribution, and customer service. In this case, the cycle may be defined as the life span of the patent on the product or the life span of its marketability.

Life-cycle costing is sometimes used on a strategic basis for cost planning and product pricing. It is designed to allow a firm to focus on the overall costs for a product or service. Poor early design could lead to much higher marketing costs, lower sales, and higher service costs. The total costs for a product's life cycle have three phases.

1. Upstream costs: costs that are prior to the manufacturing of the product or sale of the service, such as research and development or design (prototypes, tests, and engineering).
2. Manufacturing costs: costs involved in producing a product or service, such as purchasing and direct and indirect manufacturing costs.
3. Downstream costs: costs subsequent to (or coincident with) manufacturing costs, such as marketing, distribution (packaging, shipping and handling, promotions, and advertising), service costs, and warranty costs (defect recalls, returns, and liability)

Life-cycle costing places its strategic focus on improving costs in all three phases. Improving product design is the key to the upstream phase. Improving the manufacturing process and relationships with suppliers is highlighted in the manufacturing phase. Improving the first two phases is the key to lowering downstream costs because actions taken in these phases limit the downstream choices. In other words, life-cycle costing attempts to make managers proactive in the earlier phases so they do not have to be reactive later.

Other Costing Methods

Two other costing methods are **operation costing**—which combines job costing with process costing—and **backflush costing**—which is used in just-in-time production systems.

Operation Costing

Operation costing is a costing system that combines job costing with process costing. Similar to job costing, operation costing assigns direct materials to each job or batch, but direct labor and overhead (conversion costs) are assigned similarly to process costing. This hybrid system is most suitable for manufacturers that have similar processes for high-volume activities but that need to use different materials for different jobs. Clothing manufacturers, for example, have standard operations—choosing patterns, cutting, and sewing—but the fabrics used vary by item, size, color and price, among other factors. Other industries that are suitable for operation costing include textiles, metalworking, furniture, shoes, and electronic equipment.

For example: A metalworking company produces handrails that are either unfinished (for painting) or chrome-plated. The company has one department create all of the metal rails and then transfers some to the chrome-plating department.

Assume that the company produced 1,000 unfinished rails and 500 chrome rails during a month and that it had no beginning or ending inventory for the month. Operation costing tracks direct materials by job and tracks conversion costs (direct labor and overhead) by department, as shown in Figure 1C-20.

Figure 1C-20 Total Cost Calculation

Direct Materials		$30,000
Job 1 — Unfinished Rails (1,000)		
Job 2 — Chrome Rails (500)		
Materials for Rails in Metal Department	15,000	
Chrome Plating Added to Rails in Chrome Department	10,000	25,000
Total Direct Materials		$55,000
Conversion Costs		
Metal Department		$45,000
Chrome Department		10,000
Total Conversion Costs		$55,000
Total Costs		$110,000

The product costs for unfinished rails and chrome rails are calculated in Figure 1C-21. Note that the conversion costs for the metal department groups all rails together because they are all processed the same in that department.

Note that the total cost of $110,000 is the same as in Figure 1C-20, proving that the calculations are correct.

Backflush Costing

Backflush costing is a costing system tailored to just-in-time production systems. A **just-in-time (JIT)** system produces materials just as they are needed for the next step in production. The trigger for manufacturing at a particular work area is the demand from the next station down the line. As a result, organizations using JIT production have very little inventory, making the choice of inventory valuation methods (FIFO or weighted-average) and inventory costing methods (absorption costing or variable costing) irrelevant because the costs flow directly to cost of goods sold during an accounting period.

Backflush costing contrasts with traditional costing systems that use sequential tracking to record purchases and movements of costs between inventories and

Figure 1C-21 Product Cost Calculation

	Unfinished Rails	Chrome Rails
Direct Materials		
$\text{Job 1}\left(\dfrac{\$30,000}{1,000}\right)$	$30/Rail	
$\text{Job 2}\left(\dfrac{\$25,000}{500}\right)$		$50/Rail
$\text{Conversion} - \text{Metal Department}\left(\dfrac{\$45,000}{1,500}\right)$	$30/Rail	$30/Rail
$\text{Conversion} - \text{Chrome Department}\left(\dfrac{\$10,000}{500}\right)$		$20/Rail
Total Cost per Rail	$60/Rail	$100/Rail

Total Product Cost

$$\text{Unfinished Rails } \$60 \times 1,000 = \$60,000$$
$$\text{Chrome Rails } \$100 \times 500 = 50,000$$
$$\text{Total} = \$110,000$$

accounts in the order in which they occur. Sequential tracking tracks costs through a four-stage cycle:

Stage A: Purchase of direct materials (journal entry in materials inventory)

Stage B: Production (journal entry in WIP inventory)

Stage C: Completion of a good finished unit (journal entry in finished goods inventory)

Stage D: Sale of finished good (journal entry in cost of goods sold)

The journal entries made at each stage are called trigger points. Backflush costing omits some or all of the journal entries for the production cycle. When the journal entries are omitted from certain stages of the cycle, normal or standard costs are used to work backward and flush out the costs and then make the required journal entries for the missing steps.

Backflush costing skips the journal entry for WIP inventory, because JIT systems reduce the time that materials remain in this stage.

The use of backflush costing may not be in strict accordance with GAAP because backflush costing entries ignore WIP inventory, which still exists and should be recorded as an asset. However, many companies justify the use of backflush costing because under JIT production, such items are immaterial. When they are material, these unrecorded costs need to be approximated and adjusting entries made.

Backflush costing can save a company money on accounting, but some critics find the lack of a clear audit trail to be a risk because it limits the ability to pinpoint resources at each stage of the manufacturing process. Many inventories are so low under JIT production, however, that managers can track operations by simple observation and computer monitoring.

Companies that use JIT production systems are prime candidates for using backflush costing, but any industry that has fast manufacturing lead times and/or very stable inventory levels can use backflush costing.

**Knowledge Check:
Costing Systems**

The next questions are intended to help you check your understanding and recall of the material presented in this topic. They do not represent the type of questions that appear on the CMA exam.

Directions: Answer each question in the space provided. Correct answers and section references appear after the knowledge check questions.

1. Which of the following costing systems would work best for a firm that spends a considerable percentage of its overall costs on research and development?
   - ☐ **a.** Job order costing
   - ☐ **b.** Process costing
   - ☐ **c.** Activity-based costing
   - ☐ **d.** Life-cycle costing

2. A post office wants to implement a cost accumulation system for its bulk mail sorting warehouse. Which of the following methods would be best suited to this situation?
   - ☐ **a.** Life-cycle costing
   - ☐ **b.** Activity-based costing
   - ☐ **c.** Process costing
   - ☐ **d.** Job costing

3. Which of the following terms refers to an item with little economic value for the firm?
   - ☐ **a.** Abnormal spoilage
   - ☐ **b.** Normal spoilage
   - ☐ **c.** Rework
   - ☐ **d.** Scrap

4. A company is using process costing with FIFO. For a particular period, there is no beginning WIP inventory, the ending WIP inventory includes 10,000 physical units that are 60% complete, and there are 20,000 units completed during the period. How many equivalent units are there in total at the end of the period?
   - ☐ **a.** 20,000
   - ☐ **b.** 26,000
   - ☐ **c.** 32,000
   - ☐ **d.** 34,000

5. Five steps are used to develop a production cost report using the weighted-average method. Number the steps in the correct order:

   Assign total manufacturing costs to units.

   Calculate total manufacturing costs.

   Calculate unit costs.

   Determine the equivalent units.

   Determine the flow of physical units.

6. When a company moves from a traditional cost system in which manufacturing overhead is applied based on machine hours to an activity-based costing system in which there are batch-level and product-level costs, the unit product costs of high-volume products typically will _____ while the unit product costs of low-volume products typically will _____.

Knowledge Check Answers: Costing Systems

1. Which of the following costing systems would work best for a firm that spends a considerable percentage of its overall costs on research and development? *[See Life-Cycle Costing.]*

   ☐ **a.** Job order costing

   ☐ **b.** Process costing

   ☐ **c.** Activity-based costing

   ☑ **d.** Life-cycle costing   .

2. A post office wants to implement a cost accumulation system for its bulk mail sorting warehouse. Which of the following methods would be best suited to this situation? *[See Job Order versus Process Costing.]*

   ☐ **a.** Life-cycle costing

   ☐ **b.** Activity-based costing

   ☑ **c.** Process costing

   ☐ **d.** Job costing

3. Which of the following terms refers to an item with little economic value for the firm? *[See Scrap.]*

   ☐ **a.** Abnormal spoilage

   ☐ **b.** Normal spoilage

   ☐ **c.** Rework

   ☑ **d.** Scrap

4. A company is using process costing (with FIFO). For a particular period, there is no beginning WIP inventory, the ending WIP inventory includes 10,000 physical units that are 60% complete, and there are 20,000 units completed during the period. How many equivalent units are there in total at the end of the period? *[See Equivalent Units in Process Costing.]*

   ☐ **a.** 20,000

   ☑ **b.** 26,000

   ☐ **c.** 32,000

   ☐ **d.** 34,000

5. Five steps are used to develop a production cost report using the weighted average method. Number the steps in the correct order: *[See Steps in Preparing a Production Cost Report.]*

    (5) Assign total manufacturing costs to units.

    (3) Calculate total manufacturing costs.

    (4) Calculate unit costs.

    (2) Determine the equivalent units.

    (1) Determine the flow of physical units.

6. When a company moves from a traditional cost system in which manufacturing overhead is applied based on machine hours to an activity-based costing system in which there are batch-level and product-level costs, the unit product costs of high-volume products typically will **decrease** while the unit product costs of low volume products typically will **increase**. *[See Differences Between ABC and Traditional Costing.]*

Overhead Costs

MANUFACTURING OVERHEAD COSTS CAN BE very significant for a business because they include all manufacturing costs except direct materials and direct labor. Overhead costs are product costs, which flow through inventory accounts such as raw materials inventory, work-in-process inventory, and finished goods inventory. Product costs flow to the income statement once the product has been sold.

This topic covers fixed and variable overhead, plant-wide versus departmental overhead, and activity-based costing overhead allocation. It also discusses determining an allocation base (i.e., choosing a cost driver) and the allocation of service department costs.

 READ the Learning Outcome Statements (LOS) for this topic as found in Appendix A and then study the concepts and calculations presented here to be sure you understand the content you could be tested on in the CMA exam.

Fixed and Variable Overhead Expenses

All overhead expenses are either fixed or variable costs. **Fixed costs** include depreciation on assets, rentals, leasing costs, and indirect labor incurred in manufacturing. These costs do not change during an accounting period, provided the relevant range is consistent with the level of production. **Variable costs** include power, water, sewage, engineering support, machine maintenance, and indirect materials. Variable costs change in proportion to the changes in a particular cost driver and the cost drivers can be either volume or activity based.

Fixed Overhead Costs

Most fixed costs are set for a certain performance period, so, by definition, the day-to-day operations of a business have little effect on fixed costs. The time frame for planning fixed overhead costs has two phases: setting priorities and being efficient in the pursuit of those priorities. Setting priorities means that the firm should determine which fixed overhead costs should or must be undertaken, which fixed costs add no value and should be eliminated, and which fixed costs are most important to get right.

The second phase is pursuing efficiency in the fixed overhead costs that are on the list of priorities and determining which costs are most likely to be reduced through more careful planning.

For example: An auto rental company might set its highest fixed cost priority as the leasing or purchase of the proper number of rental vehicles for a period so that each facility has enough cars to satisfy demand without leaving too much unused capacity. The rental company can decide whether leasing or purchasing is the most cost-effective option, by choosing the most trouble-free brands of cars, or negotiating the best deals with the auto manufacturers.

Variable Overhead Costs

The time frame for planning variable overhead costs has the same two phases: setting priorities and being efficient in the pursuit of those priorities. Setting priorities for variable costs involves determining which activities add value for customers and which can be eliminated. Unlike fixed costs, variable costs can be influenced on a day-to-day basis, so the efficient pursuit of priorities can be an ongoing process.

For example: The car rental company might eliminate several paperwork steps for customers or automate the entire process to both reduce its variable administrative costs and improve customer service. It could then implement efficiency measures, such as scheduling car maintenance activities during times of low rental demand, so that these activities do not hamper business.

Fixed Overhead Cost Allocation Rates

Fixed overhead costs are a lump-sum amount that will not change over the course of a period even if wide variations occur in activity. The four steps in determining the budgeted fixed allocation rate are:

1. Determine the proper accounting period. A year basis is usually preferable to a monthly basis because most companies want to smooth over variations due to seasonality or different numbers of days per month. Using an annual period also keeps managers from having to create a new budget each month.
2. Determine the allocation base (cost driver) to use when allocating fixed overhead. A firm could use a volume- or activity-based cost driver. Although fixed costs do not vary, they still must be allocated in proportion to the value they are providing to each cost pool.
3. Determine the fixed overhead costs associated with each cost allocation base (cost driver). Fixed overhead costs could be grouped into any number of pools divided according to which allocation base best measures the value provided by the set of fixed costs.

4. Calculate the rate per unit of each allocation base used when allocating fixed overhead costs to cost objects:

$$\text{Fixed Overhead Application Rate} = \frac{\text{Total Cost in Fixed Overhead Cost Pool}}{\text{Total Quantity of Allocation Base}}$$

In this way, more of the fixed cost is assigned to operations that use more of the allocation base than other operations.

For example: A tennis ball manufacturer uses machine hours as its fixed cost driver (step 2, above). The company budgets 40,000 machine hours annually to produce 200,000 cans of tennis balls.

All fixed manufacturing overhead costs relate to the machine hours allocation base (step 3, above). The fixed overhead costs total $1,000,000 for the year. The rate per unit is calculated as:

$$\text{Fixed Overhead Application Rate} = \frac{\$1,000,000}{40,000 \text{ Machine Hours}} = \$25/\text{Machine Hour}$$

Planning for fixed overhead expenses is similar to planning for variable overhead expenses. Managers must attempt to eliminate activities that do not add value to a product or service to effectively plan fixed overhead costs and fixed overhead rates. Common fixed overhead costs include plant leasing costs, machine depreciation costs, and plant manager salaries. Management should select the appropriate allocation base for fixed overhead expenses based on operations. Common appropriate allocation bases may include machinehours, labor hours, or labor dollars.

Budgeted Variable Overhead Cost Allocation Rates

The steps and calculations listed for budgeting fixed overhead cost allocation rates are the same for variable rates. Simply substitute "variable" in place of "fixed" in the text to determine how to develop an applicable rate.

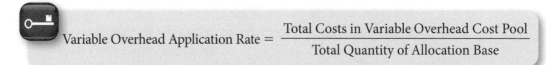

$$\text{Variable Overhead Application Rate} = \frac{\text{Total Costs in Variable Overhead Cost Pool}}{\text{Total Quantity of Allocation Base}}$$

Managers must attempt to eliminate activities that do not add value to a product or service to effectively plan variable overhead costs and variable overhead rates. Common variable overhead costs include indirect materials, indirect labor, utility costs, maintenance costs, and engineering support. Management should select the appropriate allocation base for variable overhead expenses based on operations. Common appropriate allocation bases may include machinehours, labor hours, or labor dollars.

Job Costing Using the High-Low Method

The high-low method is a cost accounting technique that separates fixed costs from variable costs. It uses the highest and lowest observed cost driver (i.e., machine hours) values within the relevant range and their respective costs to estimate the slope coefficient and the constant of the cost function. By performing a high-low analysis, interested parties gain an initial understanding of the relationship between a cost driver and costs (semivariable cost).

To illustrate the use of the high-low method, consider the next scenario.

Plate, Inc. has the following four months' worth of wage activity associated with production:

Month	Production Activity	Wages
July	2,000 units	$30,000
August	1,800 units	$28,000
September	1,900 units	$29,000
October	2,100 units	$31,000

The highest production for Plate, Inc. is 2,100 units. The lowest production for Plate, Inc. is 1,800 units. The difference in production is 300 units.

The highest wage cost for Plate, Inc. is $31,000. The lowest wage cost is $28,000. The difference in wage costs is $3,000.

Now we use the high-low method to determine the variable costs associated with production. We take the $3,000 difference in wage cost and divide by the difference in production of 300 units, arriving at variable costs per unit of $10.

The fixed costs assigned can then be calculated by subtracting variable costs from total costs. In September, for example, the total cost was $29,000. Variable costs were $19,000 ($10 × 1,900 units). Therefore, fixed costs for the month of September are $10,000.

High-Low Method and Regression Analysis

We can also use the high-low method using regression analysis. This quantitative analysis will show the best fit line associated with the data points. Using the same example, we can compute the regression coefficient in this way:

$$y = a + bX$$

or

$$a = y - bX$$

To compute the constant, we can use either the highest or the lowest observation of the cost driver.

At the highest observation of the cost driver, the constant, *a*, is calculated as:

Constant = $31,000 − ($10.00 per machine hours × 2,100 units) = $10,000

And at the lowest observation of the cost driver, the constant, *a*, is calculated as:

Constant = $28,000 − ($10 × 1,800) = $10,000

Thus, the high-low estimate of the cost function is:

$$y = a + bX$$
$$y = \$10,000 + (10 \times \text{Number of production units})$$

Advantage and Disadvantage of the High-Low Method

The advantage of the high-low method is that it is simple to use and, from a logical standpoint, easy to understand. The speed and initial understanding provided into how the cost driver affects indirect manufacturing labor costs is beneficial. The disadvantage is that this method relies on only two observations to estimate a cost function. The method ignores information that may change the results going forward.

Plant-Wide, Departmental, and Activity-Based Costing Overhead Costing

Firms with two or more production departments can assign factory overhead costs to jobs or products in these ways:

- Plant-wide overhead rate
- Departmental overhead rate
- Activity-based overhead costing

Plant-Wide Overhead Rate

A **plant-wide overhead rate** is a single rate used for all overhead costs incurred at a production facility. The total plant factory overhead is determined using the next calculation:

$$\text{Plant-Wide Overhead} = \frac{\text{Total Plant Overhead}}{\substack{\text{Total Units of Cost Driver (Allocation Base)} \\ \text{Common to All Jobs}}}$$

Because plant-wide allocation is, by its nature, very general, it can be used only by facilities that have a strong single cost driver that relates to all types of production.

If one department in a plant is highly automated and another department is labor-intensive, different cost drivers should be used for each department instead of a plant-wide overhead rate.

Departmental Overhead Rate

A **departmental overhead** rate is a single overhead rate calculated for a particular department. Departmental overhead rates are more accurate than plant-wide rates.

Each department could have its own rate calculated based on its own cost drivers. The departmental overhead rate is calculated as shown:

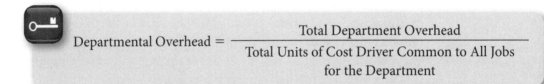

$$\text{Departmental Overhead} = \frac{\text{Total Department Overhead}}{\substack{\text{Total Units of Cost Driver Common to All Jobs} \\ \text{for the Department}}}$$

Accounting for each overhead amount is tracked by keeping separate factory overhead and applied overhead accounts for each department. As with the plant-wide rate, the departmental overhead rate is still a fairly general rate, so misallocations of costs can occur if the cost driver chosen does not truly relate to all activities for a department.

Departmental overhead rates should be used only if the department is homogeneous and if a cause-and-effect relationship can be defined between each job and the selected cost driver. When this is not true, several sets of cost drivers and associated cost pools should be used. The dangers of improperly allocating costs have been elaborated on earlier—that is, certain products will appear less profitable than they really are and vice versa, thereby risking mismanagement of the product lines.

Activity-Based Costing Overhead Costing

When plant-wide and departmental overhead allocation methods are not accurate enough, an **activity-based costing** (ABC) method can be used. ABC assigns factory overhead costs to products or services using multiple cost pools and multiple cost drivers. The cost drivers are selected based on a cause-and-effect relationship and can be both activity based and volume based.

For example: Figure 1C-22 shows the cost pools and cost drivers for a sample production facility.

Figure 1C-22 Cost Pools, Drivers, and Predetermined Driver Rate

Overhead Cost Pool	Budgeted Overhead Cost	Cost Driver	Units	Predetermined Driver Rate
Utilities	$100,000	Machine hrs.	10,000	$10/machine hr.
Materials handling	120,000	Materials weight (pounds)	40,000	$3/pound
Setups	90,000	Number of setups	300	$300/setup
	$310,000			

In the table, the predetermined driver rate is calculated by dividing the budgeted overhead cost by the total number of units of the cost driver. The precision in this system is apparent when two or more jobs or products share these costs.

Assume that the facility described has two jobs for the current period. Job 1 uses 4,000 machine hours and 30,000 pounds in direct materials weight and has 100 setups. Job 2 uses 6,000 machine hours and 10,000 pounds in direct materials weight and has 200 setups. The costs assigned to each job are calculated as shown in Figure 1C-23.

Figure 1C-23 ABC versus Plant-Wide Overhead Allocation

	ABC	Plant-Wide
Job 1 Utilities $10/machine hr. × 4,000 hrs. =	$40,000	
Job 1 Materials handling $3/lb. × 30,000 lbs. =	90,000	
Job 1 Setups $300/setup × 100 setups =	30,000	
Total =	$160,000	124,000
Job 2 Utilities $10/machine hr. × 6,000 hrs. =	$60,000	
Job 2 Materials handling $3/lb. × 10,000 lbs. =	30,000	
Job 2 Setups $300/setup × 200 setups =	60,000	
Total =	$150,000	186,000
	$310,000	$310,000

For comparison, if a plant-wide rate had been used with machine hours as the sole cost driver, the total overhead of $310,000 divided by 10,000 machine hours would be $31/machine hour, multiplied by 4,000 hours for job 1 ($124,000) and 6,000 hours for job 2 ($186,000).

Note that the ABC method produces very different costs for the two products compared to the plant-wide method.

Benefits of ABC

Activity-based overhead allocation may help management identify inefficient products, departments, and activities when it attempts to eliminate activities that do not provide value to products and services. Activity-based overhead allocation may encourage focusing resources on profitable products, departments and activities, and controlling costs.

Allocation of Service Department Costs

There are two basic types of departments in a company: production departments and service departments. In contrast to production departments (which have been the focus of the discussion to this point), service departments do not directly perform operating activities. Instead, they assist production departments, customers, and employees. Examples of service departments include maintenance, internal auditing, cafeterias, information technology, human resources, purchasing, company stores, customer service, engineering, and cost accounting.

Allocation of service department costs has three phases:

Phase 1: Trace all direct costs and allocate overhead costs to all departments (production departments and other service departments).

Phase 2: Allocate service department costs to production departments or other service departments.

Phase 3: Allocate production department costs to products.

Service department costs are allocated because most service departments do not generate any revenue (i.e., they are cost centers). When a service department does generate revenue, such as the cafeteria or a repairs department, these revenues offset the costs, and any net cost is transferred to the production departments, which are revenue-producing departments. Managers must decide whether they should allocate service department costs to operating departments. If costs are allocated, the fixed and variable costs should be allocated in the same way.

Although a service department may not directly add value to a product, a service department provides a service to other departments within a company that may directly add value to the products and services that the company offers. Managers may determine that service department costs should be allocated back to the operating departments because an operating department may not be able to provide its products without the support of the service department.

Phase 1: Trace Direct Costs and Allocate Overhead Costs to Departments

The first activity in Phase 1 is to trace direct costs to production and service departments. This is the same process as tracing direct costs to production departments.

Similarly, overhead costs can be allocated to service departments in the same way as they are allocated to production departments. However, the cost drivers (allocation bases) may be slightly different in type. Common cost drivers for various service departments are listed next.

Cost accounting—labor hours, customers served

Data processing—number of personal computers, central processing unit minutes, disk storage used

Janitorial services—square feet of building space

Maintenance—machine hours

Materials handling—labor hours, volume handled

Medical facilities—cases handled

Shipping and receiving—units handled, number of requisitions, labor hours

Overall, the cost drivers selected should be easily understood by the managers who will have these costs allocated to them. Note that both the cost driver rate selected and the total units of the cost drivers can use actual or standard (budgeted) rates or units (or some combination, such as standard cost driver rate times actual units of the cost driver). Use of standard amounts for cost driver rates can motivate service department managers to control costs because the amounts can be calculated during a period. However, variances between standard and actual results will cause amounts to be underapplied or overapplied. Using actual cost drivers or actual amounts will allow for precise cost allocation but can be done only after the period is complete, so the method cannot be used for control purposes during the period.

There are two basic methods of allocating costs: the single-rate method and the contribution margin method.

Single-Rate Cost Allocation Method

The **single-rate cost allocation method** creates a single allocation base for a service department's combined fixed and variable costs, providing a single rate per unit for cost allocation. However, when fixed costs are grouped with variable costs, the entire cost seems to be a variable cost, and managers might be tempted to outsource to a provider with a lower rate. Because the fixed department costs would be incurred regardless of use (at least in the short term), outsourcing would cause the department to add new external costs while still continuing to incur the original fixed portion of the internal costs.

For example: If a project has $1 million in fixed costs plus variable costs of $50/machine hour and 5,000 machine hours, the total rate per machine hour would be [$1,000,000 + (5,000 × $50)]/5,000 = $250/machine hour. The single-rate cost can appear to overstate the rate.

Contribution Margin Cost Allocation Method

The **contribution margin cost allocation method**, also called the dual-rate method, creates separate fixed and variable cost pools for allocation of service department costs. Each pool can have its own allocation base, such as labor hours for variable costs and machine hours for fixed costs. By using different cost drivers and different rates, and using standard or actual amounts for each variable, the contribution margin method may produce a different estimate of total costs than if the single-rate method were used.

For example: By this method, with $1,000,000 in fixed costs allocated based on labor hours, and with 4,900 labor hours used, then the fixed allocation rate would be about $204/labor hour. The variable allocation rate would be $50/machine hour.

Each type of cost would be separately calculated using one of the allocation methods detailed in Phase 2 (discussed next), thus doubling the number of calculations required to find the total costs allocated. This method should lead to more precise allocation of costs and allow better managerial decision making, but it could also result in higher administrative costs due to more complex calculations and difficulty in determining proper classification of costs.

Phase 2: Allocate Service Department Costs to Production Departments or Other Service Departments

The second phase is to allocate the service department costs to the production departments or to other service departments. Allocating costs to other service departments, such as the cost for janitorial services to clean the cafeteria, are called interdepartmental or reciprocal services. Three methods can be used to allocate service costs to other departments: the direct method, the step-down method, and the reciprocal method. To keep the focus on the allocation methods, the single-rate method is used in all of the next examples. However, the contribution method can be applied to any of the methods.

Direct Method

The direct method, as its name implies, is the most direct and simple method of allocating service department costs. This method cannot be used to allocate costs to other service departments; it can be used only to allocate costs to production departments. Even when one service department does perform a significant amount of service for another department, this method bypasses such considerations and assigns all costs directly to the production departments. The direct method ignores the cost drivers that are related to the service departments and concentrates only on the cost drivers attributable to the production departments.

For example: Consider Figure 1C-24, showing four individual departments in a metalworking company.

Figure 1C-24 Department Costs and Cost Drivers

	Service		Production	
	HR	**Janitorial**	**Metal Department**	**Chrome Department**
Dept. Costs before Allocation	$200,000	$80,000	$400,000	$100,000
Labor Hours	10,000	5,000	20,000	5,000
Space (sq. ft.)	15,000	500	60,000	20,000

In this example, the human resources (HR) department's costs use the production department's labor hours, and the janitorial department uses the production department's space measurements, as calculated next:

$$\frac{\text{Department}}{\text{Allocation}} = \frac{\text{Production Department Units}}{\text{Total Units for All Production Departments}} \times \frac{\text{Department}}{\text{Costs}}$$

$$\text{HR Costs to Metal Dept.} = \frac{20,000}{20,000 + 5,000} \times \$200,000 = 0.8 \times \$200,000 = \$160,000$$

$$\text{HR Costs to Chrome Dept.} = 0.2 \times \$200,000 = \$40,000$$

$$\text{Janitorial Costs to Metal Dept.} = \frac{60,000}{60,000 + 20,000} \times \$80,000 = 0.75 \times \$80,000 = \$60,000$$

$$\text{Janitorial Costs to Chrome Dept.} = 0.25 \times \$80,000 = \$20,000$$

The total cost to the metal department is $620,000 ($400,000 + $160,000 + $60,000), and the total cost to the chrome department is $160,000 ($100,000 + $40,000 + $20,000). These allocations assume that there are only two production departments. Even so, the direct method does not take into account the services performed for other service departments. For example, the janitorial service also cleans the HR department, which means that the two production departments are receiving an inaccurate percentage of these costs.

Step-Down Method

The step-down method allocates a service department's costs to service departments and production departments. This method sequentially allocates service department costs, starting with the department that provides the most services to other service departments and finishing with the department that provides the least services to other service departments. Each successive department's allocation is a step down in costs that need to be allocated.

The step-down method also takes into account the proportion of work performed for each of the other service departments. As with the direct method, only the departments receiving the allocation are included in the calculation of cost driver proportions to be allocated.

For example: For the metalworking shop, the HR costs would be allocated first, followed by janitorial services. An actual company might have hundreds of service departments.

Figure 1C-25 illustrates allocation using the step-down method.

Figure 1C-25 Step-Down Method Allocation

	Service		Production	
	HR	**Janitorial**	**Metal Department**	**Chrome Department**
Dept. Costs before Allocation	$200,000	$80,000	$400,000	$100,000
First Step	(200,000)	33,333	133,334	33,333
Subtotal	0	113,333	533,334	133,333
Second Step		(113,333)	85,000	28,333
Total	$0	$0	$618,334	$161,666
Labor Hours	10,000	5,000	20,000	5,000
Space (sq. ft.)	15,000	500	60,000	20,000

Some figures are rounded.

The HR department costs are allocated to the three other departments in this way:

Step 1. A factor (or percentage) is created for each of the receiving departments by taking each of the receiving department's labor hours and dividing that number by the total number of labor hours for the three departments that will receive the allocation from the HR department.

- The janitorial department's allocation percentage is calculated by using 5,000 hours as the numerator and 30,000 (5,000 + 20,000 + 5,000 = 30,000) as the denominator, to create an allocation factor of 5,000/30,000, or 0.167.
- The factors for the metal and chrome departments are 0.667 and 0.167, respectively.
- These factors are then applied to the $200,000 in HR department costs that need to be allocated to the three departments. The HR department's service costs are then allocated to each of the three departments that benefit from its services.
- The janitorial department receives an allocation of $33,333 in costs from the HR department.
- The metal department receives an allocation of $133,334 in costs from the HR department.
- The chrome department receives an allocation of $33,333 in costs from the HR department.

Step 2. The new total of $113,333 for the janitorial costs is allocated to the two production departments based on square feet.

Comparing these costs to those provided by the direct method, the costs are slightly higher for the metal department and slightly lower for the chrome department. The step-down method provides a more accurate measure of how costs should be allocated. However, as can be seen, some costs still can be distorted. For example, janitorial costs still are not allocated to the HR department, even though it has many square feet of space that are cleaned.

In a realistic situation, these costs would be allocated to many service departments (ones with lower costs) other than just the production departments. However, all of the costs eventually end up in the revenue-producing production departments.

Reciprocal Method

The reciprocal method fully recognizes all interdepartmental service costs using simultaneous equations. In contrast, the step-down method provides only partial recognition because it does not allocate costs backward, only forward. Although the reciprocal method is a true recognition method and is most accurate, it is rarely used because of the complexity of its calculations and because the step-down method provides a more cost-effective and reasonable approximation of costs. Software applications make the reciprocal method easier to calculate, but most companies still do not use it.

For example: Apply the reciprocal method to the metalworking shop.

Step 1. Set up a system of equations beginning with the total service department costs and the portions for each of the other departments.

$$HR = \$200,000 + \left(\frac{15,000}{15,000 + 60,000 + 20,000} \times \text{Janitorial} \right)$$

$$\text{Janitorial (J)} = \$80,000 + \left(\frac{5,000}{5,000 + 20,000 + 5,000} \times HR \right)$$

$$HR = \$200,000 + 0.15789(J)$$

$$J = \$80,000 + 0.16667(HR)$$

$$HR = \$200,000 + 0.15789\big[\$80,000 + 0.16667(HR)\big]$$

$$HR = \$200,000 + \$12,631.20 + 0.02632(HR)$$

$$1(HR) - 0.02632(HR) = \$212,631.20$$

$$0.97368(HR) = \$212,631.20$$

$$HR = \frac{\$212,631.20}{0.97368} = \$218,378.93$$

$$HR \approx \$218,379$$

Step 2. Solve for HR's total cost and allocate this to the janitorial, metal, and chrome departments. This amount will be more than the $200,000 department costs.

Step 3. Allocate the new total in janitorial to HR, metal, and chrome departments. At this point, all costs will be allocated to production departments only.

	HR Department	Janitorial Department	Metal Department	Chrome Department
Costs	$200,000	$80,000	$400,000	$100,000
Step 1	(218,379)	36,397	145,586	36,397
Step 2	18,379*	(116,397)	73,514*	24,505*
	$0	$0	$619,100	$160,902

*Slightly off due to rounding.

Phase 3: Allocate Production Department Costs to Products

This phase has already been covered under the various costing methods described in this section.

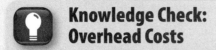

Knowledge Check: Overhead Costs

The next questions are intended to help you check your understanding and recall of the material presented in this topic. They do not represent the type of questions that appear on the CMA exam.

Directions: Answer each question in the space provided. Correct answers and section references appear after the knowledge check questions.

1. To calculate a department's overhead rate that is based on machine hours, which of the following would be used in the numerator and denominator?

	Numerator	Denominator
☐ **a.**	Actual manufacturing overhead	Actual machine hours
☐ **b.**	Actual manufacturing overhead	Estimated machine hours
☐ **c.**	Estimated manufacturing overhead	Actual machine hours
☐ **d.**	Estimated manufacturing overhead	Estimated machine hours

2. Which of the terms below would make the next sentence correct? Multiple overhead rate costing systems are usually more _____ than plant-wide overhead rates.

   ☐ **a.** accurate and complex

   ☐ **b.** accurate

   ☐ **c.** complex

3. Which of the following allocates service department costs sequentially to both production and other service departments, starting with the department that provides the most services, and finishes in a single pass (does not allocate costs to items higher in the sequence)?

   ☐ **a.** Direct method

   ☐ **b.** Step-down method

   ☐ **c.** Reciprocal method

   ☐ **d.** Indirect method

4. Complete the following formula for calculating the fixed overhead application rate.

   $$\text{Fixed Overhead Application Rate} = \left[\frac{\rule{3cm}{0.4pt}}{\text{Total Quantity of Allocation Base}} \right]$$

5. Select the appropriate rate calculation method for each of these firms:

	Plant-wide overhead rate	Departmental overhead rate	ABC overhead costing
A firm manufactures and installs playground equipment			
A firm converts wastewater sludge into fertilizer			
A firm produces 17 types of power tools			

6. Determine if each of the following statements regarding allocation of service department costs is true or false.

	True	False
The reciprocal method provides a highly accurate view of costs.		
The direct method provides a simple means of allocating costs to production departments and to other service departments.		
The step-down method is used because of its relative ease of implementation, even if it is less accurate than other methods.		

Knowledge Check Answers: Overhead Costs

1. To calculate a department's overhead rate that is based on machine hours, which of the following would be used in the numerator and denominator? *[See Departmental Overhead Rate.]*

	Numerator	**Denominator**
☐ **a.**	Actual manufacturing overhead	Actual machine hours
☐ **b.**	Actual manufacturing overhead	Estimated machine hours
☐ **c.**	Estimated manufacturing overhead	Actual machine hours
☐ **d.**	Estimated manufacturing overhead	Estimated machine hours

2. Which of the terms below would make the next sentence correct? *[See Phase 2: Allocate Service Department Costs to Production Department or Other Service Departments]*
   Multiple overhead rate costing systems are usually more _____ than plant-wide overhead rates.

   ☑ **a.** accurate and complex

   ☐ **b.** accurate

   ☐ **c.** complex

3. Which of the following allocates service department costs sequentially to both production and other service departments, starting with the department that provides the most services, and finishes in a single pass (does not allocate costs to items higher in the sequence)? *[See Step-Down Method.]*

   ☐ **a.** Direct method

   ☑ **b.** Step-down method

   ☐ **c.** Reciprocal method

   ☐ **d.** Indirect method

4. Complete the following formula for calculating the fixed overhead application rate. *[See Fixed Overhead Cost Allocation Rates.]*

$$\text{Fixed Overhead Application Rate} = \frac{\textbf{Total Costs in Fixed Overhead Cost Pool}}{\text{Total Quantity of Allocation Base}}$$

5. Select the appropriate rate calculation method for each of these firms: *[See Plant-Wide, Departmental, and ABC Overhead Costing.]*

	Plant-wide overhead rate	Departmental overhead rate	ABC overhead costing
A firm manufactures and installs playground equipment		X	
A firm converts wastewater sludge into fertilizer	X		
A firm produces 17 types of power tools			X

6. Determine if each of the following statements regarding allocation of service department costs is true or false. *[See Phase2: Allocate Service Department Costs to Production Department or Other Service Departments.]*

	True	False
The reciprocal method provides a highly accurate view of costs.	X	
The direct method provides a simple means of allocating costs to production departments and to other service departments.		X
The step-down method is used because of its relative ease of implementation, even if it is less accurate than other methods.	X	

Operational Efficiency

A PARADIGM IS AN EXAMPLE OR a model, and a paradigm shift refers to a significant change in the model that people use to organize or understand what they are doing. At their inception, just-in-time production systems, theory of constraints, and outsourcing represented paradigm shifts in manufacturing. These manufacturing practices changed the type of information needed for decision making and the methods used to collect that data. Ultimately, these practices changed the role of the management accountant and improved the efficiency and effectiveness of information reporting.

This topic looks at the traditional material requirement planning system as well as just-in-time and outsourcing systems and systems built on the theory of constraints. It also discusses capacity concepts and other production management theories.

 READ the Learning Outcome Statements (LOS) for this topic as found in Appendix A and then study the concepts and calculations presented here to be sure you understand the content you could be tested on in the CMA exam.

Material Requirements Planning

The system of production traditionally used in manufacturing is **materials requirements planning** (MRP). Taking a product from raw material through delivery often is treated as a series of discrete events. The concept is to "push" the product through production to reach a market.

The premises underlying MRP push-through systems include:

- Demand forecasts
- A materials order specifying the materials, components, and subunit tasks required to produce a final product
- A production order specifying the quantities of materials, components, subunits, and product inventories needed to meet the demand forecast

In MRP systems, a master production schedule indicates the quantities and timing of each part to be produced. Once the scheduled production run begins, departments push output through a system, regardless of whether that output is needed.

For example: Using an MRP system, here is how a company might calculate subunits (parts) to produce Product P and offset lead times.

Product P is made from:	Part A is made from:	Part B is made from:
2 parts A	1 part C	2 parts C
3 parts B	2 parts D	2 parts E

If 100 units of Product P are required:

Part A	2 × number of Ps	= 2 × 100	= 200
Part B	3 × number of Ps	= 3 × 100	= 300
Part C	1 × number of As	= 1 × 200	
	+ 2 × number of Bs	+ 2 × 300	= 800
Part D	2 × number of As	= 2 × 200	= 400
Part E	2 × number of Bs	= 2 × 300	= 600

The lead times required are:

Product P	1 week
Part A	2 weeks
Part B	2 weeks
Part C	3 weeks
Part D	1 week
Part E	1 week

Once the date for Product P delivery is known, a schedule can be created, specifying when all the parts must be ordered and received to meet the demand for Product P.

		\multicolumn{7}{c}{Weeks}	
		1	2	3	4	5	6	7	
P	Required date							100	P lead time = 1 week
	Order placement						100		
A	Required date						200		A lead time = 2 weeks
	Order placement				200				
B	Required date						300		B lead time = 2 weeks
	Order placement				300				
C	Required date				800				C lead time = 3 weeks
	Order placement	800							
D	Required date				400				D lead time = 1 week
	Order placement			400					
E	Required date				600				E lead time = 1 week
	Order placement			600					

In this example, the MRP is based on the demand for P, the parts or subunits that compose P, and the lead times needed to obtain each part either internally or from an outside supplier.

Benefits of MRP Systems

The benefits of MRP systems include:

- Less coordination required between functional areas; everyone follows the bill of materials.
- Scheduling improvements; levels load when demand is variable or relatively unpredictable.
- Predictable raw material needs; can take advantage of bulk purchasing and other price breaks.
- More efficient inventory control; schedules to use up raw materials or build finished goods.
- Additional inventory on hand to cover orders should product be damaged or lost in transit to a customer.
- Quick response to new customer demand; can supply new customers from existing inventory rather than building product after the order is received.
- Better manufacturing process control; minimizes retooling and machine setup time.

The primary disadvantage of an MRP environment is potential inventory accumulation. Workstations may receive parts that they are not ready to process.

Just-in-Time Manufacturing

A **just-in-time (JIT) system** refers to a comprehensive production and inventory control methodology in which materials arrive exactly as they are needed for each stage in a production process. The goal of JIT is to create lean manufacturing, reducing or eliminating waste of resources by producing production line components as they are required rather than holding large safety stocks of inventory. Nothing is produced until it is needed.

In a JIT system, need is created by demand for a product. Theoretically, the market "pulls" a replacement product from the last position in the system. Demand triggers every step and pulls a product through production—from customer demand for a finished product at one end working all the way back to the demand for raw materials at the other end. This "demand-pull" feature of a JIT system requires high levels of quality at each point in the system because only the minimum number of items demanded will be produced. Close coordination is required among all participants to ensure a smooth flow of goods and operations.

Characteristics of JIT Systems

The major characteristics of a JIT environment are:

- Production organized into manufacturing work cells. Organization of the related manufacturing processes necessary to create a final product into clusters and then logical grouping of clusters into small groups for close proximity, improved communication, and immediate feedback.
- Multiskilled workers. Cross-functional training of workers so they can perform a variety of operations and tasks on an as-needed basis to maintain smooth production flow.
- Reduced setup times. Reduction of the time required to get tools, equipment, and materials ready for a production run.
- Reduced manufacturing lead times. Reduction of the time from when an order is initiated to when a finished good is produced.
- Reliable suppliers. Careful screening of suppliers to ensure on-time deliveries of high-quality goods for JIT use possibly within a day or less.

Use of Kanban in JIT Implementation

Kanban is a Japanese term that describes a visual record or a card and is one of the most common methods used to implement JIT systems. In JIT environments, workers use a kanban to signal the need for a specified quantity of materials or parts to move from one work cell operation or department to another in sequence. Workers respond only after receiving a kanban. When production is complete, the kanban is attached to the finished order and sent downstream to the next work cell.

A kanban traditionally was a card with information identifying the part, the number needed, the delivery location, and similar information. E-kanban applications provide an automated approach that can be integrated with communications and enterprise resource planning (ERP) systems.

JIT Benefits and Limitations

Some of the general benefits of JIT are:

- Obvious production priorities
- Reduced setup and manufacturing lead time
- No overproduction occurrences
- Improved quality control (faster feedback) and less materials waste
- Easier inventory control (low or even zero inventory)
- Less paperwork
- Strong supplier relationships

JIT systems focus on controlling total manufacturing costs versus individual costs, such as raw materials or direct manufacturing labor. Typically, manufacturing costs decline, and cash flow and working capital levels improve. Specific financial benefits are possible; these include:

- Lower inventory investments.
- Reduced costs for carrying and handling inventories.
- Reduced risk of inventory obsolescence, damage, or "shrinkage. "
- Lower investments in space (for production and inventories).
- Higher revenues resulting from a quicker response time to customers.
- Direct tracing of some costs that would otherwise be classified as overhead is also possible. Labor, shipping, and other costs arbitrarily allocated under another method are potentially traceable.

For all the benefits, JIT systems are not without their limitations, which may include:

- No buffer inventory; potential for increased idle time if production needs to wait for materials.
- Reliance on suppliers to maintain adequate stock to meet unpredictable demands; highly dependent on supply chain.
- Potential stockouts at suppliers; critical parts shortages can shut down an entire line.
- Potential overtime expenses from unanticipated orders.

It should be noted that in some markets and under certain conditions, occasional stockouts are preferable to the alternatives.

Outsourcing

Outsourcing describes a company's decision to purchase a product or service from an outside supplier rather than producing it in house. Through this option, an organization can concentrate resources on its core business competencies while capitalizing on the expertise of other firms that are more efficient, effective, or knowledgeable at specialized tasks that are peripheral to those core business competencies. Today, many firms outsource significant parts of their support services, such as information technology, customer service, and human resource functions.

The term *make versus buy* is often used in reference to outsourcing. Make-versus-buy analysis examines the relevant costs of keeping activities in-house versus outsourcing to external suppliers. Some firms have extended the idea of outsourcing to **contract manufacturing,** in which another company actually manufactures a portion of the first firm's products. Contract manufacturing can provide a win-win relationship if one firm has excess capacity or expertise and another company lacks capacity or knowledge.

Benefits and Limitations of Outsourcing

There are many strategic reasons an organization may choose to outsource work. For smaller business, outsourcing may provide access to resources and expertise for capabilities they may not have internally. For larger businesses, outsourcing can improve specific functions. Outsourcing may provide these benefits:

- Can allow management and employees to focus on core competencies and strategic revenue-generating activities
- Can improve efficiency and effectiveness by gaining outside expertise or scale
- Can provide access to current technologies at reasonable cost without the risk of obsolescence
- Can reduce expenses by gaining capabilities without incurring overhead costs (e.g., staffing, benefits, space)
- May improve the quality and/or timeliness of products or services

Despite many attractive advantages, outsourcing is not the answer for all activities or functions. Companies thinking of outsourcing should consider these key cautions:

- May cost more to go outside for specific expertise
- Can result in a loss of in-house expertise and capabilities
- Can reduce process control
- May reduce control over quality
- May lead to less flexibility (depending on the external supplier)
- May result in less personalized service
- Creates privacy and confidentiality issues
- Can result in giving knowledge away and lead to competitors obtaining expertise, scale, customers, and the like.
- Potential for employee morale and loyalty issues

Theory of Constraints

In the 1990s, Dr. Eliyahu Goldratt, a physicist turned business management consultant, countered the adage of "A penny saved is a penny earned" with "The goal is not to save money but to make money. "

Goldratt developed the **theory of constraints (TOC)** as an overall management philosophy with a basis in the manufacturing environment. The overriding goal of the TOC is to improve speed in the manufacturing process by optimizing throughput rather than simply measuring output.

The premise behind the TOC is that every system is pursuing a goal and that every goal is constrained by a limit. If a system is a series of connecting processes that work together to accomplish some aim, a constraint is a limiting factor, bottleneck, or barrier that slows a product's total cycle time. Cycle time is the time it takes to complete a process from beginning to end. Constraint management is the process of identifying process barriers, analyzing and understanding the barriers, and removing them so as to reduce cycle time and optimize the system's efficiency.

Goldratt maintains that that there is only one constraint in a system at any given time but that this bottleneck limits the output of the entire system. The remaining components of the system are known as nonconstraints (non-bottlenecks). Overall, the TOC emphasizes fixing the system constraint and temporarily ignoring the nonconstraints. In this way, the theory has a profound impact on cycle time and process improvement rather than spreading limited time, energy, and resources across an entire system, which may or may not have tangible results.

However, when one constraint is strengthened, the system does not become infinitely stronger. The constraint simply migrates to a different component of the system (i.e., some other factor becomes a bottleneck or barrier). The system is stronger than it was but still not as strong as it could be.

Basic Principles in the Theory of Constraints

Inventory, operational expenses, throughput contribution, and the drum-buffer-rope system are the principal concepts underlying the TOC.

Inventory

Inventory refers to all the money the system invests in purchasing items it intends to resell. Typically, this referred to all physical inventory items, but the term now is more broadly defined to include all assets.

Operating Expenses

In the TOC, *operating* (or operational) *expenses* refer to the money the system spends to convert inventory into throughput. Operating expenses include expenditures such as direct and indirect labor, supplies, outside contractors, interest payments, and depreciation. Employees are responsible for turning inventory into throughput.

Throughput Contribution

Throughput contribution, also known as throughput margin or simply throughput, is a TOC measure of product profitability. It is the rate at which the entire system generates money through product and/or service sales.

Throughput contribution is represented by the next formula:

Throughput Contribution = Sales Revenue – Direct Material Costs

Throughput contribution assumes that the material costs include all purchased components and material handling costs. TOC analysis also assumes that labor is a fixed cost, not a direct and variable cost. The relationship between TOC and throughput contribution is explained in further detail later in this section.

Drum-Buffer-Rope System

The drum-buffer-rope (DBR) system is a TOC method for balancing the flow of production through the constraint. The drum connotes the constraint, the rope is the sequence of processes prior to and including the constraint, and the buffer is the minimum amount of work-in-process input needed to keep the drum busy. The objective of the drum-buffer-rope system is to keep the process flow running smoothly through the constraint by careful timing and scheduling of the processes in the rope leading up to the constraint.

Steps in the Theory of Constraints

The TOC includes five focusing steps designed to concentrate improvement efforts on the constraint most likely to have a positive impact on a system. Figure 1C-26 summarizes the five steps.

Figure 1C-26 Five Focusing Steps of the Theory of Constraints

Step 1	**Identify the system constraint.**
	In the first step, an organization identifies what part of the system constitutes the weakest link, or the constraint, and determines whether it is a physical constraint or a policy constraint.
	Example: A management accountant works with managers and engineers to flowchart a manufacturing process for a product line. They identify the sequence and the amount of time each step requires. A system constraint is identified where one step in the process is taking too long to complete or is idle too long.
Step 2	**Decide how to exploit the constraint.**
	The organization "exploits" the constraint by utilizing every bit of the constraining component without committing to potentially expensive changes and/or upgrades.
	Example: Scheduling of key machine time is changed, and employees are redeployed.
Step 3	**Subordinate everything else.**
	With a plan in place for exploiting the constraint, an organization adjusts the rest of the system to enable the constraint to operate at maximum effectiveness and then evaluates the results to see if the constraint is still holding back system performance. If it is, the organization proceeds to Step 4. If it is not, the constraint has been eliminated, and the organization skips ahead to Step 5.
	Example: Further analysis looks at actions to maximize flow through the constraint. With a focus on throughput, the review team suggests ways to speed up the process, such as reduced setup times and use of the DBR system. Non-value-added activities are eliminated. The idea is to keep the constraint busy without accumulating inventory or accumulating work in the process.
Step 4	**Elevate the constraint.**
	If an organization reaches Step 4, it means that Steps 2 and 3 were not sufficient in eliminating the constraint. At this point, the organization elevates the constraint by taking whatever action is needed to eliminate it. This may involve major changes to the existing system, such as reorganization, divestiture, or

Figure 1C-26 (Continued)

capital improvements. Because these typically require a substantial up-front investment, the organization should be certain that the constraint cannot be broken in Steps 1 through 3 before proceeding.

Example: Management considers how to increase capacity of the system (should Steps 2 and 3 prove unsatisfactory in alleviating the constraint). Additional labor or more/new equipment may be necessary.

Step 5   **Go back to Step 1, but beware of inertia.**

After a constraint is broken, the organization repeats the steps all over again, looking for the next thing constraining system performance. At the same time, it monitors how changes related to subsequent constraints may impact the constraints that are already broken, thus preventing solution inertia.

Example: The organization considers a strategic response to the constraint. The goal is to improve throughput. The product or the process may be redesigned or hard-to-manufacture products may be eliminated, and so on.

In the theory of constraints, throughput (T), inventory (I), and operating expenses (OE) link operational and financial measures. As discussed in Statement on Management Accounting No. 4HH, "Theory of Constraints (TOC) Management System Fundamentals" *(Copyright © 1999 Institute of Management Accountants)*:

- Net profit increases when throughput goes up or operating expenses go down.
- Throughput can go up by increasing sales revenues or reducing variable costs of production.
- Measures that increase net profit increase return on investment—as long as inventory remains the same.
- If inventory can be decreased then ROI will increase even without an increase in net profit.
- Cash flow increases when either throughput goes up or the time to generate throughput is reduced, assuming the time save is applied toward generating more throughput.

The TOC attempts to maximize throughput while decreasing inventory, operational expenses, and other investments. Unlike traditional performance measures, which focus on direct labor efficiency and unit costs and how efficiently the company must produce a product, TOC emphasizes how efficiently an organization must manufacture products for optimum market success. The flow of product is dictated by market demand, not by the forces influencing traditional mass production: cheap sources of materials, machine efficiencies, or low direct labor.

Stated another way, T, I, and OE measurements enable a company to understand how much money it is making and how to best leverage capabilities to improve profitability.

Theory of Constraints Reports

The TOC focuses on eliminating constraints and decreasing cycle time or delivery time. Performance measures used in implementing the TOC also will identify critical success factors (CSFs). Organizations often prepare a TOC report to high-light select operating data and the throughput margin. TOC reports are valuable in identifying both profitability and CSFs.

Figure 1C-27 presents a sample TOC report.

Figure 1C-27 Sample Theory of Constraints Report

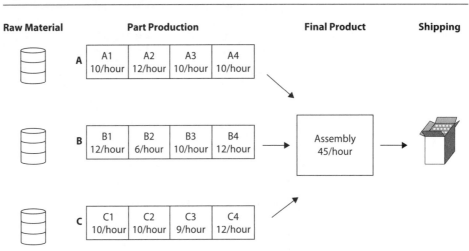

Various formats are possible for TOC reports. In looking at this sample, the key points include:

- The final product is assembled from three component parts: A, B, and C.
- Each part is the result of a different series of linear operations. For example, part A starts with the raw material and goes through operations A1, A2, A3, and A4; raw material for part B goes through B1, B2, B3, B4, and so forth.
- The slowest operation is B2 (six per hour); therefore, the output of this operation is the weakest link and is constraining the output of the entire system.

Having successfully identified the system constraint, steps can be taken to lessen or eliminate it. The organization may "exploit" the constraint by changing how it uses the constraint without spending more money—such as by reducing setup times to improve efficiency and optimize the activity. The organization may "elevate" the constraint by investing money to increase the capacity of the constrained resources—such as buying another piece of equipment or outsourcing an activity.

Naturally, an organization should spend additional money to elevate a constraint only after exploiting the constraint to the fullest potential.

Theory of Constraints and Activity-Based Costing

Organizations that implement the TOC often use activity-based costing (ABC) as well. TOC and ABC are both used by organizations to assess product profitability, but there are a few differences in how these two cost management methods are used.

- TOC takes a short-term approach to profitability analysis with an emphasis on materials-related costs. ABC examines long-term costing, including all product costs.
- TOC considers how to improve short-term profitability by focusing on production constraints and plausible short-term product mix adjustments.
- ABC does not consider resource constraints and process capability; it analyzes cost drivers and accurate unit costs for long-term strategic pricing and profit planning decisions.
- ABC is generally used as a tool for planning and control.

The short-term aspects of TOC and the long-range focus of ABC make them complementary profitability analysis methods.

Although the TOC has its roots in the manufacturing environment, applications have been developed for service industries. Measures of speed and cycle time must be defined appropriately for the nature of the enterprise. Additionally, specific TOC implications for management accounting have been assessed to consider the benefits of throughput accounting in business rather than using traditional cost accounting methods.

Theory of Constraints and Throughput Costing

The TOC focuses on improving a company's profits by managing its operating constraints. Companies that employ a TOC approach use a form of variable costing called throughput costing. Throughput costing, also called super-variable costing, is a costing method where the only costs included in inventory are the costs of direct materials. All other costs are classified as period costs. In many companies, it is quite accurate to say that direct labor behaves like a committed fixed cost in the shortrun, not like a variable cost that adjusts to changes in output. The TOC has a short-time focus; an assumption is made that all operating costs are fixed in the short-term and are therefore categorized as fixed costs. Like variable costing, throughput costing is an internal reporting tool.

Three items that are measured in the TOC are **throughput contribution**, **inventory (or investments)**, and **operating expenses**.

Throughput Contribution = Sales Revenue − Direct Material Costs

Inventory = (Materials Costs in Direct Materials, Work-in-Process, and Finished Goods Inventories) + (R & D Costs) + (Costs of Equipment and Buildings)

Operating Expenses = All Costs of Operations, Not Including Direct Materials

Using this method, the objective is to maximize throughput contribution while reducing investments and operating costs.

Capacity Concepts

A key issue in costing is choosing the capacity level for computing the allocation of manufacturing overhead. Determining the correct level of capacity to use is a difficult strategic decision for managers. The choice of capacity level used to allocate overhead can have a great effect on product cost information used by managers. If a company has capacity in excess of what it needs, it will incur large costs of unused capacity. Likewise, if a company has too little capacity to meet demand, it may have trouble filling customer orders.

Theoretical capacity (also known as ideal capacity) is the level of capacity that can be achieved under ideal conditions, when there are no machine breakdowns or maintenance, delays, or the like. Theoretical capacity represents the largest volume of output possible but is unattainable and unrealistic.

Practical capacity represents the highest level of capacity that can be achieved while allowing for unavoidable losses of productive time, such as machine breakdowns, employee vacations, maintenance, and so on. Unlike theoretical capacity, it is the level of capacity that can realistically be achieved.

Using theoretical capacity when calculating overhead allocations would mean that a large denominator activity level would be used, resulting in a lower overhead allocation to individual units of product. This would distort the allocated costs (making them too low) and provide management with product cost information that is not representative of actual costs. Practical capacity does not take into consideration the amount of unused capacity in allocating costs. The benefit of this approach is that it encourages managers to focus their attention on the amount of unused capacity, and user departments are not overcharged for a portion of costs related to unused capacity.

Practical capacity is a better choice to use as the denominator activity level for allocating overhead because it is realistic and will generate product costs that accurately reflect the cost of the product. By using practical capacity to calculate product costs, the company is not over- or underallocating costs to each unit of product. Instead, a "practical" or "realistic" amount of overhead is allocated to each unit produced. As a result, many companies prefer to use practical capacity as the denominator to calculate the allocated overhead rate.

Other Production Management Theories

Competitiveness . . . productivity . . . continuous improvement . . . profitability . . .

Organizations constantly strive to improve on what they already do well and to capitalize on growth opportunities. Beyond the manufacturing paradigms previously discussed, organizations have a wide array of other production management techniques to consider in their quest for better, faster, and more profitable operations.

Many organizations have adopted some or all of the approaches listed in Figure 1C-28 in an attempt to reduce costs, increase productivity, improve quality, and increase their overall responsiveness to customers.

Figure 1C-28 Contemporary Productivity Approaches

Technique	Description
Automation/robots	Uses reprogrammable, multifunctional robots (machines) designed to manipulate materials, parts, tools, or specialized devices through variable programmed motions
	Applies robots to the performance of a variety of repetitive tasks
Capacity management and analysis (capacity planning)	Represents an important decision-making area involving strategic, tactical, and operational aspects
	Includes an iterative procedure that:
	• Reviews long-term demand forecasts
	• Translates forecasts into capacity requirements
	• Matches the capacity requirements to present facilities
	• Identifies mismatches between capacity requirements and projected availability
	• Devises plans to overcome mismatches and selects the best alternative
Computer-aided design (CAD)	Uses computers in product development, analysis, and design modification to improve the quality and performance of the product
	Usually entails the drawing or physical layout steps of engineering design
Computer-aided manufacturing (CAM)	Applies the computer to the planning, control, and operation of a production facility
Computer-integrated manufacturing (CIM)	Involves a manufacturing system that completely integrates all factory and office functions within a company via a computer-based information network
	Uses computers to control the integration and flow of information between design, engineering, manufacturing, logistics, warehousing and distribution, customers and suppliers, sales and marketing activities, and accounting
	Facilitates hour-by-hour manufacturing management
Concurrent engineering (simultaneous engineering)	Integrates product or service design with input from all business units and functions throughout a product's or service's life cycle
	Emphasizes upstream prevention versus downstream correction
	Attempts to balance the needs of all parties in product or service design while maintaining customer requirements
Flexible manufacturing system (FMS)	Uses a computerized network of automated equipment that produces one or more groups of parts or variations of a product in a flexible manner

Knowledge Check: Operational Efficiency

The next questions are intended to help you check your understanding and recall of the material presented in this topic. They do not represent the type of questions that appear on the CMA exam.

Directions: Answer each question in the space provided. Correct answers and section references appear after the knowledge check questions.

1. What is the primary benefit of just-in-time (JIT) systems compared with traditional materials requirement planning systems?

   ☐ **a.** Increased stock quantities at all levels in a system

   ☐ **b.** Maximization of production runs to accommodate complete product lines

   ☐ **c.** Replacement of a push-through manufacturing strategy with a demand-pull strategy

   ☐ **d.** Reduced risk of overproduction and savings from holding less inventory

2. A large semiconductor manufacturer plans to apply the theory of constraints methodology to increase production capacity. How could a management accountant **best** support the initiative?

   ☐ **a.** Determine outsourcing costs to offload long-term critical constraints.

   ☐ **b.** Design buffer management worksheets to facilitate quantitative analysis.

   ☐ **c.** Provide net profit, return on investment, and cash flow data.

   ☐ **d.** Supply activity-based cost data.

   Match the following terms to their appropriate description.

   a. An iterative decision-making process intended to overcome supply and demand mismatches

   b. A decision to purchase a product or service from an external supplier rather than producing it in-house

   c. JIT system feature requiring close coordination to ensure a smooth flow of goods and operations despite low inventory quantities

   d. A visual signal indicating the need for a specified quantity of materials or parts to move from one operation or department to another in sequence

3. _____ Demand-pull

4. _____ Kanban

5. _____ Outsourcing

6. _____ Capacity management

7. An organization will directly gain all of the following benefits from the TOC methodology **except:**

   ☐ **a.** reduced bottlenecks.

   ☐ **b.** increased profitability.

   ☐ **c.** improved long-term planning and control.

   ☐ **d.** improved quality of products and services.

8. In a TOC model, what does this calculate?

   Sales Revenue − Direct Material Costs = _____

9. In TOC, what factors link operational and financial measures?

   a. _____

   b. _____

   c. _____

10. What concern would there be in using theoretical capacity to allocate overhead? What should be used instead?

    _____

Knowledge Check Answers: Operational Efficiency

1. What is the primary benefit of just-in-time (JIT) systems compared with traditional materials requirement planning systems? *[See JIT Benefits and Limitations.]*

    ☐ **a.** Increased stock quantities at all levels in a system

    ☐ **b.** Maximization of production runs to accommodate complete product lines

    ☐ **c.** Replacement of a push-through manufacturing strategy with a demand-pull strategy

    ☑ **d.** Reduced risk of overproduction and savings from holding less inventory.

2. A large semiconductor manufacturer plans to apply the theory of constraints methodology to increase production capacity. How could a management accountant **best** support the initiative? *[See Theory of Constraints and Activity-Based Costing.]*

    ☐ **a.** Determine outsourcing costs to offload long-term critical constraints.

    ☐ **b.** Design buffer management worksheets to facilitate quantitative analysis.

    ☐ **c.** Provide net profit, return on investment, and cash flow data.

    ☑ **d.** Supply activity-based cost data.

    Match the following terms to their appropriate description. *[See Just-in-Time- Manufacturing, Outsourcing and Capacity Concepts.]*

    a. An iterative decision-making process intended to overcome supply and demand mismatches

    b. A decision to purchase a product or service from an external supplier rather than producing it in-house

    c. JIT system feature requiring close coordination to ensure a smooth flow of goods and operations despite low inventory quantities

    d. A visual signal indicating the need for a specified quantity of materials or parts to move from one operation or department to another in sequence

3. __c__ Demand-pull

4. __d__ Kanban

5. __b__ Outsourcing

6. __a__ Capacity management

7. An organization will directly gain all of the following benefits from the TOC methodology **except:** *[See Theory of Constraints.]*

    ☐ **a.** reduced bottlenecks.

    ☐ **b.** increased profitability.

    ☑ **c.** improved long-term planning and control.

    ☐ **d.** improved quality of products and services.

8. In a TOC model, what does this calculate? *[See Theory of Constraints and Throughput Costing.]*

    Sales Revenue − Direct Material Costs = **Throughput Contribution**

9. In TOC, what factors link operational and financial measures? *[See Steps in the Theory of Constraints.]*

    a. **Throughput (T)**

    b. **Inventory (I)**

    c. **Operating expenses (OE)**

10. What concern would there be in using theoretical capacity to allocate overhead? What should be used instead? *[See Capacity Concepts.]*

    Using theoretical capacity results in a lower overhead allocation to individual units of product. Practical capacity reduces theoretical capacity by including unavoidable interruption, such as machine maintenance, plant shutdowns, and the like. Therefore, practical capacity is more realistic and will generate product costs that more accurately reflect the cost of the product than if theoretical capacity is used to allocate overhead.

Business Process Performance

BUSINESS PERFORMANCE HAS ORGANIZATIONAL RAMIFICATIONS beyond matching or surpassing the competition in your industry. Customers are generally better informed and have virtually unlimited sources of quality goods and services at acceptable prices. Customers today demand more for less. Organizations are constantly challenged to address these rising customer expectations, and the analysis of business process performance is one way to meet those challenges.

This topic addresses some of the techniques used to analyze business process performance: value chain analysis, process analysis, process reengineering, benchmarking, activity-based management, continuous improvement, best practice analysis, and cost-of-quality analysis.

READ the Learning Outcome Statements (LOS) for this topic as found in Appendix A and then study the concepts and calculations presented here to be sure you understand the content you could be tested on in the CMA exam.

Value Chain Analysis

How do organizations make intelligent choices about where to focus their energy and how to best create value in the eyes of their customers? Many organizations have found success through value chain analysis, which has become an integral part of the strategic planning process. Similar to strategic planning, value chain analysis is a continuous process of gathering, evaluating, and communicating information. The basic intent of value chain analysis is to help managers envision an organization's future and implement business decisions to gain and sustain competitive advantage.

The concept underlying this system is **value**, which is generally used to describe the worth, desirability, or utility of a particular asset. It may be applied to an individual product or a service rendered, to a group of assets, or to an entire business unit. Value may also be applied as a metric, such as in market value, shareholders' value, and so on.

Value activities describe the collective activities performed by organizations in a given industry, from the processing of raw material (in a manufacturing industry) to the production and servicing of a final product. Depending on the industry, some firms may be involved in several activities whereas others may have responsibility for only a single activity. Within an organization, business units may be a further subset. A clothing company, for example, may start with the raw textiles, design and manufacture clothing articles, and contract advertising and sales to retailers. Another clothing company may contract out manufacturing, concentrate on sales and marketing through organizational business units, and rely on retailers for distribution.

A **cost driver** is any factor that causes a change in the cost of an activity. Direct labor hours, machine hours, computer time, and beds occupied in a hospital are all examples of cost drivers. For more meaningful analysis, beyond the total costs of each value-creating activity, the causes for significant costs need to be identified. Firms examine structural cost drivers and executional cost drivers. Structural cost drivers are long-term organizational decisions that determine the economic structure driving the cost of the firm's product or service. Executional cost drivers reflect a firm's operational decisions on how to best use its resources, both human and physical, to achieve organizational goals and objectives.

A **supply chain** is the extended network of distributors, transporters, storage facilities, and suppliers that participate in the production, design, sale, delivery, and use of a company's product or service. During value chain analysis, an organization examines the entire supply chain.

A **value chain** is a system of interdependent activities, each of which is intended to add value to the final product or service. Naturally, the development of a value chain depends on the industry. Figure 1C-29 shows a typical value chain for a manufacturing environment. In a service environment, the acquisition of raw materials would be absent, and other activities and operations might vary and/or assume different degrees of importance.

Value chain analysis (VCA) is a strategic analysis tool organizations use to assess the importance of their customers' value perceptions. It consists of an integrated set of tools and processes that define current costs and performance measures and evaluate where customer value can be increased and where costs can be reduced throughout the supply chain.

The distinct benefit of VCA is that it looks at the entire value chain, not just the activities in which the organization participates. Suppliers, distributors, and others involved in a value chain each have costs and profit margins, which affect the final price to end users and the marketing strategy for the product or service.

Steps in Value Chain Analysis

The purpose of a VCA is to focus on the total value chain of each product or service and to determine which selected part or parts support the firm's competitive advantage and strategy. Theoretically, competitive advantage and competitive strategy cannot be examined meaningfully at the organizational level as a whole or even at the business unit level. Because a value chain separates the firm into distinct

Figure 1C-29 Typical Value Chain for a Manufacturing Environment

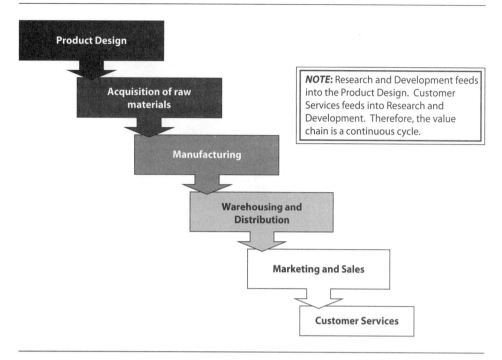

NOTE: Research and Development feeds into the Product Design. Customer Services feeds into Research and Development. Therefore, the value chain is a continuous cycle.

strategic activities, organizations are able to use VCA to determine where in the operations—from design to distribution and customer service—customer value can be enhanced and costs lowered. In this way, VCA helps to identify sources of profitability and to understand the costs of the related activities and processes.

VCA requires a strategic framework as a starting point for organizing and analyzing internal and external information and for summarizing findings and recommendations.

There is no one standard process to conduct a VCA, and practices will vary among companies. The general steps in VCA discussed on the IMA Web site in Statement on Management Accounting No. 4X, "Value Chain Analysis for Assessing Competitive Advantage," *(Copyright © 1996 Institute of Management Accountants)* are summarized in Figure 1C-30.

Figure 1C-30 Value Chain Approach for Assessing Competitive Advantage

Step 1	Internal cost analysis
	This step determines the sources of profitability and the relative cost of internal processes or activities. An internal cost analysis will:
	Identify the firm's value-creating processes.
	Determine the portion of the total cost of the product or service attributable to each value-creating process.
	Identify the cost drivers for each process.
	Identify the links between processes.
	Evaluate opportunities for achieving relative cost advantages.

(Continued)

Figure 1C-30 (Continued)

Step 2	**Internal differentiation analysis**

During this part of the analysis, sources for creating and sustaining superior differentiation are examined. The primary focus is the customer's value perceptions of the firm's products and services. Similar to Step 1, an internal differentiation analysis first requires identifying internal value-creating processes and cost drivers. With this information, a firm can perform a differentiation analysis to:

Identify customers' value-creating processes.

Evaluate differentiation strategies for enhancing customer value.

Determine the best sustainable differentiation strategies.

Step 3	**Vertical linkage analysis**

Vertical linkage analysis is a broader application of Steps 1 and 2; it includes all upstream and downstream value-creating processes in an industry. Vertical linkage can identify which activities are the most/least critical to competitive advantage or disadvantage. It considers all links, from the source of raw materials to the disposal and/or recycling of a product. A vertical linkage analysis will:

Identify the industry's value chain and assign costs, revenues, and assets to value-creating processes.

Diagnose the cost drivers for each value-creating process.

Evaluate the opportunities for sustainable competitive advantage.

These three types of analysis—internal cost analysis, internal differentiation analysis, and vertical linkage analysis—are complementary. Organizations begin by examining their internal operations and then broaden their focus to evaluate their competitive position within their industry.

Typically, a large amount of data is generated during a VCA study, and these data require careful interpretation to discern the key messages of how to best create customer-perceived value.

Value-Added Concepts and Quality

Quality, like strategy and strategic planning, has many definitions and descriptions and a variety of approaches. The customer ultimately defines what constitutes product or service quality, but this is not a static perception; instead, it is constantly evolving based on factors such as product innovation and market changes.

Internal and External Customers

In quality terms, a customer is anyone who is affected by an organization's processes, products, and services. Therefore, a firm has both internal and external customers.

An **internal customer** is an employee, department, or business unit that receives an output in the form of information, a product, or a service from another employee, department, or business unit. Even the next person in a work process is an internal customer. Based on this concept, all work-related activities may be considered as a series of transactions between employees or between internal customers and internal suppliers.

An **external customer** is a person or entity outside of the organization who receives information, a product, or a service. Generally, external customers are thought of as being end users outside the organization.

Value Chain Analysis and Quality Performance

As organizations strive for quality performance, everyone, from the top executives to an employee on the front line, has a responsibility to create or contribute to the value of the firm's processes, products, and services for the external customer or end user.

Suppliers also have a crucial role. An organization starts with external customer requirements as determined by its industry analysis and/or strategies. The firm proceeds to identify internal customer–supplier relationships and requirements and continues with external suppliers. A chain of operations produces the final product or service. The external customer is best served when every internal customer and supplier receives what they need along the chain.

Figure 1C-31 illustrates the customer-supplier value chain as represented in IMA Statement on Management Accounting No. 4R "Managing Quality Improvements." *(Copyright © 1993 Institute of Management Accountants).*

Figure 1C-31 Customer–Supplier Value Chain

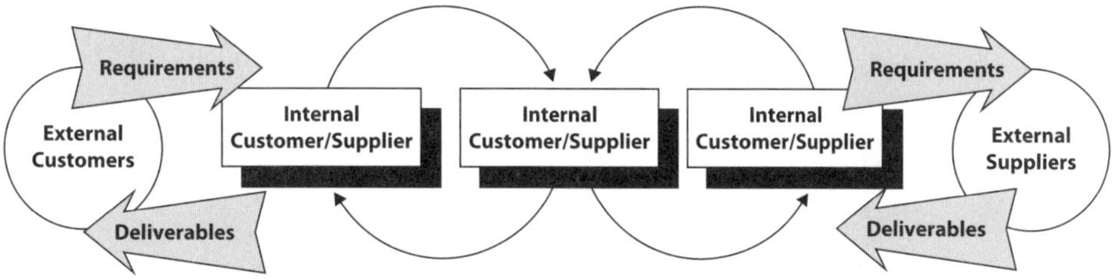

The concept of **value added** refers to activities that convert resources into products and services consistent with external customer requirements. Non-value-added activities can be eliminated with no deterioration in product or service functionality, performance, or quality in the eyes of the end user. In industries in which product and service parity is prevalent or outputs are perceived as commodities, examples of value-added activities might be some extra fabrication or customization before the sale to a customer or providing more service with the sale. Activities related to materials movement or rework would most likely be non-value-added.

The goal of the customer–supplier value chain is to integrate value into every aspect of a work process. By removing non-value-added activities, work processes can be more efficient and ultimately yield a better-quality product or service.

Process Analysis

A **process** is an activity or a group of interrelated activities that takes an input of materials and/or resources, adds value to it, and provides an output to internal or external customers. A process often spans several departmental units, such as accounting, sales, production, and shipping.

A firm should recognize and understand the array of business processes that contribute to its business profitability. One way to do this is through process analysis. **Process analysis** refers to a collection of analytic methods that can be used to examine and measure the basic elements for a process to operate. It can also identify those processes with the greatest need for improvement.

Process Characteristics

Three characteristics that help to identify a good process fit are:

1. **Effectiveness.** A process is effective when it produces the desired result and meets or exceeds customers' requirements. Customers perceive an effective process as being of high quality.
2. **Efficiency.** A process is efficient when it achieves results with minimal waste, expense, and/or cycle time. It has a high ratio of output to input.
3. **Adaptability.** A process is adaptable when it is flexible and can react quickly to changing requirements or new competition.

A process needs to address all three areas: A cost-efficient process is of little use if it does not produce an effective product, or if it cannot adapt to changing needs.

An assumption from the early days of quality improvement programs was that process improvements could be gained only at the expense of productivity. Although experience has shown that quality improvements usually increase productivity by decreasing waste and the need for rework, the fact is that quality does have a cost, but it is a cost that management can influence and control.

A quality-oriented approach to product design, manufacturing, and service will consider upstream and downstream effects of all decisions. Cost drivers from all the company's departments, plus additional outside costs, must be accurately understood to ensure that sufficient resources are available for the transition to a quality enterprise.

Process Reengineering/Business Process Reengineering

Process improvements and productivity gains achieved through total quality management (TQM) generally are incremental gains achieved by tweaking a system and reducing inputs. In contrast, process reengineering and business process reengineering offer deeper, more sweeping gains.

Process reengineering diagrams a process in detail, evaluates and questions the process flow, and then completely redesigns the process to eliminate unnecessary steps, reduce opportunities for errors, and reduce costs. All activities that do not add value are eliminated.

Business process reengineering (BPR) is the fundamental analysis and radical redesign of business processes within and between enterprises to achieve dramatic improvements in performance (e.g., cost, quality, speed, and service). Michael Hammer and James Champy brought BPR to the forefront in the early 1990s with their book *Reengineering the Corporation* (HarperBusiness, 2003). BPR promotes the idea that sometimes wiping the slate clean and radically redesigning and reorganizing an enterprise is necessary to lower costs and increase the quality of a product or service.

According to Hammer and Champy, BPR involves changes that are:

Fundamental. BPR forces people to look at tacit rules and assumptions underlying the way they currently do business. Firms must answer two questions: Why do we do what we do? Why do we do it the way we do it?

Radical. BPR is about reinvention, not improvement or modification. A radical redesign means disregarding existing processes and inventing new ways of doing work.

Dramatic. BPR is not for the faint of heart. It should be used when "heavy blasting" is needed to alleviate a dire situation. If you need only a slight bump in process improvement, there is no need to reengineer.

Process. BPR is about a process orientation with a heavy emphasis on the chain of activities that take input and create output of value to the customer.

The BPR model espouses that process workflow in most large corporations is based on assumptions about technology, people, and organizational goals that are no longer valid. It also maintains that information is a key enabler to achieve radical change.

Figure 1C-32 lists the common tools and tactics underpinning successful BPR efforts.

Figure 1C-32 Fundamentals of Business Process Reengineering

Process orientation	Organizations look at entire processes that cut across organizational boundaries, not narrowly defined tasks with predefined organizational boundaries.
Ambition	Companies aim for breakthroughs, not minor improvements.
Rule breaking	Old traditions and assumptions are deliberately abandoned.
Creative use of technology	Current/state-of-the-art technology serves as an enabler that allows organizations to do work in radically different ways.

Process reengineering and BPR are strong medicine. Many well-intended reengineering efforts have failed for any number of reasons. In a bit of a backlash to Hammer and Champy's initial foray, reengineering was even accused of being a cover for downsizing and layoffs. Yet the success stories show that although boldness may have perils and may create some pain, the end gains of reengineering can be dramatic.

Process analysis looks at the linkage of quality, productivity, and process improvements:

1. Productivity implies trying to improve on what already exists.
2. Improving productivity requires continuous quality improvement.
3. Continuous improvement necessitates ongoing organizational learning, process improvements, and reengineering.

These continuous productivity improvements, then, can help an organization be competitive in the long term.

Business Process Reengineering Cycle

Identify Processes

Review, Update, Analyze

Design

Test & Implement

Benchmarking

Benchmarking can be used in coordination with process analysis to develop measures to use in assessing an organization's effectiveness, efficiency, and adaptability. The term **benchmarking** describes a continuous, systematic process of measuring products, services, and practices against the best levels of performance. Many people think of benchmarking as simply capturing best-in-class information, but the practice has a much wider application. Quite often, best-in-class levels are comparisons to external benchmarks of industry leaders. However, they may also be based on internal benchmarking information or measures from other organizations (outside an industry) that have similar processes.

Benchmarking Process Performance

Best-in-class levels may be financial or nonfinancial measures. Statement on Management Accounting No. 4V, "Effective Benchmarking," *(Copyright © 1995 Institute of Management Accountants)* describes benchmarking as having seven phases with associated activities, as illustrated in Figure 1C-33.

Figure 1C-33 Benchmarking Phases and Activities

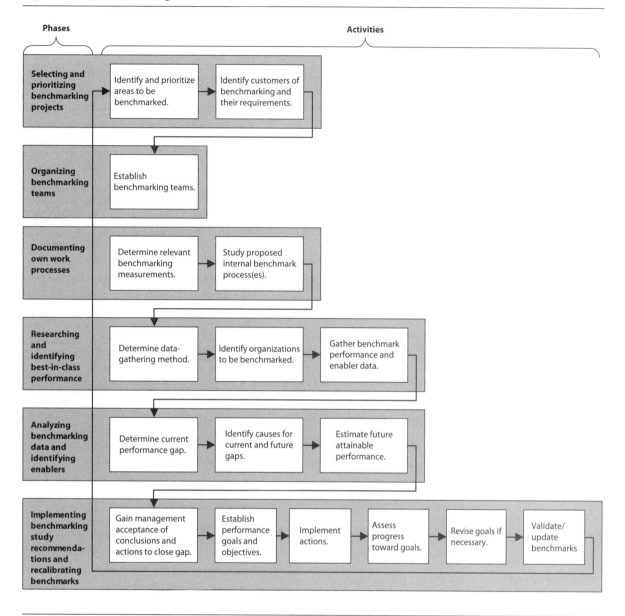

Benchmarking and Creating Competitive Advantage

The 1990s saw a proliferation in benchmarking studies, but, unfortunately, many organizations misused benchmarking. Benchmarking studies in various forms (best practice, functional, process, and competitive) were freely conducted, generally without a context. Invalid comparisons were often made (e.g., comparing the growth of a highly leveraged company to one internally financed from earnings, or comparing the growth of a company in a low-cost environment to one in Silicon Valley). Given such misapplications, most of these benchmarking studies were not particularly cost-effective.

However, well-designed and properly applied benchmarking can be a powerful tool in helping an organization to be competitive. Through benchmarking, a firm identifies best-in-class levels and conducts a study to determine how those levels can be adopted and lead to improved performance. It provides a rational method for setting performance goals and gaining market leadership; important decisions are based on facts and data rather than on emotions. Because benchmarking is based on what the best are doing, it provides an accurate assessment of what needs to change.

Strategic Benchmarking

Although many benchmarking studies have an operational focus, a benchmarking project also may have a strategic focus. Strategic benchmarking applies process benchmarking to the level of business strategy by incorporating benchmarking results in the strategic planning process. As such, it helps an organization develop an increased understanding and ability to address strategic business issues such as:

- Building core competencies to help sustain competitive advantage
- Developing a new business line
- Targeting a specific shift in strategy (e.g., entering new markets or developing a new service)
- Making an acquisition
- Creating an organization that can quickly respond to uncertainties

Activity-Based Management

Activity-based management is another type of strategic analysis aimed at yielding process improvements.

Activity-based costing and activity-based management are related concepts. **Activity-based costing (ABC)** is a measure of the costs and performance of activities, resources, and cost objects. It assigns resources to activities and assigns activities to cost objects. It focuses on a causal relationship between cost drivers and activities.

- **Activity-based management (ABM)** focuses on the management of activities as the way of improving the value received by the customer and the profit achieved by providing this value. ABC provides the data used by ABM for cost driver analysis, activity analysis, and performance measurement.
- While ABC designates and uses cost drivers for each activity, ABM analyzes these cost drivers for their effectiveness in defining the root causes of activity costs. To explain the effects of cost drivers, ABM uses internal interviews, observation, and quality control tools such as theory of constraints benchmarking, and other analytical tools. The result will be an assessment of how well cost drivers reflect actual costs and actual areas of profitability.

- Another aspect of ABM is performance measurement. ABM helps make performance evaluation measures relate to the factors that drive the element being measured (i.e., costs drivers and revenue drivers). Such measures include revenue, manufacturing cost, nonmanufacturing cost, and profit as well as nonfinancial measures.

The bottom line is that both ABC and ABM are valuable practices for any firm striving to maintain or improve its competitive position. ABC answers the question "What do things cost?" ABM takes a process view and asks "What causes costs to occur?"

ABM Principles and Process Improvements

ABM is forward-looking and change-oriented. It seeks ways to avoid unnecessary costs and put existing resources to maximum use.

Based on ABM information, organizations generally can:

- Make better decisions.
- Improve performance.
- Increase earnings on total resources deployed.

Overall, ABM supports both process reengineering and BPR by analyzing the organizational processes and by facilitating the measurement of the impact of reengineering efforts, thereby increasing the value created for the resources consumed.

Organizations implement ABM for a variety of reasons. Figure 1C-34 summarizes general situations where a firm can benefit from ABM, depending on its stage of evolution.

Figure 1C-34 General Applications for ABM

If a firm's operations are . . .	Then ABM can be useful to . . .
Growing	Redeploy non-value-added work.
	Improve processes and activities.
Flat	Identify non-value-added costs.
	Set priorities for improvement and effect improvement.
	Isolate/eliminate cost drivers.
	Determine product/service costs.
Declining	Cut costs.
	Downsize.
	Effect layoffs.
Constrained as to capacity	Determine product/service costs.
	Make product/service decisions.
	Determine activity capacity.
	Identify bottlenecks.

ABM and Quality Improvements

ABM is sometimes erroneously thought of as a replacement for quality efforts, just-in-time systems, process reengineering, BPR, and benchmarking. To the contrary, ABM supports quality management and the other initiatives by providing an integrated information system that:

- Establishes accountability
- Facilitates measuring of results
- Enables setting of priorities
- Specific to quality, an ABM system facilitates quality implementation by:
  - Identifying activity costs
  - Increasing the visibility of associated costs of quality
  - Providing quality cost measures that can be easily incorporated in cost-of-quality reports

Because traditional accounting systems focus on functions (e.g., research and design, production, sales and marketing, etc.), collecting data about the costs of quality is more problematic. With ABM, activity costs resulting from poor quality are more readily identifiable.

Advantages and Disadvantages of ABM

ABM has six advantages over traditional cost management techniques:

1. It uses continuous improvement to maintain the firm's competitive advantage.
2. It allocates more resources to activities, products, and customers that add more value, strategically redirecting management focus.
3. It eliminates non-value-added activities.
4. It measures process effectiveness and identifies areas to reduce costs or increase customer value.
5. It works well with just-in-time processes.
6. It ties performance measurement to ABC to provide consistent incentives for using ABC.

ABM has three disadvantages when compared to traditional cost management:

1. Changing to ABC/ABM will result in different pricing, process design, manufacturing technology, and product design decisions. The company must be prepared to support managers who embrace these methods and discourage managers who continue to use the older methods.
2. ABC/ABM is not used for external financial reporting. The need to prepare reports using traditional methods may influence management decision making enough to dilute the impact of ABC/ABM.
3. Implementing ABC/ABM is expensive and time-consuming, so a cost-benefit analysis should be done to identify all hidden costs and benefits.

Continuous Improvement (Kaizen) Concepts

Kaizen is a Japanese term used to describe continuous improvement at all levels in an organization. The premise is that as every process, beginning with the most important, is examined, worked on, and improved, the total enterprise improves. Kaizen acknowledges that innovation is valuable, but it also maintains that innovations do not collectively contribute as much as continuous incremental improvements.

The kaizen process is often described as a staircase of improvement. Moving from step to step, an organization uses a continuous process of following an improvement, maintaining an improvement, following an improvement, maintaining an improvement, and so on. Although the steps may be small, each step moves the organization upward toward sustained improvements.

Continuous improvements often are based on standards, which become organizational performance expectations and goals. Standards allow an enterprise to identify the cost to manufacture and sell a product or a service and to determine the causes of cost overruns.

Organizations can develop standards based on:

- Activity analysis
- Historical data
- Benchmarking
- Market expectations
- Strategic decisions

Company benchmarking, for example, could be used to compare a firm's current cost structure to that of similar businesses and to develop appropriate standards. Once standards are determined, a series of continuous improvements could be implemented to increase efficiency and effectiveness and minimize variances.

Best Practice Analysis

The term **best practice** generally refers to a process or technique that has produced outstanding results in one situation and that can be applied and/or adapted to improve effectiveness, efficiency, quality, safety, innovativeness, and/or some other performance measure in another situation. Best practice analysis refers to the collective steps in a gap analysis. A gap analysis is generally described as the difference between the current state and a desired state, or the space between what is and what an organization hopes to be. The current state is defined by current practices, and the desired state is defined by best practices.

Best practice analysis involves assessing how a firm's given performance level measures up to a best practice and then defining the logical next steps in transitioning to the desired performance level.

Typical activities are:

- Defining the gap (through a comparison to internal operational data)
- Determining the reasons for the gap
- Examining the factors that contribute to the existence of the best practice(s)
- Developing recommendations and an approach to implement the best practice(s)

Techniques and tools for conducting a best practice analysis vary. Qualitative and quantitative tools are used, but most of the tools are common to TQM and kaizen.

It may be said that best practice analysis tools—such as VCA, process analysis, BPR, benchmarking, TQM, and kaizen—are the clout behind business process improvement initiatives. Best practice analysis enables firms to identify and undertake performance improvements.

Costs of Quality Analysis

Process improvement teams need to know the specific costs for each part of the production process in order to determine how changes in a quality design affect profitability. The costs of quality (COQ) are broken down into four categories:

1. **Prevention costs** are the costs of quality system design, implementation, and maintenance, including audits of the quality system itself. Examples include quality planning, review of new products, surveys of supplier capabilities, team meetings for quality, and training for quality, as well as those related to ensuring the quality or quality improvement of the product: market research, product testing, and product design.

2. **Appraisal costs** are the costs of auditing processes for quality, including formal and informal measurements and evaluations of quality levels and setting quality standards and performance requirements. Examples include inspection and testing of raw materials, work-in-process and finished goods testing, calibration of equipment, and audits or operations or services. In addition, they address more externally focused costs, such as monitoring market reaction and competitors' products.

3. **Internal failure costs** include the costs involved with defective products and components that are caught before shipping them to the customer. Examples include scrap, rework, spoilage, retesting, and reinspection. They also include systemic problems, such as the inability to meet the design, manufacturing, and service standards identified for the product.

4. **External failure costs** are the costs involved with shipping a defective product to a customer. Examples include customer complaints, returns, product recalls, and warranty claims. Overall, these costs relate to an inability to meet customer perceptions for product quality and service.

A quality-oriented approach can achieve gains in productivity and profit, but only if the company makes a long-term commitment to implement and sustain the effort.

Knowledge Check:
Business Process Performance

The next questions are intended to help you check your understanding and recall of the material presented in this topic. They do not represent the type of questions that appear on the CMA exam.

Directions: Answer each question in the space provided. Correct answers and section references appear after the knowledge check questions.

1. Which of the following statements best characterizes value chain analysis?

   ☐ **a.** It emphasizes a firm's functional structure.

   ☐ **b.** It examines a firm's hierarchal structure.

   ☐ **c.** It examines distinct strategic activities.

   ☐ **d.** It promotes product/service differentiation.

Match the following business process concepts to the appropriate application.

   a. Noncompetitive firms exchanging information about similar manufacturing processes

   b. An airline removing seats in a plane to give coach passengers more leg room

   c. An internal system examining past, current, and future performance

2. _____ Value chain analysis

3. _____ Benchmarking

4. _____ Activity-based management

5. Which of the following statements accurately differentiates activity-based costing (ABC) and activity-based management (ABM)?

   ☐ **a.** ABC provides information on process, product, and market performance; ABM finds ways to improve them.

   ☐ **b.** ABC provides actionable information; ABM is a source of explanatory data.

   ☐ **c.** ABC seeks to change costs and their drivers; ABM focuses on understanding them.

   ☐ **d.** ABC is predominately forward-looking; ABM is primarily historical.

6. The four categories used for cost of quality analysis are:

   a. _____

   b. _____

   c. _____

   d. _____

Knowledge Check Answers: Business Process Performance

1. Which of the following statements best characterizes value chain analysis? *[See Steps in Value Chain Analysis.]*

   ☐ **a.** It emphasizes a firm's functional structure.

   ☐ **b.** It examines a firm's hierarchal structure.

   ☑ **c.** It examines distinct strategic activities.

   ☐ **d.** It promotes product/service differentiation.

   Match the following business process concepts to the appropriate application. *[See Value Chain Analysis, Benchmarking, and Activity-Based Management.]*

   a. Noncompetitive firms exchanging information about similar manufacturing processes

   b. An airline removing seats in a plane to give coach passengers more leg room

   c. An internal system examining past, current, and future performance

2. __b__ Value chain analysis

3. __a__ Benchmarking

4. __c__ Activity-based management

5. Which of the following statements accurately differentiates activity-based costing (ABC) and activity-based management (ABM)? *[See Activity-Based Management.]*

   ☑ **a.** ABC provides information on process, product, and market performance; ABM finds ways to improve them.

   ☐ **b.** ABC provides actionable information; ABM is a source of explanatory data.

   ☐ **c.** ABC seeks to change costs and their drivers; ABM focuses on understanding them.

   ☐ **d.** ABC is predominately forward-looking; ABM is primarily historical.

6. The four categories used for cost of quality analysis are: *[See Cost of Quality Analysis.]*

   a. prevention costs

   b. appraisal costs

   c. internal failure costs

   d. external failure costs

Directions: This sampling of questions is designed to emulate actual exam questions. Read each question and write your response on another sheet of paper. See the "Answers to Section Practice Questions" section at the end of this book to assess your response. Validate or improve the answer you wrote. For a more robust selection of practice questions, access the **Online Test Bank** found on the IMA's Learning Center Web site.

Question 1C1-CQ01
Topic: Measurement Concepts

A company employs a just-in-time (JIT) production system and utilizes back-flush accounting. All acquisitions of raw materials are recorded in a raw materials control account when purchased. All conversion costs are recorded in a control account as incurred, while the assignment of conversion costs are from an allocated conversion cost account. Company practice is to record the cost of goods manufactured at the time the units are completed using the estimated budgeted cost of the goods manufactured.

The budgeted cost per unit for one of the company's products is as shown:

Direct materials	$15.00
Conversion costs	35.00
Total budgeted unit cost	$50.00

During the current accounting period, 80,000 units of product were completed, and 75,000 units were sold. The entry to record the cost of the completed units for the period would be which of the following?

a. Work-in-Process—Control   4,000,000
        Raw Material—Control   1,200,000
        Conversion Cost Allocated   2,800,000

b. Finished Goods—Control   4,000,000
        Raw Material—Control   1,200,000
        Conversion Cost Allocated   2,800,000

c. Finished Goods—Control   3,750,000
        Raw Material Control   1,125,000
        Conversion Cost Allocated   2,625,000

d. Cost of Goods Sold   3,750,000
        Raw Material—Control   1,125,000
        Conversion Cost Allocated   2,625,000

Question 1C1-CQ02

Topic: Measurement Concepts

From the budgeted data shown, calculate the budgeted indirect cost rate that would be used in a normal costing system.

Total direct labor hours	250,000
Direct costs	$10,000,000
Total indirect labor hours	50,000
Total indirect labor-related costs	$5,000,000
Total indirect non-labor-related costs	$7,000,000

- ☐ **a.** $20
- ☐ **b.** $28
- ☐ **c.** $40
- ☐ **d.** $48

Question 1C2-CQ03

Topic: Costing Systems

Loyal Co. produces three types of men's undershirts: T-shirts, V-neck shirts, and athletic shirts. In the Folding and Packaging Department, operations costing is used to apply costs to individual units, based on the standard time allowed to fold and package each type of undershirt. The standard time to fold and package each type of undershirt is shown next.

T-shirt	40 seconds per shirt
V-neck shirt	40 seconds per shirt
Athletic shirt	20 seconds per shirt

During the month of April, Loyal produced and sold 50,000 T-shirts, 30,000 V-neck shirts, and 20,000 athletic shirts. If costs in the Folding and Packaging Department were $78,200 during April, how much folding and packaging cost should be applied to each T-shirt?

- ☐ **a.** $0.5213
- ☐ **b.** $0.6256
- ☐ **c.** $0.7820
- ☐ **d.** $0.8689

Question 1C1-CQ05

Topic: Measurement Concepts

Chassen Company, a cracker and cookie manufacturer, has these unit costs for the month of June.

Variable Manufacturing Cost	Variable Marketing Cost	Fixed Manufacturing Cost	Fixed Marketing Cost
$5.00	$3.50	$2.00	$4.00

A total of 100,000 units were manufactured during June, of which 10,000 remain in ending inventory. Chassen uses the first-in, first-out (FIFO) inventory method, and the 10,000 units are the only finished goods inventory at month-end. Using the full absorption costing method, Chassen's finished goods inventory value would be

- ☐ **a.** $50,000
- ☐ **b.** $70,000
- ☐ **c.** $85,000
- ☐ **d.** $145,000

Question 1C1-CQ11
Topic: Measurement Concepts

During the month of May, Robinson Corporation sold 1,000 units. The cost per unit for May was as shown:

	Cost per Unit
Direct materials	$5.50
Direct labor	3.00
Variable manufacturing overhead	1.00
Fixed manufacturing overhead	1.50
Variable administrative costs	0.50
Fixed administrative costs	3.50
Total	$15.00

May's income using absorption costing was $9,500. The income for May, if variable costing had been used, would have been $9,125. The number of units Robinson produced during May was

- ☐ **a.** 750 units
- ☐ **b.** 925 units
- ☐ **c.** 1,075 units
- ☐ **d.** 1,250 units

Question 1C1-CQ12
Topic: Measurement Concepts

Tucariz Company processes Duo into two joint products, Big and Mini. Duo is purchased in 1,000 gallon drums for $2,000. Processing costs are $3,000 to process the 1,000 gallons of Duo into 800 gallons of Big and 200 gallons of Mini. The selling price is $9 per gallon for Big and $4 per gallon for Mini.

The 800 gallons of Big can be processed further into 600 gallons of Giant if $1,000 of additional processing costs are incurred. Giant can be sold for $17 per gallon. If the net-realizable-value (NRV) method were used to allocate costs to the joint products, the total cost of producing Giant would be:

- ☐ **a.** $5,600
- ☐ **b.** $5,564
- ☐ **c.** $5,520
- ☐ **d.** $4,600

Question 1C1-CQ13
Topic: Measurement Concepts

Tucariz Company processes Duo into two joint products, Big and Mini. Duo is purchased in 1,000 gallon drums for $2,000. Processing costs are $3,000 to process the 1,000 gallons of Duo into 800 gallons of Big and 200 gallons of Mini. The selling price is $9 per gallon for Big and $4 per gallon for Mini.

If the sales value at split-off method is used to allocate joint costs to the final products, the per gallon cost (rounded to the nearest cent) of producing Big is:

- ☐ **a.** $5. 63 per gallon
- ☐ **b.** $5. 00 per gallon
- ☐ **c.** $4. 50 per gallon
- ☐ **d.** $3. 38 per gallon

Question 1C1-CQ14
Topic: Measurement Concepts

Tempo Company produces three products from a joint process. The three products are sold after further processing as there is no market for any of the products at the split-off point. Joint costs per batch are $315,000. Other product information is shown next.

	Product A	Product B	Product C
Units produced per batch	20,000	30,000	50,000
Further processing and marketing cost per unit	$0.70	$3.00	$1.72
Final sales value per unit	$5.00	$6.00	$7.00

If Tempo uses the net realizable value method of allocating joint costs, how much of the joint costs will be allocated to each unit of Product C?

- ☐ **a.** $2.10
- ☐ **b.** $2.65
- ☐ **c.** $3.15
- ☐ **d.** $3.78

Question 1C1-CQ15

Topic: Measurement Concepts

Fitzpatrick Corporation uses a joint manufacturing process in the production of two products, Gummo and Xylo. Each batch in the joint manufacturing process yields 5,000 pounds of an intermediate material, Valdene, at a cost of $20,000.

Each batch of Gummo uses 60% of the Valdene and incurs $10,000 of separate costs. The resulting 3,000 pounds of Gummo sells for $10 per pound.

The remaining Valdene is used in the production of Xylo, which incurs $12,000 of separable costs per batch. Each batch of Xylo yields 2,000 pounds and sells for $12 per pound.

Fitzpatrick uses the net realizable value method to allocate the joint material costs. The company is debating whether to process Xylo further into a new product, Zinten, which would incur an additional $4,000 in costs and sell for $15 per pound. If Zinten is produced, income would increase by:

- ☐ **a.** $2,000
- ☐ **b.** $5,760
- ☐ **c.** $14,000
- ☐ **d.** $26,000

Question 1C2-CQ04

Topic: Costing Systems

During December, Krause Chemical Company had these selected data concerning the manufacture of Xyzine, an industrial cleaner.

Production Flow	Physical Units
Completed and transferred to the next department	100
Add: Ending work-in-process inventory	10 (40% complete as to conversion)
Total units to account for	110
Less: Beginning work-in-process inventory	20 (60% complete as to conversion)
Units started during December	**90**

All material is added at the beginning of processing in this department, and conversion costs are added uniformly during the process. The beginning work-in-process inventory had $120 of raw material and $180 of conversion costs incurred. Material added during December was $540, and conversion costs of $1,484 were incurred. Krause uses the weighted-average process-costing method. The total raw material costs in the ending work-in-process inventory for December are:

☐ **a.** $120

☐ **b.** $72

☐ **c.** $60

☐ **d.** $36

Question 1C2-CQ08

Topic: Costing Systems

Oster Manufacturing uses a weighted-average process costing system and has these costs and activity during October:

Materials	$40,000
Conversion cost	32,500
Total beginning work-in-process inventory	$72,500
Materials	$700,000
Conversion cost	617,500
Total production costs—October	$1,317,500
Production completed	60,000 units
Work-in-process, October 31	20,000 units

All materials are introduced at the start of the manufacturing process, and conversion cost is incurred uniformly throughout production. Conversations with plant personnel reveal that, on average, month-end in-process inventory is 25% complete. Assuming no spoilage, how should Oster's October manufacturing cost be assigned?

Production Completed	**Work in Process**
a. $1,042,500	$347,500
b. $1,095,000	$222,500
c. $1,155,000	$235,000
d. $1,283,077	$106,923

Question 1C2-CQ10

Topic: Costing Systems

During December, Krause Chemical Company had these selected data concerning the manufacture of Xyzine, an industrial cleaner:

Production Flow	Physical Units
Completed and transferred to the next department	100
Add: Ending work-in-process inventory	10 (40% complete as to conversion)
Total units to account for	110
Less: Beginning work-in-process inventory	20 (60% complete as to conversion)
Units started during December	**90**

All material is added at the beginning of processing in this department, and conversion costs are added uniformly during the process. The beginning work-in-process inventory had $120 of raw material and $180 of conversion costs incurred. Material added during December was $540, and conversion costs of $1,484 were incurred. Krause uses the weighted-average process-costing method. The total conversion cost assigned to units transferred to the next department in December was

- ☐ **a.** $1,664
- ☐ **b.** $1,600
- ☐ **c.** $1,513
- ☐ **d.** $1,484

Question 1C3-CQ01

Topic: Overhead Costs

During December, Krause Chemical Company had these selected data concerning the manufacture of Xyzine, an industrial cleaner.

Production Flow	Physical Units
Completed and transferred to the next department	100
Add: Ending work-in-process inventory	10 (40% complete as to conversion)
Total units to account for	110
Less: Beginning work-in-process inventory	20 (60% complete as to conversion)
Units started during December	**90**

All material is added at the beginning of processing in this department, and conversion costs are added uniformly during the process. The beginning work-in-process inventory had $120 of raw material and $180 of conversion costs incurred. Material added during December was $540, and conversion costs of

$1,484 were incurred. Krause uses the first-in, first-out (FIFO) process-costing method. The equivalent units of production used to calculate conversion costs for December was:

- ☐ **a.** 110 units
- ☐ **b.** 104 units
- ☐ **c.** 100 units
- ☐ **d.** 92 units

Question 1C2-CQ12

Topic: Costing Systems

Waller Co. uses a weighted-average process-costing system. Material B is added at two different points in the production of shirts; 40% is added when the units are 20% completed, and the remaining 60% of Material B is added when the units are 80% completed. At the end of the quarter, there are 22,000 shirts in process, all of which are 50% completed. With respect to Material B, the ending shirts in process represent how many equivalent units?

- ☐ **a.** 4,400 units
- ☐ **b.** 8,800 units
- ☐ **c.** 11,000 units
- ☐ **d.** 22,000 units

Question 1C2-CQ14

Topic: Costing Systems

The Chocolate Baker specializes in chocolate baked goods. The firm has long assessed the profitability of a product line by comparing revenues to the cost of goods sold. However, Barry White, the firm's new accountant, wants to use an activity-based costing system that takes into consideration the cost of the delivery person. Listed are activity and cost information relating to two of Chocolate Baker's major products.

	Muffins	Cheesecake
Revenue	$53,000	$46,000
Cost of goods sold	$26,000	$21,000
Delivery Activity		
Number of deliveries	150	85
Average length of delivery	10 minutes	15 minutes
Cost per hour for delivery	$20.00	$20.00

Using activity-based costing, which one of the following statements is correct?

- ☐ **a.** The muffins are $2,000 more profitable.
- ☐ **b.** The cheesecakes are $75 more profitable.
- ☐ **c.** The muffins are $1,925 more profitable.
- ☐ **d.** The muffins have a higher profitability as a percentage of sales and, therefore, are more advantageous.

Question 1C2-CQ16

Topic: Costing Systems

Baldwin Printing Company uses a job order costing system and applies overhead based on machine hours. A total of 150,000 machine hours have been budgeted for the year. During the year, an order for 1,000 units was completed and incurred:

Direct material costs	$1,000
Direct labor costs	$1,500
Actual overhead	$1,980
Machine hours	450

The accountant calculated the inventory cost of this order to be $4.30 per unit. The annual budgeted overhead in dollars was:

- ☐ **a.** $577,500
- ☐ **b.** $600,000
- ☐ **c.** $645,000
- ☐ **d.** $660,000

Question 1C3-CQ03

Topic: Overhead Costs

Cynthia Rogers, the cost accountant for Sanford Manufacturing, is preparing a management report that must include an allocation of overhead. The budgeted overhead for each department and the data for one job are shown next.

	Department	
	Tooling	Fabricating
Supplies	$ 690	$ 80
Supervisor's salaries	1,400	1,800
Indirect labor	1,000	4,000
Depreciation	1,200	5,200
Repairs	4,400	3,000
Total budgeted overhead	$8,690	$14,080
Total direct labor hours	440	640
Direct labor hours on Job #231	10	2

Using the departmental overhead application rates and allocating overhead on the basis of direct labor hours, overhead applied to Job #231 in the Tooling Department would be:

- ☐ **a.** $44.00
- ☐ **b.** $197.50
- ☐ **c.** $241.50
- ☐ **d.** $501.00

Question 1C3-CQ05

Topic: Overhead Costs

Atmel Inc. manufactures and sells two products. Data with regard to these products are given next.

	Product A	Product B
Units produced and sold	30,000	12,000
Machine hours required per unit	2	3
Receiving orders per product line	50	150
Production orders per product line	12	18
Production runs	8	12
Inspections	20	30

Total budgeted machine hours are 100,000. The budgeted overhead costs are shown next.

Receiving costs	$450,000
Engineering costs	300,000
Machine setup costs	25,000
Inspection costs	200,000
Total budgeted overhead	$975,000

The cost driver for engineering costs is the number of production orders per product line. Using activity-based costing, what would the engineering cost per unit for Product B be?

- ☐ **a.** $4.00
- ☐ **b.** $10.00
- ☐ **c.** $15.00
- ☐ **d.** $29.25

Question 1C3-CQ08

Topic: Overhead Costs

Logo Inc. has two data services departments (the Systems Department and the Facilities Department) that provide support to the company's three production departments (Machining Department, Assembly Department, and Finishing Department). The overhead costs of the Systems Department are allocated to other departments on the basis of computer usage hours. The overhead costs of the Facilities Department are allocated based on square feet occupied (in thousands). Other information pertaining to Logo is as shown next.

Department	Overhead	Computer Usage Hours	Square Feet Occupied
Systems	$200,000	300	1,000
Facilities	100,000	900	600
Machining	400,000	3,600	2,000
Assembly	550,000	1,800	3,000
Finishing	620,000	2,700	5,000
		9,300	11,600

Logo employs the step-down method of allocating service department costs and begins with the Systems Department. Which one of the following correctly denotes the amount of the Systems Department's overhead that would be allocated to the Facilities Department and the Facilities Department's overhead charges that would be allocated to the Machining Department?

	Systems to Facilities	Facilities to Machining
☐ a.	$0	$20,000
☐ b.	$19,355	$20,578
☐ c.	$20,000	$20,000
☐ d.	$20,000	$24,000

Question 1C3-CQ09
Topic: Overhead Costs

Adam Corporation manufactures computer tables and has this budgeted indirect manufacturing cost information for next year:

	Support Departments		Operating Departments		
	Maintenance	Systems	Machining	Fabrication	Total
Budgeted Overhead	$360,000	$95,000	$200,000	$300,000	$955,000
Support work furnished					
From Maintenance		10%	50%	40%	100%
From Systems	5%		45%	50%	100%

If Adam uses the direct method to allocate support department costs to production departments, the total overhead (rounded to the nearest dollar) for the Machining Department to allocate to its products would be which of the following?

☐ **a.** $418,000

☐ **b.** $422,750

☐ **c.** $442,053

☐ **d.** $445,000

 To further assess your understanding of the concepts and calculations covered in Part 1, Section C: Cost Management, practice with the **Online Test Bank** for this section. REMINDER: See the "Answers to Section Practice Questions" section at the end of this book.

Internal Controls

Internal controls are designed to ensure that the goals and objectives of a business are achieved efficiently. As a business grows, management becomes removed from the firm's operations and increasingly depends on reports to evaluate the business's performance. Management must have assurance that the reports are accurate and that subordinates carry out management's directives. An internal control system provides a higher level of confidence in these matters.

This section looks at several interrelated approaches to control: the assessment and management of risk; the process of internal auditing and responsibilities of auditors; and measures taken to ensure the security and reliability of systems and the information they provide.

An emphasis on controls has grown from several policy and legislative initiatives. The Sarbanes-Oxley Act of 2002 (SOX) created the Public Company Accounting Oversight Board (PCAOB) as a part of the Securities and Exchange Commission. The PCAOB is responsible for the setting of standards for audits of publicly held corporations. The PCAOB has adopted the Committee of Sponsoring Organizations (COSO) internal control model as its guide. The original COSO model, which was put into effect in 1992, is called the *Internal Control—Integrated Framework*, and contains five elements. It defines internal control and the criteria for determining the effectiveness of an internal control system. The five elements of the 1992 COSO model on internal controls are:

1. The control environment
2. Risk assessment
3. Control activities
4. Information and communication
5. Monitoring

The model was eventually updated and expanded in 2004 to include eight elements in total, and is called the *Enterprise Risk Management—Integrated Framework*. It serves as a guide for successful enterprise risk management implementation. The 1992 COSO model is covered in this section of the CMA body of knowledge.

The 2004 COSO model is discussed in Part 2, Section C, which covers risk management topics.

Sections 302 and 404 of SOX instituted specific requirements for chief executive officers and chief financial officers of publicly held corporations relative to the financial reports and internal controls of the organization. The result of this legislation is that greater responsibility is placed on high-level management for establishing and maintaining adequate internal control policies. The external auditor must also provide input on the internal control structure.

PCAOB Auditing Standard No. 5 requires auditors to follow a risk-based approach to the development of auditing procedures. Auditors are also required to scale the audit to the size of the organization and to follow other prescribed approaches to perform the audit.

Risk Assessment, Controls, and Risk Management

THE PRIMARY OBJECTIVE OF A system of internal controls is to reduce risk to an acceptable level. The internal control system is designed to provide reasonable (but not absolute) assurance regarding the achievement of an entity's objectives. Specifically, the control activities are a set of policies and procedures established and implemented to assign authority for the day-to-day operations, provide a system of authorizations and documentations, protect company assets, require independent verifications, and accomplish effective separation of duties. The board of directors is charged with the hiring of managers who will create, implement, and monitor these activities in order to promote the effectiveness and efficiency of operations, the reliability of financial reporting, the safeguarding of assets, and the firm's compliance with applicable laws and regulations. When determining internal control policies and procedures, management must weigh the cost of suggested controls against the risks that the policies and procedures are intended to reduce. The controls should be cost beneficial.

This topic begins by defining risk and the types of risks auditors must assess. It looks at design controls to address risk and the role of management philosophy and internal control structure on its risk control efforts. It also addresses the controls imposed by the U. S. government through the Sarbanes-Oxley Act and the Foreign Corrupt Practices Act and discusses types of internal controls and methods of control.

 READ the Learning Outcome Statements (LOS) for this topic as found in Appendix A and then study the concepts and calculations presented here to be sure you understand the content you could be tested on in the CMA exam.

Risk

Risk is defined as exposure to circumstances that may increase the likelihood of loss. From an internal control perspective, it can be defined as the probability of a threat multiplied by the probability that the control to prevent or detect the threat fails, multiplied by the amount of the loss from the threat.

$$\text{Risk} = P(t) \times P(f) \times (\text{Amount of Loss})$$

where:
P = probability
t = threat
f = failure of a control

The level of risk is a combination of both the total dollar value of assets that are exposed to loss and the probability that such a loss will occur. Management seeks to minimize risks by:

- Preventing threats from occurring
- Increasing systems controls
- Insuring or otherwise reducing possible losses

The design of controls should be driven by risk assessments. Controls should be established to limit risk of a potential loss of assets or misstatements of material information. Greater risks warrant more extensive control.

Factors affecting risk include:

- Frequency of independent checks on performance
- Adequacy of organizational control methods
- Adequacy of communication of authority and responsibility
- Consistency of enforcement of controls
- Adequacy of systems controls that limit access to or physical control of assets, records, software, or data

When considering risk, there is need for regular monitoring of control policies and procedures as well as regular independent audits to monitor compliance with internal controls.

Types of Risk

Auditors assess risk as part of an audit. Auditors divide risk into three types:

1. **Inherent risk (IR)** is the susceptibility of financial statements to material misstatement when there are no internal controls. It is the probability of an error or irregularity (fraud). Errors are unintentional and relate to the competence of the organization's personnel. Fraud is intentional and relates to the integrity of the organization's personnel. Competence and integrity of personnel are the cornerstones of effective internal control.
2. **Control risk (CR)** is the likelihood that misstatements exceeding an acceptable level will not be prevented or detected by the firm's internal controls. It is the probability of a control failure.
3. **Detection risk (DR)**, or planned detection risk, is a measure of the risk that audit evidence will fail to detect misstatements exceeding an acceptable audit

risk. It is the risk the auditor is willing to take that an error or fraud goes undetected by audit procedures.

Acceptable Audit Risk

Acceptable audit risk (AAR) is the probability of an audit failure and is a function of the three types of risk that were just defined. It is the probability that the auditor will conclude that the financial statements "fairly present" and issues an unqualified opinion when, in fact, the statements are materially misleading. It represents the risk the auditor is willing to take that the audit will fail.

AAR is a function of three things:

1. Management integrity
2. The number of financial statement users
3. The auditee's financial condition

If auditors want to have greater certainty that the financial statements are not materially misstated, they will lower the acceptable audit risk. The lower the management integrity, the lower the AAR. The more financial statement users, the lower the AAR. The worse the auditee's financial condition, the lower the AAR.

$$AAR = IR \times CR \times DR$$

$$DR = AAR / (IR \times CR)$$

where:
AAR = acceptable audit risk
IR = inherent risk
CR = control risk
DR = detection risk

The auditor sets the AAR based on factors noted earlier, and assesses the IR and CR. The combination of IR and CR is normally either high or low, because lack of integrity and/or competence normally results in weaker controls. The lower the calculated DR, the more evidence the auditor would require to support the audit.

Design Controls to Address Risks

The most broadly accepted model for designing and assessing internal control is the *Internal Control—Integrated Framework*, established in 1992 by the Committee of Sponsoring Organizations (COSO) of the Treadway Commission (the National Committee on Fraudulent Financial Reporting)—a framework now considered by the PCAOB and the American Institute of Certified Public Accountants (AICPA) as a basis for U. S. auditing standards. In 2004, COSO incorporated the original model into the *Enterprise Risk Management—Integrated Framework*, which, as the name implies, goes beyond internal controls to provide guidelines for managing risk across the enterprise.

The original COSO framework comprises five mutually reinforcing components. They are meant to be integrated with an organization's management processes and applied in successive iterations to adapt to changing conditions. Each component may have an impact on any or all of the others. The next summary outlines the five components.

1. **Control environment.** The control environment refers to the organization's management philosophy and appetite for risk and includes integrity, ethical values, and the environment in which an organization operates.

2. **Risk assessment.** The model included a component for assessing risk—determining its probability and degree of importance. Risks are classified as either inherent or residual. Inherent risks are those that the organization will face unless management takes action to avoid or mitigate them. They are the first to be assessed. Residual risks are those that remain after any actions management might take with regard to inherent risks.

3. **Control activities.** Policies and procedures are established and implemented to help ensure that the risk responses are effectively carried out. The COSO model lists six control activities:

    a. The assignment of authority and responsibility (job descriptions), which requires the board of directors to hire the chief executive officer [CEO] and other managers who will hire, train, and appropriately compensate competent, reliable, ethical employees to accomplish the day-to-day operations of the company.

    b. A system of transaction authorizations, which helps to avoid duplicate and fictitious payments, safeguard assets, and generate reliable accounting information. These controls include signatures of approval, reconciliations, and the forms that document those actions.

    c. Adequate documentation and records, which are necessary because documents provide the details of the company's operations. Documents, such as invoices and orders, may be paper or electronic. The prenumbering of documents, such as invoices, purchase orders, and checks, helps to prevent theft and inefficiencies by drawing attention to gaps in sequences.

    d. Security of assetsis enabled by a good system of authorizations and segregation of duties in order to reduce the opportunities for fraud and theft. Production activities and sales activities should not be performed by accounting personnel.

    e. Independent verifications may be internal (such as the internal audit staff) or external (such as an independent certified public accountant who audits financial statements or a regulator who audits regulatory issues).

    f. Adequate separation of duties requires the separation of the authorization for a transaction from the execution of the transaction, from the recording of the transaction, and from the custody of the assets resulting from the transaction.

For example: A purchase is authorized by a purchase requisition originating in inventory control. The purchase is executed by the purchasing agent and is recorded by the information technology department. The raw materials are received by the receiving department. Receiving validates the receipt to the purchase order by counting, inspecting, and preparing the receiving report. The materials are then released to inventory control.

    1. **Information and communication.** The COSO model recognizes that relevant information must be identified, captured, and communicated in a form and time frame that enables people to do their jobs successfully. This assumes that the data communicated are secure and accurate.

    2. **Monitoring.** All aspects of internal controls are monitored, and modifications made as necessary. Monitoring is accomplished through ongoing management activities, separate evaluations, or both. Internal auditors, the audit committee, and the disclosure committee, as well as management, may all be involved in monitoring controls.

The original COSO model encompasses internal control and emphasizes the role of managing risk in order to achieve success. It includes the internal environment in which risks are evaluated and managed, objective setting to allow the assessment of risks that may hinder success, identification of risks (as well as positive events), and methods of responding to risks once they have been assessed.

When management encounters situations in which controls might add to the efficiency of operations, it must weigh the risk of loss or inefficiency against the cost of the controls.

Effective Control Principles

Controls are designed to prevent unintentional errors due to carelessness or lack of knowledge. Fraud, however, is intentional, and it is difficult to prevent collusion and management override. No matter how well internal controls are designed, they cannot provide complete assurance against intentional fraud. Moreover, human error, carelessness in executing control procedures, fatigue or stress, and the tendency to let familiarity supersede control procedures can result in errors or even fraud. In addition, even a well-designed control system is subject to obsolescence over time if not adjusted to changes in operations. There is a twofold risk in designing controls. On one hand, they may be too lax, thus failing to ensure compliance or to provide reliable information to help management achieve the goals of the organization. On the other hand, they may be so complex and detailed as to increase the difficulty of processing transactions, reducing productivity without adding value.

The four principles of accounting system design apply to the creation of effective controls:

1. **Control principle.** Requires that an accounting system provide internal control features in order to protect a firm's assets and ensure that data is reliable.
2. **Compatibility principle.** Holds that the design of an accounting system must be in harmony with the organizational and human factors of the business.
3. **Flexibility principle.** Holds that an accounting system must be flexible enough to allow the volume of transactions to grow and organizational changes to be made.
3. **Cost-benefit principle.** Holds that the benefits derived from an accounting system and the information it generates must be equal to or greater than the system's costs, both tangible and intangible. Tangible costs include personnel, forms, and equipment. Intangible costs include the cost of wrong decisions.

Internal Control Structure and Management Philosophy

A company's organizational structure, policies, objectives, and goals, as well as its management philosophy and style, influence the scope and effectiveness of the control environment. The organizational structure defines lines of responsibility and authority. Formal communication about these lines of responsibility, as well as about control procedures, plays an important role in the organization's overall adherence to internal controls.

Management organizes resources into various functions, such as financial management, production, and so on. Separation of responsibility establishes a structure within which the goals of the business may be accomplished. An organization's structure identifies individual components and the operational and informational interrelationships among the various components. The most common method of documenting organizational structure is through the organizational chart.

The next level of organizational structure outlines the key decisions for which each organizational component is responsible. For example, the controller will determine the financial controls and accounting principles the firm will employ. The production manager will be responsible for determining the best means of fulfilling production commitments.

The internal control structure consists of three components:

1. Control environment
2. Accounting system
3. Control procedures

Control Environment

Management and the board of directors of a company set the environment for the business, including its control environment. Management's philosophy and operating style send signals to employees about the importance of internal controls. Management behavior—for example, whether it is prone to taking risks or conservative—sends signals to employees, as well as the auditor, about management's attitude toward internal control.

If management and the board project an attitude that controls are not important, others in the business will act accordingly and management's control objectives are unlikely to be met. If management and the board of directors send a message that internal control is important to them, employees will respond by carefully observing the established controls.

The same holds true for the firm's overall integrity and ethical values. Management's actions to remove or reduce temptation that might prompt personnel to engage in dishonest, illegal, or unethical acts set the tone for the firm's integrity. Management also communicates the entity's values and behavioral standards to personnel through policy statements and codes of conduct, and also by example.

The sum of the components of a firm's control procedures can provide an external auditor a picture of management's attitude toward internal control. As this topic progresses, the control environment will continue to be mentioned in relation to the components of the firm's control procedures, such as hiring and training policies covered under control policies.

Board of Directors and Audit Committee

The board of directors bears final responsibility for business practices and results; it sets broad purposes of operations that guide how control systems should be designed and monitored. The primary responsibility of the board of directors is to ensure that the company operates in the best interest of shareholders. The board of directors is elected by the shareholders, and is charged with establishing corporate policies and hiring the major officers (such as the CEO) to set the tone of the organization and to manage day-to-day affairs.

For firms that have an internal audit function , the internal auditor provides that assurance to the board of directors by verifying that control procedures are adequate and being followed. The organizational chart should show the audit director reporting directly to the CEO and the audit committee of the board of directors.

Audit committees have not always been effective. Investors have blamed such committees for lacking the independence or financial expertise to uncover financial reporting failures. Audit committees have also fallen short in cases where a CEO has picked members willing to "go with the flow. "

Audit committees need independent directors with sophisticated financial backgrounds. The Sarbanes-Oxley Act of 2002 (SOX) requires that the audit committee consist entirely of directors who are independent of the issuer, meaning that they cannot accept any consulting, advisory, or other compensatory fee from the issuer or be affiliated with the issuer or any of its subsidiaries. At least one of the audit committee members should qualify as a "financial expert" within the meaning and rules of the Securities and Exchange Commission (SEC).

Management Responsibility Under Sarbanes-Oxley Act of 2002

Section 404 of SOX requires that public companies establish and maintain a system of internal controls which is then audited by external auditors. The act requires that corporate officers annually certify that (1) management is responsible for internal controls, (2) the internal controls have been designed to provide adequate disclosure of financial activities, and (3) the internal controls have been evaluated as to their effectiveness. Section 404 requires that management produce a report as to their responsibilities and the adequacy of the controls to generate reliable financial information.

Auditor Responsibility Under SOX

Section 404 of SOX requires an external auditor to attest to and report on the adequacy of financial reporting internal controls.

The cost of compliance with Section 404 is significant. Therefore, the PCAOB approved PCAOB Auditing Standard No. 5 in 2007, which provides guidance to management and the external auditor in complying with Section 404 requirements. PCAOB Auditing Standard No. 5 requires auditors to perform their internal control assessment using a top-down, risk assessment (TDRA) approach. TDRA is a hierarchical approach that applies specific risk factors to determine the scope of work and evidence required in the assessment of internal controls.

The steps in TDRA are:

1. Identifying significant accounts or disclosures.
2. Identifying material misstatement risks within these accounts or disclosures. Doing this requires the determination as to whether an account/disclosure is significant and, if significant, to rate the misstatement risk as low, medium, or high. Management is charged with developing a list of assertion-level control objectives for each significant account/disclosure and from those objectives to develop the risks that have a reasonably possible likelihood to cause material misstatement risk (MMR) in the financial statements.
3. Determining which entity-level controls sufficiently address the risk.
4. Determining which transaction-based controls compensate for possibly entity-level control failures. For each MMR, controls (either entity-level controls or transaction-based controls) are identified that will sufficiently mitigate the risk, which is defined as reducing the risk to a remote level.
5. Determining the nature, extent, timing of evidence gathering tests needed to complete the assessment of the internal controls. This is the final step based upon the assessments in Steps 3 and 4.

The TDRA is a principle-based approach that provides management significant flexibility as it designs the scope of the controls to test and the nature, timing, and extent of testing procedures to be performed.

Accounting System

Information systems typically are divided into two functions: financial accounting systems and operating information systems. The financial accounting system contains data used to produce the company's financial statements. The operating information system accepts and stores data from various operations of the company and provides reports on activities and functions.

The objective of internal control to maintain reliability and integrity of the information system is important for management's decision-making processes. Incorrect information could lead management to take action in a particular direction that diverts resources from more profitable activities.

Control Procedures

General controls relating to the control environment are different from specific controls directed at detailed procedures and activities. Examples of specific controls include requiring competitive bids on projects and requiring use of only authorized vendors. Examples of general controls include procedures such as segregating purchasing responsibilities from responsibility for custody of assets. The general control environment can offset or render ineffective the potential effectiveness of such controls.

Each general control has at least one corresponding specific control. For example, a general control regarding purchases requires authorization by a specified officer and corresponding specific controls for accuracy. Design of control policies and procedures must consider potential risk, stated risk, and actual risk exposure when selecting which specific controls to employ.

Internal controls are designed to provide reasonable assurance regarding achievement of an entity's objectives involving five areas, which can be remembered by the acronym SCARE :

Safeguarding of assets

Compliance with applicable laws and regulations

Accomplishment of organizational goals and objectives

Reliability of financial reporting records

Efficiency of operations

Safeguarding of Assets

Internal controls designed to protect the firm's assets are often the most visible safeguarding controls. Such controls include door locks, security systems, computer passwords, and requirements for dual control of valuable assets. Assets can be stolen, misused, or accidentally destroyed unless protected by adequate controls. Controls for safeguarding of assets include segregation of functions in processing transactions. For example, the person who writes up an order should not have access to the assets for fulfillment of the order.

Multiple levels of access controls should be built into an organization's operations and information systems. For example, users with authority to arrange shipments are able to update the inventory system, but sales staff is given read-only access to the data.

Compliance with Applicable Laws and Regulations

To comply with externally imposed laws and regulations, the firm establishes internal controls in the form of policies, plans, and procedures. Failure to comply with such controls jeopardizes the firm's compliance with the associated laws and regulations.

Accomplishment of Organizational Goals and Objectives

The focus of controls and organizational activities is on the accomplishment of the business's goals and objectives. Effectiveness is the accomplishment of goals and objectives.

If an organization fails in this area, how well it does anything else is irrelevant.

Reliability of Financial Reporting

Management has legal and professional responsibility to ensure that information in financial statements is fairly represented and prepared in accordance with generally accepted accounting principles (GAAP). Examples of controls for reliability of financial reporting include control procedures for budgeting, internal performance reports, accounting groups to which transactions are posted, and control over account balances. These controls have importance not only for financial reporting but also for ensuring that management decisions are based on accurate information.

Efficiency of Operations

Internal controls are designed to promote efficient use of resources. The economic principle of scarcity of resources applies to the firm's desire to produce with as little waste as possible. If facilities are underutilized, if work is nonproductive, if procedures are not cost-justified, or if the company is overstaffed or understaffed, the organization will not realize maximum profits.

Operating standards provide a basis for measuring economy and efficiency that will ultimately be reflected in the financial statements. Internal auditors as well as others in the firm, including production workers, should continue to watch for opportunities for improvements in efficiency.

Foreign Corrupt Practices Act

The U. S. Congress passed the **Foreign Corrupt Practices Act** (FCPA) in 1977 as a result of SEC investigations in the mid-1970s revealing that hundreds of companies admitted to making questionable or illegal payments to foreign government officials to secure favorable action. The act forbids an American company doing business overseas to pay bribes to a foreign government for obtaining contracts or business.

Firms and/or any officer or director of a firm that violate provisions of the FCPA are subject to criminal and civil penalties. Criminal penalties allow for fines of up to $2 million and imprisonment for up to five years.

Every issuer of securities subject to the FCPA is required to make and keep books, records, and accounts that, in reasonable detail, accurately and fairly reflect the transactions and dispositions of the assets of the issuer. In addition, the issuer must devise and maintain a system of internal accounting controls sufficient to provide reasonable assurances that:

- Transactions are executed in accordance with management's general or specific authorization.
- Transactions are recorded as necessary to permit preparation of financial statements in conformity with GAAP or any other criteria applicable to such statements and to maintain accountability for assets.
- Access to assets is permitted only in accordance with management's general or specific authorization.
- The recorded accountability for assets is compared with the existing assets at reasonable intervals, and appropriate action is taken with respect to any differences.

These objectives should be related to specific internal control procedures in order to evaluate controleffectively. Such procedures may include requirements for completion and supervision of expense reports, defining who is authorized to approve expense reports, and obtaining cash and documenting its use. Internal control procedures should include a routine accounting for agreement between totals on expense reports and cash advances.

The SEC is responsible for monitoring compliance with the internal controls provisions of the FCPA.

Types of Internal Controls

Internal controls can be classified as preventive, detective, corrective, directive, or compensating.

Preventive Controls

Preventive controls are intended to prevent errors and misappropriation of assets. For example, a control may create an obstacle that prevents the processing of a particular type of transaction. Credit checks on potential clients (intended to prevent sales to clients with poor credit risk) or guards at exit points (intended to prevent employee theft) are other types of preventive controls.

Transactional controls are a specific type of preventive control designed to ensure that every transaction is documented, that false transactions are not entered into the system, and that all valid exchanges are accurately recorded. The types of controls selected in large part will depend on the quantity and the nature of the transactions the firm completes.

Preventive controls that depend on functions or people performing their roles effectively may include:

- Separation of duties.
- Supervisory review, such as a supervisor approving a purchase transaction.
- Dual control, such as two authorizations for every transaction above a certain threshold.

- Edit and accuracy checks, such as reconciling of invoice amounts against original warehouse receipt records before an invoice is paid.
- Reasonableness checks, such as verifying the total of a transaction against a customer's credit limit. (Reasonableness checks are often built into software systems.)
- Completeness checks, such as a computer form that will not allow the operator to continue until required fields are completed. (If during data entry a data entry screen insists on complete fields before it permits processing, the screen itself operates as a preventive control to ensure completeness.)

As with internal controls in general, no preventive control can be expected to be foolproof. Thus, it is important for a firm to recognize the dependence of preventive controls upon detective controls.

Detective Controls

Detective controls are intended to back up preventive controls by detecting errors after they have occurred. Reconciliation of bank statements is an example of a detective control over cash assets. Detective controls complement preventive controls and are essential components of a well-designed control system. In some cases, detective controls may be less costly than preventive controls because random transactions, rather than every transaction, can be examined.

Corrective Controls

Corrective controls correct problems identified using detective controls. For example, an ordering system's routine edit function may detect an inaccurate account number on a sales order, read the client's name, search the database for the correct account number, and correct the original record. In some cases, if a record cannot be found on the database matching the customer name, the computer may generate an error report, which an employee can use to follow up on and resolve the discrepancy.

Directive Controls

In contrast to controls that prevent, detect, and correct negative results, directive controls are designed to produce positive results. For example, a firm may have a policy to use local vendors as often as possible. Directive controls may be intended to create a favorable image for the company in the community.

Compensating Controls

Compensating controls, also called mitigating controls, are designed to compensate for shortcomings elsewhere in the control structure. For example, a bank reconciliation process performed by a party independent of accounting and cash handling can compensate for a number of flaws in the controls over cash transactions. Similarly, a hands-on owner-manager's supervision of operations might compensate for a lack of segregation of duties in a small business.

Compensating controls are an approach to limiting risk exposure. Risk exposure must be analyzed in the context of what could happen, given particular system weaknesses. Compensating controls may include redundancy. Data entry verification often has been achieved by having two entry points, reconciliation of resulting records, and generation of exceptions reports on any detected differences.

Methods of Internal Control

Internal control methods can be placed into five categories: organizational controls, operational controls, controls for personnel management, review controls or monitoring controls, and controls for facilities and equipment.

Organizational Controls

Organizational controls establish statements of purpose, authority, and responsibility for each division in the company. These statements include such controls as authorized range of activities and reporting responsibilities. A firm's organizational structure—such as separate departments for financial management, production, marketing, engineering, and so on—identifies the operational and informational relationships and decision authority among components. The primary organizational control is the adequate separation of duties.

Operational Controls

Operational controls include activities such as planning, budgeting, documentation, and controls for the accounting and information systems. Transaction controls are critical. An organization should have a transaction control system that provides reasonable assurance that all transactions are authorized, complete, accurate, and timely.

Controls for Personnel Management

Hiring and other human resource policies affect adherence to internal controls. Competent and trustworthy employees, combined with timely and effective training, minimize the corrective need of internal control. Part of the firm's control procedures may relate to methods used for hiring, evaluating, and training employees.

Recruitment and Selection of Suitable Personnel

Businesses generally define qualifications for personnel in various positions. Staff is recruited, screened, and hired based on these qualifications, such as educational requirements, work experience, and professional certifications. Hiring practices may include reference and credit checks, security checks, and drug testing. Employers should also screen for conflicts of interest. Organizational structure, lines of authority, and job descriptions, while important, do not substitute for good employees. Personnel who are unsuitable to perform their assigned tasks can threaten even the best-designed internal control policies and procedures.

Orientation, Training, and Development

Even the most qualified and skilled employees require an orientation to the business's goals, objectives, policies, and procedures. Job orientation should be given immediately at the start of employment. Ongoing training and development is usually desirable, and, in some fields, is required by law or certification requirements. Most organizations recognize the importance of training and development to the overall success of the enterprise, and many provide or compensate employees for attending training sessions.

Supervision

Most employees require some degree of supervision. Supervisory responsibilities include observation of the work process and examination of the work product. The amount of supervision each employee or position requires varies depending on the abilities and experience of the employee and the complexity of the work.

Bonding and Personnel Practices

Personnel controls often include the bonding of those having custody of money and other assets. Rotation of duties and rotation of shifts can be an important control, especially for personnel with financial responsibilities. Requiring that each employee takes occasional vacation time is another means of helping ensure that one individual has not compromised the controls. Having another employee handle the same tasks during an employee's vacation provides a check on the processes.

Review Controls or Monitoring Controls

Periodic reviews help firms assess the performance of individual employees and the achievement of corporate goals and objectives. In fact, monitoring (or reviewing) controls is one of the components of COSO's *Enterprise Risk Management—Integrated Framework*. Monitoring can be carried out on a formal, continuous basis in addition to periodic reviews and audits.

Most firms provide for regularly scheduled reviews for individual employees, usually conducted by the employee's supervisor. Employee reviews examine the employee's performance in relation to his or her goals and identify skills or functions in which the employee could improve. The employee review often sets goals and identifies methods for achieving them.

Most firms also provide for regular review of operations and projects. These review (or monitoring) controls might include any or all of the following:

- Internal audits carried out by employees working independently of accounting and other departments and charged with responsibility to assess financial, operational, and other aspects of the organization.
- Management reviews carried out by company managers in formal meetings.
- Audit committee reviews performed by a committee appointed by the board of directors to oversee audit operations. The audit committee prepares

SEC-mandated reports for the proxy statement issued to investors, provides a point of contact between the board and independent auditors, and is generally responsible for the integrity of the company's financial statements and its compliance with laws and regulations.

- Activities of a disclosure committee chartered to ensure that the organization's reporting standards are in compliance with SOX and that all information released to shareholders and investors is complete and accurate. Disclosure committees may design controls relating to investment reporting, monitor the disclosure controls, review financial reports, and perform other related duties.

Any firm that issues public securities is required to have an external audit, which is an external review by an independent party. Many firms that do not issue public securities also provide for annual external audits.

Controls for Facilities and Equipment

Facilities and equipment represent the fixed assets of the corporation. Controls for maintaining suitable equipment and facility standards include such things as design, cleanliness, and repair and maintenance schedules. Controls for protecting fixed assets from theft or damage include security systems, fire and smoke alarms, locked doors, and affixing permanent identification tags on equipment to facilitate inventory and identify assets in the case of theft.

Inherent Limitations on Internal Controls

Certain human factors or exceptions may present inherent limitations to otherwise well-designed and well-supported control policies and procedures. The major ones are management override of controls and collusion between employees and between employees and outsiders. Other inherent weaknesses are errors, misunderstandings, mistakes in judgment, and the cost-benefit nature of controls.

Management Override

Management override can be a threat to any control system. If a well-designed control structure can be overridden at management's discretion, the resulting risk exposure can be the same as having no controls in place. Circumstances sometimes justify management override. However, the control environment can be maintained only if management overrides are monitored and limited. For example, a control may be set in place to automatically trigger an exception report any time there is a management override of a control procedure.

Conflicts of Interest

Employees' conflicts of interest pose a threat to any business. For example, a purchasing agent for a clothing retailer who has a financial interest in a clothing design and manufacturing company has a conflict of interest when deciding which supplier to use.

Documenting Control Policies and Procedures

Internal control policies and procedures need to be documented. Documentation serves a number of purposes, including use in training and for audits. At the most detailed level, written job descriptions outline the specific requirements of each job in the firm, including job qualifications, specific responsibilities, and reporting relationships.

The most common methods used to document control policies and procedures include written narratives accompanied by flowcharts that graphically depict a step-by-step process. Section 404 of SOX requires that publicly held companies document their internal controls.

Knowledge Check: Risk Assessment, Controls, and Risk Management

The next questions are intended to help you check your understanding and recall of the material presented in this topic. They do not represent the type of questions that appear on the CMA exam.

Directions: Answer each question in the space provided. Correct answers and section references appear after the knowledge check questions.

1. Which of the following is **not** a type of risk?

    ☐ **a.** Inherent risk

    ☐ **b.** Detection risk

    ☐ **c.** Safeguarding risk

    ☐ **d.** Control risk

2. Which of the following is true of control risk?

    ☐ **a.** Control risk is an assessment of the likelihood that misstatements exceeding an acceptable level will not be detected by internal controls.

    ☐ **b.** Control risk is an assessment of the likelihood that misstatements exceeding an acceptable level will not be detected by an internal audit.

    ☐ **c.** Control risk is dependent on detection risk.

    ☐ **d.** Control risk is measured in combination with safeguarding risk to determine overall risk.

3. The primary authority over the internal audit is:

    ☐ **a.** departmental managers.

    ☐ **b.** senior management.

    ☐ **c.** the external auditor.

    ☐ **d.** the audit committee.

4. Internal controls are designed to provide reasonable assurance regarding which of the following?

    I.   Efficiency of operations

    II. Reliability of financial reporting

    III. Compliance with applicable laws and regulations

    IV. Feasibility of project completion

    ☐ **a.** I

    ☐ **b.** II and III

    ☐ **c.** I, II, and III

    ☐ **d.** I, II, III, and IV

5. The audit committee can contain all of the following **except**:

   ☐ **a.** the company president.

   ☐ **b.** the chair of the board of directors.

   ☐ **c.** a member of the board of directors who owns a separate business not related to the business of the company.

   ☐ **d.** the president of the local chamber of commerce.

6. Which of the following are types of internal controls?

   I. Preventive

   II. Detective

   III. Corrective

   IV. Compensating

   ☐ **a.** I

   ☐ **b.** II and III

   ☐ **c.** I, II, and III

   ☐ **d.** I, II, III, and IV

7. Detective controls

   ☐ **a.** serve as a backup for corrective controls.

   ☐ **b.** are the procedures the internal auditor follows to detect flaws in the control process.

   ☐ **c.** serve as a backup for preventive controls.

   ☐ **d.** are the procedures the external auditor follows if fraud is suspected

8. Directive controls

   ☐ **a.** serve as a backup for corrective controls.

   ☐ **b.** relate to the override of controls by management.

   ☐ **c.** serve as a backup for preventive controls.

   ☐ **d.** are designed to create positive results.

9. Name the five components of the *Internal Control—Integrated Framework* established in 1992 by COSO:

   a. _____

   b. _____

   c. _____

   d. _____

   e. _____

10. Which of the following are required under the Foreign Corrupt Practices Act?

   I. A firm must design internal control procedures.

   II. A firm must have an internal audit department.

III. Transactions must be executed with management's authorization.

IV. Access to assets must be authorized.

☐ **a.** I and II

☐ **b.** III

☐ **c.** I, III, and IV

☐ **d.** I, II, III, and IV

Knowledge Check Answers: Risk Assessment, Controls, and Risk Management

1. Which of the following is **not** a type of risk? *[See Types of Risk.]*

   ☐ **a.** Inherent risk

   ☐ **b.** Detection risk

   ☑ **c.** Safeguarding risk

   ☐ **d.** Control risk

2. Which of the following is true of control risk? *[See Types of Risk.]*

   ☑ **a.** Control risk is an assessment of the likelihood that misstatements exceeding an acceptable level will not be detected by internal controls.

   ☐ **b.** Control risk is an assessment of the likelihood that misstatements exceeding an acceptable level will not be detected by an internal audit.

   ☐ **c.** Control risk is dependent on detection risk.

   ☐ **d.** Control risk is measured in combination with safeguarding risk to determine overall risk.

3. The primary authority over the internal audit is: *[See Board of Directors and Audit Committee.]*

   ☐ **a.** departmental managers.

   ☐ **b.** senior management.

   ☐ **c.** the external auditor.

   ☑ **d.** the audit committee.

4. Internal controls are designed to provide reasonable assurance regarding which of the following? *[See Control Procedures.]*

   I. Efficiency of operations

   II. Reliability of financial reporting

   III. Compliance with applicable laws and regulations

   IV. Feasibility of project completion

   ☐ **a.** I

   ☐ **b.** II and III

   ☑ **c.** I, II, and III

   ☐ **d.** I, II, III, and IV

5. The audit committee can contain all of the following **except**: *[See Board of Directors and Audit Committee.]*

    ☑ **a.** the company president.

    ☐ **b.** the chair of the board of directors.

    ☐ **c.** a member of the board of directors who owns a separate business not related to the business of the company.

    ☐ **d.** the president of the local chamber of commerce.

6. Which of the following are types of internal controls? *[See Types of Internal Control.]*

    I. Preventive

    II. Detective

    III. Corrective

    IV. Compensating

    ☐ **a.** I

    ☐ **b.** II and III

    ☐ **c.** I, II, and III

    ☑ **d.** I, II, III, and IV

7. Detective controls *[See Detective Controls.]*

    ☐ **a.** serve as a backup for corrective controls.

    ☐ **b.** are the procedures the internal auditor follows to detect flaws in the control process.

    ☑ **c.** serve as a backup for preventive controls.

    ☐ **d.** are the procedures the external auditor follows if fraud is suspected

8. Directive controls *[See Directive Controls.]*

    ☐ **a.** serve as a backup for corrective controls.

    ☐ **b.** relate to the override of controls by management.

    ☐ **c.** serve as a backup for preventive controls.

    ☑ **d.** are designed to create positive results.

9. Name the five components of the *Internal Control–Integrated Framework* established in 1992 by COSO: *[See Design Controls to Address Risks.]*

    a. **Control environment**

    b. **Risk assessment**

    c. **Control activities**

    d. **Information and communication**

    e. **Monitoring**

10. Which of the following are required under the Foreign Corrupt Practices Act? *[See Foreign Corrupt Practices Act.]*

I. A firm must design internal control procedures.

II. A firm must have an internal audit department.

III. Transactions must be executed with management's authorization.

IV. Access to assets must be authorized.

☐ **a.** I and II

☐ **b.** III

☑ **c.** I, III, and IV

☐ **d.** I, II, III, and IV

Internal Auditing

THE PRIMARY PURPOSE OF AN internal audit is to appraise the design of, effectiveness of, and adherence to internal control policies and procedures and to assess the firm's quality of performance. The internal auditor ensures that any risk to the business is addressed and verifies that the firm's goals and objectives are met efficiently and effectively. The scope of internal auditing is broad and may include: the efficacy of operations; the reliability of financial reporting; deterring, detecting, and investigating fraud; safeguarding assets; and compliance with laws and regulations.

This topic discusses standards that apply to the internal audit function, management of the internal audit department, reporting and recommendations, and audit evidence. It also looks at the types of audits conducted by internal auditors.

 READ the Learning Outcome Statements (LOS) for this topic as found in Appendix A and then study the concepts and calculations presented here to be sure you understand the content you could be tested on in the CMA exam.

Responsibility and Authority of the Internal Audit Function

The internal audit function receives professional guidance from the Institute of Internal Auditors (IIA). Like the American Institute of Certified Public Accountants, the IIA has established standards for internal auditors. The IIA's standards fall into three categories: attribute standards, performance standards, and implementation standards. According the organization's Web site (www. theiia .org), "The attribute standards address the characteristics of organizations and parties performing internal audit activities. The performance standards describe the nature of internal audit activities and provide quality criteria against which the performance of these services can be evaluated. " The implementation standards provide more specific guidance on how particular attribute or performance standards should be applied within different types of engagements or activities. The implementation standards have been established for assurance and consulting activities.

Attribute Standards

The attribute standards provide guidance in these areas:

- Purpose, authority, and responsibility
- Independence and objectivity
- Proficiency and due professional care
- Quality assurance and improvement programs

Purpose, Authority, and Responsibility

The purpose, authority, and responsibility of the internal audit function should be defined in a formal charter consistent with IIA standards and signed by the board of directors.

Independence and Objectivity

To maintain organizational independence, the chief audit executive (CAE) should report to a level within the organization that allows the internal audit activity to fulfill its responsibilities without feeling biased toward one area or function of the organization. The internal audit activity should be free from interference in determining the scope of internal auditing, performing work, and communicating results. To ensure individual objectivity, internal auditors should maintain an impartial, unbiased attitude and avoid conflicts of interest. Internal auditors should not assess operations for which they had any responsibility during the past year. A person outside the internal audit activity should oversee any assurance engagements in functions over which the CAE has responsibility. Any impairments of independence or objectivity affecting internal auditors should be reported to appropriate parties.

Proficiency and Due Professional Care

Each internal auditor should possess the knowledge, skills, and other competencies necessary to his or her individual responsibilities. Collectively, the internal audit function should possess all the proficiencies required by its responsibilities. The internal auditor should be able to identify the indicators of fraud but need not have the same level of expertise of someone whose primary responsibility is detecting and investigating fraud. All internal auditors need some knowledge of information technology, but not all need to have the same expertise as an auditor who specializes in information technology.

Internal auditors need not be infallible, but they should exercise the care and skill of a "reasonably prudent and competent internal auditor. " This includes considering the use of computers and data analysis when performing audits.

Internal auditors should enhance proficiency through continuing professional development.

Quality Assurance and Improvement Programs

A quality assurance and improvement program should cover all aspects of the internal audit activity and should be subject to continuous internal monitoring as well as periodic internal and external quality assessments. The program should help the internal auditing activity add value and improve the organization's operations in conformity with the IIA's standards and the code of ethics. The CAE should be responsible for developing and maintaining the program and for communicating results of external assessments of the program to the board.

Performance Standards

The IIA performance standards provide descriptions of activities that internal auditing should perform and indicate appropriate levels of quality. The next summary touches on the main points in the performance standards.

Managing the Internal Audit Activity

The CAE's role is to manage the internal audit activity effectively, ensuring that it adds value to the organization. The responsibilities of this role include:

- Establishing risk-based plans
- Communicating plans to senior management and the board
- Ensuring that sufficient resources are available to carry out the plans
- Establishing policies and procedures to guide audit activity
- Coordinating activities and sharing information
- Reporting relevant information periodically to senior management and the board
- Defining the nature of work

The internal audit should evaluate and contribute to the improvement of risk management, control, and governance using a systematic and disciplined approach. Assessing governance and recommending improvements involves promoting ethics and values within the organization as well as ensuring performance management, communicating risk and control information throughout the organization, and coordinating and sharing information among stakeholders. The objectives of the engagement should be consistent with the overall goals of the organization.

Engagement Planning

When planning an engagement, the internal auditor should consider:

- The objectives and performance controls of the activity.
- Significant risks to the activity and means of keeping the risk level acceptable.
- Adequacy and effectiveness of the activity's risk management and control systems compared with a relevant model.
- Opportunities to improve the activity's risk management and controls.

Objectives should be developed for each engagement, and the scope should be sufficient to satisfy the objectives. Consultant engagements that develop during an assurance engagement should be based on a written understanding of objectives, scope, and so on, and the results should be communicated in accordance with consulting standards. Engagement with parties outside the organization should also be based on a written understanding.

Performing the Engagement

Internal auditors should identify, analyze, evaluate, and record sufficient information to achieve the objectives of the engagement. The CAE should control access to the records and develop retention requirements and policies to govern custody.

Communicating Results

Internal auditors should communicate the results of the engagement, including objectives and scope, as well as conclusions, recommendations, and action plans.

Monitoring Progress

The senior audit executive should develop a follow-up process to ensure that management implements the recommendations of the audit report or accepts the risks of not taking actions.

Resolution of Management's Acceptance of Risks

Assurance engagements conclude with the development of a residual risk profile for the organization. If the CAE believes that senior management has accepted an unacceptably high level of risk for the organization's risk appetite, then the CAE and senior management should report the matter to the board.

Management of the Internal Auditing Department

The director of internal auditing should manage the auditing department, including establishing the next controls:

- Statement of purpose, authority, and responsibility for the internal auditing department
- Plans to carry out the department's responsibilities
- Written policies and procedures to guide the audit staff
- Program for selecting and developing the human resources of the audit department
- Coordination of internal and external audit efforts
- A quality assurance program to evaluate the operation of the internal auditing department

Reporting Audit Results

Potential audiences for the audit report include divisional and operational managers as well as top management and the board of directors. The internal auditor should inform management of all problems. Because of the possible use of the internal audit report by external auditors, legal counsel may need to be consulted before highly sensitive information is included in a written audit report. According to IIA Standard 2440. A2:

> If not otherwise mandated by legal, statutory, or regulatory requirements, prior to releasing results to parties outside the organization, the chief audit executive should:
>
> - assess the potential risk to the organization,
> - consult with senior management and/or legal counsel as appropriate, and
> - control dissemination by restricting the use of the results.

Such discussions minimize misunderstandings.

The auditor's report identifies conditions as findings, or issues to address or recognize. One audit report may include several specific findings, and each finding, which may be positive or negative, should be documented on a separate summary findings sheet. Negative findings are called exceptions. Findings are performance or actions as measured against the firm's policies, procedures, standards, or external laws and regulations and against risks such as inadequate safeguarding of company assets.

Each summary findings sheet should report the condition and the policy, legal criteria, or expectation regarding the finding. The auditor's report should include conclusions regarding the effect of the condition and the cause of the condition. The auditor should also provide recommendations that offer alternatives relative to the specific control objective for each finding. A recommendation does not necessarily represent a solution for the condition.

Recommendations should:

- Identify the internal control breakdown and the associated risks involved.
- Identify what needs to be achieved by the change and leave the details of strategy and tactics to management.
- Be stated clearly and succinctly but should be detailed enough to require no further explanation.
- Be fully supported by evidence.
- Be action-oriented and achievable, with reasonable expenditures, deadlines, staffing, and so on, in relation to the problem addressed.

Types of Recommendations

The auditor can make four types of recommendations:

1. **Make no changes.** If the audit determines that the activities investigated do not represent any significant problems—such as noncompliance with regulations, failure to safeguard assets, insufficient control of transactions, and so on—the auditor will recommend no change. It is also possible that recommending change is not the most effective way to achieve a desired result in the organization. In such cases, the auditor may seek an exception to the standard and instead submit an analysis to management.

2. **Modify internal control policies and/or procedures** If the auditor does uncover problems, the audit report should recommend changes in the areas of risk or poor performance.

3. **Add insurance for potential risks discovered during the audit.** Rather than suggesting new policies or procedures to address a potential risk, the auditor may suggest insuring against the liability involved. The auditor must be certain that insurance is an appropriate as well as cost-effective measure. Whether to eliminate a potential liability or insure against its occurrence may involve ethical as well as practical considerations, depending on the nature of the risk.

4. **Adjust the required rate of return on an activity to match the associated risk.** In assessing the nature of potential risks in light of the organization's attitudes and risk appetite, the auditor may report that one of the organization's activities involves more potential risk than is justified by its current projected return.

General and Specific Findings

An internal auditor may report a number of findings to management. General findings may include such items as inadequate control procedures, lack of adherence to control procedures (e. g., disorganized records), inadequate safeguarding of assets, inefficient allocation of resources, and so on. The auditor can provide a service by prioritizing the various risks in terms of their potential costs.

Each general finding should be supported by specific findings and backed up by solid evidence. For example, an internal auditor conducting a compliance audit might provide managers with a report indicating which employees failed to have their timecards up-to-date. An internal auditor conducting an audit of the physical security of assets might report anyone whose sensitive files were found unlocked during an after-hours check. A software audit might result in a report of computers on which unlicensed software had been loaded.

Audit Evidence

Audit evidence can take a number of forms. Evidence gathered by auditors is called **primary evidence** and might be gathered by observation, surveys, interviews, inspection of documents (canceled checks to verify disbursements, timecards to verify hours worked, etc.), or other means. Primary evidence is the least open to question from the viewpoint of the auditor who gathered it. Evidence gathered and submitted by the subject of the audit, or by third parties, constitutes **secondary evidence** . Auditors will assign credibility to this evidence according to their assessment of the internal controls relevant to it. The weaker the controls, the more corroborating evidence the auditors will require.

Evidence can also be considered according to legal categories. Primary evidence is direct; secondary evidence from the subject of the audit is hearsay. Checks, stock certificates, timecards, and the like are documentary evidence, useful in corroborating direct testimony or hearsay. Expert opinion can be used in audits as in courtrooms. An internal auditor is not expected to be an ultimate expert in all relevant matters. Computer programmers may, for example, be useful in reviewing computer systems controls. **Circumstantial evidence** is not direct, hearsay, or opinion. Rather, it is a set of conditions—circumstances—that make one suspect the existence of a particular problem. The suspected problem must be verified by harder evidence.

Analytical evidence includes such things as financial ratios and vertical and horizontal financial statement analysis. This type of evidence can be useful in testing the success of financial operations in supporting corporate objectives. Analysis can include period-to-period comparisons of results (this quarter against last quarter or the same quarter of one or more previous years). Budgets can be compared to forecasts. The organization's performance—in terms of profits, revenues, sales, margins, and so on—can be compared to industry averages. Financial ratios are used by analysts and investors, as well as financial auditors, to assess a company's performance and prospects.

Types of Audits Conducted by Internal Auditors

Internal audits are conducted for a number of reasons, including financial control, assurance of compliance with regulations, and assessment of internal control policies and procedures. An internal auditor could conduct one or more of several types of audits: financial, operational, performance, electronic data processing, contract, compliance, and special investigations (such as fraud). A data processing audit might include running special mapping software that scans computer systems searching for malicious, hidden code designed to steal data, crash the computer, or provide access to outsiders. Internal auditors have concentrated less on financial audits and more on operational audits. Over half of the average internal auditor's time is spent on operational audits. The compliance audit is another key type of audit.

Financial Audit

A **financial audit** is an audit of the firm's financial statements. The objective is to determine whether the overall financial statements fairly represent the firm's operations and financial condition. The internal auditor may conduct an audit of financial reports for a department or a segment of a department. The audience for a financial audit is the board of directors and senior management. The direction of a financial audit conducted by an internal auditor is forward-looking, in contrast to the external audit, which is backward-looking.

When designing a financial audit, the auditor assesses the adequacy of internal controls as they relate to financial activities. The nature, timing, and extent of substantive testing will depend on the auditor's assessment of the amount of control risk and the credibility of assertions regarding the company's transactions. Substantive tests in the financial audit might focus on the details of account balances, analytical procedures, transactions, and the physical security of assets, among other matters.

Operational Audit

An **operational audit** is a nonfinancial audit that is intended to evaluate the effectiveness and efficiency of the organization or one of its divisions, departments, or processes. Businesses often combine financial and operational audits.

The operational audit is an organized search for improvements in efficiency and effectiveness of operations and often takes on the form of constructive criticism. It is a tool for regularly and systematically appraising the effectiveness of the firm against organizational and industry standards, organizational goals and objectives, and applicable laws and regulations. The objectives of this type of audit are to ensure the board of directors and senior management that the organization's goals and objectives are being met and to identify conditions that can be improved. In an operational audit, the auditor has the responsibility of discovering operating problems, informing the board of directors and management of the problems, and recommending realistic courses of action for resolving the problems.

Compliance Audit

During a **compliance audit**, the auditor determines whether the firm has complied with applicable laws and regulations as well as professional or industry standards or contractual responsibilities. A compliance audit can be part of a financial or operational audit or undertaken separately. Compliance audits can be initiated by management or may be required by law or regulation.

The auditor first needs to determine whether management has a system in place for identifying applicable policies, procedures, standards, laws, and regulations. Then the auditor evaluates whether controls are being applied and followed properly. This testing should lead to conclusions as to whether the firm is in compliance.

Internal Audit Assistance Provided to Management

To assist management, the internal audit function provides analyses, appraisals, recommendations, counsel, and information concerning activities reviewed.

The organization's operating management, such as department heads or supervisors, is accountable for the effectiveness and efficiency of operations. Audit reports support operating management in this regard by identifying areas needing improvement and stimulating action in the appropriate direction. In addition, the results of an internal audit may provide objective support to the operations manager for issues that will require the support of upper management to address and improve. An audit may bring to a manager's attention activities or practices of which he or she was not aware—for example, the shipping manager needing to recheck all the sales orders because of repeated inaccuracies by sales staff. Expectations of the internal audit, as well as lessons learned from previous internal audits, ultimately may serve to promote more disciplined operations.

Audit reports serve to identify for the board of directors and senior management the changing level and types of risks that management needs to address. Due to the nature or scope of the audit or the independence and objectivity of the internal auditor, an internal audit report can provide senior management with details about operations as well as controls that are not included in other reports.

Knowledge Check: Internal Auditing

The next questions are intended to help you check your understanding and recall of the material presented in this topic. They do not represent the type of questions that appear on the CMA exam.

Directions: Answer each question in the space provided. Correct answers and section references appear after the knowledge check questions.

1. Which of the following are categories of standards for internal auditing?

    I. Attribute

    II. Characteristic

    III. Performance

    IV. Implementation

    ☐ **a.** I and III

    ☐ **b.** II and IV

    ☐ **c.** I, III, and IV

    ☐ **d.** I, II, III, and IV

2. A compliance audit in a manufacturing firm could verify which of the following?

    ☐ **a.** Compliance with GAAP

    ☐ **b.** Compliance with employment laws

    ☐ **c.** Compliance with worker safety and health laws

    ☐ **d.** All of the above

3. Which of the following would **not** be a type of recommendation an internal auditor would make?

    ☐ **a.** Add a procedure for ensuring that transactions cannot be placed by unauthorized personnel.

    ☐ **b.** Controls should be implemented to ensure that unauthorized personnel cannot access payroll files.

    ☐ **c.** Controls should be implemented that ensure increasing compensation for production managers.

    ☐ **d.** Add a procedure for ensuring that key files cannot be accidentally deleted from the computer system.

4. The auditor can make four types of recommendations. Complete the next list.

    a. Make no changes.

    b. Modify internal control policies and/or procedures.

     c. _____.

     d. _____.

5. Which of the following is **not** something that would be done by the chief audit executive prior to releasing results about an audit?

    ☐ **a.** Provide a summary report to the external auditors.

    ☐ **b.** Assess the potential risk to the organization.

    ☐ **c.** Control dissemination by restricting the use of the results.

    ☐ **d.** Consult with senior management and/or legal counsel as appropriate.

Knowledge Check Answers: Internal Auditing

1. Which of the following are categories of standards for internal auditing? *[See Responsibility and Authority of the Internal Audit Function.]*

    I. Attribute

    II. Characteristic

    III. Performance

    IV. Implementation

    ☐ **a.** I and III

    ☐ **b.** II and IV

    ☑ **c.** I, III, and IV

    ☐ **d.** I, II, III, and IV

2. A compliance audit in a manufacturing firm could verify which of the following? *[See Compliance Audit.]*

    ☐ **a.** Compliance with GAAP

    ☐ **b.** Compliance with employment laws

    ☐ **c.** Compliance with worker safety and health laws

    ☑ **d.** All of the above

3. Which of the following would **not** be a type of recommendation an internal auditor would make? *[See Types of Recommendations.]*

    ☐ **a.** Add a procedure for ensuring that transactions cannot be placed by unauthorized personnel.

    ☐ **b.** Controls should be implemented to ensure that unauthorized personnel cannot access payroll files.

    ☑ **c.** Controls should be implemented that ensure increasing compensation for production managers.

    ☐ **d.** Add a procedure for ensuring that key files cannot be accidentally deleted from the computer system.

4. The auditor can make four types of recommendations. Complete the next list. *[See Types of Recommendations.]*

    a. Make no changes.

    b. Modify internal control policies and/or procedures.

    c. **Add insurance for potential risks discovered during the audit.**

    d. **Adjust the required rate of return on an activity to match the associated risk.**

5. Which of the following is **not** something that would be done by the chief audit executive prior to releasing results about an audit? *[See Reporting Audit Results.]*

    ☑ **a.** Provide a summary report to the external auditors.

    ☐ **b.** Assess the potential risk to the organization.

    ☐ **c.** Control dissemination by restricting the use of the results.

    ☐ **d.** Consult with senior management and/or legal counsel as appropriate.

Systems Controls and Security Measures

INFORMATION IS A KEY ASSET of any company, and internal controls are imperative for the protection of this asset. Information stored on a computer system is subject to loss or inaccuracy resulting from:

- Computer or network crashes
- Natural disaster or theft
- Human error in input or application
- Manipulation of input data
- Intentional alteration of records or programs
- Sabotage
- Software bugs
- Computer viruses and worms
- Trojan horse programs and other computer system threats

A company must consider all of these very real risks in establishing internal controls to prevent or minimize losses of sensitive information assets. Systems controls enhance the accuracy, validity, safety, security, and adaptability of systems input, processing, output, and storage functions.

This topic deals with the risks associated with information systems and the controls that companies can put in place to reduce these risks, including organizational controls, personnel policies, and systems development controls. It describes some of the network, hardware, and facility controls organizations put in place, strategies used to help prevent loss of business information and ensure operations in case of a system failure, and accounting controls that are incorporated into computer systems and manual processes. Finally, the topic looks at the use of flowcharting to assess controls and identify gaps.

 READ the Learning Outcome Statements (LOS) for this topic as found in Appendix A and then study the concepts and calculations presented here to be sure you understand the content you could be tested on in the CMA exam.

General Information Systems Controls

Information systems are usually divided into two functions: financial accounting and operating information systems.

1. **Financial accounting information systems** generate an organization's financial statements, budgets, and cost reports for managers.
2. **Operating information systems** gather information relating to various operational activities and generate reports for managers.

Having internal controls to maintain the reliability and integrity of the information system is critical to management's decision-making processes. Protecting the information system and the information in its databases is essential for accurate and reliable financial reports as well as for the operating reports that management uses to make decisions.

Information system controls consist of general and application controls. **General controls**, sometimes called pervasive controls, are controls related to the computer, technology, or information technology (IT) function. They include:

- Organizational, personnel, and operations controls
- Systems development controls
- Network, hardware, and facility controls
- Backup and disaster recovery controls
- Accounting control

General systems controls include a plan for the organization of the information system and the methods and procedures that apply to the systems operations in a business. General controls, as a basis for effective application controls, are vital in the protection of information systems.

Application controls consist of input, process, and output controls. These controls are covered in greater detail in the discussion of accounting controls, later in this topic. As with other controls, the control environment plays a vital role in the effectiveness of information systems controls. The actions that management and the board of directors take regarding oversight of systems controls and involvement with key decisions regarding the information systems provide clear signals to the rest of the company.

Risks Associated with Information Systems

Computers and networks present risks that are specific to their nature within the company's operations:

- There is less visibility of the audit trail, with the reduction or elimination of source documents and records that auditors can use to trace accounting information. Other controls must be put into place to replace the traditional ability to compare output information with hard copy data.
- Hardware or software may malfunction.

- Human involvement is reduced and, along with it, the possibility that human intervention could identify mistakes that the software may not be designed to catch.
- Systematic errors may occur because of flaws in the program design.
- Unauthorized users may accidentally alter or delete data.
- Data may be lost or stolen, which could result in costly business interruptions or errors. Stolen personal information can create substantial public relations and financial risks for a company.
- Systems may be damaged by malicious code.
- Segregation of duties may be reduced, so that functions that traditionally were separated as a control are made more accessible.
- There may be a lack of traditional authorization when transactions are initiated automatically.
- The risk of information loss and fraud should be of great concern to organizations. Threats to an information system can occur both internally and externally. Internal threats to an information system can come from systems personnel including computer maintenance persons, programmers, computer operators, computer and information systems administrative personnel, and data control clerks. External threats to an information system can come from intruders. Losses can occur from input manipulation, program alteration, direct file alteration, data theft, and sabotage.
- Input manipulation requires the least amount of technical skill and is the most common threat in practice. Common input manipulation examples are hacking into a Web site to steal credit card numbers or data processing clerks altering supporting documents and entering inaccurate information into the computer system.
- Program alteration requires programming skills and knowledge and may be the least common method used to commit computer fraud. Program alterations can occur by using trapdoors to enter a computer program while bypassing its normal security systems. For example, a programmer could make unauthorized program changes to divert monies to accounts that he or she created. Companies with good internal control systems can prevent this type of fraud by carefully reviewing, testing, approving, and logging all program changes before they are implemented.
- In some cases, individuals find ways to bypass the normal process for inputting data into computer programs. An example of direct file alteration is when an employee uses special software tools to modify files or databases directly. Direct file alteration is easily prevented by limiting access and encrypting the files and databases.
- Data theft fraud is difficult to detect because it is often performed by trusted employees who have routine access to data. Further, in highly competitive industries, quantitative and qualitative information about competitors is constantly being sought.
- Sabotage is a deliberate action aimed at weakening an organization through subversion, obstruction, disruption, or destruction. Sabotage often is carried out by disgruntled or recently fired employees to interrupt operations and destroy software and electronic files.

Organization Controls and Personnel Policies

Some general information systems controls include personnel policies that apply to the structuring of duties and use of systems.

Segregation of Duties and Functions

Segregation of duties and functions in IT begins with the separation of the IT function from the rest of the organization. The head of IT or chief information officer should report to the firm's chief executive officer. IT belongs to the entire organization, not to any one function.

There should also be a separation of systems development, operations, and technical support within the IT function. Systems development covers the application programmers and analysts—those responsible for application software development or selection. IT operations include computer operators, the input/output function, and the library function. Technical support includes the network administrator, the database administrator, the security administrator, and the systems programmers. Systems programmers are responsible for the systems programs. Systems programs include the operating system, the library system, and systems utilities. Systems utilities are housekeeping programs for common functions, such as sorts, merges, compilers, and translators.

Controls for information systems should clearly define the responsibilities associated with the accounting and operating subsystems and ensure that these responsibilities are appropriately segregated. Authorizations for all transactions should be outside IT. IT's role is the processing, storage, and dissemination of information and data. The information and data belong to the users only. For example, authorization for issuance of paychecks should be initiated within the accounting or payroll department, not by data processing personnel.

Any changes made to the master file or transaction files should be authorized by the appropriate accounting person before they are implemented. Many firms implement control policies that require change request forms that document information about the origin of the change, including the date and a supervisor's approval. Some systems may provide a log of file request changes.

Controls for segregation of duties should include separation of responsibilities within the information processing department. For example, employees involved in the design, development, and maintenance of the information system should not be involved in day-to-day processing of transactions. Conversely, employees doing data entry should not be provided with access to program documentation or source code. The database is the responsibility of the database administrator. The network administrator is responsible for all data communication hardware and software and usage. The security administrator is responsible for the assignment and control of user access.

Each application should include functions for tracking program changes and for controlling access to the production version of the application. The controls should also include a supervisory review of program maintenance and revisions.

Vacation Rule

Many fraud schemes require constant action by the perpetrator, who juggles (or laps) accounts to keep the fraud from being detected. For this reason, many firms require personnel in certain positions to take vacation for a certain length of time to help detect this or similar types of fraudulent activity.

Computer Access Controls

Only approved users should be allowed to access systems. Administrators can control the rights of individual users as well as their access to information within the system. System usage can be tracked by time of day, duration of access, and location of access. This tracking provides administrators with information regarding unusual access or usage of the system.

Systems Development Controls

Systems development controls begin with an appropriate set of systems development standards that cover the various stages of the systems development life cycle, which include analysis, design, implementation, and maintenance.

Analysis

The purpose of analysis is twofold: to understand the system and to develop appropriate design specifications. Design consists of general design (gross or conceptual design) and detailed design (physical design). Detailed design can involve either software selection or software development. Software selection involves purchasing off-the-shelf software and using it as is or modifying it to suit the needs of the organization. Software development consists of design specifications, prototyping, and programming. Implementation consists of quality assurance, pilot (beta) and parallel testing, conversion, and user acceptance.

A firm planning to purchase or develop a large computer system usually assembles a team that oversees the design, development (or selection), and implementation of the new system . This team should be made up of employees from the information systems department as well as others, including managers and end users of the system.

In support of segregation of duties, an auditor assigned to direct the development, installation, and testing of a new information system should be excluded from the team that audits the accounting system and related functional areas.

Design

The system specifications must be documented in detail before development begins. Team members should study the functionality of the current system, identify needs not met by the current system, and identify other features the new system must or should have. Having personnel from different areas of the company on the team helps ensure that the new system design incorporates usability, appropriate reporting capabilities, and internal controls.

Prototype

Making changes to a system or program that is near completion is costly. Therefore, most development projects include the creation of a prototype that shows the interface design and general features. Changes usually are expected during the prototype stage.

Programming/Development

In the development phase, control policies should ensure that no individual programmer or systems analyst is responsible for the design or development of the complete information system. The design, development, and implementation of a new computer system program should be subject to strict controls that will ensure system reliability and data integrity.

Quality Assurance

A quality assurance program must test the new system with realistic data to ensure that it functions as expected and is compatible with existing programs and hardware.

Prior to testing the entire system, modular testing is performed. **Modular testing** is the testing of individual modules of the system to see that they are functioning properly.

End user testing of the system often includes both pilot testing and parallel testing. **Pilot testing**, also called beta testing, is the initial testing of the system by a select group while most of the company continues to use the old software. Pilot testing is conducted at the stage at which the programming is completed and the system is largely is ready for production. Testing by end users is aimed at identifying both system bugs and usability issues. **Parallel testing** involves inputting and processing identical information on both the old and new systems and comparing the output.

After successful testing, user acceptance should be documented by appropriate user management sign-offs.

Implementation

Once the system has been tested, accepted, and approved for release, the programming staff will provide the system files and documentation to the system administrator for release (with data converted from the old system).

Maintenance

System maintenance involves monitoring the system over time to make sure performance is maintained at the desired level. Version control software tracks all changes and maintenance to the program. System maintenance and upgrades usually are scheduled for off-peak hours.

Network, Hardware, and Facility Controls

To protect the information on a system, controls must be in place to protect the hardware and the facility that houses it.

Facility and Hardware Controls

Protecting systems and information assets begins with controlling access to the building. Within the building, the data center should be in a location away from public spaces. Access should be granted only to specifically authorized personnel. Many data centers use individual keycodes or biometrics to control entrance to the facility. In addition to protection from unauthorized entry, computer equipment must also be protected from environmental threats, such as fire and floods, and from human sabotage or attack. Environmental controls, including air conditioning and humidity control, are also required.

Computer equipment must be protected from power surges and outages through the use of surge protectors and backup power supplies. The system and its supporting network should be designed to handle periods of peak volume. Additional protection with redundant components should be put in place so the system can switch to a backup unit in the event of hardware failure.

Finally, the controls must extend to the individual users. Software controls can be implemented to require users to have strong passwords and change them frequently. However, users must take responsibility for securing their equipment and the information on it. This is especially important with the growing use of laptops, tablets, and smart phones.

Network Controls

The objective of a network is to enable authorized employees to access and work with the firm's data and programs. However, without well-designed and strictly enforced control policies and procedures, unauthorized people both within and outside the company may access and alter critical information.

Even the smallest organizations are likely to use **local area networks** (LANs), either wired or wireless, to share data, applications, and other network resources.

Larger organizations may implement a **wide area network** (WAN), a private network connecting multiple LANs over a broad geographic area. Many organizations also use virtual private networks (VPNs) that permit secure communications over public or shared network facilities, including the Internet.

The Internet has introduced risks to computer systems that do not exist on private networks. Among the threats is a greatly increased risk of unauthorized access, as hackers have grown both numerous more sophisticated in their attacks. Internet presence also exposes systems to "malware"—including virus, worms, spyware, spam, and Trojan horses .

Companies must use a variety of controls to protect their systems and data, beginning, at the most basic, with passwords. Software-based access controls allow the system administrators to manage access privileges. An additional step many firms take is to encrypt data so that unauthorized users who have been able to bypass first-level controls are not able to read, change, add to, or remove the data.

Data Encryption and Transmission

Data Encryption

Data encryption converts data from an easily read local language into a code that can be read only by those with the correct decryption key. The data are encoded during the input or transmission stage, then decrypted at output by the person authorized to receive them. Other controls designed to reduce the risk of interception and to detect errors or alterations in data transmissions include routing verification and message acknowledgment.

Routing Verification

Routing verification procedures add assurance that transactions are routed to the correct computer address. A transaction transmitted over a network contains a header label identifying its destination. When the transaction is received, the sending system verifies that the identity of the receiving computer matches the transaction's destination code. Routing verification is assisted by dual transmissions and echo checks. An echo check is a verification by the receiving node that what the sending node sent is in fact what was received.

Message Acknowledgment

Message acknowledgment procedures require a trailer message that the receiving computer can use to verify that the entire transmission was received. The receiving computer signals the sending computer regarding the successful completion of the transmission. If the receiving computer detects an error, data are retransmitted.

Virus Protection and Firewalls

Network information needs to be protected from both corruption and intruders. Antivirus software scans files to detect viruses and other malicious code. Many companies have policies that prohibit employees from installing any programs not approved by the information systems department.

A **firewall**—a combination of hardware and software—is used to help prevent unauthorized access from the Internet. Within the company network, firewalls may be used to prevent unauthorized access to specific systems, such as the payroll or personnel. Multiple firewalls are recommended in order to improve security.

A number of different controls or control alerts can be contained within a firewall system. The firewall may include an automated disconnect if a user enters a specified number of wrong passwords. Change control software provides an audit trail showing the sources of all changes made to files. And the network or firewall software may produce a network control log that lists all transmissions to or from a computer. This log can be useful for identifying the source of errors or attempts at unauthorized access.

Intrusion Detection System

If someone gains unauthorized access to a company's network, intrusion detection systems analyze network activity for aberrant or unauthorized activity and keep a centralized security event log that includes event logs from servers and workstations and provides alerts to security breaches. Event logs also can be used to detect misuse from internal sources.

Backup and Disaster Recovery Controls

Control policies and procedures are essential to prevent loss of critical business information and to ensure continued operation in the face of a major system failure or destruction of the facility. Two levels of policies and procedures must be set in place to protect from these eventualities: data backup policies and procedures and disaster recovery policies and procedures.

Data Backup Policies and Procedures

Backup policies and procedures are instituted to ensure that data that are lost due to malware, natural disasters, hardware failures, theft, deletions, and software malfunctions can be recovered. Most firms institute procedures for backing up all files on the network daily, during slow processing times. Backup is normally achieved by copying files to tape or other offline media that may be kept in the data processing center or stored off-site. Off-site storage should be considered mandatory, because data can be recovered in the event of a disaster that affects the data center. Backup files also can be electronically transferred to off-site locations. This is called electronic vaulting.

Many firms institute a procedure called the grandfather-father-son (GFS) method. With this method, the most recent three generations (e. g. , days) of backup files are secured at all times. If data are lost or altered, they may be retrieved from the most recent "clean" backup file.

Some firms that employ a master file and transaction files institute the checkpoint procedure, which runs at intervals throughout the day and facilitates recovery from a system failure. Using this procedure, the network system temporarily does not accept new transactions while it finishes updating procedures for transactions entered since the last checkpoint and then generates a backup copy of all data values and other information. Should a system failure occur, the system can be restarted by reading in the last checkpoint from the backup.

The control policies also should provide for backup of system configurations. Significant time may be lost before backup files can be recovered from storage tapes if a network first must be reformatted and reconfigured to its previous status.

Disaster Recovery Policies and Procedures

Disaster recovery policies and procedures—also called business continuance plans—are designed to enable the firm to carry on business in the event that an emergency, such as a natural disaster, disrupts normal function. A company's disaster recovery plan should define the roles of all members of the disaster recovery team, appointing both a primary leader and an alternate leader for the process.

The plan should specify backup sites for alternate computer processing. This site may be another location owned by the firm or may be owned by another organization.

A "hot site" is a location that includes a system configured like the firm's production system. Hot sites are often called duplex systems. Duplex systems run simultaneously with the regular system, and a failure in the main system can trigger an automatic switchover to the backup. A "warm site" is a backup site that has hardware and software available and can be made operational within a short timeframe. A "cold site" provides a location where the company can install equipment and personnel on fairly short notice and begin operations using backup files. If a cold site is the designated recovery site, additional arrangements must be in place for obtaining computer equipment matching the lost system's configuration requirements.

The disaster recovery plan should be tested, documented, reviewed regularly, and updated as required. All relevant personnel must be thoroughly trained in the procedures.

Accounting Controls

The accounting system should contain controls that readily confirm or question the reliability of recorded data. Types of controls that can be implemented in an accounting system include those listed next.

Batch totals. The input preparer reports the total amount in the batch; this amount is also listed on the cover sheet of the group of transaction documents. This number can be the total number of records or the total dollar value of all the transactions being entered.

Control accounts. This type of control allows only authorized personnel into particular accounts on the system. For example, a payroll professional may not have access to accounts that do not involve payroll.

Voiding/cancellation. This type of control involves proper voiding or cancellation of invoices and supporting documents after payment.

Feedback controls. Feedback controls provide information about system performance, especially information selected to see that the system, or model, is performing as intended. Feedback can be delivered in different ways depending on the nature of the organization and the system; it may consist of written or oral reports or it may be automated. To allow effective corrective action, feedback information must be delivered quickly (depending on the problem's size, severity, and difficulty of correction). It is essentially diagnostic, and any amelioration occurs after problems arise and then are discovered, reported, and analyzed. In a sense, all monitoring controls are feedback controls, because they are designed to collect, analyze, and report data that can be used to determine the success of all other controls.

Feedforward and preventive controls. Feedforward controls are based on predictions about future events. They are less common and more complicated to manage than feedback controls. Feedforward controls based on current actions are predictions of future events with some degree of probability. Because feedforward controls are based on predictions of future occurrences, they may be designed to prevent anticipated problems. Setting up an off-site location ready for use in an emergency is an example of feedforward, preventive controls.

Application and Transaction Controls

Application and transaction controls are designed to prevent, detect, and correct errors and irregularities in transactions that are processed by accounting systems. Application controls can be divided into three categories: input controls, processing controls, and output controls. The purpose of application controls is to provide reasonable assurance that all processing is authorized, complete, and timely.

Input Controls

Input controls are designed to provide a system of checks and balances over the input of data or transactions into the system. Input controls are designed to prevent or detect errors in the time information is data entered into the computer system. Often this involves conversion of transaction data into a machine-readable format. The capability of these control procedures to correct errors early helps ensure accuracy and reliability of reporting data.

Among the manual methods used to increase the accuracy of input are:

- Batch controls, which include a batch number, record count, control totals, and a hash total. (A hash total is a total of nonsignificant numbers, such as customer numbers and part numbers, that is used to detect deletions or insertions in a batch.)
- Approval mechanisms.
- Dual observation, to review data before input.
- Supervisory procedure to confirm accuracy of data gathered by the employee before input.

Well-designed source documents are an important input control. Data should be organized on the input form in a way that facilitates accurate input. Many accounting systems contain built-in edit tests, such as an accounting input control that requires that debits equal credits before the system will accept a journal entry. A full edit check should be performed on all transactions before they are entered as updates to the master file.

Other input control procedures include redundant data checks, unfound records tests, anticipation checks, preformatted screens, interactive edits, and check digits.

- **Redundant data checks** encode repetitious data on a transaction record, enabling a later processing test to compare the two data items for compatibility. For example, a grocery store system may compare the bar code on the product and an alpha description of the item. If they do not match, an exceptions report is produced.
- **Unfound records tests** (also called validity tests or master file checks) are run as data are input. Any transaction with no master file will be rejected. Note, however, that computers process data on two different time schedules: real time and batch processing. With real-time processing, data in master files are updated as each transaction is entered. Batch processing systems collect data throughout a time period, such as a day, and then process the group of transactions together. An operator inputting to a batch system must wait until the new information appears in the master file. With a real-time system, the new account information appears as soon as it is entered, after which the transaction can be input.
- **Anticipation checks** are dependence or consistency checks and look for a relationship between two items or conditions. An example of this type of check could be that sales tax is not included when a sale is made to a nonprofit or governmental organization.
- **Preformatted screens** with logical content groupings and "forced choices" when only certain options are available improve the efficiency and accuracy of input entry.
- **Interactive edits** are performed as the data are entered to check that the data in a particular field meet specified requirements, such as:
  - Character checks. A character in a particular field has to be alphabetic, numeric, or some particular symbol.
  - Completeness checks. All fields requiring characters are filled.
  - Limit, range, or reasonable checks. Values in a field are neither too large nor too small and are reasonable. Examples would be not allowing a paycheck above a certain amount or not allowing a purchase or shipment quantity greater than a certain amount.

  A transaction should not be entered until it passes ("clears") all of the edit checks.
- **Check digit** is derived from an operation on all the digits in a number (e. g. , a sum). The sum of digits in the account number 5678, for example, would be 26 $(5 + 6 + 7 + 8)$; the check digit would be the last digit of the sum, or 6.

Processing Controls

Processing controls address the system's manipulation of the data after they are input. Processing controls often are interdependent with input controls and output controls, as in the example of check digits. They involve the reediting of data and the resulting error correction and reentry routines. Processing controls include run-to-run totals. Such totals help ensure that the output from one application agrees to the input to an application it feeds. An example is the output of cash disbursements equaling the input to the vouchers payable system. The sum is meaningless except for the computer's batch control in processing checks. Typical processing controls include the next items:

Mechanization. Consistency is provided by machine processing. An example of mechanization is when cash deposits are totaled by adding machine or calculator.

Standardization. Consistent procedures are developed for all processing. An example of standardization is the use of a chart of accounts to identify the normal debits and credits for each account.

Default option. The automatic use of a predefined value for input transactions that are left blank. An example of default option is automatically paying salaried employees for 40 hours each week.

Batch balancing. A comparison of the items or documents actually processed against a predetermined control totals. An example of batch balancing is when a cashier balances deposit tickets to control totals of cash remittances.

Run-to-run totals. The use of output control totals resulting from one process as input control totals over subsequent processing. The control totals are used as links in a chain to tie one process to another in a sequence of processes over a period of time. An example of run-to-run totals are when beginning accounts receivable balance less payments plus new purchases should equal ending accounts receivable.

Balancing. A test for equality between the values of two equivalent sets of items or one set of items and a control total. An example of balancing is confirming that the balance of the accounts payable subsidiary ledger equals the balance of the general ledger control account.

Matching. Matching items with other items received from independent sources to control the processing of transactions. An example of matching occurs when an accounts payable clerk matches vendor invoices to receiving reports and purchase orders.

Clearing account. An amount that results from the processing of independent items of equivalent value. After all items are processed, the net control value should equal zero. An example is imprest checking, which should have a zero balance after all paychecks have been cashed by employees for the week.

Tickler file. A control file consisting of items sequenced by date for processing or follow-up purposes. An example of a tickler file is invoices received and filed by due date.

Redundant processing. Duplicate processing and comparison of individual results for equality. An example of redundant processing is when two clerks compute the gross and net pay of each employee for comparison purposes.

Trailer label. A record providing a control total for comparison with accumulated counts or values of records processed. An example of a trailer label is the last record of a receivable file containing a record count of the number of records in the file.

Automated error correction. Automatic error correction of transactions or records that violate a detective control. An example of an automated error correction is the automatic initiation of a credit memo when customers overpay their account balances.

Output Controls

Output controls are designed to check that input and processing resulted in accurate and valid output. Output includes data files and reports produced after computer processing is completed. Two types of output controls are required to ensure accuracy and validity of information: controls for validating processing results and controls regulating the distribution and disposal of the output.

Controls for Validating Processing Results

The validity, accuracy, and completeness of output from accounting systems can be verified by activity reports that provide detailed information about all changes to the master files. File changes can be tracked to the events or documents that initiated the changes, and the accuracy can be verified. Where the volume of transactions makes verification using activity reports impractical, exception reports showing material changes to files can be used.

Controls Regulating Distribution of Output

There are a number of concerns regarding controls for output from computers—printed or electronic. Forms controls can be used for printed output along with precautions on how and by whom the materials are distributed, stored, and disposed of. Appropriate controls also need to be put in place for electronic distribution, including password protection of the document, encryption, controlled distribution lists, and access restrictions.

Additionally, specific output controls include:

Reconciliation. An identification and analysis of differences between the values contained in a detail file and a control total. Reconciliation is completed to identify errors rather than the existence of a difference between the balances. An example of reconciliation is completing a monthly reconciliation of a checking account.

Aging. Identification of unprocessed or retained items in files according to their date, usually the transaction date. The aging classifies items according to various date ranges. An example of aging is to complete a report to identify delinquent accounts within 30 days, 60 days, 90 days or more.

Suspense file. A file containing unprocessed or partially processed items that need further action. An example of a suspense file is a file of back-ordered raw materials awaiting receipt.

Suspense account. A control total for items that need further processing. An example of a suspense account is when the total of the accounts payable subsidiary ledger should equal the general ledger control account.

Periodic audit. Periodic verification of a file or process to detect control problems. An example of a periodic audit is sending confirmations to customers and vendors to verify account balance.

Discrepancy reports. A listing of items that have violated some control and require further investigation. An example of a discrepancy report is a list of employees who have exceeded overtime limits.

Flowcharting to Assess Controls

Documenting an organization's information system and related control procedures often can be done most effectively through flowcharting. A flowchart visually depicts the flow of transactions through the process from initiation to storage of data. Diagramming the process can help identify gaps or flaws in the controls.

Flowcharts can be useful not only for summarizing the internal auditor's information about processes but also to aid in design, development, and implementation of new accounting information systems or new control procedures.

Standard flowcharting symbols are recognized by the American National Standards Institute and the International Organization for Standardization. A few of the basic symbols are shown in Figure 1D-1.

Figure 1D-1 Flowchart Symbols

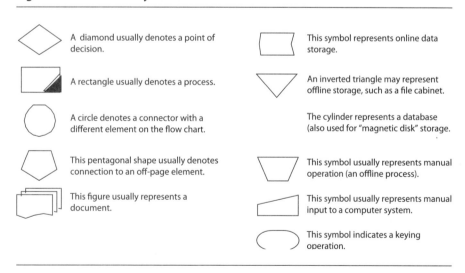

Thus, an internal auditor's flowchart of a transaction process may look something like that shown in Figure 1D-2.

Some computer programs have the ability to create an automated flowchart of a program's functionality and processes.

Figure 1D-2 Flowchart of Transaction Process

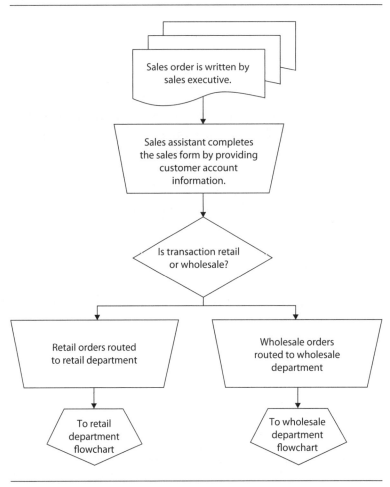

Flowcharts can help the auditor and management analyze a set of internal controls to find both strengths and weaknesses and to develop recommended corrections. Analysis might begin by matching a flowchart submitted as data to see if it corresponds to the reality of the system it purports to describe. Are retail orders actually routed as the flowchart claims, or are there perhaps unnecessary intervening procedures that are not identified on the chart? At each control point, the auditor might ask, "Is there sufficient oversight by a qualified person?" For example, in Figure 1D-2, management may see inefficiency in the fact that input of transaction orders is done by two different input operators. Management may want to examine whether it can be more efficient by routing all orders to the same input area and subsequently providing the retail and wholesale departments with reports regarding their transactions.

Flowcharts ultimately can be used to depict any process or other relationships in the firm, to illustrate relationships between different data elements, or to depict the movement of a single document throughout the process.

Knowledge Check: Systems Controls and Security Measures

The next questions are intended to help you check your understanding and recall of the material presented in this topic. They do not represent the type of questions that appear on the CMA exam.

Directions: Answer each question in the space provided. Correct answers and section references appear after the knowledge check questions.

1. Which of the following is a risk specifically associated with computer systems?
   - ☐ **a.** Risk of information assets being stolen
   - ☐ **b.** Risk of errors caused by careless input
   - ☐ **c.** Risk of limited visibility of the audit trail
   - ☐ **d.** Risk of break-in to the facility

2. Which of the following control procedures can be used to uncover a fraud scheme?
   - ☐ **a.** Prototype
   - ☐ **b.** Vacation rule
   - ☐ **c.** Disaster recovery procedures
   - ☐ **d.** Backup procedures

3. Which of the following are effective systems development controls?
   - I. Designate a team involving end users and representatives from various departments to create a thorough design.
   - II. Develop a prototype for the design team and end users to test and approve before full production.
   - III. Conduct thorough pilot and parallel testing.
   - IV. Each programmer should be responsible for placing the final version of his or her program into the final version of the system.
   - ☐ **a.** I
   - ☐ **b.** II and III
   - ☐ **c.** I, II, and III
   - ☐ **d.** I, II, III, and IV

4. Which of the following are true regarding accounting controls?
   - I. Batch totals are calculated when the transaction is output.
   - II. Control accounts should be accessed only by authorized personnel.
   - III. Invoices and supporting documents should be subject to controls for appropriate voiding after payment is received.
   - IV. Input should be processed only by management accountants.

- ☐ **a.** I
- ☐ **b.** II and III
- ☐ **c.** II and IV
- ☐ **d.** I, II, III, and IV

5. Which of the following is an example of computerized input control procedures?

- ☐ **a.** Unfound records test
- ☐ **b.** Dual observation
- ☐ **c.** Processing controls
- ☐ **d.** Backup procedures

6. Which of the following is true regarding network controls?

I. Data encryption helps protect information from unauthorized access.

II. Routing verification procedures ensure that transmissions are routed to the correct address.

III. Electronic funds transfer transmissions require strict control procedures to protect from unauthorized funds transfers.

IV. Firewalls are designed principally to detect unauthorized access from the Internet.

- ☐ **a.** I
- ☐ **b.** II and III
- ☐ **c.** I, II, and III
- ☐ **d.** I, II, III, and IV

7. Which of the following statements about backup and disaster recovery procedures is true?

- ☐ **a.** Disaster recovery procedures are recommended in the situation where backups are run only on a weekly basis.
- ☐ **b.** Disaster recovery procedures ensure the uninterrupted operation of the business.
- ☐ **c.** Backup procedures protect the company from complete loss of data.
- ☐ **d.** Backup procedures ensure the uninterrupted operation of the business in the event of a natural disaster that destroys the computer system.

8. Which of the following statements about flowcharting is **not** correct?

- ☐ **a.** Flowcharts can help the auditor and management analyze a set of internal controls.
- ☐ **b.** Flowcharts can be useful for summarizing the internal auditor's information about processes.
- ☐ **c.** Flowcharts can be used to depict the movement of a single document through a process.
- ☐ **d.** All of the above are correct.

Knowledge Check Answers: Systems Controls and Security Measures

1. Which of the following is a risk specifically associated with computer systems? *[See Risks Associated with Information Systems.]*
   - ☐ **a.** Risk of information assets being stolen
   - ☐ **b.** Risk of errors caused by careless input
   - ☑ **c.** Risk of limited visibility of the audit trail
   - ☐ **d.** Risk of break-in to the facility

2. Which of the following control procedures can be used to uncover a fraud scheme? *[See Vacation Rule.]*
   - ☐ **a.** Prototype
   - ☑ **b.** Vacation rule
   - ☐ **c.** Disaster recovery procedures
   - ☐ **d.** Backup procedures

3. Which of the following are effective systems development controls? *[See Systems Development Controls.]*
   - I. Designate a team involving end users and representatives from various departments to create a thorough design.
   - II. Develop a prototype for the design team and end users to test and approve before full production.
   - III. Conduct thorough pilot and parallel testing.
   - IV. Each programmer should be responsible for placing the final version of his or her program into the final version of the system.
   - ☐ **a.** I
   - ☐ **b.** II and III
   - ☑ **c.** I, II, and III
   - ☐ **d.** I, II, III, and IV

4. Which of the following is (are) true regarding accounting controls? *[See Accounting Controls.]*
   - I. Batch totals are calculated when the transaction is output.
   - II. Control accounts should be accessed only by authorized personnel.
   - III. Invoices and supporting documents should be subject to controls for appropriate voiding after payment is received.
   - IV. Input should be processed only by management accountants.
   - ☐ **a.** I
   - ☑ **b.** II and III

☐ **c.**   II and IV

☐ **d.**   I, II, III, and IV

5. Which of the following is an example of computerized input control procedures? *[See Input Controls.]*

☑ **a.**   Unfound records test

☐ **b.**   Dual observation

☐ **c.**   Processing controls

☐ **d.**   Backup procedures

6. Which of the following is (are) true regarding network controls? *[See Network Controls.]*

I.   Data encryption helps protect information from unauthorized access.

II. Routing verification procedures check that data is delivered to the correct address.

III. Electronic funds transfer transmissions require strict control procedures to protect from unauthorized funds transfers.

IV. Firewalls are designed principally to detect unauthorized access from the Internet.

☐ **a.**   I

☐ **b.**   II and III

☑ **c.**   I, II, and III

☐ **d.**   I, II, III, and IV

7. Which of the following statements about backup and disaster recovery procedures is true? *[See Disaster Recovery Policies and Procedures.]*

☐ **a.**   Disaster recovery procedures are recommended in the situation where backups are run only on a weekly basis.

☐ **b.**   Disaster recovery procedures ensure the uninterrupted operation of the business.

☑ **c.**   Backup procedures protect the company from complete loss of data.

☐ **d.**   Backup procedures ensure the uninterrupted operation of the business in the event of a natural disaster that destroys the computer system.

8. Which of the following statements about flowcharting is **not** correct? *[See Flowcharting to Assess Controls.]*

☐ **a.**   Flowcharts can help the auditor and management analyze a set of internal controls.

☐ **b.**   Flowcharts can be useful for summarizing the internal auditor's information about processes.

☐ **c.**   Flowcharts can be used to depict the movement of a single document through a process.

☑ **d.**   All of the above are correct.

Practice Questions: Internal Controls

Directions: This sampling of questions is designed to emulate actual exam questions. Read each question and write your response on another sheet of paper. See the "Answers to Section Practice Questions" section at the end of this book to assess your response. Validate or improve the answer you wrote. For a more robust selection of practice questions, access the **Online Test Bank** found on the IMA's Learning Center Web site.

Question 1D1-CQ01

Topic: Risk Assessment, Controls, and Risk Management

A firm is constructing a risk analysis to quantify the exposure of its data center to various types of threats. Which one of the following situations would represent the highest annual loss exposure after adjustment for insurance proceeds?

	Frequency of Occurrence (years)	Loss Amount	Insurance (% coverage)
☐ a.	1	$ 15,000	85
☐ b.	8	$75,000	80
☐ c.	20	$200,000	80
☐ d.	100	$400,000	50

Question 1D1-AT09

Topic: Risk Assessment, Controls, and Risk Management

When management of the sales department has the opportunity to override the system of internal controls of the accounting department, a weakness exists in which of the following?

- ☐ **a.** Risk management
- ☐ **b.** Information and communication
- ☐ **c.** Monitoring
- ☐ **d.** Control environment

Question 1D1-AT01

Topic: Risk Assessment, Controls, and Risk Management

Segregation of duties is a fundamental concept in an effective system of internal control. Nevertheless, the internal auditor must be aware that this safeguard can be compromised through

- ☐ **a.** lack of training of employees.
- ☐ **b.** collusion among employees.

☐ **c.**   irregular employee reviews.

☐ **d.**   absence of internal auditing.

Question 1D1-AT02

Topic: Risk Assessment, Controls, and Risk Management

A company's management is concerned about computer data eavesdropping and wants to maintain the confidentiality of its information as it is transmitted. The company should utilize:

☐ **a.**   data encryption.

☐ **b.**   dial-back systems.

☐ **c.**   message acknowledgment procedures.

☐ **d.**   password codes.

Question 1D3-AT11

Topic: Systems Controls and Security Measures

Which one of the following would **most** compromise the use of the grandfather-father-son principle of file retention as protection against loss or damage of master files?

☐ **a.**   Use of magnetic tape

☐ **b.**   Inadequate ventilation

☐ **c.**   Storing of all files in one location

☐ **d.**   Failure to encrypt data

Question 1D3-AT12

Topic: Systems Controls and Security Measures

In entering the billing address for a new client in Emil Company's computerized database, a clerk erroneously entered a nonexistent zip code. As a result, the first month's bill mailed to the new client was returned to Emil Company. Which one of the following would most likely have led to discovery of the error at the time of entry into Emil Company's computerized database?

☐ **a.**   Limit test

☐ **b.**   Validity test

☐ **c.**   Parity test

☐ **d.**   Record count test

Question 1D3-AT07

Topic: Systems Controls and Security Measures

In the organization of the information systems function, the most important separation of duties is:

☐ **a.**   assuring that those responsible for programming the system do not have access to data processing operations.

☐ **b.** not allowing the data librarian to assist in data processing operations.

☐ **c.** using different programming personnel to maintain utility programs from those who maintain the application programs.

☐ **d.** having a separate department that prepares the transactions for processing and verifies the correct entry of the transactions.

Question 1D2-AT09

Topic: Internal Auditing

There are three components of audit risk: inherent risk, control risk, and detection risk. Inherent risk is described as:

☐ **a.** the risk that the auditor may unknowingly fail to appropriately modify his or her opinion on financial statements that are materially misstated.

☐ **b.** the susceptibility of an assertion to a material misstatement, assuming that there are no related internal control structure policies or procedures.

☐ **c.** the risk that a material misstatement that could occur in an assertion will not be prevented or detected on a timely basis by the entity's internal control structure policies or procedures.

☐ **d.** the risk that the auditor will not detect a material misstatement that exists in an assertion.

Question 1D3-AT01

Topic: Systems Controls and Security Measures

Accounting controls are concerned with the safeguarding of assets and the reliability of financial records. Consequently, these controls are designed to provide reasonable assurance that all of the following take place except:

☐ **a.** executing transactions in accordance with management's general or specific authorization.

☐ **b.** comparing recorded assets with existing assets at periodic intervals and taking appropriate action with respect to differences.

☐ **c.** recording transactions as necessary to permit preparation of financial statements in conformity with generally accepted accounting principles and maintaining accountability for assets.

☐ **d.** compliance with methods and procedures ensuring operational efficiency and adherence to managerial policies.

Question 1D1-AT05

Topic: Risk Assessment, Controls, and Risk Management

Preventive controls are:

☐ **a.** usually more cost beneficial than detective controls.

☐ **b.** usually more costly to use than detective controls.

☐ **c.** found only in general accounting controls.

☐ **d.** found only in accounting transaction controls.

Question 1D2-AT02

Topic: Internal Auditing

In planning an audit, the auditor considers audit risk. Audit risk is the

☐ **a.** susceptibility of an account balance to material error assuming the client does not have any related internal control.

☐ **b.** risk that a material error in an account will not be prevented or detected on a timely basis by the client's internal control system.

☐ **c.** risk that the auditor may unknowingly fail to appropriately modify his or her opinion on financial statements that are materially misstated.

☐ **d.** risk that the auditor's procedures for verifying account balances will not detect a material error when in fact such error exists.

Question 1D2-AT03

Topic: Internal Auditing

Control risk is the risk that a material error in an account will not be prevented or detected on a timely basis by the client's internal control system. The **best** control procedure to prevent or detect fictitious payroll transactions is

☐ **a.** to use and account for prenumbered payroll checks.

☐ **b.** personnel department authorization for hiring, pay rate, job status, and termination.

☐ **c.** internal verification of authorized pay rates, computations, and agreement with the payroll register.

☐ **d.** storage of unclaimed wages in a vault with restricted access.

Question 1D2-AT10

Topic: Internal Auditing

Of the following, the **primary** objective of compliance testing is to determine whether

☐ **a.** procedures are regularly updated.

☐ **b.** controls are functioning as planned.

☐ **c.** financial statement line items are properly stated.

☐ **d.** collusion is taking place.

Question 1D3-AT05

Topic: Systems Controls and Security Measures

A critical aspect of a disaster recovery plan is to be able to regain operational capability as soon as possible. In order to accomplish this, an organization can have an arrangement with its computer hardware vendor to have a fully operational facility available that is configured to the user's specific needs. This is **best** known as a(n)

- ☐ **a.** uninterruptible power system.
- ☐ **b.** parallel system.
- ☐ **c.** cold site.
- ☐ **d.** hot site.

Question 1D1-AT07

Topic: Risk Assessment, Controls, and Risk Management

Which of the following is **not** a requirement regarding a company's system of internal control under the Foreign Corrupt Practices Act of 1977?

- ☐ **a.** Management must annually assess the effectiveness of its system of internal control.
- ☐ **b.** Transactions are executed in accordance with management's general or specific authorization.
- ☐ **c.** Transactions are recorded as necessary (1) to permit preparation of financial statements in conformity with GAAP or any other criteria applicable to such statements, and (2) to maintain accountability for assets.
- ☐ **d.** The recorded accountability for assets is compared with the existing assets at reasonable intervals, and appropriate action is taken with respect to any differences.

To further assess your understanding of the concepts and calculations covered in Part 1, Section D: Internal Controls, practice with the **Online Test Bank** questions for this section. REMINDER: See the "Answers to Section Practice Questions" section at the end of this book.

Professional Ethics

Management accountants and financial managers confront unique ethical challenges arising from their particular organizational responsibilities. To help accountants in these roles assess the specific ethical demands of their situations, the Institute of Management Accountants has developed the *IMA Statement of Ethical Professional Practice*. This statement, which is available from IMA's Web site in Statement on Management Accounting and is reproduced here, is the basis for this section.

Note to students: The Ethics section in Part 1 of the CMA exam addresses the subject from the perspective of individual behavior and in particular how individuals use the *IMA Statement of Ethical Professional Practice*. Students will see the topic of ethics covered again in Part 2 of the CMA exam. The Ethics section in Part 2 addresses the subject from the perspective of the organization. Students should be aware of and focused on the different perspectives being covered in each part of the exam. Be sure to carefully review the Learning Outcome Statements related to ethics for each part.

IMA Statement of Ethical Professional Practice

Members of IMA shall behave ethically. A commitment to ethical professional practice includes overarching principles that express our values, and standards that guide our conduct.

Principles

IMA's overarching ethical principles include: Honesty, Fairness, Objectivity, and Responsibility. Members shall act in accordance with these principles and shall encourage others within their organizations to adhere to them.

Standards

A member's failure to comply with the following standards may result in disciplinary action.

I. Competence

Each member has a responsibility to:

- Maintain an appropriate level of professional expertise by continually developing knowledge and skills.
- Perform professional duties in accordance with relevant laws, regulations, and technical standards.
- Provide decision support information and recommendations that are accurate, clear, concise, and timely.
- Recognize and communicate professional limitations or other constraints that would preclude responsible judgment or successful performance of an activity.

II. Confidentiality

Each member has a responsibility to:

- Keep information confidential except when disclosure is authorized or legally required.
- Inform all relevant parties regarding appropriate use of confidential information. Monitor subordinates' activities to ensure compliance.
- Refrain from using confidential information for unethical or illegal advantage.

III. Integrity

Each member has a responsibility to:

- Mitigate actual conflicts of interest, and regularly communicate with business associates to avoid apparent conflicts of interest. Advise all parties of any potential conflicts.

- Refrain from engaging in any conduct that would prejudice carrying out duties ethically.
- Abstain from engaging in or supporting any activity that might discredit the profession.

IV. Credibility

Each member has a responsibility to:

- Communicate information fairly and objectively.
- Disclose all relevant information that could reasonably be expected to influence an intended user's understanding of the reports, analyses, or recommendations.
- Disclose delays or deficiencies in information, timeliness, processing, or internal controls in conformance with organization policy and/or applicable law.

Resolution of Ethical Conflict

In applying the Standards of Ethical Professional Practice, you may encounter problems identifying unethical behavior or resolving an ethical conflict. When faced with ethical issues, you should follow your organization's established policies on the resolution of such conflict. If these policies do not resolve the ethical conflict, you should consider the following courses of action:

- Discuss the issue with your immediate supervisor except when it appears that the supervisor is involved. In that case, present the issue to the next level.
- If you cannot achieve a satisfactory resolution, submit the issue to the next management level. If your immediate superior is the chief executive officer or equivalent, the acceptable reviewing authority may be a group such as the audit committee, executive committee, board of directors, board of trustees, or owners. Contact with levels above the immediate superior should be initiated only with your superior's knowledge, assuming he or she is not involved. Communication of such problems to authorities or individuals not employed or engaged by the organization is not considered appropriate, unless you believe there is a clear violation of the law.
- Clarify relevant ethical issues by initiating a confidential discussion with an IMA Ethics Counselor or other impartial advisor to obtain a better understanding of possible courses of action.
- Consult your own attorney as to legal obligations and rights concerning the ethical conflict.

Ethical Considerations for Management Accounting and Financial Management Professionals

ETHICAL CHALLENGES CAN DERAIL THE career of a management accountant or financial management professional. Therefore, these individuals have an obligation to the public, their profession, the organizations they serve, and themselves to maintain the highest standards of ethical conduct.

This topic addresses the elements and application of the *IMA Statement of Ethical Professional Practice*. By knowing and applying the *IMA Statement of Ethical Professional Practice*, not only will professionals be able to meet their obligations, they also will be perceived as trustworthy sources of information and partners in the organization.

 READ the Learning Outcome Statements (LOS) for this topic as found in Appendix A and then study the concepts and calculations presented here to be sure you understand the content you could be tested on in the CMA exam.

Introduction

What should an accountant do if instructed by an immediate superior to record the physical inventory at original cost even though obsolescence has clearly reduced its value? The *IMA Statement of Ethical Professional Practice* is intended to provide guidance to an accountant in this example as well as many other situations that will challenge how accountants do their work.

Ethics is the intellectual discipline that attempts to distinguish right from wrong in human conduct. It is also a practical endeavor that proposes standards of perfect behavior as points of comparison when individuals must choose among various courses of action. Applying perfect standards in an imperfect world is rarely easy or straightforward.

In the situation just described, for example, two opposing ethical principles apply. On one hand, the accountant has a duty under an employment contract to carry out the instructions of a supervisor. On the other hand, it would be unethical for the accountant to record the inventory at cost rather than at its depreciated value. The accountant cannot satisfy both principles at once and must choose between them. Ethics, then, consists of making morally defensible choices within the sometimes ethically ambiguous, perhaps even threatening, conditions of real life.

Two good questions to ask when faced with an ethical dilemma are: "Have I gathered all the information and insight I need to take responsible and objective action?" and "Would I be pleased to have my closest friends learn of my actions?"

IMA Statement of Ethical Professional Practice

Much of this section is excerpted directly from the *IMA Statement of Ethical Professional Practice*. It is recommended that candidates study this statement thoroughly and commit the principles, standards, and resolution of ethical conflict to memory.

Ethical Behavior for Practitioners of Management Accounting and Financial Management

Practitioners of management accounting and financial management have an obligation to the public, their profession, the organizations they serve, and themselves to maintain the highest standards of ethical conduct. In recognition of this obligation, the Institute of Management Accountants has promulgated standards of ethical professional practice. Adherence to these standards, both domestically and internationally, is integral to achieving the objectives of management accounting. Practitioners of management accounting and financial management shall not commit acts contrary to these standards nor shall they condone the commission of such acts by others within their organizations.

IMA Statement of Ethical Professional Practice

Practitioners of management accounting and financial management shall behave ethically. A commitment to ethical professional practice includes overarching principles that express our values and standards that guide our conduct.

Principles

IMA's overarching ethical principles include:

1. Honesty
2. Fairness

3. Objectivity
4. Responsibility

Practitioners shall act in accordance with these principles and shall encourage others within their organizations to adhere to them.

Honesty

The first principle, honesty, requires conscientious application to the task at hand and truthfulness in all analyses and communications. Honesty is one of the key attributes people look for in an accountant or financial professional: "If you can't trust your accountant, who can you trust?" Examples of honesty include: disclosing all necessary and relevant information to outside auditors; refusing to record information that is anything less than accurate; and providing factual information to others so that they can make decisions based on truthful information.

Fairness

Fairness requires empathetic, and just consideration of the needs of others involved in a particular situation and full disclosure of all necessary contextual information. The organization deserves adequate and full disclosure in context so that appropriate actions can be taken within a reasonable time frame. To be fair, that context should be fully spelled out. Examples of fairness include: providing information and feedback objectively; identifying and fixing mistakes; and selecting vendors without bias, prejudice, or favoritism.

Objectivity

Objectivity requires impartial and dispassionate evaluation of conflicting points of view before arriving at a conclusion. For many years, organizations have depended on the objectivity of internal and external financial professionals to support them in making critical business decisions. "Let's ask our accountants" is often the course of action when businesspeople want to determine a reasoned, thorough, dispassionate, legally defensible course of action. Examples of objectivity are stating relevant financial and legal guidelines, maintaining standards for documenting information, and making recommendations on existing data despite pressures to favor one course over another.

Responsibility

Responsibility requires actions to be performed with faithfulness and loyalty. Responsibility to the client and the profession is one of the most important underpinnings for the ethical behavior of financial professionals. This includes not just loyalty to the short-term interests of the client but also to the long-term impact of financial decisions. Examples of responsibility include conveying information at the appropriate time, ensuring information on reports and statements is accurate, and gathering enough information to make an informed decision.

Standards

The *IMA Statement of Ethical Professional Practice* identifies and explains four standards that help define a member's ethical responsibility:

1. Competence
2. Confidentiality
3. Integrity
4. Credibility

A member's failure to comply with these standards may result in disciplinary action.

Competence

Each member has a responsibility to:

1. Maintain an appropriate level of professional expertise by continually developing knowledge and skills.
2. Perform professional duties in accordance with relevant laws, regulations, and technical standards.
3. Provide decision support information and recommendations that are accurate, clear, concise, and timely.
4. Recognize and communicate professional limitations or other constraints that would preclude responsible judgment or successful performance of an activity.

The rules in accounting are as diverse as they are dynamic. Keeping up to date with changes in regulations and the adoption of new laws and standards in the industry is essential. Failing to do so may unknowingly lead to unethical behavior.

Confidentiality

Each member has a responsibility to:

1. Keep information confidential except when disclosure is authorized or legally required.
2. Inform all relevant parties regarding the appropriate use of confidential information. Monitor subordinates' activities to ensure compliance.
3. Refrain from using confidential information for unethical or illegal advantage.

While the confidentiality standard is fairly straightforward, today's technological advances actually may hinder management accountants from following it as diligently as they must. Not only should paper and electronic documents be properly secured, but all conversations, especially those on cell phones, should be conducted only in a private setting and never in public locations, such as airports and cafés.

Integrity

Each member has a responsibility to:

1. Mitigate actual conflicts of interest. Regularly communicate with business associates to avoid apparent conflicts of interest. Advise all parties of any potential conflicts.
2. Refrain from engaging in any conduct that would prejudice carrying out duties ethically.
3. Abstain from engaging in or supporting any activity that might discredit the profession.

Integrity includes the responsibility to communicate both the good and the bad, whether it is news, analysis, judgment, or professional opinion.

Credibility

Each member has a responsibility to:

1. Communicate information fairly and objectively.
2. Disclose all relevant information that could reasonably be expected to influence an intended user's understanding of the reports, analyses, or recommendations.
3. Disclose delays or deficiencies in information, timeliness, processing, or internal controls in conformance with organization policy and/or applicable law.

Credibility ties in closely with the competence standard. In order to be credible, an individual must be competent. Underlying credibility is the management accountant's duty to plan ahead and assess potential risks, gather enough information to be fully informed about all relevant facts, and communicate unfavorable news promptly.

Resolution of Ethical Conflict

Resolving an ethical conflict can be a difficult and often stressful task. Unfortunately, there is no magic formula that will result in the right decision. Each situation is different, and the circumstances are often complex. The *IMA Statement of Ethical Professional Practice* advises:

> In applying the Standards of Ethical Professional Practice, you may encounter problems identifying unethical behavior or in resolving an ethical conflict. When faced with ethical issues, you should follow your organization's established policies on the resolution of such conflict. If these policies do not resolve the ethical conflict, you should consider the following courses of action.
>
> 1. Discuss such problems with the immediate supervisor except when it appears that the supervisor is involved. In that case, present the issue to the next managerial level.

2. If the immediate supervisor is the chief executive officer or equivalent, the acceptable reviewing authority may be a group such as the audit committee, executive committee, board of directors, board of trustees, or owners. Contact with levels above the immediate superior should be initiated only with the superior's knowledge, assuming he or she is not involved. Communication of such problems to authorities or individuals not employed or engaged by the organization is not considered appropriate, unless the member believes there is a clear violation of the law.

3. Clarify relevant ethical issues by initiating a confidential discussion with an IMA Ethics Counselor or other impartial advisor to obtain a better understanding of possible courses of action.

4. Consult your own attorney as to legal obligations and rights concerning the ethical conflict.

Addressing any ethical conflict requires careful consideration and an examination of all the facts before proceeding. This may require:

- Checking data and source material
- Confirming rumors
- Asking more detailed questions
- Probing other people for more information
- Disregarding preconceived ideas

Any of these steps must be done with regard to ethical responsibilities for confidentiality in accordance with the Standards of Ethical Professional Practice.

The next question to consider when faced with an ethical conflict is "What are the alternatives?" Defining the alternatives will provide a framework within which to examine the merits and drawbacks of each option. Attempting to clearly define the choices may reveal a new option.

Consider any rules, laws, or regulations that may apply. What do the rules say? How do they apply to each of the alternatives? Depending on the situation, many different rules and regulations may need to be examined, including the company's code of conduct; local, state and federal laws; generally accepted accounting principles and Financial Accounting Standards Board (FASB) standards, and the IMA's Standards of Ethical Professional Practice.

The company's policies provide a starting point. The IMA Ethics Helpline (1-800-245-1383) is available for members and can offer an outside perspective. It may be necessary to consult with the company's legal or compliance department and, if necessary, a personal attorney, regarding interpretation of laws and regulations as well as the management accountant's legal obligations and rights. When interpreting the rules, it is always best to err on the conservative side.

When someone feels pressured in a particular direction, the human factor of an ethical conflict comes into play. Individuals may feel pressured by professional obligations and personal values, which, in some cases, may conflict. A person's morals, background, experiences, social and economic circumstances, and the ethical culture of the organization all may contribute to an ethical conflict. Professional obligations related to customer expectations, investor goals, departmental quotas, delivery schedules, and many internal and external factors also may compel an individual to choose one option over another. Personal and professional factors differ, so each individual is likely to respond differently to pressure. One strategy is to try to pinpoint the reasons the decision is difficult to make, considering each side.

Finally, the consequences of each alternative need to be considered carefully, including who else will be affected and how they will be affected.

Practice Ethical Scenario

The board of directors of Arivan Corporation recently learned that some members of the senior management team had circumvented the company's internal controls for personal gain. The board appointed a special task force of external auditors and outside legal counsel to investigate the situation.

After extensive review, the task force concluded that for a period of several years, the expenses of the company's chief executive officer, president, and vice president for public relations were charged to an account called the Limited Expenditure Account (LEA). The account was established five years before and was not subject to the company's normal approval and authorization process. Approximately $2,000,000 of requests for reimbursement were routinely processed and charged to LEA. Accounting personnel were advised by the controller to process such requests based on the individual approval of the three executives, even when the requests were not adequately documented.

The vice president for public relations and his department were in charge of political fundraising activities. The task force determined, however, that only a small portion of the $1,000,000 raised in the previous year actually was used for political purposes. In addition, departmental resources were used for personal projects of the three identified executives. The task force also uncovered an additional $4,000,000 of expenditures that were poorly documented so that even the amounts for proper business purposes could not be identified.

The task force noted that these payment practices, as well as LEA, were never disclosed in the internal audit department's audit reports even though company disbursements were tested annually. References to these practices and LEA were included on two occasions in recent years' work papers. The director of internal audit, who reports to the controller, advised that he reviewed these findings with the controller who, in turn, advised that he mentioned these findings to the president. The president recommended that they not be included in the internal audit reports. The task force also noted that the company did not have a formal, published ethics policy.

1. Discuss whether the controller has acted unethically. Reference the relevant standards of ethical practice in your answer.
2. If you were one of the accounting personnel directed to process these transactions, what steps would you take to resolve the ethical conflict?

Think about how you would apply the IMA Statement of Ethical Professional Practice to answer these questions. Write your ideas on a separate sheet of paper, then read the solutions provided to assess your answers.

Solution: Question 1

Referring to the *IMA Statement of Ethical Professional Practice,* the controller has acted unethically. Even though the company does not have an ethics policy, members must act in accordance with the principles of honesty, fairness, objectivity, and responsibility. The controller also should encourage others in the organization to adhere to these same principles. Furthermore, the controller has violated specific standards of ethical conduct by advising accounting personnel to process payments with individual authorizations, even when the transactions were not adequately documented, and by advising the director of the internal audit department to not include any references to these improprieties in the audit reports. The specific standards violated are discussed next.

Competence

Perform professional duties in accordance with relevant laws, regulations, and technical standards.

Integrity

- Mitigate actual conflicts of interest. Regularly communicate with business associates to avoid apparent conflicts of interest. Advise all parties of any potential conflicts.
- Refrain from engaging in any activity that would prejudice their ability to carry out their duties ethically.
- Refrain from engaging in or supporting any activity that would discredit the profession.

Credibility

Communicate information fairly and objectively.

Confidentiality

Not an issue in this situation.

Solution: Question 2

Given that the company does not have a formal ethics policy, Arivan most likely does not have an established policy for resolving ethical conflicts. However, if a policy does exist, a management accountant should follow the company's procedures. In the absence of an established ethics policy, or if the procedures fail to resolve the ethical conflict, the management accountant should consider these actions:

- Because the accountant's superior appears to be the cause of this ethical dilemma, the accountant should present the issue to the next highest-level manager in the organization and then proceed to successively higher levels (e.g., audit committee, board of directors, etc.), until the matter is satisfactorily resolved.
- The accountant should not communicate the situation to individuals or authorities outside of Arivan unless there is a clear violation of the law.
- The accountant should clarify the ethical issues with an impartial advisor to obtain a better understanding of possible courses of action.
- The accountant should consult his or her own attorney about personal legal obligations and rights concerning this situation.

Resolving an ethical conflict can be a challenging and often stressful task. In this scenario, there are many levels of authority to transcend before reaching someone who is not involved.

Knowledge Check: Professional Ethics

The next questions are intended to help you check your understanding and recall of the material presented in this topic. They do not represent the type of questions that appear on the CMA exam.

Directions: Answer each question in the space provided. Correct answers and section references appear after the knowledge check questions.

1. The *IMA Statement of Ethical Professional Practice* includes four overarching ethical principles. Name the four principles.

    a. _____

    b. _____

    c. _____

    d. _____

2. The *IMA Statement of Ethical Professional Practice* includes four standards. Name the four standards.

    a. _____

    b. _____

    c. _____

    d. _____

    Match the following rules to the IMA standards of ethical responsibility. More than one standard may apply.

    a. Competence

    b. Integrity

    c. Confidentiality

    d. Credibility

3. _____ Refuse any gift that might influence your actions in your capacity as an accountant.

4. _____ Prepare complete and clear reports.

5. _____ Disclose fully all relevant information that could influence a user's understanding of a report.

6. _____ Communicate unfavorable as well as favorable information.

7. _____ Perform your duties in accordance with applicable laws, regulations, and standards.

8. If an accountant's immediate supervisor instructs the accountant to withhold essential but unpleasant information in a management report, the accountant should:

    ☐ **a.** do as the supervisor asks and tell no one.

    ☐ **b.** refuse to do as the supervisor asks and alert an investigative reporter to the problem.

    ☐ **c.** take the matter to the supervisor's immediate supervisor.

    ☐ **d.** take the matter directly to the corporate ombudsman.

Knowledge Check Answers: Professional Ethics

1. The *IMA Statement of Ethical Professional Practice* includes four overarching ethical principles. Name the four principles. *[See IMA Statement of Ethical Professional Practice Principles.]*

   a. **Honesty**

   b. **Fairness**

   c. **Objectivity**

   d. **Responsibility**

2. The *IMA Statement of Ethical Professional Practice* includes four standards. Name the four standards. *[See IMA Statement of Ethical Professional Practice - Standards.]*

   a. **Competence**

   b. **Confidentiality**

   c. **Integrity**

   d. **Credibility**

   Match the following rules to the IMA standards of ethical responsibility. More than one standard may apply.

   a. Competence

   b. Integrity

   c. Confidentiality

   d. Credibility

3. <u>**b**</u> Refuse any gift that might influence your actions in your capacity as an accountant.

4. <u>**a and d**</u> Prepare complete and clear reports.

5. <u>**d**</u> Disclose fully all relevant information that could influence a user's understanding of a report.

6. <u>**b and d**</u> Communicate unfavorable as well as favorable information.

7. <u>**a**</u> Perform your duties in accordance with applicable laws, regulations, and standards.

8. If an accountant's immediate supervisor instructs the accountant to withhold essential but unpleasant information in a management report, the accountant should: *[See Resolution of Ethical Conflict.]*

   ☐ a. do as the supervisor asks and tell no one.

   ☐ b. refuse to do as the supervisor asks and alert an investigative reporter to the problem.

   ☑ c. take the matter to the supervisor's immediate supervisor.

   ☐ d. take the matter directly to the corporate ombudsman.

? Practice Questions: Professional Ethics

Directions: This sampling of questions is designed to emulate actual exam questions. Read each question and write your response on another sheet of paper. See the "Answers to Section Practice Questions" section at the end of this book to assess your response. Validate or improve the answer you wrote. For a more robust selection of practice questions, access the **Online Test Bank** found on the IMA's Learning Center Web site.

Question 1E1-AT01

Topic: Ethical Considerations for Management Accounting and Financial Management

As management accountants progress in the profession, they often have the responsibility to supervise the work of less experienced workers. Which of the following is an ethical responsibility of the supervisor?

- ☐ **a.** Hire new workers who will fit in socially with existing staff.
- ☐ **b.** Maximize the profit or minimize the cost of the department.
- ☐ **c.** Ensure that workers handle confidential information appropriately.
- ☐ **d.** Encourage the workers to develop relations with customers.

Question 1E1-AT02

Topic: Ethical Considerations for Management Accounting and Financial Management

Sam Smith has been offered a pair of tickets to the pro football team if Smith purchases a computerized inventory control system from a specific vendor. Which of the following steps should Smith take?

- ☐ **a.** Refuse any further conversations with the vendor.
- ☐ **b.** Review his company's policies on gifts from vendors.
- ☐ **c.** Sign the contract for the system if the price of the ticket is less than $50.
- ☐ **d.** Consult with the Audit Committee of the board of directors.

Question 1E1-AT03

Topic: Ethical Considerations for Management Accounting and Financial Management

John Moore was recently hired as assistant controller of a manufacturing company. The company controller, Nancy Kay, has forecasted a 16% increase in annual earnings. However, during the last quarter of the year, John estimates that the company will report only a 12% increase in earnings. When he reports this to Nancy, she tells him that meeting the numbers won't be a problem. She explains that there are several jobs in production that will finish after the end of the fiscal year, and she will record the associated revenue in the accounting system for the current year.

What is the first step that John Moore should take at this time?

a. Notify the audit committee of the issue.

b. Contact his lawyer to determine his rights.

c. Discuss the issue with the chief financial officer of another company, who does not know any employees at John's company.

d. Follow his organization's established policies regarding the resolution of this type of conflict.

 To further assess your understanding of the concepts covered in Part 1, Section E: Professional Ethics, practice with the **Online Test Bank** for this section. REMINDER: See the "Answers to Section Practice Questions" section at the end of this book.

Essay Exam Support Materials

Writing an effective essay exam is a special challenge. It tests your written communication skills in addition to your knowledge of the content. Essay questions also test your understanding of how specific pieces of information relate to one another, and your ability to apply your knowledge to real-life situations. The next information is included to help you learn more about how to respond to the exam part content in written essay form.

Preparing for the Essay Portion of the Exam

The essay portion of the CMA exam can draw from any of the LOS and content from Part 1: Financial Planning, Performance and Control. It requires understanding the content and being prepared to evaluate the issues presented as well as making recommendations for the resolution of specific situations.

Your study plan should help you learn the content, learn how to respond to the content in multiple-choice questions, and learn to respond to essay questions presented on the content. This is a significant part of the challenge of the CMA exams. One way to meet this challenge is to break it down into smaller challenges—learn the content first, then practice multiple-choice exam-type questions, then learn how to respond to essay questions.

How to Write Essay Answers

The CMA exam essay questions require you to discuss the main points of a specific topic and then examine their implications. When developing your responses, you must support your answers with evidence of your thinking in order to demonstrate your knowledge and comprehension of a topic and your ability to apply that knowledge via thoughtful analysis.

You will be expected to present written answers that:

- Directly respond to the questions asked.
- Are presented in a logical manner.
- Demonstrate an appropriate understanding of the subject matter.

Clues within the questions can be used to help you formulate and organize your responses. Verbs such as *analyze*, *apply*, *explore*, *interpret*, and *examine* can help delineate the requirements of the question. Using the same verbs within your answer will help ensure that you are responding directly and completely to the specific questions being asked.

Candidates are expected to have a working knowledge of using word processing and electronic spreadsheets. They are also expected to have an understanding of basic financial statements, time value of money concepts, and elementary statistics. The essay portion of the exam is computer driven. Answers are entered using a text editor similar to Microsoft Notepad. Some questions may require a spreadsheet similar to, but not exactly the same as, Microsoft Excel. Become familiar with the essay exam format by trying the online demo as part of your studies. You can find the demo at: www. prometric. com/ICMA/Demo. htm.

Writing Skills

The essay section of the CMA exam is a way to assess your ability to analyze, evaluate, and effectively communicate about business situations. Written communication is an important skill required in today's business environment.

The Institute of Certified Management Accountants (ICMA) assesses your writing skills in the essay portion of the CMA exam. The assessment is based on these criteria:

- Use of standard English
- Organization
- Clarity

Use of Standard English

The use of standard English is an integral part of expressing ideas in a business environment. Assessment of the use of clear and concise terminology as is standard to the English language will be administered on the essay portion of the exam.

Organization

When answering essay questions, organizing your answers in a logical manner is important to effective business writing skills. As you read through the question, order your thoughts in a manner that exercises your process of thinking. Make sure that your answer has a clear beginning, outlining what you will be answering, followed by the answer, backed up by CMA content-specific facts, and a summary of what you just described.

Clarity

Being clear in your response is as important as the use of standard English and organization of your response on the CMA exam. Assessors of the essay portion of the CMA exam will look at the answer and critique based on whether the answer is clearly expressed and that the answer is supported by CMA content-specific rationale. When answering, make sure that you read your answer thoroughly to make sure that your response is clear and that the reader will understand how you are attempting to answer the questions.

Using Standard English, Organization, and Clarity in Your Responses to the Essays

When reading through the essay examples, work through the problems as if you were actually answering the questions on the actual CMA exam. When working through the essays, pay close attention to the key words in the question, organize your response, and start writing the answer to the question. When answering, make sure that you are answering the question in a clear and concise manner and make sure that you use standard English. Once complete, compare your answer to the answer provided in the textbook. Pay close attention to the way the answer is organized, the key words that are used, and way the answer is presented. Compare the textbook answer to your answer to see how you did.

Essay Exam Study Tips

ON THE ACTUAL FOUR-HOUR CMA exam, the essay portion of the exam will begin once you complete the multiple-choice section or after three hours, whichever comes first. This means you will have at least one hour to complete the two essay questions presented.

To make the best use of your time to complete the essay portion:

- Prior to taking the exam, take the online tutorial to become familiar with the testing screens. The tutorial is not part of your testing time and may be repeated. However, total tutorial time is limited to 20 minutes.
- Briefly skim through both essay questions and get an idea what each question is asking you to do (i.e., describe, analyze, calculate, etc.)
- You have one hour to complete the full essay exam (more if you have finished the multiple-choice section earlier than the three-hour limit). Determine how much time you will dedicate to each essay question.
- Start with the question you know best. Begin by writing key words, thoughts, facts, figures, and anything else that can be used to answer the question.
- As you answer one question, issues related to the other may occur to you. Write that information next to the appropriate question. This will build your confidence and give you a starting place when you begin to the second question.

To answer each question:

- Read the entire question for requirements.
- Be aware of the verb clues that delineate what is being asked. This will help you formulate and organize your answer. Note that you may have more than one task—for example, define abc and interpret its applicability to xyz.
- Write the basic requirements in the answer space so that you are sure to address them.
- Begin your answer with one or two sentences that directly answer the question. If possible, rephrase the question's essential terms in a statement that directly answers the question.

- Use bullet points to show main ideas, and support each point with sufficient detail to show that you understand all the issues relevant to the question.
- Make it as easy as possible for graders to give you points. The goal in grading is to award you points, so show your thinking clearly and effectively. Do not write too little or too much.
- Finish your essay with one or two sentences that summarize your main point(s).
- Proofread your answer for logic, thoroughness, and clarity.
- Keep track of time. Do not spend too much time on one question.
- If you do not have enough time to write a full essay, write an outline of your main points to show what you know in order to get partial credit.

Examples of Essay Question Answers

Each essay question actually consists of several related questions based on one scenario. The question as a whole is worth a set number of points and is graded against a scorecard to ensure consistent grading. The scorecard lists appropriate terms, topics, and ideas that address the answer. Presented here are two essay questions drawn from previous exams. The first essay question is followed by an example of an answer that would be awarded maximum points—a "best" answer. How these points are awarded is shown on a scorecard similar to ones used by the Institute of Certified Management Accountants (ICMA).

Following the second essay question are two answers that were awarded fewer points because they do not address all the issues. The "good" answer meets some but not all of the criteria. The "better" answer covers more of the requested information, as shown on the scorecard, and receives more points.

As you will see, the goal of the graders is to give test takers points rather than taking them away. If test takers earn more credits than the maximum allowable points, they can be awarded only the maximum allowable number of points.

There are two types of essay questions: questions that ask for a **written response** and questions that ask for a **series of calculations, tables, or charts for a response**. For essay questions that require a purely written answer (i.e., no calculations), you will have a box in which to type your response. For problems that require quantitative responses, a spreadsheet may be be available in which to present your calculations.

Note: The questions, answers, and scorecards used in these examples were provided by the ICMA and are used with their permission.

Example Question 1: Amur Company

Amur Company manufactures three lawn care component parts: fuel systems, transmission assemblies, and electrical systems. For the past five years, manufacturing overhead has been applied to products on standard direct labor hours for the units actually produced. The standard cost information is shown next.

Exhibit A shows standard cost information.

Exhibit A Standard Cost Information

	Fuel Systems	Transmission Assemblies	Electrical Systems
Units produced and sold	10,000	20,000	30,000
Standard labor hours	2.0	1.5	1.0
Standard direct material cost per unit	$25.00	$36.00	$30.00
Budgeted and actual manufacturing overhead		$3,920,000	

The current direct labor rate is $10 per hour. New machinery that highly automates the production process was installed two years ago and greatly reduced the direct labor time to produce the three products. The selling price for each of the three products is 125% of the manufacturing cost.

Amur's segment of the lawn care component industry has become very competitive, and the company's profits have been decreasing. Eric West, Amur's controller, has been asked by the president of the company to analyze the overhead allocations and pricing structure. West thinks that future allocations should be based on machine hours and direct labor hours rather than the current allocation method, which is based on direct labor hours only. West has determined the additional product information shown in Exhibit B.

Exhibit B Additional Product Information

	Fuel Systems	Transmission Assemblies	Electrical Systems
Standard machine hours	2.0	4.0	6.0
Manufacturing overhead:			
Direct labor cost		$ 560,000	
Machine cost		$3,360,000	

Questions

1. By allocating all of the budgeted overhead based on direct labor hours, calculate the unit manufacturing cost and unit sales price for each of the three products manufactured at Amur Company.
2. Prepare an analysis for Amur Company using the appropriate cost driver(s) determined by Eric West for manufacturing overhead. Calculate the unit manufacturing cost and unit sales price for each of the three products.
3. Based on your calculations in Questions 1 and 2, prepare a recommendation for the president at Amur Company to increase the firm's profitability.

Sample "Best" Answer for Amur Business Scenario

Question 1

The allocation of all of Amur Company's budgeted manufacturing overhead based on direct labor hours results in the unit manufacturing costs and unit sales prices for its three products is calculated as follows:

Fuel systems

Units: 10,000
Standard labor hour/unit: 2.0
Total standard labor hours: 20,000

Direct material: $25.00
Direct labor at $10/hour: $20.00
Overhead at $49/DLH[1]: $98.00
Total cost: $143.00
Sales price (125% of cost): $178.75

Transmission Assemblies

Units: 20,000
Standard labor hour/unit: 1.5
Total standard labor hours: 30,000

Machine hours per unit: 4.0
Total machine hours: 80,000

Direct material: $36.00
Direct labor at $10/hour: $15.00
Overhead at $49/DLH[1]: $73.50
Total cost: $124.50
Sales price (125% of cost): $155.63

Electrical Systems

Units: 30,000
Standard labor hour/unit: 1.0
Total standard labor hours: 30,000

Direct material: $30.00
Direct labor at $10/hour: $10.00
Overhead at $49/DLH[1]: $49.00
Total cost: $89.00
Sales price (125% of cost): $111.25

Note:

[1] Total manufacturing overhead of $3,920,000 / 80,000 total direct labor hours = $49.00 per direct labor hour.

Question 2

When the cost drivers identified by Eric West are used to allocate manufacturing overhead, the unit manufacturing costs and unit sales prices for the three products manufactured at Amur Company are calculated as follows:

Fuel systems

Units: 10,000
Standard labor hour/unit: 2.0
Total standard labor hours: 20,000

Machine hours per unit: 2.0
Total machine hours: 20,000

Direct material: $25.00
Direct labor at $10/hour: $20.00
Overhead (DLH at $7/hr[1]): $14.00
Overhead (Machine hrs at $12/hr[2]): $24.00
Total cost: $83.00
Sales price (125% of cost): $103.75

Transmission Assemblies

Units: 20,000
Standard labor hour/unit: 1.5
Total standard labor hours: 30,000

Machine hours per unit: 4.0
Total machine hours: 80,000

Direct material: $36.00
Direct labor at $10/hour: $15.00
Overhead (DLH at $7/hr[1]): $10.50
Overhead (Machine hrs at $12/hr[2]): $48.00
Total cost: $109.50
Sales price (125% of cost): $136.88

Electrical Systems

Units: 30,000
Standard labor hour/unit: 1.0
Total standard labor hours: 30,000

Machine hours per unit: 6.0
Total machine hours: 180,000

Direct material: $30.00
Direct labor at $10/hour: $10.00
Overhead (DLH at $7/hr[1]): $7.00
Overhead (Machine hrs at $12/hr[2]): $72.00

Total cost: $119.00

Sales price (125% of cost): $148.75

Notes:

[1] Direct labor overhead of $560,000 / 80,000 total direct labor hours = $7.00 per direct labor hour.

[2] Machine overhead of $3,360,000 / 280,000 total machine hours = $12.00 per machine hour.

Question 3

The summary of the revised margins for each of Amur Company's three products, assuming the sales prices developed in Question 1 (allocation of all manufacturing overhead based on direct labor hours) is compared to revised costs developed in question 2 (allocation of manufacturing overhead based on cost drivers), is as follows:

Fuel Systems

Current price: $178.75

Revised cost: $83.00

Gross profit (loss): $95.75

Margin: 54%

Transmission Assemblies

Current price: $155.63

Revised cost: $109.50

Gross profit (loss): $46.13

Margin: 30%

Electrical Systems

Current price: $111.25

Revised cost: $119.00

Gross profit (loss): ($7.75)

Margin: NA

Based on this analysis, fuel systems and transmission assemblies are producing a higher return than Amur Company previously thought. Fuel systems are the most profitable (54% gross margin) followed by transmission assemblies; however, electrical systems are losing money on a full-cost basis.

Recommendations for improving profitability include:

- Focus on fuel systems, through actions such as increasing marketing expenditures and reducing the price to increase sales.
- Improve profitability of electrical systems through changes to the manufacturing process to reduce the machine hours required.
- Decrease marketing of this electrical system, and increase the selling price if possible.

Scoring of "Best" Answer for Amur Business Scenario

The Amur question would be graded against a scorecard similar to the one shown next. Note that:

- The scorecard addresses more issues than is required by the question. This is done to accommodate variations between test takers and to provide the greatest opportunity for a maximum score. The goal of the graders is to give test takers points rather than taking them away. If test takers earn more credits than the maximum allowable points, they will be awarded only the maximum allowable points.
- At times, the process is more important than the numeric answers. Test takers should show all work/calculations to earn the maximum allowable points.
- Explanations add points.
- Formatting is not an issue. You will be using simple text editing, such as Microsoft Notepad, so you may not be able to make charts and should use dashes for bullets.

Amur Scorecard

Amur—Total allowable points 17

Question 1: Maximum allowable points = 5

Issues to address

Unit manufacturing cost and price (DLH allocation) =

Total labor hrs = Standard Hr/Unit $\times$ Units for each product

Totals all product labor hrs/ (80,000)

Overhead of \$3,920,000/ 80,000 DLH = Overhead rate

Includes unit direct materials cost in product cost

Direct labor = \$10 $\times$ Standard DLH per unit

OH/Unit for each product = OH rate $\times$ standard DLH/Unit

DM + DL + OH = Product cost/ (\$143(\$89)) / (\$124.5)

Sales price = 125% $\times$ Product cost

Question 2: Maximum allowable points = 5

Unit manufacturing cost and price (Cost driver allocation) =

Total machine hours = (Standard hour / Unit) $\times$ Units for each product

Totals all product machine hours / (280.000)

Machine OH = \$3,360,000 / 280,000

DL OH = \$560,000 / 80,000 hours / (\$7 per DHL)

OH / unit for each product = OH rate $\times$ standard MH / unit

OH / unit for each product = OH rate $\times$ standard DLH / unit

Includes DM and DLH for each product

Totals all costs / (\$83) / (\$109.50) / (\$119)

Sales price = 125% $\times$ Product cost

Question 3: Maximum allowable points = 7

Issues to address

Recommendation

Increase emphasis on fuel systems

   Margin/Profit highest

Increase emphasis on Transmission

   Margin/Profit is high

Increase marketing to generate sales

Decrease price to stimulate sales

Other recommendations to leverage profitability

Decrease emphasis on electrical systems

   Margin is lower/losing money

Improve manufacturing process

Raise price if market will bear it

Other recommendations to deal with electrical systems

Example Question 2: Zylon Corporation

Business Scenario

Jeff Frankie is the chief financial officer of Zylon Corporation, a manufacturer and distributor of electronic security devices primarily suited for residential applications. Frankie is currently in the process of preparing the Y2 annual budget and implementing an incentive plan to reward the performance of key personnel. The final operating plans will then be presented to the board of directors for approval.

Frankie is aware that next year may be very difficult due to announced price increases to major customers. Zylon's president has put pressure on management to achieve the current year's earnings per share amounts. Frankie is, therefore, considering introducing zero-based budgeting in order to bring costs into line with revenue expectations.

Duke Edwards, Zylon's manufacturing director, is attempting to convince Frankie to build budgetary slack into the operating budget. Edwards contends that productivity is burdened by an abnormal amount of product design changes and small lot size production orders that incur costly setup times.

Questions

1. Explain at least three advantages and at least three disadvantages of budgetary slack from the point of view of Zylon Corporation's management group as a whole.

2. Describe how zero-based budgeting could be advantageous to Zylon Corporation's overall budget process.

Sample "Better" Answer for Zylon Business Scenario

Question 1

At least three advantages and three disadvantages of budgetary slack from the point of view of Zylon Corporation's management group as a whole include the following:

Advantages

1. It provides flexibility for operating under unknown circumstances, such as an extra margin for discretionary expenses in case budget assumptions on inflation are incorrect, or adverse circumstances arise.
2. Additional slack may be included to offset the costly setups from design changes and/or small lot size orders.
3. The increased pressure to meet Y1 earnings per share targets may result in postponing expenditures into Y2 or aggressively pulling sales into Y1. Budgetary slack in Y2 may compensate for shifting those earnings from Y2 into Y1.

Disadvantages

1. It decreases the ability to highlight weaknesses and take timely corrective actions on problem areas.
2. It decreases the overall effectiveness of corporate planning. Actions such as pricing changes or reduced promotional spending may be taken from a perceived need to improve earnings, when eliminating the budgetary slack could accomplish the same objective without marketplace changes.
3. It limits the objective evaluation of departmental managers and performance of subordinates by using budgetary information.

Question 2

Zero-based budgeting (ZBB) could be advantageous to Zylon Corporation's overall budget process for the following reasons:

- The ZBB process evaluates all proposed operating and administrative expenses as if they were being initiated for the first time. Each expenditure is justified, ranked, and prioritized according to its order of importance to the overall corporation, not just its role in one department.
- The focus is on evaluation of all activities rather than just incremental changes from the prior year. This allows addressing activities that have been ongoing to determine if they are still useful in the current environment. The objectives, operations, and costs of all activities are evaluated, and alternative means of accomplishing the objectives are more likely to be identified.

Scoring of "Better" Answer for Zylon Business Scenario

The Zylon question would be graded against a scorecard similar to the one shown following. Note that:

- The scorecard addresses more issues than is required by the question. This is done to accommodate variations between test takers and to provide the greatest opportunity for a maximum score. The goal of the graders is to give test takers points rather than taking them away. If test takers earn more credits than the maximum allowable points, they can be awarded only the maximum allowable points.

- At times, the process is more important than the numeric answers. Test takers should show all work/calculations to earn the maximum allowable points.
- Explanations add points.
- Formatting is not judged. You will be using simple text editing such as Microsoft Notepad, so you may not be able to make charts and should use dashes for bullets.

Zylon Scorecard

Zylon Total allowable points 12

Question 1: Maximum allowable points = 6
Issues to address
Advantages
Provides flexibility under uncertainty
Extra margin for discretionary expenses
If assumptions wrong or adverse circumstances
Offsets unexpected setup costs
  Design changes
  Small lot sizes
Can compensate for earnings timing shifts
  Pressure to meet EPS
  Postponing expenses or accelerating sales
Other
  Explanation
Disadvantages
Decreases ability to ID weakness and take action
  Expenses are overstated in budget
Decreases effectiveness of overall planning process
Unnecessary actions taken such as
  Price changes or promotional spending cuts
  When eliminating slack would have solved problem
Limits objective evaluation of employees
  Measured against inflated budget
Other
Explanation

Question 2: Maximum allowable points = 6
Issues to address
Advantages
Each expense is justified and ranked
  Each exp is evaluated as it were first time
Unnecessary activities can be eliminated
  All activities are evaluated
  Ongoing activities must be justified

(Continued)

(Continued)

Slack can be reduced

    Expenses must be grounded in realistic assumptions

Alternative means can be identified

    Are forced to evaluate processes

Other

    With explanation

Sample "Good" Answer for Zylon Business Scenario

A good answer would address enough of the identified three issues on the Zylon scorecard to earn a sore of 70% or 80% of the maximum allowable points. A good answer for the Zylon scenario is shown next. It addresses the issues but does not go beyond the question to provide explanations and clarification.

Question 1

At least three advantages and three disadvantages of budgetary slack from the point of view of Zylon Corporation's management group as a whole include the following:

Advantages

- It provides operating flexibility.
- Additional slack may be included to offset costs.
- Zylon will need to postpone expenditures.

Disadvantages

- It decreases the ability to highlight weaknesses and take timely corrective actions on problem areas.
- It decreases the overall effectiveness of corporate planning.
- It limits the objective evaluation of departmental managers and performance of subordinates.

Question 2

Zero-based budgeting (ZBB) could be advantageous to Zylon Corporation's overall budget process for these reasons:

- The ZBB process evaluates all proposed operating and administrative expenses as if they were being initiated for the first time.
- The focus is on evaluation of all activities.

Practice Essay Questions and Answers

The next essay questions, and the answers that appear at the end, were adapted from the *Revised CMA Exam, Questions and Answers: Part 4* (2005 and 2008) books supplied by the Institute of Certified Management Accountants and are used with their permission.

The focus of the questions will be on the test taker's ability to apply concepts presented in the part being tested to a business scenario.

The answers supplied are meant to serve as samples of answers that address 80% or more of the points listed on the question grading guide. There are generally more points on the grading guide than points that can be awarded (i.e., there may be 110 possible points but only 100 that can be awarded in total), so answers scoring 80% may vary among test takers. Thus, the answers presented here represent one possible answer, not a definitive correct answer.

Part 1 Section A Questions

Question 1A-ES01

Rein Company, a compressor manufacturer, is developing a budgeted income statement for the calendar year 2006. The president is generally satisfied with the projected net income for 2005 of $700,000 resulting in an earnings per share figure of $2.80. However, next year he would like earnings per share to increase to at least $3. Rein Company employs a standard absorption cost system. Inflation necessitates an annual revision in the standards as evidenced by an increase in production costs expected in 2006. The total standard manufacturing cost for 2005 is $72 per unit produced.

Rein expects to sell 100,000 compressors at $110 each in the current year (2005). Forecasts from the sales department are favorable, and Rein Company is projecting an annual increase of 10% in unit sales in 2006 and 2007. This increase in sales will occur even though a $15 increase in unit selling price will be implemented in 2006. The selling price increase was absolutely essential to compensate for the increased production costs and operating expenses. However, management is concerned that any additional sales price increase would curtail the desired growth in volume.

Standard production costs are developed for the two primary metals used in the compressor (brass and a steel alloy), the direct labor, and manufacturing overhead.

The following schedule represents the 2006 standard quantities and rates for material and labor to produce one compressor.

Brass	4 pounds	@	$5.35/pound	$21.40
Steel alloy	5 pounds	@	$3.16/pound	15.80
Direct labor	4 hours	@	$7.00/hour	28.00
			Total prime costs	$65.20

The material content of the compressor has been reduced slightly, hopefully without a noticeable decrease in the quality of the finished product. Improved labor productivity and some increase in automation have resulted in a decrease in labor hours per unit from 4.4 to 4.0. However, the significant increases in material prices and hourly labor rates more than offset any savings from reduced input quantities. The manufacturing overhead cost per unit schedule has yet to be completed. Preliminary data is as follows:

	Activity Level (units)		
	100,000	110,000	120,000
Overhead items			
Supplies	$475,000	$522,000	$570,000
Indirect labor	530,000	583,000	636,000
Utilities	170,000	187,000	204,000
Maintenance	363,000	378,000	392,000
Taxes and insurance	87,000	87,000	87,000
Depreciation	421,000	421,000	421,000
Total overhead	$2,046,000	$2,178,000	$2,310,000

The standard overhead rate is based on direct labor hours and is developed by using the total overhead costs from the above schedule for the activity level closest to planned production. In developing the standards for the manufacturing costs, the following two assumptions were made.

- The cost of brass is currently selling at $5.65/pound. However, this price is historically high, and the purchasing manager expects the price to drop to the predetermined standard early in 2006.
- Several new employees will be hired for the production line in 2006. The employees will be generally unskilled. If basic training programs are not effective and improved labor productivity is not experienced, then the production time per unit of product will increase by 15 minutes over the 2006 standards.

Rein employs a LIFO inventory system for its finished goods. Rein's inventory policy for finished goods is to have 15% of the expected annual unit sales for the coming year in finished goods inventory at the end of the prior year. The finished goods inventory at December 31, 2005, is expected to consist of 16,500 units at a total carrying cost of $1,006,500.

Operating expenses are classified as selling, which are variable, and administrative, which are all fixed. The budgeted selling expenses are expected to average 12% of sales revenue in 2006, which is consistent with the performance in 2005. The administrative expenses in 2006 are expected to be 20% higher than the predicted 2005 amount of $907,850.

Management accepts the cost standards developed by the production and accounting department. However, it is concerned about the possible effect on net income if the price of brass does not decrease, and/or the labor efficiency does not improve as expected. Therefore, management wants the budgeted income statement to be prepared using the standards as developed but to consider the worst possible situation for 2006. Each resulting manufacturing variance should be separately identified and added to or subtracted from budgeted cost of goods sold at standard. Rein is subject to a 45% income tax rate.

Questions

A. Prepare the budgeted income statement for 2006 for Rein Company as specified by management. Round all calculations to the nearest dollar.
B. Review the 2006 budgeted income statement prepared for Rein Company and discuss whether the president's objectives can be achieved.

Question 1A-ES02

Gleason Company, a manufacturer of children's toys and furniture, is beginning budget preparation for next year. Jack Tiger, a recent addition to the accounting staff at Gleason, is questioning Leslie Robbins and James Crowe, sales and production managers, to learn about Gleason's budget process.

Crowe says that he incorporates Robbins's sales projections when estimating closing inventories but that the resulting numbers aren't completely reliable because Robbins makes some "adjustments" to her projections. Robbins admits that she does indeed lower initial sales projections by 5% to 10% to give her department some breathing room. Crowe admits that his department makes adjustments not unlike Robbins's; specifically, production adds about 10% to its estimates. "I think everyone here does something similar," he says, and Robbins nods assent.

Questions

A. What benefits do Robbins and Crowe expect to realize from their budgetary practices?
B. What are possible adverse effects of introducing budgetary slack for Robbins and Crowe?

Question 1A-ES03

Eugene Logan is the chief financial officer of Artech Corporation, a manufacturer and distributor of electronic security devices primarily suited for residential applications. Logan is currently in the process of preparing next year's annual budget and implementing an incentive plan to reward the performance of key personnel. The final operating plans will then be presented to the board of directors for approval.

Logan is aware that next year may be difficult due to announced price increases to major customers. Artech's president has put pressure on management to achieve the current year's earnings per share amounts. Logan is, therefore, considering introducing zero-based budgeting in order to bring costs into line with revenue expectations.

Leonard Drake, Artech's manufacturing director, is attempting to convince Logan to build budgetary slack into the operating budget. Drake contends that productivity is burdened by an abnormal amount of product design changes and small lot size production orders that incur costly setup times.

Questions

A. Explain at least three advantages and at least three disadvantages of budgetary slack from the point of view of Artech Corporation's management group as a whole.

B. Describe how zero-based budgeting could be advantageous to Artech Corporation's overall budget process.

Question 1A-ES04

Matchpoint Racquet Club (MRC) is a sports facility that offers tennis, racquetball, and other physical fitness facilities to its members. MRC owns and operates a large club with 2,000 members in a metropolitan area. The club has experienced cash flow problems over the last five years, especially during the summer months when both court use and new membership sales are low. Temporary bank loans have been obtained to cover the summer shortages.

The owners have decided to take action to improve MRC's net cash flow position. They have asked the club's financial manager to prepare a projected cash budget based on a proposed revised fee structure. The proposal would increase membership fees and replace the hourly tennis and racquetball court fees with a quarterly charge that would allow unlimited usage of the courts. The new rates would remain competitive when compared to the rates of other clubs in the area. Although there will be some members who do not renew because of the increase in price, management believes that the offer of unlimited court time will increase membership by 10%.

The proposed fee structure is shown next, along with the current membership distribution. The membership distribution is assumed to remain unchanged. All members would be required to pay the quarterly court charges.

Proposed Fee Structure

Membership Category	Annual Membership Fees	Quarterly Court Charges
Individual	$300	$50
Student	$180	$40
Family	$600	$90

Membership Distribution	
Individual	60%
Student	10%
Family	30%

Projected Membership Payment Activity

			Court Time in Hours	
Quarter	New	Renewed	Prime	Regular
1	100	700	5,000	7,000
2	70	330	2,000	4,000
3	50	150	1,000	2,000
4	200	600	5,000	7,000

The average membership during the third quarter is projected to be 2,200 people. Fixed costs are $157,500 per quarter, including a quarterly depreciation charge of $24,500. Variable costs are estimated at $15 per hour of total court usage time.

Questions

A. Prepare MRC's cash budget for the third quarter. Assume the opening cash balance is $186,000, that membership at the beginning of the quarter is 2,000, and that the change to the new pricing structure will be implemented. Include supporting calculations where appropriate.

B. How would sensitivity analysis help MRC management in the decision-making process?

C. Identify at least four factors that MRC should consider before implementing this decision.

Part 1 Section B Questions

Question 1B-ES01

Handler Company distributes two power tools to hardware stores—a heavy duty ½-inch hand drill and a table saw. The tools are purchased from a manufacturer where the Handler private label is attached. The wholesale selling prices to the hardware stores are $60 each for the drill and $120 each for the table saw. The 2005 budget and actual results are presented next. The budget was adopted in late 2004 and was based on Handler's estimated share of the market for the two tools.

**Handler Company Income Statement for the Year Ended December 31, 2005
(000s omitted)**

	Hand Drill		Table Saw		Total		
	Budget	Actual	Budget	Actual	Budget	Actual	Variance
Sales in units	120	86	80	74	200	160	40
Revenue	$7,200	$5,074	$9,600	$8,510	$16,800	$13,584	$(3,216)
Cost of goods sold	6,000	4,300	6,400	6,068	12,400	10,368	2,032
Gross margin	$1,200	$774	$3,200	$2,442	4,400	3,216	(1,184)
Unallocated costs							
Selling					1,000	1,000	—
Advertising					1,000	1,060	(60)
Administration					400	406	(6)
Income taxes (45%)					900	338	562
Total unallocated costs					3,300	2,804	496
Net income					$1,100	$412	$(688)

During the first quarter of 2005, Handler's management estimated that the total market for these tools actually would be 10% below its original estimates. In an attempt to prevent Handler's unit sales from declining as much as industry projections, management developed and implemented a marketing program. Included in the program were dealer discounts and increased direct advertising. The table saw line was emphasized in this program.

Questions

A. Analyze the unfavorable gross margin variance of $1,184,000 in terms of:
   1. Sales price variance
   2. Cost variance
   3. Volume variance
B. Discuss the apparent effect of Handler Company's special marketing program (i.e., dealer discounts and additional advertising) on 2005 operating results. Support your comments with numerical data where appropriate.

Question 1B-ES02

The Jackson Corporation is a large manufacturing company where each division is viewed as an investment center and has virtually complete autonomy for product development, marketing, and production. Performance of division managers is evaluated periodically by senior corporate management. Divisional return on investment is the sole criterion used in performance evaluation under current corporate policy. Corporate management believes return on investment is an adequate measure because it incorporates quantitative information from the divisional income statement and balance sheet in the analysis.

Some division managers complained that a single criterion for performance evaluation is insufficient and ineffective. These managers have compiled a list of criteria that they believe should be used in evaluating division managers' performance. The criteria include profitability, market position, productivity, product leadership, employee development, employee attitudes, public responsibility, and balance between short-range and long-range goals.

Questions

A. Jackson management believes that return on investment is an adequate criterion to evaluate division management performance. Discuss the shortcomings or possible inconsistencies of using return on investment as the sole criterion to evaluate divisional management performance.

B. Discuss the advantages of using multiple criteria versus a single criterion to evaluate divisional management performance.

C. Describe the problems or disadvantages which can be associated with the implementation of the multiple performance criteria measurement system suggested to Jackson Corporation by its division managers.

Question 1B-ES03

George Nickles has recently been appointed vice president of operations for Merriam Corporation. The company's business segments include manufacture of heavy equipment, food processing, and financial services. Nickles has suggested to Merriam's chief financial officer, Karen Schilling, that segment managers should be evaluated on segment data contained in the company's annual report, which presents revenues, earnings, identifiable assets, and depreciation for each segment for a five-year period. Nickles reasons that segment managers may be appropriately evaluated by the same criteria used to evaluate top management. Schilling has doubts about using information from the annual report for that purpose and suggests that Nickles consider other ways of evaluating the segment managers.

Questions

A. What legitimate concerns might Karen Schilling have regarding the evaluation of segment managers using segment information prepared for public reporting?

B. What could the possible behavioral impact be on Merriam Corporation's segment managers if their performance evaluations are based on information published in the annual report?

C. What types of financial information would be more appropriate for George Nickles to use in evaluating the performance of segment managers?

Question 1B-ES04

ARQ Enterprises was formed by the merger of Andersen, Rolvaag, and Quie Corporations. Its three divisions retain the names of the former companies and operate with complete autonomy. Corporate management evaluates the divisions and division management according to return on investment.

The Rolvaag and Quie divisions are currently negotiating a transfer price for a component that Quie manufactures and Rolvaag needs. Quie, which sells the component already into a market that it expects to grow rapidly, currently has excess capacity. Rolvaag could buy the component from other suppliers.

Three transfer prices are under consideration:

1. Rolvaag has bid $3.84 for the component, which is Quie's standard variable manufacturing cost plus a 20% markup.
2. Quie has offered the component to Rolvaag at $5.90, which is its regular selling price in the marketplace ($6.50) minus variable selling and distribution expenses.
3. ARQ management, which has no established policy on transfer pricing, has offered the compromise price of $5.06, which is the standard full manufacturing cost plus 15%.

Both the Quie and Rolvaag divisions have rejected the compromise price. Refer to the pricing chart for a summary of this information.

Pricing Chart	
Regular selling price	$6.50
Standard variable manufacturing cost	$3.20
Standard full manufacturing cost	$4.40
Variable selling and distribution expenses	$0.60
Standard variable manufacturing cost plus 20% ($3.20 × 1.20)	$3.84
Regular selling price less variable selling and distribution expenses ($6.50−$0.6)	$5.90
Standard full manufacturing cost plus 15% ($4.40 × 1.15)	$5.06

Questions

A. What effect might each of the three proposed prices have on the Quie division management's attitude toward intracompany business?
B. Would a negotiation of a price between Quie and Rolvaag be a satisfactory method to establish a transfer price in this situation? Explain your decision.
C. Should ARQ corporate management become involved in resolving this transfer price controversy? Explain your decision.

Question 1B-ES05

Within Sparta Enterprises, the extraction division transfers 100% of its total output of 500,000 units of a particular type of clay to the pet products division, which treats the clay and sells it as cat litter for $42 a unit. The pet products division currently pays a transfer price for the clay of cost plus 10%, or $22 a unit. The clay has many other uses and could be sold in the marketplace for $26 in virtually unlimited quantities. If the extraction division did sell the clay into the wider market, it would incur a variable selling cost of $1.50 per unit.

The extraction division recently hired a new manager, Keith Richardson, who immediately complained to top management about the disparity between the transfer price and the market price. For the most recent year, the pet products division's contribution margin on the sale of 500,000 units of cat litter was $5,775,000. The extraction unit's contribution margin on the transfer of an equal number of units of clay to the pet products division was $1,625,000.

Refer to the Unit Cost Structure chart for more information.

	Unit Cost Structure	
	Extraction Division	**Pet Products Division**
Transfer price for clay	—	$22.00
Material cost	$4.00	2.00
Labor cost	6.00	4.00
Overhead	11.00[*]	7.00[†]
Total cost per unit	$21.00	$35.00

[*]Overhead in the extraction division is 25% fixed and 75% variable.
[†]Overhead in the pet products division is 65% fixed and 35% variable.

Questions

A. Why don't cost-based transfer prices provide an appropriate measure of divisional performance?

B. Using the market price for the clay, what is the contribution margin for the two divisions for the most recent year?

C. What price range for the clay would be acceptable to both divisions if Sparta instituted negotiated transfer pricing and allowed the divisions to buy and sell clay on the open market? Explain your answer.

D. Why should a negotiated transfer price result in desirable behavior from the management of the two divisions?

Question 1B-ES06

4-Cycle, Inc., manufactures small engines for recreational vehicles, motorcycles, boats, and stationary equipment. Each line has its own product manager. The company chief financial officer, Stan Downs, prepares divisional budgets on a per-month basis using a standard cost system. Each product line occupies its own space, with square footage varying considerably among lines. Fixed production costs are allocated on the basis of square feet using a factory-wide rate. Variable factory overhead is based on machine hours. Other costs are based on revenue.

At the company's quarterly meeting, Laura Fleur, the new product manager for marine engines, received an unpleasant surprise. When distributing the performance report (shown next) to each manager, Stan Downs remarked aloud that Fleur would need to see him after the meeting to discuss ways to improve her line's lackluster performance. Since she thought her first quarter's performance was impressive, she was taken aback by Downs's comments. The performance report provided her with no clue to what had gone wrong.

4-Cycle, Inc. Marine Engine Quarterly Performance Report			
	Actual	**Budget**	**Variance**
Units	10,500	8,500	2,000 F
Revenue	$17,500,000	$14,700,000	$2,800,000 F
Variable production costs			
Direct materials	2,500,000	2,164,750	335,250 U
Direct labor	2,193,000	1,790,000	403,000 U
Machine time	2,300,000	1,950,000	350,000 U
Factory overhead	4,500,000	3,825,000	675,500 U
Fixed production costs			
Indirect labor	925,000	580,250	344,750 U
Depreciation	500,000	500,000	—
Taxes	232,500	220,000	12,500 U
Insurance	437,000	437,000	—
Administrative expense	1,226,000	919,500	306,500 U
Marketing expense	848,000	540,000	308,000 U
Research and development	613,000	460,000	153,000 U
Operating profit	$1,225,000	$1,313,500	$88,500 U

Questions

A. What are at least three weaknesses in 4-Cycle's quarterly performance report? Explain your answer.

B. What are some ways in which 4-Cycle can eliminate the weaknesses in the way it reports quarterly performance to its managers? Revise the quarterly report accordingly.

Question 1B-ES07

SieCo is a sheet metal manufacturer whose customers are mainly in the automobile industry. The company's chief engineer, Steve Simpson, has recently presented a proposal for automating the Drilling Department. The proposal recommended that SieCo purchase from Service Corp. two robots that would have the capability of replacing the eight direct labor workers in the department. The cost savings in the proposal included the elimination of the direct labor costs plus the elimination of manufacturing overhead cost in the Drilling Department as SieCo charges manufacturing overhead on the basis of direct labor costs using a plant-wide rate.

SieCo's controller, Keith Hunter, gathered the information shown in Exhibit 1 to discuss the issue of overhead application at the management meeting at which the proposal was approved.

Exhibit 1

Date	Average Annual Direct Labor Cost	Average Annual Manufacturing Overhead Cost	Average Manufacturing Overhead Rate
Current Year	$4,000,000	$20,000,000	500%

Category	Cutting Department	Grinding Department	Drilling Department
Average Annual Direct Labor	$2,000,000	$1,750,000	$250,000
Average Annual Overhead Cost	11,000,000	7,000,000	2,000,000

Simpson met the chief accountant, Leslie Altman, in the lunchroom and inquired about the status of the proposal. Altman told Simpson that the project had been approved. Simpson said, "That's great. Be sure to make the payment as soon as possible as my brother-in-law owns Service Corp."

Altman was puzzled by the fact that there had been no competitive bidding and spoke to his supervisor, Keith Hunter. Hunter told Altman not to worry; Service Corp will do a great job.

Required:

A. Using the information from Exhibit 1, describe the shortcomings of the system for applying overhead that is currently used by SieCo.

B. Recommend two ways to improve SieCo's method for applying overhead in the Cutting and Grinding Departments.

C. Recommend two ways to improve SieCo's method for applying overhead to accommodate the automation of the Drilling Department.

D. Explain the misconceptions underlying the statement that the manufacturing overhead cost in the Drilling Department would be reduced to zero if the automation proposal were implemented.

E. Referring to the specific standards outlined in IMA's Statement of Ethical Professional Practice, identify and discuss the ethical conflicts that Altman needs to resolve.

F. According to IMA's Statement of Ethical Professional Practice, identify the steps that Altman should take to resolve this situation

Question 1B-ES08

For many years, Lawton Industries has manufactured prefabricated houses where the houses are constructed in sections to be assembled on customers' lots. The company expanded into the precut housing market in 2006 when it acquired Presser Company, one of its suppliers. In this market, various types of lumber are precut into the appropriate lengths, banded into packages, and shipped to customers' lots for assembly. Lawton decided to maintain Presser's separate identity and, thus, established the Presser Division as an investment center of Lawton.

Lawton uses return on average investment (ROI) as a performance measure the investment defined as operating assets employed. Management bonuses are based in part on ROI. All investments in operating assets are expected to earn a minimum return of 15% before income taxes. Presser's ROI has ranged from 19.3% to 22.1% since it was acquired in 2006. The division had an investment opportunity in the year just ended that had an estimated ROI of 18%, but Presser's management decided against the investment because it believed the investment would decrease the division's overall ROI.

Presser's operating statement for the year just ended is presented next. The division's operating assets employed were $12,600,000 at the end of the year, a 5% increase over the balance at the end of the previous year.

Presser Division Operating Statement
for the Year Ended December 31
($000 omitted)

Sales revenue		$24,000
Cost of goods sold		15,800
Gross profit		$8,200
Operating expenses		
Administrative	$2,140	
Selling	3,600	5,740
Income from operations		
before income taxes		$2,460

Required

A. Calculate these performance measures for the year just ended for the Presser Division of Lawton Industries:
   1. Return on average investment in operating assets employed (ROI).
   2. Residual income calculated on the basis of average operating assets employed.

B. Would the management of Presser Division have been more likely to accept the investment opportunity it had during the year if residual income were used as a performance measure instead of ROI? Explain you answer.

C. The Presser Division is a separate investment center with Lawton Industries. Identify and describe the items Presser must control if it is to be evaluated fairly by either the ROI or residual income performance measures.

Part 1 Section C Questions

Question 1C-ES01

Many companies recognize that their cost systems are inadequate for today's powerful global competition. Managers in companies selling multiple products are making important product decisions based on distorted cost information, as most cost systems designed in the past focused on inventory valuation. In order to elevate the level of management information, it has been suggested that companies should have as many as three cost systems for (1) inventory valuation, (2) management control of operations, and (3) an activity-based costing system for decision making.

Questions

A. Discuss why the traditional cost system, developed to value inventory, distorts product cost information.

B. 1. Describe the benefits that management can expect from activity-based costing.

　　2. List the steps that a company, using a traditional cost system, would take to implement activity-based costing.

Question 1C-ES02

TruJeans, a new start-up company, plans to produce blue jean pants, customized with the buyer's first name stitched across the back pocket. The product will be marketed exclusively via an Internet Web site. For the coming year, sales have been projected at three different levels: optimistic, neutral, and pessimistic. TruJeans does keep inventory on hand but prefers to minimize this investment.

The controller is preparing to assemble the budget for the coming year and is unsure about a number of issues, including:

- The level of sales to enter into the budget
- How to allocate the significant fixed costs to individual units
- Whether to use job order costing or process costing

In addition, the controller has heard of kaizen budgeting and is wondering if such an approach could be used by TruJeans.

Questions

A. How could the use of variable (direct) costing mitigate the problem of how to allocate the fixed costs to individual units?

B. Which cost system seems to make more sense for TruJeans, job order costing or process costing? Explain your answer.

Question 1C-ES03

Sonimad Sawmill Inc. (SSI) purchases logs from independent timber contractors and processes the logs into three types of lumber products:

1. Studs for residential building (e.g., walls, ceilings)
2. Decorative pieces (e.g., fireplace mantels, beams for cathedral ceilings)
3. Posts used as support braces (e.g., mine support braces, braces for exterior fences around ranch properties)

These products are the result of a joint sawmill process that involves removal of bark from the logs, cutting the logs into a workable size (ranging from 8 to 16 feet in length), and then cutting the individual products from the logs, depending on the type of wood (pine, oak, walnut, or maple) and the size (diameter) of the log. The joint process results in the following costs and output of products for a typical month.

Joint production costs

Materials (rough timber logs)	$500,000
Debarking (labor and overhead)	50,000
Sizing (labor and overhead)	200,000
Product cutting (labor and overhead)	250,000
Total joint costs	$1,000,000

Product yield and average sales value on a per unit basis from the joint process are shown next.

Product	Monthly Output	Fully Processed Sales Price
Studs	75,000	$8
Decorative pieces	5,000	100
Posts	20,000	20

The studs are sold as rough-cut lumber after emerging from the sawmill operation without further processing by SSI. Also, the posts require no further processing. The decorative pieces must be planed and further sized after emerging from the SSI sawmill. This additional processing costs SSI $100,000 per month and normally results in a loss of 10% of the units entering the process. Without this planning and sizing process, there is still an active intermediate market for the unfinished decorative pieces where the sales price averages $60 per unit.

Required

A. Based on the information given for Sonimad Sawmill Inc., allocate the joint processing costs of $1,000,000 to each of the three product lines using the
   1. Relative sales value method at split-off
   2. Physical output (volume) method at split-off
   3. Estimated net realizable value method

B. Prepare an analysis for Sonimad Sawmill Inc. to compare processing the decorative pieces further, as the company currently does, with selling the rough-cut product immediately at split-off, and recommend which action the company should take. Be sure to provide all calculations.

Question 1C-ES04

Alyssa Manufacturing produces two items in its Trumbull plant: Tuff Stuff and Ruff Stuff. Since inception, Alyssa has used only one manufacturing overhead pool to accumulate costs. Overhead has been allocated to products based on direct labor hours.

Until recently, Alyssa was the sole producer of Ruff Stuff and was able to dictate the selling price. However, last year Marvella Products began marketing a comparable product at a price below the standard costs developed by Alyssa. Market share has declined rapidly, and Alyssa must now decide whether to meet the competitive price or to discontinue the product line. Recognizing that discontinuing the product line would place additional burden on its remaining product, Tuff Stuff, Alyssa is using activity-based costing to determine if it would show a different cost structure for the two products.

The two major indirect costs for manufacturing the products are power usage and setup costs. Most of the power usage is used in fabricating, while most of the setup costs are required in assembly. The setup costs are predominantly for the Tuff Stuff product line. A decision was made to separate the Manufacturing Department costs into two activity centers: (1) fabricating using machine hours as the cost driver (activity base) and (2) assembly using the number of setups as the cost driver (activity base).

		Manufacturing Department	
		Annual Budget Before Separation of Overhead	
	Total	Product Line	
		Tuff Stuff	Ruff Stuff
Number of units		20,000	20,000
Direct labor*		2 hrs./unit	3 hrs./unit
Total direct labor	$800,000		
Direct material		$5.00/unit	$3.00/unit
Budgeted overhead:			
Indirect labor	$24,000		
Fringe benefits	5,000		
Indirect material	31,000		
Power	180,000		
Setup	75,000		
Quality assurance	10,000		
Other utilities	10,000		
Depreciation	15,000		

*Direct labor hourly rate is the same in both departments.

Manufacturing Department

Cost Structure after Separation of Overhead into Activity Pools

	Fabrication	Assembly
Direct labor	75%	25%
Direct material	100%	0%
Indirect labor	75%	25%
Fringe benefits	80%	20%
Indirect material	$20,000	$11,000
Power	$160,000	$20,000
Setup	$5,000	$70,000
Quality assurance	80%	20%
Other utilities	50%	50%
Depreciation	80%	20%
Activity Base	**Tuff Stuff**	**Ruff Stuff**
Machine hours per unit	4.4	6.0
Number of setups	1,000	272

Required

A. By allocating overhead based on direct labor hours, calculate the
1. Total budgeted cost of the Manufacturing Department
2. Unit standard cost of Tuff Stuff
3. Unit standard cost of Ruff Stuff

B. After separation of overhead into activity pools, compute the total budgeted cost of the
1. Fabricating Department
2. Assembly Department

C. Using activity-based costing, calculate the unit standard costs for
1. Tuff Stuff
2. Ruff Stuff

D. Discuss how a decision by Alyssa Manufacturing regarding the continued production of Ruff Stuff will be affected by the results of your calculations in Requirement C.

Part 1 Section D Questions

Question 1D-ES01

Superior Co. manufactures automobile parts for sale to major automakers. Superior's internal audit staff is reviewing the internal controls over machinery and equipment and making recommendations for improvements where appropriate.

The internal auditors obtained the information presented next during this review.

- Purchase requests for machinery and equipment normally are initiated by the supervisor in need of the asset. The supervisor discusses the proposed acquisition with the plant manager. A purchase requisition is submitted to the purchasing department when the plant manager determines that the request is reasonable and that there is a remaining balance in the plant's share of the total corporate budget for capital acquisitions.
- Upon receiving a purchase requisition for machinery or equipment, the purchasing department manager looks through the records for an appropriate supplier. A formal purchase order is then completed and mailed. When the machine or equipment is received, it is immediately sent to the user department for installation. This allows the economic benefits from the acquisition to be realized at the earliest possible date.
- The property, plant, and equipment ledger control accounts are supported by lapsing schedules organized by year of acquisition. These lapsing schedules are used to compute depreciation as a unit for all assets of a given type that are acquired in the same year. Standard rates, depreciation methods, and salvage values are used for each major type of fixed asset. These rates, methods, and salvage values were set ten years ago during the company's initial year of operation.
- When machinery or equipment is retired, the plant manager notifies the accounting department so that the appropriate entries can be made in the accounting records.
- There has been no reconciliation since the company began operations between the accounting records and the machinery and equipment on hand.

Question

Identify the internal control weaknesses and recommend improvements that the internal audit staff of Superior Co. should include in its report regarding the internal controls employed for fixed assets. Use the following format in preparing your answer.

Weaknesses	Recommendations
1.	1.

Question 1D-ES02

The board of directors of a Large Corporation recently learned that some members of the senior management team had circumvented the company's internal controls for personal gain. The board appointed a special task force of external auditors and outside legal counsel to investigate the situation.

After extensive review, the task force has concluded that for a period of several years the expenses of the company's chief executive officer, president, and vice president-public relations were charged to an account called the Limited Expenditure

Account (LEA). The account was established five years ago and was not subject to the company's normal approval authorization process. Approximately $2,000,000 of requests for reimbursement were routinely processed and charged to LEA. Accounting personnel were advised by the controller to process such requests based on the individual approval of any of the three executives, even when the requests were not adequately documented.

The vice president-public relations and his department were in charge of political fundraising activities. The task force determined, however, that only a small portion of the $1,000,000 raised last year was actually used for political purposes. In addition, departmental resources were used for personal projects of the three identified executives. The task force also uncovered an additional $4,000,000 of expenditures that were poorly documented so that even the amounts for proper business purposes could not be identified.

The task force noted that these payment practices, as well as LEA, were never disclosed in the Internal Audit Department's audit reports even though company disbursements were tested annually. References to these practices and LEA were included on two occasions in recent year's work papers. The director of internal audit, who reports to the controller, advised that she reviewed these findings with the controller who, in turn, advised that he mentioned these findings to the president. The president recommended that they not be included in the internal audit reports. Furthermore, the external auditors, who reviewed the internal audit work papers, did not mention LEA or these payment practices in their recommendations for improved internal control procedures to management or in their external audit reports. The task force also noted that the company did not have a formal, published ethics policy.

Questions

A. Identify at least three internal control weaknesses in the company's internal control system.
B. Identify at least three illegal or improper practices uncovered at the company.
C. Identify at least four important steps the company should take, both procedurally and organizationally, to correct the problems that were uncovered in order to prevent a similar situation in the future.

Question 1D-ES03

Brawn Technology, Inc. is a manufacturer of large wind energy systems. The company has its corporate headquarters in Buenos Aires and a central manufacturing facility about 200 miles away. Since the manufacturing facility is so remote, it does not receive the attention or the support from the staff that the other units do. The president of Brawn is concerned about whether proper permits have been issued for new construction work being done to handle industrial waste at the facility. In addition, he wants to be sure that all occupational safety laws and environmental issues are being properly addressed. He has asked the company's internal auditor to conduct an audit focusing on these areas of concern.

Questions

A. Identify the seven types of internal audits and describe the two most common types of internal audits. Using examples, describe two situations where each type of common audit would be applicable.

B. Referring to Brawn Technology:
1. Identify the type of audit that would best address the concerns of the president.
2. Identify the objective of this audit.
3. Give two reasons why this type of audit would best address the concerns of the president.

C. Recommend two procedures that could be implemented at Brawn's manufacturing plant that would lessen the president's concerns. Explain each of your recommendations.

Question 1D-ES04

Ted Crosby owns Standard Lock Inc., a small business that manufactures metal door handles and door locks. When he first started the company, Crosby managed the business by himself, overseeing purchasing and production as well as maintaining the financial records. The only employees he hired were production workers.

As the business expanded, Crosby decided to hire John Smith as the company's financial manager. Smith had an MBA and ten years of experience in the finance department of a large company. During the interview, Smith mentioned that he was considering an offer from another company and needed to know of Crosby's decision within the next couple of days. Since Crosby was extremely impressed with Smith's credentials, he offered him the job without conducting background checks. Smith seemed to be a dedicated and hard-working employee. His apparent integrity quickly earned him a reputation as an outstanding and trusted manager.

Later in the year, Crosby hired another manager, Joe Fletcher, to oversee the production department. Crosby continued to take care of purchasing and authorized all payments.

Fletcher was highly qualified for the position and seemed to be reliable and conscientious. After observing Fletcher's work for one year, Crosby concluded that he was performing his duties efficiently. Crosby believed that Fletcher and Smith were both good managers whom he could trust and gave them expanded responsibilities. Fletcher's additional responsibilities included purchasing and receiving; Smith paid all the bills, prepared and signed all checks, maintained records, and reconciled the bank statements.

Soon Crosby began taking a hands-off approach to managing his business. He frequently took long vacations with his family and was not often at the office to check on the business. He was pleased that the company was profitable and expected that it would continue to be profitable in the future under the supervision of two qualified and trusted managers. One year after Crosby left the management of the company to Smith and Fletcher, business began to experience a decline in profits.

Crosby assumed that it was due to a cyclical downturn in the economy. When Standard continued to decline even as the economy improved, Crosby began to investigate. He noticed that revenues were increasing but profits were declining. He also discovered that purchases from one vendor had increased significantly as compared to the other five vendors. Crosby is concerned that fraud may be occurring in the company.

Required

A. Identify and describe four internal control deficiencies within Standard Lock Inc.

B. For each of the internal control deficiencies identified, recommend an improvement in procedures that would mitigate these deficiencies.

C. If the company were to implement an ideal internal control system, can it guarantee that fraud would not occur in future? Explain your answer.

Question 1D-ES05

Sam Pierce is a division controller with Med Direct, Inc., a publicly traded multinational corporation that manufactures large-scale medical equipment and also provides financing services to its customers. Pierce has seen many news stories recently of competitors having severe financial difficulty, including bankruptcy. He has also seen other corporations suffer from regulatory indictments and fines. Pierce not only wants to avoid such problems, but he also wants his company to report stable earnings and a rising stock price. Pierce's goal is to integrate enterprise risk management into the culture and operations of his division, and throughout the whole corporation. He also wants to make sure the company is in compliance with the requirements of the Sarbanes-Oxley Act of 2002.

Required

A. Identify and explain two risks that a multinational firm such as Med Direct may encounter in each of these three areas:
   1. Buying raw materials from other countries
   2. Selling on credit terms to customers in foreign countries
   3. Developing and manufacturing high-tech equipment

B. Identify two reasons why each of the next three elements is important for a risk assessment and control program to be effective. Provide one example of each element.
   1. Understanding your business
   2. Implementing checks and balances
   3. Developing procedures that set limits or establish standards

C. Explain how a company's organizational policies and management style impact the effectiveness of the control environment and its management of risk.

D. Identify and explain the compliance requirements with respect to internal controls in the Sarbanes-Oxley Act of 2002 (SOX 404).

Part 1 Section E Questions

Question 1E-ES01

Borealis Industries has three operating divisions: Sandstone Books, Corus Games, and Sterling Extraction Services. Each division maintains its own accounting system and method of revenue recognition.

Sandstone Books

Sandstone Books sells novels to regional distributors, which then sell to independent bookstores and retail chains in their territory. The distributors are allowed to return up to 25% of their purchases to Sandstone, and the distributors have the same return allowance with the bookstores. The returns from distributors have averaged 20% over the past five years. During the fiscal year just ended, Sandstone's sales to distributors totaled $15,000,000. At year-end, $6,800,000 of sales are still subject to return privileges over the next six months. The balance of the book sales, $8,200,000, had actual returns of 19%. Sales from the previous fiscal year totaling $5,500,000 were collected in the current fiscal year, with 21% of sales returned. Sandstone records revenue in accordance with the method referred to as revenue recognition when the right of return exists as the company's operations meet all the applicable criteria for use of this method.

Corus Games

Corus Games supplies video arcades with new games and updated versions of standard games. The company works through a network of sales agents in various cities. Orders are received from the sales agents along with down payments; Corus then ships the product directly to the customer, f.o.b. shipping point. The customer is billed for the balance due plus the actual shipping costs. During the fiscal year just ended, Corus received orders for $12,000,000 from the sales agents along with $1,200,000 in down payments. Customers were billed $150,000 in freight costs and $9,180,000 for goods shipped. After an order has been shipped, the sales agent receives a 12% commission on the product price. The goods are warranted for 90 days after sales, and warranty returns have been about 3% of sales. Corus recognizes revenue at the point of sale.

Sterling Extraction Services

Sterling specializes in the extraction of precious metals. During the fiscal year just ended, Sterling entered into contracts worth $36,000,000 and shipped metals worth $32,400,000. One quarter of the shipments was made from inventories on hand at the beginning of the year, and the remaining shipments were made from metals that were mined during the year. Sterling uses the completion-of-production method to recognize revenue, because the operations meet the specified criteria (i.e., reasonably assured sales prices, interchangeable units, and insignificant distribution costs).

Questions

The chief executive officer (CEO) of Sterling Extraction Services has asked the controller, "How do you know which orders were filled from inventory? I want you to take another look at the revenue calculation. At the current level, our incentive payments will be much lower than expected. Besides, I promised the board of directors that this year's revenue would exceed last year's by at least 12%; I don't like not keeping my promises."

The controller is very uncomfortable with the implications of the CEO's statement and has turned to the *IMA Statement of Ethical Professional Practice* for guidance. According to this guidance:

A. Identify the principles that should guide the work of a management accountant.
B. Identify and describe the standards that would be violated if the controller of Sterling were to manipulate the revenue calculation.
C. Identify the steps the controller should take to resolve this situation.

Question 1E-ES02

Alex Raminov is a management accountant at Carroll Mining and Manufacturing Company (CMMC), a large processor of ores and minerals. While working late one night to complete the footnotes for the financial statements, Raminov was looking for a file in his supervisor's office and noticed a report regarding procedures for disposing of plant wastes. According to handwritten notes on the face of the report, CMMC had been using a residential landfill in a nearby township to dump toxic coal cleaning fluid wastes over a considerable period of time. The report stated that locating a new dump site was urgent because the current one was nearing capacity.

Raminov realized that it was possible CMMC had been improperly disposing of highly toxic fluids in a landfill that was restricted to residential refuse. In addition to the obvious hazards to residents of the area, there could be legal problems if and when the authorities were notified. The financial consequences of cleanup actions, as well as the loss of CMMC's generally good environmental reputation, could be catastrophic for the company.

Raminov asked his supervisor how this item was to be included in the footnotes and inquired whether an accrual for cleanup costs was anticipated. His supervisor told him to "forget about this matter" and that he had no intention of mentioning one word about waste disposal in this year's financial statements.

Questions

A. Using the categories outlined in *IMA Statement of Ethical Professional Practice*, identify the standards that are specifically relevant to Alex Raminov's ethical conflict and explain why the standards are applicable to the situation.
B. According to the *IMA Statement of Ethical Professional Practice*, what further steps, if any, should Raminov take in resolving his ethical dilemma?

C. If he continues to be rebuffed by his employer, should Raminov notify the appropriate authorities? Should he anonymously release the information to the local newspaper? Explain your answers.

Question 1E-ES03

Amy Kimbell was recently hired as an accounting manager for Hi-Quality Productions Inc., a publicly held company producing components for the automotive industry. One division, Alpha, uses a highly automated process that had been outsourced for a number of years because the capital investment required was high and the technology was constantly changing. Two years ago, the company decided to make the necessary capital investment and bring the operation in house. Since all major capital investments must be approved by the board of directors, the budget committee for the Alpha Division recommended the $4 million investment to the board, projecting a significant cost savings.

In her new job as accounting manager, Kimbell is on the budget committee for the Alpha Division. The board has requested from the committee a postaudit review of the actual cost savings. While working on the review, Kimball noted that several of the projections in the original proposal were very aggressive, including an unusually high salvage value and an excessively long useful life. If more realistic projections had been used, Kimbell doubts that the board would have approved the investment.

When Kimbell expressed her concerns at the next meeting of Alpha's budget committee, she was told that it had been the unanimous decision of the committee to recommend the investment because it was thought to be in the best long-term interest of the company. According to the committee members, the postaudit report would not discuss these issues; the committee members believe that certain adjustments to the review are justified to ensure the success of the Alpha division and the company as a whole.

Questions

A. Using the categories outlined in the *IMA Statement of Ethical Professional Practice*, identify the standards that are specifically relevant to Kimbell's ethical conflict and explain why the identified standards are applicable to the situation.
B. According to the *IMA Statement of Ethical Professional Practice*, what specific actions should Kimbell take to resolve her ethical conflict?

Question 1E-ES04

Pro-Kleen specializes in cleaning carpets and upholstery for residences and businesses. Three years ago, the company upgraded its equipment in order to remain competitive and take advantage of new technology. At that time, Pro-Kleen purchased two truck-mounted steam cleaners; the details are shown next.

Purchase date	March 15, 2005
Cost	$200,000
Estimated life	8 years
Salvage value	$20,000

Pro-Kleen takes one-half year's depreciation in both the year of acquisition and the year of disposal and uses the straight-line method for calculating depreciation expense.

Based on recent information, John Morgan, Pro-Kleen's assistant controller, has changed the estimated useful lives of the equipment to five years. The salvage value of the equipment has been reduced to $10,000 due to unexpected obsolescence. These revisions are effective January 1, 2008. After revising the depreciation amounts for the current year's financial reporting, Morgan was told by the controller, Eileen Ryan, that the revision was significant enough to change the small profit projected for the year into a loss. As a result, Ryan has asked Morgan to reduce by half the total depreciation expense for the current year.

Questions

A. Referring to the specific standards outlined in the *IMA Statement of Ethical Professional Practice*, identify and discuss the specific ethical conflicts that Ryan's instruction presents to Morgan.

B. According to the *IMA Statement of Ethical Professional Practice*, identify the steps that Morgan should take to resolve this situation.

Question 1E-ES05

United Forest Products (UFP) is a $1 billion corporation with many large timber and wood processing plants. The company is decentralized into divisions that operate as profit centers. The majority of the centers are evaluated on cost control and the achievement of budgeted output and profits. If target numbers are met, all division employees participate in a profit-sharing plan, and senior management potentially can receive substantial bonuses.

Charlene White is the controller of the Allegheny Division of UFP. Over the past six months, she discussed the division's performance several times with the president of the Allegheny Division, William Jefferson, and it became apparent that the division would not meet its targeted goals unless drastic changes were made. The Allegheny Division is actually a cost center that has been required to use a non-market-based transfer price, but it is evaluated as a profit center. Jefferson realized this problem and told White that the only way to meet budget was "to maximize output and make some serious changes in our cost control." Several weeks later, White noted a dramatic increase in the profitability of the division.

When analyzing the monthly profit and loss details, White noted only a slight increase in output but a significant decrease in the purchase cost of raw timber. She knew her responsibilities required her to understand fully how this sudden change was taking place and began investigating. At the log yard where timber is received and scaled to determine its price, she noticed that a trucker-timber contractor was quite aggravated when he was given the scale report (board feet and quality). When she asked one of the employees what was bothering the contractor, he said, "Are you kidding? You wouldn't believe how much we've been lowering scale measures the last three months!" Further conversations revealed that Jefferson had apparently told the division's mill workers to significantly reduce both the size scale (in inches of log diameter) and quality measures of logs sold to the mill. The impact has been a significant reduction in the price paid to contractors for timber purchased by the division.

White suspects that Jefferson has instructed employees to deliberately give logging contractors arbitrary and inaccurate evaluations of raw material quantity and quality, an unethical business practice.

Questions

A. Identify and discuss Charlene White's ethical conflict, and determine if she has an obligation to act. Be sure to refer to the relevant standards outlined in IMA's Standards of Ethical Professional Practice to support your answer.
B. According to IMA's Standards of Ethical Professional Practice, what steps should White take to resolve the perceived ethical dilemma?
C. Explain how the performance evaluation system affected behavior at the Allegheny Division, and recommend improvements to the system.

Question 1E-ES06

GRQ Company is a privately held entity that refines a variety of natural raw materials used as primary inputs for the steel industry. The firm has done well over the last several years, and most members of senior management have received bonuses well in excess of 60% of their base salaries. Also, both the chief financial officer and the chief executive officer have earned bonuses in excess of 100% of their base salaries. GRQ has projected this trend of successful earnings and bonuses to continue.

All-American Steel Company (AAS) has tendered a very generous offer to acquire GRQ. At the same time, several top GRQ executives, who own over 40% of GRQ's stock, have learned that the primary supplier of their major raw material will not renew their contract at the end of the current fiscal year. GRQ has no other vendors available within the United States to competitively provide this raw material in the amount needed to support their continued record of profitable operations.

As part of the due diligence process, an analyst with AAS has asked John Spencer, controller of GRQ, if he knows of any material event that would impact earnings over the next several years. Spencer, who also participates in the bonus program, is aware that GRQ's primary supplier will no longer provide raw materials to the firm beyond the end of the current fiscal year. He spoke with Bob Green, the CFO of GRQ, telling him that while the profit projections for the remainder of the current year will match the earnings of prior years, it is obvious that projected earnings for the next year will be greatly reduced. Green informed Spencer that the executive committee had met and decided that only members of top management were to be made aware of the situation with their key supplier. Accordingly, Spencer should not inform AAS of the situation with the supplier.

Required

  A. Referring to the specific standards outlined in *IMA Statement of Ethical Professional Practice*, identify and discuss Spencer's ethical obligations.
  B. According to *IMA Statement of Ethical Professional Practice*, identify the steps that Spencer should take to resolve the dilemma.

Question 1E-ES07

CenturySound, Inc. produces cutting-edge high-end audio systems that are sold primarily through major retailers. Any production overruns are sold to discount retailers, under CenturySound's private label SoundDynamX. The discount retail segment appears very profitable because the basic operating budget assigns all fixed expenses to production for the major retailers, the only predictable market.

Several years ago, CenturySound implemented a 100% testing program. On average approximately 3% of production is found to be substandard and unacceptable. Of this 3%, approximately two thirds are reworked and the remaining one third are scrapped. However, in a recent analysis of customer complaints, George Wilson, the cost accountant, and Barry Ross, the quality control engineer, have ascertained that normal rework does not bring the audio systems up to standard. Sampling shows that about 25% of the reworked audio systems will fail after extended operation within one year.

Unfortunately, there is no way to determine which reworked audio systems will fail because testing will not detect this problem. CenturySound's marketing analyst has indicated that this problem will have a significant impact on the company's reputation and customer satisfaction if the problem is not corrected. Consequently, the board of directors would interpret this problem as having serious negative implications on the company's profitability.

Wilson has included the audio system failure and rework problem in his written report that has been prepared for the upcoming quarterly meeting of the board of directors. Due to the potential adverse economic impact, Wilson has followed a long standing practice of highlighting this information.

After reviewing the reports to be presented, the plant manager was upset and said to the controller, "We can't trouble the board with this kind of material. Tell Wilson to tone that down. People cannot expect their systems to last forever."

The controller called Wilson into his office and said, "George, you'll have to bury this one. The probable failure of reworks can be referred to briefly in the oral presentation, but it should not be mentioned or highlighted in the advance material mailed to the board."

Wilson feels strongly that the board will be misinformed on a potentially serious loss of income if he follows the controller's orders. Wilson discussed the problem with Ross, the quality control engineer, who simply remarked, "That's your problem, George."

Required:

A. Identify and discuss the ethical considerations that George Wilson should recognize in deciding how to proceed in this matter. Support your answer by referring to the specific standards outlined in the *IMA Statement of Ethical Professional Practice.*

B. According to the *IMA Statement of Ethical Professional Practice*, what are the steps Wilson should take in order to resolve the situation?

Part 1 Section A Answers

Answer to Question 1A-ES01

Answer A:

<table>
<tr><td colspan="3" align="center">**Rein Company**
Budgeted Income Statement
for the Year Ended December 31, 2006</td></tr>
<tr><td>Sales [100,000 × 1.1 × ($110 + 15)]</td><td></td><td>$13,750,000</td></tr>
<tr><td>Cost of goods sold at standard [110,000 × (65.20 + 19.80)[1]]</td><td></td><td>9,350,000</td></tr>
<tr><td>Gross margin at standard</td><td></td><td>$4,400,000</td></tr>
<tr><td>   Variances</td><td></td><td></td></tr>
<tr><td>   Material-brass—unfavorable
            [(111,650 compressors[2]) ×
            (4 lbs/compressor) × ($.30/lb)]</td><td>$(133,980)</td><td></td></tr>
<tr><td>   Labor efficiency—unfavorable
            [(111,650 compressors) ×
            (0.25 hours/compressor) × ($7/hr)]</td><td>(195,388)</td><td></td></tr>
<tr><td>   Variable overhead efficiency—unfavorable
            [(111,650 compressors) ×
            (0.25 hrs/compressor) × ($3.30/hour[3])]</td><td>(92,111)</td><td></td></tr>
<tr><td>   Fixed overhead volume—favorable
            [(111,650 − 110,000
            compressors) × $6.60/compressor[4])]</td><td>10,890</td><td>(410,589)</td></tr>
<tr><td>Gross margin at actual</td><td></td><td>$3,989,411</td></tr>
<tr><td>Operating expenses</td><td></td><td></td></tr>
<tr><td>   Selling expense ($13,750,000 × .12)</td><td>$1,650,000</td><td></td></tr>
<tr><td>   Administrative expense ($907,850 × 1.2)</td><td>1,089,420</td><td>2,739,420</td></tr>
<tr><td>Income before taxes</td><td></td><td>$1,249,991</td></tr>
<tr><td>   Income tax expense (45%)</td><td></td><td>562,496</td></tr>
<tr><td>Net income</td><td></td><td>$687,495</td></tr>
<tr><td></td><td></td><td></td></tr>
<tr><td>Earnings per share (250,000 shares)</td><td></td><td>$2.75</td></tr>
</table>

Supporting Calculations

---

1 Standard cost of compressor

Brass 4 lbs. @ $5.35/lb.	$21.40
Steel alloy 5 lbs. @ $3.16/lb.	15. 80
Direct labor 4 hrs. @ $7.00/hr.	28. 00
Overhead (2,178,000 ÷ 110,000)	19. 80
Total cost per compressor	$85. 00

2 Production schedule

2006 sales	110,000
Desired ending inventory 12/31/06 (110,000 × 1.1 × .15)	18,150
Required inventory	128,150
Beginning inventory 1/1/06 (110,000 × .15)	16,500
2006 production	111,650

3 Determination of the variable overhead rate and total fixed overhead

Variable overhead rate per compressor $= \dfrac{\text{Change in Overhead}}{\text{Change in Activity}}$

$\dfrac{(\$2,178,000 - \$2,046,000)}{110,000 - 100,000} = \dfrac{\$132,000}{10,000}$

$= \$13.20/\text{compressor}$

Variable overhead rate/direct labor hour $= \dfrac{\$13.20/\text{compressor}}{4 \text{ hrs./compressor}}$

$= \$3.30/\text{direct labor hour}$

Total overhead at 110,000 compressors	$2,178,000
Total variable overhead at 110,000 compressors (110,000 × $13.20)	− 1,452,000
Total budgeted fixed overhead	$726,000

4 Normal activity level and fixed overhead rate

Fixed overhead rate $= \dfrac{\text{Budgeted fixed overhead (See note 3)}}{\text{Normal production activity level}}$

$= \dfrac{\$726,000}{110,000}$

$= \$6.60/\text{compressor}$

Answer B:

Based on the results of the 2006 budgeted income statement, the president's objective cannot be achieved. A review of the statement highlights these circumstances:

- A 2006 income statement prepared using the worst situation gives a net income of $687,495 and earnings per share of $2.75, which is a decrease from the 2005 income of $700,000 and earnings per share of $2.80. These budgeted figures are also considerably below the president's objective of $750,000 net income and $3 earnings per share.

- If the unfavorable variances do not occur, net income will increase by $231,813 after taxes ($421,479 × .55), resulting in an increase in earnings per share of $.927, giving a total earnings per share of $3.677 which is well above the president's objective.
- Manufacturing costs are 65. 5% of the selling price ($72 / $110) in 2005, and 68% of the selling price in 2006. Administrative expenses increased 20% in 2006. Therefore, the 13. 6% sales price increase in 2006 was not sufficient to cover the increases in manufacturing cost and increases in administrative expense.

Answer to Question 1A-ES02

Answer A:

Robbins and Crowe introduce slack into their budgets for these reasons:

- To hedge against uncertainties that might cause actual results to differ markedly from their projections.
- To allow their employees to exceed expectations, show consistent performance, or both. This becomes especially significant if their performance is evaluated by comparing actual results to budget projections.
- To bring the organization's goals into alignment with their own goals by using budgetary slack to improve the organization's assessment of their performance, thus earning higher salaries, better bonuses, or promotions.

Answer B:

Slack might adversely affect Robbins and Crowe in these ways:

- By limiting the usefulness of the budget to motivate top performance from their employees
- By affecting their ability to identify trouble spots and take appropriate corrective action
- By reducing their credibility in the eyes of management

The use of budgetary slack also may affect management decisions, since the budgets will show lower contribution margins (fewer sales, higher expenses). Decisions regarding profitability of product lines, staffing levels, incentives, and other matters could adversely affect Robbins's and Crowe's departments.

Answer to Question 1A-ES03

Answer A:

At least three advantages and three disadvantages of budgetary slack from the point of view of Artech Corporation's management group as a whole include those listed.

Advantages

- It provides flexibility for operating under unknown circumstances, such as an extra margin for discretionary expenses in case budget assumptions on inflation are incorrect or adverse circumstances arise.

- Additional slack may be included to offset the costly setups from design changes and/or small lot size orders.
- The increased pressure to meet current-year earnings per share targets may result in postponing expenditures into the next year or aggressively pulling sales into the current year. Budgetary slack in the next year may compensate for shifting those earnings from next year into the current year.

Disadvantages

- It decreases the ability to highlight weaknesses and take timely corrective actions on problem areas.
- It decreases the overall effectiveness of corporate planning. Actions such as pricing changes or reduced promotional spending may be taken from a perceived need to improve earnings when eliminating the budgetary slack could accomplish the same objective without marketplace changes.
- It limits the objective evaluation of departmental managers and performance of subordinates by using budgetary information.

Answer B:

Zero-based budgeting (ZBB) could be advantageous to Artech Corporation's overall budget process for these reasons:

- The ZBB process evaluates all proposed operating and administrative expenses as if they were being initiated for the first time. Each expenditure is justified, ranked, and prioritized according to its order of importance to the overall corporation, not just its role in one department.
- The focus is on evaluation of all activities rather than just incremental changes from the prior year. This allows addressing activities which have been ongoing to determine if they are still useful in the current environment. The objectives, operations, and costs of all activities are evaluated, and alternative means of accomplishing the objectives are more likely to be identified.

Answer to Question 1A-ES04

Answer A:

MRC Cash Budget Proposed	
Third Quarter (only)	
Beginning cash balance (given)	$186,000
Add: Third-quarter cash receipts[1]	200,650
Less: Third-quarter cash expenditures[2]	178,000
Ending cash balance	$208,650

Supporting Calculations

1 Third-quarter cash receipts

Fee			Distribution	
Memberships				
	Individual	$300	60%	$36,000	*[(50 new + 150 renew) × 0.60 × $300]*
	Student	180	10%	3,600	*[(50 + 150) × 0.10 × $180]*
	Family	600	30%	36,000	*[(50 + 150) × 0.30 × $600]*
	Total			$75,600	
Court Fees				
	Individual	$50	60%	$61,500	*[(50 new + 2,000 reg.) × 0.60 × $50]*
	Student	40	10%	8,200	*[2,050 × 0.10 × $40]*
	Family	90	30%	55,350	*[2,050 × 0.30 × $90]*
	Total			125,050	
	Total Third-Quarter Cash Receipts:			$200,650	

2 Cash expenditures

Fixed costs	$157,500	
Less: Depreciation	24,500	
Add: Variable costs	45,000	*[(1000 hours + 2000 hours) × $15]*
Total Costs:	$178,000	

Answer B:

Sensitivity analysis would help MRC management by testing the assumed projections and seeing how sensitive the cash flows are to changes in the number of members or the distribution of members.

Answer C:

Other factors that MRC should consider include:

- Communication strategy to current members
- Market acceptance of the new pricing strategy
- Cost associated with the change
- Timing of the change
- Effect on the mix of membership class
- Anticipated rate of return for excess cash and the costs of borrowing funds
- Reliability of the projections
- Capacity of the tennis and racquetball courts
- Price elasticity for memberships in similar clubs
- Reaction of the competition
- Quality of its facilities and staff
- Cost of advertising/communicating this price change

Part 1 Section B Answers

Answer to Question 1B-ES01

Answer A:

Sales Price Variance	Budget Sales Price	Actual Sales Price	Unit Variance	Actual Unit Sales	Sales Price Variance	Total
Hand Drills	$60	$59	$1 U	86,000	$86,000	
Table Saws	$120	$115	$5 U	74,000	$370,000	$456,000 U

Cost Price Variance	Budgeted Cost	Actual Cost	Unit Variance	Actual Unit Purchases	Cost Price Variance	
Hand Drills	$50	**$50**	$0	86,000	None	
Table Saws	$80	**$82**	$2 U	74,000	$148,000	$148,000 U

Volume Variance	Budgeted Volume in Units	Actual Volume in Units	Unit Variance	Budgeted[1] Contribution Margin/Unit	Volume Variance	
Hand Drills	120,000	86,000	34,000 U	$10	$340,000	
Table Saws	80,000	74,000	6,000 U	$40	240,000	$580,000 U
Total Gross Margin Variance						**$1,184,000 U**

[1]Budgeted total margin ÷ Budget unit sales	Hand Drills	Table Saws
	$1,200,000	$3,200,000
	120,000	80,000
	$10/unit	$40/unit

Answer B:

The effectiveness of Handler's marketing program is difficult to judge in the absence of actual industry-wide performance data. If the industry estimate of a 10% decline in the market for these tools is used as a basis for comparison, then Handler's gross margin should have fallen to $3,960,000 ($4,400,000 × .9) as summarized next ($000 omitted).

	Hand Drill	Table Saw	Total
Budgeted gross margin	$1,200	$3,200	$4,400
Budget adjusted for 10% industry decline	$1,080	$2,880	$3,960
Less: Actual gross margin	774	2,442	3,216
Shortage	$ 306	$ 438	$ 744

Handler's gross margin actually fell to $3,216,000, which is $744,000 lower than might have been expected. To have been considered a success, the marketing program should have generated a gross margin above $4,020,000 (the original budget minus the projected industry decline plus the incremental cost of the marketing program, i.e., $4,400 − 440 + 60).

Handler hoped to do better than the industry average by giving dealer discounts and increasing direct advertising. However, to be successful, the discounts and advertising must be offset by an increase in volume. Handler was not successful in this regard in total; sales volume dropped 7.5% in the table saw line as compared to a 28.3% decline in hand drill volume. Note that the table saw price was dropped by 4.2% as against a price decline of only 1.7% on hand drilled. Apparently the discounts and advertising did not generate enough unit sales volume to offset and compensate for the promotion.

Answer to Question 1B-ES02

Answer A:

The shortcomings or possible inconsistencies of using return on investment (ROI) as the sole criterion to evaluate divisional management performance include:

- ROI tends to emphasize short-run performance at the possible expense of long-run profitability.
- ROI is not consistent with cash flow models used for capital expenditure analysis.
- ROI frequently is not controllable by the division manager because many components included in the computation are committed in amount or are the responsibility of others.
- Reliance on ROI as the only measurement indicator could lead to an inaccurate decision or investment at either the divisional or corporate level.

Answer B:

The advantages of using multiple criteria to evaluate divisional management performance include:

- Multiple performance measures provide a more comprehensive picture of performance by considering a wider range of responsibilities.
- Multiple performance measures emphasize both the short-term and long-term results, thereby emphasizing the total performance of the division.
- Multiple performance measures may highlight nonquantitative as well as quantitative-oriented aspects.
- Multiple performance criteria will enhance goal congruence and reduce the importance of the dysfunctional short-run goal of profit maximization.

Answer C:

The problems or disadvantages of implementing a multiple performance criteria measurement system include:

- The measurement criteria are not all equally quantifiable.
- Management may have difficulty applying the criteria on a consistent basis, some criteria may be subjectively more heavily weighted than other criteria, and some criteria may be in conflict with each other.
- A multiple performance measurement system may be confusing to division management.
- Overemphasis on multiple evaluation criteria may lead to diffusion of effort and the failure to perform as well as expected in any one area.

Answer to Question 1B-ES03

Answer A:

Segment information prepared for public reporting may be inappropriate for evaluation of segment managers for these reasons:

- An allocation of common costs incurred for the benefit of more than one segment must be included for public reporting purposes.
- Common costs generally are allocated on an arbitrary basis.
- Segments identified for public reporting may not coincide with actual management responsibilities.
- Information in the annual report does not distinguish between a segment that is a poor investment and one in which the manager has done well despite adverse circumstances.

Answer B:

Segment managers may become frustrated and dissatisfied if their performance is evaluated on the basis of information in the annual financial report. Using that information may lead to their being held responsible for earnings figures that include the arbitrary allocation of common costs and costs that are traceable to them but are not under their control. Such evaluations reduce motivation and may even cause managers to seek other employment.

Answer C:

Merriam Corporation should define responsibility centers that coincide with managers' actual responsibilities rather than using segment rules developed for public reporting. All reports should be prepared using the contribution approach, which separates costs by behavior and assigns costs only to segments that control them. The report should disclose contribution margin, contributions controllable by segment managers, and contribution by each segment after the allocation of common costs.

Answer to Question 1B-ES04

Answer A:

Because Quie's management apparently has excess capacity, it should be positive toward each suggested price in decreasing order. Each price exceeds variable costs and thus will increase Quie's ROI, which is the basis of its evaluation by corporate management.

Answer B:

Negotiating a price between the two divisions is the best method to resolve the controversy in this situation. ARQ is highly decentralized and exhibits all four conditions required for negotiating a transfer price:

1. Outside markets exist to give both parties alternatives to dealing with each other.
2. Both parties have access to market price information.
3. Both parties are free to buy and sell outside the corporation.
4. Top management supports the continuation of the decentralized arrangement.

Answer C:

ARQ management should not become involved in resolving the controversy. This would violate the autonomous relationship of the divisions, which ARQ intends to maintain. Imposing conditions on the pricing will adversely affect the current ROI-based evaluation system, since the two divisions will no longer be in control of their profits. Finally, division management would most likely respond negatively to a loss of the autonomy it is used to exercising.

Answer to Question 1B-ES05

Answer A:

Transfer prices based on cost are not appropriate measures of divisional performance for several reasons, including these:

- The selling division has little incentive to control costs if all costs will be recovered in the transfer price.
- The company as a whole often makes poor decisions when one division is covering another's full costs.

Answer B:

The next table shows the results for both the extraction and pet products divisions of using the market price as the transfer price.

Results of Using Market-Based Transfer Pricing

	Extraction Division	Pet Products Division
Selling price	$26.00	$42.00
Less variable costs		
Material cost	$4.00	$2.00
Labor cost	$6.00	$4.00
Overhead (variable)	$8.25 *	$2.45†
Transfer price	–	$26.00
Unit contribution margin	$7.75	$7.55
Volume	× 500,000	× 500,000
Total contribution margin	$3,875,000.00	$3,775,000.00

*Variable overhead = $11 × 75% = $8.25.

†Variable overhead = $7 × 35% = $2.45.

Answer C:

If Sparta Enterprises lets its divisions buy and sell in the open market and also allows them to negotiate an acceptable transfer price, the result would be as shown:

- Any price between $24. 50 and $26 will result in an overall benefit to the company.
- The extraction division would prefer to sell its clay to the pet products division at the same price it receives in the market: $26 per unit. But it would be willing to sell at $24. 50, because it saves $1. 50 in selling costs per unit by selling within the company.
- Similarly, the pet products division would like to continue paying $22 per unit for the clay, but if it cannot purchase the clay within the company, it will have to pay the full $26 market price. Therefore, it will be willing to pay the $24.50 transfer price it can negotiate with the extraction division.

Answer D:

Using a negotiated transfer price should result in desirable management behavior because it will:

- Encourage the management of the extraction division to control costs.
- Benefit the pet products division by providing the clay at a below-market price.
- Provide a more realistic measure of divisional performance.

Answer to Question 1B-ES06

Answer A:

The quarterly performance report that 4-Cycle provides to its managers includes at least these three weaknesses:

1. It is based on a static budget. The company should switch to a flexible budget that compares the same levels of activity and shows variances between the actual budget and the flexible budget.

2. The report includes costs that supervisors cannot control, such as fixed production costs and overhead.

3. The report allocates fixed production costs using a single rate for all lines. Since the amount of space occupied by production may not, in fact, determine fixed production costs, the company should select an appropriate base to determine the rate for each product line.

Answer B:

To remove the weaknesses in the performance report, you could recommend that the CFO at 4-Cycle, Inc. :

- Use flexible rather than static budgeting.
- Stop holding product managers responsible for costs they cannot control.
- Include footnotes to make the report easier to understand.

A revised quarterly report that incorporates these suggested changes is shown next.

4-Cycle, Inc.
Marine Engine Quarterly Performance Report

	Actual	Flexible Budget	Flexible Budget Variance
Units	10,500	10,500	
Revenue	17,500,000	$18,158,805[1]	$658,805 U
Variable production costs			
Direct material	2,500,000	2,674,140[2]	174,140 F
Direct labor	2,193,000	2,211,195[3]	18,195 F
Machine time	2,300,000	2,408,805[4]	108,805 F
Factory overhead	4,500,500	4,725,000[5]	224,500 F
Total variable costs	11,493,500	12,019,140	525,640 F
Contribution margin	$6,006,500	$6,139,665	$133,165 U

(1) ($14,700,000 budget ÷ 8,500 budgeted units) × 10,500 actual units
(2) ($2,164,750 budget ÷ 8,500 budgeted units) × 10,500 actual units
(3) ($1,790,000 budget ÷ 8,500 budgeted units) × 10,500 actual units
(4) ($1,950,000 budget ÷ 8,500 budgeted units) × 10,500 actual units
(5) ($3,825,000 budget ÷ 8,500 budgeted units) × 10,500 actual units
Note: All calculations rounded amounts to two decimal places.

Answer to Question 1B-ES07

A. SieCo is currently using a plant-wide overhead rate that is applied on the basis of direct labor costs. In general, a plant-wide manufacturing overhead rate is acceptable only if a similar relationship between overhead and direct labor exists in all departments or the company manufactures products that receive proportional services from each department.

In most cases, departmental overhead rates are preferable to plant-wide overhead rates because plant-wide overhead rates do not provide:

- A framework for reviewing overhead costs on a departmental basis, identifying departmental cost overruns, or taking corrective action to improve departmental cost control
- Sufficient information about product profitability, thus increasing the difficulties associated with management decision making

B. In order to improve the allocation of overhead costs in the Cutting and Grinding Departments, SieCo should:

- Establish separate overhead accounts and rates for each of these departments.
- Select an application basis for each of these departments that best reflects the relationship of the departmental activity to the overhead costs incurred (i.e., machine hours, direct labor hours, etc.).
- Identify, if possible, fixed and variable overhead costs and establish fixed and variable overhead rates for each department.

C. In order to accommodate the automation of the Drilling Department in its overhead accounting system, SieCo should:

- Establish separate overhead accounts and rates for the Drilling Department.
- Identify, if possible, fixed and variable overhead costs and establish fixed and variable overhead rates.
- Apply overhead costs to the Drilling Department on the basis of robot or machine hours.

D. Because SieCo uses a plant-wide overhead rate applied on the basis of direct labor costs, the elimination of direct labor in the Drilling Department through the introduction of robots may appear to reduce the overhead cost of the Drilling Department to zero. However, this change will not reduce fixed manufacturing expenses, such as depreciation, plant supervision, and the like. In reality, the use of robots is likely to increase fixed expenses because of increased depreciation expense. Under SieCo's current method of allocating overhead costs, these costs merely will be absorbed by the remaining departments.

E. Under competence, Altman has a responsibility to "provide decision support information and recommendations that are accurate, clear, concise and timely." It is possible that the decision was made with less than optimal decision support.

Under confidentiality, he must keep information confidential except when disclosure is authorized or legally required, and he must inform his subordinates of the same requirement.

No information is presented that indicates that this standard has been or may be violated.

Under integrity, Altman must "avoid actual or apparent conflicts of interest and advise all appropriate parties of any potential conflict." He must also "refrain from engaging in any activity that would prejudice his ability to carry out his duties ethically." He should also "refrain from engaging in any activity that would discredit the profession." There appears to be a conflict of interest here when Simpson's brother-in-law has won the contract.

Finally, under credibility, Altman must "communicate information both fairly and objectively." He should "disclose fully all relevant information that could reasonably be expected to influence an intended user's understanding of the reports and recommendations presented." The ownership by Simpson's brother-in-law should be disclosed to Hunter.

F. According to the *IMA Statement of Ethical Professional Practice*, Altman should first follow the established policies of the organization he is employed by in an effort to resolve the ethical dilemma. If such policies do not exist or are not effective, he should follow the steps as outlined in "Resolution of Ethical Conflict."

First, he should discuss the problems with his immediate superior. except when it appears the superior is involved. In this case, it is not clear if Hunter is involved. If this step is not successful in solving the dilemma, he should proceed up the chain of command, which in this case would appear to be the president and then the board of directors.

However, he should note that except where legally prescribed, communication of such internal problems should not be discussed with authorities or individuals not employed or engaged by the organization.

Spencer should clarify relevant ethical issues by confidential discussion with an objective advisor (e.g., an IMA ethics counselor) to obtain a better understanding of possible courses of action. He should consult his own attorney as to his legal obligations and rights concerning the ethical conflict.

Answer to Question 1B-ES08

A. Average investment in operating assets employed:

Balance end of current year	$12,600,000
Balance end of previous year*	12,000,000
Total	$24,600,000
Average operating assets employed†	$12,300,000

*$12,600,000 ÷ 1.05
†$24,600,000 ÷ 2

ROI = Income from operations ÷ Average operating assets employed
= $2,460,000 ÷ $12,300,000
= .20 or 20%

Residual Income:

Income from operations	$2,460,000
Minimum return on assets employed*	1,845,000
Residual income	$615,000

*$12,300,000 × .15

B. Yes, Presser's management probably would have accepted the investment if residual income were used. The investment opportunity would have lowered Presser's ROI because the expected return (18%) was lower than the division's historical returns as well as its actual ROI (20%) for the year just ended. Management rejected the investment because bonuses are based in part on the performance measure of ROI. If residual income was used as a performance measure (and as a basis for bonuses), management would accept any and all investments that would increase residual, including the investment opportunity rejected in the year just ended.

C. Presser must control all items related to profit (revenues and expenses) and investment if it is to be evaluated fairly as an investment center by either the ROI or residual income performance measures. Presser must control all elements of the business except the cost of invested capital, that being controlled by Lawton Industries.

Part 1 Section C Answers

Answer to Question 1C-ES01

Answer A:

The traditional cost system, developed to value inventory, distorts product cost information because the cost system:

- Was designed to value inventory in the aggregate and not relate to product cost information.
- Uses a common departmental or factory-wide measure of activity, such as direct labor hours or dollars (now a small portion of overall production costs) to distribute manufacturing overhead to products.
- Deemphasizes long-term product analysis (when fixed costs become variable costs).
- Causes managers, who are aware of distortions in the traditional system, to make intuitive, imprecise adjustments to the traditional cost information without understanding the complete impact.

Answer B:

1. The benefits that management can expect from activity-based costing include:

   - It leads to a more competitive position by evaluating cost drivers (e.g., costs associated with the complexity of the transaction rather that the production volume).

- It streamlines production processes by reducing non-value-adding activities (e.g., reduced setup times, optimal plant layout, and improved quality).
- It provides management with a more thorough understanding of product costs and product profitability for strategies and pricing decisions.

2. The steps that a company, using a traditional cost system, would take to implement activity-based costing include these:

- Evaluation of the existing system to assess how well the system supports the objective of an activity-based cost system
- Identification of the activities for which cost information is needed with differentiation between value-adding and non-value-adding activities.

Answer to Question 1C-ES02

Answer A:

Under direct costing, fixed manufacturing costs are expensed rather than being added to the inventoriable cost of each unit. Thus, it is not necessary to determine the allocation of fixed costs to individual units.

Answer B:

At first glance, job order costing appears to make more sense, as each pair of jeans is literally unique, given that the buyer's name is stitched on the back pocket. However, in reality, process costing should be used, because jeans will be produced continually and for cost purposes, will be same for each pair.

Answer to Question 1C-ES03

A. 1. Relative sales value method at split-off:

Product	Monthly Output	Sales Price	Split-Off Value	% of Sales	Allocated Costs
Studs	75,000	$8	$600,000	46.15%	$461,539
Decorative Pieces	5,000	60	300,000	23.08%	230,769
Posts	20,000	20	400,000	30.77%	307,692
Totals			**$1,300,000**	**100%**	**$1,000,000**

2. Physical output (volume) method at split-off:

Product	Monthly Output	% of Output	Allocated Costs
Studs	75,000	75.00%	$ 750,000
Decorative pieces	5,000	5.00%	50,000
Posts	20,000	20.00%	200,000
Totals	**100,000**	**100.00%**	**$1,000,000**

3. Estimated net realizable value method:

Product	Monthly Output	Sales Price	Split-Off Value	% of Sales	Allocated Costs
Studs	75,000	$ 8	$600,000	46.15%	$461,539
Decorative Pieces	4,500[1]	100	350,000[2]	23.08%	230,769
Posts	20,000	20	400,000	30.77%	307,692
Totals			**$1,300,000**	**100%**	**$1,000,000**

(1) 5,000 monthly units of output − 10% normal spoilage = 4,500 good units
(2) 4,500 good units × $100 = $450,000 − further processing costs of $100,000 = $350,000

B. Presented next is an analysis for Sonimad Sawmill comparing the processing of decorative pieces further versus selling the rough-cut product immediately at split-off. Based on this analysis, it is recommended that Sonimad further process the decorative pieces as this action results in an additional contribution of $50,000.

	Units	Dollars
Monthly unit output	5,000	
Less: Further normal processing shrinkage	500	
Units available for sale	4,500	
Final sales value (4,500 units × $100 each)		$450,000
Less: Sales value at split-off		300,000
Differential revenue		$150,000
Less: Further processing costs		100,000
Additional contribution from further processing		$50,000

Answer to Question 1C-ES04

Answer A:

1. The total budgeted costs for the Manufacturing Department at Alyssa Manufacturing are presented next.

Direct material
    Tuff Stuff ($5.00/unit × 20,000 units) $100,000
    Ruff Stuff ($3.00/unit × 20,000 units)   60,000
Total direct material $160,000
Direct labor   800,000
Overhead
    Indirect labor $ 24,000
    Fringe benefits   5,000
    Indirect material   31,000
    Power   180,000
    Setup   75,000
    Quality assurance   10,000
    Other utilities   10,000
    Depreciation   15,000
Total overhead   350,000
Total budgeted cost $1,310,000

A. 2&3. The unit standard costs of Tuff Stuff and Ruff Stuff, with overhead allocated based on direct labor hours, are calculated as shown.

Tuff Stuff

Direct material	$5.00
Direct labor ($8.00/hour × 2 hours)*	16.00
Overhead ($3.50hour × 2 hours)*	7.00
Tuff Stuff unit standard cost	$28.00

Ruff Stuff

Direct material	$3.00
Direct labor ($8.00/hour × 3 hours)*	24.00
Overhead ($3.50/hour × 3 hours)*	10.50
Ruff Stuff unit standard cost	$37.50

*Budgeted direct labor hours

Tuff Stuff (20,000 units × 2 hours)	40,000
Ruff Stuff (20,000 units × 3 hours)	60,000
Total budgeted direct labor hours	100,000

Direct labor rate: $800,000 ÷ 100,000 hours = $8.00/hour

Overhead rate: $350,000 ÷ 100,000 hours = $3.50/hour

Answer B:

B. 1&2. The total budgeted cost of the Fabricating and Assembly Departments, after separation of overhead into the activity pools, is calculated as shown.

	Total	Fabricating Percent	Fabricating Dollars	Assembly Percent	Assembly Dollars
Direct material	$160,000	100%	$160,000		
Direct labor	800,000	75%	600,000	25%	$200,000
Overhead					
Indirect labor	24,000	75%	18,000	25%	6,000
Fringe benefits	5,000	80%	4,000	20%	1,000
Indirect material	31,000		20,000		11,000
Power	180,000		160,000		20,000
Setup	75,000		5,000		70,000
Quality assurance	10,000	80%	8,000	20%	2,000
Other utilities	10,000	50%	5,000	50%	5,000
Depreciation	15,000	80%	12,000	20%	3,000
Total overhead	350,000		232,000		118,000
Total budget	$1,310,000		$992,000		$318,000

Answer C:

C. 1&2. The unit standard costs of the products using activity-based costing are calculated next.

Fabricating Department

Total cost	$992,000
Less: Direct material	160,000
Less: Direct labor	600,000
Pool overhead cost for allocation	$232,000
Hours: Tuff Stuff (4.4 hours $\times$ 20,000 units)	88,000
Ruff Stuff (6.0 hours $\times$ 20,000 units)	120,000
Total machine hours	208,000

Overhead cost/machine hour: $232,000 \div 208,000 = \$1.1154$/hour

Fabrication cost per unit: Tuff Stuff $\$1.1154 \times 4.4$ hours $= \$4.91$ per unit
Ruff Stuff $\$1.1154 \times 6.0$ hours $= \$6.69$ per unit

Assembly Department

Total cost $-$ Direct labor $=$ Pool overhead cost for allocation
$\$318,000 - \$200,000 = \$118,000$

Setups $= 1,000$ (Tuff Stuff) $+ 272$ (Ruff Stuff) $= 1,272$
Cost per setup: $\$118,000 \div 1,272 = \$92.77$ per setup

Setup cost per unit:

Tuff Stuff: $(\$92.77 \times 1,000) \div 20,000$ units $= \$4.64$ per unit
Ruff Stuff: $(\$92.77 \times 272) \div 20,000$ units $= \$1.26$ per unit

Tuff Stuff Standard Activity-Based Cost

Direct material	$ 5.00
Direct labor	16.00
Fabrication Department overhead allocation	4.91
Assembly Department overhead allocation	4.64
Total cost	$30.55

Ruff Stuff Standard Activity-Based Cost

Direct material	$ 3.00
Direct labor	24.00
Fabrication Department overhead allocation	4.91
Assembly Department overhead allocation	6.69
Total cost	$34.95

Answer D:

When compared to the old standard cost ($37. 50), the new activity-based standard cost for Ruff Stuff ($34. 95) should lead the company to decide to lower the price for Ruff Stuff in order to be more competitive in the market and continue production of the product. Using ABC for allocating overhead costs generally leads to a more accurate estimate of the costs incurred to produce a product, and Alyssa should be able to make better informed decisions regarding pricing and production.

Part 1 Section D Answers

Answer to Question 1D-ES01

	Weaknesses	Recommendations
1.	An authorization document that describes the item to be acquired, indicates the benefits to be derived, and estimates its cost is not prepared and reviewed with management.	To obtain approval for the purchase of machinery and equipment, an appropriations request should be prepared, describing the item, indicating why it is needed, and estimating its expected costs and benefits. The document also could include the item's accounting classification, expected useful life, depreciation method and rate, and name the approving company executives.
2.	There is no control over authorized acquisitions. The purchase requisitions and purchase orders for fixed assets are interspersed with other requisitions and purchase orders and handled through normal purchasing procedures.	Authorized acquisitions should be processed using special procedures and purchase orders. These purchase orders should be subjected to numerical control. Copies of purchase orders should be distributed to all appropriate departments so that the acquisition can be monitored.
3.	Plant engineering does not appear to be inspecting machinery and equipment upon receipt.	Purchases of machinery and equipment should be subject to normal receiving inspection routines. In the case of machinery and equipment, plant engineering is usually responsible for reviewing the receipt to make certain the correct item was delivered and that it was not damaged in transit. All new machinery and equipment would be assigned a control number and tagged at the time of receipt.
4.	The lapsing schedules are not reconciled periodically to general ledger control accounts to verify agreement.	At least once each year, machinery and equipment lapsing schedules, which provide information on asset cost and accumulated depreciation, should be reconciled to general ledger control accounts. Furthermore, an actual physical inventory of existing fixed assets should be taken periodically and reconciled to the lapsing schedules and general ledger control account to assure accuracy.
5.	Machinery and equipment accounting policies, including depreciation, have not been updated to make certain that the most desirable methods are being used.	Machinery and equipment accounting procedures, including depreciation, must be updated periodically to reflect actual experience, and changes in accounting pronouncements and income tax legislation.

Answer to Question 1D-ES02

Answer A:

At least three weaknesses in the company's internal control system include:

1. The Limited Expenditure Account (LEA) not being subject to normal accounting controls.
2. The lack of adequate supporting documentation for personal and other expenditures. There is an improper or inadequate identification of the use of these resources, which makes proper accounting classification difficult or impossible. This increases the possibility of illegal use and material misstatements.
3. The Internal Audit Department not reporting its findings in connection with the payment practices and the LEA.

Answer B:

At least three illegal or improper practices uncovered at the company include:

1. Funds raised for political purposes were diverted to other uses. This misappropriation of funds included Public Relations Department resources being used for personal projects and the authorizing of payments to vendors for personal services and goods.
2. Management fraud. Senior management advised the Internal Audit Department to conceal findings; this act is detrimental to the company. There also appears to be a senior management conspiracy.
3. The external auditors not reporting these practices in their recommendations for improved internal control procedures.

Answer C:

At least four important steps that the company should take, both procedurally and organizationally, to correct the problems that were uncovered in order to prevent a similar situation in the future include:

1. Terminating the employment of the chief executive officer, president, vice president-public relations, as well as the controller and director of the Internal Audit Department.
2. Strengthening the company's internal controls, including:

   - The establishment of a company policy that all payments and reimbursements must be supported by appropriate documentation and, also, approved by at least one higher level of authority.
   - Establishing dollar limits that can be approved at each level of authority.

3. Issuing a strong formal company-wide code of ethics.
4. Restructuring the organization so that the Internal Audit Department reports to the audit committee of the board of directors.

Answer to Question 1D-ES03

Answer A:

The seven types of internal audits are financial, operational, performance, information systems, contract, compliance, and special investigation (e.g., fraud). The two most common types of internal audits are operational audits and compliance audits.

An operational audit is a comprehensive review of the varied functions within an enterprise to appraise the efficiency and economy of operations and the effectiveness with which those functions achieve their objective. An example would be an audit to assess productivity. Other examples could include an evaluation of processes to reduce rework, or reduce the time required to process paperwork or goods.

A compliance audit is the review of both financial and operating controls to see how they conform to established laws, standards, regulations, and procedures. An environmental audit would be an example of a compliance audit. Other examples of compliance audits could include the review of controls over industrial wastes or the review of procedures ensuring that proper disclosure is made regarding hazardous materials on site.

Answer B:

1. A compliance audit would best fit the requirements of the president of Brawn.
2. The objective of this compliance audit is to assure the president that the manufacturing facility has appropriate policies and procedures in place for obtaining the needed permits, has obtained all the required permits in accordance with the law, and that environmental and safety issues are being properly addressed.
3. The assignment specifically is to address the proper use of permits, compliance with safety regulations, and compliance with environmental standards. These issues can be properly addressed only by conducting a compliance audit. Although financial and operational areas might be involved, they would be secondary to the compliance issues. For example, a financial impact could result from the evaluation of compliance with safety regulations. The findings might result in additional expenditures for safety precautions or a reduction in the company's risk of being fined for lack of compliance.

Answer C:

To mitigate the president's concern, these activities and procedures could be implemented.

- Set the tone at the top. The president should communicate to all employees that the company expects appropriate business practices on the part of all employees in all divisions.
- Ensure that all employees have the necessary information to perform their duties. Keep the lines of communication open. For example, involve senior mangers from the manufacturing facility in monthly operational meetings for the whole company.

- Conduct regularly scheduled audits of compliance with applicable laws, regulations, and standards.
- Periodically review and update policies, rules, and procedures to ensure that internal controls prevent or help to detect material risks. Make sure all employees have access to the relevant policies and procedures. For example, post the policies and procedures on the company's intranet.

Answer to Question 1D-ES04

Answer A:

A.1. Crosby, the owner is taking a hands-off approach. He is hardly around to check on the business.

A.2. The two managers, Smith and Fletcher, have too much control without any independent checks on them.

A.3. Hiring policies to hire the right kind of employees are lacking; Crosby does not screen the job applicants; he did not check any background references for Smith and Fletcher.

A.4. Proper internal controls such as segregation of duties, authorizations, independent checks are not in place. Fletcher places purchase orders, and also receives materials. Crosby is in charge of collecting the payments, maintaining records, reconciling the bank accounts, preparing and signing checks, and approving payments. Lack of basic internal controls seems to have opened the door for employees to commit fraud.

Answer B:

Proper internal controls must be in place so that opportunities to commit, and/or conceal fraud are eliminated. In this case, the internal controls needed are: (1) segregation of duties; (2) system of authorizations; (3) independent checks; and (4) proper documentation. No one department or individual should handle all aspects of a transaction from beginning to end. No one person should perform more than one function recording transactions, and reconciling bank accounts (as done by Crosby in this case). In a similar manner, Fletcher should not authorize purchases, receive inventory, and issue materials for production. The company also should separate the duties of preparing and signing checks, especially because the same person has the authority to approve payment.

There is a failure to enforce authorization controls. Crosby should authorize purchases and approve payments. He might consider hiring another person so that the two tasks, record keeping and bank reconciliation, can be separated.

In addition to that, the company must have better hiring policies in place, may require vacations, conduct internal audits, and have good oversight over employees.

Require vacations, conduct internal audits, owner/board oversight.

Answer C:

Even the best internal controls do not guarantee that fraud will be eliminated. These controls provide reasonable, not absolute, assurance against fraud. Internal controls are not fraud-proof, internal controls never provide absolute insurance that fraud will be prevented. Effectiveness depends on competency and dependability of people enforcing the controls.

Answer to Question 1D-ES05

Answer A:

A.1. Buying raw materials from other countries will expose the company to market risk, including the exposure to potential loss that would result from changes in market prices or rates. Examples include foreign exchange valuation, interest rate changes, and the volatility of crude oil prices. If a company has a contract to purchase products in a foreign currency, the cost of those products may increase drastically due to depreciation of the home currency. Foreign products may increase in price, or become unavailable, due to political events, such as expropriation or inflation.

A.2. Credit risk is the economic lost suffered due to the default of a borrower or counterparty. Default can be legal bankruptcy or failure to fulfill contractual obligations in a timely manner, due to inability or unwillingness. Credit risk includes loan default, failure to pay accounts receivable, or the inability of a business partner to fulfill agreed-on actions or payments. These conditions may be worsened when dealing with international counterparties, due to differences in legal systems, accounting systems, and credit reporting services.

A.3. International companies may have additional operational risk, defined as the risk of direct or indirect loss resulting from inadequate or failed internal processes, people, and systems or from external events. An example is failure to follow quality standards resulting in the shipment of deficient products, customer dissatisfaction, and reputation damage. Other examples include failure to properly monitor financial transactions, the hacking of computer files, and failure to follow loan approval controls.

Answer B:

B.1. Without a thorough understanding of your business, it is not possible to (1) identify the risks associated with daily operations, (2) understand the external risks associated with elements such as competitors or changes in technology, or (3) to assign individual accountability for risk management. If you do not understand your business position, decisions can be made that would undermine that position. For example, if your customers buy your service or good because of its quality and they don't care about price, you need to know this to mitigate the risk of damaging this relationship.

B.2. A system of checks and balances (1) prevents any individual or group from gaining the power to take unplanned risks on behalf of an organization, and

(2) safeguards assets, and (3) prevents fraudulent activities. Examples include the segregation of duties to safeguard financial transactions and the use of passwords to limit access to records and programs.

B.3. Procedures that set limits and set standards can (1) prevent inappropriate behavior, and (2) tell a business when to stop. Examples might include standards for sales practices and product disclosures, standards for hiring practices regarding background checks on prospective employees, or termination policies for violation of company policy.

Answer C:

Management should be involved with:

- Setting the tone from the top and building awareness through demonstration of senior management commitment
- Establishing the principles that will guide the company's risk culture and values
- Facilitating open communication for discussing risk issues, escalating exposures, and sharing lessons learned and best practices
- Providing training and development programs
- Selecting appropriate performance measures to promote desired behavior
- Setting compensation policies that reward desired behavior

Answer D:

Management should be involved with:

- Section 404 of the Sarbanes-Oxley Act of 2002 (SOX 404) requires management to "take ownership" of internal controls over financial reporting by assessing and publicly reporting on their effectiveness.
- Each annual report of an issuer (of public securities) will contain an "internal control report." This report contains a statement that management is responsible for maintaining adequate internal controls. The report also contains an assessment of the effectiveness of the internal control structure.
- Each issuer is required to disclose the content of its code of ethics for senior financial officers.
- The auditor's report will evaluate management's assessment of the internal controls and issue an opinion as to the effectiveness of the internal controls.

Part 1 Section E Answers

Answer to Question 1E-ES01

Answer A:

The overarching principles identified in the *IMA Statement of Ethical Professional Practice* that should guide the work of a management accountant are honesty, fairness, objectivity, and responsibility.

If the controller were to manipulate the revenue in accordance with the implied wishes of the chief executive officer, these standards would be violated:

Competence

- Perform professional duties in accordance with relevant laws, regulations, and technical standards.

Integrity

- Mitigate actual conflicts of interest, regularly communicate with business associates to avoid apparent conflicts of interest. Advise all parties of potential conflicts.
- Refrain from engaging in any conduct that would prejudice carrying out duties ethically.
- Abstain from engaging in or supporting any activity that might discredit the profession.

Credibility

- Communicate information fairly and objectively.
- Disclose all relevant information that could reasonably be expected to influence an intended user's understanding of the reports, analyses, or recommendations.
- Disclose delays or deficiencies in information, timeliness, processing, or internal controls in conformance with organization policy and/or applicable law.

To resolve this situation, the controller should follow Sterling's policy for resolving ethical issues. If there is no policy or the policy does not resolve the situation, the controller should consider:

- Discussing the issue with the immediate supervisor unless the supervisor is involved, in which case the issue should be presented to the next higher level. If the CEO is the controller's immediate supervisor, the acceptable reviewing authority may be the audit committee or the board of directors. Communication with those outside the organization is not appropriate unless there is a clear violation of the law.
- Having a confidential discussion of the issues with an IMA ethics counselor or other impartial advisor and may consult an attorney to discuss legal obligations and rights concerning the ethical conflict.

Answer to Question 1E-ES02

Answer A:

The standards from the *IMA Statement of Ethical Professional Practice* that specifically relate to Alex Raminov and the situation at Carroll Mining and Manufacturing are these:

Competence

- Perform professional duties in accordance with relevant laws, regulations, and technical standards. It appears that CMMC is not in compliance with the relevant laws and regulations regarding the dumping of toxic materials; at a minimum, Raminov has an obligation to report this situation to higher authorities in the company.

Confidentially

- Keep information confidential except when disclosure is authorized or legally required. This standard may or may not relate to the CMMC situation, depending on the requirements of the environmental regulations in effect in the jurisdiction where CMMC is operating. Raminov may be required by law to disclose the information.

Integrity

- Refrain from engaging in any conduct that would prejudice carrying out duties ethically.
- Abstain from engaging in or supporting any activity that might discredit the profession.
- If Raminov does not report the apparent illegal dumping to those in authority at CMMC, his behavior would not be considered ethical under these standards, and his lack of action would discredit the profession.

Credibility

- Communicate information fairly and objectively.
- Disclose all relevant information that could reasonably be expected to influence an intended user's understanding of the reports, analyses, or recommendations.
- Disclose delays or deficiencies in information, timeliness, processing, or internal controls in conformance with organization policy and/or applicable law.
- All of these standards make it clear that Raminov has an obligation to act objectively in this matter and report the situation to those in authority at CMMC. The risks and exposures of illegal dumping should be disclosed in the financial reports that Raminov is preparing.

Answer B:

Initially, Raminov should follow CMMC's policy regarding the resolution of an ethical conflict. If there is no policy or the policy does not resolve the issue, he should consider the courses of action recommended in the *IMA Statement of Ethical Professional Practice*.

Since Raminov's immediate supervisor appears to be involved in the dumping situation, he should submit the issue to the next higher level. If the situation is not satisfactorily resolved, Raminov should approach successive levels of authority (e.g., chief financial officer, audit committee, board of directors). He can also contact an IMA ethics counselor or other impartial advisor to discuss possible courses of action.

Raminov should consult an attorney regarding his legal obligations and rights in this ethical conflict.

Answer C:

It is not considered appropriate for Raminov to inform authorities or individuals not employed or engaged by CMMC unless he believes there is a clear violation of the law. In discussions with his attorney, Raminov should clarify his obligations under the law. If CMMC does not take action after Raminov has informed the appropriate in-house authorities, he may be obligated to inform the regulatory agency involved. He should not under any circumstances anonymously release this information to the local newspaper.

Answer to Question 1E-ES03

Answer A:

The standards from the *IMA Statement of Ethical Professional Practice* that specifically relate to Amy Kimbell and the situation at Hi-Quality Productions are these:

Competence

- Provide decision support information and recommendations that are accurate, clear, concise, and timely.
- Recognize and communicate professional limitations or other constraints that would preclude responsible judgment or successful performance of an activity.
- Amy Kimbell has an ethical conflict because she has been told to keep quiet about errors she has discovered in the original budgeting process. The incorrect data used make the decision support data provided suspect and the decisions made based on that data risky.

Integrity

- Refrain from engaging in any conduct that would prejudice carrying out duties ethically.
- Abstain from engaging in or supporting any activity that might discredit the profession.
- Amy Kimball has an ethical conflict as she has an obligation to disclose the errors in the budgets presented but has been told not to. If she does not correct the situation, she will not be carrying out her duties ethically and therefore will discredit her profession.

Credibility

- Communicate information fairly and objectively.
- Disclose all relevant information could reasonably be expected to influence an intended user's understanding of the reports, analyses, or recommendations.
- It is clear that the budget committee has not been objective in its presentation of information and therefore has distorted the decisions based on that information. Kimbell should correct the information so that future expectations are realistic.

Answer B:

Initially, Kimbell should follow Hi-Quality Productions' policy regarding the resolution of an ethical conflict. If there is no policy or the policy does not resolve the issue, she should consider the courses of action recommended in the *IMA Statement of Ethical Professional Practice*.

Kimbell should present her findings to her immediate supervisor. If her immediate supervisor is involved in the incorrect budgeting situation or if the supervisor takes no action, she should submit the issue to the next higher level. If the situation is not satisfactorily resolved, Kimbell should approach successive levels of authority (e.g., chief financial officer, audit committee, board of directors). She can also contact an IMA ethics counselor or other impartial advisor to discuss possible courses of action. Kimbell should consult an attorney regarding her legal obligations and rights in this ethical conflict.

Answer to Question 1E-ES04

Answer A:

The standards from the *IMA Statement of Ethical Professional Practice* that specifically relate to John Morgan and the situation at Pro-Kleen are these:

Competence

- Perform professional duties in accordance with relevant laws, regulations, and technical standards.

Integrity

- Refrain from engaging in any conduct that would prejudice carrying out duties ethically.
- Abstain from engaging in or supporting any activity that might discredit the profession.

Credibility

- Communicate information fairly and objectively.
- Disclose all relevant information that could reasonably be expected to influence an intended user's understanding of the reports, analyses, or recommendations.

Answer B:

Initially, Morgan should follow Pro-Kleen's policy regarding the resolution of an ethical conflict. If there is no policy or the policy does not resolve the issue, he should consider the courses of action recommended in the *IMA Statement of Ethical Professional Practice*.

Since Morgan's immediate supervisor appears to be involved in the situation, he should submit the issue to the next higher level. If the situation is not satisfactorily resolved, Morgan should approach successive levels of authority (e.g., chief financial officer, audit committee, board of directors). He can also contact an IMA ethics counselor or other impartial advisor to discuss possible courses of action. Morgan should consult an attorney regarding his legal obligations and rights in this ethical conflict.

Answer to Question 1E-ES05

Answer A:

Management accountants should not condone the commission of unethical acts by others within their organizations. It is stated that the low-quality, low-size estimates sought by Jefferson were unethical business practices. Therefore, Charlene White should take action to resolve this situation. Specific standards that relate to this situation include these:

Competence

- Perform professional duties in accordance with relevant laws, regulations, and technical standards.

Integrity

- Mitigate actual conflicts of interest, regularly communicate with business associates to avoid apparent conflicts of interest. Advise all parties of any potential conflicts.
- Refrain from engaging in or supporting any activity that might discredit the profession.

Credibility

- Communicate information fairly and objectively.
- Disclose fully all relevant information that could reasonably be expected to influence an intended user's understanding of the reports, analyses, or recommendations.

Answer B:

Initially, White should follow UFP's policy regarding the resolution of an ethical conflict. If there is no policy or the policy does not resolve the issue, she should consider the courses of action recommended in the *IMA Statement of Ethical Professional Practice*.

Since White's immediate supervisor appears to be involved in the situation, she should submit the issue to the next higher level. If the situation is not satisfactorily resolved, White should approach successive levels of authority (e.g., corporate chief financial officer, audit committee, board of directors). She can also contact an IMA ethics counselor or other impartial advisor to discuss possible courses of action. White should consult an attorney regarding her legal obligations and rights in this ethical conflict.

Answer C:

The performance evaluation system directly affected performance at the Allegheny Division. The employees were paid bonuses on the basis of profitability but had no control over revenue because of the transfer pricing that was negotiated elsewhere. The division should be evaluated as a cost center only. The evaluation criteria should include quality standards that must be met in order to preclude the behavior exhibited.

Answer to Question 1E-ES06

Answer A:

Under *competence*, Spencer has a responsibility to "maintain an appropriate level of professional competence." He must perform his duties in accordance with relevant laws, regulations and technical standards (e.g., FASB No. 5, *Accounting for Contingencies*).

Under *confidentiality*, he must keep information confidential except when disclosure is authorized or legally required and inform his subordinates of the same requirement. He must refrain from using or appearing to use confidential information for unethical or illegal advantage personally.

Under *integrity*, Spencer must "avoid actual or apparent conflicts of interest and advise all appropriate parties of any potential conflict." He must also "refrain from engaging in any activity that would prejudice his ability to carry out his duties ethically." He should also "refrain from engaging in any activity that would discredit the profession."

Finally, under *credibility*, Spencer must "communicate information both fairly and objectively." He should "disclose fully all relevant information that could reasonably be expected to influence an intended user's understanding of the reports and recommendations presented."

Answer B:

According to *IMA Statement of Ethical Professional Practice* Spencer should first follow the established policies of the organization he is employed by in an effort to resolve the ethical dilemma. If such policies do not exist or are not effective, he should follow the steps as outlined in "Resolution of Ethical Conflict."

First, he should discuss the problems with his immediate superior except when it appears the superior is involved. Since his superior is the chief financial officer, who gave him the instructions to ignore the situation and not consider the financial ramifications of nondisclosure, he should proceed to the next higher level, which is the chief executive officer of GRQ Company. If this step is not successful in solving the dilemma, he should proceed up the chain of command, which in this case would appear to be the board of directors of GRQ.

However, he should note that except where legally prescribed, communication of such internal problems should not be discussed with authorities or individuals not employed or engaged by the organization.

Spencer should clarify relevant ethical issues by confidential discussion with an objective advisor (e.g., IMA ethics counselor) to obtain a better understanding of possible courses of action. He should consult his own attorney as to his legal obligations and rights concerning the ethical conflict.

According to the provisions of the Sarbanes-Oxley Act of 2002 (SOX), employees are to be provided with a means to report such matters to top management of the organization. When deemed appropriate, they may report these matters to the appropriate external parties (e.g., the Securities and Exchange Commission, Justice Department, Environmental Protection Agency, etc.) as the matter dictates. Candidates should be given some credit for being aware of this provision made by SOX.

Answer to Question 1E-ES07

Answer A:

According to the *IMA Statement of Ethical Professional Practice*, Wilson in this situation has a responsibility to demonstrate:

- Competence by preparing complete and clear reports and recommendations after appropriate analyses of relevant and reliable information.
- Confidentiality by refraining from disclosing confidential information acquired in the course of their work except when authorized, unless legally obligated to do so.
- Integrity by communicating unfavorable as well as favorable information and professional judgments or opinions as well as refraining from engaging in or supporting any activity that would discredit the profession.
- Objectivity by communicating information fairly and objectively and disclose fully all relevant information that could reasonably be expected to influence an intended user's understanding of the reports, comments, and recommendations presented.

Answer B:

Wilson should first discuss this matter with his superior, the controller, unless his superior is involved; in that case, he should go to the next managerial level. If a satisfactory solution cannot be reached with his superior, Wilson should move up the chain of command. Unless his superior is involved, Wilson should inform his superior when he goes to higher levels of management. If his superior is the chief executive officer, Wilson should go to an acceptable reviewing authority, such as the audit committee, executive committee, board of directors. Wilson can clarify ethical issues by having a confidential discussion with an objective advisor (e.g., an IMA ethics counselor) to determine a possible course of action. He may also consult with his own attorney. If Wilson is unable to resolve the ethical dilemma, there may be no other course than to resign and submit an informative memorandum to an appropriate representative of the organization.

Answers to Section Practice Questions

Section A: Planning, Budgeting, and Forecasting Answers and Explanations

Question 1A4-CQ02

Topic: Annual Profit Plan and Supporting Schedules

Troughton Company manufactures radio-controlled toy dogs. Summary budget financial data for Troughton for the current year are shown next.

Sales (5,000 units at $150 each)	$750,000
Variable manufacturing cost	400,000
Fixed manufacturing cost	100,000
Variable selling and administrative cost	80,000
Fixed selling and administrative cost	150,000

Troughton uses an absorption costing system with overhead applied based on the number of units produced, with a denominator level of activity of 5,000 units. Underapplied or overapplied manufacturing overhead is written off to cost of goods sold in the year incurred.

The $20,000 budgeted operating income from producing and selling 5,000 toy dogs planned for this year is of concern to Trudy George, Troughton's president. She believes she could increase operating income to $50,000 (her bonus threshold) if Troughton produces more units than it sells, thus building up the finished goods inventory.

How much of an increase in the number of units in the finished goods inventory would be needed to generate the $50,000 budgeted operating income?

a. 556 units

b. 600 units

c. 1,500 units

d. 7,500 units

Explanation: The correct answer is: **a.** 1,500 units.

Increasing production over sales allows the company to bury fixed overhead costs in the ending inventory, resulting in an increase in net income. The increase in net income from the extra production can be calculated as shown:

Increase in Net Income = (Fixed Overhead Rate) (Excess of Production over Sales)
= $30,000

Fixed Overhead Rate = (Fixed Manufacturing Costs) /
(Denominator Activity Level)

Fixed Overhead Rate = $100,000 / 5,000 Units = $20 per Unit

Therefore, the increase in production over sales = $30,000 / $20 per unit = 1,500 units.

Question 1A4-CQ04

Topic: Annual Profit Plan and Supporting Schedules

Hannon Retailing Company prices its products by adding 30% to its cost. Hannon anticipates sales of $715,000 in July, $728,000 in August, and $624,000 in September. Hannon's policy is to have on hand enough inventory at the end of the month to cover 25% of the next month's sales. What will be the cost of the inventory that Hannon should budget for purchase in August?

a. $509,600

b. $540,000

c. $560,000

d. $680,000

Explanation: The correct answer is: **b.** $540,000.

Sales = 1.3 (Cost of Sales), which can also be stated as:

Cost of Sales = (Sales) / 1.3

Expected Ending Inventory for Each Month = 0.25 (Next Month's Sales)

The purchases in a given month can be computed as shown:

Inventory Purchased for a Month = (Sales for the Month / 1.3)
+ (Expected Ending Inventory / 1.3)
− (Expected Beginning Inventory / 1.3)

Inventory Purchased for August = [($728,000) / 1.3] + [(0.25) ($624,000) / 1.3]
− [(0.25) ($728,000) / 1.3]

Inventory Purchased for August = $560,000 + $120,000 − $140,000 = $540,000

Question 1A4-CQ06

Topic: Annual Profit Plan and Supporting Schedules

Tyler Company produces one product and budgeted 220,000 units for the month of August with these budgeted manufacturing costs:

	Total Costs	Cost per Unit
Variable costs	$1,408,000	$6.40
Batch setup cost	880,000	4.00
Fixed costs	1,210,000	5.50
Total	$3,498,000	$15.90

The variable cost per unit and the total fixed costs are unchanged within a production range of 200,000 to 300,000 units per month. The total for the batch setup cost in any month depends on the number of production batches that Tyler runs. A normal batch consists of 50,000 units unless production requires less volume. In the prior year, Tyler experienced a mixture of monthly batch sizes of 42,000 units, 45,000 units, and 50,000 units. Tyler consistently plans production each month in order to minimize the number of batches. For the month of September, Tyler plans to manufacture 260,000 units. What will be Tyler's total budgeted production costs for September?

a. $3,754,000

b. $3,930,000

c. $3,974,000

d. $4,134,000

Explanation: The correct answer is: **b.** $3,930,000.

September Budgeted Production Costs = (Fixed Costs) + (Variable Costs) + (Batch Setup Costs)

Variable Costs = (260,000 Units) ($6.40 per Unit) = $1,664,000

Batch setup costs: 260,000 units require a minimum of 6 batches.

In August, 220,000 units were produced in 5 batches for a total of $880,000. The cost per batch was $880,000 / 5 = $176,000.

6 Batches at $176,000 per Batch = $1,056,000

September Budgeted Production Costs = ($1,210,000) + ($1,664,000) + ($1,056,000) = $3,930,000

Question 1A4-CQ08

Topic: Annual Profit Plan and Supporting Schedules

Savior Corporation assembles backup tape drive systems for home microcomputers. For the first quarter, the budget for sales is 67,500 units. Savior will finish the fourth quarter of last year with an inventory of 3,500 units, of which 200 are obsolete. The target ending inventory is 10 days of sales (based on 90 days in a quarter). What is the budgeted production for the first quarter?

a. 75,000

b. 71,700

c. 71,500

d. 64,350

Explanation: The correct answer is: **b.** 71,700.

The expected beginning inventory is calculated as shown:

$$\text{Expected Beginning Inventory} = (3,500 \text{ Units} - 200 \text{ Obsolete Units})$$
$$= 3,300 \text{ Units}$$

The expected ending inventory is 10 days' sales, which is calculated as shown:

$$\text{Expected Ending Inventory} = [(67,500 \text{ Units}) / 90] (10) = 7,500 \text{ Units}$$

Therefore, budgeted production $= 67,500$ Units $+ 7,500$ Units $- 3,300$ Units
$$= 71,700 \text{ Units}.$$

Question 1A4-CQ09

Topic: Annual Profit Plan and Supporting Schedules

Streeter Company produces plastic microwave turntables. Sales for the next year are expected to be 65,000 units in the first quarter, 72,000 units in the second quarter, 84,000 units in the third quarter, and 66,000 units in the fourth quarter.

Streeter usually maintains a finished goods inventory at the end of each quarter equal to one half of the units expected to be sold in the next quarter. However, due to a work stoppage, the finished goods inventory at the end of the first quarter is 8,000 units less than it should be.

How many units should Streeter produce in the second quarter?

a. 75,000 units

b. 78,000 units

c. 80,000 units

d. 86,000 units

Explanation: The correct answer is: **d.** 86,000 units.

Budgeted production is calculated as shown:

Budgeted Production = (Expected Sales) + (Expected Ending Inventory)
$\qquad$ − (Expected Beginning Inventory)

The expected ending inventory for each quarter equals 50% of the next quarter's expected sales. Since the finished goods inventory at the end of the first quarter is 8,000 less than it should be, the budgeted production for the second quarter is calculated as shown:

Budgeted Production, Second Quarter = 72,000 Units + 0.5(84,000 Units)
$\qquad$ − [0.5(72,000 Units) − 8,000 Units]

Budgeted Production, Second Quarter = 72,000 Units + 42,000 Units
$\qquad$ − [36,000 Units − 8,000 Units]

Budgeted Production, Second Quarter = 114,000 Units − 28,000 Units
$\qquad$ = 86,000 Units

Question 1A4-CQ10

Topic: Annual Profit Plan and Supporting Schedules

Data regarding Rombus Company's budget are shown next.

Planned sales	4,000 units
Material cost	$2.50 per pound
Direct labor	3 hours per unit
Direct labor rate	$7 per hour
Finished goods beginning inventory	900 units
Finished goods ending inventory	600 units
Direct materials beginning inventory	4,300 units
Direct materials ending inventory	4,500 units
Materials used per unit	6 pounds

Rombus Company's production budget will show total units to be produced of:

a. 3,700.

b. 4,000.

c. 4,300.

d. 4,600.

Explanation: The correct answer is: **a.** 3,700.

Budgeted production is calculated as shown:

Budgeted Production = (Expected Sales) + (Expected Ending Inventory)
− (Expected Beginning Inventory)

Budgeted Production = 4,000 Units + 600 Units − 900 Units = 3,700 Units

Question 1A4-CQ11
Topic: Annual Profit Plan and Supporting Schedules

Krouse Company is in the process of developing its operating budget for the coming year. Given next are selected data regarding the company's two products, laminated putter heads and forged putter heads, sold through specialty golf shops.

	Putter Heads	
	Forged	**Laminated**
Raw materials		
Steel	2 pounds @ $5/pound	1 pound @ $5/pound
Copper	None	1 pound @ $15/pound
Direct labor	1/4 hour @ $20/hour	1 hour @ $22/hour
Expected sales	8,200 units	2,000 units
Selling price per unit	$30	$80
Ending inventory target	100 units	60 units
Beginning inventory	300 units	60 units
Beginning inventory (cost)	$5,250	$3,120

Manufacturing overhead is applied to units produced on the basis of direct labor hours. Variable manufacturing overhead is projected to be $25,000, and fixed manufacturing overhead is expected to be $15,000.

The estimated cost to produce one unit of the laminated putter head (PH) is:

a. $42.

b. $46.

c. $52.

d. $62.

Explanation: The correct answer is: **c.** $52.

Production Costs = Direct Materials + Direct Labor + Manufacturing Overhead

Direct Materials = (1 Pound Steel) ($5/Pound) + (1 Pound Copper) ($15/Pound)
= $5 + $15 = $20

Direct Labor = (1 Hour) ($22/Hour) = $22

Manufacturing overhead is calculated as shown:

Manufacturing Overhead = (Total Expected Overhead) /
(Total Expected Direct Labor Hours)

Manufacturing Overhead = ($25,000 Variable Overhead + $15,000 Fixed
Overhead) / 4,000 Direct Labor Hours
= $10

Use the next calculation to determine direct labor hours for the overhead calculation:

Direct Labor Hours = (# Laminated PHs Produced) (# Hours/Laminated PH)
+ (# Forged PHs Produced) (# Hours/Forged PH)

Production of PHs = (Expected Sales) + (Expected Ending Inventory)
− (Expected Beginning Inventory)

Production of Laminated PHs = 2,000 + 60 − 60 = 2,000 Units

Production of Forged PHs = 8,200 + 100 − 300 = 8,000 Units

Direct Labor Hours = (2,000 Units) (1 Hour/Unit)
+ (8,000 Units) (0.25 Hours/Unit)

Direct Labor Hours = 2,000 Hours + 2,000 Hours = 4,000 Hours

Question 1A4-CQ12

Topic: Annual Profit Plan and Supporting Schedules

Tidwell Corporation sells a single product for $20 per unit. All sales are on account, with 60% collected in the month of sale and 40% collected in the following month. A partial schedule of cash collections for January through March of the coming year reveals these receipts for the period:

	\multicolumn{3}{c}{Cash Receipts}		
	January	February	March
December receivables	$32,000		
From January sales	$54,000	$36,000	
From February sales		$66,000	$44,000

Other information includes:
- Inventories are maintained at 30% of the following month's sales.
- Assume that March sales total $150,000.

The number of units to be purchased in February is

a. 3,850 units.

b. 4,900 units.

c. 6,100 units.

d. 7,750 units.

Explanation: The correct answer is: **c.** 6,100 units.

The expected unit purchases for any month are calculated as shown:

$$\text{Expected Purchases} = (\text{Expected Sales in Units}) + (\text{Expected Ending Inventory}) - (\text{Expected Beginning Inventory})$$

The expected ending inventory for a month is 30% of the next month's expected sales.

Expected sales are calculated as shown:

$$\text{Expected Sales} = (\text{Sales in \$}) / (\$20 \text{ Selling Price per Unit})$$

$$\text{Number of Units to Be Purchased in February} = (\$110,000 / \$20 \text{ per Unit}) + [0.3(\$150,000 / \$20 \text{ per Unit})] - [0.3(\$110,000 / \$20 \text{ per Unit})]$$

$$\text{Number of Units to Be Purchased in February} = 5,500 \text{ Units} + [0.3 (7,500 \text{ Units})] - [0.3 (5,500 \text{ Units})]$$

$$\text{Number of Units to Be Purchased in February} = 5,500 \text{ Units} + 2,250 \text{ Units} - 1,650 \text{ Units} = 6,100 \text{ Units}$$

Question 1A4-CQ13

Topic: Annual Profit Plan and Supporting Schedules

Stevens Company manufactures electronic components used in automobile manufacturing. Each component uses two raw materials, Geo and Clio. Standard usage of the two materials required to produce one finished electronic component, as well as the current inventory, are shown next.

Material	Standard Usage per Unit	Price	Current Inventory
Geo	2.0 pounds	$15/pound	5,000 pounds
Clio	1.5 pounds	$10/pound	7,500 pounds

Stevens forecasts sales of 20,000 components for each of the next two production periods. Company policy dictates that 25% of the raw materials needed to produce the next period's projected sales be maintained in ending direct materials inventory.

Based on this information, what would the budgeted direct material purchases for the coming period be?

	Geo	Clio
a.	$450,000	$450,000
b.	$675,000	$300,000
c.	$675,000	$400,000
d.	$825,000	$450,000

Explanation: The correct answer is: **b.** $675,000 and $300,000.

The expected material purchases in units for any month can be calculated as shown:

Expected Material Purchases = (Production Needs for the Month)
    + (Expected Ending Inventory) − (Expected Beginning Inventory)

The expected ending inventory for any month is 25% of the next month's expected sales.

Since 2 pounds of Geo are used per unit, the expected purchase of Geo can be calculated as shown:

Expected Purchases of Geo = (2 Pounds) (20,000) + (0.25) (2 Pounds) (20,000)
    − 5,000 Pounds

Expected Purchases of Geo = 40,000 Pounds + 10,000 Pounds − 5,000 Pounds
    = 45,000 Pounds

Total Cost of Geo = (45,000 Pounds) ($15/Pound) = $675,000

Since 1.5 pounds of Clio are used per unit, the expected purchase of Clio can be calculated as shown:

Expected Purchase of Clio = (1.5 Pounds) (20,000) + (0.25) (1.5 Pounds) (20,000)
    −7,500 Pounds

Expected Purchase of Clio = 30,000 Pounds + 7,500 Pounds − 7,500 Pounds
    = 30,000 Pounds

Total Cost of Clio = (30,000 Pounds) ($10/Pound) = $300,000

Question 1A4-CQ14

Topic: Annual Profit Plan and Supporting Schedules

Petersons Planters Inc. budgeted these amounts for the coming year:

Beginning inventory, finished goods	$ 10,000
Cost of goods sold	400,000
Direct material used in production	100,000
Ending inventory, finished goods	25,000
Beginning and ending work-in-process inventory	Zero

Overhead is estimated to be two times the amount of direct labor dollars. The amount that should be budgeted for direct labor for the coming year is:

a. $315,000.

b. $210,000.

c. $157,500.

d. $105,000.

Explanation: The correct answer is: **d.** $105,000.

Since there was no change in work-in-process inventory, cost of goods manufactured equals total manufacturing costs.

Cost of goods manufactured is calculated as shown:

$$\text{Cost of Goods Manufactured} = (\text{Ending Finished Goods}) + (\text{Cost of Goods Sold}) - (\text{Beginning Finished Goods})$$

$$\text{Cost of Goods Manufactured} = \$25,000 + \$400,000 - \$10,000 = \$415,000$$

Since cost of goods manufactured is equal to total manufacturing costs, use the next formula to solve for direct labor costs:

$$\text{Total Manufacturing Costs} = (\text{Direct Material}) + (\text{Direct Labor}) + (\text{Manufacturing Overhead})$$

$$\$415,000 = \$100,000 + \text{Direct Labor} + 2\,(\text{Direct Labor})$$

$$\$415,000 = \$100,000 + 3\,(\text{Direct Labor})$$

$$\$315,000 = 3\,(\text{Direct Labor})$$

$$\text{Direct Labor} = \$105,000$$

Question 1A4-CQ15

Topic: Annual Profit Plan and Supporting Schedules

Over the past several years, McFadden Industries has experienced the costs shown regarding the company's shipping expenses:

Fixed costs	$16,000
Average shipment	15 pounds
Cost per pound	$0.50

Shown next are McFadden's budget data for the coming year.

Number of units shipped	8,000
Number of sales orders	800
Number of shipments	800
Total sales	$1,200,000
Total pounds shipped	9,600

McFadden's expected shipping costs for the coming year are:

a. $4,800.

b. $16,000.

c. $20,000.

d. $20,800.

Explanation: The correct answer is: **d.** $20,800.

Total shipping costs include both fixed and variable shipping costs.

$$\text{Total Shipping Costs} = \text{Fixed Shipping Cost} + \text{Variable Shipping Cost}$$

$$\text{Total Shipping Costs} = \$16,000 + (\$0.50)(\text{Number of Pounds Shipped})$$

$$\text{Total Shipping Costs} = \$16,000 + (\$0.50)(9,600 \text{ Pounds})$$

$$\text{Total Shipping Costs} = \$16,000 + \$4,800 = \$20,800$$

Question 1A4-CQ18

Topic: Annual Profit Plan and Supporting Schedules

In preparing the direct material purchases budget for next quarter, the plant controller has this information available:

Budgeted unit sales	2,000
Pounds of materials per unit	4
Cost of materials per pound	$3
Pounds of materials on hand	400
Finished units on hand	250
Target ending units inventory	325
Target ending inventory of pounds of materials	800

How many pounds of materials must be purchased?

a. 2,475

b. 7,900

c. 8,700

d. 9,300

Explanation: The correct answer is: **c.** 8,700.

The direct material purchases budget is calculated as shown:

Direct Materials Purchases = (Production Requirement) + (Expected Ending Inventory in Pounds) − (Expected Beginning Inventory in pounds)

Direct Materials Purchases = 8,300 Pounds + 800 Pounds − 400 Pounds = 8,700 Pounds

Production Requirement = (4 Pounds per Unit) (Expected Production)

Production Requirement = (4 Pounds per Unit) (2,075 Units) = 8,300 pounds

Expected Production = (Sales) + (Expected Ending Finished Goods Inventory) − (Expected Beginning Finished Goods Inventory)

Expected Production = 2,000 Units + 325 Units − 250 Units = 2,075 Units

Question 1A4-CQ22

Topic: Annual Profit Plan and Supporting Schedules

Given the next data for Scurry Company, what is the cost of goods sold?

Beginning inventory of finished goods	$100,000
Cost of goods manufactured	700,000
Ending inventory of finished goods	200,000
Beginning work-in-process inventory	300,000
Ending work-in-process inventory	50,000

a. $500,000

b. $600,000

c. $800,000

d. $950,000

Explanation: The correct answer is: **b.** $600,000.

Cost of goods sold is calculated as shown:

Cost of Goods Sold = (Cost of Goods Manufactured) + (Beginning Finished Goods Inventory) − (Ending Finished Goods Inventory)

Cost of Goods Sold = $700,000 + $100,000 − $200,000

Cost of Goods Sold = $600,000

Question 1A4-CQ23

Topic: Annual Profit Plan and Supporting Schedules

Tut Company's selling and administrative costs for the month of August, when it sold 20,000 units, were:

	Cost per Unit	Total Cost
Variable costs	$18.60	$372,000
Step costs	4.25	85,000
Fixed costs	8.80	176,000
Total selling and administrative costs	$31.65	$633,000

The variable costs represent sales commissions paid at the rate of 6.2% of sales.

The step costs depend on the number of salespersons employed by the company. In August there were 17 persons on the sales force. However, 2 members have taken early retirement effective August 31. It is anticipated that these positions will remain vacant for several months.

Total fixed costs are unchanged within a relevant range of 15,000 to 30,000 units per month.

Tut is planning a sales price cut of 10%, which it expects will increase sales volume to 24,000 units per month. If Tut implements the sales price reduction, the total budgeted selling and administrative costs for the month of September would be:

a. $652,760.

b. $679,760.

c. $714,960.

d. $759,600.

Explanation: The correct answer is: **a.** $652,760.

Total budgeted selling and administrative costs in this problem can be calculated as shown:

Total Budgeted Selling and Administrative Costs = (Variable Costs) + (Step Costs) + (Fixed Costs)

Total Budgeted Selling and Administrative Costs = $401,760 + $75,000 + $176,000

Total Budgeted Selling and Administrative Costs = $652,760

Rearrange the next formula to determine sales for August, then sales price per unit.

Variable Costs = (6.2%) (Sales)

Sales = (Variable Costs) / (0.062) = \$372,000 / 0.062 = \$6,000,000

Sales Price per Unit = (Sales) / (# Units Sold) = \$6,000,000 / 20,000 = \$300

Expected Sales in September = (90%) (August Sales Price per Unit)
(September Sales Volume)
= (0.9) ((\$300) (24,000) = \$6,480,000

Budgeted Variable Costs = (0.062) (\$6,480,000) = \$401,760

Step Costs per Salesperson = \$85,000 / 17 Salespeople = \$5,000

Due to the retirement of two salespeople, the budgeted step costs are reduced and are calculated as shown:

Budgeted Step Costs = (15 Salespeople) (\$5,000 Cost per Salesperson)
= \$75,000

Total Budgeted Selling and Administrative Costs = \$401,760 + \$75,000
+ \$176,000

Total Budgeted Selling and Administrative Costs = \$652,760

Question 1A4-CQ36

Topic: Annual Profit Plan and Supporting Schedules

Data regarding Johnsen Inc. 's forecasted dollar sales for the last seven months of the year and Johnsen's projected collection patterns are shown next.

Forecasted sales

June	\$700,000
July	600,000
August	650,000
September	800,000
October	850,000
November	900,000
December	840,000

Types of sales

Cash sales	30%
Credit sales	70%

Collection pattern on credit sales (5% determined to be uncollectible)

During the month of sale	20%
During the first month following the sale	50%
During the second month following the sale	25%

Johnsen's budgeted cash receipts from sales and collections on account for September are:

a. $635,000.

b. $684,500.

c. $807,000.

d. $827,000.

Explanation: The correct answer is: **b.** $684,500.

The budgeted cash receipts from sales and collections on account for September are calculated as shown:

Budgeted Cash Receipts from Sales and Collections on Account, September
= (September Cash Sales) + (Collections from September Credit Sales)
+ (Collections from August Sales) + (Collections from July Sales)

September Cash Sales = (30%) (September Sales)
= (0.3) ($800,000) = $240,000

Collections from September Credit Sales = (20%) (70%) (September Sales)

Collections from September Credit Sales = (0.2) (0.7) ($800,000) = $112,000

Collections from August Sales = (50%) (70%) (August Sales)

Collections from August Sales = (0.5) (0.7) ($650,000) = $227,500

Collections from July Sales = (25%) (70%) (July Sales)

Collections from July Sales = (0.25) (0.7) ($600,000) = $105,000

Budgeted Cash Receipts from Sales and Collections on Account, September
= $240,000 + $112,000 + $227,500 + $105,000
= $684,500

Question 1A4-CQ37

Topic: Annual Profit Plan and Supporting Schedules

The Mountain Mule Glove Company is in its first year of business. Mountain Mule had a beginning cash balance of $85,000 for the quarter. The company has a

$50,000 short-term line of credit. The budgeted information for the first quarter is shown next.

	January	February	March
Sales	$60,000	$40,000	$50,000
Purchases	$35,000	$40,000	$75,000
Operating costs	$25,000	$25,000	$25,000

All sales are made on credit and are collected in the second month following the sale. Purchases are paid in the month following the purchase while operating costs are paid in the month that they are incurred. How much will Mountain Mule need to borrow at the end of the quarter if the company needs to maintain a minimum cash balance of $5,000 as required by a loan covenant agreement?

a. $0

b. $5,000

c. $10,000

d. $45,000

Explanation: The correct answer is: **c.** $10,000.

The projected cash balance, without borrowing, at the end of the quarter is calculated as shown:

Projected Cash Balance, Without Borrowing, End of Quarter
= (Beginning Cash Balance) + (Projected Cash Receipts)
– (Projected Cash Disbursements)

Beginning Cash Balance for the Quarter = $85,000

Projected cash receipts for the quarter are equal to the January sales amount, because all sales are made on credit and are collected in the second month following business.

Projected Cash Receipts for the Quarter = $60,000

Projected cash disbursements for the quarter will include the purchases from January and February (March purchases are not included, because they will be paid for in April), plus the operating costs for the months of January, February, and March.

Projected Cash Disbursements = $35,000 + $40,000 + $25,000
+ $25,000 + $25,000
= $150,000

The projected cash balance, without borrowing, for the end of the quarter can be calculated as shown:

Projected Cash Balance, Without Borrowing, End of Quarter
        $= \$85,000 + \$60,000 - \$150,000$
        $= -\$5,000$

Therefore, $10,000 will have to be borrowed to maintain a minimum cash balance of $5,000.

Question 1A2-CQ05

Topic: Forecasting Techniques

Aerosub, Inc. has developed a new product for spacecraft that includes the manufacture of a complex part. The manufacturing of this part requires a high degree of technical skill. Management believes there is a good opportunity for its technical force to learn and improve as it becomes accustomed to the production process. The production of the first unit requires 10,000 direct labor hours. If an 80% learning curve is used, the cumulative direct labor hours required for producing a total of eight units would be:

a. 29,520 hours.

b. 40,960 hours.

c. 64,000 hours.

d. 80,000 hours.

Explanation: The correct answer is: **b.** 40,960 hours.

Using a cumulative average time learning curve, as the cumulative output doubles, the cumulative average direct labor hours per unit becomes the learning curve percentage times the previous cumulative average direct labor hours per unit. So, if the direct labor hours for the first unit are 10,000 and an 80% learning curve is used, the cumulative average direct labor hours for 2 units would be calculated as shown:

Cumulative Average Direct Labor Hours for 2 Units
        $= 0.8 \ (10,000 \ \text{Direct Labor Hours})$
        $= 8,000 \ \text{Direct Labor Hours}$

When output doubles to 4 units, the cumulative average direct labor hours would be calculated as shown:

Cumulative Average Direct Labor Hours for 4 Units $= 0.8 \ (8,000 \ \text{Direct Labor Hours})$
        $= 6,400 \ \text{Direct Labor Hours}$

When output doubles again, this time to 8 units, the cumulative average direct labor hours would be calculated as shown:

Cumulative Average Direct Labor Hours for 8 Units $= 0.8 \ (6,400 \ \text{Direct Labor Hours})$
        $= 5,120 \ \text{Direct Labor Hours}$

Therefore, the cumulative direct labor hours for 8 units = (5,120 direct labor hours) (8 units) = 40,960 direct labor hours.

Question 1A2-CQ09

Topic: Forecasting Techniques

Sales of big-screen televisions have grown steadily during the past five years. A dealer predicted that the demand for February would be 148 televisions. Actual demand in February was 158 televisions. If the smoothing constant is $\alpha = 0.3$, the demand forecast for March, using the exponential smoothing model, will be:

a. 148 televisions.

b. 151 televisions.

c. 153 televisions.

d. 158 televisions.

Explanation: The correct answer is: **b.** 151 televisions.

The formula for exponential smoothing is:

$$F(t + 1) = \alpha[A\,(t)] + (1 - \alpha)[F\,(t)]$$

where:
F = forecast
t = current time period
α = smoothing constant
A = actual

February Forecast = F(t) = 148
February Actual = A(t) = 158
March Forecast = F(t + 1) = (0.3) (158) + (1 – 0.3) (148)
F(t + 1) = 47.4 + 0.7 (148)
F(t + 1) = 47.4 + 103.6 = 151

Question 1A2-CQ14

Topic: Forecasting Techniques

Scarf Corporation's controller has decided to use a decision model to cope with uncertainty. With a particular proposal, currently under consideration, Scarf has two possible actions: invest or not invest in a joint venture with an international firm. The controller has determined this information:

Action 1: Invest in the Joint Venture

Events and Probabilities:

Probability of success = 60%

Cost of investment = $9.5 million

Cash flow if investment is successful = $15.0 million

Cash flow if investment is unsuccessful = $2.0 million

Additional costs to be paid = $0

Costs incurred up to this point = $650,000

Action 2: Do Not Invest in the Joint Venture

Events:

Costs incurred up to this point = $650,000

Additional costs to be paid = $100,000

Which one of the next alternatives correctly reflects the respective expected values of investing versus not investing?

a. $300,000 and ($750,000)

b.   ($350,000) and ($100,000)

c. $300,000 and ($100,000)

d.   ($350,000) and ($750,000)

Explanation: The correct answer is: **c.** $300,000 and ($100,000).

The expected value of not investing is ($100,000), since this is the additional cost that would be incurred if no investment is made.

The expected value of investing can be calculated by adding together the expected value of when the investment is successful and adding to it the expected value of when the investment is unsuccessful and then subtracting the initial investment cost.

Expected Value of Investing = (Expected Value When Successful) + (Expected Value When Unsuccessful) − (Initial Investment Cost)

Expected Value of Investing = (0.6) ($15,000,000) + (0.4) ($2,000,000) − $9,500,000

Expected Value of Investing = $9,000,000 + $800,000 − $9,500,000

Expected Value of Investing = $300,000

Note that the $650,000 in costs incurred up to this point are sunk costs and are irrelevant to the analysis.

Section B: Performance Management
Answers and Explanations

Question 1B1-CQ01

Topic: Cost and Variance Measures

The following performance report was prepared for Dale Manufacturing for the month of April.

	Actual Results	Static Budget	Variance
Sales units	100,000	80,000	20,000 F
Sales dollars	$190,000	$160,000	$30,000 F
Variable costs	125,000	96,000	29,000 U
Fixed costs	45,000	40,000	5,000 U
Operating income	$20,000	$ 24,000	$ 4,000 U

Using a flexible budget, Dale's total sales-volume variance is:

a. $4,000 unfavorable.

b. $6,000 favorable.

c. $16,000 favorable.

d. $20,000 unfavorable.

Explanation: The correct answer is: **c.** $16,000 favorable.

The sales-volume variance is the difference between the static budget profit of $24,000 and the flexible budget profit at the actual volume of 100,000 sales units.

The Flexible Budget Profit at 100,000 Units = Budgeted Sales – Budgeted Variable Costs – Budgeted Fixed Costs all at 100,000 Units.

Budgeted Sales = (Budgeted Price) (Actual Sales in Units)

Budgeted Sales = ($160,000 / 80,000 Units) (100,000 Units)

Budgeted Sales = $200,000

Budgeted Variable Costs = (Unit Variable Cost) (Actual Sales in Units)

Budgeted Variable Costs = ($96,000 / 80,000 Units) (100,000 Units)

Budgeted Variable Costs = $120,000

Budgeted Fixed Costs = $40,000 at Any Volume in the Relevant Range.

Flexible Budget Profit = $200,000 – $120,000 – $40,000
= $40,000

Total Sales-Volume Variance = $24,000 – $40,000
= $(16,000), or $16,000 Favorable

Question 1B1-CQ02

Topic: Cost and Variance Measures

MinnOil performs oil changes and other minor maintenance services (e. g. , tire pressure checks) for cars. The company advertises that all services are completed within 15 minutes for each service.

On a recent Saturday, 160 cars were serviced resulting in the following labor variances: rate, $19 unfavorable; efficiency, $14 favorable. If MinnOil's standard labor rate is $7 per hour, determine the actual wage rate per hour and the actual hours worked.

	Wage Rate	Hours Worked
a.	$6.55	42.00
b.	$6.67	42.71
c.	$7.45	42.00
d.	$7.50	38.00

Explanation: The correct answer is: **d.** $7.50 and 38.00.

The labor efficiency variance of $(14), or $14 favorable, is used in the next formula to determine the actual hours (AH):

Labor Efficiency Variance = (Standard Rate) (Actual Hours – Standard Hours)

$$-\$14 = (\$7) \, [AH - (160 \text{ Units}) (1/4 \text{ Hour per Unit})]$$

$$-\$14 = \$7(AH - 40)$$

$$-\$14 = \$7AH - \$280$$

$$-\$14 = \$7AH - \$280$$

$$\$266 = \$7AH$$

$$AH = 38$$

The labor rate variance of $19, or $19 unfavorable, is used in the next formula to determine the actual wage rate (AR):

Labor Rate Variance = (Actual Hours) (Actual Wage Rate – Standard Wage Rate)

$$\$19 = (38 \text{ Hours})(AR - \$7)$$

$$\$19 = (38 \text{ Hours})(AR - \$7)$$

$$\$19 = 38AR - \$266$$

$$\$285 = 38AR$$

$$AR = \$7.50$$

Question 1B1-CQ03

Topic: Cost and Variance Measures

Frisco Company recently purchased 108,000 units of raw material for $583,200. Three units of raw materials are budgeted for use in each finished good manufactured, with the raw material standard set at $16.50 for each completed product.

Frisco manufactured 32,700 finished units during the period just ended and used 99,200 units of raw material. If management is concerned about the timely reporting of variances in an effort to improve cost control and bottom-line performance, the materials purchase price variance should be reported as

a. $6,050 unfavorable.

b. $9,920 favorable.

c. $10,800 unfavorable.

d. $10,800 favorable.

Explanation: The correct answer is: **d.** $10,800 favorable.

The material purchase price variance is calculated as shown:

Material Purchase Price Variance = (Actual Quantity Purchased) (Actual Price) – (Actual Quantity Purchased) (Standard Price)

Material Purchase Price Variance = ($583,200) – (108,000 Units) ($16.50 / 3 Units)

Material Purchase Price Variance = $583,200 – $594,000
= $(10,800) Favorable

Question 1B1-CQ04

Topic: Cost and Variance Measures

Christopher Akers is the chief executive officer of SBL Inc. , a masonry contractor. The financial statements have just arrived showing a $3,000 loss on the new stadium job that was budgeted to show a $6,000 profit. Actual and budget information relating to the materials for the job are shown next.

	Actual	Budget
Bricks – number of bundles	3,000	2,850
Bricks – cost per bundle	$7.90	$8.00

Which one of the following is a **correct** statement regarding the stadium job for SBL?

a. The price variance was favorable by $285.

b. The price variance was favorable by $300.

c. The efficiency variance was unfavorable by $1,185.

d. The flexible budget variance was unfavorable by $900.

Explanation: The correct answer is: **b.** The price variance was favorable by $300.

The material price variance is calculated as shown:

Material Price Variance = (Actual Quantity Purchased)
(Actual Price – Standard Price)

Material Price Variance = (3,000) ($7.90 – $8.00) = $(300) favorable.

The other available answer choices are incorrect. Note that the flexible budget variance includes all variable cost variances (material, direct labor, and variable overhead) as well as the fixed overhead budget variance.

Question 1B1-CQ05

Topic: Cost and Variance Measures

A company isolates its raw material price variance in order to provide the earliest possible information to the manager responsible for the variance. The budgeted amount of material usage for the year was computed as shown:

150,000 Units of Finished Goods $\times$ 3 Pounds/Unit $\times$ $2.00/Pound = $900,000

Actual results for the year were the following:

Finished goods produced	160,000 units
Raw materials purchased	500,000 pounds
Raw materials used	490,000 pounds
Cost per pound	$2.02

The raw material price variance for the year was

a. $9,600 unfavorable.

b. $9,800 unfavorable.

c. $10,000 unfavorable.

d. $20,000 unfavorable.

Explanation: The correct answer is: **c.** $10,000 unfavorable.

The raw material price variance is calculated as shown:

Raw Material Price Variance = (Actual Quantity Purchased) (Actual Price
− Standard Price)

Raw Material Price Variance = (500,000) ($2.02 − $2.00)
= $10,000 Unfavorable.

Question 1B1-CQ06

Topic: Cost and Variance Measures

Lee Manufacturing uses a standard cost system with overhead applied based on direct labor hours. The manufacturing budget for the production of 5,000 units for the month of May included the following information.

Direct labor cost (10,000 hours at $15/hour)	$150,000
Variable overhead	$30,000
Fixed overhead	$80,000

During May, 6,000 units were produced and the direct labor efficiency variance was $1,500 unfavorable. Based on this information, the actual number of direct labor hours used in May was:

a. 9,900 hours.

b. 10,100 hours.

c. 11,900 hours.

d. 12,100 hours.

Explanation: The correct answer is: **d.** 12,100 hours.

The labor efficiency variance is calculated as shown:

Labor Efficiency Variance = (Standard Rate) (Actual Hours − Standard Hours)

Actual Hours = AH

Standard Hours = (6,000 Units) (10,000 Hours / 5,000 Units) = 12,000 Hours

$1,500 = ($15) (AH − 12,000 Hours)

$1,500 = $15AH − $180,000

$181,500 = $15AH

AH = 12,100

Question 1B1-CQ07

Topic: Cost and Variance Measures

At the beginning of the year, Douglas Company prepared this monthly budget for direct materials.

Units produced and sold	10,000	15,000
Direct material cost	$15,000	$22,500

At the end of the month, the company's records showed that 12,000 units were produced and sold and $20,000 was spent for direct materials. The variance for direct materials is:

a. $2,000 favorable.

b. $2,000 unfavorable.

c. $5,000 favorable.

d. $5,000 unfavorable.

Explanation: The correct answer is: **b.** $2,000 unfavorable.

The variance for direct materials is calculated as shown:

Variance for Direct Materials = (Actual Direct Material Cost)
$\qquad$ − (Budgeted Direct Material Cost at
$\qquad$ Actual Level Of Production)

Variance for Direct Materials = ($20,000) − (12,000 Units)
$\qquad$ ($15,000 / 10,000 Units)

Variance for Direct Materials = $20,000 − $18,000
$\qquad$ = $2,000 unfavorable

Question 1B1-CQ08

Topic: Cost and Variance Measures

A company had a total labor variance of $15,000 favorable and a labor efficiency variance of $18,000 unfavorable. The labor price variance was:

a. $3,000 favorable.

b. $3,000 unfavorable.

c. $33,000 favorable.

d. $33,000 unfavorable.

Explanation: The correct answer is: **c.** $33,000 favorable.

The total labor variance is given as −$15,000 favorable and is calculated as shown:

Total Labor Variance = (Labor Rate Variance) + (Labor Efficiency Variance)

Labor Rate Variance = LRV

−$15,000 = (LRV) + ($18,000)

−$15,000 − $18,000 = LRV

LRV = −$33,000 which makes the labor price (rate) variance $33,000 favorable

Question 1B1-CQ09

Topic: Cost and Variance Measures

Lee Manufacturing uses a standard cost system with overhead applied based on direct labor hours. The manufacturing budget for the production of 5,000 units for the month of June included 10,000 hours of direct labor at $15 per hour, or $150,000. During June, 4,500 units were produced, using 9,600 direct labor hours, incurring $39,360 of variable overhead, and showing a variable overhead efficiency variance of $2,400 unfavorable. The standard variable overhead rate per direct labor hour was:

a. $3.85.

b. $4.00.

c. $4.10.

d. $6.00.

Explanation: The correct answer is: **b.** $4.00.

The variable overhead efficiency variance is given as $2,400 unfavorable.

The standard variable overhead rate per direct labor hour (SRV) can be calculated by rearranging the next formula:

Variable Overhead Efficiency Variance = (SRV) (Actual Direct Labor Hours − Standard Direct Labor Hours)

Variable Overhead Efficiency Variance = (SRV) (9,600 Hours − [(4,500 Units) (10,000 Hours / 5,000 Direct Labor Hours per Unit)]

Variable Overhead Efficiency Variance = (SRV) (9,600 Hours − 9,000 hours)

Variable Overhead Efficiency Variance = 600 SRV

$2,400 = 600 SRV

SRV = $4.00

Question 1B1-CQ10

Topic: Cost and Variance Measures

Cordell Company uses a standard cost system. On January 1 of the current year, Cordell budgeted fixed manufacturing overhead cost of $600,000 and production at 200,000 units. During the year, the firm produced 190,000 units and incurred fixed manufacturing overhead of $595,000. The production volume variance for the year was:

a. $5,000 unfavorable.

b. $10,000 unfavorable.

c. $25,000 unfavorable.

d. $30,000 unfavorable.

Explanation: The correct answer is: **d.** $30,000 unfavorable.

The fixed overhead volume variance is calculated as shown:

Fixed Overhead Volume Variance (FOVV) = (Fixed Overhead Rate) (Normal Base Level of Production – Actual Production Level)

Fixed Overhead Rate = SRF

FOVV = (SRF) (200,000 Units – 190,000 Units)

FOVV = 10,000 SRF

The fixed overhead rate (SRF) is equal to the budgeted fixed overhead of $600,000, divided by the normal (budgeted) base of 200,000 units, which comes to $3.00 per unit.

Therefore, the FOVV = (10,000) ($3) = $30,000 unfavorable.

Question 1B1-CQ11

Topic: Cost and Variance Measures

Harper Company's performance report indicated this information for the past month:

Actual total overhead	$1,600,000
Budgeted fixed overhead	$1,500,000
Applied fixed overhead at $3 per labor hour	$1,200,000
Applied variable overhead at $. 50 per labor hour	$200,000
Actual labor hours	430,000

Harper's total overhead spending variance for the month was:

a. $100,000 favorable.

b. $115,000 favorable.

c. $185,000 unfavorable.

d. $200,000 unfavorable.

Explanation: The correct answer is: **b.** $115,000 favorable.

The overhead spending variance is calculated as shown:

Overhead Spending Variance (OSV) = (Actual Overhead) – (Budgeted Overhead at Actual Direct Labor Hours Used)

OSV = ($1,600,000) – (Budgeted Overhead at Actual Direct Labor Hours Used)

Budgeted Overhead at the Actual Direct Labor Hours Used = (Fixed Overhead) + (Actual Direct Labor Hours) (Rate of Labor Hours Used to Apply Variable Overhead)

Budgeted Overhead at the Actual Direct Labor Hours Used = $1,500,000 + (430,000 Hours $\times$ $0.50 per Direct Labor Hour)

Budgeted Overhead at the Actual Direct Labor Hours Used = $1,500,000 + $215,000 = $1,715,000

OSV = $1,600,000 – $1,715,000 = $(115,000) Favorable

Question 1B1-CQ12

Topic: Cost and Variance Measures

The JoyT Company manufactures Maxi Dolls for sale in toy stores. In planning for this year, JoyT estimated variable factory overhead of $600,000 and fixed factory overhead of $400,000. JoyT uses a standard costing system, and factory overhead is allocated to units produced on the basis of standard direct labor hours. The denominator level of activity budgeted for this year was 10,000 direct labor hours, and JoyT used 10,300 actual direct labor hours.

Based on the output accomplished during this year, 9,900 standard direct labor hours should have been used. Actual variable factory overhead was $596,000, and actual fixed factory overhead was $410,000 for the year. Based on this information, the variable overhead spending variance for JoyT for this year was:

a. $24,000 unfavorable.

b. $2,000 unfavorable.

c. $4,000 favorable.

d. $22,000 favorable.

Explanation: The correct answer is: **d.** $22,000 favorable.

The variable overhead spending variance is calculated as shown:

Variable Overhead Spending Variance (VOSV) = (Actual Variable Overhead) – (Budgeted Variable Overhead at the Actual Level of Direct Labor Hours Used)

VOSV = ($596,000) – (Budgeted Variable Overhead at the Actual Level of
        Direct Labor Hours Used)

The budgeted variable overhead at the actual level of direct labor hours used is
calculated as shown:

Budgeted Variable Overhead at the Actual Level of Direct Labor Hours Used
    = (Variable Overhead Rate, or SRV) (Actual Direct Labor Hours Used)

Budgeted Variable Overhead at the Actual Level of Direct Labor Hours Used
    = (SRV) (10,300 Direct Labor Hours)

SRV = (Estimated Variable Overhead) / (Budgeted Direct Labor Hours)

SRV = ($600,000) (10,000 Budgeted Direct Labor Hours)
    = $60 per Direct Labor Hour

Budgeted Variable Overhead at the Actual Level of Direct Labor Hours
    = $60 (10,300 Hours)

Budgeted Variable Overhead at the Actual Level of Direct Labor Hours
    = $618,000

VOSV = $596,000 – $618,000 = –$22,000, or, $22,000 Favorable

Question 1B1-CQ13

Topic: Cost and Variance Measures

Johnson Inc. has established per unit standards for material and labor for its
production department based on 900 units normal production capacity as
shown.

3 pounds of direct materials @ $4 per pound	$12
1 direct labor hour @ $15 per hour	15
Standard cost per unit	$27

During the year, 1,000 units were produced. The accounting department has
charged the production department supervisor with the next unfavorable
variances.

Material Quantity Variance		Material Price Variance	
Actual usage	3,300 pounds	Actual cost	$4,200
Standard usage	3,000 pounds	Standard cost	4,000
Unfavorable	300 pounds	Unfavorable	$200

Bob Sterling, the production supervisor, has received a memorandum from his boss stating that he did not meet the established standards for material prices and quantity and corrective action should be taken. Sterling is very unhappy about the situation and is preparing to reply to the memorandum explaining the reasons for his dissatisfaction.

All of the following are valid reasons for Sterling's dissatisfaction **except** that the:

a. material price variance is the responsibility of the purchasing department.

b. cause of the unfavorable material usage variance was the acquisition of substandard material.

c. standards have not been adjusted to the engineering changes.

d. variance calculations fail to properly reflect that actual production exceeded normal production capacity.

Explanation: The correct answer is: **d.** variance calculations fail to properly reflect that actual production exceeded normal production capacity.

Production variances (cost, spending, and efficiency variances) are based on *actual production volumes.* They are not based on normal production, capacity production, budgeted production, estimated production, projected production, expected production, or any other measure of production. Therefore, the difference between actual production and any other measure of production is irrelevant.

Question 1B2-CQ01

Topic: Responsibility Centers and Reporting Segments

Manhattan Corporation has several divisions that operate as decentralized profit centers. At the present time, the Fabrication Division has excess capacity of 5,000 units with respect to the UT-371 circuit board, a popular item in many digital applications. Information about the circuit board is presented next.

Market price	$48
Variable selling/distribution costs on external sales	$5
Variable manufacturing cost	$21
Fixed manufacturing cost	$10

Manhattan's Electronic Assembly Division wants to purchase 4,500 circuit boards either internally or else use a similar board in the marketplace that sells for $46. The Electronic Assembly Division's management feels that if the first alternative is pursued, a price concession is justified, given that both divisions are part of the same firm. To optimize the overall goals of Manhattan, the minimum price to be charged for the board from the Fabrication Division to the Electronic Assembly Division should be:

a. $21.

b. $26.

c. $31.

d. $46.

Explanation: The correct answer is: **a.** $21.

The optimal transfer price is calculated as shown:

Optimal Transfer Price, T(o) = (Manufacturing Division's Opportunity
Cost of Production) + (Any Avoidable
Fixed Costs) + (Any Forgone Contribution from
Manufacturing the Product)

The Manufacturing Division's opportunity cost of production is equal to its relevant unit variable cost per unit, or $21 in this case.

Since the Fabrication Division has excess capacity, the forgone contribution is $0.

There is no mention of avoidable fixed costs.

T(o) = $21 + $0 + $0 = $21

Question 1B3-CQ01

Topic: Performance Measures

Performance results for four geographic divisions of a manufacturing company are shown next.

Division	Target Return on Investment	Actual Return on Investment	Return on Sales
A	18%	18.1%	8%
B	16%	20.0%	8%
C	14%	15.8%	6%
D	12%	11.0%	9%

The division with the **best** performance is:

a. Division A.

b. Division B.

c. Division C.

d. Division D.

Explanation: The correct answer is: **b.** Division B.

Division B exceeded its target return on investment (ROI) by 25%, which is calculated as shown:

Percent of ROI Achieved = (Actual ROI − Target ROI) / (Actual ROI)

Percent of ROI Achieved = (20 − 16) / 16
= 25%

Divisions A and C exceeded their targets by much less. Division D's actual ROI was lower than its target ROI.

Question 1B3-CQ02

Topic: Performance Measures

KHD Industries is a multidivisional firm that evaluates its managers based on the return on investment (ROI) earned by its divisions. The evaluation and compensation plans use a targeted ROI of 15% (equal to the cost of capital), and managers receive a bonus of 5% of basic compensation for every one percentage point that the division's ROI exceeds 15%.

Dale Evans, manager of the Consumer Products Division, has made a forecast of the division's operations and finances for next year that indicates the ROI would be 24%. In addition, new short-term programs were identified by the Consumer Products Division and evaluated by the finance staff as shown.

Program	Projected ROI
A	13%
B	19%
C	22%
D	31%

Assuming no restrictions on expenditures, what is the optimal mix of new programs that would add value to KHD Industries?

a. A, B, C, and D

b. B, C, and D only

c. C and D only

d. D only

Explanation: The correct answer is: **b.** B, C, and D only.

KHD would want to invest in any project whose ROI exceeds the corporate target of 15%. Programs B, C, and D all have ROI's that exceed 15%.

Question 1B1-AT03

Topic: Cost and Variance Measures

Franklin Products has an estimated practical capacity of 90,000 machine hours, and each unit requires two machine hours. The next data apply to a recent accounting period.

Actual variable overhead	$240,000
Actual fixed overhead	$442,000
Actual machine **hours** worked	88,000
Actual finished **units** produced	42,000
Budgeted variable overhead at 90,000 machine hours	$200,000
Budgeted fixed overhead	$450,000

Of the following factors, the production volume variance is **most** likely to have been caused by:

a. acceptance of an unexpected sales order.

b. a wage hike granted to a production supervisor.

c. a newly imposed initiative to reduce finished goods inventory levels.

d. temporary employment of workers with lower skill levels than originally anticipated.

Explanation: The correct answer is: **c.** a newly imposed initiative to reduce finished goods inventory levels.

Volume variances are caused by a difference in the budgeted fixed overhead and the amount allocated on the basis of actual output. A newly imposed initiative to reduce finished goods inventory levels is consistent with the change in production compared to budget.

A wage hike would affect the spending variance, not the volume variance.

Since the volume variance in this case is unfavorable (amount allocated less than budget), acceptance of an unexpected sales order would not be correct because an unexpected sales order would increase the amount allocated.

Question 1B3-AT03

Topic: Performance Measures

Which one of the following **best** identifies a profit center?

a. A new car sales division for a large local auto agency

b. The Information Technology Department of a large consumer products company

c. A large toy company

d. The Production Operations Department of a small job-order machine shop company

Explanation: The correct answer is: **a.** A new car sales division for a large local auto agency.

A profit center is a responsibility center whose manager is responsible for revenues as well as costs. Profit is used to measure performance of a new car sales division of a local auto agency, which best identifies a profit center as it has its own costs and revenues.

Question 1B3-AT20

Topic: Performance Measures

Teaneck Inc. sells two products, Product E and Product F, and had these data for last month:

	Product E		Product F	
	Budget	**Actual**	**Budget**	**Actual**
Unit sales	5,500	6,000	4,500	6,000
Unit contribution margin (CM)	$4.50	$4.80	$10.00	$10.50

The company's sales mix variance is:

a. $3,300 favorable.

b. $3,420 favorable.

c. $17,250 favorable.

d. $18,150 favorable.

Explanation: The correct answer is: **a.** $3,300 Favorable.

CM = Contribution Margin

Budgeted mix:

55% E × $4.50 CM	$2.475
45% F × $10.00 CM	4.500
Per unit CM	$6.975

Actual mix:

50% E × $4.50 CM	$2.250
50% F 3 $10.00 CM	5.000
Per unit CM	$7.250

Increase in CM 0.275 × Actual Units of 12,000 = $3,300 favorable

Question 1B3-AT05

Topic: Performance Measures

The balanced scorecard provides an action plan for achieving competitive success by focusing management attention on critical success factors. Which one of the following is *not* one of the critical success factors commonly focused on in the balanced scorecard?

a. Financial performance measures

b. Internal business processes

c. Competitor business strategies

d. Employee innovation and learning

Explanation: The correct answer is: **c.** Competitor business strategies.

The critical success factors used in the balanced scorecard are:

- Financial performance
- Customer satisfaction
- Internal business processes
- Innovation and learning

Section C: Cost Management
Answers and Explanations

Question 1C1-CQ01
Topic: Measurement Concepts

A company employs a just-in-time (JIT) production system and utilizes back-flush accounting. All acquisitions of raw materials are recorded in a raw materials control account when purchased. All conversion costs are recorded in a control account as incurred, while the assignment of conversion costs are from an allocated conversion cost account. Company practice is to record the cost of goods manufactured at the time the units are completed using the estimated budgeted cost of the goods manufactured.

The budgeted cost per unit for one of the company's products is as shown:

Direct materials	$15.00
Conversion costs	35.00
Total budgeted unit cost	$50.00

During the current accounting period, 80,000 units of product were completed, and 75,000 units were sold. The entry to record the cost of the completed units for the period would be which of the following?

a. Work-In-Process—Control	4,000,000	
Raw Material—Control		1,200,000
Conversion Cost Allocated		2,800,000
b. Finished Goods—Control	4,000,000	
Raw Material—Control		1,200,000
Conversion Cost Allocated		2,800,000
c. Finished Goods—Control	3,750,000	
Raw Material Control		1,125,000
Conversion Cost Allocated		2,625,000
d. Cost of Goods Sold	3,750,000	
Raw Material—Control		1,125,000
Conversion Cost Allocated		2,625,000

Explanation: The correct answer is:

b. Finished Goods—Control	4,000,000	
Raw Material—Control		1,200,000
Conversion Cost Allocated		2,800,000

With JIT, there is no work-in-process inventory. To record the cost of the completed units during the period, the next entries would be made:

Credit the Raw Material—Control account for $1,200,000 (80,000 units @ $15 direct materials each) to show the transfer of raw materials to finished goods. The offsetting debit would go to the Finished Goods—Control account.

Credit the Conversion Cost Allocated account for $2,800,000 (80,000 units @ $35 conversion costs each) to show the transfer of conversion costs to finished goods. The offsetting debit would go to the Finished Goods—Control account.

In total, the Finished Goods—Control account would receive a debit in the amount of $4,000,000, which is made up of $1,200,000 of raw materials and $2,800,000 of conversion costs.

Question 1C1-CQ02

Topic: Measurement Concepts

From the budgeted data shown, calculate the budgeted indirect cost rate that would be used in a normal costing system.

Total direct labor hours	250,000
Direct costs	$10,000,000
Total indirect labor hours	50,000
Total indirect labor-related costs	$ 5,000,000
Total indirect non-labor-related costs	$ 7,000,000

a. $20

b. $28

c. $40

d. $48

Explanation: The correct answer is: **d.** $48.

The budgeted indirect cost rate per direct labor hour is calculated as shown.

Budgeted Indirect Labor Cost Rate per Direct Labor Hour
= (Budgeted Indirect Costs) / (Budgeted Direct Labor Hours)

Budgeted Indirect Labor Cost Rate per Direct Labor Hour
= ($5,000,000 + $7,000,000) / $250,000

Budgeted Indirect Labor Cost Rate per Direct Labor Hour
= $12,000,000 / $250,000

Budgeted Indirect Labor Cost Rate per Direct Labor Hour
= $48 per Direct Labor Hour

Question 1C2-CQ03
Topic: Costing Systems

Loyal Co. produces three types of men's undershirts: T-shirts, V-neck shirts, and athletic shirts. In the Folding and Packaging Department, operations costing is used to apply costs to individual units, based on the standard time allowed to fold and package each type of undershirt. The standard time to fold and package each type of undershirt is shown next.

T-shirt	40 seconds per shirt
V-neck shirt	40 seconds per shirt
Athletic shirt	20 seconds per shirt

During the month of April, Loyal produced and sold 50,000 T-shirts, 30,000 V-neck shirts, and 20,000 athletic shirts. If costs in the Folding and Packaging Department were $78,200 during April, how much folding and packaging cost should be applied to each T-shirt?

a. $0.5213

b. $0.6256

c. $0.7820

d. $0.8689

Explanation: The correct answer is: **d.** $0.8689.

The folding and packaging cost applied to each T-shirt can be calculated as shown.

Folding and Packaging Cost Applied = (40 Seconds) (Cost Rate per Second)

Cost Rate per Second = ($78,200) / (Total Seconds)

Cost Rate per Second = ($78,200) / [(50,000 T-Shirts) (40 Seconds per Shirt) + (30,000 V-Neck Shirts) (40 Seconds per Shirt) + (20,000 Athletic Shirts) (20 Seconds per Shirt)]

Cost Rate per Second = ($78,200) / (2,000,000 Seconds + 1,200,000 Seconds + 400,000 Seconds)

Cost Rate per Second = $78,200 / 3,600,000 Seconds

Cost Rate per Second = $0.0217222 per Second

Cost Applied to Each T-Shirt = (40 Seconds) (0.0217222 per Second) = $0.8689

Question 1C1-CQ05

Topic: Measurement Concepts

Chassen Company, a cracker and cookie manufacturer, has these unit costs for the month of June.

Variable Manufacturing Cost	Variable Marketing Cost	Fixed Manufacturing Cost	Fixed Marketing Cost
$5.00	$3.50	$2.00	$4.00

A total of 100,000 units were manufactured during June, of which 10,000 remain in ending inventory. Chassen uses the first-in, first-out (FIFO) inventory method, and the 10,000 units are the only finished goods inventory at month-end. Using the full absorption costing method, Chassen's finished goods inventory value would be

a. $50,000.

b. $70,000.

c. $85,000.

d. $145,000.

Explanation: The correct answer is: **b.** $70,000.

The full absorption cost inventory consists of variable and fixed manufacturing costs per unit multiplied by the number of units in the inventory.

Full Absorption Cost Inventory = ($5 + $2) (10,000 Units)
= $7(10,000 Units) = $70,000

Question 1C1-CQ11

Topic: Measurement Concepts

During the month of May, Robinson Corporation sold 1,000 units. The cost per unit for May was as shown:

	Cost per Unit
Direct materials	$ 5.50
Direct labor	3.00
Variable manufacturing overhead	1.00
Fixed manufacturing overhead	1.50
Variable administrative costs	0.50
Fixed administrative costs	3.50
Total	$15.00

May's income using absorption costing was $9,500. The income for May, if variable costing had been used, would have been $9,125. The number of units Robinson produced during May was

a. 750 units.

b. 925 units.

c. 1,075 units.

d. 1,250 units.

Explanation: The correct answer is: **d.** 1,250 units.

Use the next formula to solve for the production units:

Full Absorption Cost Operating Income = (Variable Cost Operating Income) + (Fixed Manufacturing Cost per Unit) (Production Units – Sales Units)

Full absorption cost operating income is given as $9,500.

Variable cost operating income is given as $9,125.

$9,500 = $9,125 + ($1.50) (Production Units – 1,000 Units)

$9,500 = $9,125 + $1.50 (Production Units) – $1,500

$9,500 = $7,625 + $1.50 (Production Units)

$1,875 = $1.50 (Production Units)

1,250 = Production Units

Question 1C1-CQ12
Topic: Measurement Concepts

Tucariz Company processes Duo into two joint products, Big and Mini. Duo is purchased in 1,000 gallon drums for $2,000. Processing costs are $3,000 to process the 1,000 gallons of Duo into 800 gallons of Big and 200 gallons of Mini. The selling price is $9 per gallon for Big and $4 per gallon for Mini.

The 800 gallons of Big can be processed further into 600 gallons of Giant if $1,000 of additional processing costs are incurred. Giant can be sold for $17 per gallon. If the net-realizable-value (NRV) method were used to allocate costs to the joint products, the total cost of producing Giant would be:

a. $5,600.

b. $5,564.

c. $5,520.

d. $4,600.

Explanation: The correct answer is: **a.** $5,600.

The NRV of a product at split-off is its market value less the costs to complete and dispose of the product.

The NRV of Giant at split-Off is calculated as shown:

NRV of Giant at Split-Off = (Market Value) – (Separable Processing Costs)

Market Value of Giant = (600 Gallons) ($17 Each) = $10,200

NRV of Giant at Split-Off = $10,200 – $1,000 = $9,200

The NRV of Mini at split-Off is calculated as shown:

NRV of Mini at Split-Off = (Market Value) – (Separable Processing Costs)

NRV of Mini at Split-Off = (200 Gallons) ($4 Each) = $800

NRV of Giant and Mini = $9,200 + $800 = $10,000

Therefore, Giant's share of the joint costs is ($9,200 / $10,000) ($5,000) = $4,600.

Cost of Using NRV at Split-Off, Giant = (Separable Costs)
                                      + (Share of Joint Processing Costs)

Cost of Using NRV at Split-Off, Giant = $1,000 + $4,600 = $5,600

Question 1C1-CQ13

Topic: Measurement Concepts

Tucariz Company processes Duo into two joint products, Big and Mini. Duo is purchased in 1,000 gallon drums for $2,000. Processing costs are $3,000 to process the 1,000 gallons of Duo into 800 gallons of Big and 200 gallons of Mini. The selling price is $9 per gallon for Big and $4 per gallon for Mini.

If the sales value at split-off method is used to allocate joint costs to the final products, the per gallon cost (rounded to the nearest cent) of producing Big is:

a. $5.63 per gallon.

b. $5.00 per gallon.

c. $4.50 per gallon.

d. $3.38 per gallon.

Explanation: The correct answer is: **a.** $5.63 per gallon.

The per gallon cost of Big, using the relative sales value at split-off method, is calculated by finding Big's share of the joint costs and dividing it by the 800 gallons produced.

Sales Value of Big at Split-Off = (800 Gallons) ($9) = $7,200

Sales Value of Mini at Split-Off = (200 Gallons) ($4) = $800

Total Sales Value (Big + Mini) at Split-Off = $7,200 + $800 = $8,000

Big's Share of the Joint Costs = ($7,200/$8,000) ($5,000) = $4,500

Big's Cost per Gallon = $4,500 / 800 Gallons = $5.625, or $5.63 rounded

Question 1C1-CQ14

Topic: Measurement Concepts

Tempo Company produces three products from a joint process. The three products are sold after further processing as there is no market for any of the products at the split-off point. Joint costs per batch are $315,000. Other product information is shown next.

	Product A	Product B	Product C
Units produced per batch	20,000	30,000	50,000
Further processing and marketing cost per unit	$0.70	$3.00	$1.72
Final sales value per unit	$5.00	$6.00	$7.00

If Tempo uses the net realizable value method of allocating joint costs, how much of the joint costs will be allocated to each unit of Product C?

a. $2.10

b. $2.65

c. $3.15

d. $3.78

Explanation: The correct answer is: **d.** $3.78.

The joint cost per unit assigned to Product C using the net realizable value (NRV) at split-off method is calculated by taking the product's share of the joint costs of $315,000 and dividing it by the 50,000 units produced.

NRV at Split-Off for Product A = (Product A Market Value) – (Separable Costs)

NRV at Split-Off for Product A = (20,000 Units) ($5 per Unit)
                                        – (20,000) ($0.70 per Unit)

NRV at Split-Off for Product A = $100,000 – $14,000 = $86,000

NRV at Split-Off for Product B = (Product B Market Value) – (Separable Costs)

NRV at Split-Off for Product B = (30,000 Units) ($6 per Unit) – (30,000 Units)
($3.00 per Unit)

NRV at Split-Off for Product B = $180,000 – $90,000 = $90,000

NRV at Split-Off for Product C = (Product C Market Value) – (Separable Costs)

NRV at Split-Off for Product C = (50,000 Units) ($7 per Unit) – (50,000 Units)
($1.72 per Unit)

NRV at Split-Off for Product C = $350,000 – $86,000
= $264,000

Sum of the Three NRVs = $86,000 + $90,000 + $264,000 = $440,000

Product C's Share of Total Costs = ($264,000 / $440,000) ($315,000) = $189,000

Product C's Cost per Unit Using NRV at Split-Off Method = $189,000/50,000 Units

Product C's Cost per Unit Using NRV at Split-Off Method = $3.78

Question 1C1-CQ15

Topic: Measurement Concepts

Fitzpatrick Corporation uses a joint manufacturing process in the production of two products, Gummo and Xylo. Each batch in the joint manufacturing process yields 5,000 pounds of an intermediate material, Valdene, at a cost of $20,000.

Each batch of Gummo uses 60% of the Valdene and incurs $10,000 of separate costs. The resulting 3,000 pounds of Gummo sells for $10 per pound.

The remaining Valdene is used in the production of Xylo, which incurs $12,000 of separable costs per batch. Each batch of Xylo yields 2,000 pounds and sells for $12 per pound.

Fitzpatrick uses the net realizable value method to allocate the joint material costs. The company is debating whether to process Xylo further into a new product, Zinten, which would incur an additional $4,000 in costs and sell for $15 per pound. If Zinten is produced, income would increase by:

a. $2,000.

b. $5,760.

c. $14,000.

d. $26,000.

Explanation: The correct answer is: **a.** $2,000.

The increase in income from producing Zinten is calculated by taking the $30,000 market value of Zinten (2,000 pounds at $15 per pound) and subtracting both the $24,000 market value of Xylo (2,000 pounds at $12 per pound) and the $4,000 in additional processing costs.

Increase in Income = $30,000 − $24,000 − $4,000 = $2,000

The joint costs and their allocation are sunk and are therefore irrelevant.

Question 1C2-CQ04

Topic: Costing Systems

During December, Krause Chemical Company had these selected data concerning the manufacture of Xyzine, an industrial cleaner.

Production Flow	Physical Units
Completed and transferred to the next department	100
Add: Ending work-in-process inventory	10 (40% complete as to conversion)
Total units to account for	110
Less: Beginning work-in-process inventory	20 (60% complete as to conversion)
Units started during December	90

All material is added at the beginning of processing in this department, and conversion costs are added uniformly during the process. The beginning work-in-process inventory had $120 of raw material and $180 of conversion costs incurred. Material added during December was $540, and conversion costs of $1,484 were incurred. Krause uses the weighted-average process-costing method. The total raw material costs in the ending work-in-process inventory for December are:

a. $120.

b. $72.

c. $60.

d. $36.

Explanation: The correct answer is: **c.** $60.

The total raw material cost in the ending inventory is calculated by taking the equivalent units of raw material in the ending inventory and multiplying it by the raw material costs per equivalent unit.

Total Raw Material Cost, Ending Inventory = (Equivalent Units, Raw Material Ending Inventory) (Raw Material Costs per Equivalent Unit)

The weighted-average method assumes that all units and costs are current (i. e. , there is no beginning inventory). Therefore, 110 equivalent units of raw material are required to yield a transfer-out of 100 units and 10 units in the ending inventory.

Raw Material Cost per Equivalent Unit = (Total Material Cost) / (Equivalent Units)

Raw Material Cost per Equivalent Unit = ($120 + $540) / (110 Equivalent Units)

Raw Material Cost per Equivalent Unit = $660 / 110 Units
$$= \$6 \text{ per Unit}$$

Therefore, the total raw material cost, ending inventory = (10 equivalent units) ($6 per unit) = $60.

Question 1C2-CQ08

Topic: Costing Systems

Oster Manufacturing uses a weighted-average process costing system and has these costs and activity during October:

Materials	$40,000
Conversion cost	32,500
Total beginning work-in-process inventory	$72,500
Materials	$700,000
Conversion cost	617,500
Total production costs—October	$1,317,500
Production completed	60,000 units
Work-in-process, October 31	20,000 units

All materials are introduced at the start of the manufacturing process, and conversion cost is incurred uniformly throughout production. Conversations with plant personnel reveal that, on average, month-end in-process inventory is 25% complete. Assuming no spoilage, how should Oster's October manufacturing cost be assigned?

Production Completed	**Work in Process**
a. $1,042,500	$347,500
b. $1,095,000	$222,500
c. $1,155,000	$235,000
d. $1,283,077	$106,923

Explanation: The correct answer is: **c.** $1,155,000 and $235,000.

The cost of the units completed is calculated as shown:

Cost of Units Completed = (Number of Units) (Total Cost per Equivalent Unit)

Cost of Units Completed = (60,000 Units) (Total Cost per Equivalent Unit)

Because all materials are introduced at the start of the manufacturing process, the equivalent units of material for October consist of the completed units and the work-in-process units.

The Equivalent Units of Material for October = (Completed Production Units)
+ (Work-in-Process Units)
= 60,000 + 20,000 = 80,000.

The Equivalent Units for Conversion are calculated by adding together the units that were started and finished to the equivalent units that were in work-in-process inventory.

Equivalent Units for Conversion = (Units Started and Finished)
+ (% Complete for Conversion) (Ending Work-in-Process Inventory)

Equivalent Units for Conversion = (60,000) + (0.25) (20,000)
= 65,000 Equivalent Units for Conversion

Cost per Equivalent Unit for Materials = ($40,000 + $700,000) / 80,000 Equivalent Units

Cost per Equivalent Unit for Materials = $740,000 / 80,000 Equivalent Units
= $9.25

Cost per Equivalent Unit for Conversion = ($32,500 + $617,500) / 65,000 Equivalent Units

Cost per Equivalent Unit for Conversion = $650,000 / 65,000 Equivalent Units
= $10

Total Cost per Equivalent Unit = ($9.25 + $10) = $19.25

The cost of the 60,000 units completed would be calculated as shown:

Cost of Units Completed = (60,000 Units) ($19.25) = $1,155,000

Cost of the Ending Inventory = (Equivalent Units for Materials)
(Materials Cost per Equivalent Unit) +
(Equivalent Units for Conversion Costs) (Conversion Cost per Equivalent Unit)

Cost of the Ending Inventory = (20,000 Equivalent Units for Materials)
($9.25 per Unit) + (5,000 Equivalent Units for Conversion) ($10 per Unit)
= $235,000

Question 1C2-CQ10

Topic: Costing Systems

During December, Krause Chemical Company had these selected data concerning the manufacture of Xyzine, an industrial cleaner:

Production Flow	Physical Units
Completed and transferred to the next department	100
Add: Ending work-in-process inventory	10 (40% complete as to conversion)
Total units to account for	110
Less: Beginning work-in-process inventory	20 (60% complete as to conversion)
Units started during December	**90**

All material is added at the beginning of processing in this department, and conversion costs are added uniformly during the process. The beginning work-in-process inventory had $120 of raw material and $180 of conversion costs incurred. Material added during December was $540, and conversion costs of $1,484 were incurred. Krause uses the weighted-average process-costing method. The total conversion cost assigned to units transferred to the next department in December was

a. $1,664.

b. $1,600.

c. $1,513.

d. $1,484.

Explanation: The correct answer is: **b.** $1,600.

The total conversion cost assigned to the units transferred to the next department can be calculated as shown:

Total Conversion Cost Assigned to Units Transferred to Next Department
= (Number of Units Transferred) (Conversion Cost per Equivalent Unit)

Number of Units Transferred = 100

The weighted-average method assumes that all units and costs are current (i. e., there is no beginning inventory).

Therefore, the Equivalent Units for Conversion Cost
= (Units Completed) + (Units in Ending Inventory) (% Complete).

Equivalent Units for Conversion Cost = (100) + (10) (40%) = 104

Conversion Cost per Equivalent Unit = ($180 + $1,484) / 104 Equivalent Units

Conversion Cost per Equivalent Unit = $1,664 / 104 = $16 per Equivalent Unit

Total Conversion Cost Assigned to the Units Transferred to the Next Department
= (100 Units) ($16) = $1,600

Question 1C3-CQ01

Topic: Overhead Costs

During December, Krause Chemical Company had these selected data concerning the manufacture of Xyzine, an industrial cleaner.

Production Flow	Physical Units
Completed and transferred to the next department	100
Add: Ending work-in-process inventory	10 (40% complete as to conversion)
Total units to account for	110
Less: Beginning work-in-process inventory	20 (60% complete as to conversion)
Units started during December	90

All material is added at the beginning of processing in this department, and conversion costs are added uniformly during the process. The beginning work-in-process inventory had $120 of raw material and $180 of conversion costs incurred. Material added during December was $540, and conversion costs of $1,484 were incurred. Krause uses the first-in, first-out (FIFO) process-costing method. The equivalent units of production used to calculate conversion costs for December was:

a. 110 units.

b. 104 units.

c. 100 units.

d. 92 units.

Explanation: The correct answer is: **d.** 92 units.

FIFO follows the actual flow of the units through the process. Therefore, the equivalent units of production used to calculate conversion costs for December can be calculated as shown:

Equivalent Units, Conversion Costs = (Units in Beginning Inventory)
(1 − Completion Rate at the Beginning of the Period) + (Units Started
and Finished) + (Units in Ending Inventory) (Completion %)

Equivalent Units, Conversion Costs = (20 Units) (1 − 0.6) + (80 Units)
+ (10 Units) (0.4)

Equivalent Units, Conversion Costs = 8 Units + 80 Units + 4 Units = 92 Units

Question 1C2-CQ12

Topic: Costing Systems

Waller Co. uses a weighted-average process-costing system. Material B is added at two different points in the production of shirts; 40% is added when the units are 20% completed, and the remaining 60% of Material B is added when the units are 80% completed. At the end of the quarter, there are 22,000 shirts in process, all of which are 50% completed. With respect to Material B, the ending shirts in process represent how many equivalent units?

a. 4,400 units

b. 8,800 units

c. 11,000 units

d. 22,000 units

Explanation: The correct answer is: **b.** 8,800 units.

The ending inventory of 22,000 shirts is only 50% complete. Therefore, the inventory units have only 40% of the Material B.

This equates to 8,800 equivalent units, which is calculated by multiplying the number of units in ending inventory (22,000) by the percent of Material B (40%).

$$\text{Equivalent Units, Shirts} = (22{,}000 \text{ Units}) (0.4) = 8{,}800 \text{ Units}$$

Question 1C2-CQ14

Topic: Costing Systems

The Chocolate Baker specializes in chocolate baked goods. The firm has long assessed the profitability of a product line by comparing revenues to the cost of goods sold. However, Barry White, the firm's new accountant, wants to use an activity-based costing system that takes into consideration the cost of the delivery person. Listed are activity and cost information relating to two of Chocolate Baker's major products.

	Muffins	Cheesecake
Revenue	$53,000	$46,000
Cost of goods sold	$26,000	$21,000
Delivery Activity		
Number of deliveries	150	85
Average length of delivery	10 minutes	15 minutes
Cost per hour for delivery	$20.00	$20.00

Using activity-based costing, which one of the following statements is correct?

a. The muffins are $2,000 more profitable.

b. The cheesecakes are $75 more profitable.

c. The muffins are $1,925 more profitable.

d. The muffins have a higher profitability as a percentage of sales and, therefore, are more advantageous.

Explanation: The correct answer is: **c.** The muffins are $1,925 more profitable.

The gross profit for muffins after assigning delivery costs would be calculated as shown:

Gross Profit, Muffins = Revenue – Cost of Goods Sold – Assigned Delivery Costs

Gross Profit, Muffins = $53,000 – $26,000 – Assigned Delivery Costs

Gross Profit, Muffins = $27,000 – Assigned Delivery Costs

The assigned delivery costs are calculated as shown:

Assigned Delivery Costs, Muffins = (Number of Deliveries) (Cost per Delivery)

Assigned Delivery Costs, Muffins = (150 Deliveries) (10 Minutes / 60 Minutes) ($20 per Hour)
= $500

Gross Profit for Muffins = $27,000 – $500 = $26,500.

The gross profit for cheesecake after assigning delivery costs would be calculated as shown:

Gross Profit, Cheesecake = Revenue – Cost of Goods Sold – Assigned Delivery Costs

Gross Profit, Cheesecake = $46,000 – $21,000 – Assigned Delivery Costs

Gross Profit, Cheesecake = $25,000 – Assigned Delivery Costs

The assigned delivery costs are calculated as shown:

Assigned Delivery Costs, Cheesecake = (Number of Deliveries) (Cost per Delivery)

Assigned Delivery Costs, Cheesecake = (85 Deliveries) (15 Minutes/ 60 Minutes) ($20 per Hour)
= $425

Gross Profit for Cheesecake = $25,000 – $425 = $24,575

The gross profit for cheesecake is $1,925 less than the gross profit for muffins.

$26,500 – $24,575 = $1,925

Question 1C2-CQ16

Topic: Costing Systems

Baldwin Printing Company uses a job order costing system and applies overhead based on machine hours. A total of 150,000 machine hours have been budgeted for the year. During the year, an order for 1,000 units was completed and incurred:

Direct material costs	$1,000
Direct labor costs	$1,500
Actual overhead	$1,980
Machine hours	450

The accountant calculated the inventory cost of this order to be $4.30 per unit. The annual budgeted overhead in dollars was:

a. $577,500.

b. $600,000.

c. $645,000.

d. $660,000.

Explanation: The correct answer is: **b.** $600,000.

The total inventory cost, or total manufacturing cost, per unit of $4.30, is made up of direct materials cost, direct labor cost, and manufacturing overhead cost.

$$\text{Total Manufacturing Cost} = \text{Direct Materials Cost} + \text{Direct Labor Cost} + \text{Manufacturing Overhead Cost}$$

$$\text{Direct Materials Cost per Unit} = \$1,000 / 1,000 \text{ Units} = \$1.00 \text{ per Unit}$$

$$\text{Direct Labor Cost per Unit} = \$1,500 / 1,000 \text{ Units} = \$1.50 \text{ per Unit}$$

Therefore,

$$\$4.30 = \$1.00 + \$1.50 + \text{Manufacturing Overhead Cost}$$

$$\text{Manufacturing Overhead Cost} = \$1.80 \text{ per Unit}$$

Use the next formula to calculate the overhead rate, which you will then use to calculate the budgeted overhead cost:

$$\text{Manufacturing Overhead Cost per Unit} = (\text{Machine Hours}) (\text{Overhead Rate}) / (\# \text{Units})$$

$$\$1.80 = (450 \text{ Machine Hours}) (\text{Overhead Rate}) / (1,000 \text{ Units})$$

($1.80) (1,000 Units) = (450 Machine Hours) (Overhead Rate)

1,800 = (450 Machine Hours) (Overhead Rate)

Overhead Rate = 1,800 / 450 = $4

Now calculate the budgeted overhead cost:

Overhead Rate = (Budgeted Overhead Cost) / (Total Budgeted Machine Hours)

$4 = (Budgeted Overhead Cost) / (150,000 Machine Hours)

Budgeted Overhead Cost = $4 × 150,000 = $600,000

Question 1C3-CQ03
Topic: Overhead Costs

Cynthia Rogers, the cost accountant for Sanford Manufacturing, is preparing a management report that must include an allocation of overhead. The budgeted overhead for each department and the data for one job are shown next.

	Department	
	Tooling	**Fabricating**
Supplies	$ 690	$ 80
Supervisor's salaries	1,400	1,800
Indirect labor	1,000	4,000
Depreciation	1,200	5,200
Repairs	4,400	3,000
Total budgeted overhead	$8,690	$14,080
Total direct labor hours	440	640
Direct labor hours on Job #231	10	2

Using the departmental overhead application rates and allocating overhead on the basis of direct labor hours, overhead applied to Job #231 in the Tooling Department would be:

a. $44.00.

b. $197.50.

c. $241.50.

d. $501.00.

Explanation: The correct answer is: **b.** $197.50.

The overhead applied to Job #231 in the Tooling Department is calculated as shown:

Tooling Overhead Applied, Job #231 = (Tooling Overhead Rate) (Number of Direct Labor Hours Used by Job #231)

Tooling Overhead Rate = (Total Tooling Overhead Costs) / (Total Direct Labor Hours Used in Tooling Department)

Tooling Overhead Rate = ($8,690) / (440 Direct Labor Hours)
= $19.75 per Direct Labor Hour

Tooling Overhead Applied, Job #231 = ($19.75) (10 Direct Labor Hours) = $197.50

Question 1C3-CQ05

Topic: Overhead Costs

Atmel Inc. manufactures and sells two products. Data with regard to these products are given next.

	Product A	Product B
Units produced and sold	30,000	12,000
Machine hours required per unit	2	3
Receiving orders per product line	50	150
Production orders per product line	12	18
Production runs	8	12
Inspections	20	30

Total budgeted machine hours are 100,000. The budgeted overhead costs are shown next.

Receiving costs	$450,000
Engineering costs	300,000
Machine setup costs	25,000
Inspection costs	200,000
Total budgeted overhead	$975,000

The cost driver for engineering costs is the number of production orders per product line. Using activity-based costing, what would the engineering cost per unit for Product B be?

a. $4.00

b. $10.00

c. $15.00

d. $29.25

Explanation: The correct answer is: **c.** $15.00.

The engineering cost per unit for Product B is calculated as shown:

Engineering Cost per Unit, Product B
    = [(Engineering Cost per Production Order) (Number of Production Orders
    for Product B)] / (Number of Units of Product B)

Engineering Cost per Production Order = ($300,000) / 30 Total Production Orders

Engineering Cost per Production Order = $10,000 per Production Order

Engineering Cost per Unit, Product B = [($10,000) (18)] / (12,000 Units)
                                     = $15 per Unit

Question 1C3-CQ08

Topic: Overhead Costs

Logo Inc. has two data services departments (the Systems Department and the Facilities Department) that provide support to the company's three production departments (Machining Department, Assembly Department, and Finishing Department). The overhead costs of the Systems Department are allocated to other departments on the basis of computer usage hours. The overhead costs of the Facilities Department are allocated based on square feet occupied (in thousands). Other information pertaining to Logo is as shown next.

Department	Overhead	Computer Usage Hours	Square Feet Occupied
Systems	$200,000	300	1,000
Facilities	100,000	900	600
Machining	400,000	3,600	2,000
Assembly	550,000	1,800	3,000
Finishing	620,000	2,700	5,000
		9,300	11,600

Logo employs the step-down method of allocating service department costs and begins with the Systems Department. Which one of the following correctly denotes the amount of the Systems Department's overhead that would be allocated to the Facilities Department and the Facilities Department's overhead charges that would be allocated to the Machining Department?

	Systems to Facilities	Facilities to Machining
a.	$0	$20,000
b.	$19,355	$20,578
c.	$20,000	$20,000
d.	$20,000	$24,000

Explanation: The correct answer is: **d.** $20,000 and $24,000.

The amount of the Systems Department's overhead that would be allocated to the Facilities Department is calculated as follows:

Systems Department Overhead Allocated to Facilities Department
 = [(Number of Facilities Computer Usage Hours) (Systems Department Overhead Cost)] / (Number of Computer Usage Hours Used by All Departments Except System)

System's Department Overhead Allocated to Facilities Department
 = [(900 Hours) ($200,000)] / (9,000 Hours) = $20,000

The Facilities Department now has $120,000 to allocate to the three production departments.

The Facilities Department's overhead charges that would be allocated to the Machining Department are:

Facilities Department Overhead to Be Allocated to Machining Department
 = ($120,000) (2,000 Square Feet Occupied by Machining) / (10,000 Square Feet Occupied by the Three Production Departments)

Facilities Department Overhead to Be Allocated to Machining Department
 = $24,000

Question 1C3-CQ09

Topic: Overhead Costs

Adam Corporation manufactures computer tables and has this budgeted indirect manufacturing cost information for next year:

	Support Departments		Operating Departments		
	Maintenance	Systems	Machining	Fabrication	Total
Budgeted Overhead	$360,000	$95,000	$200,000	$300,000	$955,000
Support work furnished					
From Maintenance		10%	50%	40%	100%
From Systems	5%		45%	50%	100%

If Adam uses the direct method to allocate support department costs to production departments, the total overhead (rounded to the nearest dollar) for the Machining Department to allocate to its products would be which of the following?

a. $418,000

b. $422,750

c. $442,053

d. $445,000

Explanation: The correct answer is: **d.** $445,000.

The direct method of cost allocation assumes service departments serve production only. There are no interservice department services. Therefore, the total overhead for the Machining Department to allocate to its products is calculated as:

Total Overhead, Machining Department
= (Machining Department Overhead) + (Machining Department Share of Maintenance Overhead) + (Machining Department Share of Systems' Overhead)

Total Overhead, Machining Department
= ($200,000) + [(0.50) / (0.50 + 0.40)] ($360,000) + [(0.45) / (0.45 + 0.50)] ($95,000)

Total Overhead, Machining Department = $200,000 + $200,000 + $45,000
= $445,000

Section D: Internal Controls Answers and Explanations

Question 1D1-CQ01

Topic: Risk Assessment, Controls, and Risk Management

A firm is constructing a risk analysis to quantify the exposure of its data center to various types of threats. Which one of the following situations would represent the highest annual loss exposure after adjustment for insurance proceeds?

	Frequency of Occurrence (years)	Loss Amount	Insurance (% coverage)
a.	1	$ 15,000	85
b.	8	$75,000	80
c.	20	$200,000	80
d.	100	$400,000	50

Explanation: The correct answer is: **a.** 1, $15,000, 85.

The exposure is the same as the expected loss, which is calculated by dividing 1 by the "Frequency of Occurrence," multiplying it by the loss amount, and then multiplying that by 1 minus the "Insurance % coverage" rate.

Expected Loss = (Frequency of Occurrence) (Loss Amount) (1 – % Insurance Coverage)

For answer a, the Expected Loss = (1/1) ($15,000) (1– 0.85) = $2,250.

For answer b, the Expected Loss = (1/8) ($75,000) (1– 0.8) = $1,875.

For answer c, the Expected Loss $= (1/20)\ (\$200{,}000)\ (1-0.8) = \$2{,}000$.

For answer d, the Expected Loss $= (1/100)\ (\$400{,}000)\ (1-0.5) = \$2{,}000$.

Answer a represents the highest annual loss exposure after adjusting for insurance proceeds.

Question 1D1-AT09

Topic: Risk Assessment, Controls, and Risk Management

When management of the sales department has the opportunity to override the system of internal controls of the accounting department, a weakness exists in which of the following?

a. Risk management

b. Information and communication

c. Monitoring

d. Control environment

Explanation: The correct answer is: **d.** Control environment. The control environment includes attitude of management toward the concept of controls.

Question 1D1-AT01

Topic: Risk Assessment, Controls, and Risk Management

Segregation of duties is a fundamental concept in an effective system of internal control. Nevertheless, the internal auditor must be aware that this safeguard can be compromised through

a. lack of training of employees.

b. collusion among employees.

c. irregular employee reviews.

d. absence of internal auditing.

Explanation: The correct answer is: **b.** collusion among employees.

Effective segregation of duties means that no single employee has control over authorization, recording, and custody. If two or more employees are in collusion, these controls can be overridden.

Question 1D1-AT02

Topic: Risk Assessment, Controls, and Risk Management

A company's management is concerned about computer data eavesdropping and wants to maintain the confidentiality of its information as it is transmitted. The company should utilize:

a. data encryption.

b. dial-back systems.

c. message acknowledgment procedures.

d. password codes.

Explanation: The correct answer is: **a.** data encryption.

Data encryption, which uses secret codes, ensures that data transmissions are protected from unauthorized tampering or electronic eavesdropping.

Question 1D3-AT11

Topic: Systems Controls and Security Measures

Which one of the following would **most** compromise the use of the grandfather-father-son principle of file retention as protection against loss or damage of master files?

a. Use of magnetic tape

b. Inadequate ventilation

c. Storing of all files in one location

d. Failure to encrypt data

Explanation: The correct answer is: **c.** Storing of all files in one location.

Storing all files in one location undermines the concept of multiple backups inherent in the grandfather-father-son principle.

Question 1D3-AT12

Topic: Systems Controls and Security Measures

In entering the billing address for a new client in Emil Company's computerized database, a clerk erroneously entered a nonexistent zip code. As a result, the first month's bill mailed to the new client was returned to Emil Company. Which one of the following would **most** likely have led to discovery of the error at the time of entry into Emil Company's computerized database?

a. Limit test

b. Validity test

c. Parity test

d. Record count test

Explanation: The correct answer is: **b.** Validity test.

A validity test compares data against a master file for accuracy. Data that cannot possibly be correct (e. g. , a nonexistent zip code) would be discovered at that time.

Question 1D3-AT07

Topic: Systems Controls and Security Measures

In the organization of the information systems function, the **most** important separation of duties is:

a. assuring that those responsible for programming the system do not have access to data processing operations.

b. not allowing the data librarian to assist in data processing operations.

c. using different programming personnel to maintain utility programs from those who maintain the application programs.

d. having a separate department that prepares the transactions for processing and verifies the correct entry of the transactions.

Explanation: The correct answer is: **a.** assuring that those responsible for programming the system do not have access to data processing operations.

The information technology (IT) function should be separate from the other functional areas in the organization. In addition, within IT, there should be a separation between programmers/analysts, operations, and technical support.

Question 1D2-AT09

Topic: Internal Auditing

There are three components of audit risk: inherent risk, control risk, and detection risk. Inherent risk is described as:

a. the risk that the auditor may unknowingly fail to appropriately modify his or her opinion on financial statements that are materially misstated.

b. the susceptibility of an assertion to a material misstatement, assuming that there are no related internal control structure policies or procedures.

c. the risk that a material misstatement that could occur in an assertion will not be prevented or detected on a timely basis by the entity's internal control structure policies or procedures.

d. the risk that the auditor will not detect a material misstatement that exists in an assertion.

Explanation: The correct answer is: **b.** the susceptibility of an assertion to a material misstatement, assuming that there are no related internal control structure policies or procedures.

Inherent risk is the probability of an error or irregularity causing a material misstatement in an assertion. This is also referred to as the probability that a threat to the system will occur.

Question 1D3-AT01

Topic: Systems Controls and Security Measures

Accounting controls are concerned with the safeguarding of assets and the reliability of financial records. Consequently, these controls are designed to provide reasonable assurance that all of the following take place **except:**

a. executing transactions in accordance with management's general or specific authorization.

b. comparing recorded assets with existing assets at periodic intervals and taking appropriate action with respect to differences.

c. recording transactions as necessary to permit preparation of financial statements in conformity with generally accepted accounting principles and maintaining accountability for assets.

d. compliance with methods and procedures ensuring operational efficiency and adherence to managerial policies.

Explanation: The correct answer is: **d.** compliance with methods and procedures ensuring operational efficiency and adherence to managerial policies.

An internal control system is concerned with safeguarding assets, accuracy and reliability of records, operational efficiency, adherence to policy, and compliance with laws and regulations. The first two are called accounting controls. The latter three are referred to as administrative controls.

Question 1D1-AT05

Topic: Risk Assessment, Controls, and Risk Management

Preventive controls are:

a. usually more cost beneficial than detective controls.

b. usually more costly to use than detective controls.

c. found only in general accounting controls.

d. found only in accounting transaction controls.

Explanation: The correct answer is: **a.** usually more cost beneficial than detective controls.

The three types of controls designed into information systems are preventive, detective, and corrective. Preventive controls are designed to prevent threats, errors, and irregularities from occurring. They are more cost beneficial than detecting and correcting the problems that threats, errors, and irregularities can cause.

Question 1D2-AT02

Topic: Internal Auditing

In planning an audit, the auditor considers audit risk. Audit risk is the

a. susceptibility of an account balance to material error assuming the client does not have any related internal control.

b. risk that a material error in an account will not be prevented or detected on a timely basis by the client's internal control system.

c. risk that the auditor may unknowingly fail to appropriately modify his or her opinion on financial statements that are materially misstated.

d. risk that the auditor's procedures for verifying account balances will not detect a material error when in fact such error exists.

Explanation: The correct answer is: **c.** risk that the auditor may unknowingly fail to appropriately modify his or her opinion on financial statements that are materially misstated.

Audit risk is the probability of an audit failure. An audit failure occurs when the auditor's opinion states that the financial statements "fairly present, in all material respects, in accordance with GAAP (generally accepted accounting principles)" when, in fact, they are materially misstated.

Question 1D2-AT03

Topic: Internal Auditing

Control risk is the risk that a material error in an account will not be prevented or detected on a timely basis by the client's internal control system. The **best** control procedure to prevent or detect fictitious payroll transactions is

a. to use and account for prenumbered payroll checks.

b. personnel department authorization for hiring, pay rate, job status, and termination.

c. internal verification of authorized pay rates, computations, and agreement with the payroll register.

d. storage of unclaimed wages in a vault with restricted access.

Explanation: The correct answer is: **b.** personnel department authorization for hiring, pay rate, job status, and termination.

An independent personnel department responsible for hiring personnel, maintaining personnel records, and processing and documenting personnel terminations is a key control needed to prevent or detect fictitious personnel.

Question 1D2-AT10

Topic: Internal Auditing

Of the following, the **primary** objective of compliance testing is to determine whether

a. procedures are regularly updated.

b. controls are functioning as planned.

c. financial statement line items are properly stated.

d. collusion is taking place.

Explanation: The correct answer is: **b.** controls are functioning as planned.

A compliance audit is a review of controls to see how they conform to established laws, standards, and procedures.

Question 1D3-AT05

Topic: Systems Controls and Security Measures

A critical aspect of a disaster recovery plan is to be able to regain operational capability as soon as possible. In order to accomplish this, an organization can have an arrangement with its computer hardware vendor to have a fully operational facility available that is configured to the user's specific needs. This is **best** known as a(n)

a. uninterruptible power system.

b. parallel system.

c. cold site.

d. hot site.

Explanation: The correct answer is: **d.** hot site.

A hot site is a backup site in another location that has the company's hardware and software and is ready to run on a moment's notice.

Question 1D1-AT07

Topic: Risk Assessment, Controls, and Risk Management

Which of the following is **not** a requirement regarding a company's system of internal control under the Foreign Corrupt Practices Act of 1977?

a. Management must annually assess the effectiveness of its system of internal control.

b. Transactions are executed in accordance with management's general or specific authorization.

c. Transactions are recorded as necessary (1) to permit preparation of financial statements in conformity with GAAP or any other criteria applicable to such statements, and (2) to maintain accountability for assets.

d. The recorded accountability for assets is compared with the existing assets at reasonable intervals, and appropriate action is taken with respect to any differences.

Explanation: The correct answer is: **a.** Management must annually assess the effectiveness of its system of internal control.

Management's annual assessment of internal control is not a requirement of the Foreign Corrupt Practices Act. It became a requirement with the passage of the 2002 Sarbanes-Oxley Act.

Section E: Professional Ethics Answers and Explanations

Question 1E1-AT01

Topic: Ethical Considerations for Management Accounting and Financial Management

As management accountants progress in the profession, they often have the responsibility to supervise the work of less experienced workers. Which of the following is an ethical responsibility of the supervisor?

a. Hire new workers who will fit in socially with existing staff.

b. Maximize the profit or minimize the cost of the department.

c. Ensure that workers handle confidential information appropriately.

d. Encourage the workers to develop relations with customers.

Explanation: The correct answer is: **c.** Ensure that workers handle confidential information appropriately.

Per the *IMA Statement of Ethical Professional Practice,* a management accountant has the responsibility to keep information confidential except when disclosure is authorized or legally required. A management accountant also has the responsibility to inform all relevant parties regarding appropriate use of confidential information. This includes monitoring subordinates' activities to ensure compliance.

Question 1E1-AT02

Topic: Ethical Considerations for Management Accounting and Financial Management

Sam Smith has been offered a pair of tickets to the pro football team if Smith purchases a computerized inventory control system from a specific vendor. Which of the following steps should Smith take?

a. Refuse any further conversations with the vendor.

b. Review his company's policies on gifts from vendors.

c. Sign the contract for the system if the price of the ticket is less than $50.

d. Consult with the Audit Committee of the board of directors.

Explanation: The correct answer is: **b.** Review his company's policies on gifts from vendors.

According to the *IMA Statement of Ethical Professional Practice,* when faced with ethical issues, an individual should follow his or her organization's established policies on the resolution of such a conflict.

Question 1E1-AT03

Topic: Ethical Considerations for Management Accounting and Financial Management

John Moore was recently hired as assistant controller of a manufacturing company. The company controller, Nancy Kay, has forecasted a 16% increase in annual earnings. However, during the last quarter of the year, John estimates that the company will report only a 12% increase in earnings. When he reports this to Nancy, she tells him that meeting the numbers won't be a problem. She explains that there are several jobs in production that will finish after the end of the fiscal year, and she will record the associated revenue in the accounting system for the current year.

What is the first step that John Moore should take at this time?

a. Notify the audit committee of the issue.

b. Contact his lawyer to determine his rights.

c. Discuss the issue with the chief financial officer of another company, who does not know any employees at John's company.

d. Follow his organization's established policies regarding the resolution of this type of conflict.

Explanation: The correct answer is: **d**. Follow his organization's established policies regarding the resolution of this type of conflict.

Before taking any steps, John Moore should check to see if his organization has established policies regarding how to handle this type of conflict. If such policies exist, he should follow them.

ICMA Learning Outcome Statements—Part 1

Revised April 2012

Source: Institute of Certified Management Accountants

PART 1—Financial Planning, Performance and Control

Section A. Planning, Budgeting, and Forecasting (30%)

Part 1—Section A.1. Budgeting concepts

The candidate should be able to:

a. describe the role that budgeting plays in the overall planning and performance evaluation process of an organization.
b. explain the interrelationships between economic conditions, industry situation, and a firm's plans and budgets.
c. identify the role that budgeting plays in formulating short-term objectives and planning and controlling operations to meet those objectives.
d. demonstrate an understanding of the role that budgets play in measuring performance against established goals.
e. identify the characteristics that define successful budgeting processes.
f. explain how the budgeting process facilitates communication among organizational units and enhances coordination of organizational activities.
g. describe the concept of a controllable cost as it relates to both budgeting and performance evaluation.
h. explain how the efficient allocation of organizational resources are planned during the budgeting process.
i. identify the appropriate time frame for various types of budgets.
j. identify who should participate in the budgeting process for optimum success.
k. describe the role of top management in successful budgeting.
l. identify best practice guidelines for the budget process.
m. demonstrate an understanding of the use of cost standards in budgeting.
n. differentiate between ideal (theoretical) standards and currently attainable (practical) standards.
o. differentiate between authoritative standards and participative standards.

p. identify the steps to be taken in developing standards for both direct material and direct labor.

q. demonstrate an understanding of the techniques that are used to develop standards such as activity analysis and the use of historical data.

r. discuss the importance of a policy that allows budget revisions that accommodate the impact of significant changes in budget assumptions.

s. explain the role of budgets in monitoring and controlling expenditures to meet strategic objectives.

t. define *budgetary slack* and discuss its impact on goal congruence.

Part 1—Section A.2. Forecasting techniques

The candidate should be able to:

a. demonstrate an understanding of a simple regression equation and the measures associated with it.

b. define a *multiple regression equation* and recognize when multiple regression is an appropriate tool to use for forecasting.

c. calculate the result of a simple regression equation.

d. demonstrate an understanding of learning curve analysis.

e. calculate the results under a cumulative average-time learning model and under an incremental unit-time learning model.

f. demonstrate an understanding of moving averages, weighted moving averages, and exponential smoothing, and calculate forecasts using these methods.

g. demonstrate an understanding of time series analyses, including objectives and patterns (i.e., trend, cyclical, seasonal, and irregular).

h. list the benefits and shortcomings of regression analysis, learning curve analysis, and time series analysis.

i. calculate the expected value of random variables.

j. identify the benefits and shortcomings of expected value techniques.

k. use probability values to estimate future cash flows.

l. identify the uses of sensitivity analysis.

m. perform a sensitivity analysis with different values for the probabilities of the states of nature and/or the payoffs.

n. identify the benefits and shortcomings of sensitivity analysis.

Part 1—Section A.3. Budget methodologies

For each of the budget systems identified (annual/master budgets, project budgeting, activity-based budgeting, zero-based budgeting, continuous (rolling) budgets, and flexible budgeting), the candidate should be able to:

a. define its purpose, appropriate use, and time frame.

b. identify the budget components and explain the interrelationships among the components.

c. demonstrate an understanding of how the budget is developed.

d. compare and contrast the benefits and limitations of the budget system.

e. evaluate a business situation and recommend the appropriate budget solution.

f. prepare budgets on the basis of information presented.

g. calculate the impact of incremental changes to budgets.

Part 1—Section A.4. Annual profit plan and supporting schedules

The candidate should be able to:

a. explain the role of the sales budget in the development of an annual profit plan.

b. identify the factors that should be considered when preparing a sales forecast and evaluate the feasibility of the sales forecast based on business and economic information provided.

c. identify the components of a sales budget and prepare a sales budget based on relevant information provided.

d. explain the relationship between the sales budget and the production budget.

e. identify the role that inventory levels play in the preparation of a production budget and define other factors that should be considered when preparing a production budget.

f. prepare a production budget based on relevant information provided.

g. demonstrate an understanding of the relationship between the direct materials budget, the direct labor budget, and the production budget.

h. explain how inventory levels and procurement policies affect the direct materials budget.

i. prepare direct materials and direct labor budgets based on relevant information and evaluate the feasibility of achieving production goals on the basis of these budgets.

j. identify and describe alternative ways of allocating employee benefit expense.

k. demonstrate an understanding of the relationship between the overhead budget and the production budget.

l. separate costs into their fixed and variable components.

m. prepare an overhead budget based on relevant information provided.

n. identify the components of the cost of goods sold budget and prepare a cost of goods sold budget based on relevant information provided.

o. demonstrate an understanding of contribution margin per unit and total contribution margin, identify the appropriate use of these concepts, and calculate both unit and total contribution margin.

p. identify the components of the selling and administrative budget.

q. explain how specific components of the selling and administrative budget may affect the contribution margin.

r. prepare an operational (operating) budget.

s. prepare a capital expenditure budget.

t. demonstrate an understanding of the relationship between the capital expenditure budget, the cash budget, and the pro forma financial statements.

u. define the purposes of the cash budget and describe the relationship between the cash budget and all other budgets.

v. demonstrate an understanding of the relationship between credit policies and purchasing (payables) policies and the cash budget.

w. prepare a cash budget.

Part 1—Section A.5. Top-level planning and analysis

The candidate should be able to:

a. define the purpose of a pro forma income statement, a pro forma statement of financial position, and a pro forma cash flow statement and demonstrate an understanding of the relationship among these statements and all other budgets.

b. prepare pro forma income statements based on several revenue and cost assumptions.

c. evaluate whether a company has achieved strategic objectives based on pro forma income statements.

d. use financial projections to prepare a pro forma balance sheet and a statement of cash flows.

e. identify the factors required to prepare medium- and long-term cash forecasts.

f. use financial projections to determine required outside financing and dividend policy.

g. determine the effect of financial forecasts on debt covenants, including debt ratio and coverage ratios (no calculations required).

h. forecast basic earnings per share (EPS) based on pro forma financial statements and other relevant information (calculation of basic EPS required).

Section B. Performance Management (25%)

Part 1—Section B.1. Cost and variance measures

The candidate should be able to:

a. analyze performance against operational goals using measures based on revenue, manufacturing costs, nonmanufacturing costs, and profit depending on the type of center or unit being measured.

b. explain the reasons for variances within a performance monitoring system.

c. prepare a performance analysis by comparing actual results to the master budget, calculate favorable and unfavorable variances from budget, and provide explanations for variances.

d. identify and describe the benefits and limitations of measuring performance by comparing actual results to the master budget.

e. prepare a flexible budget based on actual sales (output) volume.

f. calculate the sales-volume variance and the sales-price variance by comparing the flexible budget to the master (static) budget.

g. calculate the flexible-budget variance by comparing actual results to the flexible budget.

h. investigate the flexible-budget variance to determine individual differences between actual and budgeted input prices and input quantities.

i. explain how budget variance reporting is utilized in a Management by Exception environment.

j. define a *standard cost system* and identify the reasons for adopting a standard cost system.

k. demonstrate an understanding of price (rate) variances and calculate the price variances related to direct material and direct labor inputs.

l. demonstrate an understanding of efficiency (usage) variances and calculate the efficiency variances related to direct material and direct labor inputs.

m. demonstrate an understanding of spending and efficiency variances as they relate to fixed and variable overhead.

n. calculate a sales-mix variance and explain its impact on revenue and contribution margin.

o. demonstrate an understanding that the efficiency (usage) variances can be further analyzed as mix and yield variances.

p. explain how a mix variance results and calculate a mix variance.

q. calculate and explain a yield variance.

r. demonstrate how price, efficiency, spending, and mix variances can be applied in service companies as well as manufacturing companies.

s. analyze factory overhead variances by calculating variable overhead spending variance, variable overhead efficiency variance, fixed overhead spending variance, and production volume variance.

t. analyze variances, identify causes, and recommend corrective actions.

Part 1—Section B.2. Responsibility centers and reporting segments

The candidate should be able to:

a. identify and explain the different types of responsibility centers.

b. recommend appropriate responsibility centers given a business scenario.

c. demonstrate an understanding of contribution margin reporting as used for performance evaluation and calculate a contribution margin.

d. analyze a contribution margin report and evaluate performance.

e. identify segments that organizations evaluate, including product lines, geographical areas, or other meaningful segments.

f. explain why the allocation of common costs among segments can be an issue in performance evaluation.

g. identify methods for allocating common costs, such as stand-alone cost allocation and incremental cost allocation.

h. define *transfer pricing* and identify the objectives of transfer pricing.

i. identify the methods for determining transfer prices and list and explain the advantages and disadvantages of each method.

j. identify and/or calculate transfer prices using variable cost, full cost, market price, negotiated price, and dual-rate pricing.

k. explain how transfer pricing is affected by business issues such as the presence of outside suppliers and the opportunity costs associated with capacity usage.

l. describe how special issues, such as tariffs, exchange rates, taxes, currency restrictions, expropriation risk, and the availability of materials and skills, affect performance evaluation in multinational companies.

Part 1—Section B.3. Performance measures

The candidate should be able to:

a. explain why performance evaluation measures should be directly related to strategic and operational goals and objectives; why timely feedback is critical; and why performance measures should be related to the factors that drive the element being measured (e.g., cost drivers and revenue drivers).

b. explain the issues involved in determining product profitability, business unit profitability, and customer profitability, including cost measurement, cost allocation, investment measurement, and valuation.

c. calculate product-line profitability, business unit profitability, and customer profitability, given a set of data and assumptions.

d. evaluate customers and products on the basis of profitability and recommend ways to improve profitability and/or drop unprofitable customers and products.

e. define and calculate *return on investment* (ROI).

f. analyze and interpret ROI calculations and evaluate performance on the basis of the analysis.

g. define and calculate *residual income* (RI).

h. analyze and interpret RI calculations and evaluate performance on the basis of the analysis.

i. compare and contrast the benefits and limitations of ROI and RI as measures of performance.

j. explain how revenue and expense recognition policies may affect the measurement of income and reduce comparability among business units.

k. explain how inventory measurement policies, joint asset sharing, and overall asset measurement may affect the measurement of investment and reduce comparability among business units.

l. demonstrate an understanding of the effect international operations can have on performance measurement.

m. define *critical success factors* and discuss the importance of these factors in evaluating a firm.

n. define the concept of a balanced scorecard and identify its components.

o. identify and describe financial measures, customer satisfaction measures, internal business process measures, and innovation and learning measures and evaluate their relevance for a specific organization using the balanced scorecard.

p. identify and describe the characteristics of successful implementation and use of a balanced scorecard.

q. analyze and interpret a balanced scorecard and evaluate performance on the basis of the analysis.

r. recommend performance measures and a periodic reporting methodology, given operational goals and actual results.

Section C. Cost Management (25%)

Part 1—Section C.1. Measurement concepts

The candidate should be able to:

a. demonstrate an understanding of the behavior of fixed and variable costs in the long and short term and how a change in assumptions regarding cost type or relevant range affects these costs.
b. identify cost objects and cost pools and assign costs to appropriate activities.
c. demonstrate an understanding of the nature and types of cost drivers and the causal relationship that exists between cost drivers and costs incurred.
d. demonstrate an understanding of the various methods for measuring costs and accumulating work-in-process and finished goods inventories.
e. identify and define cost measurement techniques, such as actual costing, normal costing, and standard costing; calculate costs using each of these techniques; identify the appropriate use of each technique; and describe the benefits and limitations of each technique.
f. demonstrate an understanding of the characteristics of variable (direct) costing and absorption (full) costing and the benefits and limitations of these measurement concepts.
g. calculate inventory costs, cost of goods sold, and operating profit using both variable costing and absorption costing.
h. demonstrate an understanding of how the use of variable costing or absorption costing affects the value of inventory, cost of goods sold, and operating income.
i. prepare summary income statements using variable costing and absorption costing.
j. determine the appropriate use of joint product and by-product costing.
k. demonstrate an understanding of concepts such as split-off point and separable costs.
l. determine the allocation of joint product and by-product costs using the physical measure method, the sales value at split-off method, constant gross profit (gross margin) method, and the net realizable value method; and describe the benefits and limitations of each method.

Part 1—Section C.2. Costing systems

For each cost accumulation system identified (job order costing, process costing, activity-based costing, life-cycle costing), the candidate should be able to:

a. define the nature of the system, understand the cost flows of the system, and identify its appropriate use.
b. calculate inventory values and cost of goods sold.
c. demonstrate an understanding of the proper accounting for normal and abnormal spoilage.
d. discuss the strategic value of cost information regarding products and services, pricing, overhead allocations, and other issues.

e. identify and describe the benefits and limitations of each cost accumulation system.

f. demonstrate an understanding of the concept of equivalent units in process costing and calculate the value of equivalent units.

g. define the elements of activity-based costing, such as cost pool, cost driver, resource driver, activity driver, and value-added activity.

h. calculate product cost using an activity-based system and compare and analyze the results with costs calculated using a traditional system.

i. explain how activity-based costing can be utilized in service firms.

j. demonstrate an understanding of the concept of life-cycle costing and the strategic value of including upstream costs, manufacturing costs, and downstream costs.

Part 1—Section C.3. Overhead costs

The candidate should be able to:

a. distinguish between fixed and variable overhead expenses.

b. determine the appropriate time frame for classifying both variable and fixed overhead expenses.

c. demonstrate an understanding of the different methods of determining overhead rates (e.g., plant-wide rates, departmental rates, and individual cost driver rates).

d. describe the benefits and limitations of each of the methods used to determine overhead rates.

e. identify the components of variable overhead expense.

f. determine the appropriate allocation base for variable overhead expenses.

g. calculate the per-unit variable overhead expense.

h. identify the components of fixed overhead expense.

i. identify the appropriate allocation base for fixed overhead expense.

j. calculate the fixed overhead application rate.

k. describe how fixed overhead can be over- or underapplied and how this difference should be accounted for in the Cost of Goods Sold, Work-in-Process, and finished goods accounts.

l. compare and contrast traditional overhead allocation with activity-based overhead allocation.

m. calculate overhead expense in an activity-based costing setting.

n. identify and describe the benefits derived from activity-based overhead allocation.

o. explain why companies allocate the cost of service departments, such as human resources or information technology, to divisions, departments, or activities.

p. calculate service or support department cost allocations using the direct method, the reciprocal method, the step-down method, and the dual allocation method.

q. estimate fixed costs using the high-low method and demonstrate an understanding of how regression can be used to estimate fixed costs.

Part 1—Section C.4. Operational Efficiency

The candidate should be able to:

a. define a *just-in-time system* and describe its central purpose.

b. identify and describe the operational benefits of implementing a just-in-time system.

c. define the term *kanban* and describe how Kanban is used in a just-in-time system.

d. demonstrate an understanding of work cells and how they relate to just-in-time processes.

e. define *material requirements planning* (MRP).

f. identify and describe the benefits of an MRP system.

g. calculate subunits needed to complete an order for a finished product using MRP.

h. explain the concept of outsourcing and identify the benefits and limitations of choosing this option.

i. demonstrate a general understanding of the theory of constraints.

j. identify the five steps involved in theory of constraints analysis.

k. define *throughput costing* (super-variable costing) and calculate inventory costs using throughput costing.

l. define and calculate *throughput contribution*.

m. discuss how the theory of constraints and activity-based costing are complementary analytical tools.

n. describe how capacity level affects product costing, capacity management, pricing decisions, and financial statements.

o. explain how using practical capacity as a denominator for fixed costs rate enhances capacity management.

p. calculate the financial impact of implementing the above-mentioned methods.

Part 1—Section C.5. Business process performance

The candidate should be able to:

a. define *value chain analysis.*

b. identify the steps in value chain analysis.

c. explain how value chain analysis is used to better understand a firm's competitive advantage.

d. define, identify, and provide examples of a *value-added activity* and explain how the value-added concept is related to improving performance.

e. demonstrate an understanding of process analysis and business process reengineering.

f. demonstrate an understanding of benchmarking process performance.

g. identify the benefits of benchmarking in creating a competitive advantage.

h. apply activity-based management principles to recommend process performance improvements.

i. explain the relationship among continuous improvement techniques, activity-based management, and quality performance.

j. explain the concept of continuous improvement and how it relates to implementing ideal standards and quality improvements.

k. define *best practice analysis* and discuss how it can be used by an organization to improve performance.

l. describe and identify the components of the costs of quality, commonly referred to as prevention costs, appraisal costs, internal failure costs, and external failure costs.

m. calculate the financial impact of implementing the above-mentioned processes.

Section D. Internal Controls (15%)

Part 1—Section D.1. Risk assessment, controls, and risk management

The candidate should be able to:

a. demonstrate an understanding of internal control risk and the management of internal control risk.

b. identify and describe internal control objectives.

c. explain how a company's organizational structure, policies, objectives, and goals, as well as its management philosophy and style, influence the scope and effectiveness of the control environment.

d. identify the board of directors' responsibilities with respect to ensuring that the company is operated in the best interest of shareholders.

e. describe how internal controls are designed to provide reasonable (but not absolute) assurance regarding achievement of an entity's objectives involving (i) effectiveness and efficiency of operations, (ii) reliability of financial reporting, and (iii) compliance with applicable laws and regulations.

f. explain why personnel policies and procedures are integral to an efficient control environment.

g. define and give examples of *segregation of duties.*

h. explain why these four types of functional responsibilities should be performed by different departments or different people within the same function: (i) authority to execute transactions, (ii) recording transactions, (iii) custody of assets involved in the transactions, and (iv) periodic reconciliations of the existing assets to recorded amounts.

i. demonstrate an understanding of the importance of independent checks and verification.

j. list examples of safeguarding controls.

k. explain how the use of prenumbered forms, as well as specific policies and procedures detailing who is authorized to receive specific documents, is a means of control.

l. define *inherent risk, control risk,* and *detection risk.*

m. describe the major internal control provisions of the Sarbanes-Oxley Act (Sections 201, 203, 302, and 404).

n. identify the role of the Public Company Accounting Oversight Board (PCAOB) in providing guidance on the auditing of internal controls.

o. differentiate between a top-down (risk-based) approach and a bottom-up approach to auditing internal controls.

p. identify the PCAOB preferred approach to auditing internal controls as outlined in Auditing Standard No. 5.

q. identify and describe the major internal control provisions of the Foreign Corrupt Practices Act.

r. identify and describe the five major components of the COSO's Internal Control Framework (the 92 model).

s. assess the level of internal control risk within an organization and recommend risk mitigation strategies.

t. define and distinguish between *preventive controls* and *detective controls*.

Part 1—Section D.2. Internal auditing

The candidate should be able to:

a. define the *internal audit function* and identify its functions and scope.

b. identify how internal auditors can test compliance with controls and evaluate the effectiveness of controls.

c. explain how internal auditors determine what controls to audit, when to audit, and why.

d. identify and describe control breakdowns and related risks that internal auditors should report to management or to the board of directors.

e. define and identify the objectives of a *compliance audit* and an *operational audit*.

Part 1—Section D.3. Systems controls and security measures

The candidate should be able to:

a. describe how the segregation of accounting duties can enhance systems security.

b. identify threats to information systems, including input manipulation, program alteration, direct file alteration, data theft, sabotage, viruses, Trojan horses, and theft.

c. demonstrate an understanding of how systems development controls are used to enhance the accuracy, validity, safety, security, and adaptability of systems input, processing, output, and storage functions.

d. identify procedures to limit access to physical hardware.

e. identify means by which management can protect programs and databases from unauthorized use.

f. identify input controls, processing controls, and output controls and describe why each of these controls is necessary.

g. identify and describe the types of storage controls and demonstrate an understanding of when and why they are used.

h. identify and describe the inherent risks of using the Internet as compared to data transmissions over secured transmission lines.

i. define *data encryption* and describe why there is a much greater need for data encryption methods when using the Internet.

j. identify a firewall and its uses.

k. demonstrate an understanding of how flowcharts of activities are used to assess controls.

l. explain the importance of backing up all program and data files regularly and storing the backups at a secure remote site.

m. define the objective of a disaster recovery plan and identify the components of such a plan.

Section E. Professional Ethics (5%)

Part 1—Section E.1. Ethical considerations for management accounting and financial management professionals

Ethics may be tested in conjunction with any topic area.

1. Provisions of IMA's Statement of Ethical Professional Practice
2. Evaluation and resolution of ethical issues

Using the standards outlined in **IMA's Statement of Ethical Professional Practice**, the candidate should be able to:

a. identify and describe the four overarching ethical principles.

b. evaluate a given business situation for its ethical implications.

c. identify and describe relevant standards that may have been violated in a given business situation and explain why the specific standards are applicable.

d. recommend a course of action for management accountants or financial managers to take when confronted with an ethical dilemma in the business environment.

e. evaluate and propose resolutions for ethical issues such as fraudulent reporting, and manipulation of analyses, results, and budgets.

Bibliography

American Institute of Certified Public Accountants, www.aicpa.org.

Anderson, David R., Dennis J. Sweeney, and Thomas A. Williams. *Quantitative Methods for Business*, 9th ed. Mason, OH: Thomson/South-Western, 2004.

Arens, Alvin A. , and James K. Loebbecke. *Auditing: An Integrated Approach*, 8th ed. Upper Saddle River, NJ: Prentice Hall, 1999.

Bergeron, Pierre G. *Finance: Essentials for the Successful Professional.* Independence, KY: Thomson Learning, 2002.

Bernstein, Leopold A. *Financial Statement Analysis: Theory, Application, and Interpretation*, 3rd ed. Homewood, IL: Irwin, 1983.

Blocher, Edward J., Kung H. Chen, and Thomas W. Lin. *Cost Management: A Strategic Emphasis,* 2nd ed. New York: McGraw-Hill Irwin, 2002.

Bodnar, George H., and William S. Hopwood. *Accounting Information Systems*, 3rd ed. Boston: Allyn & Bacon, 1987.

Boockholdt, J. L. *Accounting Information Systems.* Boston: Irwin/McGraw-Hill, 1999.

Brealey, Richard A., and Stewart C. Myers. *Principles of Corporate Finance*, 4th ed. New York: McGraw-Hill, 1991.

Brigham, Eugene F., Louis C. Gapenski, and Michael C. Ehrhardt. *Financial Management: Theory and Practice*, 9th ed. Hinsdale, IL: Dryden Press, 1999.

Campanella, Jack (ed.). *Principles of Quality Costs,* 2nd ed. Milwaukee: ASQ Quality Press, 1990.

Committee of Sponsoring Organizations of the Treadway Commission (COSO), www. coso.org

Daniels, John D., and Lee H. Radebaugh. *International Business: Environments and Operations*, 4th ed. Reading, MA: Addison-Wesley, 1986.

Evans, Matt H. Course 11: The Balanced Scorecard, www.exinfm.com/training/pdfiles/course11r.pdf

Flesher, Dale. *Internal Auditing: Standards and Practices.* Altamonte Springs, FL: Institute of Internal Auditors, 1996.

Financial Accounting Standards Board, www.fasb.org

Financial Accounting Standards Board. *Statements of Financial Accounting Concepts.* Norwalk, CT: Author.

Forex Directory, "U. S. Dollar Charts," www.forexdirectory.net/chartsfx.html

Garrison, Ray H., and Eric W. Noreen. *Managerial Accounting,* 12th ed. Boston: McGraw-Hill/Irwin, 2008.

Gelinas, Ulric J. Jr., Steve G. Sutton, and Allan E. Oram. *Accounting Information Systems,* 4th edition. Cincinnati, OH: South-Western College Publishing, 1999.

Gibson, Charles H. *Financial Statement Analysis: Using Financial Accounting Information*, 7th ed. Cincinnati, OH: South-Western College Publishing, 1998.

Goldratt, Elihayu M. *The Goal*, 3rd revised ed. Great Barrington, MA: North River Press, 2004.

Grant Thorton, LLP, www.grantthornton.ca

Greenstein, Marilyn, and Todd M. Feinman. *Electronic Commerce: Security, Risk Management, and Control.* Boston: McGraw-Hill Higher Education, 2000.

Hildebrand, David K., R. Lyman Ott, and J. Brian Gray. *Basic Statistical Ideas for Managers,* 2nd ed. Belmont, CA: Thomson Learning, 2005.

Hilton, Ronald W., Michael W. Maher, and Frank H. Selto. *Cost Management: Strategies for Business Decisions,* 2nd ed. Boston: McGraw-Hill Irwin, 2003.

Horngren, Charles T., George Foster, and Srikant M. Datar. *Cost Accounting,* 12th ed. Upper Saddle River, NJ: Pearson Prentice Hall, 2006.

Hoyle, Joe B., Thomas F. Schaefer, and Timothy S. Doupnik. *Advanced Accounting,* 6th ed. Boston: McGraw-Hill Irwin, 2001.

Institute of Internal Auditors. "International Standards for the Professional Practice of Internal Auditing," www.theiia.org/index.cfm?doc_id=1595

Institute of Management Accountants, www.imanet.org

Institute of Management Accountants. *Managing Quality Improvements.* Montvale, NJ: Author, 1993.

Institute of Management Accountants. *IMA Statement of Ethical Professional Practice.* Montvale, NJ: Author, 2005.

Institute of Management Accountants. *Enterprise Risk Management: Tools and Techniques for Effective Implementation.* Montvale, NJ: Author, 2007.

Institute of Management Accountants. *Value and Ethics: From Inception to Practice.* Montvale, NJ: Author, 2008.

International Accounting Standards Board, www.iasb.org

Investopedia. com, www.investopedia.com

Kaplan, Robert S., and David P. Norton. *The Balanced Scorecard: Translating Strategy into Action.* Boston: Harvard Business School Press, 1996.

Kaplan, Robert S., and David P. Norton. *The Strategy-Focused Organization.* Boston: Harvard Business School Press, 2001.

Kaplan, Robert S., and David P. Norton. "Using the Balanced Scorecard as a Strategic Management System." *Harvard Business Review* (January-February 1996).

Kieso, Donald E., Jerry J. Weygandt, and Terry D. Warfield. *Intermediate Accounting,* 10th ed. Hoboken, NJ: John Wiley & Sons, 2001.

Larsen, E. John. *Modern Advanced Accounting,* 10th ed. New York: McGraw-Hill, 2006.

Laudon, Kenneth C., and Jane P. Laudon. *Management Information Systems,* 8th ed. Upper Saddle River, NJ: Pearson Prentice Hall, 2003.

McMillan, Edward J. *Budgeting and Financial Management Handbook for Not-for-Profit Organizations.* Washington, DC: American Society of Association Executives, 2000.

Moscove, Stephen A., Mark G. Simkin, and Nancy A. Bagranoff. *Core Concepts of Accounting Information Systems,* 5th ed. New York: John Wiley & Sons, 1997.

Moyer, R. Charles, James R. McGuigan, and William J. Kretlow. *Contemporary Financial Management,* 4th ed. Mason, OH: West Group Publishing, 1990.

MSN Money, "Currency Exchange Rates," moneycentral.msn.com/investor/market/rates.asp

National Aeronautics and Space Administration, "Learning Curve Calculator," www1.jsc.nasa.gov/bu2/learn.html

Nicolai, Loren A., and John D. Bazley. *Intermediate Accounting,* 5th ed. Boston: PWS-Kent, 1991.

Olve, Nils-Göran, and Anna Sjöstrand. *The Balanced Scorecard.* Oxford: Capstone, 2002.

Potter, Gordon, Wayne J. Morse, James R. Davis, and Al L. Hartgraves. *Managerial Accounting,* 4th ed. Lombard, IL: Cambridge Business Publishers, 2006.

Ratliff, Richard L., Wanda A. Wallace, Glenn E. Sumners, William G. McFarland, and James K. Loebbecke. *Internal Auditing: Principles and Techniques.* Altamonte Springs, FL: Institute of Internal Auditors, 1996.

Rosenberg, Jerry M. *The Essential Dictionary of International Trade*. New York: Barnes & Noble Books, 2004.

Sarbanes-Oxley, www.sarbanesoxleysimplified.com/sarbox/compact/htmlact/sec406.html

Securities and Exchange Commission, www.sec.gov/rules/final/33-8177.htm

Siegel, Joel G., Jae K. Shim, and Stephen W. Hartman. *Schaum's Quick Guide to Business Formulas: 201 Decision-Making Tools for Business, Finance, and Accounting Students*. New York: McGraw-Hill, 1998.

Shim, Jae K., and Joel G. Siegel. *Schaum's Outlines:Managerial Accounting*, 2nd ed. New York: McGraw-Hill, 1999.

Stiglitz, Joseph E. *Globalization and Its Discontents*. New York: Norton, 2002.

U. S. Department of Justice. Foreign Corrupt Practices Act, Antibribery Provisions, www.usdoj.gov/criminal/fraud/fcpa/dojdocb.htm

U. S. Securities and Exchange Commission, www.sec.gov

Van Horne, James C., and John M. Wachowicz Jr. *Fundamentals of Financial Management*, 9th ed. Englewood Cliffs, NJ: Prentice-Hall, 1995.

Warren, Carl S., and James M. Reeve. *Financial and Managerial Accounting*, 2nd ed. Mason, OH: Thomson South-Western, 2007.

Wessels, Walter J. *Economics*, 3rd edition. New York: Barron's, 2000.

Woelfel, Charles J. *Financial Statement Analysis: The Investor's Self-Study Guide to Interpreting and Analyzing Financial Statements*, revised ed. New York: McGraw-Hill, 1994.

XE.com, www.xe.com

Registration for the Wiley CMA Learning System Exam Review

Thank you for your purchase of the Wiley CMA Learning System Exam Review. The Wiley CMA Learning System Exam Review products include a suite of offerings designed to help you study for the two-part CMA exam, learn strategies for taking the exam, and practice answering sample questions. Depending on your purchase selection, you will enjoy the features of some/all of the following:

- The **Parts 1 and 2 Self-Study Guides** contain over 1,200 pages and follow the ICMA's content specifications and Learning Outcome Statements for the CMA exam by section and topic. They offer a thorough review of critical concepts and calculations, knowledge-check questions/answers, 173 exam-type questions/answers, 53 retired sample essay questions/answers, bonus tips on exam preparation, and an extensive bibliography.
- The **Parts 1 and Part 2 Online Test Bank** includes over 1,850 multiple-choice questions with explanations. Included are tests covering each section as well as tests that emulate each full exam. There is also a grade book to track your progress on the practice tests and other resources, such as essay questions with sample answers. Test questions are randomized to provide a different presentation for each test you take—take them as often as you like.
- The **Parts 1 and 2 Online Intensive Review (OIR)** courses are two interactive, online self-study courses aligned with the ICMA's Learning Outcome Statements by section and topic. The OIR is designed to reinforce/clarify the key concepts and calculation covered in the CMA Learning System textbooks. These Web-based courses offer on-screen explanations, interactive exercises, and the popular "Ask the Expert" feature, which allows users to interact one-on-one with a CMA subject matter expert.

To activate the **Online Test Bank** (a part of all products) or **OIR** courses (if purchased):

1. Locate the insert card included at the back of your book or CD case.
2. Type in your unique URL located on the back of the insert card into an Internet-enabled Web browser (i.e., Firefox, Internet Explorer, etc.). The URL will take you to the IMA Product Page, where you will be able to check out your product and start your activation.

3. Add the online product to your cart by clicking on the "Add To Cart" button and then continue by following the on-screen instructions. Please note that you will not be charged.

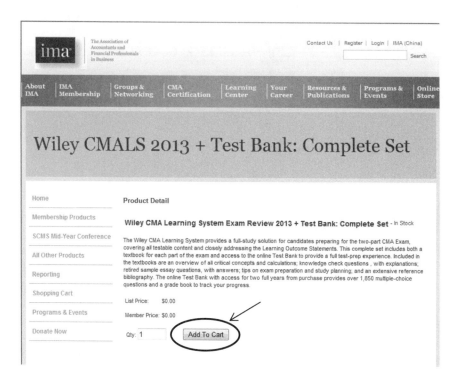

4. Review that the correct online product you purchased has been added to your cart. You are now ready to check out and register with the IMA. Click on "**shopping cart**" to complete the checkout process.

5. Click on the "Checkout" button on the Shopping Cart page.

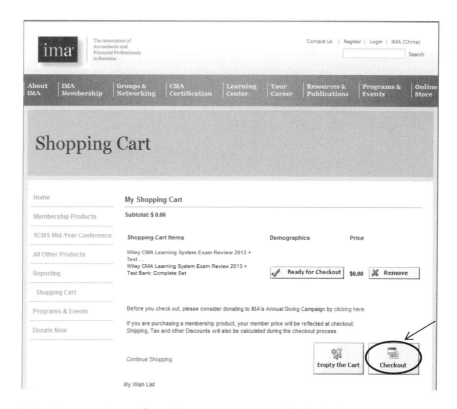

6. Login or register. If you have an account with the IMA or are a returning IMA member, please sign in with your username and password. If you are a new user, you will need to register.

Existing User

Your username is your Member number. If you are not an IMA Member, your username is your customer or Learning Center number.

Username: _____

Password: _____

☐ Remember my login information for 90 days

Forgot Password?   Sign In

New User

Please create an online account. Click here to register.

Help

Trouble signing in? Please click here to troubleshoot your account access.

Contact us for further assistance.

7. After registering with the IMA, please proceed through the checkout process and complete your order. You will receive a confirmation email after your order is complete with further instructions on how to access your product.

Once again, thank you very much for your purchase. If you need further assistance, please contact the IMA Customer Support within your region.

IMA Global Member Services
Monday through Friday 8 a.m.–6 p.m. EST
Phone: (800) 638-4427 or +1 (201) 573-9000
Fax: (201) 474-1600
ima@imanet.org

IMA China
Monday through Friday 9 a.m.–6 p.m. GMT +8
Phone: +86-4000-ima-cma (4000-462-262)
Fax: +86-10-8521-6511
imachina@imanet.org

IMA Middle East
Sunday through Thursday 9 a.m.–6 p.m. GMT +4
Phone: +971 800 IMA ME (462 63)
Fax: +971-4-311-6351
imamiddleeast@imanet.org

IMA Europe
Monday through Friday 9 a.m.–4 p.m. GMT +1 (Winter) / GMT +2 (Summer)
Phone: +41 44 500 41 69
ima@imanet.org

Index

This index identifies the page on which a key term or concept is introduced in context. It is not meant as a comprehensive index of all references to that term or concept.